Head-hunters: Black, White, And Brown

Alfred Cort Haddon

Nabu Public Domain Reprints:

You are holding a reproduction of an original work published before 1923 that is in the public domain in the United States of America, and possibly other countries. You may freely copy and distribute this work as no entity (individual or corporate) has a copyright on the body of the work. This book may contain prior copyright references, and library stamps (as most of these works were scanned from library copies). These have been scanned and retained as part of the historical artifact.

This book may have occasional imperfections such as missing or blurred pages, poor pictures, errant marks, etc. that were either part of the original artifact, or were introduced by the scanning process. We believe this work is culturally important, and despite the imperfections, have elected to bring it back into print as part of our continuing commitment to the preservation of printed works worldwide. We appreciate your understanding of the imperfections in the preservation process, and hope you enjoy this valuable book.

THE SCOTT-KELTIE FALLS, MOUNT DULIT, BARAM DISTRICT, SARAWAK

HEAD-HUNTERS

BLACK, WHITE, AND BROWN

BY

ALFRED C. HADDON, Sc.D., F.R.S.

FELLOW OF CHRIST'S COLLEGE
AND UNIVERSITY LECTURER IN ETHNOLOGY, CAMBRIDGE

WITH THIRTY-TWO PLATES, FORTY ILLUSTRATIONS IN THE TEXT
AND SIX MAPS

METHUEN & CO.
36 ESSEX STREET W.C.
LONDON
1901

All rights reserved

TO
MY WIFE
AND
TO THE MEMORY OF
MY MOTHER
WHO FIRST TAUGHT ME TO OBSERVE
I DEDICATE
THIS RECORD OF MY TRAVELS

PREFACE

IN 1888 I went to Torres Straits to study the coral reefs and marine zoology of the district; whilst prosecuting these studies I naturally came much into contact with the natives, and soon was greatly interested in them. I had previously determined not to study the natives, having been told that a good deal was known already about them; but I was not long in discovering that much still remained to be learned. Indeed, it might be truly said that practically nothing was known of the customs and beliefs of the natives, even by those who we had every reason to expect would have acquired that information.

Such being the case, I felt it to be my duty to gather what information I could when not actually engaged in my zoological investigations. I found, even then, that the opportunities of learning about the pagan past of the natives were limited, and that it would become increasingly more difficult, as the younger men knew comparatively little of the former customs and beliefs, and the old men were dying off.

On my return home I found that my inquiries into the ethnography of the Torres Straits islanders were of some interest to anthropologists, and I was encouraged to spend some time in writing out my results. Gradually this has led me to devote myself to anthropological studies, and, not unnaturally, one of my first projects was to attempt a monograph on the Torres Straits Islanders. It was soon apparent that my information was of too imperfect a nature to make a satisfactory memoir, and therefore I delayed publishing until I could go out again to collect further material.

In course of time I was in a position to organise an expedition for this purpose, which, being mainly endowed from University funds, had the honour of being closely associated with the University of Cambridge. It was my good fortune to be able to secure the co-operation of a staff of colleagues, each of whom had some special qualification.

For a long time it had appeared to me that investigations in experimental psychology in the field were necessary if we were ever to gauge the mental and sensory capabilities of primitive peoples. This expedition presented the requisite opportunity, and the organisation of this department was left to Dr. W. H. R. Rivers, of St. John's College, the University lecturer in physiological and experimental psychology. The co-operation of Dr. C. S. Myers, of Caius College, had been secured early, and as he is a good musician, he specialised more particularly in the study of the hearing and music of the natives. Mr. W. McDougall, Fellow of St. John's College, also volunteered to assist in the experimental psychology department of the expedition.

When the early arrangements were being made one of the first duties was to secure the services of a linguist, and the obvious person to turn to was Mr. Sidney H. Ray, who has long been a recognised authority on Melanesian and Papuan languages. Fortunately, he was able to join the expedition.

Mr. Anthony Wilkin, of King's College, took the photographs for the expedition, and he assisted me in making the physical measurements and observations. He also investigated the construction of the houses, land tenure, transference of property, and other social data of various districts.

When this book was being brought out the sad news arrived in England of the death by dysentery of my pupil, friend, and colleague in Cairo on the 17th of May (1901), on his return home from a second winter's digging in Upper Egypt. Poor Wilkin! barely twenty-four years of age, and with the promise of a brilliant career before him. I invited him to accompany me while he was still an undergraduate, having been struck by his personal and mental qualities. He was a man of exceptional ability and of frank, pleasing manner, and a thorough hater of humbug. Although he was originally a classical scholar, Wilkin read for the History Tripos, but his interests were wider

PREFACE

than the academic course, and he paid some attention to sociology, and was also interested in natural science. In his early undergraduate days he published a brightly written book, *On the Nile with a Camera*. Immediately after his first winter's digging in Egypt with Professor Flinders Petrie, he went with Mr. D. Randall-Maciver to Algeria to study the problem of the supposed relationship, actual or cultural, of the Berbers with the Ancient Egyptians. An interesting exhibition of the objects then collected was displayed at the Anthropological Institute in the summer (1900), and later in the year Wilkin published a well-written and richly illustrated popular account of their experiences, entitled, *Among the Berbers of Algeria*. Quite recently the scientific results were published in a sumptuously illustrated joint work entitled, *Libyan Notes*. Wilkin was an enthusiastic traveller, and was projecting important schemes for future work. There is little doubt that had he lived he would have distinguished himself as a thoroughly trained field-ethnologist and scientific explorer.

Finally, Mr. C. G. Seligmann volunteered to join the party. He paid particular attention to native medicine and to the diseases of the natives as well as to various economic plants and animals.

Such was the *personnel* of the expedition. Several preliminary communications have been published by various members; but the complete account of our investigations in Torres Straits is being published by the Cambridge University Press in a series of special memoirs. The observations made on the mainland of British New Guinea and in Sarawak will be published in various journals as opportunity offers.

The book I now offer to the public contains a general account of our journeyings and of some of the sights we witnessed and facts that we gleaned.

I would like to take this opportunity of expressing my thanks to my comrades for all the assistance they have rendered me, both in the field and at home. I venture to prophesy that when all the work of the expedition is concluded my colleagues will be found to have performed their part in a most praiseworthy manner.

Our united thanks are due to many people, from H.H. the

PREFACE

Rajah of Sarawak down to the least important native who gave us information. Wherever we went, collectively or individually, we were hospitably received and assisted in our work. Experience and information were freely offered us, and what success the expedition has attained must be largely credited to these friends.

I cannot enumerate all who deserve recognition, but, taking them in chronological order, the following rendered us noteworthy service.

The Queensland Government, through the Hon. T. J. Byrnes, then Premier, sent us the following cordial welcome by telegraph on our arrival at Thursday Island :—

"Permit me on behalf of Government to welcome you and your party to Queensland and to express our sincere hope that your expedition will meet with the success which it deserves. We shall be glad if at any time we can afford any assistance towards the object of the expedition or to its individual members, and trust that you will not hesitate to advise us if we can be of service to you. Have asked Mr. Douglas to do anything in his power and to afford you any information concerning the objects of your mission he may be in a position to impart."

The Hon. John Douglas, C.M.G., the Government Resident at Thursday Island, not merely officially, but privately and of his spontaneous good nature, afforded us every facility in his power. Through his kind offices the Queensland Government made a special grant of £100 towards the expenses of the expedition, and in connection with this a very friendly telegram was sent by the late Sir James R. Dickson, K.C.M.G., who was then the Home Secretary.

The Government of British New Guinea did what it could to further our aims. Unfortunately, His Excellency Sir William Macgregor, K.C.M.G., M.D., SC.D., the then Lieutenant-Governor of the Possession, was away on a tour of inspection during my visit to the Central District; but he afterwards showed much kindness to Seligmann. The Hon. A. Musgrave, of Port Moresby, was most cordial and helpful, and we owe a great deal to him. The Hon. D. Ballantine, the energetic Treasurer and Collector of Customs, proved himself a very good friend

PREFACE

and benefactor to the expedition. The Hon. B. A. Hely, Resident Magistrate of the Western Division, helped us on our way, and we are greatly indebted in many ways to Mr. A. C. English, the Government Agent of the Rigo District.

All travellers to British New Guinea receive many benefits directly and indirectly from the New Guinea Mission of the London Missionary Society. Everywhere we went we were partakers of the hospitality of the missionaries and South Sea teachers; the same genuine friendliness and anxiety to help permeates the whole staff, so much so that it seems invidious to mention names, but the great assistance afforded us by the late Rev. James Chalmers deserves special recognition, as does also the kindness of Dr. and Mrs. Lawes. The Mission boats were also freely placed at our disposal as far as the service of the Mission permitted; but for this liberality on the part of Mr. Chalmers we should several times have been in an awkward predicament. If any words of mine could induce any practical assistance being given to the Mission I would feel most gratified, for I sadly realise that our indebtedness to the Mission can only be acknowledged adequately by proxy.

It is a sad duty to chronicle the irreparable loss which all those who are connected with British New Guinea have undergone in the tragic death of the devoted Tamate. Mrs. Chalmers died in the autumn of 1900 under most distressing circumstances in the Mission boat when on her way to Thursday Island. A few months later, when endeavouring to make peace during a tribal war on the Aird River, Chalmers crowned a life of hardship and self-sacrifice by martyrdom in the cause of peace. A glorious end for a noble life. With him were murdered twelve native Mission students and the Rev. O. Tomkins, a young, intelligent, and enthusiastic missionary, from whom much was expected.

Very pleasing is it to record the brotherly kindness that we received at the hands of the Sacred Heart Mission. None of our party belonged to their Communion, but from the Archbishop to the lowliest Brother we received nothing but the friendliest treatment. Nor would we omit our thanks to the good Sisters for the cheerful way in which they undertook the increased cares of catering which our presence necessitated. The insight which we gained into the ethnography of the

Mekeo District is solely due to the good offices of the various members of the Sacred Heart Mission.

In the course of the following pages I often refer to Mr. John Bruce, the Government Schoolmaster on Murray Island. It would be difficult to exaggerate the influence he exerts for good by his instruction, advice, and unostentatious example. His help and influence were invaluable to us, and when our researches are finally published, anthropologists will cordially admit how much their science owes to "Jack Bruce."

We found Mr. Cowling, of Mabuiag, very helpful, not only at the time but subsequently, as he has since sent us much valuable information, and he also deserves special thanks.

Our visit to Sarawak was due to a glowing invitation I received from Mr. Charles Hose, the Resident of the Baram District. I have so frequently referred in print and speech to his generosity and erudition, that I need only add here that his University has conferred on him the greatest honour it is in her power to bestow—the degree of Doctor in Science *honoris causa*.

But it was Rajah Sir Charles Brooke's interest in the expedition that made many things possible, and to him we offer our hearty thanks, both for facilities placed at our disposal and for the expression of his good-will.

At Kuching we received great hospitality from the white residents. Particular mention must be made of the Hon. C. A. Bampfylde, Resident of Sarawak; on our arrival he was administrating the country in the absence of the Rajah, who was in England; nor should Dr. A. J. G. Barker, Principal Medical Officer of Sarawak, and Mr. R. Shelford, the Curator of the Museum, be omitted.

Great kindness and hospitality were shown us by Mr. O. F. Ricketts, Resident of the Limbang District. We had a most enjoyable visit to his beautiful Residency, and he arranged for us all the details of our journey up-river.

One fact through all our journeyings has continually struck me. Travellers calmly and uninvitedly plant themselves on residents by whom they are received with genuine kindness and hospitably entertained with the best that can be offered. Experience, information, and influence are cheerfully and ungrudg-

PREFACE

ingly placed at the disposal of the guests, who not unfrequently palm off, without acknowledgment, on an unsuspecting public the facts that others have gleaned.

The warm welcome that one receives is as refreshing to the spirit as the shower-bath is to the body and daintily served food to the appetite when one has been wandering in the wilds.

In order to render my descriptions of the places and people more continuous I have practically ignored the exact order in which events happened or journeys were made. For those who care about chronology I append a bare statement of the location of the various members of the expedition at various times. I have also not hesitated to include certain of my experiences, or some of the information I gained, during my first expedition to Torres Straits in 1888-9; but the reader will always be able to discriminate between the two occasions.

1898.
March 10th.	Left London.
April 22nd.	Arrived Thursday Island, where joined by Seligmann.
April 30th.	Left Thursday Island.
May 6th.	Arrived Murray Island.
May 23rd.	Haddon, Ray, Wilkin, and Seligmann left for New Guinea.
June 25th.	Seligmann went to Rigo.
July 20th.	Haddon, Ray, and Wilkin returned from New Guinea to Murray Island.
August 24th.	Myers and McDougall left Murray Island for Sarawak.
Sept. 8th.	Haddon, Rivers, Ray, and Wilkin left Murray Island for Kiwai.
Sept. 12th.	Seligmann arrived at Saguane.
Sept. 15th.	Haddon, Rivers, Wilkin, Seligmann left Saguane for Mabuiag.
Sept. 17th.	Arrived Mabuiag.
Oct. 3rd.	Ray came from Saguane.
Oct. 19th.	Rivers left to return home.
Oct. 21st.	Wilkin left to return home.
Oct. 22nd.	Haddon, Ray, Seligmann left for Saibai, etc.
Nov. 15th.	Left Thursday Island.

1898.
Nov. 28th.   Arrived Hongkong.
Dec. 3rd.   Left Hongkong.
Dec. 9th.   Arrived Singapore.
Dec. 10th.   Left Singapore.
Dec. 12th.   Arrived Kuching.

1899.
Jan. 4th.   Left Kuching for Baram.
Jan. 8th.   Arrived Limbang.
Jan. 16th.   Left Limbang.
Jan. 28th.   Arrived Marudi (Claudetown).
April 20th. Left Marudi.
April 25th. Left Kuching.
May 31st.   Arrived in London.

THE following is the system of spelling which has been adopted in this book:—

a as in "father."
ă as in "at."
e as *a* in "date."
ĕ as in "debt."
i as *ee* in "feet."
ĭ as in "it."
o as in "own."

ŏ as in "on."
ö as German *ö* in "schön."
ò as *aw* in "law."
u as *oo* in "soon."
ŭ as in "up."
ai as in "aisle."
au as *ow* in "cow."

The consonants are sounded as in English.

ng as in "sing." | *ngg* as in "finger."

CONTENTS

PART I

CHAPTER I
THURSDAY ISLAND TO MURRAY ISLAND

Port Kennedy, Thursday Island—Passage in the *Freya* to Murray Island—Darnley Island—Arrival at Murray Island—Reception by the natives.   *Page* 1-10

CHAPTER II
THE MURRAY ISLANDS

Geographical features of the islands of Torres Straits—Geology of the Murray Islands—Climate—The Murray Islanders—Physical and other characteristics—Form of Government .   .   .   .   .   .   *Page* 11-21

CHAPTER III
WORK AND PLAY IN MURRAY ISLAND

The Expedition Dispensary—Investigations in Experimental Psychology: visual acuity, colour vision, mirror writing, estimation of time, acuity of hearing, sense of smell and taste, sensitiveness to pain—The Miriam language—Methods of acquiring information—Rain-making—Native amusements—Lantern exhibition—String puzzles—Top-spinning—Feast—Copper Maori
Page 22-41

CHAPTER IV
THE MALU CEREMONIES

Initiation ceremonies—Secret societies—Visit to Las—Representation of the Malu ceremonies—Models of the old masks—The ceremonies as formerly carried out—"Devil belong Malu" .   .   .   *Page* 42-52

CHAPTER V.
ZOGOS

The Murray Island oracle, Tomog Zogo—The village of Las—Tamar—The war-dance at Ziriam Zogo—Zabarkar—Wind-raising—Teaching Geography at Dam—Tamar again—A Miriam "play"—How Pepker made a hill—Iriam Moris, the fat man—Zogo of the girl of the south-west—Photographing zogos—The coconut zogo—A turtle zogo—The big women who dance at night—The Waiad ceremony .   .   .   .   *Page* 53-70

CONTENTS

CHAPTER VI
VARIOUS INCIDENTS IN MURRAY ISLAND

Our "boys" in Murray Island—"Gi, he gammon"—Character of some of our native friends—Ulai—Rivalry between Debe Wali and Jimmy Rice—Our Royal Guests—The Papuan method of smoking—A domestic quarrel—Debe and Jimmy fall out—An earthquake—Cause of a hurricane—The world saved from a comet by three weeks of prayer—an unaccounted-for windstorm—New Guinea magic—"A woman of Samaria"—Jimmy Rice in prison—A yam zogo—Rain-makers—A death-dealing zogo—Mummies—Skull-divination—Purchasing skulls—A funeral . . *Page* 71–94

CHAPTER VII
KIWAI AND MAWATTA

Leave Murray Island in the *Nieue*—Daru—Arrive at Saguane—Mission-work—Visit Iasa—Long clan houses—Totems and totemistic customs—Bull-roarers and human effigies as garden charms and during initiation ceremonies—Head-hunting—Stone implements—Origin of Man—Origin of Fire—Primitive dwellings at Old Mawatta—Shell hoe—Katau or Mawatta—Election of a chief—A love story—Dances—Bamboo beheading-knife
Page 95–116

CHAPTER VIII
MABUIAG

Mabuiag revisited—Character of the island—Comparison between the Murray Island and Mabuiag natives—Barter for skulls—Economic condition of Mabuiag—Present of food—Waria, a literary Papuan—Death of Waria's baby—Method of collecting relationships and genealogies—Colour-blindness—The Mabuiag language—A May Meeting followed by a war-dance
Page 117–131

CHAPTER IX
TOTEMISM AND THE CULT OF KWOIAM

Totemism in Mabuiag—Significance of Totemism—Advantage of Totemism—Seclusion of girls—The Sacred Island of Pulu—The scenes of some of Kwoiam's exploits—The Pulu Kwod—The stone that fell from the sky—The Kwoiam Auguds—Death dances—Test for bravery—Bull-roarer—Pictographs—The Cave of Skulls—The destruction of relics—Outline of the Saga of Kwoiam—Kwoiam's miraculous water-hole—The death of Kwoiam
Page 132–147

CHAPTER X
DUGONG AND TURTLE FISHING

A dugong hunt—What is a dugong?—The dugong platform—Dugong charms—Turtle-fishing—How the sucker-fish is employed to catch turtle—Beliefs respecting the *gapu*—The *agu* and bull-roarers—Cutting up a turtle. *Page* 148–157

CONTENTS

CHAPTER XI
MARRIAGE CUSTOMS AND STAR MYTHS

MARRIAGE CUSTOMS: How girls propose marriage among the western tribe—A proposal in Tut—Marital relations—A wedding in church—An unfortunate love affair—Various love-letters. STAR MYTHS: The Tagai constellation—A stellar almanack, its legendary origin—The origin of the constellations of Dorgai Metakorab and Bu—The story of Kabi, and how he discovered who the Sun, Moon, and Night were . . . . *Page* 158-169

CHAPTER XII
VISITS TO VARIOUS WESTERN ISLANDS

Our party breaks up. SAIBAI: Clan groupings—Vaccination marks turned to a new use—Triple-crowned coconut palm—A two-storied native house. TUT: Notes of a former visit—Brief description of the old initiation ceremonies—Relics of the past. YAM: A Totem shrine. NAGIR: The decoration of Magau's skull "old-time fashion"—Divinatory skulls—The sawfish magical dance—Pictographs in Kiriri. MURALUG: Visit to Prince of Wales Island in 1888—A family party—War-dance . . . *Page* 170-189

CHAPTER XIII
CAPE YORK NATIVES

Visit to Somerset—Notes on the Yaraikanna tribe—Initiation ceremony—Bull-roarer—Knocking out a front tooth—The *ari* or "personal totem"
Page 190-194

CHAPTER XIV
A TRIP DOWN THE PAPUAN COAST

The *Olive Branch*—Passage across the Papuan Gulf—Delena—Tattooing—A Papuan *amentum*—A sorcerer's kit—Borepada—Port Moresby—Gaile, a village built in the sea—Character of the country—Kappakappa—*Dubus*—The Vatorata Mission Station—Dr. and Mrs. Lawes—Sir William Macgregor's testimony to mission work—A dance . . *Page* 197-210

CHAPTER XV
THE HOOD PENINSULA

Bulaa by moonlight—Hospitality of the South Sea teachers—Geographical character of the Hood Peninsula—Kalo—Annual fertility ceremony at Babaka—Canoe-making at Keapara—The fishing village of Alukune—The Keapara bullies—Picking a policeman's pocket—Tattooing—A surgical remedy—Variations in the character of the Papuan hair—Pile-raising—Children's toys and games—Dances—Second visit to Vatorata—Visit Mr. English at Rigo . . . . . *Page* 211-234

CHAPTER XVI
PORT MORESBY AND THE ASTROLABE RANGE

Port Moresby—Ride inland—Vegetation—View from the top of Warirata—The Taburi village of Atsiamakara—The Koiari—Tree houses—The Agi chief—Contrasts—A lantern show—The mountaineers—Tribal warfare—The pottery trade of Port Moresby—The Koitapu and the Motu—Gunboats *Page* 235-251

CONTENTS

CHAPTER XVII
THE MEKEO DISTRICT

Arrival at Yule Island—The Sacred Heart Mission—Death of a Brother—A service at Ziria—The meeting of the Papuan East and West in Yule Island—The *Ibitoe*—Making a drum—Marriage customs—Omens—Tattooing—The Roro fishers and traders—The Mekeo agriculturists—The Pokao hunters—Markets—Pinupaka—Mohu—Walk across the plain and through the forest—Inawi—War and Taboo chiefs—Taboo customs—Masks—A Mission festivity—Tops—Veifaa—Women's dress—Children's games—Return to coast . . . . . . *Page* 252-277

PART II

CHAPTER XVIII
JOURNEY FROM KUCHING TO BARAM

Arrival in Sarawak—Description of Kuching—The Sarawak Museum—Visit to Sibu—Stay in Limbang—A Malay sago factory—Visit to Brunei—Method and aims of Rajah Brooke's Government . . . *Page* 279-294

CHAPTER XIX
THE WAR-PATH OF THE KAYANS

Leave Limbang—A Kadayan house at Tulu—Rapids on the Limbang—Ascent of the Madalam—The Insurrection of Orang Kaya Tumonggong Lawai—Enter the Trikan—Durian—Met by Mr. Douglas—Old Jungle—Descend the Malinau and Tutau—Kayan tattooing—Berantu ceremony in the Batu Blah House—Arrival at Marudi (Claudetown)—Kenyah drinking customs
Page 297-311

CHAPTER XX
THE COUNTRY AND PEOPLE OF BORNEO

THE GEOGRAPHICAL AND GEOLOGICAL FEATURES OF BORNEO: Arrangement of mountains—The geology of the "Mountain-land," Palæozoic—Mesozoic—the geology of the "Hill-land," Cainozoic—The geology of the Plains, Quaternary—The geology of the Marshes, Alluvium—Recent volcanic action. A SKETCH OF THE ETHNOGRAPHY OF SARAWAK: Punans—Various agricultural tribes of Indonesian and Proto-Malay stock—Land Dayaks—Kenyahs and Kayans—Iban (Sea Dayaks)—Malays—Sociological History of Sarawak—Chinese traders . . . *Page* 312-329

CHAPTER XXI
A TRIP INTO THE INTERIOR OF BORNEO

The Lelak house at Long Tru—Skull trophies—The settled Punans on the Bok—Sarcophagus in Taman Liri's house—Divination by means of a pig's liver in Aban Abit's house—Purchase of some skulls—The Panyamun Panic in Sarawak in 1894-5—Commencement of a similar scare—Administrative duties at Long Semitan—Character of the Sĕbops—The fable of the monkey and the frog—A visit to Mount Dulit—The Scott-Keltie Falls—The Himalayan affinities of the fauna of Mount Dulit and of other high mountains in Borneo . . . . . . *Page* 330-351

CONTENTS

CHAPTER XXII
A TRIP INTO THE INTERIOR OF BORNEO—*continued*

Ceremony of moving skulls into a new house at Long Puah—Naming ceremony for Jangan's boy—Peace-making—Conviviality—Malohs desire to marry some Sĕbop girls—Sĕbop dances—Scenery on the Tinjar—Burnt house at Long Dapoi—Panyamun Scare again—The Dapoi—Long Sulan—Tingan's matrimonial mishap—News from the Madangs—A Punan medicine man—Panyamun Scare settled—Discovery of stone implements—A native selling a stone implement for a loin cloth to die in—A stone hook—A visit to Tama Bulan—The unfortunate Bulan—Fanny Rapid—A Kenyah love story
Page 352-380

CHAPTER XXIII
NOTES ON THE OMEN ANIMALS OF SARAWAK

Archdeacon Perham on the omens of the Iban (Sea Dayaks)—List of the omen animals of the Kayans, Kenyahs, Punans, and Iban—Reputed origin of "Birding" . . . . . . *Page* 381-393

CHAPTER XXIV
THE CULT OF SKULLS IN SARAWAK

Reasons for collecting heads—Head required for going out of mourning for a chief—Kenyah legend of the origin of Head-hunting—How Kenyahs leave skulls behind when moving into a new house . . *Page* 394-400

CHAPTER XXV
PEACE-MAKING AT BARAM

Padi competition—Obstacle race—Speech-making—The Lirong *jawa*—Fracas and reconciliation—Tuba-fishing in Logan Ansok—Great boat-race—Monster public meeting—Enthusiastic speeches, and Madangs formally received into the Baram Administrative District . . . *Page* 401-415

INDEX . . . . . . *Page* 417-426

LIST OF ILLUSTRATIONS

The Scott-Keltie Falls, Mt. Dulit, Baram District, Sarawak. *Frontispiece*

PLATE			FACING PAGE
I.	A.	Ari, the Mamoose of Mer	18
	B.	Pasi, the Mamoose of Dauar	
II.	A.	Rain Shrine, Mer	34
	B.	Doiom with Bull-roarer	
III.	A.	Ulai	40
	B.	A Top-spinning Match, Mer	
IV.	A.	Removing Sand from a Copper Maori	41
	B.	A Murray Island Feast	
V.	A, B, C.	The Dance of the Malu Zogole	48
VI.	A.	The Malu Ceremony at Las	49
	B.	Ulai singing Malu songs into a Phonograph: Gasu is beating the Malu drum	
VII.	A.	The Shrine of Zabarker	54
	B.	Tomog Zogo	
VIII.	A.	The Islands of Waier and Dauar from the beach of Mer, with a Fish Shrine in the foreground	64
	B.	U Zogo, the Coconut Shrine of Dauar	
IX.	A.	Debe Wali and his Wife	72
	B.	Jimmy Rice and his Wife	
X.	A.	Iasa, Kiwai	99
	B.	Side view of the Soko-Korobe Clan-house at Iasa	
XI.	A.	Waria, Peter, Tom, and Gizu of Mabuiag	123
	B.	Neët, or Platform from which Dugong are harpooned	
XII.	A.	Man dressed up for the Death Dance	139
	B.	Divining Skulls: 1. Skull of Magau of Nagir; 2. A Murray Island Skull	
XIII.	A.	The Marine Village of Gaile	206
	B.	Bulaa	
XIV.	A.	Girls of Babaka dressed for the Annual Ceremony	218
	B.	Girls on the Dubu at Babaka for the Annual Ceremony	
XV.	A.	Hollowing out a Canoe with Stone Adzes at Keapara	220
	B.	A Bulaa girl being tattooed	
XVI.	A.	A Native of Bulaa	223
	B.	A Bulaa youth with Ringworm	
XVII.	A.	Dubu at Kamali	232
	B.	Dubu Dance at Gomoridobo	
XVIII.	A.	Udia and Daube, Taburi, Koiari	243
	B.	Elevara, Port Moresby, with the London Missionary Society's Station in the background	

LIST OF ILLUSTRATIONS

PLATE		FACING PAGE
XIX.	A. Gewe, Chief of Agi, when deprived of his Hat B. Gewe, with his Hat restored	245
XX.	A. Tree House at Gasiri B. Pottery-making at Hanuabada, Port Moresby	248
XXI.	A. A Mekeo Ibitoe B. Masked Man, Kaivakuku, of Waima, Mekeo District	256
XXII.	A. Mohu, Mekeo District B. Marea at Mohu	268
XXIII.	A. Regatta at Kuching B. View from Kaban Hill, with the Brunei Hills in the distance	280
XXIV.	A. Brunei B. A Family Bathe	290
XXV.	A. Orang Kaya Tummonggong Lawai, a Long Pata Chief in war costume, with a Kenyah shield B. A Sleeping-hut in the Jungle	300
XXVI.	A. Ascending a Rapid B. House of the Orang Bukits at Long Linai, Tutau River	306
XXVII.	A. Punans B. A Lelak man with typical Tattooing on shoulders and upper arms	320
XXVIII.	A. Side view of a Kayan House B. Verandah of a Kayan House at Long Lama, Baram River	331
XXIX.	A. Shrine outside Tama Bulan's House B. Bulan C. Saba Irang, the Head Chief of the Madangs	376
XXX.	A. Skull Trophy in a Kayan House B. Skull Trophies in Ahan Abit's House at Long Tisam, Barawan tribe	396
XXXI.	A. Beating Tuba and baling the Infusion out of a Canoe B. Penchallong prepared for the Great Peace-making	408

The photographs for Plates i.-iv. A., vi. B., vii. B., viii. B.-xi. A., xii. A., xiii.-xvi., xvii. A., xviii. A., xix.-xxii. were taken by the late A. Wilkin; those for Plates xvii. B., xxv. A., xxvii. B., xxx. A. were taken by C. G. Seligmann; Plate iv. B. by Dr. C. S. Myers; xii. B. by H. Oldland; and the Frontispiece and Plates v., vii. A., viii. A., xviii. B., xxiii., xxiv., xxv. B., xxvi., xxvii. A., xxviii., xxix., xxx. B., xxxi. by the Author. Plates vi. A. and xi. B. were drawn from photographs taken by the Author by his brother Trevor Haddon. With the exception of Plate xxx. B. none of the photographs have been retouched.

The skulls depicted on the cover are drawn from a photograph of a trophy collected by the Author at Mawatta, p. 115.

LIST OF ILLUSTRATIONS

LIST OF FIGURES IN THE TEXT

FIG.		PAGE
1.	The Hill of Gelam, Murray Island	15
2.	Murray Island from the south	16
3.	Waier and Dauar	17
4.	Model of the Bomai Mask of the Malu Ceremonies	47
5.	Pepker, the Hill-maker	65
6.	Ziai Neur Zogo, a Therapeutic Shrine	65
7.	Native drawings of some of the Nurumara (totems) of Kiwai	102
8.	Agricultural Charms of Kiwai	105
9.	Neur Madub, a Love Charm	106
10.	Shell Hoe used by the Natives of Parama	110
11.	Bamboo Beheading-knife and Head Carrier, Mawatta	115
12.	The Kwod, or Ceremonial Ground, in Pulu	139
13.	Drawing by Gizu of a Danilkau, the Buffoon of the Funeral Ceremonies	140
14.	Drawing by Gizu of Mŭri ascending a Waterspout	141
15.	Dugong Harpoon and Dart	149
16.	Marine Plants (*Cymodocea*) on which the Dugong Feeds	152
17.	Drawing by Gizu of the Method of Harpooning a Dugong	153
18.	Wooden Dugong Charm from Moa	154
19.	Drawing by Gizu of Dorgai Metakorab and Bu	167
20.	House on Piles at Saibai, with the lower portion screened with leaves	173
21.	Restoration of the Kwod in Tut during the Initiation Period	177
22.	Restoration of the Kwod in Yam	179
23.	Rock Pictographs in Kiriri	185
24.	Umbalako (Bull-roarers) of the Yaraikanna Tribe, Cape York	191
25.	Irupi Dance, Babaka	217
26.	Palm-leaf Toys, Bulaa	226
27.	Tattooing in the Mekeo District	260
28.	Afu, or Taboo Signal, Inawi	271
29.	Boys at Veifaa dressed up as Fulaari	275
30.	Kayan Tattoo Designs	306
31.	Berantu Ceremony of the Orang Bukit	307
32.	Butiong in a Lelak House	333
33.	Sarcophagus of a Boy in a Barawan House	334
34.	Praying to a Pig in a Barawan House	336
35.	Mount Dulit from Long Asiah Kechil	347
36.	Long Sulan	361
37.	Kedaman and Kelebong at Long Sulan	362
38.	Stone Implements from the Baram District, Sarawak	369
39.	Magical Stone Hook	371
40.	Figure-heads of Canoes, Baram District	407

All the above illustrations except Figs. 13, 14, 17, and 19 were drawn by the Author.

LIST OF MAPS

	PAGE
Map of Torres Straits	13
Sketch Map of British New Guinea	195
Map of the Central District, British New Guinea	237
Map of the Mekeo District, British New Guinea	263
Sketch Map of the Baram District, Sarawak	295
Geological Sketch Map of Borneo	313

HEAD-HUNTERS

BLACK, WHITE, AND BROWN

CHAPTER I

THURSDAY ISLAND TO MURRAY ISLAND

WE arrived at Torres Straits early in the morning of April 22nd, 1898, and dropped anchor off Friday Island, as the steamers of the Ducal Line are not allowed now to tie up at the hulk at Thursday Island. Shortly afterwards we were met by the Hon. John Douglas, the Resident Magistrate, and Dr. Salter, both of whom were old friends who had shown me much kindness during my previous expedition. They were accompanied by Seligmann, who had left London some months previously in order to visit Australia, and as a handsel had already done a little work on a hitherto unknown tribe of North Queensland natives.

The township of Thursday Island, or Port Kennedy, as it is officially termed, had increased considerably during the past decade. This was partly due to the natural growth of the frontier town of North Queensland, and partly to the fact that it has become a fortified port which commands the only safe passage for large vessels through these dangerous straits. So assiduous have been the coral polyps in defending the northern-most point of Australia, that although the straits measure some eighty miles between Cape York and the nearest coast of New Guinea, what with islands and the very extensive series of intricate coral reefs, there is only one straightforward passage for vessels of any size, and that is not more than a quarter of a mile wide.

Although the town has increased in size its character has not altered to any considerable extent. It is still the same assemblage of corrugated iron and wooden buildings which garishly broil under a tropical sun, unrelieved by that vegetation which renders beautiful so many tropical towns. It is true a little planting has been done, but the character of the soil, or perhaps the absence of sufficient water, render those efforts melancholy rather than successful.

Many of the old desert lots are now occupied by stores and lodging-houses. The characteristic mountains of eviscerated tins, kerosine cases, and innumerable empty bottles which betoken a thirsty land, have been removed and cast into the sea. Thriving two- or three-storied hotels proclaim increase in trade and comparative luxury.

There is the same medley of nationalities—British, Colonial, French, German, Scandinavian, Greek, and other European job lots, in addition to an assortment from Asia and her islands. As formerly, the Pacific islands are well represented, and a few Torres Straits islanders are occasionally to be seen. Some of the latter are resident as policemen, others visit the island to sell pearl-shell, bêche-de-mer, and sometimes a little garden produce, and to purchase what they need from the stores.

One great change in the population is very striking, and that is the great preponderance of the Japanese. So far as I remember they were few in number ten years previously, and were, I believe, outnumbered by the Manila men; now they form the bulk of the population, much to the disgust of most of the Europeans and Colonials. Various reasons are assigned for this jealousy of the Japanese, and different grounds are taken for asserting that the influx should be checked, and restrictions enforced on those who have already settled.

It appeared to me that the bed-rock of discontent was in the fact that the Japanese beat the white men at their own game, mainly because they live at a lower rate than do the white men. A good proportion of the pearl-shelling industry is now carried on by the Japanese, who further play into each other's hands as far as possible. A good example of their enterprise is shown by the fact that they have now cut out the white boat-builders. A few years ago, I was informed, some Japanese took to boat-building and built their first boats from printed directions in some English manual. Their first craft were rather clumsy, but they discovered their mistakes, and now they turn out very satisfactory sailing boats. It is impossible not to feel respect for men who combine brains with diligence, and who command success by frugality and combination.

The white men grumble that the Japanese spend so little in the colony and send their money away; but the very same white men admit they would themselves clear out as soon as they had made their pile. Their intentions are the same as are the performances of the Japanese; but the white men cannot, under the present conditions, make a fortune quickly, and certain of them cannot keep what they do make. There are white men acting as divers for coloured men's pay who some years ago owned boats of their own. The fall in value of pearl-shell a few years since is scarcely the sole reason for this change of fortune; bad management and drink have a good deal to answer for.

Some white men contend that as this is a British colony, and has been developed by British capital and industry, the Japanese should not be allowed to reap the benefit; but a similar argument might be applied to many of the industrial enterprises of the British in various parts of the world. As an outsider, it appears to me that it is some of those very qualities that have made the British colonist what he is that manifest themselves in the Japanese. In other words, the Japanese are feared because they are so British in many ways, saving perhaps the British expensive mode of life. It is probably largely this latter factor that renders the Japanese such deadly competitors.

Formerly there were in Torres Straits regular bêche-de-mer and copra industries, now there is very little of the former, and none of the latter. Large, slimy, leathery sea-slugs gorge the soft mud on the coral reefs; these when boiled and smoke-dried shrivel into hard rough rolls, which are exported in large numbers to China. These bêche-de-mer, or, as the Malays call them, "tripang," are scientifically known as Holothuria, and are related to sea-urchins and starfish. Copra is the dried kernel of the coconut.

When one walks about the township and sees the amount of capital invested, and when one considers what is spent and how much money is sent away, it is hard to realise that all this wealth comes out of pearl-shell and pearls. During the past thirty years very many thousands of pounds have been made out of pearl-shell in Torres Straits; but now the waters have been overfished, and unless measures are taken to protect the pearl oysters, the harvest will become yet scantier and scantier. In any case the time for big hauls and rapid fortunes is probably over.

About the year 1890 gold was found in some of the islands, but I believe that the working only pays in one island, though it may be resumed at Horn Island, which at one time promised to be a lucrative goldfield.

At Thursday Island we met with much helpful kindness. Mr. Douglas entertained a couple of us, and did all he could to expedite matters. Unfortunately he was then without a steamer, and so could not tranship us and our gear to Murray Island, which otherwise he would have gladly done. It took a week to overhaul our baggage, get in stores, and to arrange about transport, and eventually I arranged with Neil Andersen to take us across; but even then there was neither room for all our baggage nor accommodation for the whole of our party. Rivers, Ray, and Seligmann and myself went on in the *Freya*, leaving the others to follow in the *Governor Cairns*, an official schooner that was shortly to start for Darnley Island.

It was not till the late afternoon of Saturday, April 30th, that we actually started, and then we were only able to beat up the passage between Thursday Island and Hammond Island, and anchored about six o'clock in the lee of Tuesday Island. There are very strong tides between these islands, and I have seen even a large ocean steamer steaming full speed against a tide race, and only just able to hold her own, much less make way against it.

The *Freya* was a ketch, a kind of fore-and-aft schooner, 47 feet 6 inches long and 11 feet 2 inches in the beam, and could carry about twenty tons of cargo. We had a strange medley of races on board—European skipper and passengers, our Javanese "boy," the Japanese diver, two Polynesian sailors from Rotumah, and three Papuans from Parama, near the mouth of the Fly River. Our captain was a fine, big man, probably a good type of the Dubhgaill, or "black (dark) strangers," who a thousand years ago ravaged the southern and eastern coast of Ireland as far north as Dublin. We "turned in" early—this consisted in wrapping oneself up in a blanket, extemporising a pillow, and lying on the deck.

Left Tuesday Island at 4 a.m. in a stiff breeze and chopping sea, and so could only make Dungeness Island by 4 p.m. Twelve hours to go fifty-five miles! We landed at the mangrove swamp, but there was little of interest. We hoped to have reached Darnley Island next day, but only fetched Rennel Island by 5.30 p.m. This is a large vegetated sandbank, on which we found traces of occupation, mainly where the natives had camped when bêche-de-mer fishing. We all suffered a good deal from sunburnt feet, the scorching by the sun being aggravated by the salt water. Some of our party were still seasick; one lay on the deck as limp as damp blotting-paper, and let the seas break over him without stirring even a finger. We had a wet night of it, what with the rain from above and the sea-water swishing in at the open stern and flooding the sleepers on the deck.

We made an early start next morning and reached Erub, or Darnley Island, at three in the afternoon. Immediately on landing I went to Massacre Bay to photograph the stratified volcanic ash that occurs only at this spot in the island, and which is the sole visible remains of the crater of an old volcano. The rest of the island is composed of basalt, which rises to a height of over 500 feet, and is well wooded and fertile—indeed, it is perhaps the most beautiful island in Torres Straits. Save for rocky headlands which separate lovely little coves fringed with white coral sand, the whole coast is skirted with groves of coconut palms and occasional patches of mangroves. The almost impenetrable jungle clothes the hills, except at those spots that have been cleared for "gardens." Even the tops of the hills are covered with trees.

Very shortly after landing, a fine, honest-faced Murray Island native, Alo by name, who was visiting Erub, came up and greeted me very warmly. I regret to say I had quite forgotten him, but he perfectly remembered me, and he beamed with pleasure at seeing me. We walked along the coast to the village where the chief lives, and saw Captain H——, and I made arrangements with Koko Lifu, a South Sea man, to lighter our goods off the *Governor Cairns* and to take the cargo and our three comrades to Murray Island.

Captain H—— is one of those remarkable men one so constantly meets in out-of-the-way places. It is the common man one comes across at home. On the confines of savagery and civilisation one meets the men who have dared and suffered, rugged like broken quartz, and maybe as hard too, but withal streaked with gold—ay, and good gold too. Captain H—— started in life as a middy in the Navy; owing to a tiff with his people he quitted the Service and entered the Merchant Service. He advanced quickly, and when still very young obtained a command. He has made two fortunes, and lost both owing to bank failures, and is at present a ruined old recluse, living on a remote island along with Papuans, Polynesians, and other races that now inhabit Erub. He is a kind of Government Agent, and patrols the deep-water fishing grounds. I have previously mentioned that the ordinary fishing grounds for pearl-shell are practically exhausted, and the shellers have to go further afield or have to dive in deeper water in order to get large shells. Near Darnley Island are some good fishing grounds, but the water is so deep as to render the fishing dangerous to life, and the Queensland Government has prohibited fishing in these waters. There are, however, always a number of men who are willing to run the risk for the sake of increased gain, and it is all they can do to dodge the vigilance of the wary old sea-dog.

Captain H—— lives entirely by himself, and has no intercourse with the natives beyond what is absolutely necessary. He puts in his spare time in attending to his gardens and reading. Amongst other accomplishments he is a fluent speaker of French and Italian, and it was a strange experience to meet a weather-worn old man in frontier dishabille acting and speaking like a refined gentleman.

As on previous nights, except the first, Andersen made a tent for us on board the *Freya* out of the mainsail, the boom forming the ridge-pole. Ontong, the cook I had engaged at Thursday Island, woke us up at 2.30 a.m. to tell us tea was ready, and it was too! The pungent smell of the smoke prevented me from going to sleep for some time. In the morning Ontong said he thought it was "close up daylight"; and with an energy which is not usually credited to the Oriental character, he had made tea so as to be prepared for an early start.

We started early next morning with Alo as pilot; for the coral reefs between Darnley and Murray are extensive, intricate, and mainly uncharted. Andersen started for the "big passage" that large boats always take; but after some time it was discovered that Alo did not know this passage, but another one to the south-west of Darnley. As half the tide had by this time turned and the weather was very squally and the reefs could not be seen with certainty, we returned to our old anchorage by 9.30, and so another day was lost. We spent a lazy day to give our sore legs a rest. Alo left us in the evening, as he said he was "sick." The truth was he did not care about the job, so Andersen went ashore and brought another pilot, named Spear. His father was a native of Parama; his mother was an Erub woman. Spear told us he had first married a Murray Island girl, and then half a dozen New Guinea women; but Dr. Macfarlane, the pioneer missionary in these parts, had made him "chuck" the latter.

Next day we started betimes, and sailed down channels in the reefs not marked in the charts. The day was dull, and the little wind was southerly when we wanted it easterly, whereas the previous day the reverse was the case. Later it became squally with rain, and finding it hopeless to reach Murray Island, Spear piloted us to a sheltered spot in the lee of a reef and close to a sandbank. We were only about four miles from our destination, and we could hear the roaring of the breakers of the Pacific Ocean as they dashed themselves against the Great Barrier Reef ten miles distant.

We had a very disturbed night. About eight o'clock, whilst we were yarning, the skipper jumped up and said the anchor was dragging. Then ensued a scene of intense excitement, as we were close not only to the sandbank, but also to a jagged coral reef. It was horrid to feel the boat helplessly drifting, for not only were the sails down, but the mainsail was unlashed below to make our tent, and further, it was tied down in various places. The first thing to do was to haul up the anchor, and furl the jib and mainsail, and unship the tent. We all lent a hand to the best of our ability, and soon we were sailing down the narrow passage. Andersen's voice was hoarse and trembling with excitement, but he kept perfectly cool, and he never lost his temper, though in the confusion and babel of tongues some lost their heads through fright and did not do the right thing at the right moment, and each of the crew was ordering the others about in his own language.

After sailing about a little we made another attempt to anchor, and again the anchor dragged and we had another little cruise. Again we tried and again we failed, and it may be imagined that our sensations were not of a very cheerful nature, as we were in a really grave predicament; sometimes we actually sailed over the reef, and might any moment have knocked a hole in the ship's bottom or have become stranded. If he could not effect an anchorage, two courses were open to Andersen. One was to cruise about all night, and it was very dark, keeping the reef in sight, or rather sailing up and down the passage, for if he had sailed out into the open he would probably strike a reef or coral patch that was unnoticed. The second alternative was to run the boat on to the sandbank and let it float off at high water in the morning. The reason why we drifted was because the anchor was let down on a steep gravelly slope, and the movement of the boat, which was naturally away from the bank, prevented the flukes from getting a firm grip.

On the fourth essay the anchor was put on the sandbank in a depth of three fathoms while we swung in fourteen or fifteen fathoms. After waiting some time in anxiety, we found to our relief that the anchor held, and we wrapped ourselves up in our blankets and slept on deck, pretty well exhausted. We had such confidence in the skill and alertness of Andersen, whom we knew to be a pre-eminently safe man, that we soon composed ourselves and slept soundly.

Friday, May 6th.—Again the wind was against us and the weather was squally, and it was not till one o'clock that we dropped anchor off the Mission premises at Murray Island.

I have briefly described our tedious trip to Murray Island, not because there was anything at all unusual in it, but merely to give some idea of the difficulty and uncertainty in sailing in these waters. There is no need, therefore, for surprise at the isolation of Murray Island, a fact which had influenced me in deciding to make it the scene of our more detailed investigations.

On landing we were welcomed by Mr. John Bruce, the schoolmaster and magistrate. He is the only white man now resident on the island, and he plays a paternal part in the social life of the people. I was very affectionately greeted by Ari the Mamoose, or chief of the island, and by my old friend Pasi, the chief of the neighbouring island of Dauar, and we walked up and down the sand beach talking of old times, concerning which I found Pasi's memory was far better than mine.

I found that one of the two Mission residences on the side of the hill that were there ten years before was still standing and was empty, so I decided to occupy that, although it was rather dilapidated; and it answered our purpose admirably. The rest of the day and all the next was busily spent in landing our stuff and in unpacking and putting things to rights. We slept the first night at Bruce's house, which is on the strand. When I went up next morning to our temporary home I found that the Samoan teacher Finau and his amiable wife had caused the house to be swept, more or less, and had put down mats, and placed two brightly coloured tablecloths on the table, which was further decorated with two vases of flowers! It seemed quite homely, and was a delicate attention that we much appreciated.

I engaged two natives, Jimmy Rice and Debe Wali, to get wood and water for us and to help Ontong. We had various vicissitudes with these two "boys," but we retained them all through our stay, and they afforded us much amusement, no little instruction, and a very fair amount of moral discipline. The legs of two of our party were still so sore that they had to be carried up the hill, and on Saturday night we were established in our own quarters, and eager to commence the work for which we had come so far.

We had a deal of straightening up to do on Sunday morning, but I found time to go half-way down the hill to the schoolhouse, and was again impressed, as on my former visit, with the heartiness of the singing, which was almost deafening. The congregation waited for me to go out first, and I stood at the door and shook hands with nearly all the natives of the island as they came down the steps, and many were the old friends I greeted. I invited them to come up and see some photographs after the afternoon service.

We made the place as tidy as possible, and we had a great reception in the afternoon. Nearly all my old friends that were still alive turned up, besides many others. To their intense and hilarious delight I showed them some of the photographs I had taken during my last visit, not only of themselves, but also of other islands in the Straits. We had an immense time. The yells of delight, the laughter, clicking, flicking of the teeth, beaming faces and other expressions of joy as they beheld photographs of themselves or of friends would suddenly change to tears and wailing when they saw the portrait of someone since deceased. It was a steamy and smelly performance, but it was very jolly to be again among my old friends, and equally gratifying to find them ready to take up our friendship where we had left it.

Next morning when we were yarning with some natives others solemnly came one by one up the hill with bunches of bananas and coconuts, and soon there was a great heap of garden produce on the floor. By this time the verandah was filled with natives, men and women, and I again showed the photographs, but not a word was said about the fruit. They looked at the photographs over and over again, and the men added to the noise made by the women. On this occasion there was more crying, which, however, was enlivened with much hilarity. Then the Mamoose told Pasi to inform me in English, for the old man has a very imperfect command even of the jargon English that is spoken 'out here, that the stack of bananas and coconuts was a present to me. I made a little speech in reply, and they slowly dispersed.

On Tuesday evening McDougall, Myers, and Wilkin arrived, and our party was complete.

CHAPTER II

THE MURRAY ISLANDS

TORRES STRAITS were discovered and passed through in August, 1606, by Luis Vaez de Torres. They were first partially surveyed by Captain Cook in 1770, and more thoroughly during the years 1843-5 by Captain Blackwood of H.M.S. *Fly*, and in 1848-9 by Captain Owen Stanley of H.M.S. *Rattlesnake*. H.M. cutter *Bramble* was associated with both these ships in the survey. But in the meantime other vessels had passed through: of these the most famous were the French vessels the *Astrolabe* and *Zélée*, which in the course of the memorable voyage of discovery under M. Dumont d'Urville were temporarily stranded in the narrow passage of the Island of Tut in 1840.

Bampton and Alt, the adventurous traders and explorers of the Papuan Gulf, came in the last years of the eighteenth century, and since then there have not been wanting equally daring men who, unknown to fame, have sailed these dangerous waters in search of a livelihood.

Mr. John Jardine was sent from Brisbane in 1862 to form a settlement at Somerset, in Albany Pass; but the place did not grow, and in 1877 the islands of Torres Straits were annexed to Queensland, and the settlement was transferred from the mainland to Thursday Island.

The islands of Torres Straits, geographically speaking, fall into three groups, the lines of longitude 140° 48′ E. and 143° 29′ E. conveniently demarcating these subdivisions.

The western group contains all the largest islands, and these, as well as many scattered islets, are composed of ancient igneous rocks, such as eurites, granites, quartz andesites, and rhyolitic tuff. These islands are, in fact, the submerged northern extremity of the great Australian cordillera that extends from

Tasmania along the eastern margin of Australia, the northernmost point of which is the hill of Mabudauan, on the coast of New Guinea, near Saibai. This low granitic hill may be regarded as one of the Torres Straits islands that has been annexed to New Guinea by the seaward extension of the alluvial deposits brought down by the Fly River. Coral islets also occur among these rocky islands.

The shallow sea between Cape York peninsula and New Guinea is choked with innumerable coral reefs. By wind and wave action sandy islets have been built up on some of these reefs, and the coral sand has been enriched by enormous quantities of floating pumice. Wind-wafted or water-borne seeds have germinated and clothed the sandbanks with vegetation. Owing to the length of the south-east monsoon, the islands have a tendency to extend in a south-easterly direction, and consequently the north-west end of an island is the oldest, hence one sometimes finds that in the smaller islands a greater vegetable growth, or the oldest and largest trees, is at that end of an island; but in time the vegetation extends uniformly over the whole surface. The islands of the central division are entirely vegetated sandbanks.

The eastern division of Torres Straits includes the islands of Masaramker (Bramble Cay), Zapker (Campbell I.), Uga (Stephen's I.), Edugor (Nepean I.), Erub (Darnley I.), and the Murray Islands (Mer, Dauar, and Waier), besides several sandbanks, or "cays."

All the above-named islands are of volcanic origin. The first five consist entirely of lava with the exception of two patches of volcanic ash at Massacre Bay, in Erub, to which I have already referred. Mer, the largest of the Murray Islands, is composed of lava and ash in about equal proportions, while Dauar and Waier consist entirely of the latter rock. It is interesting to note that where the Great Barrier Reef ends there we find this great outburst of volcanic activity. It was evidently an area of weakness in one corner of the continental plateau of Australia. In pre-Carboniferous times the tuffs were ejected and the lava welled forth that have since been metamorphosed into the rocks of the Western Islands; but the basaltic lavas of the Eastern Islands belong to a recent series of earth movements, possibly of Pliocene age.

Strictly speaking, to the three islands of Mer, Dauar, and

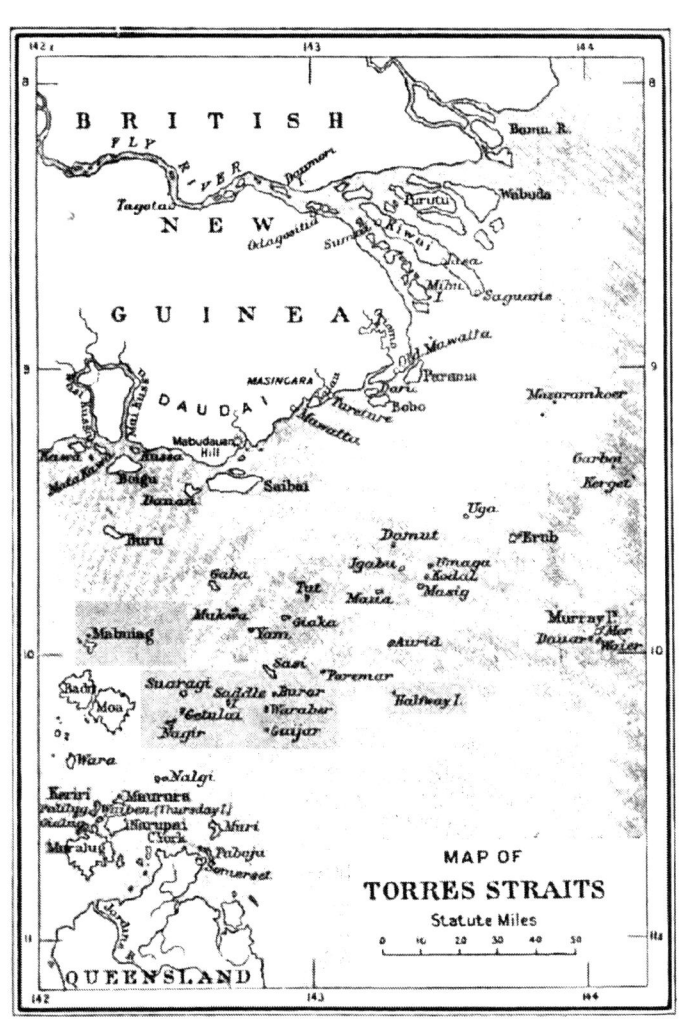

Waier should the name of Murray Islands, or Murray's Islands, be confined; but in Torres Straits the name of Murray Island has become so firmly established for the largest of them that, contrary to my usual custom, I propose to adopt the popular rather than the native name.

Mer, or Murray Island, is only about five miles in circumference, and is roughly oval in outline with its long axis running roughly north-east to south-west. The southerly half consists of an extinct crater, or caldera, which is breached to the north-east by the lava stream that forms the remainder of the high part of the island. This portion is very fertile, and supports a luxuriant vegetation, which, when left to itself, forms an almost impenetrable jungle; it is here that the natives have the bulk of their gardens, and every portion of it is or has been under cultivation. The great crescentic caldera valley, being formed of porous volcanic ash and being somewhat arid, is by no means so fertile; the vegetation, which consists of grass, low scrub, and

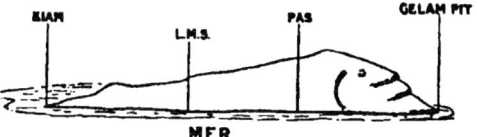

FIG. 1. THE HILL OF GELAM, MURRAY ISLAND

scattered coconut palms, presents a marked contrast to that of the rest of the island. The slopes of the hills are usually simply grass-covered.

The most prominent feature of Mer is the long steep hill of Gelam, which culminates in a peak, 750 feet in height. It extends along the western side of the island, and at its northern end terminates in a low hill named Zomar, which splays out into two spurs, the outer of which is called Upimager and the inner Měkernurnur. Gelam rises up from a narrow belt of cultivated soil behind the sand beach at an angle of 30 degrees, forming a regular even slope, covered with grass save for occasional patches of bare rock and low shrubs. At the southern end the ground is much broken. The termination of the smooth portion is marked by a conspicuous curved escarpment; beyond this is a prominent block of rock about half-way up the hill. This is known as the "eye." The whole hill seen from some distance at sea bears a strong resemblance to an animal, and the natives speak of it as having once been a dugong, the history of which is enshrined in the legend of Gelam, a youth who is fabled to have come from Moa. The terminal hill and the north end of Gelam represents the lobed tail of the dugong, the curved escarpment corresponds to the front edge of its paddle, while the "eye" and the broken ground which indicates the nose and mouth complete the head.

The highest part of Gelam on its landward side forms bold, riven precipices of about fifty feet in height. A small gorge (Werbadupat) at the extreme south end of the island drains the great valley; beyond it rises the small, symmetrical hill Dĕbĕ-mad, which passes into the short crest of Mergar. The latter

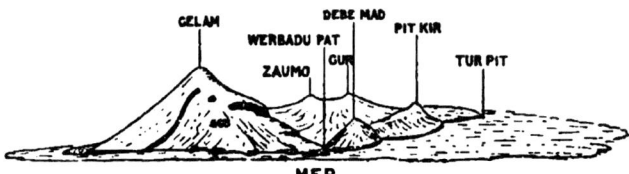

FIG. 2. MURRAY ISLAND FROM THE SOUTH, WITH ITS FRINGING REEF

corresponds to Gelam on the opposite side of the island; it terminates in the steep hill Pitkir.

Gelam and Mergar form a somewhat horseshoe-shaped range, the continuity of which is interrupted at its greatest bend, and it is here the ground is most broken up. The rock is a beautifully stratified volcanic ash, with an outward dip of 30 degrees. Within this crater is a smaller horseshoe-shaped hill, which is the remains of the central cone of the old volcano. The eastern limit of the degraded cone is named Gur; the western, which is known as Zaumo, is prolonged into a spur called Ai. In the valley (Deaudupat) between these hills and Gelam arises a stream which flows in a northerly and north-easterly direction, and after receiving two other affluents empties itself into the sea at Korog. It should be remembered that the beds of all the streams are dry for a greater portion of the year, and it is only during the rainy season—*i.e.* from November to March, inclusive—and then only immediately after the rain, that the term "stream" can be applicable to them. There are, however, some water-holes in the bed of the stream which hold water for many months.

The great lava stream extends with an undulating surface from the central cone to the northern end of the island. It forms a fertile tableland, which is bounded by a steep slope. On its west side this slope is practically a continuation of the sides (Zaumo and Ai) of the central cone, and bounds the eastern side of the miniature delta valley of the Deaudupat stream. At the northern and eastern sides of the island the lava stream forms an abrupt or steep declivity, extending either right down to the water's edge or occasionally leaving a narrow shore.

A fringing coral reef extends all round Mer, but has its greatest width along the easterly side of the island, where it forms an extensive shallow shelf which dries, or very nearly so, at spring tides, and constitutes an admirable fishing ground for the natives.

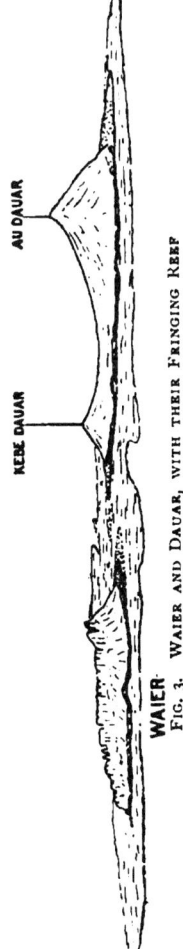

FIG. 3. WAIER AND DAUAR, WITH THEIR FRINGING REEF

A mile and a quarter to the south of Mer are the islands of Dauar and Waier. The former consists of two hills — Au Dauar, 605 feet in height, and Kebe Dauar, of less than half that height. Au Dauar is a steep, grassy hill like Gelam, but the saddle-shaped depression between the two hills supports a luxuriant vegetation. There is a sand-spit at each end.

Waier is a remarkable little island, as it practically consists solely of a pinnacled and fissured crescentic wall of coarse volcanic ash about 300 feet in height. There is a small sand-spit on the side facing Dauar, and a sand beach along the concavity of the island. At these spots and in many of the gullies there is some vegetation, otherwise the island presents a barren though very picturesque appearance.

c

Dauar and Waier are surrounded by a continuous reef, which extends for a considerable distance towards the south-east, far beyond the region that was occupied by the other side of the crater of Waier. We must regard Dauar and Waier as the remnants of two craters, the south-easterly side of both of which having been blown out by a volcanic outburst, but in neither case is there any trace of a lava stream.

The climate, though hot, is not very trying, owing to the persistence of a strong south-east tide wind for at least seven months in the year—that is, from April to October. This is the dry season, but rain often falls during its earlier half. Sometimes there is a drought in the island, and the crops fail and a famine ensues. During the dry season the temperature ranges between 72° and 87° F. in the shade, but in the dead calm of the north-west monsoon a much greater temperature is reached, and the damp, muggy heat becomes at such times very depressing.

The reading of the barograph shows that there is a wonderful uniformity of atmospheric pressure. Every day there is a remarkable double rise and fall of one degree; the greatest rise occurs between eight and ten o'clock, morning and evening, while the deepest depression is similarly between two and four o'clock. In June, that is in the middle of a dry season, the barograph records a pressure varying between 31 and 33, which gradually decreases to 28 to 30 in December, again to rise gradually to the midsummer maximum. These data are obtained from inspection of the records made on the island by Mr. John Bruce on the barograph we left with him for this purpose.

Like the other natives of Torres Straits, the Murray Islanders belong to the Melanesian race, the dark-skinned people of the West Pacific who are characterised by their black frizzly or woolly hair. They are a decidedly narrow-headed people. The colour of the skin is dark chocolate, often burning to almost black in the exposed portions. The accompanying illustrations give a far better impression of the appearance and expression of the people than can be conveyed by any verbal description. Suffice it to say, the features are somewhat coarse, but by no means bestial; there is usually an alert look about the men, some of whom show decided strength of character in the face. The old men have usually quite a venerable appearance.

Their mental and moral character will be incidentally illus-

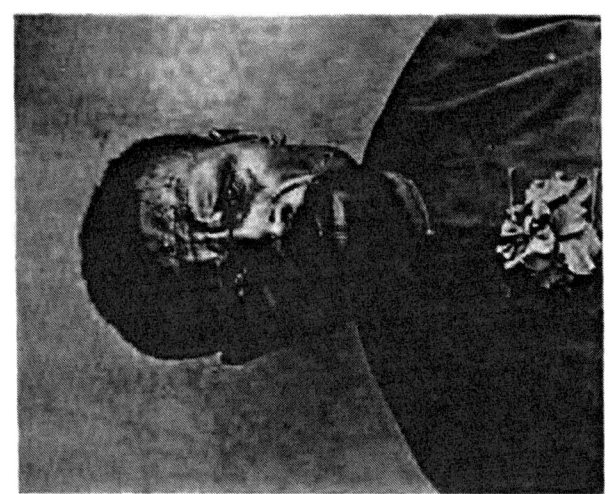

PASI, THE MAMOOSE OF DAUAR

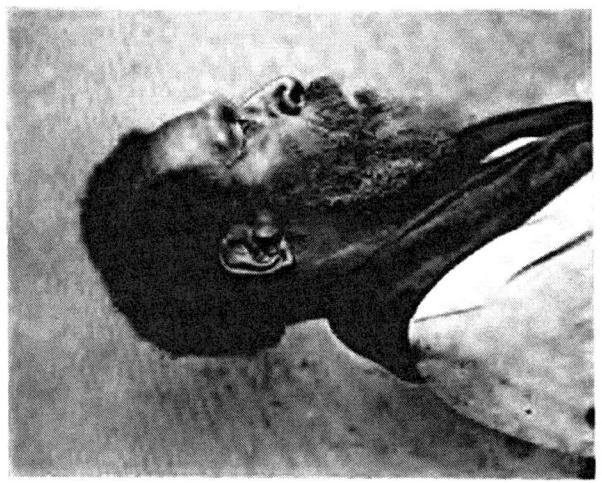

ARI, THE MAMOOSE OF NER

trated in the following pages, and considering the isolation and favourable conditions of existence with the consequent lack of example and stimulus to exertion, we must admit that they have proved themselves to be very creditable specimens of savage humanity.

The Murray Islanders have often been accused of being lazy, and during my former visit I came across several examples of laziness and ingratitude to the white missionaries. As to the first count, well, there is some truth in it from one point of view. The natives certainly do not like to be made to work. One can always get them to work pretty hard in spurts, but continuous labour is very irksome to them; but after all, this is pretty much the same with everybody. Nature deals so bountifully with the people that circumstances have not forced them into the discipline of work.

The people are not avaricious. They have no need for much money; their wants are few and easily supplied. Surely they are to be commended for not wearing out their lives to obtain what is really of no use to them. The truth is, we call them lazy because they won't work for the white man more than they care to. Why should they?

As to ingratitude. They take all they can get and, it is true, rarely appear as grateful as the white man expects; but this is by no means confined to these people. How often do we find exactly the same trait amongst our own acquaintances! They may feel grateful, but they have not the habit of expressing it. On the other hand, it is not beyond the savage mind for the argument thus to present itself. I did not ask the white man to come here. I don't particularly want him. I certainly don't want him to interfere with my customs. He comes here to please himself. If he gives me medicines and presents that is his look-out, that is his fashion. I will take all I can get. I will give as little as I can. If he goes away I don't care.

Less than thirty years ago in Torres Straits might was right, and wrongs could only be redressed by superior physical force, unless the magic of the sorcery man was enlisted. For the last fifteen years the Queensland Government has caused a court-house to be erected in every island that contains a fair number of inhabitants, and the chief has the status of magistrate, and policemen, usually four in number, watch over the public morality.

The policemen are civil servants, enjoying the following

annual emoluments—a suit of clothes, one pound sterling in cash, and one pound of tobacco. In addition, they have the honour and glory of their position; they row out in their uniforms in the Government whale-boat to meet the Resident Magistrate on his visits of inspection to the various islands, and they go to church on Sundays dressed in their newest clothes. There are doubtless other amenities which do not appear on the surface.

The Mamoose, or chief, being a great man, "all along same Queen Victoria," as they proudly claim and honestly imagine, is not supposed to receive payment. I well remember the complex emotion shown on my former visit by the Mamoose of Murray Island, who was torn by conflicting desires. Whether to share the golden reward with his subordinates, or to forego the coin on account of his being a great man, was more than he could determine; it was clear that he preferred the lower alternative—for what worth is honour if another man gets the money? I suspected he almost felt inclined to abdicate his sovereignty on the spot for the sake of one pound sterling; but the Hon. John Douglas, who was then on his tour of inspection, kept him up to the dignity of his position, and pointed out that great men in his position could not take money like policemen. Possibly the poor man thought that reigning sovereigns ruled simply for the honour and glory of it, and had no emoluments. Mr. Douglas' intention was solely to support the dignity of Ari's office, for, to do him justice, when old Ari visited the Government steamer on the following morning a little matter was privately transacted in the cabin which had the effect of making Ari beamingly happy.

But there are recognised perquisites for the Mamoose in the shape of free labour by the prisoners. It would seem as if such a course was not conducive to impartial justice, for it would clearly be to the judge's interest to commit every prisoner; this temptation is, however, checked by the fact that all trials are public, and popular opinion can make itself directly felt.

Most of the cases are for petty theft or disputes about land. It is painful to have to confess that during our recent stay in Murray Island many of the cases were for wife-beating or for wife-slanging. The Mamoose is supplied with a short list of the offences with which he is empowered to deal and the penalties he may inflict. The technical error is usually made of confusing moral and legal crimes. I gathered that very fair justice is meted out in the native courts when left to themselves.

The usual punishment is a "moon" of enforced labour on any public work that is in operation at the time, such as making a road or jetty, or on work for the chief, such as making a pigsty or erecting fences. The alternative fine used to be husking coconuts and making copra; the natives in some cases had to supply their own coconuts for this purpose—the number varied from 100 to 1,000, according to the offence. This was chiefly the punishment of the women, the copra was one of the Mamoose's perquisites. Fines are now paid in money.

At night-time the prisoners are supposed to sleep in jail—an ordinary native house set apart for this purpose—but at the present time in Murray Island, owing to the absence of a jail, they sleep at home! and during the whole of the time they are under the surveillance of one or more policemen. Very often it appeared to me that a policeman's chief duty consisted in watching a prisoner doing nothing. Very bad, or often repeated, offenders are taken to Thursday Island to be tried by the Resident Magistrate.

CHAPTER III

WORK AND PLAY IN MURRAY ISLAND

THE first thing we did after arranging the house was to convert a little room into a dispensary, and very soon numbers of natives came to get medicine and advice. McDougall, Myers, and Seligmann worked hard at this, partly because they were really interested in the various cases, and partly since it brought natives to the house who could be utilised for our other investigations.

The doctors also paid visits to bad cases in their homes. As the former white missionaries on the island in days gone by had been accustomed to dispense, to the best of their ability, from their somewhat large assortment of drugs, the natives took it for granted that we should do the same; hence there were no special signs of gratitude on their part. Bruce, too, does what he can for the natives, but his remedies are naturally of a simple, though often drastic, character.

The medical skill and gratuitous advice and drugs of our doctors did a great deal to facilitate the work of the expedition. Towards the end of our time, hearing Captain H—— of Darnley Island was seriously ill, McDougall volunteered to go over and nurse him, and he remained there for a week or two.

It was a great safeguard for us, too, having so many doctors about; but fortunately we only required their aid, or they each other's, for malarial fever or for minor ailments like sores. Only on three occasions during the time we were away, till we left Borneo, were there sufficiently bad cases of fever to cause the least anxiety. So, on the whole, we came off remarkably well on the score of health.

Although we have a fair amount of information about the external appearance, the shape of the head, and such-like data of most of the races of mankind, very little indeed is known about the keenness of their senses and those other matters that constitute the subject commonly known as experimental psychology. My colleagues were the first thoroughly to investigate primitive people in their own country, and it was the first time that a well-equipped psychological laboratory had been established among a people scarcely a generation removed from perfect savagery.

Dr. Rivers undertook the organisation of this department, and there were great searchings of heart as to what apparatus to take out and which to leave behind. There was no previous experience to go upon, and there was the fear of delicate apparatus failing at the critical time, or that the natives would not be amenable to all that might be required of them. Fortunately the latter fear was groundless. It was only in the most tedious operations, or in those in which they were palpably below the average, that the natives exhibited a strong disinclination to be experimented upon. Sometimes they required a little careful handling—always patience and tact were necessary, but taking them as a whole, it would be difficult to find a set of people upon whom more reliable and satisfactory observations could be made. I refer more particularly to the Torres Straits islanders.

In his work in Murray Island, Rivers was assisted by Myers and McDougall. During his trips to New Guinea, Seligmann made some supplemental observations of interest. The subjects investigated included visual acuity, sensitiveness to light, colour vision, including colour blindness, binocular vision, and visual space perception; acuity and range of hearing; appreciation of differences of tone and rhythm; tactile acuity and localisation; sensibility to pain; estimation of weight, smell, and taste; simple reaction times to auditory and visual stimuli, and choice reaction times; estimation of intervals of time; memory; strength of grasp and accuracy of aim; reading, writing, and drawing; the influence of various mental states on blood-pressure, and the influence of fatigue and practice on mental work.

The visual acuity of these people was found to be superior to that of normal Europeans, though not in any very marked degree. The visual powers of savages, which have excited the admiration of travellers, may be held to depend upon the faculty of observation. Starting with somewhat superior acuteness of vision, by long attention to minute details coupled with familiarity with their surroundings, they become able to recognise things in a manner that at first sight seems quite wonderful.

The commonest defect of eyesight among Europeans is myopia, or short-sightedness, but this was found to be almost completely absent amongst savages. The opposite condition, hypermetropia, which is apparently the normal condition of the European child, was very common among them.

The colour vision of the natives was investigated in several ways. A hundred and fifty natives of Torres Straits and Kiwai were tested by means of the usual wool test for colour-blindness without finding one case. The names used for colours by the natives of Murray Island, Mabuiag, and Kiwai were very fully investigated, and the derivation of such names in most cases established. The colour vocabularies of these islands showed the special feature which appears to characterise many primitive languages. There were definite names for red, less definite for yellow, and still less so for green, while a definite name for blue was either absent or borrowed from English.

The three languages mentioned, and some Australian languages investigated by Rivers, seemed to show different stages in the evolution of a colour vocabulary. Several North Queensland natives (from Seven Rivers and the Fitzroy River) appeared to be almost limited to words for red, white, and black; perhaps it would be better to call the latter light and dark. In all the islands there was a name for yellow, but in Kiwai, at the mouth of the Fly River, the name applied to green appeared to be inconstant and indefinite, while there was no word for blue, for which colour the same word was used as for black. In Torres Straits there are terms for green. In Murray Island the native word for blue was the same as that used for black, but the English word had been adopted and modified into *bŭlu-bŭlu*. The language of Mabuiag was more advanced; there was a word for blue (*maludgamulnga*, sea-colour), but it was often also used for green. In these four vocabularies four stages may be seen in the evolution of colour languages, exactly as deducted by Geiger, red being the most definitive, and the colours at the other end of the spectrum the least so. As Rivers has also pointed out, it was noteworthy, too, that the order of these people in respect to culture was the same as in regard to development of words for colours. Rivers found that though the people showed no confusion between red and green they did between blue and green. The investigation of these colour-names, he thought, showed that to them blue must be a duller and darker colour than it is to us, and indeed the experiments carried out with an apparatus known as Lovibond's tintometer afforded evidence of a distinct quantitative deficiency in their perception of blue, though the results were far from proving blindness to blue.

Numerous observations were made by Rivers on writing and drawing, the former chiefly in the case of children. The most striking result was the ease and correctness with which mirror writing was performed. Mirror writing is that reversed form of writing that comes right when looked at in a looking-glass. In many cases native children, when asked to write with the left hand, spontaneously wrote mirror writing, and all were able to write in this fashion readily. In some cases children, when asked to write with the left hand, wrote upside down.

Experiments were made on the estimation of time. The method adopted was to give signals marking off a given interval; another signal was then given as the commencement of a second interval, which the native had to finish by a similar signal when he judged it to be equal to the previous given interval. Rivers found that this somewhat difficult procedure met with unexpected success, and intervals of ten seconds, twenty seconds, and one minute, were estimated with fairly consistent results.

The conditions for testing acuity of hearing were very unfavourable on Murray Island, owing to the noise of the sea and the rustle of the coconut palms. Myers found that few Murray Islanders surpassed a hyper-acute European in auditory acuity, while the majority could not hear as far. No great weight, however, could be attached to the observations, because all the men were divers, an occupation that certainly damaged the ears to some extent. To investigate their range of hearing a Galton's whistle was used, and it was found they could hear very high notes. Twelve Murray Islanders were tested for their sense of rhythm; this was found to be remarkably accurate for 120 beats of the metronome to the minute, and somewhat less so for 60 beats.

Myers tested their sense of smell by means of a series of

tubes containing solutions, of varying strength, of odorous substances like valerian and camphor, and the results, while not altogether satisfactory, tended to show that they had no marked superiority in this respect over the members of the expedition.

With regard to taste it was very difficult to get information, as the natives, naturally enough, did not like strange substances being put into their mouths. Sugar and salt were readily recognised, acid was compared to unripe fruit, bitter is most uncertain, and there is no distinctive name for it in the Murray Island vocabulary.

Numerous time reaction experiments were made by Myers. The time of the simple reaction is not sensibly longer, but probably in many cases even shorter, than would be that given by a corresponding class of Europeans. Myers points out that the experiments clearly showed the great difference of temperament among the individuals investigated. There was at one extreme the slow, steady-going man, who reacted with almost uniform speed on each occasion; at the other extreme was the nervous, high-strung individual, who was frequently reacting prematurely.

There is a consensus of opinion that savages are less sensitive to pain than Europeans, but there is always the doubt whether they are really able to bear pain with fortitude. However, the conclusion McDougall arrived at, that the Murray Islanders were distinctly less sensitive than the Europeans in the expedition, was supported not only by their statements, but also by tests depending on simple pressure of the skin made by a small piece of apparatus. It should be understood that the degree of pain produced was in all cases so slight as not to spoil the pleasure and interest of the subjects in the proceedings.

It was found that the natives had points on their skin specially sensitive to cold, exactly as in the case with Europeans. As to touch, when tested by McDougall to see how close the points of a pair of compasses must be put on the skin before they cease to be felt as two, their sensitiveness was in general better than that of the members of the expedition.

A series of tin canisters of the same size and appearance, but variously weighted, was prepared by McDougall; another series having the same weight, but of different sizes, was also provided: the first experiment was to test the delicacy of discrimination of the differences of weight, and the second to determine the degree of their suggestibility by the effect of size, as appreciated by sight and grasp, on the judgment of weight. It was interesting to find that although the abstract idea of weight seemed entirely new to the minds of these people, who had no word to express it, and who, moreover, could have had no practice, yet they were more accurate than a practised European.

It would be tedious to recount all the work that was accomplished in the psychological laboratory; but it was most interesting to watch the different operations and to see what earnestness, I may say conscientiousness, most of the subjects exhibited in the performance of the tasks set them. We never knew what they thought of it all, or of us—perhaps it was as well that we did not.

In the preliminary report Rivers has published, he notes that our observations were in most cases made with very little difficulty, and, with some exceptions, we could feel sure that the natives were doing their best in all we asked them to do. This opinion is based not only on observation of their behaviour and expression while the tests were being carried out, but on the consistency of the results; the usually small deviations showed that the observations were made with due care and attention.

Attempts were made, but with very little success, to find out what was actually passing in the minds of the natives while making these observations.

One general result was to show very considerable variability. It was obvious that in general character and temperament the natives varied greatly from one another, and very considerable individual differences also came out in our experimental observations. How great the variations were as compared with those in a more complex community can only be determined after a large number of comparative data have been accumulated.

Another general result pointed out by Rivers is that these natives did not appear to be especially susceptible to suggestion, but exhibited a very considerable independence of opinion. This observation is of importance, as there is a widely spread idea that the reverse is the case for backward peoples. Leading questions were found not to be so dangerous as was expected.

Whenever possible I spent the mornings in measuring the natives. In this I was helped by Wilkin, who also photographed them. It is not always easy to obtain good portraits when the accessories of a well-lighted studio are absent, but the expedition is to be congratulated on the success of Wilkin's labours. Most of the Murray Island photographs were developed on the spot, and in a considerable number of cases copies of the portraits were given to the sitters in consideration for their submitting to be psychologised.

Nearly all the Torres Straits and New Guinea photographs were taken by Wilkin, and it is greatly to his credit that there were very few failures.

Wilkin also paid some attention to native architecture in Torres Straits and on the mainland of New Guinea, and to the laws regulating land tenure and inheritance of property in Torres Straits.

As Seligmann did not return with Ray, Wilkin, and myself after our trip to the Central District of British New Guinea, he had only two and a half weeks on Murray Island. During that time he collected some natural history and botanical specimens, and paid attention to native medicine and surgery as well, and he also made some clinical observations on the diseases of the natives. During his New Guinea trips, and when he rejoined us in the western islands of Torres Straits, he continued on much the same lines; so that in the end he gained a very fair insight into "folk-medicine." He also at various times made some interesting ethnological observations and measured some tribes I was not able to visit. Frequently he assisted Rivers and myself in our investigations in Mabuiag.

Myers and McDougall left Murray Island on August 24th, so as to get up the Baram River, Sarawak, before the northeast monsoon set in. The work carried on in Kiwai and Mabuiag and other of the western islands of the Straits was very much of the same character as that which we did in Murray Island. Fewer psychological observations could be made, owing to the fact that most of the apparatus had been taken on to Borneo. The subjects investigated were chiefly visual acuity and colour vision, auditory acuity, smell and touch, writing and drawing.

Ray was engaged practically the whole of every morning in studying the Miriam language with Ari, the Mamoose of Mer, and Pasi, the Mamoose of Dauar. He worked them very hard, and often I had to go into the inner room in which he studied and liberate the poor chiefs, who frequently were quite done up, while Ray himself was as keen and fresh as ever. The good men conscientiously turned up regularly, though I am sure they must often have been heartily sick of the whole concern. Giving the names of things is one matter, but it is quite a different affair to plod through empty phrases in all their possible moods and tenses, hour after hour, day after day, and week after week. They were not the first, nor will they be the last, to feel repugnance at the study of grammar.

The construction of the language was found to be very complex, modifications of sense in the verb being expressed by an elaborate system of prefixes and suffixes, for example :—

Kaka mari natageri, I tell you.	*E netat le detageri,* he tells one man.
Kaka abi detageri, I tell him.	*E neis le daratagri,* he tells two men.
E wiabi daratagereda, he tells them.	*Neis netat le abi detagridare* three men tell him.

Nouns are declined through several cases by means of suffixes: *e.g. tulik*, a knife; *tuliku*, by means of a knife; *tulikra*, of a knife; *tuliklam*, from a knife, etc.

Ray distinguishes two groups of languages in British New Guinea, which he has termed respectively "Papuan" and "Melanesian." The former he regards as indigenous to New Guinea, or at all events it may be regarded as such for all practical purposes. The latter group of languages bears such close resemblances to the language spoken in the great chain of islands in the Western Pacific (or Melanesia) that there is no doubt they are all derived from the same source. A third group of languages, current in this part of the world, is that spoken on the Australian continent. It is thus a matter of some interest to discover to which linguistic group we must assign the languages of Torres Straits.

I have to thank my colleague for giving me the following information, which will sufficiently explain the differences between these three groups of languages.

The Papuan languages agree with one another in very few characteristics, and totally differ in vocabulary and constructive particles. Consonantal sounds are very fully used, but closed syllables are not common except in the western languages.

Demonstrative words indicating the place or direction of actions are numerous. Nouns and pronouns are declined through various cases by means of suffixes. Adjectives precede substantives. The pronoun in some languages has a trial as well as a singular, dual, and plural; but the inclusion or exclusion of the person addressed is rarely indicated. The verb is very complicated, and is modified by prefixes and suffixes, its forms indicating the number of subject and object, as well as tense and mood. Numeration is limited, and rarely goes beyond two. Parts of the body are much used in counting.

The Melanesian languages have a very general agreement among themselves in grammatical construction and vocabulary. They use consonants very freely and have some consonantal sounds which are difficult to transliterate. Many syllables are closed. Demonstrative words pointing hither and thither are much used. Nouns are divided into two classes, with or without pronominal suffixes, according to the nearness or remoteness of the connection between possessor or possessed. Words may represent any part of speech without change, but the use of a word is sometimes shown by prefix or affix. Number and case are shown by separate words preceding the noun. Adjectives follow the noun. Pronouns are numerous, and often of four numbers—singular, dual, trial, and plural. The first person always has forms including or excluding the person addressed. Any word is made into a verb by the use of a preceding particle, which usually marks tense and mood, and in some languages person and number. Verbs have a causative, reciprocal, frequentative and intensive form. Numeration is extensive, and there is counting up to high numbers.

The Australian languages are in some respects similar to the Papuan, though prefixes are not commonly used. Certain consonantal sounds are rarely heard. Nouns and pronouns are declined by means of suffixes through various cases. Adjectives precede the noun. The pronoun has no trial number, and some languages have the inclusive and exclusive forms in the first person. The verb is modified as to time and mood, and sometimes number, by suffixes, and has numerous but, as a rule, simple forms. Numeration does not proceed beyond two, or three at the utmost.

The grammar of the Murray Island (or Miriam) language bears no resemblance to the Melanesian, and but little to the

Australian. It must therefore be regarded as belonging to the Papuan group. The speech used by the Mission is a debased form of the original, as Pasi told Ray "they cut it short." Ray is of opinion that as most of the young people know English, it is very probable the pure language will die out with the older folk.

Several of the elder men used to come and talk to me at various times, but they came more regularly after we had witnessed the Malu performances, and while the excitement about them was still fresh. Baton and Mamai were the first to come, they were policemen during my previous visit, and were consequently old friends. I obtained, however, more valuable information from Enocha and Wano, who were pillars of the Church, but being old men they also knew about the past; unfortunately there were very few alive at the time of our stay in the island who knew first-hand about those matters that interested us most.

These good people enjoyed describing the old ceremonies. Often they brought me something that was formerly employed in their mysteries or a model of it.

When any action was described the old fellows jumped up and danced it in the room, sometimes two or three would perform at once. I always had a drum handy to be in readiness when they broke forth into song, and for the dance they took bows and arrows or whatever may have been appropriate from the stack of implements that was in a corner of the room.

We had many interesting séances, and it enabled us to get a glimmer of the old ceremonies that was most tantalising. If only we could have seen the real thing, how different would the description be! How little, after all our efforts, could we accomplish by mere hearsay! But even an undress rehearsal or an imperfectly performed representation was better than nothing at all.

For example, Bruce and I were independently trying to work out the rain-making ceremony or charm. We obtained more or less full descriptions that agreed on the whole and which supplemented each other. He got some *zogo mer*, or "sacred words"—that is, the magical incantation employed—from Gasu, a noted and credited rain-maker. I tried these on Ulai, a somewhat disreputable old man, who has been of considerable use to us, and who at the same time gave us much amusement; he immediately reeled off a lot more words. Gasu then admitted that most of these were correct. I next tried Enocha, who had the reputation of being a great master in the art of rain-making. He passed most of Ulai's words, denied others, and gave me fresh ones. Eventually we arrived at a version that may be taken as authentic; but doubtless each rain-maker has his traditional formula, which may differ in details from that of a rival magician.

A little incident was rather curious. Late one evening, when Gasu was teaching Bruce the *zogo mer* of the rain charm, a smart little shower came suddenly and unexpectedly from an apparently cloudless sky. There was not a native next morning who had not his own opinion as to the origin of the shower.

It seemed very strange to us that our informants, however friendly and anxious to help us, so often kept back something till their hands were forced, so to speak, by information gained from another source. Then it became possible to go one step further. I think this was due in many cases simply to a lack of appreciation of what we wanted to know; in other instances there appeared to be an ingrained reticence which prevented their speaking freely about sacred or magical ceremonies. When, however, it became evident to them that we already knew something about the ceremony or formula in question, there was but little reluctance in giving information, especially when they did not know how much or how little we knew.

I mention these details in order to give some idea of the method we adopted of gaining our information. It is comparatively easy to get an account of a ceremony or custom from one man, but we invariably checked this information by inquiring from other men, always selecting the oldest men available. Even amongst ourselves no two people will describe any occurrence in the same manner, and one will emphasise a certain point which another may omit. Hence, in collecting from natives, we were very careful to obtain as many versions as possible and to sift the evidence. The results often appear meagre for the really considerable amount of time and pains we spent on attaining them; but, on the other hand, we feel fairly confident as to their accuracy. Interesting as all this was, it involved a great deal of very tedious work. One had to let the old men ramble on, and it often happened that they got on to side issues and barren narrations; but even so our patience was occasionally rewarded by a hint of something which we would not otherwise have come across, and which, followed out later, led to a really interesting record. Tact and patience are necessary in extracting reliable information from primitive folk.

I should perhaps add that although we communicated with one another in jargon, or pidgin-English, we used native words whenever there was a possibility of a misunderstanding arising, and by the context we could usually make certain as to the significance of new or obscure native terms. If the context failed to elucidate the meaning, we arrived at it by questioning all round the subject, or by allowing our informant to give his explanation in his own way. I have given several examples of the pidgin-English spoken in the Torres Straits in the course of this narrative. It is a quaint, though not an ideal mode of communication of ideas, but with practice and the employment of suitable illustrations and similes, one can get along fairly well. I found, too, one could often elucidate a statement by acting it, or by using sticks and stones as dummies; it is remarkable what can be done in that way, and the natives quite enter into the spirit of the thing.

One day Bruce surprised me by showing a minute bull-roarer that was hung round the neck of a *doiom*. A *doiom* is the stone effigy of a man that is used in the rain-making ceremony. I had all along felt that a bull-roarer should appear in the performance, but I could not hear of one. Well, here it was, worn as a neck pendant, with two seed rattles. I showed it to Ulai; he said it was not correct, and brought me another model, which was much larger. Then I showed them both to Enocha. He scoffed at Gasu's little bull-roarer, admitted that Ulai's was more correct, but added that Ulai didn't know about it. He then promised to let me have the correct thing. This was probably little more than professional jealousy, as Gasu was noted as a successful rain-maker.

That same morning Enocha and Wano were alone with me, and I turned the conversation to rain-making; then a happy inspiration seized me, and I asked them to give me a demonstration. They agreed. I provided one of the several *doioms* I had already collected, and we adjourned to the shade of a neighbouring tree, where, hidden by bushes, we would be quite unobserved and undisturbed. Although we had not the proper appurtenances, a pantomime was gone through, and I jotted down full notes. It was strange to see these dear old men doing everything half seriously, and at the same time laughing as if they were truant schoolboys at some forbidden pleasure. By a strange coincidence the school children were singing "Auld Lang Syne" in the schoolhouse down the hill, whilst the old men were rehearsing "old-time fashion" a short distance off.

A couple of days later Gasu gave us a complete demonstration at the other end of the island, with all the accessories. Four large plaited coconut leaves were erected to represent rain clouds; there was a blackened patch on each of these to mimic the blackness of a rain cloud, and one or two pendant leaves imitated the falling rain. The four screens inclosed a small space in which a hole was made in the ground. The *doiom* was decorated with certain leaves, and packed in a banana leaf with various minced leaves and numbers of red seeds; the leaf was filled with water and placed in the hole, the rain-maker all the while muttering the magical formulæ. During part of the performance a lighted brand was waved about, and at another a bamboo clapper was rattled. Thus were simulated the lightning and thunder. Several instances came to my notice during my recent and earlier visits to Murray Island of the employment of this ceremony.

When I was arranging for the purchase of Gasu's *doiom*, Jimmy Dei, the sergeant of the police—a very intelligent man and a devout churchgoer—objected to the transaction, as they might not be able to obtain rain in the future when they required it. The very day after I had bought Gasu's *doiom* he wanted it back, and would gladly have returned the goods I gave him in exchange, for his was a very famous charm, and it even had the proud distinction of having a name of its own. Sometimes even a potent charm like this will fail in its function, and once this mischance befell this particular *doiom*, whereat Gasu was much enraged and threw it on the ground, and, alas! the head broke off; then Gasu repented, and fastened the head on again with wire. I must confess I felt very sorry for Gasu when he regretted having yielded to my importunity and wanted his *doiom* back, but the collecting instinct was stronger than pure sentiment, and I had to inform him that it was then too late. Recently I have had a letter from Mr. Bruce, in which he says, "Gasu is always speaking of you and his *doiom*, and

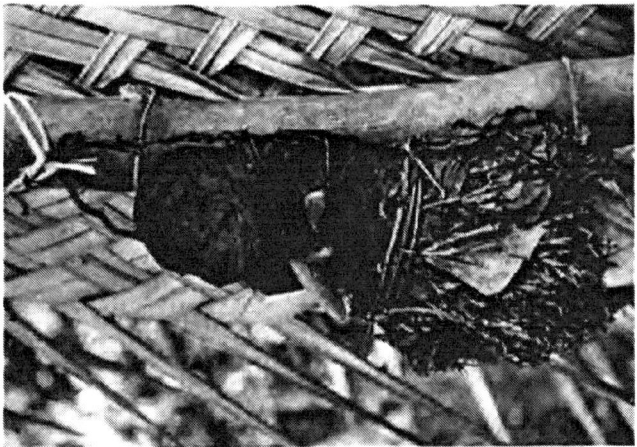

RAIN SHRINE

DOJOM WITH BULL-ROARER

adds, 'Mind you, if he had not asked for it, I would not have given it to the Professor.'" Poor old Gasu! he was half blind when we were there, now he has completely lost his eyesight, and I am afraid he does not bear a pleasing memory of our visit, but still mourns the loss of his old and powerful charm.

In the same letter Bruce writes: "We have still some very powerful *doioms* left on the island. The new church was badly injured last year by the foundations settling, owing to the rain of a very heavy thunderstorm, but all the natives maintained it was the thunder that did the damage. But the storm must have been made by someone. Enocha was first suspected, but he denied his ability to do so, as he says he does not make thunder and lightning to spoil things; he only makes good rain to make men's gardens grow, and 'besides,' he said, 'I am an *ekalesia*, I did not spoil the sacred house.' So they had to fall back on Wali, as he was not an *ekalesia*, or member of the Church, and he had been angry with Finau, the teacher, about something. They have now made Wali an *ekalesia* to protect the building from further damage."

The worthy Finau never appeared to realise the nature of our work or its effect upon the natives. He evidently thought that the interest we took in the old customs and ceremonies would tend to a recrudescence of paganism, and there is little doubt that he intentionally hindered and hampered our investigations. He was not sufficiently alert to appreciate the fact that we were really playing into his hands. We bought and took away many legendary and magical stones, including a large number of rain charms, and in having representations of the Malu ceremonies we must have stripped off some of the glamour that ignorance throws round the unknown. We doubtless revived impressions in the memory of a few old men, but the younger men would be disillusioned by what they witnessed. It is needless to add that we never undermined his influence as a teacher, nor did anything that would be a stumbling-block to the feeblest of his adherents.

Finau often preached loudly against native dancing, and consigned those who attempted a little of it to hell, where, he informed them, they would have kerosene poured over them, and then they would be burnt; but, perhaps as he was himself a Samoan, he allowed certain South Sea dances, which the natives constantly practised under the tuition of a native of

Rotumah who was living on Murray Island. These dances were to be performed at the opening of the new church in Darnley, which was to take place in several months' time, and doubtless the opening of the church Finau was building in Murray Island would be commemorated in its turn in a similar manner.

In the Rotumah dances that we saw the men stood side by side in three or four rows, and went through rather graceful movements with heads, arms, and legs. Most of the movements appeared to be conventionalised representations of hauling ropes and other nautical actions. After a series of evolutions had been performed the front rank retired behind, and the second rank took its place. All was gone through again, and so on in succession until the last rank had danced in the front row.

One evening soon after our arrival there was a "play" in a village close by. It now seems to be the fashion for the people on one side of the island to learn new songs from Thursday Island or from the crews of fishing-boats. When they consider themselves proficient they go to other villages on the opposite side of the island and there sing them. Shortly afterwards a return visit is paid.

This custom of one side of the island challenging the other in friendly rivalry is apparently an old one, and seems to point to a dual division of the population such as we found later in the western tribe, and which is of fundamental, social importance among the Australians and many Papuan and Melanesian peoples. Dr. Rivers has gathered a good deal of information on this point, but he has not yet had time to work up his material. This particular performance was certainly trivial and mean; but surely the white man and not the native must be criticised for this. The visitors from Las and other villages were all dressed in their Sunday best, the girls stood in a clump in the middle and sang Japanese and other songs. Then a man blowing a whistle walked round and round and called out, " Twenty-five cents a ride," or something to that effect. Next a number of men ranged themselves in pairs, like the spokes of a wheel radiating from a hub of girls. The latter sang, and the men walked round and round the girls, gradually going faster and faster. This was in imitation of a merry-go-round which had paid a couple of visits to Thursday Island. So popular was this merry-go-round that I was informed the owners made a profit of £1,600 for three months' work!

To a sing-song tune of "la, la, la—la, la, la," sundry very solemn couples of girls separated themselves from the throng and danced a polka—of a sort—slowly and carefully. One or two pairs of men danced more vigorously. I saw only two couples of opposite sex dancing together, and though these good people are considerably emancipated from the past and were actually copying a white-man's dance, still their feeling of delicacy was too strong to permit them to indulge in promiscuous dancing.

One funny man, dressed in a long figured-calico dressing-gown, danced by himself; his antics were greatly appreciated. Some of the girls had covered their faces with white, and had painted a dab of red pigment on each cheek, perhaps in imitation of the Japanese women of the settlement in Thursday Island, which goes by the name of "Yokohama."

A few days after our arrival we gave an evening entertainment in the schoolhouse, at which there was a large attendance. I opened the proceedings with an address in jargon English, and referred to my last visit and told them what we wanted to do this time. Ray next gave a couple of tunes on the phonograph, Myers was to have performed on his violin, but unfortunately the violin had suffered from damp, had become unglued and had fallen to pieces. I showed a number of lantern slides of local interest by means of a lantern Wilkin had brought out at my request. I commenced with a copy of the plate in Juke's *Voyage of the "Fly,"* which illustrated Captain Blackwood's reception at Murray Island in 1845. In this interesting picture the ship's boats are surrounded by a noisy, gesticulating crowd of naked savages. The second slide I showed was the present of fruit which they themselves had given me four days previously, and which Wilkin had photographed and made into a lantern-slide. After showing photographs I took ten years previously of a congregation in the building in which we were then assembled, I showed a photograph of a wedding that had taken place in the same room two days previously. Several other slides were shown made from the photographs I had taken on my last visit; these were received with great excitement, and the audience quickly recognised the various views and people, many of the latter were actually present, a few were dead. When a group of children taken ten years before was thrown on the screen I asked if any of them were present, and a lad and a lass came before the screen and stood beside their portraits. Then followed a phonographic interlude, and I gave a second lantern show, mostly of slides of native decorative art and native drawings of animals. Wilkin, who kindly acted as "operator," then showed a number of his comic slides which were much appreciated, finishing off with the children's perennial favourite of rats running down a snoring man's throat. I made a point of procuring this slide before I left England, and my anticipations of its popularity were not unfounded, it simply brought down the house, and " Man he sleep, he kaikai mokeis," was always vociferously welcomed. A couple of phonograph records concluded the performance.

Our friends were greatly pleased, and all behaved remarkably well. Of course I expected them to behave properly, but I did not think they would have so much control over their excitable feelings, and I suspected they might be carried away in the exuberance of their joy. Continually the more uproarious were called to order by various members of the audience.

Every now and again we ran one thing hard on Murray Island; for example, for a week or so some of us studied "cat's cradle" games. McDougall soon became fascinated by these, and Myers eventually succumbed. But *kamut*, as the natives call their string puzzles, is a very different matter from the uninteresting and simple performance to which we were accustomed as children.

Two distinct kinds of operations may be performed with string, namely, tricks and puzzles. The former usually are movements which appear to form knots or ties, but which really run out freely. The puzzles are complicated figures which are supposed to bear some resemblance to natural objects. Our "cat's cradle" belongs to the latter category, but we have also numerous string tricks.

Some of the string tricks are the same as those practised at home. One was intended to represent some food held in the hand which was offered to the spectator, but when the latter attempted to take it, saying, "You got some food for me?" the food disappeared as the player replied, "No got." A similar, apparently knotted puzzle terminated in two loops, which represented a mouse's ears, but on attempting to catch it the whole ran out.

Some of the string puzzles represented divers objects, as a bird's nest, coconut palm, the setting sun, a fish spear, a crab, a canoe, and many others. Quite a number were moving puzzles—working models, in fact; such were, for example, a sea-snake swimming, a man dancing, and so forth. Some of these were indelicate. The most interesting was a fight between a Dauar man and a Murray Islander. In this *kamut*, by working the strings, two loose knots collided in the centre and became mixed up, but eventually one knot returns with a loop on it, which is the successful Murray Islander returning with the head of his adversary!

Little songs are sung to many string puzzles as they are being played, which may be the relics of some magical formulæ. Several *kamut* puzzles illustrate legendary beings such as Geigi, the boy king-fish, or his mother Nageg, the trigger-fish. One represents the taboo grounds of Gazir and Kiam, where some of the Malu ceremonies were held.

We learnt a good many of these *kamut*, but they were very difficult to remember, owing to the extreme complication of the processes in making the figures, and we had to practise them constantly. Eventually we invented a system of nomenclature, by means of which we found it possible to write down all the stages of manipulation; and we found as a rule the more complex the figure the easier it was to describe. By rigorous adherence to our system it will be possible for others to reproduce the Murray Island figures and to record others from elsewhere. Generally Rivers and Ray first learnt a particular puzzle, and gradually worked out the description by slowly performing the movements and dictating the processes to me, but I did not watch what they were doing.

Then one of them read out the description while I endeavoured to reproduce the puzzle from the verbal description alone. We were never satisfied until it can be so done without any possibility of mistake. We had many fights over the descriptions, and always felt very proud of ourselves when one account was satisfactorily finished. But I can very well imagine that had we been observed some people would have thought we were demented, or, at least, were wasting our time.

One afternoon some of us went to a *kaikai*, or feast. The word *kaikai* means food, a meal, a feast, or to eat. It is in use all over the South Seas, and is derived from the Polynesian *kai*

PLATE IV

REMOVING SAND FROM A COPPER MAORI

A MURRAY ISLAND FEAST

dream of breaking it by getting food on Sunday, consequently numbers of children came to school on Monday morning without having had any breakfast. This made them peevish and inattentive, so Mr. Bruce had to complain to the Mamoose, and an edict was issued prohibiting the *kolap* matches on Saturday, and the men were told to go to their gardens on that day as heretofore.

After this particular match two "copper Maoris" were opened. A "copper Maori," or earth-oven, is a large shallow hole in the ground, in which stones are placed and a fire lighted—this makes the stones red hot. "Native food" of various kinds—yams, sweet potatoes, taro, etc.—is wrapped in banana leaves and placed on the hot stones. Small pigs are put in whole. The food is then covered over with leaves, and sometimes mats and earth are heaped over all. In an hour or two the food is cooked to perfection. It is the best method of cooking food, as the juices and flavours are retained.

The name "copper Maori," or *kŏpa Mauri*, as it is here pronounced, is now common all over the Pacific, though this method of cooking has everywhere in the West Pacific its local name, and therefore is an indigenous and not introduced custom. In Torres Straits the earth-oven is called *ame* or *amai*, but the introduced word alone is used when speaking to foreigners. The word *kopa* is the Maori name for the ordinary earth-oven, or more correctly for the hole in the ground. The similarity of sound between *kopa* and "copper" has led to the current belief that as the whalers in New Zealand used large coppers for boiling down the blubber, the native method of cooking came to be called "copper Maori," that is, the Maori copper.

By this time a mat was spread apart from the others, to which we were invited along with the two Mamooses, Ari and Pasi. We had pork, yams, pumpkins and bananas, and green coconuts to drink. Most of the men sat on each side of a long row of mats, the food being placed down the middle. They ate from the packets with their fingers, and munched chunks of roast pork with evident gusto. They gave us plates and knives and forks, but I preferred a banana leaf, native fashion, to a plate. The women and children had their food apart in various family groups.

After all was over the women placed their baskets in two rows, and the hosts filled each with an equal amount of raw native food. The party then broke up.

CHAPTER IV

THE MALU CEREMONIES

IN various parts of the world there are very important ceremonies in which the lads are formally received into the community of men. Before undergoing these initiation ceremonies they have no social position, but subsequently they are recognised as men, and are at liberty to marry. There may be numerous grades of rank through which it may take many years to pass, but the first series of ceremonies are all-important.

Initiation ceremonies are observed all over Australia and throughout the greater part of Melanesia, as well as in portions of the Indonesian Archipelago, not to mention other regions of the earth. It would take too long if I were to attempt even the briefest description and analysis of the various customs connected with these important rites in this quarter of the globe; but the following features are fairly widely spread.

When the lads show by the sprouting hair on their face that they are attaining manhood, their male relations agree that they shall be initiated. This ceremony may take place annually or at intervals of two or three years.

The lads are secluded in a tabooed spot in the bush, access to which is strictly prohibited to any non-initiated person. Sacred emblems are frequently shown to the lads; these are often masked men who symbolise some legendary or mystical person or event. Usually a flat, thin piece of wood shaped like a willow leaf is shown to them, this is the so-called bull-roarer. It is fastened to one end of a piece of string, the other being lashed on to a stick. The apparatus is whirled round and round above the head of the operator, and according to its size and shape it makes a buzzing or a humming noise; the movement may be varied by violently lashing it backwards and forwards, when it gives rise to a siren-like shriek. The weird and mysterious sounds issuing from the bush terrify the women and children, who regard them as the voices of spirits. The secret is soon learnt by the young initiate, who is given a bull-roarer and warned never to show it to a woman or child on penalty of death.

Whatever may be done, or shown, or told to the lads is to be kept secret by them, and by way of emphasising this they are usually frightened in various ways or subjected to severe treatment.

Certain restrictions, or taboos, are generally placed on the lads for a variable time, and during the probationary period they are instructed in the moral code, social customs, and sacred legends of the community, and, in fact, all that it behoves a "man" to know.

Every tribe is composed of several divisions or clans, and it is the rule in Australia and in some parts of Melanesia for each clan to be intimately associated with at least one class of animals, plants, or natural objects. This animal, or whatever it may be, is spoken of as the totem of the clan or individual, and it should be borne in mind that the totem is a species of animal, or plant, not an individual one. Thus all cassowaries, and not any one particular bird, are the totem of the whole cassowary clan, or of each member of that clan. It is the business of the clan relatives of the boy to see that he is duly instructed in the duties and prohibitions that his particular totem imposes on him.

In communities at this stage of culture there are certain definite restrictions as to marriage and intercourse with women. It is now nearly universally the rule that a man may have nothing to do with a woman who belongs to the same totem as himself. In some cases the group from which he may choose his wife is yet more restricted. Any infringement of this rule is a most heinous offence, for the perpetration of which the death penalty may be inflicted on one or both offenders.

Although a tribe may be subdivided into quite a number of clans, these usually fall into two groups. For example, the clan groups of "Eaglehawk" and "Crow" are very widely spread throughout Australia. Members of any particular clan of one tribe have friendly relations with the members of a corresponding clan in another tribe; these two clans may or may not have the same totem, but in either case they are recognised as affiliated.

In the foregoing account I have very briefly sketched some of the main features of a totemistic society. It is probable that in its more primitive stage all the members of a community had an approximately equal position according to their grade and irrespective of their particular clan or totem. We find, however, in the present day that there are various interesting stages of the disintegration of this old social system; especially is this the case in Melanesia.

Speaking in general terms, what happens is as follows. One clan or group becomes more influential than the others and arrogates privileges to its members, who thus constitute a powerful secret society. Although at first membership was restricted to those who were born into the clan, eventually it seems as if anyone who could afford to pay the charges might be admitted.

Other secret societies or clubs would be formed by ambitious men, which might in turn acquire more or less power, or, on the other hand, might prove of no account. Gradually the system breaks down—as Dr. Codrington has shown us was the case in Melanesia—and in Florida, for example, the old men sat and wept over the profanation of the ancient mysteries and the loss of their own power and privilege.

In our travels we came across peoples in various stages of culture, as will be narrated in due course. In Murray Island true totemism does not exist now, whatever may have been the case in the past; but there is an important secret society or brotherhood, the power of which was broken by the missionaries.

For a long time I had been trying to get the natives of the village of Las, on the eastern side of the island, to give us a demonstration of the ancient initiation ceremonies connected with the Malu cult. All was supposed to be ready on Thursday afternoon, July 28th, so we walked over, but found no preparations made. We were greatly disappointed, and I spoke rather strongly to some of the influential men, but I did not feel at all hopeful as to the result.

After a meal in Gododo's house, we spent the evening yarning and recording some songs on the phonograph.

Next day, after an early breakfast, I walked to Ulag to inquire after a star-shaped stone club that was used in the old Malu ceremonies; this I borrowed, and also arranged for a similar club and the sacred drum to be brought. Of all the paraphernalia appertaining to this cult only these three implements remain.

In the afternoon matters began to look more lively, and it was soon evident that something was about to happen.

We were taken to the taboo ground at Gazir, and shortly afterwards the men assembled and went through a representation of the first ceremony, at which the sacred masks were shown to the lads (*kersi*) who were to be initiated. Now no masks remain, and we had to be content with an exceedingly poor counterfeit of what must have been a very awe-inspiring ceremony. There were just sufficient echoes of it, as it were, to enable us to catch something of the old solemnity. The meaning of the reiterated couplet that was sung on this occasion is to the effect that Malu had bad teeth! Could anything be more trivial? It quite pained me when I heard the translation of the chant.

When this was over we hastened down to the sand beach at Las, and shortly afterwards the second ceremony was performed, very much as I had seen it ten years before. There were many discordant elements in the performance, but these it is now impossible to eliminate.

What threatened to be a fiasco turned out to be quite a success, and several points that were obscure to me before were cleared up. Myers helped me a great deal, and as he has noted down quite a number of the Malu songs and tunes, we can now restore the ceremonies at Gazir, Las, and Dam with a very fair degree of accuracy.

After this exhibition we spent many days in going over the details of the ceremonies and songs. Information of this kind which appears so simple when written is surprisingly difficult and tedious to collect. It is by no means easy to get the natives to understand precisely what one requires. There is also little doubt that they do not care to speak freely about the sacred rites they revered in the past. I allude, of course, to the old men, for even the middle-aged know very little of their ancient customs, and the young men nothing at all.

The habit of secrecy was too ingrained to be readily relinquished. In nearly every inquiry of this sort we found there were certain *zogo mer*, or "sacred words," which it was always very difficult to obtain. Sometimes these are magical phrases, as in the charm for making rain, or a formula that was known to but a very few men, like that employed at Tomog Zogo. Naturally the *zogo mer* of the Malu ceremonies were not to be repeated lightly.

There were some sacred words which they disliked mentioning: for example, the culture hero in the "Myth of Origin" of these ceremonies is always spoken of as *Malu*, and this name is known to women and children—it is, in fact, what they call an *au ne, i.e.* a "big" or "general" name; but his real name is *Bomai*—this is the *zogo ne* (sacred name) or *gumik ne* (secret name), which only initiates may learn, and is one of those "unspeakable words which it is not lawful for a man to utter."

On the occasion of my previous visit to Murray Island I quite failed to get models made of the Malu masks, and it was not till the close of the present visit that I could persuade anyone to make us some; but by this time we had worked up a temporary recrudescence of interest in these and other ceremonies, and eventually our good friends Wano and Enocha agreed to make the models for me, but on the understanding that I should give each of them ten shillings, which they particularly requested should be paid in gold, as they wanted to put it in the plate at the annual missionary meeting. I provided them with the requisite cardboard, as it was out of the question to get the masks constructed of turtle-shell ("tortoise-shell") like the originals. Nearly every day one or other came to tell me how well they were getting on, and how pleased I should be with the result; they were evidently hugely delighted with themselves.

One evening, on their way to the weekly prayer-meeting, they brought the masks very carefully hidden, and by this time I was almost as excited as they were. Both models were slightly different from what I expected, but there is no doubt they are as accurate representations of the old masks as it is now possible to obtain. The face-mask is of open work, painted red, and stuck on it are scattered white feathers. The raised nose is made of beeswax; the eyes are two red seeds; a ring of wax represents the lips. Cardboard models represent the beard of human lower jawbones. Above are feathers of the Torres Straits pigeon and croton leaves. Behind is a model of a turtle.

THE MALU CEREMONIES

Next morning I incautiously showed these masks to a woman who happened to be about the place. Later in the day Enocha came to me in a great hurry and besought me not to let any woman see them, and, of course, I respected his wish. This was an interesting proof of the sanctity in which the original was held. The ceremonies had not been held for a quarter of a century, the people are all Christian, and yet even now a woman may not see cardboard models of the tabooed masks!

We had many male visitors to see the masks, and it was quite pathetic to see the expressions of pleasure tempered with sadness manifested by the old men. They shook their heads and clicked, and even the tears started to their eyes. Ichabod!

I seized the opportunity of the possession of these models to induce some of my friends to give us another performance of that part of the Malu ceremony in which masks were worn. Two days before we left the island we went to Kiam, the other taboo ground where the ceremony was held. One year it was held at Gazir, and the following at Kiam, on the opposite side of the island. Gadodo, Kilerup, and another man dressed up, and I had the satisfaction of being able to take a cinematograph picture of the pro-

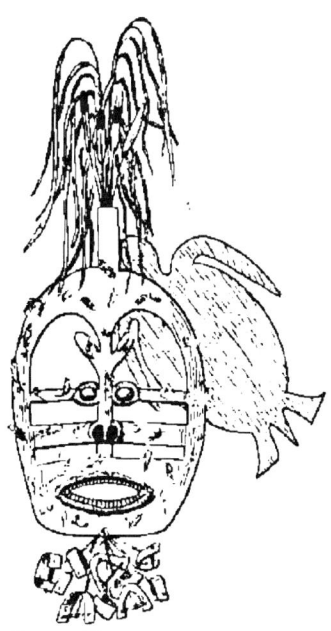

FIG. 4. MODEL OF THE BOMAI MASK OF THE MALU CEREMONIES

cessional dance. The grotesque masks worn by ruddled men, girt with leafy kilts, had a strange effect as they emerged from the jungle, and very weird was the dance in the mottled shade of the tropical foliage, a fantasy in red and green, lit up by spots of sunshine.

In order to give the reader a substantially accurate idea of the Malu ceremonies, I do not propose to describe exactly only what we saw, but I shall endeavour, as briefly as possible, to resuscitate the past. Full details will be published elsewhere. The *kersi*, painted and decorated in a peculiar manner, were marshalled on the taboo ground by some elders; beyond was the round house, in which the emblems were kept. Between the hut and the boys was an avenue of men with long staves, who performed rhythmic movements, which bore some resemblance to those made in energetically punting a boat. Near the *kersi* sat the drum-beaters, and round about in their allotted places, according to their clans, were former initiates. The *kersi* sat tailorwise in a semicircle, with hands resting on their legs, feeling very frightened. Suddenly the fearsome procession appeared at the other end of the avenue of men, and the three *Zogole* slowly marched with peculiar movements. They alone wore leafy girdles (it should be remembered that at that time the Torres Straits men invariably went nude except the performers of certain ceremonies). The head of the first *zogole* was covered with a ruddled turtle-shell mask, representing a human face, which had a beard of human jaw-bones; above the face were leaves and feathers, and hanging from it behind was a painted carapace of a turtle, the latter was supported by a long string by the second *zogole*. The third *zogole* bore a turtle-shell mask representing a hammer-headed shark, on which was a human face; it was provided with human arms and hands, and decorated with leaves, feathers, and turtle-shell figures of birds, frogs, and centipedes. When the *zogole* came to the semicircle of *kersi* they turned round and kicked out behind. They retired and advanced again, and then once more. The sacred words were uttered and the chant sung. The *kersi* were told the hidden name, and they had to make a present of food to the *zogole*.

This was certainly the essential initiation ceremony; it was followed by another, which had not the same sacred character, as women and children were allowed to be present. The latter was, in fact, a public recognition service, an acknowledgment that the *kersi* had been duly initiated, and that henceforth, after the completion of all the ceremonies, they were to rank as members of the fraternity.

The second ceremony took place in the afternoon or early evening on the sand beach between the village of Las and the sea. The spectators sat in a confused crowd along the village fence, the newly initiated lads occupying a prominent position.

PLATE V

THE DANCE OF THE MALU ZOGOLE

PLATE VI

THE MALU CEREMONY AT LAS

ULAI SINGING MALU SONGS INTO A PHONOGRAPH,
GASU IS BEATING THE MALU DRUM

THE MALU CEREMONIES

The drum-men appearing from behind a point at the southern end of the beach, ran forward and beat their drums with the characteristic staccato rhythm, and as the chant slowly augmented in sound, all the other voices were hushed, and the audience sat motionless in hushed expectancy.

Two or three pairs of *omai le* rushed forward, with bent body and trailing arms; with their hands they jerked up sand behind them as they ran, ever and again stopping and playing about and jumping over each other after the manner of the dogs they personated.

These were followed by several pairs of *daumer-le*, who, in the intervals of running forward, jumped about in a crouching attitude, and beat their chests with the palms of their hands, thereby imitating the perching and the flapping of the wings of the Torres Straits pigeon (*daumer*).

They were succeeded by a group of *girigirile*. The bird that they personified is a native of New Guinea, but what it is I was unable to discover.

With a whirl and a rush a revolving group of men next swept along the sand beach, the inner circle of young men brandished stone clubs, while the outer circle of old men carried sticks.

These operations were watched by the three *zogole*, who slowly and sedately marched along till they arrived opposite the spectators, and they then stood still. The reddened bodies of the *zogole* were entirely covered with white feathers, and their heads were similarly obscured; each carried five wands in his right hand. Although they were visible to the women, the personality of the *zogole* was supposed to be unknown to them, and should any woman divulge the name of one of the *zogole*, "she die that night."

The old women heaped up food in front of the *zogole*, and the ceremony concluded, as usual, with a big feast.

After initiation the lads underwent a long course of instruction, and had to submit to certain taboos. They were told to make a large garden and build a big house and a fence. They were also instructed in certain agricultural details; for example, one variety of yam, the *ketai*, should be planted beside a big tree and allowed to remain there for four or five years, and clusters of green bananas were to be tied up to form what is known as *sopsop*. They were cautioned not to spend all their time in fishing, and not to steal bananas and yams from other people's gardens, nor to filch anything from another man; neither were they to play any more, nor to talk too much. During the whole of that dry season they were not to cut or dress their hair, to dance or feast or smoke or behave unseemly in any way. If they divulged what happened at the mysteries to any woman or child or to a man who did not belong to the favoured clans, they were threatened with the penalty of death, and it would have been inflicted too.

One must admit that a course of instruction in the work that men have to do, in addition to information as to rules of conduct, the customs of the tribe and the traditions of the elders was a training of some importance, and I believe lasted for some eight months. Especially as it occurred at an impressionable age of life, when new ideas and sensations are surging up, and when the fuller life of adult manhood is looming in the immediate future. The emotions of the lads were quickened by the remarkable ceremonies in which they had recently participated, and their minds were kept more or less on the stretch by the knowledge of others yet to follow.

Part of the Malu ceremonies consisted in thoroughly frightening the *kersi* with "Devil belong Malu." This was accomplished by men disguised by being completely covered with coconut and banana leaves, who rushed about making noises by hitting or rubbing together two rough clam shells. The lads were beaten with clubs; sometimes they were merely bruised, but some old men still bear the scars of wounds they received at this time. Naturally the fright the boys then received left a lasting impression on them. They were informed that if they divulged any of the Malu secrets *magur* would kill them. Every man who offended against Malu would also be punished. The *kersi* were also told "no keep word close to heart, he go speak quick; but in big toe, then you keep him long, when grey hair, no speak." In other words they had to bury the secrets deep so that they would not be revealed, even should the lads grow to be old men, but otherwise the secrets might escape. The *kersi* were informed later that the *magur* were not spirits, but only men dressed up. Women and un-initiates had a great dread of *magur*, and the women and children, at all events, believed them to be spirits. They only knew of them by this name; but the *zogo ne*, known only to the initiates, was *Ib*.

THE MALU CEREMONIES

It is pretty evident that *magur* was essentially the disciplinary executive of the Malu cult. All breaches of discipline, acts of sacrilege, and the like were punished by *magur*. *Magur* was also the means of terrorising the women and thereby keeping up the fear and mystery of the Malu ceremonies. There is no doubt that this great power was often abused to pay off personal grudges or for the aggrandisement or indulgence of the Malu officials. A somewhat similar institution occurs in the Papuan Gulf and Mekeo districts of British New Guinea. The *rukruk* of North Bougainville, in the Solomon Islands, and the *dukduk* of the Gazelle Peninsula, in New Britain, are apparently also of the same nature.

The life of the Torres Straits Islanders was at all times hedged in with observances, for the powers of the unseen world are very real to savages, and most of the ordinary events in Nature have to be supplemented by magical processes. Indeed, the magic connected with planting is as essential as is the agricultural process itself, and without certain specific magical rites it would be foolish to expect abundant crops of fruit or success in fishing. In the course of this narration I incidentally allude to many of these customs, but it would be tedious to enumerate all those concerning which we have gathered some information, and we recognise that quite a number must have escaped our ken altogether.

But of all the ceremonies of the eastern tribe, that of the great and sacred Malu Mystery was certainly the most famous, for, as far as we could learn, there was nothing to approach it in Erub. The fame of it had spread to the western tribe, but doubtless the initiation ceremonies of the different islands had a similar overwhelming sanctity for their initiates.

It is difficult for us to realise the awe and reverence that was felt by these people for these sacred ceremonies, and it must be admitted that this intense feeling, combined as it was with reticence and discipline, had a strong educative effect on the people. For this reason, if for no other, these ceremonies are worthy of a very careful study. Whatever tends to take a man out of himself and to weld him into a solidarity, limited though that may be, is an upward step in the slow and laborious evolution of man, and deserves our sympathetic respect.

The paraphernalia of nearly every ceremony of all peoples

are generally foolish, and often grotesque, to the outsider; but they awaken deep religious sentiment in the true believer, who, when duly instructed, beholds in them a symbolism that visualises the sacred legends and aspirations of his community. There cannot be the least doubt that these sentiments exist among so-called savages, and those who scoff at their ceremonies thereby condemn themselves.

CHAPTER V

ZOGOS

WE all like to know what has happened recently, or what will probably take place in the immediate future, and so we read the daily paper to learn the news. Savages, after all, are not very different in many ways from ourselves, and they, too, want to know what is going on. Although our Murray Island friends had no written language, and consequently could have no newspapers, they managed to invent a system for finding out about things which appeared to answer their purpose admirably—at all events they were very proud of it. The cynical might hazard a suggestion that the news imparted by the Murray Island oracle was not appreciably more fallible than that which appears in many of our newspapers.

I discovered the old Murray Island oracle ten years ago, and being anxious to renew my acquaintance with *Tomog Zogo*, as it is called, we went to have a look at it; but we found it dreadfully overgrown with vegetation. I grubbed about for some time, but gave it up as hopeless till we had some help; so we went on to visit some other relics of the past. As we were going through the bush to see a garden *zogo* stone that had "come by itself" from Erub, thirty miles off, we came across a party of men who had been collecting wood to burn the lime for the new church. They were having a "spell" and eating in groups; then some of them began to dance the Rotumah dance that they so often practised, and which they intended to perform on the occasion of opening of the new church at Erub. It was pleasingly unexpected to come suddenly upon a convivial group of twenty to thirty men. We chatted, joked, and passed on.

Next morning I sent the sergeant, Jimmy Dei, and some policemen to cut away the bamboos and undergrowth that obstructed *Tomog Zogo*, and Ray and I spent a long afternoon in mapping it. We placed two long bamboos east and west along each side of the large group of stones that constitute the *zogo*. Then we tied taut strings across from the one to the other bamboo at intervals of two feet. Next we marked on a sheet of squared paper the positions of the bamboos and strings, each square of the paper representing six square inches on the ground; there were thus four squares between each two lines of string on the paper. Ray measured the distance of every stone from the nearest bamboo and string, and thus I was able to put down each stone on paper with a very fair degree of accuracy.

The following afternoon we all went to the *zogo*; Bruce came too. Strangely enough he had not previously seen or heard of this *zogo*. We had with us the Mamoose, Enocha, Jimmy Dei, Ulai, and Kaige, all of whom belonged to the *zogo*. We learnt the names of the stones, and then at our request the *zogo* men placed themselves in the right position and attitude for consulting the *zogo*, and then they were photographed. It was very suggestive to see the reverent affection the old men had for the *zogo*, and they seemed gratified at the care with which it had been cleaned and mapped.

This famous *zogo* consists of a collection of stones, on each of which was formerly placed a large shell, usually a great Fusus or a helmet-shell; each stone, with its shell, represented a village or a district of the island. A little way off was a single stone and shell that stood for the whole island. Divination was accomplished by the voices and movements of birds, lizards, insects, or the appearance of natural objects. Anything that happened to the separate stone and shell concerned all the inhabitants of the island; but anything that happened to one of the grouped stones and shells related only to the man or men who live in the house or district represented by that particular stone and shell. There was thus a means for both analysis and synthesis.

At the eastern end of the group of stones were a large number of giant-clam shells; many were concentrically arranged, and formerly there were more of them, the smaller within the larger, so that the whole must have looked like a huge white rosette, and safely ensconced in the centre was a small star-shaped stone, the *zogo* itself; the concentric clam shells formed the "house of the *zogo*." In other words, the small stone was the oracle, the clam shells were its shrine.

PLATE VII

THE SHRINE OF BABARKER

TOMOG ZOGO

Tomog Zogo acted as *The Police News, The Hue and Cry*, and a morning newspaper, with a little prophesying thrown in.

A very limited number of men belonged to this *zogo*, and they consulted it only at daybreak, "small fellow daylight." Those who came to inquire of the oracle would stand up in a particular spot and say, "Tomog Zogo, you know everything, tell us the truth." After they had asked the definite question for which they required an answer, they sat down on some leaves, with their legs crossed under them, with their closed fists on their knees.

It is a fixed belief amongst most savage peoples that no one gets ill or even dies from natural causes, but that all these misfortunes are due to magic, and it is necessary to find out who perpetrated this evil. Supposing, for example, someone in the island was sick, the friends of the invalid would approach the men who belonged to *Tomog Zogo*, and would ask them to find out who had brought this misfortune on their friend. Next morning the *zogo* men would start before sunrise, and would ask the *zogo*, "Who made So-and-so sick? where does he live?"

Then the inquirers would sit down in a row and wait. By-and-by a lizard might come out of one of the shells; this would indicate the house where the man lived, and later, by means of careful inquiries in the village, they would try to discover who he was. When they had satisfied themselves, they would tell him to take his sorcery stone and to put it in the sea. As the stone was cooled by the water, so the patient would recover from his illness. Whether the man had made sorcery or not, he would always own to it and do as he was told, partly to save trouble and partly because he was pleased to have the reputation of being able to perform this kind of magic.

The *Tomog Zogo* was also consulted if a man was very ill, in order to find out whether he would recover. If a dead lizard was seen, he would be expected to die, and it is pretty certain he would do so.

It was the custom to attend the *zogo* every morning to discover if anything was going to happen. If a spider's web was seen hanging on the bushes, it would foretell the appearance of a white man's ship coming from the direction in which the web was hanging.

The appearance of a certain wild fowl would foretell the approach of a canoe from that particular quarter whence the fowl emerged from the bush, and its behaviour would indicate how soon the canoe might be expected.

If a red spot was seen on a leaf it would mean a fight, and its position would show whence the danger would come.

When an evil-smelling fungus sprung up within the area of stones there would be a famine, or a scarcity of yams.

Should a stream of ants come from the bush to the northward of the *zogo*, the diviners would expect a visit from the natives of the mainland of New Guinea, and if the ants carried their cocoons (the so-called "ants' eggs") in their mouths, it would mean that the men would bring some sago with them.

If there was no "news," nothing would happen.

Supposing the *zogo* was consulted for a definite purpose and no answer was vouchsafed. The men would sit watching patiently till the sun was high, then they would consult together, and probably would agree that the silence indicated a "big sick," and that some sickness or epidemic was in store for the island.

As an illustration of the power of *Tomog Zogo* I was told the following story:—

The first missionaries to this island were Mataika and his wife; they had been brought from Lifu, in the Loyalty Islands, to Erub in 1872. Towards the end of that year, in a canoe of his own making, Mataika crossed from Darnley to convert the Murray Islanders. After Mataika had been there for some time, he wanted fresh stores, and so he went to the headquarters of the Mission, which were then at Somerset, Cape York.

Mataika was away such a long time that his wife became very anxious, and feared that he was dead. Being unable to bear the suspense any longer, she spoke to Obra, the father of Kaige the policeman, and said, "Very good; you go to your *zogo*, and ask him where Mataika he stop. I think him dead." He said, "All right; to-morrow small daylight I go."

On consulting *Tomog Zogo* at daybreak next morning, Obra could not see anything happen in the clearing in the direction of Somerset. After some time two *kead* birds came out from the bush which lay in the direction of Erub and looked at Obra, and immediately they disappeared.

Obra came back and said to the anxious wife, "Mataika, he leave Somerset long time ago; he go to Erub; close up he come." Next morning Obra went up the hill Gelam, and espied a canoe coming from Erub. He told Mataika's wife that her husband was on board, and sure enough he was, with one other man and three boys.

On his arrival Mataika was informed what had been done, and he told the natives to burn and break up all their other *zogos*, charms, and images. "They all devil-devil; but good thing you keep *Tomog Zogo;* he speak true. Ah! he all right; all same dream."

I never heard whether this oracle was ever consulted again; at all events, *Tomog Zogo* has shared the fate of all the other *zogos*, and it is now broken and partially destroyed.

When one remembers how many civilised nations have believed in and consulted oracles, one need not be surprised if these people were reluctant to give up their old sacred places. The wonder is that they have so readily embraced the new faith and the new ideas.

The Mamoose promised to give us a private rehearsal of *Tomog Zogo* the next morning at daybreak. I was up in time, but he did not come. I had a little talk with him later in the day, and the following morning he arrived, and one or two of us went just before sunrise in the "old-time fashion." We told the Mamoose we were anxious for the speedy arrival of the Mission vessel, the *Nieue*, and wanted to know when she was coming. We heard some birds twittering in the bushes, which Mamoose gravely assured us meant a boat was approaching. After sitting a long time on dew-bespangled dead leaves, we retired. The chief point of interest to me was the fact that the steady-going old chief, who had long been a deacon of the church, was still a believer in this famous *zogo* to which he and his ancestors belonged, and whilst he was sitting motionless in the old spot and intently gazing at the *zogo* and listening for the message from the birds, the church bell was ringing summoning the people to the early morning prayer-meeting.

Later in the day George Rotumah's lugger came in and brought us a mail, so the birds had not twittered in vain.

On the opposite side of Murray Island from the Mission Station is the village of Las, perhaps the largest and most important village in the island in former times. As it was the main centre of the ancient Malu ceremonies, I thought it would be well for me to stay there for a day or two. So in the afternoon of Wednesday, May 18th, Rivers and I walked over along the new road, made by prison labour, that skirts the greater part of the island. Rivers went with me, as he wanted to see if it would be practicable to take some psychological apparatus over there to test those people who would not, or could not, come across to us.

We had a pleasant walk. The faithful Pasi accompanied us, as did Gadodo, Pasi's cousin and our host. We found Gadodo had a large grass house of the now usual South Sea type—that is, oblong, with one doorway and no other opening. In the interior, along the end walls, were bamboo stagings, about three to four feet from the ground, which served as beds. All the houses of the eastern tribe of Torres Straits (*i.e.* Uga, Erub, and the Murray Islands) were formerly circular and quite small. There is only one beehive house remaining in Murray Island. After we had dumped our swag, or, as some people would say, after we had deposited our luggage in the house, we had the usual drink of coconut water, and squatted on a mat by Mrs. Gadodo's side to have a chat. Then we had a walk along the sand beach. Our dinner consisted of a plate of boiled sweet potatoes, bananas, and pumpkin, all mixed up together, with a coconut for drink.

After the evening meal we sat on mats by the light of lamps in the village inclosure, and yarned and played "cat's cradle." Soon the bell sounded for prayers, and Enocha came with his service-book, and several others gathered together. Pasi started the hymn, read the lesson, and prayed, of course, all in Murray Island language.

Very soon after this the small boys arranged themselves round some branched posts which had been planted in the sand so as to inclose an oval space, and clamoured out for *tamar*. *Tamar* is a sort of market that was introduced here by Loyalty Islanders from Lifu and Mare, and which appears now to be firmly established, though its popularity waxes and wanes from time to time. I heard of it ten years before, but never witnessed it, so I was very pleased at the present opportunity.

A crowd soon collected, made up chiefly of children, and a fire was lit in the centre of the area. We sat apart, as this was our first appearance at a *tamar*. There was a great deal of noise and fun going on. The game is as follows. The players bring firewood (*i.e.* coconut-palm leaves and other fuel) and food; the "master" (of ceremonies) goes round the circle, standing in front of each player in turn. The latter holds up the object he has brought, saying, "*Tamar*," and mentions what he holds up. The "master" asks, Where did you get this?" And a reply is made which is supposed to be a true answer, but as a laugh often followed, I suspect some humbugging went on. This took some time. Then a prayer was made!—why, I don't know; it seemed very comical in a game—and then "New man, new man!" was shouted out, and Pasi, Rivers, and I went into a circle near the fire, and a small mat was placed there too. Several brought us coconuts as a present, which were placed on the mat. Then the "master" pointed a glowing fire-stick at me, and said words to this effect: "You see this fire-stick; you go home and look after wife belong you. If you do not bring firewood and food next time, you will be thrown into the sea." The *tamar* concluded after Rivers had been similarly introduced, and Rivers and I very shortly turned in, as we were very tired; but Pasi stayed up, as he wanted to hear the small boys practise their songs!

We were up early next morning, and got the local legend of the disreputable Iruam from Pasi and Gadodo. Soon after an early breakfast of wild sweet potatoes and green coconuts, and an attendance at morning prayers, I took my camera and notebook, and went along the beach to pick up some information of which I had previously gained clues.

Soon after starting I heard about an ancient fighting custom associated with *Ziriam Zogo*, at a place called Meket. There was a turtle-shell mask, which no woman was allowed to see, that was kept in a hole in the rock. I asked Pasi to sketch the mask for me in the sand; then I asked another man to do so. Of course I did not let either look at the other man's representation until they had finished. As I found they differed, I made further inquiries, and found that an old man named Wano, who lived closed by, knew all about the ceremony; so he was fetched, and he drew a diagram on the sand. By dint of much questioning and pantomimic action, I found out something about the ceremony and the character of the mask. This consisted of a turtle-shell face, with pearl-shell eyes surmounted by a turtle-shell crescent about three feet across, decorated on each horn with a black-tipped feather of the white Torres Straits pigeon and two seed rattles. Attached to the chin of the mask was a rope about six feet long, to which a large number of human lower jawbones were tied. Before I left Murray Island Wano made a rough wooden model of the mask for me.

After a fight a number of men would come here with bows and arrows and clubs, especially with the former. The men formed a circle and danced with appropriate shooting gestures; two men painted red and wearing dance-petticoats danced in crouching attitudes in the centre, and all sang a weird song. One of the central dancers would wear the mask and would carry in his right hand a club, and in his left a bleeding, decapitated human head. The other man supported the rope of human jawbones.

At the back of my old friend Mamai's house at Warwe was a shrine of stones and shells, on which were two stones called *Zabarker*. Zabarker was formerly a woman who came from New Guinea, and Mamai told me her short, but not very edifying story. She is now a somewhat pyramidal black stone resting on a saucer-shaped stone of granite, which represents her canoe. The upper stone is a piece of the local lava, but the granite occurs only in the western islands, some hundred and twenty miles or more away, or in the hill of Mabudauan, in New Guinea, also about the same distance from Murray Island. I now find there are quite a number of these foreign stones in the island, which evidently point to some forgotten migration from, or former intercourse with, the western islands.

A little further along the coast is the ancient and efficacious *Wag Zogo*, at the small cape called Tur Pit. In a sandy-bottomed recess in a block of lava on the foreshore lie an oval and a spherical granitic boulder, named respectively *Neiu* and *Sager*. Some four or five men used to take a number of plants called *geribe* and coconut leaves, which they pointed repeatedly at the stones, and "a big wind" would immediately come from the south-east. As long as the leaves remained there, so long would the wind continue. Here again we find foreign stones, which I was informed came from New Guinea. I asked if they could make a south-east wind during the north-west monsoon, but I was informed that the ceremony could only be done during the south-east season. In this, as in other cases, I found that the impossible was never attempted. A rain charm would not be made when there was no expectation of rain coming, or a south-east wind raised during the wrong season.

ZOGOS

The sun beat fiercely on the sand beach, and the heat and glare, combined with the talking and excitement, tired us much, so we went back to Las and lay down for an hour or two in the cool, dark house. After another meal of boiled yams and a coconut drink, I went along the shore in the opposite direction and photographed an oblong stone on the beach, that was once a man named *Iruam*, who deservedly came to a bad end.

An old dancing-ground, *Dam*, associated with the Malu ceremonies, was next visited. It was situated to the north-east of Las in the bush, a few yards from the beach. This was overgrown by vegetation, so we set to work and cleared it. A quadrangular area of shells, mostly the large Fusus, amongst which were five stones, was laid bare. This had a general N.N.W. to S.S.E. direction. At right angles to this group of shells was a series of stones, arranged like a fish-hook, extending for a distance of about fourteen feet. About fifteen feet to the south-east was another stone, *Zugared*. Three of the stones were foreign; all the remainder were, I believe, local stones—two of them were blocks of coral.

When this particular ceremony was carried on, a taboo was put for some distance on each side of the sand beach to warn off all unauthorised persons. The four officiating men mixed the ashes of a scented root with oil in a couple of shells; two of them held the shells while the other two anointed the initiates between the first two toes and on the knee and shoulder of the right side. Four men next held a large Fusus shell in each hand, the first two stood side by side, the second two crouched behind them, and a number of pairs of men crouched behind these; this double row formed up between *Zugared* and the other stones. On the opposite side of the island stones the *kersi* clung in fright round the three *zogole*, who stood close together.

Finally all went and jumped in the sea; after swimming about for a short time the *kersi* were rubbed with coconut oil and painted in a particular manner and given a pigeon's feather to wear. The boys were shown the stones and told their names, and were informed that they were placed there by Malu. There can be little doubt that these stones formed a kind of map, or chart, for the instruction of the youths, and to impress upon them the wanderings of Malu on his voyage to Murray Island. I could not help recalling a parallel instance to this that occurred during my former visit to Murray Island, when the white missionary was instructing, by means of a map, the young native teachers in the three journeys of St. Paul.

We next went up the hill to Gazir, where, in a thicket of bamboos, the first of the Malu ceremonies was held. These ceremonies have already been dealt with. There is no doubt that if reliable information is to be obtained on sacred customs, one must go to the very spot where the ceremony took place in order to gain it, for not only does a right comprehension often depend on a knowledge of local conditions, but the place itself, by the association of ideas, recalls incidents to the narrator's memory.

On our way back we met Seligmann, who had come across to join us. We had the usual meal of boiled yams and coconuts. Prayers were followed by another *tamar*, which was a little better than that of the night before. Pasi and I joined the circle, and Seligmann was left outside. When the "master" came round to me I showed a piece of firewood, which I threw into the fire, then I said " *Tamar* ———" (the native name for the variety of cooked yam Pasi had given me; I have forgotten what it was). The "master" said, "Who gave it you?" and I said, "My wife in England cooked it for me," at which there was a laugh. Then I held up a coconut Gadodo had given me, and lastly some tobacco, a piece of which I gave to the "master." Thus I fulfilled the injunction laid upon me the previous night, and I was not ducked in the sea. When the round was finished a prayer was offered, and Seligmann was next admitted as Rivers and I previously had been. After this preliminary ceremony a sort of auction, or market, is supposed to take place; but these were very small *tamars*, and very little trading was done. Bruce tells me that at large *tamars* a great deal of buying and selling may occur, and good prices are often realised. As in some other matters, the natives overdo *tamar*, and rivalry in buying food results in the paralysing of ordinary routine daily work.

After *tamar* I persuaded Enocha and another man to sing to me. Both belonged to the *sügareb*, or "drum" clan, the members of which used formerly to beat the drum and sing the songs at the ceremonies; they were, in fact, the bards of the islands. One quite beautiful mournful couplet was a funeral dirge for a deceased Malu initiate.

Another Malu chant, which ran as follows—"O welwa, O lelelewar, O welwatamera, O gulabatamera, O wei—wei, wei—wei," etc., sounded most pathetic, and led one to expect a suitable meaning; but the translation, so far as I could make out, is—"O feathers! O yams! O feathered stone-club! O dry banana leaf!"

We were then interrupted by a "play." The people from our side of the island had come over to give a return performance, and with them had come Ontong, our cook. Two of the men had painted their faces a bright pale red, and one or two lads and lassies had only one side of the face so ruddled. They had but one song, the sole words of which were—

> "Oh you must be a lover of the Lord,
> Or you won't go to heaven when you die."

This was sung *ad nauseam*. Usually they sang it "You mussa be," which sounded like "You mustn't be." To this song various tricks were performed, and the serious polka which I have already described was danced to a very simple tune. The tricks consisted of string puzzles, turning round under one's arm, the hand of which was resting on a stick, and the following well-known riddle: "Add five to six and make nine." Six strokes | | | | | | were made in the sand, and the spokesman said the village would belong to him if no one could guess it. He then came up to me, and in a loud whisper said it was not meant for me, and besought me not to disclose the answer. Of course I did not dream of giving the show away. No one gave the answer, which, of course, was the addition of five strokes \ \ Ξ to the others to make N I N E. I was not sure whether the hosts did not know the answer, or whether those who did were too polite to give it. There was also a sham boxing-match. I found afterwards the Las people did not think very much of the performance.

After refreshments most of the visitors returned to their homes, and we retired to bed.

I spent most of the next morning in photographing *Dam* and in completing my notes on the ceremony there performed. I also took a group of Gadodo and his friends, as well as some views of the village of Las. We rested in the middle of the day and got more information. Gadodo gave me some stone fire- and rain-charms. When I first went to Las I showed them some photos I had taken ten years before, and they were continually asking to see them again; I also showed one or two prints of *zogos* that I had recently photographed at Dauar; and the photos of my wife and children, which I always carry about with me, were, as usual, hailed with great enthusiasm.

DAUAR

It will be remembered that the neighbouring island of Dauar consists mainly of two hills. The geologist recognises in these parts of an ancient volcano, but the natives have a different opinion concerning their origin. Two women of Dauar, named Pepker and Ziaino, had a race in the making of mud-pies with the object of deciding who could make the largest heap. Ziaino was soon tired, and called out, "You no finish? I finish now." And that is why Kebe Dauar is such a small hill. I will conclude the story in the words in which it was told to me. "Him (Pepker) he sing out, 'I no finish now.' Make him, make him, make him that hill. He finish, he sing out, 'I finish now.'" Pepker is now a rude stone figure, nearly a foot in height, and at the present time, together with several other "Lot's wife" stones, is in the collection at Cambridge.

We paid several visits to Dauar, but, not to be tedious, I will only describe one. We sailed across in the early morning with Pasi, Smoke and his wife, and one or two others. On landing we were met by Keriba, and after knocking down and eating a little wild fruit, which, by the way, was scarcely worth the effort, we sat in the welcome shade of some umbrageous trees close to the beach and listened to a couple of legends of local heroes told by Keriba. One related to an old man named Iriam Moris, whose appetite and capacity would be the envy of the most "aldermanic" of City fathers. On one occasion he ate four large shellfuls of small fish, an immense king-fish, which was really a metamorphosed lad named Geigi, and he finished off with the fish-trap, cooking-stones, firewood and ashes—in fact, all he could lay hands on; and in the terse jargon of that part of the world: "He kaikai (*i.e.* eat) so much, he can't walk about; he lay like a stone. He say 'I feel good now'"! Later Geigi's mother killed Iriam Moris and resuscitated her son. During this narration we were sitting on a slightly convex rock that was all but covered with sand, but was none other than the "big belly" of Iriam Moris.

PLATE VIII

THE ISLANDS OF WAIER AND DAUAR FROM THE BEACH OF MER, WITH A FISH SHRINE IN THE FOREGROUND

U ZOGO, THE COCONUT SHRINE OF DAUAR

We walked through beautiful and luxuriant "scrub" and native gardens and visited a *zogo* in a garden in the saddle between the two hills. The whole of the low land of the island has been more or less cultivated, so there is no old jungle anywhere; but it is all the owners of the land can do to prevent the rampant vegetation from overrunning their gardens of yams and sweet potatoes or smothering the bananas. It requires a more facile pen than I can wield and a better knowledge of plants than I possess to adequately describe such scenes. As is usually the case in most of the uncultivated tropical districts I have seen, there were but few flowers, and these were of no special beauty; but this is partly made up for by the varied form and hue of the green foliage and by the bold contrasts of light and shade that result from vertical sunshine. The smooth broad leaves of the bananas above and of aroids below give the eye welcome "areas of repose" amid the multiplicity of detail and the unceasing struggle for mastery that almost oppresses one in tropical vegetation.

FIG. 5. PEPKER, THE HILL-MAKER

The *zogo*, which was one object of our walk, was called *Ziai Neur*, that is, "the girl of the south-west," but why this was her name I could not discover. The *zogo* consisted of two images, male and female, roughly carved out of vesicular lava. When a man has a "bad sick" they take the fluid of a green coconut and wet the image with it, and the patient gets well. After Wilkin had photographed them, I tried to purchase them from a man named Billy who had been working in a garden close by, and came to see what we were about. Billy refused to part with them. Pasi quietly told me that as this garden belonged to Billy's wife and not to him, I should deal with the lady directly, and consequently Billy had nothing to do with it. The next day Pasi communicated with her, and the woman was willing to let me have the *zogo*; but the man was obdurate,

FIG. 6. ZIAI NEUR ZOGO.
A Therapeutic Shrine.

and they had a quarrel over it. Eventually I had to forego the transaction, as it did not answer my purpose to have any unfriendly feeling springing up with regard to ourselves or our work.

Most of the shrines we visited on this and other occasions looked at first sight like confused masses of shells and stones. The preliminary business was to cut down overhanging branches, creepers, and the undergrowth generally, then to clear away the dead leaves and other rubbish. When this was done a certain amount of order became apparent. Occasionally a few stones required to be placed upright, or broken ones put together. The best view for the photograph had to be carefully chosen, and further clearing of the foliage was generally necessary; sometimes branches of trees a little way off had to be lopped if they cast distracting shadows. Usually little twigs, leaves, or tiny plants had to be removed from the ground or from between the stones and shells, so as not to unnecessarily complicate the picture.

As a rule it is worth while to find out the best time of day to photograph any particular object; usually, however, these shrines were so placed that the time of day made very little difference.

Very rarely did I turn a carved stone round so as to bring out its carving more effectively; occasionally I shifted shells a little, so as to make them show up better, but only when these originally had no definite position. Attention to small details such as these are necessary to produce intelligible photographs, but care must be exercised not to overdo it or in any way to modify the object or shrine.

When all was ready the photograph was taken generally by Wilkin; and we sat down, and a native told me the "storia" connected with it. This I wrote down as nearly as I could in his own words, or at all events with some phrases verbatim. It was most interesting to hear these yarns on the spot, told by natives who believed in them. In some cases we have brought away the chief stone so that it can be exhibited in the museum along with a photograph of it *in situ*. We could not always buy the stone, as sometimes the natives were not willing to part with it, and never did we take anything without permission, or without full payment.

We crossed the island and came out in the bay named

Sauriad, which is mentioned in the chief legend of these islands as being where Malu fled after he had been entrapped on the sand spit. At one spot, named Orme, there is the important *U zogo*, or coconut shrine. Only old men officiated here; they rubbed themselves with the fluid from a coconut, and this made the palms productive. The *zogo* now consists of a few large clam shells on some rocks. One large *kaper* tree had a great Fusus stuck into it, round which the bark had partially grown; under a smaller *zom* tree were two large blocks of stone, on which were one or two giant clam shells. I do not know if there was anything further. We visited two other *zogos*, but there was nothing of interest about them or anything worth photographing.

The most satisfactory translation of the word *zogo* is "holy" or "sacred"; or a holy or sacred spot such as an oracle or a shrine for magical rites; or a potent object or charm. As in all primitive religions, holiness is not an ethical idea; indeed, as Robertson Smith points out in his *Religion of the Semites*, "at the Canaanite shrines the name of 'holy' was specially appropriated to a class of degraded wretches devoted to the most shameful practices of a corrupt religion." *Zogo* does not mean "tabooed" or "prohibited," as the Miriam word for that idea is *gelar*.

When walking along a sand beach at the western end of the island we saw, close in shore, very dense shoals of small fish, locally called *tup*. At one spot two small sharks were preying on them, and wherever a shark swam there was a band of clear water, and the yellow sand could be seen beneath; elsewhere the water was solidly black with fish. It reminded me of a certain town and gown row in my undergraduate days, when the market-place was a dense mass of men, mainly undergraduates, but wherever the proctors moved there was always a clear space around them.

We photographed the tracks of a turtle where she had gone up the sand beach to lay her eggs, and had returned to the sea. We prodded the sand about the apex of the converging tracks in the orthodox fashion, with a pointed stick, but could not find the nest.

When we had worked our way round to the side of the island from which we had started we found that Mrs. Canoe had laid out some banana leaves on the sand in an inclosure round her house. On this native tablecloth she had placed four heaps of coconut chips and a central heap of warm roasted green bananas, and four green coconuts were prepared for us to drink from. We much enjoyed this *al fresco* repast.

WAIER

I knew from various legends and other information that the island of Waier was of some importance, so I arranged for a visit there, and as part of the island belonged to our friend Smoke I endeavoured to get him to act as cicerone. We sailed across to Dauar, where Smoke was working in his garden, and we waited some time in vain for him to come to us.

Eventually Smoke's elder brother, Keriba, consented to accompany us, and as he is an old man and had officiated at the *zogos* we could not have done better. His first excuse was that already that morning he had been round Waier fishing and was tired, which was doubtless true.

We waded across the reef which joins Dauar and Waier, as it was then low tide, and went round the southern side of this extinct crater. As I have already mentioned, Waier is a remarkable island, consisting of a crescentic, greatly fissured wall of volcanic ash, with the upper edge pinnacled and battlemented like an old castle. In the hollow of the crescent is a narrow sand beach, behind which, close to the rocks, is a little vegetation.

As we went along Keriba pointed out the interesting places, and gave us names of the prominent rocks and objects. It was stimulating to see the old sacred places, many of which Wilkin and I photographed, and to hear what happened there. Keriba seemed a little nervous about touching or interfering with some of the *zogos*, but when he saw us tidying them, and removing overgrowing grass and weeds, he too gave a hand.

The first one we came to was *Zab Zogo*, which consists merely of a few giant clam shells within a recess in the cliff, and protected by a row of stones. This gives good fishing, but only for a small kind of fish, which is speared at night by the light of torches made of dry coconut leaves.

Close by is a longish oblong rock on the beach, which is called *Geigi-baur*, i.e. "Geigi's fish-spear." Geigi was a hero of Waier who lived with his mother Nageg, about whom there are legends. Later in the day I was shown a flat rock on the sand beach in the bay of Waier, which was the mother's mat. Geigi ultimately became a "king-fish," and his mother a "trigger-fish." Seligmann had already collected a specimen of the lady, and the "king-fish" is well known. One of the string puzzles represents Geigi, and another Nageg.

Shortly after we had rounded the southern point of Waier, and were walking along the bay, we came to a black stone about fifteen inches in length lying broken in the grass, on a heap of stones and shells at the foot of the cliff. We stuck it upright and cleared away the weeds, in order to get a photograph of the gentleman, who is named *Waipem*, but who after all has no particular shape, though a little pit on each side of the head does duty for the eyes. Formerly the men who belonged to this *zogo* erected in front of the image three bamboos like a football goal, on the crossbar of which was hung various kinds of fruit, and "man think inside himself, 'If we give you plenty fruit I think you give us plenty turtle.'" They would then go to the two points of the island and look out for the turtles, which would be sure to come. This little ceremony was only performed about January—that is, during the turtle season.

In a small cave a little further on were two slabs, which represented two women called *Au kosker* ("big women"). Their heads had fallen off; one had been much battered by the sea, but the other was in a better state of repair, and some white paint indicated the eyes, nose, and mouth. We replaced this head, but could not repair the other, which we placed by the side of the body. After a lot of trouble we focussed the camera and gave it an exposure of half an hour or so. When Wilkin developed it in the evening we found to our surprise that we had a fairly good negative.

So far as I could make out, all the *Au kosker* ever did was to come out in the night-time and dance in a circle on the sand beach, waving and crossing their arms. Waiad used to look at them and beat a drum; after that the two ladies retired to their cave.

I had previously heard about Waiad, and took this opportunity of finding out more about him. Whatever he was supposed to be in ancient times, Waiad was until recently represented by a turtle-shell human effigy about four feet in height that was kept in a cave high up in the *Au kes*, the large central fissure of Waier. At the time of the Waiad ceremony the fraternity assembled on the sand spit, which is also called Waier, and yarned about the lads (*kersi*) who were about to be initiated. Most of the men then walked round the southern side of the island to the tabooed ground. Three sacred men (*zogole*) took Waiad from his cave and placed him on a small column-like stone, which was pointed out to us. The stone is now overshadowed by vegetation, and there are still to be seen the great Fusus shells that radiated from it; but formerly the place was clear, and Waiad could be seen from afar. A *zogole* stood on each side of the image.

The lads who were to be initiated into this *zogo* were brought from the sand spit round by the north side of the island and hidden behind a great mass of rock that had fallen from the cliff. When the proper time came two men were sent by the *zogole* to fetch the *kersi*, who came kneeling and laden with presents of coconuts, bananas, and yams. Each *kersi* had in his mouth a large white shell painted red, which protruded from his lips. The boys had to traverse some eighty or ninety yards on their knees from their hiding-place to the shrine of Waiad. These Waiad ceremonies lasted for a fortnight, during which time there was more or less continuous singing and drum-beating.

CHAPTER VI

VARIOUS INCIDENTS IN MURRAY ISLAND

I HAVE previously mentioned that I had engaged two Murray Island natives, Debe Wali and Jimmy Rice, to assist Ontong, our Javanese cook. At first I offered them a shilling a day as wages. This they refused after much consideration, but agreed that they would take a pound a month. Later on, when they had practical experience that one pound sterling a month was not so advantageous to them as six shillings a week, they repented of their bargain, but as it was not to our interest to be hard on them, we reverted to my original offer. Our supply of silver was running short, so after a time we had to pay in half-sovereigns; at first there was some difficulty in making them understand the equity of their having to return four shillings in silver in exchange for the gold coin.

One morning during my temporary absence from the island, Jimmy Rice came up on the verandah, followed by an islander named Gi, and said, "This man want to speak along you, fellow." Gi said, "Me want sell porslin along you." My colleagues, not having at that time an instinctive knowledge of pidjin English, and forgetting that *f* and *sh* are often transmuted into *p* and *s*, awaited with some interest Gi's disclosure of the porcelain. Gi produced four shillings (por s'lin') and said, "Me want to buy ten s'lin'." A light gradually dawned on my colleagues as they recollected the Saturday night transactions with Jimmy Rice and Debe Wali.

The more obvious part of this arrangement had evidently been noised abroad, and Gi came prepared to test our readiness to give a half-sovereign in exchange for four shillings.

After introducing Gi, Jimmy Rice retired below the verandah, where he remained evidently appreciating the humour of the situation. He said afterwards, "I laugh along myself inside. I laugh, laugh, laugh. Gi he gammon."

This was by no means the only occasion on which we were humbugged, but we did not mind, for were we not studying the psychology of the natives amongst other subjects, and it was most interesting to watch the various idiosyncrasies of our friends and acquaintances.

For example the grey-bearded Ari was somewhat slow and perhaps a little stupid, but he was thoroughly conscientious and always tried to do the right thing. We were never quite sure, by the way, whether the old boy's name, which was pronounced Ari, was really a native name or merely their version of "Harry." Pasi was a man of stronger character and more intelligent; he had an alert manner and an abrupt method of speech. Debe Wali was a highly strung, nervous, voluble person, and not averse to thrusting himself forward; Jimmy Rice was much quieter and slower in his speech and thoughts; he was certainly more reliable than Debe Wali, but he had a strong instinct of acquisitiveness, scarcely a day passed without his asking for something. Myers tells me that once within twenty-four hours he asked for a pair of boots, a belt, two empty rice bags, a Jew's harp, a hat, and of course some tobacco. Jimmy Dei was a thorough gentleman, Gadodo a man of action, Alo a great, good-natured fellow who kept and carefully tended a wheezy old sick man. So I might go on, matching white men known to me with our Papuan friends; few were really disagreeable, but I call to mind one sleek, hypocritical man named Papi, who was always trying to get the better of everyone else, and in this he generally succeeded.

Old Ulai was perhaps the greatest character of the lot, a regular old heathen, who exhibited but scanty signs of grace. He gloated over the past, especially the shady parts of it, and it was this lack of reverence that made him so valuable to us. As he had but little of that reticence that is so characteristic of the Melanesian, we were able to get hints from him that we followed up with our other friends to our great advantage. For, alas! I do not think our friend was very truthful, nor did he know all about everything, and occasionally he was inclined to gammon us even in serious matters; but that did not matter, as we never trusted his word alone. Indeed, the cunning old

PLATE IX

DEBE WALI AND HIS WIFE

JIMMY RICE AND HIS WIFE

man was a great humbug, and he seemed to quite enjoy being found out, and never resented the imputation of "gammoning." He had a craving for beer and grog, and often and often he would sidle up and whisper, "You give me a little grog." A demand, needless to add, that was never satisfied.

When I went to New Guinea I took Ontong, our Malay cook, with me, and left Rivers, Myers, and McDougall with the two native "boys." My colleagues have described to me how amused they were in watching the subsequent developments. Rivers did not consider it expedient to definitely appoint one as cook and the other as helper, knowing matters would right themselves.

Naturally, Debe Wali at once took the more important post, and to Jimmy Rice fell the job of carrying water twice daily and getting firewood. Debe's active mind soon discovered that if he was doing cook's work he should have cook's pay, so he wanted a rise in wages. Then it dawned upon Jimmy Rice that he should not be left out in the cold; he argued, "Debe, he now got one job—he cook; me got two job—me cut 'im wood, me fetch 'im water. You give me more wages."

It did not take Debe Wali long to discover that Jimmy Rice had practically the whole day to himself, while he, as cook, was more occupied, though, to tell the truth, the cooking was of the most rudimentary kind possible.

Eventually an arrangement was made between Debe and Jimmy among themselves, by which they spent alternate weeks at cooking and hewing wood and drawing water. There was always considerable jealousy as to who was the better cook; once, when it was Jimmy's week to cook, and he had brought up some bread of his own making, Debe came in, looked at it, and sticking his thumb well in, blandly remarked, "I call that damper."

On another occasion, when the mind of the entire island was absorbed in the preparation of a big *kaikai* (feast), Jimmy Rice went off into the bush to bring back his contribution of yams, bananas, and coconuts, and there became so absorbed in his work that he did not return until after my colleagues had cooked their own dinner. Debe Wali was furious when he heard of his comrade's unpunctuality. "When I cook, by jingo, I give you proper *kaikai* (food); breakfast, sun there; dinner, sun up here; supper, sun over there." That same evening and the following morning Debe forgot to fill the jugs with water.

One nice thing about our helpers was that they never considered themselves as servants. They treated us as equals, much to the amusement and disgust of Ontong. They would come up from the kitchen, loll on our deck chairs, and chatter away always in the most amusing fashion.

Myers also told me the following :—" Debe astonished us one evening by the calm announcement, 'Milk he no good. Me suck (chuck) 'im away. He full plenty big black pigeon.' With no little interest we prepared to make the acquaintance of the big black 'pigeon,' ignorant at that time that the word 'pigeon' is applied by the Murray Islanders to any living thing that is not obviously a four-footed animal. We found an open tin of condensed milk swarming with large black ants."

Ten years previously, when in Mabuiag, I sent Dick, the boy who used to fetch and carry for me, to a fresh-water pool with a net and bottle to see what he could catch. He returned in high glee crying, "Doctor, I catch 'im pigeon belong waterhole." The "pigeons" happened to be some small water-beetles.

Very shortly before we left I invited the Mamoose, Pasi, who is the Mamoose of Dauar, and Jimmy Dei, the Sergeant of Police, to dinner. We gave them soup, curry and rice, rice and honey, and pancakes. Judging from the quantities they ate they enjoyed themselves very much. Afterwards we gave them songs and music on the phonograph, and I obtained their autographs, for it is not often that one has two kings to dinner.

Rivers had asked them twice before, when some of us were in New Guinea; on one occasion when Pasi went home he saw his eldest son nursing a very small infant, and he asked him, "What man belong that boy?" "Why, poppa," was the answer, "he belong you!" His wife had presented Pasi with a baby when he was out to dinner. According to the common practice of the island, Pasi had promised the unborn babe to a native named Smoke, who, having no children of his own, had expressed a wish to "look out for it," or in other words, to take care of it; a *sogo* is said to "look out garden."

I was informed by Myers that at this supper Harry, the Mamoose, and Pasi each asked for three helpings of curry, and three of rice with jam and marmalade. Pickles and marmalade proved an irresistible attraction. Even Pasi, who has travelled as far as Thursday Island, had never met with marmalade before.

When Harry began his third helping Pasi spoke to him in the Miriam tongue, "Only take a little." The hosts knew enough of the language to understand what was said, and, to the evident amusement of the two guests, persuaded Pasi also to "take a little."

Cigars were given them after dinner, which they were polite enough to pretend to relish. Harry's cigar remained almost unsmoked; a New Guinea boy finished Pasi's. Although smoking was practised in these islands before the white men came, and they grew their own tobacco, they never smoked much at a time.

The native pipe is made of a piece of bamboo from about a foot to between two and three feet in length. The natural partition at the one end, and the intermediate one, if such occurs, is perforated. At one end of the pipe there is always a complete partition, and near this a small hole is bored; into the latter a small wooden or bamboo tube, a few inches in length, is inserted. The tobacco is put in this, and the open end of the pipe applied to the mouth, and by suction the pipe is filled with tobacco smoke. I have seen them put their mouth to the bowl and blow down it. As soon as the pipe is filled with smoke, the right hand is applied to the open end and the bowl removed. This hole is applied to the mouth, and the smoke sucked through it after the withdrawal of the hand from the open end. The length of the pipe causes such a draught that the smoke is violently inhaled.

When a man has had a suck he will put his hand to the open end of the pipe to prevent the escape of the smoke and pass it on to another, who receives it, and maybe transmits it to a third in the same manner. The women usually prepare the pipes, and pass them on to the men. This method of smoking occurs over a considerable portion of New Guinea, but, so far as I am aware, it is confined to the Papuans.

The effect of this kind of smoking appears to be very severe. The men always seem quite dazed for a second or two, or even longer, and their eyes water; but they enjoy it greatly, and value tobacco very highly, they will usually sell almost anything they possess for some. I have seen an old man reel and stagger from the effects of one pull at a bamboo pipe, and I have heard of a man even dropping down on the ground from its effects.

To return to this supper party. When the guests were trying to enjoy the cigars, Jimmy Dei arrived in a very excited condition, bringing to the chiefs news of apparently no small importance. It transpired that he, in his capacity as Sergeant of the Police, had reported the assault of an islander upon his wife, who had thereupon summoned her husband to appear at the court-house on the following day. Any excitement of this kind is always most welcome to such an impressionable people as these are.

Myers has kindly given me an account of the following circumstance that happened when I was in New Guinea :—" We were awakened one morning by the sound of voices in the 'kitchen'—that is, the space below the verandah on which we slept. They were the voices of Debe Wali and his wife, between whom short and quickly answered sentences were passing. Louder and louder grew their talk. Suddenly a blow was heard, followed by a metallic noise and the sound of falling water. There was silence for a time, then softer talking, and a woman's low cry. Up came Debe Wali to us, labouring to suppress the most intense excitement. 'Woman belong me want me go bush (*i.e.* to the garden). Me I no go. I cook here. I say to woman, "You go." She say, "No, you go." I tell 'im, "You sh-sh." He no sh-sh. I tell 'im, "You be quiet: you wake 'im white man; he sleep." He talk on. I hit 'im with saucepan. Hold on. I fetch 'im.' And Debe vanished below to reappear with his weapon, which, as he put it, he had 'capsized' on to his wife. A few minutes later the little woman, one of the hardest-working on the island, came to us to be treated for a terrible gash down to the bone on the back of her head, which had to be sewn up. Debe was much alarmed on the following day, for Kaige, the policeman, insisted on roaming about the verandah and kitchen, mainly occupied in consuming our tobacco. Had Debe not been our servant, he would undoubtedly have been summoned by his wife, and, this being his fifth offence in this direction, he would have been sent a prisoner to Thursday Island. To show his penitence he wore all day a black kerchief round his head; while, to smooth the ruffled feelings of his wife, he bought from us (out of his next week's wages) some yards of red twill which he presented to her."

Mr. Bruce has informed me by letter that early in 1899 Jimmy Rice and Debe Wali had, for them, a serious quarrel. It happened in this wise. Pedro, a Manila who had married Jimmy's wife's daughter by a former husband, D. Pitt, had given Jimmy a small cutter. Jimmy's wife considered the boat was given to her as a present for her daughter's sake, so she began to "boss" the boat and crew. Debe was captain, while Jimmy remained on shore to cook the bêche-de-mer.

Jimmy's troubles now began in earnest. First his wife thought that, as she was owner of the boat, it was beneath her dignity to cook for Jimmy, and told him when he asked for his breakfast or dinner to go out and eat filth. Poor Jimmy asked Bruce for advice.

Shortly afterwards the "fish," as bêche-de-mer is colloquially termed, they obtained was demanded by Pedro, as owner of the boat. This Jimmy gave him. Then the crew wanted their wages. Jimmy said he had nothing to give them, that they were all his friends, and had promised to work for nothing to clear the boat. Debe Wali said no; he wanted wages. Jimmy and his wife had a bad time of it, so the latter went to the Mamoose and summoned Jimmy for wages.

The police then told Jimmy he was summoned; and great was the clatter of tongues and mutual abuse. Debe ran into his house and brought out a big rowlock of a boat, and stabbed Jimmy in the chest with it. Of course it did not do Jimmy the least harm, but he commenced shouting "Police! police!" knowing well enough that the police were standing by and witnessing the whole affair. Of course the police had to arrest Debe. Next day there was a cross-summons in the court—one for wages, the other for assault.

We have here an interesting example of the confusion that arises in the transition between one economic condition and another. Formerly communal labour was the rule. If a well had to be sunk or a house built, all friends would lend a hand, a feast with the concomitant excitement being a sufficient immediate reward, the reciprocity being, of course, fully recognised. Pedro's loan of a boat on the hire system of purchase is well understood. Before the white man came it was customary for the Torres Straits Islanders to purchase their canoes on what was virtually the three years hire system. The crew demanding wages belongs to the new economic custom introduced by the Europeans.

Pedro, the owner of the boat, was drowned in the hurricane that swept across Northern Australia in March, 1899, and Jimmy had to pay D. Pitt the balance due on the boat.

The new Erub (Darnley Island) church was to be opened in September; and when the Murray Island contingent was about to start to take part in the festivities, Finau could not get a passage for himself or family unless he went with the Murray Islanders; so he asked Jimmy to lend him his boat. Jimmy said he could not lend it.

Two months afterwards Jimmy's cutter went to Garboi sandbank to fish, and the crew slept on shore the first night. When they awoke next morning no cutter was to be seen; she had parted her chain in the night and had drifted away. So poor Jimmy lost his boat and all his labour, and the worst of it is, he has the haunting fear that it was the direct act of God because he did not lend his boat to the South Sea teacher when he asked for it. All the people assert this is the true explanation of his loss.

Jimmy is a happier man since his wife has ceased to be a boatowner, as she now condescends to roast yams and cook fish for him. Debe and he are as good friends as ever, and are always plotting how they can get as many shillings as they can for the least amount of work, and on the whole they succeed very well.

Debe is now the proud father of a pretty little daughter, and devotes a good deal of his time to nursing it. Occasionally he has a row with Kaima, his wife, when he considers she is not doing the nursing in a scientific manner. Then he generally takes the management of the baby for a time, but the infant does not fail to proclaim when it is Debe's watch on deck.

On Friday, August 4th, 1899, there were two earth tremors on Murray Island. I cannot do better than transcribe Mr. Bruce's vivid description of the occurrence. "I had just sat down to lunch when the iron roof and the verandah floor made such a clatter that I could not at all make out what was wrong; about five minutes later there came another and stronger shock. I jumped up and went on the verandah.

"There was a great crowd of men playing hockey on the sand beach in front of the house, and at first I thought some of them had been larking on the verandah, but when I went out everything was quiet. They were sitting down; not a word broke the deathlike stillness. I thought at first they were resting after their game, but even then they never sit still. I asked, 'What's wrong'? Then some of them came up and said, 'Why, ground he jump up and down all the same as sea'!

"Then it struck me at once what had happened. I asked them how they felt when the shock came. They said the whole beach was heaving like the sea so that they could not stand. Some said they felt sick and wanted to vomit; others said everything looked blurred and indistinct, and men's faces were all distorted when they looked at them.

"I was sorry I was in the house at the time, as I should have liked to experience the sensation. I should think each shock must have lasted about two minutes, with an interval of five minutes between them.

"After evening school I saw some of those who had been to their gardens on the top of the hill. From their description the earthquake was felt worse up there. Pasi told me he was sitting down on the ground nursing the baby when the first shock came, and he and the baby commenced to bob up and down, and he felt as if he were sitting on something that was giving way with him. When the second shock came, the coconuts on the trees were bobbing up and down, everything was trembling and swaying; a bucket on the ground opposite him was jumping up and down. He thought it was the devil, and that he was bewitched, so he got up and called his wife to come away. Soon they met other frightened people running home. Pasi said he was 'very glad to hear all man feel him all the same as myself.'

"No doubt the people received a great scare. They were going about in quite a subdued manner for a few days. When Sunday came they were told by Finau that God was angry with them. God has been very angry with them here this year; they were told the same after the hurricane took place. But then I remember the *Princess Alice* disaster on the Thames was referred to in the same manner by Mr. Spurgeon at the Tabernacle; so we cannot wonder at the coloured teacher attributing all disasters to the wrath of an offended Deity.

"I had rather an amusing reason given to me why the cyclone of the 4th and 5th of March (1899) happened. There was a crowd of boats anchored in the bay, and a South Sea man wanted to hold a service on the beach, but very few went to hear him pray. Whilst he was praying, some unregenerate nigger had the impiety to play on his concertina. That day the hurricane came. The men who told me this thoroughly believed, since the praying South Sea man had asserted it, that God had sent the hurricane because of that man playing the concertina.

"That is the kind of God they like to have described to them, and no other. Really the South Sea teachers know the kind of God to depict to the native far better than the white missionary does; his God of Love is beyond their comprehension. They look as if they believed in Him, but converse with them, and you find the God of Wrath is their ideal of what God is. He takes the place of Bomai, etc., which they have lost.

"At the opening of the new church at Erub, in September, all the South Sea teachers from the Torres Straits were gathered together. Captain H—— had just come across an article in a newspaper, written by some German scientist, that a comet was to appear in the heavens some time in October, and that it would strike our planet on the 5th of November. The Captain described the comet to the Erub Mamoose, who in his turn told the assembled teachers, and they, not unnaturally, went to Captain H—— for further information. The Captain, nothing loth, gave them what they wanted, with a practical illustration of how the comet would act when it came in collision with the earth. He got a ball of paper and a stick, making the latter violently strike the ball of paper, which flew some distance away. 'That,' said he, 'is the way our world will go, and I know that Old Nick is preparing his fires for a lot of you fellows now.'

"The teachers held a meeting, and arranged that when each teacher went home to his station he was to appoint three weeks of special prayer, and to beseech God not to allow the comet to destroy the earth. Finau arrived here full of it, and the people with him arrived equally full of influenza through living in overcrowded houses in Darnley.

"On Sunday I went as usual to church. At the close of the service Finau told all the people to remain, as a special service was to be held; so I remained along with the rest.

"After a short interval Finau told them about the comet, and that a very wise man had written in the newspaper that the world was shortly to come to an end. This was true. He then read from the Gospel of Mark, chapter xiii., from which he proved that this was the time all these things were to happen, because this wise man said so in the newspaper.

"He kept on until he had all the people in a proper state of fear. Then he directly referred to me that I knew it was all true, and would happen. I said 'No.' He took no notice, but told them that in three weeks' time, on the 5th of November, if God did not hear their prayers, they would all be destroyed.

"After praying he invited anyone to stand up and pray and speak on the subject of the comet. Immediately all the Murray Herschels and Sir Robert Balls were on their feet, one after another, expounding on comets and their destructive powers, and they also finished up by saying, 'Oh, it's true! That wise man said so in the newspaper.' The subject suited them immensely.

"After they had all had their say, which occupied nearly two hours, Finau told them from that day until the 5th of November there were to be special prayers, asking God to rebuke the comet and make it go another road away from the earth. They would all know in three weeks' time whether God had heard their prayers. If He did not destroy the world then, that would be a sign that He had heard them, and was pleased with them; but if the comet destroyed the earth on the 5th of November, then they would understand that God was angry with them, and wished to destroy them as a punishment.

"He then again referred to me as knowing it to be true. I had to get up and speak (it was the first time I ever did so on church matters). I told the people that I had not heard anything about this comet, and that they were not to be afraid; that even if there was a comet, it was not likely to interfere with our world, and even if it did, I thought no harm would arise from it. They would all find, on the 5th of November, Murray Island would be quite safe, and everyone would be going about their work as usual. I might as well have said nothing; but there was so much sickness about (mainly influenza) that I thought this frightening of the people would have an injurious effect on them.

"The 5th of November came round, and nothing extraordinary happened. So Finau appointed the 6th to be a day of thanksgiving to God, because He had heard and answered their prayers by turning the comet away from the earth.

"Thanksgiving took the form of prayers in the morning, feasting and games in the afternoon. So you may be sure I had a good time of it in school that Monday afternoon with the noise of the thanksgiving outside and the inattention of the children inside.

"You people in England ought to be truly thankful that we have such effectual fervent prayers in this part of the world. I think this answer to prayer is quite as good as any I read in Mr. Stead's *Review of Reviews* last year. All that was wanting to make the wise man in the newspapers and Finau's predictions perfect was to have had the earth tremors introduced in November instead of August, and then what a tableau!

"Captain H—— is delighted at the good work he considers he has done in stirring up the people to such a time of prayer. In his last letter he says he has been the means of leading these South Sea teachers and the natives to more earnest prayer through fear than has ever been done by any individual in the Straits before.

"The Mamoose and Pasi left for Erub to attend the memorable opening of the church a fortnight earlier than the general public, but before starting the Mamoose left strict orders with the sergeant if anyone made a storm of wind while he was away to find him out and have him punished. No sooner did he start than it blew 'old boots'; no boat could leave the island, and the Mamoose had a terrible passage.

"Kadud, the new Sergeant of Police, came to me and told me he was looking out for the person who had made the wind, as the Mamoose had given him strict orders to have him punished by a fine. One day he came, saying he had found a dry coconut leaf stuck in the creek at Kiam, and thought he would find the party. Another day he would find a similar leaf and a shell stuck in the sand on the beach. Kadud was getting furious, and all the time it was blowing a hurricane. The storm lasted four weeks, so that the majority of the people from Murray Island were late for the opening ceremony.

"For months they tried to find out the miscreant; Wali, being a church member now, is past suspicion. It would make you laugh to hear how seriously the Mamoose and Kadud talk when I ask them if they have found out who it was that made the 'big wind.' 'Oh no,' they reply; 'by-and-by we shall catch him.'

"Mappa, a Murray Islander—one of the L.M.S. teachers—is here at present on a six months' leave of absence; he is a shrewd, sharp fellow, but a thorough native. He brought with him a young fellow named Wai from his station at New Guinea, another sharper, who has already a great reputation on Murray Island of being able to make, injure, and kill, and Mappa backs him up. *Tuk* is the form of sorcery he is supposed to practise, and the Murray people are terribly frightened of it; they tell me the New Guinea men are very powerful in *tuk*, and from Kiwai they can kill a whole village full of people on Murray Island, nearly a hundred miles away.

"Wai first began practising on William, the deacon, who lives at Dio. He went with some others to Dio, and showed William two sticks of tobacco, and said '*Tuk*.' William began to shake when Wai told him to go and look in his box and see if he had lost any tobacco. William, still trembling, got his key, looked in the box, and said, 'Yes.' Wai held up the tobacco, and said, 'This is it.' William replied, 'Yes, that's it.' Wai exclaimed '*Tuk*,' and the two sticks of tobacco disappeared, much to the astonishment of the crowd. William pressed a present on Wai, to secure himself against *tuk*. When William told me about the affair I nearly exploded, trying to keep serious, and endeavouring to sympathise with him. Wai is a smiling, comedian-faced young fellow; he comes along to see me every other day, and to have a smoke. Ulai and Mappa, a good pair, are always extolling Wai's great powers.

"A fortnight ago Mappa, who is taking Finau's place, the latter having gone on a visit to Mabuiag, had a crowd round him after a Friday morning's service, and used some strong language about some men who had not attended church and about Kadud, who owns a well at Kiam, about which he and the South Sea teacher have a dispute.

"A woman named Deau went and told these men that Mappa was speaking ill of them. They hurried along to the church compound, Deau along with them. She then asked Mappa to repeat what he had said, and told him he was bad man, that he thumped the pulpit with his hand when preaching to them, and then went home and thumped his wife. Mappa then began to tell her she was a bad woman, a *Samaria kosker* —that is, a woman of Samaria. Deau could not stand that, so she went to the police and summoned Mappa for swearing at her by calling her a *Samaria kosker*. Mappa then threatened the whole of Deau's friends that he and Wai would put *tuk* on them all. They were in a great panic; the sergeant, Kadud, was nearly white when he came to see me, with some of the threatened people, and asked if they could not arrest Mappa. They all declared that Mappa had learnt *tuk* in New Guinea, and could destroy them all if he chose.

"Mappa was summoned for slandering Deau, and dismissed on this count; next he was charged with threatening the people. The witnesses all held that when Mappa went back to New Guinea he would destroy anyone he chose by using the sorcery of *tuk*. It was *tuk*, *tuk*, and nothing but *tuk*. I asked Mappa if he had threatened the people with this, and he said he had, and that he was angry. I asked him if, when he went back to New Guinea, he or the Fly River men could shoot *tuk* to Murray Island. He said they could, but he was not sure about himself. I warned him to think about what he was saying, and if he really believed that Wai could do such a thing. He hummed and hawed, and said 'No.' That was all I wanted in order to quiet the fears of the people, so I asked Mappa to tell the Mamoose and the people that the Fly River men could not injure them, and that neither he nor Wai knew *tuk*. He told them so, but at the same time they did not believe him, and would rather have heard him say that he and Wai were *au kali tuk le* (very big *tuk* people). Mappa was dismissed from court, and advised not to practise *tuk* any more whilst on his holidays. The whole *tuk* affair has been very amusing. Mappa and his wife are now teaching the Murray youths New Guinea dances, so that they may beat the Dauar men on New Year's Day."

In a letter dated September 30th, 1900, Mr. Bruce gave us the later history of some of our friends, and as it illustrates the social life of the Murray Islanders in a very interesting manner, I do not hesitate to print the greater part of it for the benefit of my readers.

"This year we are experiencing the results of a big drought. The north-west monsoon, which generally brings a young deluge with it, has been very mild this year, so mild, in fact, that but for the change of winds we might say we had no 'nor'-west.' In December of 1899 we had good rains, which gave promise of a good harvest from the gardens this year; but there has been such a dearth of rain in 1900 that all the garden stuffs died off. First the sweet potatoes went (that is, the vines), for they never got to the length of tubers; then the yams died off, but the people managed to get a few small ones out of the crop. So the people are reduced to coconuts and bananas, which are fairly plentiful. The natives are perfectly happy, carrying on play night after night, and their boats lying idle at anchor, instead of being at work getting black-lip shell, which has been a splendid price this year, to buy flour and rice for their families. Douglas Pitt's son did very well with one boat working from here; he cleared £350 in six months with a crew of mainland boys, whilst the Murray men did not clear as many shillings with seven boats which they obtained from individuals to work out and on shares. They kept on getting advances ('draws') of calico and tobacco, and do no work.

"Your two 'curry and rice *chefs*,' Debe Wali and Jimmy Rice, both got boats. Debe obtained all the draws he could out of the owner in eight months, and collected about £4 worth of shell to pay about £10 worth of draws. The consequence was, when he went to Thursday Island for more draws the owner took possession of his boat, and he was lucky to get it, because if she had remained much longer at Murray Island she would have broken up on the beach. Jimmy Rice, poor fellow, has not been quite so fortunate as his friend Debe. In the first place, he could not get so many draws out of his man as did Debe, and he had signed before the Shipping Master, with a solicitor to see that all was fair and square. When Jimmy got all the draws he could from the owner of the boat, he and his crew refused to do any work, and they were taken before the Shipping Master at Thursday Island. The Shipping Master prosecuted them in court. All the crew, beside Jimmy Rice and Toik, decided to go to work and finish the time they had signed for. Jimmy and Toik held out, thinking they would be sent back to Murray Island by the steamer, as she was coming out the day following; but they made a mistake, and each of them got two months in jail to work out their time. One of the young Pitts paid for a boat here in four months with a mainland crew, and although the Murray men have these object lessons before them, they seem to be no incentives to make them go and do likewise, which they could easily do.

"Papi has a boat on half-shares from a Manila man named Zareal, a jeweller at Thursday Island. Like the others, Papi was doing no work after getting what he could out of Zareal; but he was lucky enough to find a good pearl in a shell, so he took it to Thursday Island and sold it for £150, then went flashing about town. Zareal came to know of the pearl, and claimed half of its value for the boat; but Papi objected, and got away from Thursday Island to Murray Island with the cash. Not a bad haul for a Murray man! There is likely to be trouble about it, but I bet my boots Papi comes off the winner.

"You remember old Gasu; his eyes were bad. He is now quite blind; can only tell the difference between night and day. He looks physically well, but takes no exercise whatever, as he tells me he is ashamed to go walking about with a boy to lead him. When I visit him I give him a spin along the road, and he enjoys it immensely. Poor old Gasu! He had not his equal on the island; a thorough, genuine old gentleman, and quite free from all cant, although he had his fears of the 'White Man's Zogo' (the Church) like all the rest.

"The great drought this year has been put down to many causes. Your party came in for some of the blame for taking away the good *doioms*, so that the rain-makers were handicapped in giving a plentiful supply. But the principal cause for a time was our old friend Debe Wali; he was charged with defiling and throwing down the yam *sogo* at Dauar, named Zegnaipur—this is the principal yam *sogo*. Debe's brother, Komabre, and Harry, the Murray Mamoose, were the two head *sogo* men who prepare it every year. Komabre died last year, and Debe, of course, believes someone was the cause of his death, and the people say that he was angry at the death of Komabre and knocked down the *sogo*, hence the drought. Mamoose and Pasi came to me to have a talk about it, and wished to know if they could not prosecute Debe in court. I told them they would have to get proof that he had done the injury, well knowing they could get none. Mamoose said he was certain Debe did the thing to spoil the yams and food, and that the law should punish him. I had to cool him off as best I could. The next one accused was Joe Brown. They said, because he has a quarrel with Jimmy Dei, he burnt the coconut *sogo* at Zeub by wilfully setting fire to the grass, and that he had stopped rain from coming and blighted all the crops. It was very amusing when I asked Debe and Joe confidentially why they had been and gone and done it. A knowing smile stole all over their faces, as much as to say, 'I'll teach them to interfere with me!' Still, they would never confess to anything, but you could see how pleased they were at the prominent place they held among the people. When I represented to them how they were making me suffer too from having empty water-tanks, old Joe said, 'By-and-by, Jack, you stop; I make him all right; you see your tank full up by-and-by!' That 'by-and-by' means so much to them, and is such a handy phrase I don't know what they would do without it now!

"In the early part of the year I was pestered by the men who had boats, and also by their crews, coming every day inquiring when the big blow was to be. I told them it was impossible for me to fix any stated time, but they knew we always had strong winds in the north-west. It was of no use, they kept on coming to inquire. At last I asked if anyone had been telling them there was to be a big blow. They said yes, one man told them; but who he was they would not say. Of course it made a good excuse for not going to work, and they made the most of it and let the boats lie up.

"The following is an example of the power *sogo* men are credited with. After Debe's and Joe's reputation was on the wane and being forgotten, Mamoose and Jimmy Dei were in my house one day, and the conversation turned on the everlasting drought, which both were bewailing. I began to twit them about the powers of the rain-makers, trying to bring them out. Mamoose did not like it, and began to converse with his optics to Jimmy (Murray men do a lot of talk on the quiet with their eyes). Jimmy assented, so Mamoose got up out of his seat, looked out of the front door, then out of the back—to make sure there was no one about who would be likely to hear—sat down again, and after sundry ahems Mamoose whispered to me the real cause of the drought. He said the rain-makers were afraid to make rain and prepare the ceremony, in case they might make too much wind along with it, and therefore cause another big hurricane, like that of last March, and they feared the Government would punish them if many lives were lost;

besides, Gasu being now blind, he could not see to prepare the *zogo* properly, and they were afraid to make it! I had to condole with them on the hard luck of having to risk the chances of either a cyclone or a famine, and agreed with them that a famine was the safest, for, as Mamoose said, the hurricane might smash up the island altogether. But I assured him at the same time that the Government would on no account hold them responsible for any damage done by any cyclone in this part of the world. I never heard of any Murray man getting the credit of making the hurricane last year; no doubt they have been afraid to hint at it, and I have no doubt the people give the honour to some of the *zogo le* for having caused that disaster.

"I had a gentleman living with me for a month or so; he came from New Zealand, and is travelling all round, doing the 'grand tour of Australia, New Guinea,' etc. He was grand company, although a very strict churchman and an extreme ritualist. I had no idea colonial high churchmen could be so high! He out-ritualed everything I had ever seen or heard of, but he was one of the good sort who could give and take a joke.

"We had a trip to Dauar one Saturday; went in the whaleboat, and several passengers accompanied us. We had a walk all round, and had a nice day of it. After we had returned home and had had supper, and were sitting talking and smoking, a deputation headed by Pasi, who is Mamoose of Dauar, came to inform me that those who had accompanied us to Dauar had gone on purpose to see the *zogo* of Wiwar. This is a round stone (sandstone) about the size of a pumpkin; if it is prepared by a *zogo* man it has the power of causing constipation, and the person affected will die if there is no antidote used in the form of taking off the power of this *zogo*. Pasi had a small packet in his hand, wrapped up very carefully, like tobacco, in a dried banana leaf. He asked me if I would examine it, and spread it out, telling me this was the cause of the sickness of an old lady named Sibra. She remembered that the last time she had been over to Dauar she had passed the *zogo* Wiwar, and now knew the cause of her sickness. Her friends had gone over with us to find out if the *zogo* was prepared; they were to take away the power of the *zogo* by cleansing it with sea-water, and placing the leaf of a plant called *gebi* on top of the stone, and pouring water over the stone. Pasi wished to know if the police could apprehend old Lui, as he was the only Dauar man who knew how to prepare the *zogo*. I asked Pasi how the *zogo* was prepared; he said, 'The *zogole*, after having a stool, placed the excreta on the stone, using an incantation, in which he referred to the person he wishes to blight.' To prove the case, the friends went to the stone and found it had been prepared, and brought away a sample of the excreta with them. My visitor could not refrain from laughing, although I warned him to keep serious. Pasi said there was no chance of Sibra's recovery, as the *zogo* had been prepared too long. I was giving the old lady medicine, and thought she was going on nicely, but on the Monday afternoon she died. Of course old Lui got the credit of removing her, because they had had a quarrel of words. The friends of Sibra do not consider our law of much account, as Lui cannot be punished, even after the strong evidence they brought to me. When Lui dies, his relatives will charge Sibra's relations with using a *zogo*, appropriate to whatever sickness he may have been afflicted with.

"It was too much when Pasi asked my visitor to have a sniff, and tell him if it was the real thing or not. He fairly exploded and roared, and spoiled the whole effect, as I had to follow suit. The deputation did not remain much longer, but carefully rolled up their sacred bundle and left. They are very sensitive to ridicule, and do not like their customs laughed at. The consequence was that they would not for some time tell me anything that occurred of a similar nature. You will perhaps think I ought to rebuke them and advise them not to follow these old customs, but it is of no use doing this, as these are so engrained into their everyday existence that they could not, as yet, live without them. Their disappearance is, I think, only a matter of time.

"It is very seldom that houses are burned down on Murray Island, considering the inflammable material they are constructed of, and the carelessness of the people with fire. This year, however, three houses were burned down. The first one belonged to a widow named Nicky. The people were all at one of their night plays, and Nicky's house was burned, and nothing saved. The play was a long way from Nicky's place, but it is considered that the spirit of her deceased husband

(Arus) was angry with her for her conduct, and burned her house down. It was a serious loss to Nicky, as she has a large family. I spoke to the Mamooses about getting the people to assist her, and another widow, Anai, whose goods were also all lost in the fire. The poor women had really saved nothing except their petticoats. I gave them a start in goods, and I was really astonished at the manner in which the people assisted; some gave her a camphor-wood box, others half-bolts of calico, plates, spoons, knives, and so forth, so the camphor-wood boxes were well filled with useful articles, and calico galore. All vied in beating each other in the giving line, and of course a ceremony was made in presenting the goods. I only hope the next unfortunate will come off as well, but I fear not, as it is so foreign to the Murray Islanders to give without getting an equivalent in exchange. However, they deserve all credit for the way in which they assisted Nicky and Anai, and ought to make Arus's *lamar* (spirit) leave the widow's house alone in future. The other houses were burned down in the daytime, and all the contents saved.

"This year (1900) has been a fairly healthy year. Up to the present there have been five deaths—two adults and three children. Matey is dead; he was a young man about thirty years old; he died of consumption, I think, and was ill for a long time. I tried to get him to go to the hospital at Thursday Island, but he would not go. There is a Queensland Aboriginal working in the boats at Darnley, who has quite a reputation as a medicine-man. When Matey was very weak he wished to be taken to Darnley to see this mainland boy. He was taken over in a dying state. The mainlander had a look at him and told him, 'You fellow, you die; no more blood stop along you; two day, three day, you finish!' This consultation was quite satisfactory to Matey and his friends, so Matey requested them to take him back to Murray Island to die there. They started back with him, and as soon as the anchor was dropped at Murray, poor Matey's spirit took flight to Boigu (an island to the west of Murray, where spirits are supposed to live in a very happy state without any fears of brimstone).

"Murray Islanders have a great dread of dying anywhere than on Murray, and no people have a greater love of their native land than they have. Since this mainland boy on

Darnley gave so good a prognosis in Matey's case, his reputation has gone up like a rocket, and has not yet come down, several have gone over to consult him."

The natives of Erub and the Murray Islands frequently used to make mummies of their dead relations. The details of the process are not particularly edifying, and need not be narrated here. The wizened corpse, which might almost have been made of papier-mâché, so light was it, was lashed to a bamboo framework. To be made more presentable it was painted red and pieces of mother-of-pearl from a nautilus shell were inserted in the orbits, a round spot of black beeswax serving for a pupil. Finally the mummy was decked with various ornaments. When it was complete and inodorous a final feast would be provided, and it would be suspended in the house. There the mummy would remain, swinging with every breath of wind and turning its gleaming eyes with each movement of the head, until it fell to pieces with old age.

When the body crumbled away word was sent to the friends to come and assist in cutting off the head. A big feast was held, and a man who was skilled in making portrait faces in beeswax on skulls was also present. Later the artist made the wax model of the deceased's face; anyhow, the length of the nose was accurate, as immediately after death the length of the nose was measured with a piece of wood, which was safely kept for the purpose of securing the right proportion of the imitation nose.

When the face was finished the head was given to the nearest male relative. The men then cried. Later it was taken to the women, who also had a good cry. The inevitable feast followed, at which the artist received a large share of food.

The modelled and decorated skulls of relatives were kept probably partly for sentimental reasons, as the people are of an affectionate disposition, and like to have memorials of deceased friends, but mainly for divinatory purposes.

A duly decorated skull when properly employed became a divining *zogo* of remarkable powers, and was mainly used in discovering a thief, or the stolen article, or a man who had by means of sorcery made someone sick. But this could only be done by *bezam le*, or members of the shark clan, who were also members of the Malu fraternity. All who engaged in this hunt went in the early evening to the *zogo* house, and one of the *zogole* took the Malu mask and put it on, repeating a certain formula. After leaving the house, the *zogole* carried the skull in front of him, and all marched with a particular gait till they heard a kind of grasshopper called *kitoto*, and they rushed in the direction from which the noise proceeded. One particular *kitoto* was believed to guide the men to the house of the offender. Should the men lose the right direction the *kitoto* would wait for them to come up, ever and again making its sound, "Sh, sh." Ultimately they were led to a house, and this must, of course, according to their ideas, be the house of the malefactor.

It was of no use for the man to deny the evil deed, for *kitoto* had found him out; and, moreover, the *bezam le* were so powerful that it was as much as his life was worth to resist. If he happened to be a *bezam le* himself he might try to brazen it out among his friends; but if he was an outsider it would be useless, and he would have to pay the fine.

I was naturally anxious to obtain one of these divining heads; even by the time of my former visit they had all been done away with, at least, so I was informed. I had therefore to be content to have a model made for me. (Plate XII., B, No. 2; p. 139.)

First a skull had to be procured—and for other reasons I was very desirous of making a collection of skulls; but it was long before I could obtain any (I am referring now to my former visit), though I constantly said, "Me fellow friend belong you fellow. 'Spose you get me head belong dead man, I no speak. 'Spose you get him, I no savvy what name you catch him, that business belong you fellow. What for I get you fellow trouble?"

Eventually I came across a man who volunteered to get me some, and I promised to give him sixpence per head; or, as I put it to him, "One head belong dead man he sixpence, one head belong dead man he sixpence; you savvy?" and as I spoke I touched and turned down, native fashion, the fingers of the left hand, beginning with the little finger. He understood perfectly.

Next day he brought me a basket of skulls, and he could tell me the names of some of them, too! As he handed out one skull and mentioned a man's name, I noticed that the nursemaid of the missionary's wife, who was standing by, looked rather queer; but as it was none of my business, I took no notice. Later I found that the skull in question belonged to the girl's uncle! I do not believe she objected to my having the skull, but that the other man should have the sixpence—the money had gone out of the family. When paying the man I ticked off each skull on the fingers of my left hand, and paid for it; but I had not enough sixpences, and so gave him half a crown for five skulls. At this he looked very askance, although I assured him the payment was quite correct. Fortunately Bruce was standing by, and said he would give him five sixpences for it at the store. My friend Baton made me one or two divining heads from these skulls in the "old-time fashion."

Hearing one day, during my former stay at Murray, that a woman had died, and being grieved at the particular circumstances attending her death, I determined to pay my visit of condolence. After dark I went to the village where she had lived, and found her laid on the beach with her head to the sea, and clothed in her best dress and wearing her new hat, all her fancy calico being laid on the body. The husband was sitting at the head, and close by were several men, women, and children laughing and chattering over their evening meal. Then the brother came up and bent over the body, wailing and sobbing.

Shortly afterwards a canoe was brought to convey the corpse to a more populous village, so that they might have a good cry.

Then I saw one of the most impressive sights it has yet been my lot to witness. It was a beautiful tropical moonlight night, the sand beach being illuminated with soft whiteness by the moon, and countless stars glittered overhead. On one side the strand was bordered by the gently lapping waves of the calm ocean, and on the other by a grove of coconut palms, their grey stems, arising from a confused shadow of undergrowth, topped by sombre feathery crowns, a peaceful adjunct to a scene of sorrow, and the antithesis of the ghastly mockeries of the funeral plumes of the professional upholstery, which have only lately been abolished in England. A small crowd of some twenty or so of us were walking along the beach with the noiseless footfall of bare feet, keeping abreast of the canoe which, with its sad freight, was poled along by the husband at one end, and the brother at the other. As I saw the black silhouette of the canoe and its crew against the moonlit sky and sea, silently gliding like a veritable shadow of death, and heard the stillness of the air broken by the moaning of the bereaved ones, my mind wandered back thousands of years, and called up ancient Egypt carrying its dead in boats across the sacred Nile—there with pomp, ceremony, and imagery, here with simplicity, poverty, and stern realism.

At length we came to the village, the inclosure of which was covered with family groups, mothers with babies surrounded by their families, and many a little one was laid asleep upon the sand, well wrapped up to keep off the flies.

The corpse was carried to a clear space, and again the gay trappings of life were spread over the dead. An old woman, I believe the deceased's mother, came to the head, and sitting down, bent over the body and commenced wailing. Then on all sides the cry was taken up mainly by the groups of women who by this time had taken their places round the dead. As one dropped out, another would join in, and so with varying accessions in volume, occasionally dying away to all but silence, the mournful sound continued through the night, rising and falling in weird manner, recalling to my memory the keening I had heard in far-away Kerry eighteen months previously.

Then I left them. The dead one surrounded by a changing circle of weeping women; beyond, the family groups each illumined by its own flickering fire, babies asleep, children playing, adults talking, young men laughing, and a little love-making taking place in the background; and above all the quiet, steady, bright face of the moon impassively gazing, like Fate, on the vicissitudes of human life.

CHAPTER VII

KIWAI AND MAWATTA

WE left Murray Island at 10 a.m., September 8th, by the *Nieue*, which the Rev. James Chalmers very kindly sent to us. A small crowd assembled to bid us farewell, and I know many of the natives were genuinely sorry that we were leaving. We spent such a happy and profitable time there, that we shall always have a soft corner in our hearts for this beautiful island.

We reached Erub (Darnley Island) about 3 p.m., landed, and called on Captain H——, who entertained us with his reminiscences of New Guinea. We sailed at daybreak next morning, and reached Daru in the early afternoon. About midday we ran on to a sandbank, but as the tide was rising this did not much matter; in fact, it was rather convenient, as we were thus enabled to have a meal on a *steady* boat, a matter of importance to some of our party.

At Daru we were boarded by Mr. H. W. de Lange, the Sub-Collector of Customs. Our little formal business was soon over, and we then called on the Hon. Bingham A. Hely, the very efficient Resident Magistrate. He kindly asked us to dinner, and we had an interesting talk about the natives of his division. Mr. Hely has lately made some observations on the important subject of totemism. On Sunday, September 11th, we arrived at Saguane in the forenoon, and Tamate, my old friend the Rev. James Chalmers, who has been described as the Livingstone of New Guinea, gave us a hearty welcome.

Unfortunately Mrs. Chalmers was ill with fever, which had prostrated her for some time. Tamate, as he likes to be called by his black and white friends, had also been quite ill from the effects of a nasty fall from a verandah in the dark, and he was scarcely well yet; indeed, it appeared to me that his health was much shaken, and no wonder, when one remembers all the hardships and privations he has undergone during his strenuous life of self-sacrifice.

Saguane is a small village at the southern extremity of Kiwai Island. The native village is dilapidated, and has a poverty-stricken appearance, probably owing to the fact that the village is only occupied for part of the year.

The Mission premises were adequate, but as little money as possible had been spent upon them, as even then it was by no means certain that Saguane would remain the permanent headquarters of the Fly River branch of the London Missionary Society. The buildings consisted of the Chalmers' comfortable house, the church, which was also used as a schoolroom, a good schoolroom for the seniors, a study, and other rooms, also the South Sea teachers' houses, the students' houses, and various offices.

Saguane was a central and convenient spot for the Mission, but that is about all that could be said in its favour. The whole island is but little above sea-level; it is malarial, and the water-supply is poor. Although the place does not look healthy, Chalmers says it is the healthiest part of the district, except Daru. A considerable amount of Mission land had already been washed away by the sea, that end of the island having been greatly reduced in size of late years; indeed, since this account was written, the Mission station had practically been devastated by the sea, and Mr. Chalmers had commenced to build a new station on Daru.

From many points of view it was a disheartening place, and it was a wonder Tamate bore up so cheerfully. He had great difficulties with teachers, South Sea men are often unsatisfactory, and the Torres Straits islanders are practically useless as native teachers; so Tamate was endeavouring to educate his own men as teachers, but it was a long and wearisome task. Tamate had a very large area under his charge, his district was undermanned, and he was greatly in need of money help, as he was naturally very anxious to have a steam-launch for river work. Alas! Tamate will never require the steamer for which he was longing. In order to keep out as far as possible the gloom which subsequent events have cast over our memory of Chalmers, I will continue my narrative in the form in which it was written prior to the tragedies to which I refer.

Like other mission stations, the instruction of the young

KIWAI AND MAWATTA

plays a prominent, one might fairly say the prominent, part in the work of the missionaries. Here it is especially needed, as these semi-migratory natives are ruder in culture than those we had met with in the east, and even the energy, enthusiasm, and sympathy of Mr. Chalmers can make relatively little impression on the adult population; but, indeed, this is pretty much the case with adults everywhere.

There are two schools in Saguane. A lower school for the village children, who reside with their parents. These are taught in the Kiwai language by the South Sea teacher and his wife. The attendance leaves much to be desired, as the children have to follow their parents in their annual migration to Iasa, and thus they lose two or three months in the year; and even during the time they reside at Saguane, neither the parents nor the children sufficiently appreciate the advantages of the instruction so freely offered to them.

The students of the upper school are all resident, and both sexes attend; I believe there are about a score in all. The English language is exclusively used. They learn reading, writing, easy arithmetic, geography, and Scripture. It is usual with Papuan children for their writing to be very good, and they have quite a remarkable knowledge of geography. The highest class can read English fairly well at sight. As in Murray Island, the change from one subject to another in school-time is made the occasion of marching and singing, which affords a welcome opportunity for blowing off steam. The children are neatly clothed, but wisely they are not overclothed. It is to be hoped that many of the students will volunteer as teachers to the various stations that Tamate is anxious to establish. Some will, doubtless, become Government servants; and there can be no question that they will render the Government great assistance in the future. Sir William Macgregor has often referred to the efficiency of the Mission schools.

Shortly after our visit Mr. de Lange was sailing with a native crew from Kiwai to Daru, when he was overtaken by a squall and his boat capsized. The boatmen were very plucky, and did all they could to save Mr. de Lange; but this promising officer was unfortunately drowned. The natives proved themselves in this emergency to be brave and faithful followers.

In addition to the instruction given in the school, the students are introduced to a more civilised mode of life; and the raising of the standard of cleanliness and comfort will of itself tend to improve the condition of the people. Perhaps the home life of the South Sea teachers is in this respect of more value than that of the white missionaries, for the latter are so obviously above the natives, and have access to what must appear to them to be limitless resources, that a real comparison can scarcely be made.

That this was the case was proved to me in an amusing, but at the same time pathetic, manner a day or two later. When I was at Iasa my opinion was confidentially asked by the chief about the missionaries, as Mr. Chalmers had persuaded them to accept a South Sea teacher, who was then at Saguane learning the language. My friends had been describing to me certain ceremonies they employ for the purpose of making the crops grow, and they were really anxious about the wisdom of adopting the new religion, which they fully realised would require them to give up these practices; for if they did not do as their fathers had done, how could the yams and sago grow? "It's all very fine," they urged, "for Tamate, as everything he eats comes out of tins which he gets from the store at Thursday Island; but how about us?"

The native teachers, on the other hand, live largely on "native food," and cultivate their own gardens. The students are trained to do the same, and the girls are taught to sew and make simple garments, and to be clean and orderly.

Mr. Hely, in his last Annual Report, states that "there has been a great demand for teachers; in fact, what amounts to a religious revival has taken place at Mawatta, Tureture, Parama, and elsewhere. It is to be hoped that it will continue. Mr. Chalmers has been hampered by the seeming difficulty of procuring teachers for this portion of the possession. Men of good culture are required at such places as Mawatta and Tureture.

"At Parama the Darnley Islander, Edagi, has worked hard. He has built a very creditable church, with the aid of the people, with whom he is very popular, and has a large school attendance. At Giavi there is a Murray Islander, but I think that the results of his ministrations are small."

We spent a quiet Sunday; the rest and comfort of the Mission station was most refreshing. I showed photographs and rubbings of patterns to some natives in the afternoon, and obtained a little information from them.

PLATE X

IASA, KIWAI ISLAND

SIDE VIEW OF THE SOKO-KOROBE CLAN HOUSE AT IASA

KIWAI AND MAWATTA

These mission stations are oases of kindness and comfort in savage lands. When one has been knocking about for days in a boat, with uncomfortable, and often unpalatable meals, and being always wet, and having broken nights, the rest in a haven of a clean mission-house is delightful.

Ray, Wilkin, and I started next morning in the *Nieue* for Iasa, the chief village and virtually the native capital of Kiwai Island, some twelves miles away. The whole district is very flat, and the shore fringed with a monotonous row of mangroves, a line only broken at Iasa by a grove of coconut palms. As at Saguane, the river is eating away the land which it had previously deposited, and we noticed large numbers of prostrate coco palms which had been uprooted by the encroaching water. Also as at Saguane, an extensive flat bank runs out a long way into the river, and thus the *Nieue* had to anchor a considerable distance from the shore.

The village consists of sixteen houses, all of large size. Five of the houses belong to local natives; the others are owned by natives from other districts. Each house is occupied solely by members of one clan, but there were two instances of one clan owning a couple of houses.

We took up our quarters at the west end-room of the longest house. This house was 285 feet in length, and was built on piles about seven feet from the ground; there was a broad ladder at each end leading up to the main entrances. Along the side facing the river were five small doors, each provided with a slight ladder, and it is only by these that the women and children may enter or leave the house. There were two doorways on the opposite side of the house, which at the time of our visit were not in use, as there were no ladders to them.

There is a separate room at each end of a house, which is evidently merely the deep verandah of the typical house of the Papuan Gulf walled in close to the gable. These end-rooms are the men's quarters, and correspond to the club-houses and tabooed erections of other parts of New Guinea.

Over a considerable portion of New Guinea the men have a social life which is distinct from the family life, and is hedged round with observances and taboos. In a given community there are usually several societies or fraternities into which entrance can only be gained by undergoing certain initiation ceremonies. These are jealously guarded, and the mysteries are performed in sacred spots in the bush, which are tabooed to all women, children, and non-initiates, or they may take place in houses set apart for the purpose, such as the large *erabo* (*elamo* or *eramo*) of the Gulf District described by Mr. Chalmers. In these the sacred emblems are kept, and although I prefer to speak of them as "club-houses," Mr. Chalmers was perhaps justified in originally calling them "temples." The end-rooms of the Kiwai houses are to be regarded rather as club-houses than temples, as are also the *marea* of the Mekeo District, and the *dubu* of the Central District.

The long central portion of the house constitutes the dwelling of all the members of the clan, each family having its own compartment with a separate fireplace. Owing to the absence of windows, it was difficult to see any details when looking down the tunnel-like house; for the doorways let in but very little light. At night, when the family fires were burning and there was plenty of smoke reflecting and dispersing the lights, one could more readily gather an impression of the weird scene. Into, and out from, the sombre shadows there passed lank women and jolly children, whose bronze skins were picturesquely lit up by the flickering yellow flames.

We traded a little with natives, and Ray gave some tunes on the phonograph. At night-time we found much difficulty in getting back to the *Nieue*, as it was low water and a strong tide was running. We waded out a long way on the mud-flats, till the water was nearly up to our waists, and the breakers completely drenched us. After getting into water deep enough to float our boat we had a long wearisome pull to the *Nieue*, but we feared we should have to put back for land after all, as the current was strongly against us. However, the captain of the *Nieue* noticed our difficulties and, weighing anchor, sailed to meet us, but for this we should not have been able to get aboard. Dry clothes and a meal soon restored us to comfort.

Next morning we returned to Iasa. Wilkin made a careful study of the long house. I measured ten men and did some trading. We were allowed to appropriate the eastern end-room of the long house, and towards evening lighted a fire, sitting by which we had our dinner, a crowd of natives watching our every action with great interest. We afterwards bought some specimens, whilst Ray gave a phonographic exhibition, and secured two good records. The pungent wood smoke was very trying to the eyes, but this was preferable to returning to the boat; later we wrapped ourselves in blankets and passed the night on a native mat.

The following morning we took some photographs, and I sketched the interior of the long house. Whilst the others were embarking I sent the small boys away, and had a confidential chat with the men about several of their customs, and obtained some most interesting information from them. We became very friendly, and the men expressed sorrow when it was time for us to leave. One man said to me, "You master good master; you master no same other master." By which he meant to express his gratitude for the sympathy I had given them and the interest I had taken in their affairs. I must confess that I was much touched by this unconsciously pathetic revelation of the apartness of the two races. Altogether they were very nice to me, and one or two of us walked to the boat with arms round one another.

The Kiwai people are somewhat different from the Torres Straits islanders in appearance and customs; their skin is very slightly lighter, and the nose is more arched; they do not use ceremonial masks except for the final stage of initiation, and they build long houses. There are other differences which need not now be mentioned. I think it is very probable that they came down the Fly River and drove some at least of the pre-existing population before them.

A very interesting feature about the Kiwai natives is that they are still in a totemistic stage of culture; in other words, their social life is bound up with a reverence for certain natural objects. A community is composed of certain clans, each of which is associated with a particular class of object; it may be a crocodile, a croton, or a pandanus tree. The animal or bird, or even an inanimate object, is the *nurumara*, as they call it, of every member of that clan, and a representation of that *nurumara* or totem is often worn on the person or carved on objects or otherwise employed as a kind of armorial bearings.

The following is a list of all the totems I have been able to record from Kiwai Island :—

Sibara, crocodile.
Diwari, cassowary.
Demauru-uru, a cat-fish.
Soko, nipa palm.
Abiomabio, mangrove.
Oso, croton or dracæna.
Oi, coconut palm.
Dudu-mabu, a reed.

Korobe, a crab that lives in the nipa palm.	*Gagari-mabu*, a small variety of bamboo.
Mabere-uru, a tree.	*Duboro-mabu*, pandanus.
Bud-uru, a kind of fig tree.	*Nowai-dua*, Polynesian chestnut.
	Noora, a stone.

There is a remarkably disproportionate number of plant to animal totems, which is very unusual, and even one of these, *korobe*, is associated with *soko*, the nipa palm being the main totem, while the crab that inhabits it appears to be subsidiary.

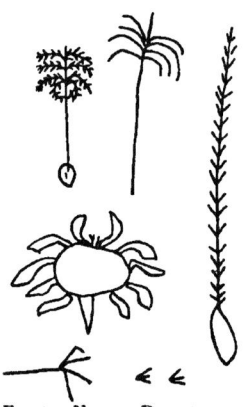

FIG. 7. NATIVE DRAWINGS OF SOME OF THE NURUMARA (TOTEMS) OF KIWAI

Oi (coconut palm), *oso* (croton or dracæna), *soko* (nipa palm), *korobe* (the crab that lives in the latter), *sibara* (crocodile), *diwari* (cassowary). The crocodile is represented by a leg only, and the cassowary by its footprint.

I have previously drawn attention to the large number of decorative designs on objects from the Fly River and neighbouring coast of New Guinea that are derived from plants. As we had then no information on the subject, I did not venture to offer an explanation, though I did suggest that the decorative employment of animals in Torres Straits and in the Louisiades and neighbouring islands was due to totemism. The distinctive character of the decorative art of this region can now be similarly explained.

Totemism has a restricted distribution in British New Guinea. We could find no trace of it in the Central District either among the Motu stock or among the hill-tribes that we visited. Sir William Macgregor has recently stated that it is prevalent all over the east end of the Possession, but it disappears at Mairu or Table Bay. There is no true totemism in the eastern tribe of Torres Straits. It is true that there were dog and pigeon men in Murray Islands, but the dog and pigeon dances during one of the Malu ceremonies were admitted to have been introduced by ancient culture heros from the western tribe, where I discovered totemism twelve years ago.

There do not appear now to be any ordinary totem restrictions on Murray Island, as there certainly were till very recently in Tut, Mabuiag, and other of the western islands of Torres Straits, and as certainly there are still in Kiwai.

In Kiwai a man may not kill or eat his *nurumara*. The children inherit the father's *nurumara*, and the wife assumes that of her husband, as she has to go and live with him in the clan house. This custom accounts for the exchange of women when a man marries; thus it is usual for a man's family to give a suitable girl in exchange for his bride, and so the balance of the sexes is approximately maintained.

Dedeamo, my interpreter, was a croton; his wife was originally a coconut, their little boy was a croton. When I asked Dedeamo what was his wife's name he refused to tell me. One frequently finds that people in a low stage of culture decline to tell you their own names, lest you should obtain power over them, but one can generally get from them the names of other people; this good man evidently thought it was wiser to be on the safe side.

The Hon. B. A. Hely, the Resident Magistrate of the Western Division, has recently published a memorandum (Annual Report B. N. G., July, 1897, to June, 1878, C. A., 119-1898) on totemism in Kiwai and elsewhere in the neighbourhood, in which he says that when a tree is the *nurumara* of a clan, the members of that clan do not eat the fruit of that tree or use it for building or other purposes. For instance, the *soko* people roof their houses with sago leaves instead of the customary nipa palm. He adds: this custom is broken through in Kiwai villages, but it is maintained on the mainland. The *duboro-mabu* people make their mats of banana leaves instead of employing the leaves of the pandanus. The *gagari-mabu* people do not use bamboo. It is believed that the killing, eating, or using for any purpose of a *nurumara* would result in severe eruptions on the body.

Mr. Hely also informs us that in fighting or dancing the representation of the man's *nurumara* is painted on his chest or back with clay or coloured earth, and it is a fixed law in battle that no man should attack or slay another who bore the same cognisance as himself. A stranger from hostile tribes can visit in safety villages where the clan of his *nurumara* is strong, and visitors from other tribes are fed and lodged by the members of the *nurumara* to which they severally belong.

At Iasa we bought an oval board about three feet in length that has a face carved on one side. It is called *gope*, and is hung up in houses to bring good luck; it is sometimes placed in the bow of a canoe for the same purpose. During the evening we spent there a similar but much smaller one (seventeen and a half inches in length) was pointed out to me by a native in the east end-room, and I managed to secure it also; but in the course of my confidential talk the following day I discovered that this was not a *gope*, but a *madubu*, or bull-roarer; they had previously spoken of it as a *gope* as some boys were near, and these were not permitted to know about the *madubu*. In my memoir on *The Decorative Art of British New Guinea* I had hazarded the suggestion that the *gope* is derived from the bull-roarer, and the evidence now appears fairly conclusive on this point.

One function of the *madubu* is to ensure good crops of yams, sweet potatoes, and bananas. I was not able to find out the whole ceremony, but gathered that a fence is made in the bush—one man goes first and makes a hole, and others come later with the *madubus*. When the natives were telling me about this I asked to be allowed to see a *madubu*, and one was brought. It was a thin ovoid slat of wood, very roughly made. I offered a round metal looking-glass for it, which was accepted. Two others were brought me on the same terms, one being a smaller specimen. I was particularly requested not to let women or children see them, and not to show them to the Saguane people, as "they no savvy that thing." Of course, I carefully kept my promise to this effect.

A few years ago Chalmers sent a bull-roarer to England from the mouth of the Fly River, which was labelled "*Burumamaramu*, a bull-roarer: when used, all women and children leave the village and go into the bush. The old men swing it and show it to the young men when the yams are ready for digging (May and June)." The name evidently signifies "the mother of the yams," *buruma* being a variety of yam, and *maramu* is "mother."

The bull-roarer is also employed in the initiation of boys into manhood. I gather that there are two initiation ceremonies; at the first the *madubu* is shown to the initiates in a tabooed and fenced-in portion of the bush. The second *moguru* ceremony takes place in the rainy season or north-west monsoon. The boys to be initiated, *koiameri*, are taken to the bush, and the *orara* is shown to them. This is a wooden image of a nude woman, which was described to me as "god belong *moguru*"; a smaller form of it is known as *umuruburo*, this is a thin flat board cut into the shape of a human being. During the ceremony the men are decorated, and wear a head-dress made of cuscus skin; or some wear on their heads long, doubled-up strips of the skin, decorated with feathers. The skin head-dresses, *marari*, like the images, must not be seen by women. I managed to secure both forms of headgear.

Women and uninitiated boys may not see an *orara*, nor an

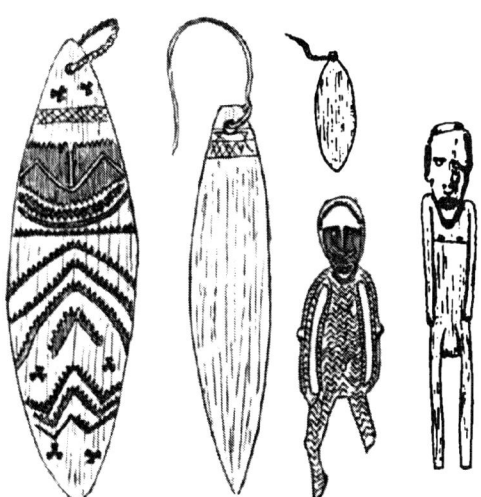

FIG. 8. AGRICULTURAL CHARMS OF KIWAI
(One-sixth natural size)
Three *madubu* (bull-roarers) for yams, and two *umuruburo* (female effigies) for sago

umuruburo. These, together with the *madubu* and *marari*, are carried at night-time from the house to the bush, and returned to their hidden receptacles in the end-rooms of the long houses. Between the *moguru* ceremony and the yam harvest the men make pandean pipes, and every young man carries and plays one.

I was informed of one fact which may throw some light on initiation ceremonies. The human effigies "look after" sago in the same way as the bull-roarers "look after" yams, sweet potatoes, and bananas. According to some notes made by Ray, the *orara* is shown to the initiates during the north-west monsoon, at the time when the sago is planted; but the *madubu* is swung and shown to the initiates when yams are planted in the south-east monsoon.

When food is scarce or of bad quality, if, for instance, a sago palm is split and found to be "no good," the natives make *moguru* and put "medicine along *moguru* for *kaikai*," that is, perform *moguru* magic for food. Unfortunately there was not time for me to follow up this line of inquiry, but probably it will be found that the *moguru* ceremony is primarily a fertility ceremony, perhaps originally agricultural, and later social. The younger members of the community had to be initiated, some time or other, into the processes necessary for producing a good harvest. The time when the lad was growing into a man would suggest itself as being a suitable time for this, and for being instructed about his *nurumara*, and being recognised as a member of the clan.

In several parts of the world certain rites connected with agriculture were, or are, performed by nude women, and it is possible that these nude female effigies may have an analogous significance. Later I shall allude to the association of girls with the annual agricultural ceremonies in the Hood Peninsula. Probably a secondary sexual element has crept into the significance of these effigies in Kiwai. Similar effigies were said to have been employed as love charms in Murray Island, and I did not find out that there they had any agricultural significance; but this may merely have been due to the fact that a specialisation had taken place, owing to insular conditions.

It is, however, significant that the name of the Murray Island love charm was *neur madub*, that is "girl *madub*." When I was in Erub in 1888 I obtained a *neur madub* (Fig. 9), which originally came from the island of Masig; it is a wooden image of a girl with scarification markings; the length is eight inches. I was informed when a young man wanted to marry a girl who would have nothing to say to him, he would go to a magician, and the latter would apply "poison medicine" to this figure and the girl would become insane. The *sugob madub* was a slat of wood, roughly shaped into a male figure, which was used

FIG. 9.
NEUR MADUB, OR LOVE CHARM

to make tobacco (*sugob*) grow. In Mabuiag wooden human effigies, called *madub*, were kept in a small hut along with bull-roarers (*bigu*). The Madub used to "turn devil" (*tartaian markai*) at night-time, and go round the gardens and swing the bull-roarers to make the yams grow. They also danced and repeatedly sang—

"*O ari ina, ina dauaiia mule.*"
("Oh! the rain is here, here by the bananas it passes along.")

In the daytime the *madub* turn into wood.

A wooden image, called *Uvio Moguru*, is used, according to Mr. Chalmers, at the initiation of the young men, and it must not be seen by women or children. He says it is also called *Oraoradubu* (which is usually translated as "God.") I suppose this is the same sort of image as that which was given to me as *orara*, but of the male sex (*dubu* means "male" or "man"). "*Oraoradubu* makes everything grow, and they bring him presents of food when the planting season comes. They place food alongside of him, and then return and carry it away and eat it. He is always consulted before fighting, and presents are given to him, and he is appealed to for help to enable them to secure heads. If anyone is sick, food is given to Uvio, who is placed on the top of a big house (*darimo*), and he is addressed, 'Oh, Uvio, finish the sickness of our dear one, and give life.' The food is left there. Uvio is also taken and placed on the sick one when asleep, and he or she will get better. Uvio is always brought at night, because he is then a living being; during the day he is only a piece of wood. He cannot cause the dead to live."

Until very recently these people were head-hunters; when an enemy was killed, the head was cut off with a bamboo knife and carried home on a rattan sling, which was inserted under the jawbone. The head was hung over a fire and all the hair singed off. During this process all the young girls of the village assembled and danced in a ring near—but not round the fire—singing all the while. The head was then taken away and all the flesh removed; after the skull was washed a carved peg was stuck in the skull, by means of which it was hung up on the main post of the house. This information was obtained from Mr. Chalmers, who also states that a young man could not marry if he had not a skull trophy, as no young woman would have him. Sometimes a young man would go to his friends at a distance—say to Mawatta or Tureture—and would remain there some months. On his return home he would bring with him several skulls which he had bought from, or through, his friends, but whatever his relatives might have been told in confidence, they gave out that he was a great brave, and the lady he loved would soon be his. A canoe has often been given in exchange for a skull.

In this island a number of very large, well-shaped, polished stone implements are found in the bush; the largest I have seen was in Mr. Chalmers' house—it measured 18¾ inches in length. These stones are now placed at the head and foot, or all round the graves, and the natives do not appear to know anything about their former use. A small stone adze-head (*tapi*) was bought at Iasa, and when I asked who made it, I was gravely informed, "He make himself, he stop along ground all time." The large implements are so cumbersome and heavy that it is difficult to understand how some of them could ever have been used, and I suspect the largest ones were in reality symbols of wealth or possibly of authority. As no stone occurs *in situ* for a distance of many miles, and none of this kind is known in the district, the implements have in all probability come down the Fly River. It is quite possible that stone implements have been out of use in this district for perhaps a century, owing to natives getting iron from wrecks and passing ships, and then bartering it to their neighbours; thus in two or three generations the knowledge of the use of stone implements would easily die out.

The natives say that Kiwai was first a small sandbank, but grew large; eventually trees and other vegetation sprang up on it. The first man came from a bird's egg. The bird left the egg in the nest, and a maggot came out of it, which developed into a man.

Mr. Chalmers also tells the following legend concerning the origin of fire. At first it was not known how to make fire, and all the animals, and then the birds tried in turn to bring it across from the mainland. Eventually the black cockatoo succeeded, but dropped it at Iasa, as he burnt himself with it; and he bears the mark of his accident to this day in the red scar round his bill.

Fire is usually produced by the groove method, as is commonly done in Eastern New Guinea and Polynesia, but it is also got by friction of a strip of cane, as among the Koiari of the Central District. In the islands of Torres Straits it is produced by the drill method.

Although the Kiwaians cultivate the soil, they do not always live in the same spot. During the "nor'-west" most of the islanders live at Iasa, which appears to be regarded as the original home of the natives of the southern portion of the island. The temporary migrations are due to the collection and preparation of sago, the people having to go periodically to the places where the sago palm grows, and elsewhere they have gardens of yams and sweet potatoes. This fact renders it difficult for the missionaries to make much headway among the natives here.

On our return to Saguane we found that Seligmann had arrived. He had made several interesting trips in the Rigo and Mekeo districts, and had acquired a good deal of valuable information; he had fortunately escaped fever or other illness. Rivers had employed his time mainly in psychologising the Kiwaians. As Ray wanted to gain some information about the Kiwaian language, he decided to remain at Saguane for a fortnight, and to join us at Mabuiag, accompanying Mr. Chalmers when he paid his promised visit to that island.

We left Saguane shortly before midday on September 15th, had a roughish spin across the mouth of the Fly River, and early in the afternoon we glided through the narrow mangrove-bordered channel between Parama and the mainland of New Guinea. We ran on a mudbank at the western entrance, and as we had to wait till the tide rose we all went ashore at Old Mawatta. Here we found a temporary village of simple huts built on the ground. The people had come over from Parama to make gardens, and among them was the only Murray Island teacher in New Guinea. We soon purchased a decorated bamboo pipe, and by dumbshow and pidgin English I asked for a shell hoe. D'Albertis obtained some of these very primitive implements at Katau, or New Mawatta, and I bought one from the same village ten years before; but Mr. Hely told me that they had since then gone out of use. But to my joy one was brought to us, for which I gave a fish-hook; and in a very short time we had half a dozen on the same terms. Hardly anything pleased me more during this trip than to secure some specimens of this very rude and primitive agricultural implement, especially as there seemed previously no chance of obtaining it. The blade is made from part of a bailer-shell (*Melo diadema*), which is jammed into the perforation in the handle and wedged tight with pieces of wood.

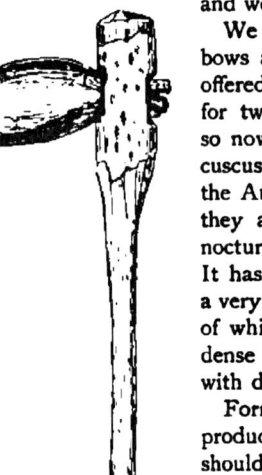

FIG. 10. SHELL HOE
Used by the natives of Parama.
About one-seventh natural size.

We bought several petticoats and some bows and arrows. A living cuscus was also offered for sale in a basket, and was bought for two fish-hooks and a stick of tobacco; so now for the first time we had a pet. The cuscus is the New Guinea representative of the Australian phalangers, or "opossums," as they are popularly called, and is a gentle nocturnal creature that feeds mainly on fruit. It has a face something like a lemur's, and a very long prehensile tail, the terminal third of which is pink and destitute of fur. The dense fur is of a creamy yellow colour mottled with dark brown.

Formerly most of the men of Torres Straits produced scars in elaborate patterns on their shoulders, and the practice is still maintained by certain tribes on the neighbouring coast of New Guinea. I had paid some attention to this kind of form of scarification, and was always on the look-out for fresh examples. On inquiry I found that the custom had quite died out, but there was one old man left who had this mark, and he was much amused when I sketched it.

These Western Papuans have such very dark skins that ordinary tattooing would not show on them. Like the Negroes, Australians, and other very dark peoples, they produce large and often prominent scars which, being lighter in colour than the skin, are fairly conspicuous. It is evident from the appearance of many of these scars that the process of producing them must have been very painful.

Wilkin made notes of and photographed a number of the huts, which were very simple in construction, and which I at once saw were very like the former dwellings of the Western Torres Straits islanders. The islanders have all adopted the kind of house introduced by South Sea men, so the evidently very primitive character of these huts and the diversity they exhibited was of especial interest to us, as they gave us an idea of what had elsewhere passed away. The leaf petticoats also of the women of these primitive people were quite the same as were the petticoats of the Torres Straits women before they adopted the hideous calico gowns they all wear now.

We parted on the best of terms with our new friends, and a number came off in canoes and swarmed aboard the *Nieue*, peering into the cabin whilst we ate our dinner.

This place is called Old Mawatta, as it was the home of the original inhabitants of Katau, or Mawatta, as it is more generally called. These people were driven from their home by the hostility and constant raids made on them by more powerful tribes from Kiwai and Parama, so they established themselves some thirty miles to the west, as they found the proprietors of the district to be friendly disposed.

When I visited Mawatta ten years previously, I accompanied Mr. H. Milman, who was Acting Resident Magistrate of Torres Straits. On landing we were met by Mr. E. Beardmore, who employed natives in fishing for pearl-shell and bêche-de-mer, and by a host of natives, all of whom came up and shook hands with us. Amongst these was the chief, or Mamoose, as he is termed. The title was engraved on a crescentic brass plate, and hung on the old man's chest like the label of a bottle of wine. This strange outward and visible sign was given to the man by Beardmore as a symbol of chieftainship. There was at the time a dispute as to the office of chief, the candidates being Billy, the son of the late chief, Gamea, a young man, who did not appear to be very popular, and Gabia, whom the majority wanted. I believe that Gabia's chief distinction was that he was the most successful hunter of wild pigs in the neighbourhood.

We adjourned to Beardmore's house, shaking hands *en route* with men, women, and children. Everybody was "decently" clothed, the women wearing long calico gowns, a disappointing sight, as the previous year when Mr. Milman was here the women wore only their characteristic small fore-and-aft leaf petticoat.

On coming out of the house all the people were marshalled. Those of the upper portion of this double village were on one side, those of the lower village on the other, while a few totally unclothed Masingara, "bushmen," who happened to be there, formed a group by themselves. These latter were absolute savages who lived a few miles inland, whereas the natives of Mawatta have been in contact with Europeans for twenty-five years or more.

Then Mr. Milman made a speech to the assembled people. I did not write it down, but this is part of what he said: "No good you fellow have two Mamooses. Good thing you have one Mamoose, one man, Gabia; him Mamoose of two villages." Then Mr. Milman formally presented him with a staff of office, which was a carved Japanese cane walking-stick, in the handle of which a shilling was inserted with the Queen's head uppermost, and the Union Jack, which Billy had hitherto flown, was given to Gabia. The ejaculations and remarks of the crowd were expressive, but quite unintelligible to me.

The new chief was then told to build a court-house in the middle of the village, and a quantity of tobacco was given him to help pay for labour and materials. When it was built the staff of office was to be kept inside, and the flag was to fly on official occasions from a pole on the roof, and when there were any disputes the people would have to go to the court-house, and it would be the chief's business to settle the quarrels, aided by the advice of the old men of the village.

The people in New Guinea usually bury their dead in very shallow graves, close to, or even underneath, the dwelling-houses. The Government puts a stop to this unhealthy arrangement, and so Gabia was told to prevent this in future, and to fix on a spot for a cemetery some distance off.

Next a social matter demanded attention, which strangely resembled a situation that is common enough at home. There was a young man named Kasawi, a fine industrious young fellow, who wanted to marry a certain young girl, and she wanted to marry him; but Kasawi was poor, and the parents of the girl tried to force her to marry a richer man.

Here also it is the custom for the man to give his own sister as a wife to the brother of the girl whom he wants to marry, but Kasawi had no sister. The old people were firm, but the girl would not do as they wished and marry an elderly Malay man who lived there, and who could afford to give good presents to her parents.

For a long time there had been considerable excitement in the village about this little love affair, as no one would give way.

KIWAI AND MAWATTA

Mr. Milman told Gabia to decide in this matter, and there was a great palaver. Then the chief proclaimed that Kasawi might marry the girl, but when he was paid off by Mr. Beardmore, for whom he was then working, he would have to give the parents of his bride certain presents from his wages. A murmur of applause went round the crowd, who appeared to highly approve of this decision, and so the young people were made happy.

After the meeting broke up I took several photographs. The first business was to get the women to exuviate, and to appear in their native dress, for, as I explained to them, if I wanted to photograph calico I could do that at home. After a little time they retired to their houses with much laughing and giggling, and reappeared dressed solely in the national costume. Many of the women had a raised scar which extended from breast to breast—this is said to be made when a brother spears his first turtle or dugong; some had cicatrices on their upper arms and shoulders; most had scars on various parts of their bodies, but these were the result of cuts made for the purpose of removing pain by bleeding.

A native dance was got up for our benefit; owing to the shortness of time at the disposal of the dancers their costume was not so elaborate as is usually the case. On this occasion only the men danced, and of these there were about twenty or thirty. The usual dress consisted only of a pair of short pants; in the belt a tail was fastened behind, either of leaves or a flap of red or gaily coloured calico. The head was ornamented with a head-dress of white or black feathers or a band of bright-coloured calico; sometimes leaves or flowers only were inserted in the hair. Some put flowers in the large holes they make in the lobes of their ears. On their arms they wore woven cane armlets or bands, generally decorated with tassels or the gaily coloured leaves of the croton; on the left forearm they wore a long cane arm-band, which is used to protect the arm from the bow string when they shoot with bow and arrow, a long bunch of cassowary feathers was usually stuck in this arm-guard. Finally, there were bands of pale yellow leaves on their legs.

It is very difficult to describe the dancing, which was always accompanied with the beating of drums. Sometimes the men danced in a circle in single file, going either from right to left or the reverse, there was a pause after each turn. One figure was somewhat more complicated: the men advanced in a line up each side of the dancing-ground, the first pair who met retreated a little in the middle line, still facing the spectators; when the next two arrived, the first pair separated to allow them to pass between, and the new-comers took up their position behind the former, and so on, until the last pair passed between the gradually lengthened avenue of standing men. Several of the dances imitated actions in real life, such as planting yams or picking up pearl-shell from the bottom of the sea, or animals were represented, and a man would mimic the movements of a crab, a lizard, or a pelican.

The Pelican dance was the last; a couple of men came forward, jumped up into the air, and alighted on the tips of their toes. As the drum-beats became more rapid, so was their jumping quicker; so active were they, that we could hardly follow their movements. When they were tired other pairs came up, until all had danced. It was really a fine sight, and, of course, we duly clapped each set of dancers, and well they deserved it.

Mr. Beardmore said that his men often broke off in the middle of their work to practise a favourite step, and work might be knocked off for an afternoon in order to have a dance; sometimes one was carried on right through the night. Where missionary influence is strong enough, the native dances are discouraged or altogether stopped. I once saw an illustration of the change that has taken place in Warrior Island. Some of the younger performers were rather ashamed to dance, others were imperfectly acquainted with the steps, but the old women danced splendidly, and thoroughly enjoyed it. The natives were beginning to care less for their old customs and more for trade, as the men can earn quite a lot of money by fishing.

After the dancing we gave scrambles for tobacco, first to the children only, then to the women only. It was amusing for all of us, and there was great screeching and laughing. Then the barter commenced, and I was fortunate enough to obtain a number of interesting objects.

For a scrub-knife, that is, a knife with a very long blade that is used for cutting down the underwood when they make their gardens, I obtained a mask in the shape of a crocodile's head made of tortoise-shell. This mask was worn during certain

KIWAI AND MAWATTA

religious dances, and when I asked the man from whom I bought it to put it on in order that I might see how it was used, he refused, as he said if he did so he would die by a slow and painful illness, and he did not want to run the risk of this to please me, nor even for a stick of tobacco. Evidently it would be regarded as sacrilege to wear a mask of this kind on any other occasion than the sacred ceremony to which it belonged.

Below one of the large houses there were clusters of human skulls hanging like bunches of grapes or strings of onions; these were the skulls of enemies killed in battle, and they were hung up as trophies.

The possession of skulls is a sign of bravery, and so the men like to have them, and the women are very proud of their husbands if they have several. In fighting they use the bow and arrow and stone clubs. The most common kind of stone club is that which has a perforated disc of hard stone, finely polished and brought to a sharp edge, which is mounted usually on a short length of rattan, but there are others which have knobbed or star-shaped heads. Some of the skulls I obtained had holes in them that clearly showed with which kind of club the men had been killed.

After a man is killed his head is cut off with a bamboo knife; the blade is made of a split piece of bamboo, the handle being bound round with plaited string. When the knife is to be used a nick is made on the edge, close to the handle, with a small shell; then a strip is peeled off from the other end, the nick preventing the handle from splitting.

The rind of bamboo is full of minute flinty particles, so much so that a freshly-cut edge is very sharp, and will cut off a man's head; but it will suffice for only one occa-

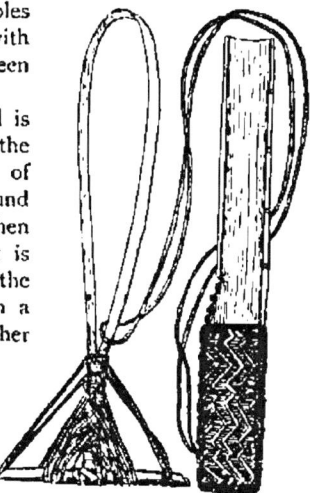

FIG. 11. BAMBOO BEHEADING-KNIFE AND HEAD-CARRIER, MAWATTA
One-fifth natural size

sion, and a fresh edge has to be made for each head that is cut off. One knife I bought had five nicks, which means it had been used for the purpose of cutting off the heads of five people, and another had nine notches.

Along with the knife I bought a cane loop, or sling; this is used for carrying home the heads after they have been cut off.

CHAPTER VIII

MABUIAG

THE day after we left Parama we had a long, disagreeable run against the tide to Dauan, only reaching a comparatively sheltered anchorage near this island late at night. In the morning we made an early start, and arrived at Mabuiag in the afternoon. It was rough till we got in the lee of the extensive Orman's reef. When the shelter of that was passed we had to do a lot of beating up against a strong tide, for in the narrow channels between the reefs, or between the reefs and the islands, there is often a tidal race.

I was very pleased to visit Mabuiag once more. During my former expedition I spent five weeks in this island, and its inhabitants happened to be the first natives I had studied and made friends with. After interviewing Mr. Cowling, the local trader, we went on to the Mission Station, and the rest of the day was spent in landing our stuff and putting up the camp beds, and otherwise establishing ourselves in the mission-house. Cowling invited us to dinner, for which we were grateful, as our domestic arrangements were all sixes and sevens. After a yarn we returned to the Mission camp; it felt quite chilly at night, as a strong south-east wind was blowing. Fortunately there were no mosquitoes nor sandflies, so there was no need to be cooped up in mosquito nets.

The Mission Station on Murray Island is on the leeward or western side of the island; but when we went across the island —to Las, for example—we found the continuous wind very refreshing. In Mabuiag the Mission Station is on the windward or south-east side of the island, and we at once felt braced by the change of air. There is no doubt that, owing to this, we could work better, and there was less temptation to slackness than was the case in Murray Island.

Mabuiag is a larger island than Murray, and consists of several hills three or four hundred feet in height, some are about five hundred feet high. It is, roughly speaking, triangular in outline, each side measuring about a couple of miles. Owing to the character of ancient igneous rocks the island is only moderately fertile, and the vegetation has more of an Australian character than has that of Murray Island. There are also small grassy plains with scattered pandanus trees, and here and there a cycad. The somewhat conical rocky hills are mostly covered with trees, with grassy patches on their summits. Water is rather scarce.

The little harbour, with its jetty, is situated at the most easterly point of the island. It is here Cowling has his store. The Mission Station is on the beach on the south-eastern side of the island, at one end of the only village in the island. Formerly the houses were more or less scattered over the island, but the missionaries have induced the natives to congregate in one spot.

Compared with the Murray Islanders, the people of Mabuiag are much better off so far as clothes and European commodities are concerned; but, as already stated, the island is much less fertile—indeed, little native food is now grown, barely enough for daily use.

Mabuiag has been for a longer time, and also far more thoroughly, under the influence of the white man than has Murray Island. Consequently the social and economic conditions have been more modified, and one immediately perceives that the people are more civilised, and it does not take long to find out that they are more intelligent as a whole. The men do more fishing, and are altogether more industrious than are the Murray Islanders.

At first sight one would be inclined to put all this down to the credit of the influence of the white men, but I am by no means sure that this is entirely the case. When the results of our investigations are completed and published it will, we suspect, be evident that the Mabuiag people are naturally more intelligent than the Murray Islanders.

Mabuiag is situated half-way between New Guinea and Australia, and it was the intermediate trading station between the natives of the Prince of Wales group and those of Saibai, who, on the other hand, had trading relations with the coastal people of Daudai, as the neighbouring part of New Guinea is locally termed.

The Mabuiag men were skilful sailors and fishermen, and they combined with this a little head-hunting and a fair amount of trading, all of which occupations tend to develop the intelligence. They also had the advantage of not having a very fertile soil. It was therefore necessary for them to till the ground fairly assiduously if they were to have enough garden produce to sustain life in comfort; this probably assisted towards making them industrious.

Muralug, the largest island in Torres Straits, and one of the nearest to Australia, has very similar physical conditions, but the people were at a much lower social grade. My impression is that they were not so enterprising on the sea as the Mabuiag men, and certainly they were greatly inferior to them so far as general culture and tilling of the soil were concerned. Indeed, most of their time was spent wandering about in the bush and living on what fruit happened to be in season. Macgillivray states that none of the land "by cultivation has been rendered fit for the permanent support of man." It is possible that the Muralug people, although of the same stock as the Mabuiag folk, were influenced for bad by their neighbours on the Cape York peninsula, while the Mabuiag men were braced by contact with the Papuans of the mainland of New Guinea.

Murray Island, as we have seen, was so fertile that very little labour was necessary for supplying garden produce; and though the men were good sailors, and often visited Erub, and even occasionally Parama or Kiwai, yet their isolation prevented much intercourse, and they remained less intelligent than the Mabuiag people, but more so than the Muralug folk.

There is another circumstance that must not be overlooked, although we do not yet know its full bearing. From the measurements we made of the living natives, and from those I have made on the skulls, it appears that the Torres Straits Islands were inhabited by a branch of the Western Papuans, who had the very dark skin, black woolly hair, and long, narrow heads that characterise that group of peoples. This stock alone occurs in Murray Island, whereas in the western tribe, from Saibai to Muralug, there is superimposed on this ground-stock another stem with a similar skin and hair, but with broader heads. This broader-headed population can also be traced along the Daudai coast to Kiwai Island, and for at least seventy miles up the Fly River.

It is generally admitted that a broadening of the head is advantageous, especially if associated with an increase in total capacity. However this may be, human progress is usually directly connected with a mixture of peoples, and apparently the mixture of even a very slightly different people has somewhat improved the mental activity of the western islanders.

There is a large collection of skulls in the British Museum (Natural History Museum) which came from the island of Pulu, about which I shall have more to say immediately. They are consequently the skulls of enemies of the Mabuiag folk, probably mainly natives of Moa. These skulls, which have been described by Mr. Oldfield Thomas, are very narrow. Of one exceptionally narrow skull, with a very protruding muzzle, Mr. Thomas writes: "This skull may be taken as a type of the lowest and most simian human cranium likely to occur at the present day."

The skulls I obtained at Mabuiag during my two visits to that island belonged to natives of that island, and they are markedly broader than those collected by Dr. Macfarlane.

In 1888 I was very anxious to obtain some skulls, but for some time could not get any. One morning my boy Dick said to me, "Doctor, I savvy where head belong dead man he stop; he stop in hole." I promised the boy a jew's-harp to show me the spot, and on going there I took from a crevice in a rock a beautifully perfect skull that had been painted red. I told Dick to inform his friends that I would give a jew's-harp for a skull or for some bones.

That afternoon a crowd of small boys marched up, holding in their hands a number of human bones. I suspected I was being somewhat imposed upon, as probably one boy had collected the lot and distributed them among his friends; but I had learned the lesson that if you want to start a trade you must not mind paying extravagantly, if needs be, at first. Once the trade has started it is quite a different matter. I paid each boy a jew's-harp for the worthless broken bones he brought. The boys were hugely delighted, and strutted up and down the village strumming their jew's-harps.

The young men of the village then began to yearn for jew's-harps, and that same evening they came to me, and said, "Doctor, I want jewsarp." I replied, "I want head belong dead man." "I no got head belong dead man," they urged. "You savvy where he stop. You get him," was my reply.

The following evening the skulls began to arrive, and I duly gave a jew's-harp for each one. Unfortunately by this time my small stock of jew's-harps was exhausted, save for two. Then one young man said, "Doctor, I want jewsarp." "I want head belong dead man." "I no got head belong dead man." "You savvy where he stop; good thing you catch him." To my surprise the man replied, "I no got wife."

At first I could not make it out. In those days I had not paid any attention to craniology, but I knew enough to satisfy myself that the skulls were those of people who had been dead a long time, and many were obviously the skulls of men. Consequently the young men had not been killing their wives for the sake of a jew's-harp. No savage I ever came across would make such a bad bargain as that.

Then I discovered that the young men had sent their wives to procure the skulls; and, as not unfrequently happens elsewhere, the women did the work, and the men got the reward.

The advent of the white man has upset the former economic conditions on Mabuiag. The men now spend all their time "swimming diving" as it is called, that is, they go in parties in sailing boats, and dive by swimming for pearl-shell in shallow water. Some natives own their own boats, and make up crews on a system of sharing; others hire themselves out to white men. They generally start out on Monday and return on Friday or Saturday. All the time they are away they feed on tinned meat, biscuits, flour, and other white man's food. They get accustomed to this food, and as they are away from home so much, they cannot "make" their gardens. Thus it comes about that agriculture, as well as fishing, is greatly neglected, and a considerable portion—and in some instances the bulk—of their food has to be bought from the stores. Should the supply of pearl-shell fall off, or the price be lowered, the natives would suffer greatly; and if the storekeepers left the island, the people would practically starve. As it is, many are considerably in debt to the traders, and often the traders have to advance supplies of flour and food to ward off starvation. With all their apparent prosperity, the people are really in a false economic condition, and their future may yet be temporarily deplorable.

The Mabuiag people have a very superior new timber church, which was built, as they are proud of stating, "by contract for £250." The natives of other islands built their churches themselves, but here they could afford to pay others to do it for them; and no false modesty causes them to be behindhand in making the most of this fact. Some time ago a large quantity of pig copper was found by the natives on a reef close by, and they sold this to the traders for about £500. With some of the money thus obtained they built their church. The copper must have formed part of the cargo of a ship that struck on the reef, and the copper was jettisoned to lighten her.

We very soon annexed the old church building as a storehouse and laboratory, and found it most convenient. Some of us slept in it, and found it a cool, airy bedroom. The roof was considerably dilapidated, the thatch having come off in many spots; but fortunately there was no rain. The walls were broken in places, and the doors and window-frames were all giving way; still it suited our purposes admirably.

A day or two after our arrival a procession of men, women, and children came from the village very early in the morning, singing hymns as they marched, and deposited in front of our door a present of a large number of coconuts, four water melons, one yam, some taro, several eggs, two cocks, and a hen. Most of the parents with characteristic kindliness let their little children put their presents on the heap. The spokesman said the island was poor (in garden produce), and they could not give us much. In replying, I said we knew they had not much produce, and that they had given us a good present. I added also that no one had given us fowls and eggs before. After the little speechifying was over, the people and the heaped-up food were photographed.

It was much easier to get information from these people than from the Murray Islanders, for they know English very much better, were further removed from their past, and did not appear to have the scarcely veiled affection and respect for their old customs that the Murray Islanders certainly retain. They were less unwilling, therefore, to tell what they remembered of their former customs. There were still a few old men alive who

PLATE XI

WARIA, PETER, TOM, AND GIZU

NEĔT OR PLATFORM FROM WHICH DUGONG ARE HARPOONED

knew the "old-time fashion," and they often acted as referees, so that it was possible to get definite information upon points about which the younger men were uncertain; but the old men knew very little English, and the young men had to interpret for them.

Owing to the industrious habits of the men and their professed desire to get money for the forthcoming "May," they went out diving for pearl-shell, and we were during our first week occasionally left without "subjects." To obviate this I engaged two men, Peter and Tom, at ten shillings a week each to come and talk to us whenever we wanted them. I also engaged a man named Waria to help Ontong. After engaging Waria as literally our drawer of water and hewer of wood, I discovered that he was the hereditary chief of the island! So he was promoted to be my special instructor in the old native customs, and help Ray with his study of the language. Waria's father died when he was a lad, so the present Mamoose was elected by the Hon. John Douglas. Since we left Waria has "come into his own." We soon found out that Waria was making a translation of the Gospel of St. Matthew, and he turned out to be a very accomplished person. He was genuinely interested in our work, and quite grasped what our objects were. One day, on his own initiative, he wrote the following:—

ANTHROPOLADIKO EKSIPIDISIN
tana mun   nel   itabo   Mabaigan   nel
their   name   in the   of Mabuiag   name

Very early one morning, hearing the sound of wailing in the village, we went to inquire who had died. To our sorrow we heard it was the infant son of Waria. The child was quite well the day before, except for a stomach-ache; probably he had been overlaid in the night. There was a great exhibition of grief, and many people came in all through the day to sit in Waria's house and weep by the poor little corpse. These people are really most affectionate and sympathetic; everything was disorganised that day on account of the infant's death. Even old men sat about doing nothing. Waria was very desirous to have a photograph of his dead baby in order that he might not forget what he was like. Of course we did this for him.

When he was in Murray Island, Rivers wanted to find out

whether any of the psychological traits or aptitudes that he had investigated ran in certain families, and consequently he commenced to record the relationships of the various subjects. Before he commenced on the inquiry he had absolutely no interest in the subject of genealogy, but he soon became literally fascinated with it. In the end he had tabulated the genealogies of every native of Murray Island as far back as could be remembered.

It was very amusing to see Rivers closeted with some old man ferreting out the family history of various people, and he often surprised the natives by the width and accuracy of his knowledge. A tremendous amount of secrecy had to be exercised in these inquiries in Murray Island, and one never knew in what odd corner or retired spot one might not come upon the mysterious whispering of Rivers and his confidant. The questions one overheard ran mostly in this wise, "He married?" "What name wife belong him?" "Where he stop?" "What piccaninny he got?" "He boy, he girl?" "He come first?" and so forth.

All this is not so simple as it appears, as everyone has one or two names, and sometimes a man will casually assume a new name. Some men have married several times, often to widows with children; but the most confusing point of all is the very general custom in Murray Island of adopting children. In many cases children do not find out till they are grown up who their parents were; often they never know.

Their system of naming relationships is very different from ours; for example, a mother's sisters, that is the maternal aunts, are called "mothers." In the usual method of collecting names of relationships confusion would often arise, owing to the very varied ways of regarding kinship; but according to Rivers' system mistakes could practically never arise. All the terms he used were: "father," "mother," "husband," "wife," "boy," "girl," or "man" and "woman," and for the first of these he always asked, "He proper father?" "He proper mother?" Once a genealogy was fairly complete it was only necessary to ask, "What A call B?" "What A call F?" "What B call A?" and so on, to find out what were the relationships acknowledged by them, and the names by which they were called.

Finding that this line of inquiry led to such good results

in Murray Island, Rivers immediately started similar investigations when he arrived at Mabuiag. The collection of genealogies here was in one respect more difficult than in Murray Island, as the families were larger and the prevalence of polygamy, until quite recently, further complicated matters. Intermarriages between natives of different islands were naturally much more common than in Murray Island; indeed the intermarriage between the inhabitants of Mabuiag and Badu have been so frequent that they must be regarded as one people.

Not only did Rivers record the islands the various people came from, but their totems as well. By this laborious work a great deal of valuable information will result that could not be obtained in any other way or with anything like the same accuracy. The clan marriages of the population of Mabuiag for several generations will not fail to reveal the rules that regulated marriage and descent.

There was an interesting psychological difference between the Mabuiag folk and those of Murray Island. As has just been pointed out, great secrecy had to be maintained in the latter island when pursuing genealogical inquiries; but quite the opposite condition prevailed in Mabuiag. Here the information was obtained in public, and a doubtful point in genealogy was frankly discussed by men and women. This enabled Rivers to make more rapid progress than in Murray Island, and at the same time he was equally sure of his facts: what in Murray Island required private confabulations with various men at different times could here be settled practically offhand.

Much varied sociological information can be obtained by recording genealogies in this way. For example, one can get definite facts on the number of children in a family, the proportion of the sexes, the number that die before they themselves have children, the number of adopted children, the idea on which relationship is based, the relationship nomenclature, the relation of totems to individuals or communities, the personal or group restrictions as to marriage, the relative fertility of related or unrelated stock, the effect of crossing between different races, and so forth.

Without entering into further detail, I would like to emphasise the fact that by this system Rivers has supplied anthropologists with a new method of research, by means of which important data can be collected with absolute accuracy on subjects concerning which it has hitherto been very difficult to obtain reliable information.

Some white men resident on Mabuiag had crews of mainland (Queensland) blacks, and we took this opportunity to measure, psychologise, and photograph some dozen of these men. This was a fortunate chance for us, as we wanted to make a few comparative observations on the North Queensland aborigines.

There were also a few South Sea men living on Mabuiag, who had married native women, and we studied several of them, and their half-caste children as well. My old friend Billy Tanna was still on Mabuiag with his numerous progeny, and three or four other Tanna men besides, whom we also measured. Tanna is one of the New Hebrides group.

One Lifu man, Sŭni or Charley, had the longest head I have ever measured. It was 215 mm. ($8\frac{1}{2}$ inches) in length. It was also narrow and high; the length, breadth (or cephalic) index was 66·9. Rivers found in Sŭni the first example of true colour blindness he had yet come across. It was amusing to see Sŭni's total inability to discriminate between pink and blue and red and green, and his other attempted matches were very quaint. There were two other Lifu men on the island, and great was Rivers' delight to find that one of them was also red-green blind. One felt tempted to frame all sorts of wild theories about a colour-blind race. During his return home, both at Thursday Island and at Rockhampton, in Queensland, Rivers investigated four other Lifu men, but only one of these was colour-blind. Still, it is an interesting fact that not a single other case of colour-blindness was found among one hundred and fifty natives of Torres Straits and Kiwai, or among some eighty members of other races, including Australians, Polynesians, Melanesians, Tamils, and half-castes, and yet three out of seven Lifu men were colour-blind. Lifu is one of the Loyalty group in the South Pacific. The inhabitants are Melanesians, with, in some instances, a little Polynesian admixture.

Ray pursued his philological studies in Mabuiag, and found that there was a very marked difference, both structurally and in vocabulary, between it and the Murray Island tongue. From

Saibai to Muralug and from Badu to Tut one language is spoken, but there are at least four closely allied dialects corresponding to as many groups of islands. The grammar of this language is decidedly of the Australian type, though there is no marked connection in structure or vocabulary with languages of the neighbouring mainland of Australia.

Later, Ray had an opportunity of verifying this conclusion by a partial investigation of the language of the Yaraikanna tribe of Cape York, which is, however, totally distinct from that of the islanders of either the eastern or western tribes.

A marked peculiarity of the Mabuiag language is the extremely indefinite signification of the verbs, which require to be made definite by prefixes indicating the part of the body concerned, the direction of the action, or the place concerned. For example, *palan* apparently indicates the putting forth of something; and thus we have *poi-palan*, to shake off dust; *gagai-palan*, to fire gun or arrow; *minar-palan*, to make marks, to write; *ibelai-palan*, to cover as with a blanket; *balbalagi-palan*, to make not crooked, to straighten; *berai-palan*, to make like a rib, to slacken a rope; *dan-pali* (an intransitive), to open the eyes, to awake; *aka-pali*, to show fear. Another peculiarity is the partiality of the language for noun constructions; indeed, as all the verb suffixes are the same as those of nouns, it may be doubted whether the verb exists as it is understood in European languages. "I have seen you," is in Mabuiag *ngau ninu imai-zinga*, literally, "mine your seeing"; the imperative plural "Fear not" is *nitamun akagi*, "Your not (being) afraid."

The Mabuiag people have been under Christian teaching for over a quarter of a century, and in most respects they may be regarded as civilised and Christianised as country-folk at home. For about half this period the islanders were under the influence of the Rev. Dr. S. Macfarlane, but the actual teaching has always been done by South Sea teachers.

The new church was opened with great ceremony in 1897, and crowds of natives arrived from all parts of Torres Straits, even from the far-distant Darnley and Murray Islands.

It was amusing to find that these Mabuiag folk believe that the Murray Islanders are more savage, or less advanced than themselves, just as the Murray Islanders in their turn look down upon all the other islanders. We were told in all soberness that at the opening of the new church one of the Murray

Islanders tried to make sorcery on a Mabuiag man, but God was too powerful, and He made an example of a Murray Island boy who died mysteriously and was buried on a small island to windward. I believe our wicked old friend Ulai was the suspected sorcerer. On Mabuiag they say the Murray and Darnley people still keep up magic, and they contemptuously speak of these foreigners as eating frogs. Really, people are much alike all the world over! Here is another instance of the fact that is always striking us—the essential identity of the human mind under all varying conditions of race and climate.

Our good friend Mr. Chalmers arrived on Monday, October 3rd, from Saguane, bringing Ray with him, various mishaps having delayed his expected arrival on the previous Saturday. His main object in visiting Mabuiag was to hold a "May Meeting." Murray Island and Saibai each have their own "Mei," as they call it; but Mabuiag is the central station for all the other western islands.

Tamate employed one day in examining the school children, and some of us went to the distribution of prizes in the afternoon, the scissors, knives, pens, and pencils giving great pleasure to the little winners.

According to their custom everywhere the South Sea teachers put a stop to all native dancing in Torres Straits, and as I much wanted to see a dance in Mabuiag, there was some danger of the Mabuiag teacher misunderstanding my expressed desire to get up one. Tamate, however, soon arranged matters, and a native dance was included in the programme.

In the forenoon of Saturday, October 8th, a service was held in the church. Most of the congregation arrived in procession headed by Tamate, Isaiah, the Samoan teacher of Mabuiag, and Morris, the Niuie teacher of Badu.

After these came two broad rows of men and boys, then two rows of women and girls, all singing hymns. During the singing of the second hymn in church, it was discovered that the all-important plate for the collection had been forgotten, so a deacon went out and returned with two enamelled iron plates.

In his address Tamate said he was sorry to see that fewer people had come from the other islands than in former years. The Prince of Wales Islanders were few in number, but they (the Mabuiag people) had promised to subscribe money to help the Prince of Wales Islanders. The Mabuiag people earned plenty of money diving for pearl-shell; perhaps they made too much money, for when they went to Thursday Island they often squandered it on drink and other indulgences, and so had no reserve for bad seasons. Tamate appealed for more money to support new teachers in the Fly River district, and also for an annual contribution of clothes and calico and other things for their fellow-countryman Mugala, the teacher at Kunini. Finally he asked them to send young men to his station at Saguane to learn to read the Bible in English, and eventually to go out as teachers.

Before the meeting actually began, but after we entered the church, Mr. Chalmers, greatly to my surprise, said he would like me to speak to the natives. On finishing his address, therefore, he called upon me for a "talk." After some general remarks I spoke a little about our work, and that we found the differences between white, black, brown, and yellow men were mainly external, but in reality all were very much alike. I went on to tell them about prehistoric man in Britain, how, like themselves thirty years ago, he went naked, and only had stone implements. I described briefly the difference between palæolithic and neolithic implements, and how man gradually improved; how they themselves had *auguds* (totems) and our ancestors had too—theirs were dugong, shark, cassowary, etc., while ours had been the white horse, seal, and wild boar, and so on; how they cut representatives of their totems on their bodies, whilst our forbears used to paint their *auguds* in blue on their bodies; how tomahawks and knives came to us from another place, just as white men brought them theirs; how we formerly made sorcery just as they did—they made magic with wooden figures of men, and we stuck pins into clay figures. Then missionaries came to Britain and taught the people about God, just as missionaries come to them. The people in New Guinea are still what they themselves were like a few years ago, and it was now their turn to send missionaries to New Guinea. This address of mine given in pidgin English was the first, as it will probably be the last, given by me at a "May Meeting."

Then followed prayers and addresses in the vernacular by teachers, chiefs, and deacons, with hymns interspersed; and all the time, as in home churches, only more so, there was a continual dropping by the children of the coins they were to contribute to the collection, only, as *not* at home, the sound was the clink of silver, and not the clank of copper.

Afterwards the five young men with their wives, who were going to Chalmers' Mission Station at Saguane, were asked to come on the platform, and each gave a short address. Finally the collection was made as the congregation passed out of church in island groups. Mabuiag contributed £8 10s.; Badu and Moa, £8 0s. 9d.; Prince of Wales Island, £1; and the South Sea men of Mabuiag, £11 2s., making a total of £28 12s. 9d. During the year £64 15s. 1d. has been collected at the Sunday offertory at Mabuiag, consequently Chalmers took back as the Mabuiag subscription to the London Missionary Society £40 10s., this amount being the local "May" collection and half the weekly offerings for the year, a very creditable amount.

Mabuiag is the only native church which has a collection every Sunday; during the four months we were in Murray Island there was no collection, they have one only during their "May," and I was told that their last collection amounted to less than 10s.!

Isaiah invited all our party to luncheon with Tamate, and he gave us a first-rate midday dinner of pig, fowl, ham, yams, and sago cooked in an earth-oven; cake, tinned fruit, bananas, and water-melon, with ginger ale and coconut water to drink.

After dinner a large quantity of food was heaped in front of the mission house by the natives, and a speech was made stating that the island was so unfertile that they could not give so much as they would like. There was one large live turtle, and a cooked and cut-up one, dugong meat, fish, dampers, tins of meat, yams, taro, sweet potatoes, two bunches of bananas, and plenty of coconuts. When we had photographed the heaps of food, "Teapot," a Samoan, gave a very clever dance to the beating of an empty kerosine tin. Teapot flung an axe backward and forwards, up and down, and every possible way, catching and twisting it with great dexterity.

The present of food was then distributed. To Tamate was given the live turtle, a lot of coconuts, and other fruit; to the "Doctor," twenty coconuts and five sweet potatoes. I was very pleased at this further proof of the friendliness of the natives; other people also received a share of the present.

Later in the afternoon a dance was performed by some thirty

men in the palm grove within the Mission compound. This was the *Pibi kap*, sometimes called "Kwoiam's dance," after the legendary warrior of the island—it was a war dance performed after a successful fight. Some of the men had variously painted themselves with red and black and yellow ochre; they wore chaplets of young coconut leaves or white feathers in their hair, crossed shoulder-belts and petticoats of the same yellow, or yellowish green coconut leaves, streaming armlets to match, and bands round their legs and ankles. They held bows and arrows in their left hands, and in their right each carried a coco-nut, or pawpaw, to represent a decapitated human head.

It would be tedious to describe in detail the various movements of the dancers. Usually they advanced in single file, with a skipping movement, holding the body somewhat bent, then, resting for a moment on one leg, would beat the air two or three times with the other leg, then stoop, resting on both feet, and trail the "head" on the ground, then advance with various skipping movements; occasionally they would rapidly dance on the tips of their toes, as if they were boring into the ground, sometimes the bow would be held horizontally, at others vertically, and almost continuously the "head" would be trailed backwards and forwards in the sand; every now and again the cry of victory would be raised. Some old women excited by the memory of former days could not refrain joining also in the dance.

Imagine a "May Meeting" in Exeter Hall closing with a war dance!

CHAPTER IX

TOTEMISM AND THE CULT OF KWOIAM

IT was very interesting living among a people in the totemistic stage of culture, but this custom is now gradually dying out, and the young men do not know much about it. An old man, named Gizu, whose services I secured as referee, was a great authority on various old customs, beliefs, and legends, and we found his knowledge invaluable when Waria, or our other informants, were at fault, but his knowledge of English was too imperfect for us to rely on his services alone.

There appear to have been five chief clans in Mabuiag: *kodal* (crocodile), *tabu* (snake), *sam* (cassowary), *dungal* (dugong), and *kaigas* (shovel-nose skate), to which subsidiary or small totems were added. The members of the first three clans were called *koi augŭd kadzi*, or children of the great *augŭd*, or totem; and those of the two latter were the *mŭgi augŭd kadzi*, or children of the small *augŭd*. These two clans formerly had their headquarters on the windward or south-east side of Mabuiag, whereas the three others were mainly located on the opposite side of the island.

I was informed that the hammer-headed shark (*kursi*), the shark (*baidam*), the sting-ray (*tapimul*), and the turtle (*waru* or *surlal*) totems were associated with the skate-dugong group, the phrase used was, "They all belong water; they all friends." On the other hand, the dog (*umai*) was a subsidiary totem to the snake-cassowary-crocodile group; with the exception of the amphibious crocodile, these are all land animals.

There undoubtedly was supposed to be an intimate connection between the totem and its clansmen. For example, the crocodile-men were bloodthirsty, lusty, and always ready to fight any number of the water group; they had "no pity for people." If a crocodile-man killed a crocodile, the other members of the clan would kill him ; a member of another clan might kill a crocodile with impunity, but the *kodal*-men would mourn for it.

The snake-men were always ready for a row, and were handy with stone clubs. They used to put out their tongues and wag them as snakes do, and they had two small holes in the tip of their noses, which were evidently made to represent the nostrils of the snake.

The shark-men, like those previously mentioned, were "spoiling" for a fight. Sometimes the dog-men were fierce, at other times friendly, and "glad to see other people." If a dog-man killed a dog, his fellow-clansmen would "fight" him, but they would not do anything if an outsider killed one. A member of this clan was supposed to have great sympathy with dogs, and to understand them better than did other men.

No cassowary-man would kill a cassowary; if one was seen doing so, his clansmen would "fight" him, as they felt sorry. "*Sam*, he all same as relation ; he belong same family." The members of the cassowary clan prided themselves on being specially good runners. If there was to be a fight a *sam*-man would say to himself, "My leg is long and thin; I can run and not feel tired ; my legs will go quickly, and the grass will not entangle them." It is worth noting that the cassowary does not occur in the islands of Torres Straits; if it ever did, it must have been exterminated very shortly after the islands were inhabited. Possibly Mabuiag men occasionally visited the mainland of New Guinea; but the adoption of the cassowary as a totem points to a time when the ancestors of the Mabuiag people actually inhabited New Guinea. The same argument applies, though with less force, to the crocodile. It is true crocodiles occur sparsely on some of the islands, and that reptile might thus be, so to speak, an indigenous totem, but they are very common and dangerous in the swamps of the New Guinea coast.

On certain occasions each of the dugong-men was painted with a red line from the tip of his nose up his forehead and down his spine to the small of the back. I obtained in this island a wooden model of a dugong that was used as a charm, and which was painted with a red line in a corresponding manner. The men's foreheads were decked with upright leaves to represent the spouting of the dugong when it comes to the surface of the water to breathe, and leaves were also inserted in the arm-bands like water splashing off the dugong when it comes into very shallow water. This decoration was made when the dugong-man performed a magical rite in the *kwod* (or taboo ground) that was situated in their particular region of the island. A number of different plants were put on the ground, and a dugong was placed on the top. Several men took the dugong by the tail and hoisted up the tail in such a way as to make the dugong face the rest of the island—for the *kwod* was near the seashore, and faced the great reefs on which the dugong abound. There can be little doubt that this was a magical rite performed by the dugong-men to make the dugong come towards the island of Mabuiag. The dugong used in this ceremony was given to the turtle-men.

When only one turtle was obtained on a turtle expedition it was taken to the *kwod* of the turtle-men, who performed a pantomimic ceremony which symbolised the increase of turtle.

The origin and significance of totemism is still very obscure, and it is possible that quite different social, magical, and semi-religious institutions have been grouped together somewhat artificially as totemistic.

A very plausible hypothesis that Australian totemism is mainly an economic custom has recently been suggested independently by Dr. J. G. Frazer and Professor Baldwin Spencer. According to this view it is the business of certain groups of people, or clans, to preserve, or increase by means of magical rites, particular foodstuffs or objects of especial utility for the benefit of the whole tribe or community.

The behaviour of the dugong-men and turtle-men in Mabuiag certainly seems to support this very suggestive explanation, and I am inclined to think that it will receive additional corroboration when the Papuan evidence is forthcoming. It might be mentioned in this connection that though rain is not a totem, the office of *aripuilaig*, or "rain-maker," was hereditary in Mabuiag, and consequently rain-making would be the function of a particular family.

In Mabuiag a woman kept her totem when she married, and I was informed that children inherited their father's and mother's totems, but the father's was the chief one. I was also informed that though a man might not marry a Mabuiag or Badu woman belonging to the same *augŭd* as himself, this restriction did not apply to women from other islands.

In dealing with totemism in Kiwai I have already pointed out the value of belonging to a totemistic clan when visiting another village, and we found the same to apply among the western islands of Torres Straits. A man visiting another island would naturally be looked after and entertained by the residents who belonged to the same *augŭd* as he did. In warfare a man would never willingly or intentionally kill an enemy who he knew belonged to the same totem as himself. So that apart from its supposed economic use, totemism was undoubtedly an ameliorating influence in social intercourse, and tended to minimise inter-tribal antagonism.

During my former visit to Mabuiag, and on the present occasion, I failed to discover any very important ceremonies in connection with the initiation of the boys into their respective clans, though I have published an account of some initiation ceremonies that were held at Tut, or Warrior Island, during which the lads were secluded for a month in tents made of mats.

Seligmann discovered in Mabuiag a very interesting custom relative to the seclusion of girls on attaining womanhood. Remarkable as this practice was, very similar customs from various parts of the world have been recorded by Dr. J. G. Frazer in his erudite study in comparative religion, *The Golden Bough*. The following is from the preliminary account already published by my colleague:—

"When the signs of puberty appeared, a circle of bushes was made in a dark corner in the house of the girl's parents. The girl was fully decked with leaves, and she sat in the centre of the bushes, which were piled so high round her that only her head was visible. This seclusion lasted for three months, the bushes being changed nightly, at which time the girl was allowed to slip out of the hut. She was usually attended by two old women, the girl's maternal aunts, who were especially appointed to look after her. These women were called *mowai* by the girl; one of them cooked food for the girl at a special fire in the bush. The girl might not feed herself nor handle her food, it being put into her mouth by her attendant women. No man—not even the girl's father—might come into the house. If he did see his daughter during this time he would certainly have had bad luck with his fishing, and probably smash his canoe the first time he went out. The girl might not eat turtle or turtle eggs; no vegetable food was forbidden. The sun was not allowed to shine on her. 'He can't see day time; he stop inside dark,' said my informant.

"At the end of three months the girl was carried to a freshwater creek by her *mowai*, she hanging on to their shoulders so that not even her feet touched the ground, the women of the village forming a ring round the girl and her *mowai*, thus escorting them to the creek. The girl's ornaments were removed, and the *mowai* with their burden staggered into the creek, where the girl was immersed, all the women joining in splashing water over the three. On coming out of the water one of the *mowai* made a heap of grass for her charge to sit on, while the other ran to the reef and caught a small crab. She tore off its claws, and with these she ran back to the creek, where a fire had meanwhile been made, at which the claws were roasted. The girl was then fed on these by the *mowai*. She was then freshly decorated, and the whole party marched back to the village in one row, the girl being in the centre, with the *mowai* at her side, each of them holding one of the girl's wrists. The husbands of the *mowai* (called by the girl *waduam*) received her, and led her into the house of one of them, where all ate food, the girl being then allowed to feed herself in the usual manner. The rest of the commuuity had meanwhile prepared and eaten a feast, and a dance was held, in which the girl took a prominent part, her two *waduam* dancing, one on each side of her. When the dance was finished, the *mowai* led the girl into their house and stripped her of her ornaments. They then led her back to her parents' house."

One day Cowling invited us to go in his centre-board cutter to Pulu, as he knew we were anxious to visit that sacred islet, and we took with us Gizu, Tom, and Peter to act as guides. We had a spanking sail round the eastern and southern sides of Mabuiag, and soon reached Pulu, a small rocky island on the reef on the western side of Mabuiag. We landed at Mumugubut, a pretty little sandy bay surrounded by granitic rocks, which were fissured and undercut in an extraordinary manner. To the right, projecting high from massive boulders, was a gigantic Γ-shaped rock, which is called Kwoiam's throwing-stick. This redoubtable hero implanted his weapon here after the slaughter of a number of Badu men who had humbugged him. Kwoiam had followed these men from Mabuiag, and landing elsewhere on the island, walked close to this tiny bay. Natives point out a rock lying on the ground against which Kwoiam pressed his foot when preparing to throw his spear against his sleeping foes, but concluding this spot was not suitable he made a détour inland, and took up a position whence he commanded a better view of the unconscious Badu men. He again prepared to hurl his spear, pressing hard with his right foot against the ground, which immediately became a shelf of rock to give him a better purchase for his foot. A little inland from the bay are a number of large slabs of rock which represent the bodies of the men killed and decapitated by Kwoiam.

To the left of Mumugubut are some smoothed rocks on which are perched immense boulders. A casual observer seeing similar rocks in Europe would not hesitate to describe these also as glaciated rocks and *blocs perchés*. As a matter of fact, they are due to the same kind of weathering that carves out the Devonshire tors, and which leaves the large granite boulders on the flanks of Dartmoor.

We passed round these rocks, and then struck inland. A short way from the beach is a cleft in the rocks, which in some places is very narrow, but in others widens out to leave two or three various-sized but small open spaces, which were utilised in former days as the retiring-rooms of the men engaged in certain ceremonies. One compartment was the cooking place, another the "green-room"; and in this latter was a great overhanging rock, under the shelter of which were kept the "properties." No women were allowed to come near this spot.

We scrambled over rocks and through scrub, and soon came to an open bay, with a fair amount of level ground below it.

The southerly end of this area was the *kwod*, or tabooed camp of the men. To the left, and at high-water mark, is a huge boulder with an overhanging smooth surface facing the *kwod*. On this smooth surface are some nearly effaced paintings in red of various animals, also some handprints made by placing the outstretched palm and fingers on the rock, and splashing the rock with powdered charcoal mixed with water. The handprint thus appears white on a black background. The legend of the origin of this rock is as follows.

Once upon a time, when the Mabuiag people were camping

there, the boys and girls, in spite of the prohibition of their parents, were fond of continually twirling round on the beach with their arms extended. They played in this way every night till this great rock fell from the sky as a punishment, and killed every man, woman, and child on the island, with the exception of two sweethearts, who fled and crossed over to Mabuiag at Kakalug. They bit a piece of a *kowai* tree that grew there, and "that medicine stop that stone." This pair of lovers became the progenitors of the present population. Parents still tell their children never to play this game (*gugabidĕ tiai*) at night, lest a similar catastrophe should recur. The rock is called *menguzikula*, or "the stone that fell."

Near the centre of the *kwod* is a large oblong heap of dugong bones, *koi siboi*. At short distances from this were the fire-places of the five chief clans. These were so arranged that the *Sam* (cassowary), *Kodal* (crocodile), and *Tabu* (snake) fire-places were comparatively close together, whereas the *Kaigas* (shovel-nose skate) and *Dungal* (dugong) were much further apart. This corresponds to a grouping of the three first as the "children of the big *augŭd*," the name of which was named *kotibu*.

The two last were the "children of the little *augŭd*," which was called *giribu*. *Kotibu* and *giribu* were two crescentic ornaments, or insignia, made by Kwoiam of turtle-shell; the former was worn on the upper lip, and the latter on the chest.

It appears to me that we here have a most interesting stage in the transformation of totemism, since we have the two main groups of the old totem (*augŭd*) clans associated with relics of a national hero. There are other facts which point to the rise of a local hero cult, the hero himself (although he belonged to the *Kaigas* clan) being *augŭd*, as were also *kotibu* and *giribu*.

It is very rarely that artificial objects are adopted as totems, and I believe this is the only instance of an individual man being spoken of as a totem. Although the natives called him *augŭd*, they were evidently extending the use of that term to a point beyond which it could logically be applied; but having no name for the idea they were striving after, they were forced to employ an old term, though the meaning was strained.

At the back of the *kwod* are two heaps of Fusus shells—one slightly larger than the other—the *koi mat* and the *mŭgi mat*

PLATE XII

MAN DRESSED UP FOR THE DEATH-DANCE

DIVINING SKULLS

1 SKULL OF MAGAU OF NAGIR
2 A MURRAY ISLAND SKULL

(*koi* means "large," and *mŭgi* is "small"). A short distance to the side of these are two small heaps of shells called respectively *koi augŭdau kupar* and *mŭgi augŭdau kupar*, and beyond the latter is a double row of dugong ribs called *mŭgi siboi*.

FIG. 12. THE KWOD OR CEREMONIAL GROUND IN PULU

These five shrines are close to the bushes and rocks that form the south-easterly border of the *kwod*.

The great annual ceremonies were held here at the rising of the star *Kek* (Achernar, α of Eridanus, of our constellations).

The annual death-dance first took place, at which men with leafy masks and bodies covered with the yellow sprouting leaves of the coco-palm danced with bow and arrow, and mimicked in their gait and attitudes persons recently deceased. The women, who sat a long way off, recognised the individuals who were personified, and with tears and lamentations called out, "That's my husband!" "Oh, my son!" according to their relationship with the deceased.

Women, too, have spirits that live after death, but, as that sex is by universal consent tabooed from performing sacred ceremonies, they could not personate deceased women; so men performed that office clad in a woman's petticoat, and carried brooms in their hand, their faces being hidden with the customary head-dress of leaves.

It was a remarkable fact that these people appear to have noticed that hilarity is a natural reaction at funerals, and this was provided for in the person of a sort of masked buffoon, the *danilkau*, who "played the fool" behind the back of some of the more serious performers.

The adoption of the lads into their respective clans took place immediately after the death-dances. So far as I could gather, there were not such important ceremonies on this occasion as in the case of the Malu cult of Murray Island. I believe that masks were not employed at this time.

The only initiation ceremony, if such it can be called, that I could hear of was the chastising or torturing of the lads, more particularly the bad ones, in the *kwod*. The good boys were let off very easily, but a naughty one might be speared in the hollow of the knee by a stick armed with the spine of a sting-ray, or scraped with the rough, spiny skin of a ray, or be beaten about the ears and elsewhere with the nests of green ants, who bite ferociously, or chastised with wasps' nests.

FIG. 13.

Drawing by Giru of a *danilkau*, the buffoon of the funeral ceremonies. He wore a leafy head-dress, in which is inserted a long feathered filament; on his chest are two crossed shoulder-belts and a shell ornament; a fringed belt is round his waist, from which depends in front an empty coconut water-vessel; his legs are provided with ornamental bands.

So far as we could learn, neither here nor in Murray Island was the bull-roarer employed at the initiation ceremonies. Here it was swung in connection with turtle ceremonies; it was also useful in making garden produce grow, but it was not used to make wind or rain.

The *kernge*, or lads to be initiated, were grouped on the further side of the *koi siboi*. They remained in the *kwod* for several days, during which time they are instructed by their uncles (mothers' brothers only) in the moral code and customs of the community.

At the end of the *kwod* was a forked post; on this were hung, after the war-dance, the decapitated heads of the enemy that had been slain in battle. In front of this post are stones which mark the spot where the wedding-gifts were heaped of a certain legendary spirit named Tapĕbu who married a Mabuiag girl.

On some of the rocks beyond the ceremonial camp we found a few simple pictographs; we photographed and sketched some of these. One group consists of two *mūri* dancing, and another

TOTEMISM

beating a drum. A *mūri* is a spirit that descends and ascends waterspouts. It has only two front teeth in each jaw. The waterspout is called in Mabuiag *klak markai*, or "the spear of the spirits." It is with these that the spirits (*markai*) catch dugong and turtle.

FIG. 14.

Drawing by Gizu of Mūri ascending a water-spout (*baiu*). The black cloud above is called *baib*, and the spray *sap*. One water-spout is spearing a dugong.

Under some of the boulders were a few human bones in a very bad state of repair.

Later on we struggled towards the centre of the island, scrambling up and over boulders, and forcing our way through dense tangled bush. Finally we came to an immense block of stone, the eastern face of which overhung to a considerable extent, forming a small, low cave, which some fifteen or twenty years ago had been nearly filled up with earth by a South Sea teacher. In the old days, this cave was the storehouse of the skulls that were obtained in the forays. Most of the skulls were placed in heaps at the back of the cave, while some were kept in two long baskets. In this cave were also kept the two ceremonial stone clubs and the sacred emblems, the mysterious *kotibu* and *giribu*. The skulls in the baskets were painted red, and were said to have been provided with noses made of beeswax and eyes of mother-of-pearl, but this was probably done in only a few cases. Forty-nine of the skulls from this cave were obtained by the British Museum (Natural History Museum) from the Rev. S. Macfarlane, and the collection has been described by Mr. Oldfield Thomas in the *Journal of the Anthropological Institute*, vol. xiv. p. 328.

The mouth of the cave was built up on each side with large Fusus shells. Now the glory and mystery have departed, and earth and stones almost entirely fill up the space beneath the overhanging rock. We obtained one or two broken skulls and a number of fragments of skulls.

When any man was on his way to visit the *augŭds kotibu* and *giribu*, the latter left their respective baskets in which they were kept and came to the entrance of the cave, but when the visitor came close, the *augŭds* returned to their baskets and made a scraping noise; but the man never saw them moving, he only found them lying in their baskets.

Outside the cave are two oblong patches of Fusus shells, called respectively *koi mat* and *mŭgi mat;* the former belonged to the big *augŭd*, and the latter to the little one. Each *mat* was called the *mari* of the *augŭd*. A *mari* is a spirit, shadow, or reflection.

When the baskets showed signs of decay, new ones were made at the next *kek* season. The men belonging to each *augud* gathered a plant called *boz*, the stem of which forms a kind of rope, and placed it on the *koi-* and *mŭgi-augŭdau kupar* in the *kwod*, and later transferred each bundle of *boz* respectively to the *koi mat* and the *mŭgi mat*. A *mat*, it will be remembered, is a heap of Fusus shells. The symbolism of the operation is pretty obvious. The material of which the sacred baskets were to be made was dedicated or sanctified by first placing it on the "navel" of the *augŭd* and then on its "shadow." I found afterwards that a heap of shells, *augŭdau kupar*, or "navel of the *augŭd*," occurred in the *kwod* of the islands of Tut, Yam, and Muralug; the Kwoiam cult also extended to the latter island.

A large plaited mat was placed opposite the *koi mat* and *mŭgi mat;* on these the men of each division sat, and not one of them could budge from his mat for any purpose until the basket was finished. This was accomplished at sundown, and "every one feel glad, time to spell and walk about." The following day the baskets were taken to the cave, and the contents of the old baskets transferred to the new. There were other details that need not be mentioned here.

All the sacred relics of Kwoiam were burned at the instigation of Hakin, a Lifu teacher at the time when the Rev. S. Macfarlane was on Murray Island. The Mamoose gave his consent to their destruction, but only a South Sea man, Charley Mare, dared destroy these *augŭds*, he burnt them on the spot.

The natives say that when the Mission party started for home the water was quite smooth, there being no wind whatever. As their boat rounded Sipungar Point, on their return, a sudden gust of wind made the boat heel over and nearly capsize, and that same night Charley's body swelled up, and he was sick for a fortnight.

Kwoiam is such a central feature in the legendary lore of Mabuiag that it is desirable that a brief outline of his story should be told, since the saga of Kwoiam is too long to be here narrated in full.

Kwoiam lived with his mother, who was blind, and he had an uncle for his henchman. One day, when his mother was plaiting a mat, Kwoiam abstracted with his toes a strip of leaf his mother was about to use, and missing it she asked who had taken it. Kwoiam confessed, and his mother cursed him; this made him angry, and he went outside the hut and called to his uncle to get the sprouting leaf of a coconut palm that he might deck himself for the war-path. When he was so accoutred he killed his mother, and then went on the rampage to avenge her death, or as it was told to me, "to pay for mother."

He went to several islands and to the mainland of New Guinea, sometimes slaying the population of a whole village, at other times merely requesting food or a new canoe. Eventually Kwoiam returned with a canoe-load of human heads, and he ordered his uncle to clean them for him.

On one occasion certain Badu men fooled him, refusing to give him some fish for which he had civilly asked them. These men retired to the island of Pulu for a midday siesta; Kwoiam followed them there and killed them all except two, who made their escape, but one of them had his leg transfixed by a javelin hurled by Kwoiam. The two survivors died on reaching Badu immediately after they had narrated the fate of the others.

An expedition of Moa and Badu men was sent to retaliate; but Kwoiam killed all who were sent against him except four men. A second very large avenging expedition was sent, but when fighting against these Kwoiam's throwing-stick broke, and he was helpless. He slowly retreated backwards up his hill, and when the enemy pressed too closely upon him, he rushed forward, unarmed as he was, and frightened back his foes; this happened several times.

As soon as Kwoiam reached the summit of the hill he crouched in a prone position and gave up the ghost. A Moa man rushed up to him and began to cut off his head with a bamboo knife, but he had only made a small incision when he was stopped by another Badu man, who said, "No cut him head; he great man. Let him lie where he stop; he master over all these islands." So instead of insulting the dead warrior they did him honour, and piled over his body their bows, arrows, javelins, and stone clubs, saying that now Kwoiam was dead all the fighting was over. The cairn erected over his grave remains to this day, and on it are placed three ancient shell trumpets.

The informant closed his narrative of this saga with the following sentiment: The fame of Kwoiam caused the island of Mabuiag to be feared for many a long day, and although the island is rocky and comparatively unfertile, Kwoiam covered it with honour and glory. Thus showing how the deeds of a single man can glorify a place in itself of little worth.

We spent one very pleasant day in visiting the spots associated with this legendary hero. On the plain near the sea is a large oval boulder, the head of the luckless mother. As we ascended the hill called Kwoiamantra (I think this means "Kwoiam's ridge") we passed between a long double row of stones that represented the heads taken by Kwoiam on the famous voyage when he paid the blood-price for the death of his mother. A short distance up the hill were some rocks, from out of a cleft in which a perennial stream flows. It arose in this wise. One day Kwoiam was thirsty, and he drove his spear into the rock, and water gushed forth and has never ceased to flow. The water fills a rock basin, and from this it trickles into a lower pool, and thence the stream flows down the hill. Ten years before I was informed that only old and important men might drink from the upper pool, whereas the lower was free to all; the penalty of unworthily drinking from the upper pool was premature greyness. I asked if I might drink there, and they were good enough to think that my claims were sufficiently strong. Apparently I was presumptuous, as the penalty has been inflicted!

On a rock between the two pools is a slight concavity in which Kwoiam used to sit, and in front of it are several transverse grooves in the rock, caused, it is stated, by Kwoiam straightening his javelins there by rubbing them across the rock.

Near the top of the hill is a rough U-shaped wall of stones about two feet in height, which marks the site of Kwoiam's house; his mother lived on the flat land near the sea. Behind Kwoiam's house is a tor which commands an extensive view, not only of Mabuiag and of some of the islets around, but there is a fine panorama of the great islands of Moa and Badu some five miles distant. This was the favourite lookout of Kwoiam, and it was from here that he saw the fleets of canoes from Badu and Moa that were crossing over to attack him.

As I sat there I thought of the deeds of the berserker. Below to the left was the grassy plain studded with pandanus and other trees where he was born and where he had his gardens. The site of his mother's hut is now occupied by a South Sea man, who has married a native woman, and aliens till Kwoiam's garden lands.

Far away was the prosperous village by the sand beach, nestling under the shade of a grove of coconut palms, the new church witnessing to the change that has come over the island.

In the old days, scattered throughout the island, were the hamlets of an agricultural fisher-folk, who, though fierce and savage, regulated their conduct by a code of morals that, so far as it went, was unimprovable. The emotions of awe, veneration, and mystery were cultivated by bizarre and sacred ceremonies; and the custom and sanction of ages had imbued their rude life with a richness of sentiment and a significance that we can scarcely realise.

Now the people are all gathered into one place under the

ægis of a new religion, and are held together by an alien form of government. There is no glory, no independence, nothing to be proud of—except a church built by contract. Fishing is mainly practised to gain money to purchase the white man's goods and the white man's food. The dull and respectable uniformity of modern civilisation has gripped these poor people; but, to their credit be it spoken, they are still proud of the apotheosised Kwoiam.

Behind low-lying land were wooded hills that sent a spur forming the northern limit of the bay, and beyond this again were several low rocky islands. The pale green water fringed the bay with white surf, and beyond the limit of the fringing reef the deeper water assumed a fine blue hue. It was a pretty sight. The sear colours of the parched plain relieved with patches of the various green of coconut palm, banana, scrub, or garden plots. The red rocks variegated with green foliage, and the greens and blues of the sea relieved by a frill of white where the waves encircled the island shores.

On turning round one saw the long sky-line of the islands of Moa and Badu toothed with high hills, all colour being lost in the grey distance of a moisture-laden atmosphere. Here and there, along the coast, could be seen clouds of smoke, as the natives burnt the dead undergrowth to make their gardens. To the right various islets relieved the monotony of the waste of waters.

On the other side of the crest, overlooking Pulu and other islands, was the grave of Kwoiam. The low cairn was nine feet in height, with the head due east; it was surmounted by three reputed shell trumpets of the hero. How I longed to excavate the site! But I could not get permission from the natives, and I unwillingly gave way rather than rough-ride over their sentiment.

One little incident was very amusing as illustrating the change that has of recent years come over the people. I wanted one of the natives who had accompanied us to put himself in the attitude of the dying Kwoiam, so that I might have a record of the position he assumed, photographed on the actual spot. It took an incredible amount of persuasion to induce the man to strip, although he was a friend of ours, who knew us well. Eventually we succeeded, but the prudery he exhibited was ludicrous, and he managed to do all that we required without bringing a blush to the most sensitive cheek. There were, of course, only ourselves, and no women were present.

The bushes on the side of Kwoiam's hill have most of their leaves blotched with red, and not a few are entirely of a bright red colour. This is due to the blood that spurted from Kwoiam's neck when it was cut at his death; to this day the shrubs witness to this outrage on the dead hero.

CHAPTER X

DUGONG AND TURTLE FISHING

DURING my former visit to Mabuiag I had an opportunity of witnessing the method of catching dugong. It was a morning in October, 1888, when I accompanied the Mamoose on a dugong expedition; the crew of his lugger numbered some dozen men, all natives of his island. A few of the most wealthy of the Torres Straits islanders own, wholly or in part, craft of that particular type, as these Australian-made vessels are more convenient than their own dug-out canoes. All the natives appear to be good sailors, and they can handle boats of European rig with considerable dexterity.

On our way to the fishing-ground, which was on the extensive and uncharted Orman's Reef between Mabuiag and the New Guinea coast, the gear was put in order. This consisted of the dugong harpoon and its rope.

The harpoon is a handsome weapon usually some fourteen feet in length, and made of a hard and heavy wood. One end is ornamented with the sable plumes of the cassowary, the other extremity is swollen, and into a terminal hole is loosely inserted a dart to which the rope is lashed.

The dart was formerly always fashioned out of hard wood, but since the arrival of the white man it has usually been replaced by one made out of a file. The latter is softened by heating in a fire, and is allowed to cool slowly; the angles of the triangular rasping end are then cut into barbs by means of another file. As the bright surface would speedily rust when exposed to the action of the salt water, the cut file is again heated so as to obtain an oxidised film over the new surface.

The rope may be either plaited or twisted, each kind being made from a different plant. Home-made rope is preferred to that of European manufacture, as it is light and floats upon

DUGONG AND TURTLE FISHING

the surface of the water, whereas hempen or manila rope sinks.

The coil of rope, thirty to fifty fathoms in length, to which the harpoon dart is attached, is laid ready at the bow of the boat, and a spare rope coiled midship.

All hands next look out for the dugong, and the chief takes his place at the further end of the bowsprit, the harpoon being placed where it can be seized without a moment's delay. Now

Fig. 15.
Dugong Harpoon and Dart

we are scudding along over the sea, the dirty green colour of which shows that we are above the reefs, the waves being crested by the continuously blowing south-east trade wind; the lavender-coloured sky is studded with clouds which ever belie their pluvial appearance.

There is a shout of "*Dungal!*" ("Dugong"), but the sea-cow is a long way off. Then the cry of "*Waru!*" ("Turtle") is heard as one of these reptiles lazily floats on the surface of the water.

After cruising about for a long time and sighting but few dugong, we at length arrive at a spot where they are plentiful, and all round they are repeatedly to be seen as they rise up to breathe. A soft grunt is heard, a glimpse caught of a brown rounded back followed by a fan-shaped tail, and the beast again disappears beneath the waves, unless one happens to float for a short time on the surface of the water. This is the hunter's opportunity, and the boat is put through movements which remind one of the method of progression of a learner on a bicycle, as it dodges about in the helmsman's endeavours to approach the floating beast.

When distant from the prey the natives shout and chatter in a very lively manner, and go through a pantomime of harpooning a dugong; but when one is observed close by, a sudden hush falls upon the crew, who are by this time in a state of highly strung and barely suppressed excitement. Directions are given to the steersman by signals only, not a word is said. The chief stands at the end of the bowsprit grasping the narrow spar with his bare toes, harpoon in one hand, and with the other steadying himself by the rigging, and well he may, for the boat is pitching and tossing considerably. Behind him in the bow stands a man whose business it is to look after the rope and see that it does not get caught anywhere. Perched a short way up the foremast is the look-out man, who makes the signals; and behind are the rest of us, following with glistening eyes the movements of the dugong, and making at most a subdued whistle or the clacking sound so characteristic of these islanders.

All of a sudden the chief springs into the water, harpoon in hand, using the latter after the manner of a leaping pole, and plunging the dart into the animal. The aim is good, and the dart is firmly embedded in the dense, thick skin of the dugong, who is by this time tearing along, followed by the trailing rope.

The repressed excitement of the spectators finds vent in shouts and in various other manifestations of delight, for my comrades are a demonstrative people. Their enthusiasm was contagious, and more than once I found myself adopting their clacking and whistling in addition to the ordinary British methods of expressing delight and surprise.

The chief regains his harpoon and clambers up into the boat, where he manifests his satisfaction by a very broad grin. Shirts are doffed, and even the universal "calico" is in many cases dispensed with, as several men dive into the water. The spare rope is thrown overboard, and the men strike out for the dugong. Amid great shouting they endeavour to make fast a rope round its tail, swimming up to it when it comes up to breathe, and diving after it in its descent, their power of holding their breath under water appearing almost to rival that of the dugong itself. The main object of tying the rope round the creature's tail is to prevent it from raising its nostrils above the level of the water by bearing down upon the rope during the animal's ascent. In time these manœuvres are successful, and death by drowning results. The lubberly carcass is towed towards the boat, and after much effort and more noise it is hauled on board.

As we are in the thick of a "school," the chief intends to have a try at another before returning, although it is near sundown and we are far from home. After some skilful steering, and the rise and fall of several vain hopes, we bear down upon another dugong. A sudden leap, a splash, and the deed is done. Away swims the dugong, rising and diving, vainly endeavouring to rid itself of the painful dart. When the ungainly brute has gone to the length of its tether and then doubled, the slack rope is hauled in, and so for a short time it is "played" as a fisherman plays a salmon. Some of the crew now dive into the water, and following the struggling dugong in its movements of ascent and descent, tie a rope round its tail, by means of which it is towed to the boat. The poor beast is, however, still alive, so by main force it is held up by the tail, head downwards in the water, until it is suffocated. This second specimen is a young female, 6 feet 9 inches in length. The previous capture is a not quite full-grown male with a length of some 8 feet 6 inches, and a girth of 6 feet 10 inches.

The dugong, or sea-cow, is an animal that looks something like a porpoise, but it has a square muzzle, and there is no fin on its back. The skin is provided with very short scattered hairs, and the flippers have a distinct elbow joint, which is absent in the porpoise and other whales. The abrupt head, with its thick, bristly lips, and horny pad on the lower jaw, is very characteristic. With these the dugong nips off the marine flowering plants (Cymodocea) upon which it feeds, and this vegetable food is masticated by means of grinding teeth—very different from the pointed conical teeth of the flesh-eating porpoise.

Porpoises that feed on swiftly-swimming fish have light porous bones, so that their own weight may not be excessive; whereas the dugong never swims far with great rapidity, and as it lies on its side on the bottom of the sea when browsing on the sea-grass, its bones are very dense and heavy, heavier, in fact, than those of any other animal.

This is not the place to compare the anatomy of these two animals, which, although both live in the sea and have somewhat the same appearance, are in reality extremely different from one another.

The skin of the dugong is very thick and tough, and as it is an inch thick on the back it is not so surprising that the small dart can hold fast. Before I had actual optical evidence I could

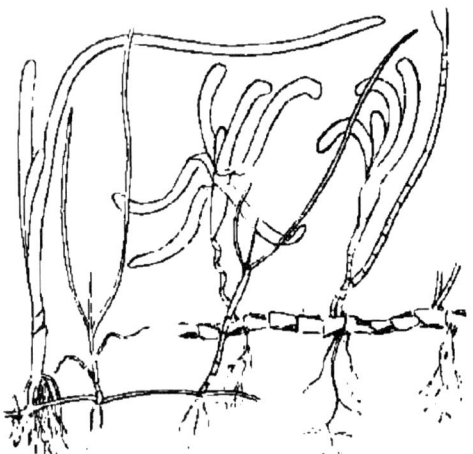

FIG. 16. MARINE PLANTS (CYMODOCEA) ON WHICH THE DUGONG FEEDS

scarcely credit the statement that this was the only weapon the natives employed. Still, it must be remembered that the harpoon is only used to secure the animal; death invariably ensues by suffocation. One day during my visit it happened that two boats went out, and several darts were broken without capturing a single dugong; in the olden days of wooden darts this probably would often happen.

Formerly dugong were harpooned from canoes, or from a bamboo platform (*nët*) erected on the reef. Both practices are now discontinued in the Straits. As I wished to know exactly how the platform was erected, I induced Waria to make one for me. This was speedily done with six bamboo poles

DUGONG AND TURTLE FISHING

lashed together, and surmounted with the steering board of a canoe. Plate XI., B (p. 123) is a drawing from the photograph I took of this erection.

The *nĕĕt* was erected at a spot where it was evident dugong had been feeding, for they habitually return to their pasture until the supply of eel-grass in that place is exhausted. It was built end-on to the wind, so that the wind, by blowing through it, should not make a noise and frighten the dugong away. The harpoon was also held in the same direction. The *nĕĕt* was

FIG. 17.

Drawings by Gizu of the process of harpooning a dugong. One man stands on the *nĕĕt* waiting for a dugong to approach. In the second sketch a man has harpooned the dugong, and has thrown himself backward in the water so as to be out of reach of the coils of the rope as it runs from the *nĕĕt*. Another man is swimming, and is tying a spare rope on to the tail of the dugong.

used at night, for it is only then that the dugong approach the shore; in the daytime they keep to the open, or on the large isolated reefs.

Charms which were supposed to ensure the approach of the dugong to the platform were often suspended to it, or hung on to a canoe. I have obtained several very small and neatly carved models of dugong at Murray Island that were employed for this purpose, but those I obtained from the western islands were of much greater size. A fine one from Moa is a foot and a half in length. This has a cavity hollowed out in the back, which, when in use, was filled up with red earth and various plants, including some eel-grass which had been chewed by the sorcerer who employed it; dugong fat completed the mixture. A bunch of eel-grass was tied to the tail, and along its back were lashed the thin leg-bones (*fibulæ*) of the sorcery man who carved the image. These were added after his death, to render the charm more effective. The whole was painted red, and fastened to a dugong platform, as in Plate XI., B (p. 123).

About the mouth of the Fly River, and I believe along the New Guinea coast and islands as far as Saibai, queer carved pegs called *agumanakai* are stuck in the canoes when going turtle or dugong hunting. I believe the word *agumanakai* means "the spirit (*manaki*) of the trophy;" the *agu* is a plat-

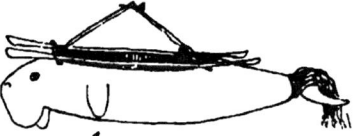

Fig. 18. Wooden Dugong Charm
Obtained at Moa in 1888

form on which the carapaces of turtle are arranged as a trophy. A dugong trophy may possibly also be called *agu*, but I am not sure of this. Some have the end carved in the form of a bird's head, while others represent a very conventional dugong's head; they were decorated with feathers. Seligmann collected a very interesting specimen of the latter class, which, in addition to the dugong, had carved on it a representation of a sting-ray, which was evidently the totem of the owner. This particular specimen not only acted as a charm to make dugong come to be harpooned, but it would turn round towards where the dugong were swimming, and thereby indicate to the owner the direction in which he should steer.

The sorcerers were credited with the power of compassing the death, by strangulation, of a dugong harpooner. In leaping into the water to harpoon a dugong care has to be taken not to get entangled in the rope. It has happened that the head of a man comes up within a coil, and as the rope is rapidly drawn out by the retreating dugong, the luckless harpooner is speedily strangled. Not unnaturally the sorcerer would claim such an

DUGONG AND TURTLE FISHING

accidental death as being due to his own powers of magic, and thus increase his reputation. This could be the more easily asserted, since all disease and death, even from old age, were firmly believed to be due to sorcery, and not to natural causes.

The dugong naturally enters into several of the native legends. One of them relates how Sesere of Badu, who was afterwards transformed into a bird, first discovered the dugong as an article of food and how to catch it, by divining with the skulls of his parents. I have already alluded to the fancied resemblance of the hill of Gelam, in Murray Island, to a dugong, for which there is, as usual, a myth of origin.

Like the dugong the turtle is an important article of food in Torres Straits. There are two periods for turtle-fishing, really lasting all the year, the one during October and November, which is the pairing season, and when turtle are easily speared, owing to their floating on the surface of the water. The pairing turtle is called *surlal*, and that season is called *surlangi*. The other turtle season extends throughout the remaining months of the year, when the turtle, then called *waru*, frequent the deeper water and the channels between the reefs.

The western islanders have a very remarkable method of obtaining turtle, which, strangely enough, is said to be also employed at Mozambique in East Africa. There is a fish belonging to the family of mackerels called the "sucker-fish," that has a large sucker on its head, by means of which it attaches itself to sharks and turtles. The species in Torres Straits is called *Echeneis naucrates* by zoologists.

When going on a turtling excursion a *gapu*, or sucker-fish, is caught, and the more experienced natives appear to have no difficulty in procuring one when required. A hole is made at the base of the tail-fin, through which the end of a very long piece of string is inserted and made fast. A short piece of string is passed through the mouth and out at the gills, securing the head. By means of these two strings the fish is retained in the water, while slung over the side of the canoe. On sighting a turtle in deep water the front string is withdrawn, plenty of slack being allowed in the hind string. The sucker-fish on perceiving the turtle immediately swims towards it, and attaches itself to the reptile's carapace. If the turtle be a little one, it is hauled in by means of the tail string of the *gapu*;

but should it be a large specimen, another mode of procedure is necessary.

A man, with the end of a long rope attached to his right upper-arm, dives into the water and follows the clue. On reaching the turtle the man gets on to its back and passes his arms behind and below the fore-flappers and his legs in front of and below the hind-flappers, thus securing a firm grip on the slippery beast. By means of the rope attached to his arm the man is rapidly drawn up to the surface of the water bearing the turtle with him. Other members of the crew dive into the water, and seizing hold of the turtle, capsize it into the canoe.

On the arrival of the diver the sucker-fish usually shifts its position from the upper to the under surface of the turtle. I was informed that at the end of the day's fishing the *gapu* was eaten, which seems hardly fair.

The natives have a great respect for the *gapu*, and firmly believe it to have supernatural powers. For example, they believe that when there is something the matter with the bow of the canoe, the *gapu* will attach itself to the neck or to the front shield-plate of the turtle; that when the lashings of the float of the outrigger of the canoe are insecure, the *gapu* will not stick fast to the turtle, but will constantly shift its position; that if the strengthening cross-ties in the centre of the canoe are faulty, the *gapu* will attach itself to the turtle, and then swim away before the turtle can be secured. More than once I was gravely assured, "Gapu savvy all same man, I think him half devil."

Formerly the shells of the captured turtle were placed on a long platform (*agu*), each canoe having its separate *agu*, and the crew that had the greatest number at the end of the season would acquire the greatest glory. Hanging round the platform were large and small bull-roarers and wooden human effigies (*wauri*).

Before going out turtling the men marched round the *agu* and whirled the bull-roarers, always circling clockwise; if they marched widdershins, the turtle would go away from them. The captain would call out, "Come along, all our crew; come with me fellow." Then they would take some bull-roarers and *wauri* to the canoe, and the captain invoked the spirits of the *wauri* that remained on the *agu* to give them luck in their enterprise so that they might get plenty of turtle.

DUGONG AND TURTLE FISHING

When the canoes were expected to return, a man would station himself on a hill to look out for them. In due time he would see the under sides of the captured turtle gleaming in the successful canoes while yet a long way off; then he whirled a small bull-roarer, and the women knew that the fishers had been lucky.

On the arrival of the canoes the men first went to the *agu* before cutting up the turtle. They marched round and swung the bull-roarers, and returned them and the *wauri* to the platform.

Several dugong and turtle were caught one week of our stay, and we had some of the meat, and found it a most welcome change. The native method of cutting up living turtle is a ghastly sight. The poor beast lies on its back and beats the air with its flappers, boys and girls, even naked little things that can scarcely toddle, stand round fingering and patting the bleeding flesh, or poke their fingers in the eyes of the turtle, or scoop up handfuls of clotted gore, ladling it into large shells. The natives have names for the various joints and for regions of the intestine much as we have; the liver and gall-bladder and some other parts have the same names in the dugong and turtle, but the heart of each has a different name. Seligmann and I noted down the names of various parts of both dugong and turtle, while Wilkin photographed some stages of the butchery.

CHAPTER XI

MARRIAGE CUSTOMS AND STAR MYTHS

MARRIAGE CUSTOMS

THERE were formerly two ways by means of which a young Torres Straits islander might find favour in the eyes of a girl—the one was skill in dancing, the other was the possession of a trophy of one or more human skulls as a token of personal bravery or prowess in war.

During the numerous and prolonged dances of former days, the young women watched the active movements of the capering youths, admired their glossy skin, their frizzly hair, their numerous gay ornaments, and took delight in their wonderful activity; and well they might, for a shapely, bronze-skinned savage is a vastly superior animal to a civilised male dancing at a ball. Pre-eminence had its reward, for, as the former chief of Mabuiag put it—" In England, if a man has plenty of money, women want to marry him; so here, if a man dances well, they want him too."

Amongst the western islanders it was customary for the young women to propose to the men. I obtained the following description of the way in which this affair was managed in Mabuiag. When a man was fancied by a girl she made a string armlet, and gave it to the man's sister or to some confidential person. On a suitable opportunity presenting itself, the confidante said to the young man, "I've got some string for you." Knowing what was meant, he replied, "Show it to me." He then learnt the girl's name and received her message. If the man was favourably inclined he accepted, and wore the *tiapururu* and sent the girl two leglets.

The girl next sent some food to the young man of her choice; he did not eat it, but gave it to his relations to eat, for, as he said, "perhaps woman he gammon." His parents also advised him not to eat the food, and his mother warned him, "You look after that armlet good, suppose you lose it, girl he wild."

The young woman again sent food, possibly the man might want to eat it, but the mother said, "Not so, or by-and-by you will get an eruption over your face and body." At all events, the relations preached caution so as to make sure that the girl was not playing false. Perhaps the young man might wait for a month, or even longer, before precipitating affairs. He also informed his parents that he was in no hurry to leave the old home, and that he did not wish to make them sorry by his absence.

While the young man, who was certainly a prudent lover, was thus "lying low," the food was coming in all the time, and as regularly he gave it to his mother. After a time the latter said, "When will you go and take her?" He then consulted his immediate relatives, and said, "Suppose you tell me to take her—I take her." All being agreeable, the "big men" of the village were consulted, and they gave their consent. One day a friend would engage the young man in conversation, and the girl, who had been previously informed that the happy moment had now arrived, quietly came behind the unsuspecting youth and gently pushed some cooked food in front of him. He turned round sharply, and to his shame-faced confusion he saw his sweetheart and fully realised the delicate situation. His friends assured him that it was all right, saying, "Good thing, you take her now." They were then man and wife. This part of the proceedings required no further ceremony.

After marriage an exchange of presents and food was made between the relatives of the two parties concerned, but the bridegroom's relations gave a great deal more than those of the bride. The bridegroom stood on a mat, and all the presents from his side of the house were heaped upon it. The bride took these presents and handed them over to her people. The bridegroom gave his father-in-law a present of perhaps a canoe, or a dugong harpoon, or something of equal value. This was the final transaction, but should the marriage result in the usual adjuncts to family life, a payment had to be paid to the wife's parents on the birth of each child.

Without going into details of custom of every island, it may not be amiss if I transcribe the account given me by my friend

Maino of Warrior Island. Here again the ring of string was a preliminary feature, and the sister, in giving it to her brother, said, "Brother, I've got some good news for you; a woman likes you." He asked who it was, and after some conversation—if he was willing to go on with the affair—he told his sister to ask the girl to go into the bush and he would follow.

When the message was delivered, the enamoured damsel informed her parents that she was going into the bush to get some food, or wood, or make some similar excuse. In due course the man met the girl, and they sat down and talked discreetly over their affairs. Any forward conduct on the part of the young man would have been regarded as bad form.

Breaking the embarrassing silence, the youth considerately asked, "You like me proper?"

"Yes," she replied, "I like you proper, with my heart inside. Eye along my heart see you. You my man."

Unwilling to give himself away rashly, he further inquired, "How you like me?"

"I like your fine leg; you got fine body, your skin good, I like you altogether," replied the girl.

Anxious to clinch the matter, the girl asked when they were to be married. "To-morrow, if you like," said the man, and they both went home and informed their respective relatives that they had arrived at an understanding. Then the girl's friends fought the man's people, "for girl more big," *i.e.* of more consequence, than boy; but the fighting did not appear to have been a serious business.

It was certainly the custom for a young man, or rather for his elders, to give a girl to the "brother" of the bride; the girl being either his own sister or a relative, who, according to their scheme of kinship, bears a similar relationship. The "brother" may similarly not be an own brother. This "swapping" of "sisters" was the usual method of getting a wife. If a young man had no "sister" he might for ever remain unmarried unless he was rich enough to purchase a wife.

After marriage the husband usually left his own people and went to live with those of his wife, even if they belonged to a different island. There is, for example, considerable intermarriage between the inhabitants of the islands of Badu and Mabuiag; in such a case the man divides his time between the two islands. It should be remembered that both the husband

and the wife own land in their respective islands, and both properties require to be cultivated and looked after. Still this is not a complete explanation of the custom. From this and other facts it would appear that these western islanders are emerging from what is usually called a "matriarchal" to a "patriarchal" system.

The husband had complete control over his wife; she was his property, for he had paid for her. In spite of the wife having asked her husband to marry her, he could kill her should she cause trouble in the house, and that without any penal consequence to himself. The payment of a husband to his wife's father gave him all rights over her, and at the same time annulled those of her father or of her family.

A rich man might have several wives, but the wife first married was chief; she was "master" over the others, and issued orders to the last married wife who conveyed the same to the intermediate wives. If the wives would not work or were inattentive to the commands of the first wife, the husband was laughed at by his friends and told he should not have so many wives. The wives all lived together.

A man might divorce his wife, in which case she returned to her parents. Incompatibility of temper was the common cause for such a step. The husband had no control over a divorced wife, who might marry again; but the new husband would have to pay the old one, and he would share the purchase goods with the woman's parents. In the case of divorce the father kept the children, but he might allow the mother temporarily to retain one, or even more, especially if they were very young.

One day during my former visit to Mabuiag there was a wedding; a widow with a baby boy had proposed to and been accepted by a young man from the island of Badu. The ceremony commenced at 7 a.m. with a full ordinary service in the church, which lasted over an hour. When this was concluded a messenger was sent to me, and I repaired to the church to witness the marriage. The bride and bridegroom were seated among their friends in different parts of the church, and on their names being called, they met and stood up in front of the Communion table. After they had repeated certain sentences and a charge had been given by the teacher, the bride and bridegroom again retired to their former places.

At the conclusion of the ceremony a Church Meeting was

held, which the bridegroom attended, and afterwards he went out dugong fishing with his friends to furnish the wedding feast. They were in luck that day, as they caught three dugong and two turtle. In the meantime I called on the bride and gave her a looking-glass, and left some tobacco for her husband. Following the usual custom, the man remained in Mabuiag and lived with his wife's people.

About the same time a native girl, who was employed as cook by the chief of the island, repeatedly asked a Loyalty Islander, Charley Lifu by name, to marry her; but he did not wish to marry a Mabuiag woman, as he would in that case have to remain permanently on the island, and he wanted to return to the South Seas. At last they arranged to have a talk in the bush to settle matters finally. The man was obdurate; and the girl was so chagrined that when she returned to the village she accused Charley of attempting to "steal" her, hoping that he would thus be forced to marry her in restitution. This caused considerable excitement, as Charley Lifu was the brother of the teacher's wife. The matter came before the chief in his capacity as judge, and after long deliberation on the part of the "old men," it was decided that the charge was unfounded, and was merely trumped up by the girl, who thus over-reached herself. I believe this was a true bill, as Charley Lifu was the gentlest and most obliging of my numerous coloured friends—a man who, I believe, would not do anyone an injury, and who would even perform a friendly act without waiting for the ordinary douceur of tobacco, but he was an incorrigible loafer.

The custom of a girl proposing marriage to a young man did not commend itself to the traditions of the missionaries, and they have tried to stop it, though I did not discover that it was necessarily at all an objectionable arrangement. It has certain definite advantages, and I was certainly given to understand that properly brought-up young men behaved with becoming bashfulness, and showed due deference to the wishes of their parents or elders.

The remarkable change that has come over the natives owing to the influence of missionary teaching is well exemplified in the fact that the girls frequently propose marriage to the men by writing; sometimes this is done by means of a letter, but I have known of a school slate being employed and sent to the young man.

MARRIAGE CUSTOMS

I managed to secure one or two examples of such love-letters. The two first were written for me by Peter when I asked him what had occurred in his own case. They purport to be Magena's proposal and his acceptance; both of them are natives of Mabuiag. The following is a transcription and literal translation:—

Okotoba 4, 1898.

Pita mido ninu ia ngai nutane ni ngözu korkak mina köi ubine mizi
Peter what your word? I try you. My heart truly big wish has

nibeka nid lak ngöna iadu turane wa sena ngozu ia Pita ni
for you. You again me tell. Yes, that my word. Peter you.

iawa   *ngai Magena.*
Good-bye.   I Magena.

Okotoba 4, 1898.

Magena ngai iauturane ni ngai lakökeda mina köi ubine meka
Magena I tell you. I again same truly big wish have

nibeka ngau ia kede mina mina ubine meka wa matamina pibeka
for you. My word thus true. True wish have. Yes, quite proper give

a ngaikika wa keda ni Magena iawa   *ngai Pita.*
then to me. Yes so. You Magena. Good-bye.   I Peter.

The following is Peter's own translation of these letters:—

"*Pita, what do you say? I try you. My heart he like very bad for you. You send me back a letter. Yes, this talk belong me. Pita, you. Good-bye. Me, Magena.*"

"*Magena, I make you know. Me just the same, I want very bad for you. My talk there. If you true like me, all right, just the same; good for you and good for me. Yes, all right. Finish. You, Magena. Good-bye. Me, Pita.*"

One informant gave the following as a typical letter of proposal from a girl to a man. Ray has kindly literally translated this for me. I also add the native's version of it.

Kake* ngau ubi gar ina mido ni ngaikika ubin meka wao mina
I say, my wish indeed this. (Sign of question) you for me wish have? Yes, true

keda ni ngaikika ubin mizi ninu na ia mido wa nagaikika modabia
that you for me wish have. Your if word what. Yes to me answer

ngapa palanekai ubil za na a ubigil za na wa matakeda
hither will write wish (thing) if and not wish (thing) if yes all-the-same

minaasin sena   *ngau ia ngau nel——*
finish that   my word, my name.

* Ray informs me that *Kake!* is a word of address to a woman; the corresponding term to a man is *Kame!* I suppose my informant, who was a Mabuiag man, made a slip, as he would himself naturally begin a love-letter with "*Kake!*"

"*I say, I tell you about what I want. What do you say, you want to come with me? Best thing you come along with me. What do you think about it? If you got something to answer back, then you let me know. 'Spose you want to come with me, let me know, then I know; 'spose you don't, you let me know, so I know. Best thing you come with me. My name——*"

The answer might be—

"*All right, I come along you,*" or "*No, I no want to come along you.*"

Another proposal is a copy of an original letter which happened to fall into my hands and which I still possess. It was from a Murray Islander named Kimel, who was then in Mabuiag offering marriage to Anuni, a Mabuiag girl.

Unfortunately I did not see her reply; but I know she received this letter, and I have no reason to believe my possession of it hindered the course of true love from running smoothly.

It is interesting to note that Kimel, being a Murray Islander, followed his tribal custom of the man proposing marriage.

Januare 1, 1899.

Peike Anuni   kara jiawali marim mama neur kaka makiriam
This   Anuni (is) my   writing to you you a girl   I   young man
nakö* ma kari lag nakö   Ad emeret detagem Adamu a Eba kosker a
(?)   you me like (?)   God formerly made Adam and Eve woman and
kimiar mokakalam kaka mari lag nakö ma kari lag nakö ma nole
man   same way   I   you like (?) you me like (?) you not
geum kak makiria abkoreb marim ma kari abkoreb   Ad emeret
afraid nothing young man suitable for you you   me suit.   God formerly
detagem kosker abkoreb ko kimiar nagiri kimiar abkoreb ko kosker
made   woman suitable for man possessing man suitable for woman
nagiri kaka mari laglag nako mer karim ma kari umele kaka nole
possessing I   you   like   what word for me you me know   I   not
mokakalam nerut le kaka dorge le peike kara mer marim   Sina
like   some other men I   work man. This   my word to you. The end.
Kara nei   *Cimell*
My name.   *Mabuiag.*

"*January* 1, 1899.

"This, Anuni, is my letter to you. You are a girl, I am a young man. Do you like me? God formerly made Adam and Eve a similar man and woman. I like you, do you like me? Don't be afraid at all of a young man suitable for you. You suit me. God formerly made woman suitable for having a man, and man suitable for having a woman. I like you. What message for me? You know me. I am not like some men, I am a man of work. This is my message to you. The end. My name

"*Cimell*

* *Nakö* is an interrogative.   "*Mabuiag.*"

STAR MYTHS

Most, perhaps all, peoples recognise certain groups of stars, or constellations, about which they tell stories. As a rule these myths of origin are not particularly instructive, except for the sidelight they cast on the people who originated them.

The constellations themselves have a very definite and practical value, as they constitute the universal sidereal almanack, by means of which the majority of primitive peoples regulate their farming operations or their festivals.

The Torres Straits islanders are no exception to this general rule, and I offer the following three myths as examples of this kind of traditional literature.

The Murray Islanders recognise a large constellation which does not coincide with any one of those mapped by our astronomers, though the canoe corresponds to part of our Scorpio.

A man named Tagai, with uplifted and outstretched hands bearing a spear, is supposed to stand upon a canoe, which is represented by the bowed row of stars that forms the scorpion's tail. Below the front end of the canoe is a single star, the anchor of the canoe, and near its other end is a red star that represents a man named Kareg. A cluster of stars is called Usiam, and another linear constellation is named Seg.

Tagai is an important constellation, not only as an indication of the approach of certain seasons, but also for navigation purposes. For example, I was told, " Usiam he *mĕk* [that is, "sign" or "mark"] for new yams." "Seg he *mĕk* next kind of yam." When Usiam is some way from the horizon at sundown, men say, "Close up new yam time," and when it is at the horizon at sunset, "Yam time he come."

"Tagai he *mĕk* for turtle season. Two hand he come first; all turtle go to islands to leeward (to the west), and they (the natives) 'kaikai' (eat) turtle first. By-and-by face belong Tagai he come up; Dauarle (the inhabitants of Dauar and of the southern end of Murray Island) get turtle, and then all the rest of Murray Island."

In sailing by night from Erub (Darnley Island) to Mer (Murray Island) they steer for the left hand of Tagai, "right hand he stop outside Mer."

The following is the reputed origin of the constellation. I give it in my informant's own words:—

THE ORIGIN OF THE TAGAI CONSTELLATION

"One man, Tagai, he got a canoe. Tagai he stop in forehead (the bow or front end of the canoe) and look out and spear fish. Kareg he stop in stern. Plenty men crew.

"They go over reef; Kareg he pole canoe. Tagai he spear fish. Sun hot on reef, all men thirsty, and steal water in canoe belong captain.

"Tagai say, 'Why you no pole canoe good? I no spear fish.' By-and-by he say, 'Where water-bamboo?' He take bamboo and shake it; it empty. 'Who drink water?'

"Men no talk.

"Tagai get wild. He get one rope and make fast round neck of six men and chuck into sea. He put name to them, 'All you fellow "Usiam."'

"Tagai take two wooden skewers and call other men in canoe, and kill plenty, and stick the skewers through their necks and chuck them in the sea, and call them 'Seg.'

"Kareg he live.

"Tagai tell Kareg, 'You stop; you no steal my water, you push canoe all time.'

"Man stop in sky all the time.

"Tagai, Kareg, and canoe stop in one place, Usiam stop in another place, and Seg stop in another place."

The next story, which was told to me in Mabuiag in 1888, refers to two constellations, one of which, a Dorgai, a sort of bogey, is followed by a cluster of stars named *Bu*, but which we call Delphin, or the dolphin, and certainly this cluster has a closer resemblance to the large Fusus or Triton shell (*bu*) than to a dolphin. The Dorgai corresponds to the star known to us as Altair, but which they call *gamu* (the body), and the adjoining stars on each side, which they name *getal* (the arms).

These constellations belong to the north-west monsoon, and when "Dorgai he come up (from the east) that time make *kap* (dance)."

A DORGAI CONSTELLATION

Once upon a time a man named Nadai, living on the Island of Boigu, went into the bush to collect the eggs of the mound-bird, a bird that lays its eggs in a great mound of earth which it scratches up with its strong feet.

STAR MYTHS

He found a large mound, and dug into it till he came to what he thought was an egg. He tried to pull it up, but it stuck fast; then he tried to get another, but neither would that come away. It so happened that a Dorgai named Metakorab was sleeping under the mound, and she was wearing several large white cowry shells, and it was these that Nadai was pulling at, mistaking them for eggs.

FIG. 19. DRAWING BY GIZU OF DORGAI METAKORAB AND BU

Nadai at last caught hold of the shell, which was tied on to the Dorgai's chin, and giving a tremendous pull he dragged the Dorgai out of the ground. He was so terrified at her appearance, that he fled back to the village and called out to the inhabitants to arm themselves and kill the Dorgai, who was sure to follow after him.

By-and-by a fly came, and behind it came the Dorgai; but the men no sooner saw her terrible face than they threw down their weapons and ran away in a fright.

Then Nadai went on to the next village, but the same thing happened again. So he went on all round the island, but it always happened as before.

At last Nadai came to a village called Kerpai, on the north side of the island, and he begged the people to stand firm and attack the Dorgai. They armed themselves, but when the fly came, and after it the Dorgai, they all took to their heels, as the others had done before, with the exception of one man named Bu. He remained in the bachelors' quarters, and armed himself with a bow and with arrows that are used for shooting wild pigs. When the Dorgai arrived, Bu shot her and killed her.

Both are now in the sky; the Dorgai going first, being continually followed by Bu.

The last story is one which was given to me by my friend Mr. Robert Bruce, who lives at Daru.

It is the story of Kăbi, a man who did not believe in much talking nor in accepting as true everything that people said; but he thought for himself, and tried to find out the truth, even if he had to make a long journey to do so. He was what we call a "scientific man."

SUN, MOON, AND NIGHT

"Plenty men sit down and yarn at Kadau (a village in the island of Dauan). All man he yarn about Sun, and Moon, and Night. All man speak, 'Sun, Moon, and Night he all the same one.' One man called Kabi he speak, 'No good you talk all the same; suppose you look. You see, Sun he come up, that time Moon he go down. Moon he come up, and Sun he go down.'

"Then all man too much wild; some man he speak, 'Very good, we kill Kabi; he talk no good.' Kabi he hear, he afraid. Kabi he then speak, 'You fellow, look, I go to-morrow; I go place belong Sun, and Moon, and Night.'

"At small daylight he go in his canoe, his woman stop behind. He go across to Saibai.

"All man in Saibai speak, 'Where you go, Kabi?' He speak, 'I go to look place where Sun he stop.'

"Him go—go—go. All islands he come up. He go big deep water. He catch him place where Sun he stop.

"Kabi he look, Sun he come out house belong him. Kabi he think, 'Sun he no good, as Sun he no got good things on.' Kabi pulled his canoe on beach and sat down. Sun then come out of door of his house and looked at Kabi. Sun then go inside house belong him and put on all flash things—one big pearl-shell he put on breast and one big shell on body.

"Sun he walk along and come close to Kabi. Kabi he very much afraid; he think inside, 'Big man he come now. I think he kill me.' Sun he speak, 'Kabi, come on, you and me go house.'

"Sun he carry canoe belong Kabi in his one hand, all same as boy carry canoe belong play; then he put canoe on top of his house.

"Then Sun he speak, 'Kabi, what name you come here for?'

"Kabi he speak, 'All man he growl for you; he all speak, "Sun, and Moon, and Night he one." Me, one fellow, speak, "No, Sun he one, Moon he one, and Night he one." Then all man he wild.'

"Sun he speak, 'All right, you come house.'

"Kabi he speak, 'What you say? Sun, Moon, you all same one?'

"Sun he speak, 'Me one, Moon another one.'

"Then Sun and Moon he bring Kabi kaikai (food). Sun he give kaikai belong Sun—bananas, yams, taro, sweet potatoes, coconuts. Moon he give him all the same.

"Sun he speak, 'All kaikai belong we fellow. Sun, Moon, and Night he all the same. We all help to make them. Sun and Moon he stop one house.'

"Sun he take canoe belong Kabi, and put it in the water; then they put all kaikai in canoe. Kabi he get afraid when he think of the long journey he got to take.

"Sun he speak, 'Kabi, I make rope fast along your head, then you and me go together; I tow you. When you come to place belong you, you shake rope; by-and-by when you loose rope, you shake it, then that time I pull up.'

"Kabi he then start in his canoe. Three big waves come; one wave lift him half-way, the next lift him along to Saibai, the next wave lift his canoe to Dauan.

"Kabi then went ashore and told all the people, 'I been to place where Sun and Moon he stop. You hear me now when I speak. He no one fellow, he two fellow. Sun he pull me here.'

"Then Kabi got all people in one place. He speak, 'You see this rope fast on top of my head. You look when I take this rope off my head. You look he go up to Sun.'

"Then all the people believe Kabi when he speak, 'Sun, Moon, and Darkness each got their own work to do.'"

CHAPTER XII

VISITS TO VARIOUS WESTERN ISLANDS

IT was sad to feel that the end of our stay in Torres Straits was drawing near. On October 19th Rivers left us, and two days later Wilkin also had to go. Ray, Seligmann, and myself alone were left.

On October 21st the Hon. John Douglas came in the *White Star* to convey us away from Mabuiag, and we made an early start next morning. Mr. Douglas made the valuable suggestion that before going on to Saibai we should run down to Yam to pick up my old friend Maino, the Mamoose of Tut and Yam, in order that he might give us information. We did so, and Maino was very pleased to come with us, and we shipped another Yam native named Kaikai.

We reached Saibai in the afternoon, and went ashore for a stroll. Saibai is a relatively large low island, but it is scarcely more than a ring-like, vegetated sandbank surrounding a huge swamp. The natives, numbering about one hundred and fifty to two hundred, are a quiet, industrious people, and grow a sufficient quantity of garden produce. We found them very intelligent, and anxious to assist us in gaining information.

We all went after breakfast on Sunday, October 23rd, to attend the morning service, which should have been held at nine o'clock, but was postponed till our arrival. This church was opened about two years ago, and is a very creditable edifice, entirely built by the natives. The walls and roof are of corrugated iron, and the architecture is of the plainest; but the people are deservedly proud of their effort, which not only represents time, energy, and money spent by themselves, but it is also the outward and visible sign of their own advance in civilisation, they feel it to be a bond of union between themselves and white Christians. It is easy to sneer at the plainness—ugliness if you will—of a tin tabernacle, but within an ungainly chrysalis there may be enshrined an incipient butterfly; the psyche of the savage, or barbarian, whether black or white, may similarly emerge from the baldest and stiffest of meeting-houses.

It is often very pathetic to see the evident strivings of these people to be like the white man; to my mind they are too ready to cast away their past, for with the crudities and social unrest of savagery there are flung aside also many of the excellent moral codes and social safeguards of the old order of things. Much native wheat is rooted up with the tares.

After the service I photographed the interior of the church, and later showed the natives photographs and sketches and chatted on various subjects, and altogether had a very profitable day. Before our midday dinner I had completed a census of the island, with the totem of every individual, and as I walked through the village the names of the residents of every house were recorded. There was no time to trace the genealogies as far back as Rivers did for Murray Island and Mabuiag, but still, what was accomplished will enable one to get some insight into the social organisation of the people. Rivers did not enumerate the inhabitants of every house in Murray Island and Mabuiag because the clans were all mixed up, but as we had found in Kiwai the houses were clan-houses, I thought the same might possibly occur here. We found that formerly this was the case, and that the snake (*Tabu*) and wild sweet potato (*Daibau*) clans lived on one side of the village, and the crocodile (*Kodal*), dog (*Umai*), and cassowary (*Sam*) lived on the other side. This division of the village into clan groups was said to tend to faction fights, and so the missionary tried to mix them up. There are still, however, distinct traces to be found of clan groupings in the village. I have previously referred to the double grouping of the clans in Mabuiag and Pulu, and a similar dual division is common throughout Australia. On the mainland of New Guinea to the east there is often a dual grouping in a village, about which more information is required, but in this case there is at present no evidence to connect it with totemism.

Ten years ago Maino, the chief of Tut, who is a crocodile-man, as a sign of friendship, exchanged names with me, and on the strength of this, on arriving at Saibai, I claimed to be a crocodile-man also, and in this assertion was supported by Maino. The other crocodile-men at once acknowledged me, for a few minutes after I landed on the island a crocodile-man made me a present of some coconuts, and stated in doing so that we were relatives.

Later on when I was sitting among a group of natives showing pictures and chatting, someone hinted a doubt as to whether an Englishman could have a crocodile *augūd*. Wherever one goes one always finds some incredulous person who will not bow unquestioningly to authority. I immediately rolled up my shirt sleeves and showed my vaccination marks, which I happen to have on both shoulders, and I pointed this out as a proof of my pretensions; the evidence at once silenced all sceptical remarks, and carried conviction. The whiteness of the skin of my upper arms, unburned as it was by the hot sun, attracted much attention, especially from the ladies.

I was chagrined to find that my clan, though formerly an important one here, was on the decline, and that a plant clan was now the most numerous. This appears to be the only true plant totem in Torres Straits, and forms another interesting link with the Fly River district. Intermarriage in the same clan is prohibited; but I believe they now kill and eat their totems.

I wanted to obtain a special kind of yellow earth that is traded as paint from this to the other islands and to New Guinea, but we were told that snakes would bite anyone who went into the bush on a Sunday. These snakes must be very degenerate subjects of the Old Serpent, the Father of Lies, if they support so strict a Sabbatarianism.

Unfortunately the triple-crowned coconut palm that I sketched on my last visit here has died, so I could not photograph it as I had hoped to do. When I was making the sketch I was, as usual, surrounded by a bevy of onlookers, and one man said to me, "I wish I could make a coconut palm grow as fast as you draw it!" As I sketched in the neighbouring palms, the bystanders mentioned the name of the owner of each, and thus I learned that every tree is owned by somebody, and in a group of palms several men or women may own various trees. It is common for a man to own land, but not to own all the trees or plants that grow on it.

SOME WESTERN ISLANDS

On the same occasion I sketched one of the houses, in which the lower portion was roughly walled up with coconut· palm leaves, so as to make a second dwelling-place beneath the house proper. At this particular time the natives of Boigu, an island some fifteen miles to the west, had come to Saibai for safety. They had heard that the Tugeri pirates were coming on a head-hunting raid, and knew they could not withstand them unaided. There was not enough house room in Saibai for these visitors, and so the under portion of this house was roughly wattled for

FIG. 20. HOUSE ON PILES AT SAIBAI
With the lower portion screened with leaves (1888)

their accommodation. This was at that time the only two-storied house in Torres Straits.

The ancient pile dwellings of Switzerland were built in the lakes for safety from attack by enemies. When the country became more settled, the pile dwellings were built on the shore instead of in the water, which is the present condition of most of the coastal villages in New Guinea. Later the Swiss put stones round the outer posts that supported their houses, and the ground floor, thus formed, was used as a shed. This is what one still finds so often in Switzerland. The real dwelling-house is supported on posts as in the prehistoric days, and the staircase is still outside the house, as was the original log ladder.

This Saibai house was temporarily in an intermediate condition between the ancient pile dwelling and the modern Swiss châlets. Not only was the final step never taken, but when the immediate need of increased accommodation was not felt, the house reverted to its previous state.

On Monday morning we measured ten natives pretty thoroughly and took a number of photographs. Ray exhibited the phonograph, and obtained some new records, whilst Seligmann worked hard at native medicine. Altogether we got through a great deal of work during these two days.

We made an early start on Tuesday in the *White Star*, and anchored off Tut in the forenoon, as I wished once more to go over the old sacred sites with Maino. No one lives on the island now, and the sacred spots are overgrown with bush, and most of the old stones are removed or broken up. This was very disappointing, and I was able to add only a very little to my previous information. It was an intensely hot day, and we were parched with thirst and soaked with perspiration.

The natives of Yam and Tut are one people. In olden days they resided part of the year in one island, and the rest in the other; now the greatly reduced population is permanently quartered on Yam. The people occasionally come across from Yam to look after their gardens, and we photographed the simple huts they had erected, which, we were informed, were like the old houses before the natives had adopted the South Sea type of house.

TUT

Tut, or Tud, or Warrior Island as it is now generally called, is situated at the southern end of the great Warrior Reefs. The island is very low, not more than ten feet above sea-level in any part, and is a true coral island, having been formed by the sea heaping coral sand and detritus on the reef, till these formed barriers which keep the sea itself at bay. As is usually the case in these parts, the soil is rendered fertile by the disintegration of pumice drifting on to the island from distant volcanoes.

Tut is evidently an island in process of formation, and is, roughly speaking, hook-shaped, the curved space being a lagoon, which is filled during the whole of the north-west monsoon, but dry except at high tide, during the south-east trade, *i.e.* during the greater portion of the year. This lagoon is evidently gradually silting up, and will ultimately form a permanent part of the island.

The vegetation is scrubby, but there are some old trees near the middle of the island. In old times the people were often short of food. At my visit in 1888 they were comfortably off, owing to the fact that most of the men were engaged in the fishing industries of the Straits, and were therefore able to buy provisions. On that occasion Maino met us, and after visiting a house and noticing a woman playing at cat's cradle, we walked across the island to the village. There was a good deal of orange-coloured dodder festooning the shrubs and grass; one coconut palm bore the inscription of **BILI FIJI**, to announce the fact of that tree being owned by Billy, a native of Fiji. A coconut lying on the ground was sending up two vigorous sprouts.

After passing the mouth of the lagoon we reached the village, and after a little persuasion the natives got up a *kŏpa-kŏpa*, or native dance, for our entertainment.

It was, however, too hurriedly arranged, and there were not enough performers for it to be very effective. Two men and about eight women and girls danced. The latter, obeying a message sent on by Maino in advance of us, had donned their garments of civilisation, from a mistaken wish to show us due honour; but after some difficulty they acceded to our request, and with much laughing and chattering retired to take off their ugly long calico gowns, and reappeared more suitably clad in their pretty native leaf petticoats, but they had added coloured girdles and wraps round their chests.

Maino played the drum for the dance, and was surrounded by his wife and children and other women and children who joined in singing a chant and encouraging the dancers. A largess of tobacco closed the proceedings.

Mr. Milman, who was then Acting Resident Magistrate, offered to take Maino to Mawatta on the New Guinea coast, as that was his wife's native place. At daybreak next morning Maino came to the steamer, and we paid him a tomahawk, five yards of calico, and some tobacco for a mask and other articles he brought us. He remarked he should give the tomahawk and calico to his mother-in-law, as he had not yet "paid" for his last baby!

The anchorage at Tut is at the opposite end of the island from Maino's camp, and a few bêche-de-mer fishermen and their staff of Australian blacks then occupied that part of the island.

Tom Randolf, a Dane, kindly lent me a small galvanised iron shed with a thatch roof; part of it was occupied by sacks of flour, rice, and miscellaneous stores. At the other end he put a couch for me, and two native mats formed a mattress, on which I was comfortable enough. The door of the shed was fastened with handcuffs, of which I kept the key, and so did not feel a prisoner. Randolf gave me some fowls, eggs, and a chunk of turtle-meat, which formed a pleasant change after a long course of tinned meats. He also allowed me to use his fresh water, of which there is a very scanty supply, there being only a very little brackish water on the island, which Europeans cannot use. The natives as well as the settlers procured their drinking water from the island of Yam, some fifteen miles away.

Maino gave me a good deal of valuable information respecting the initiation of boys into manhood, and took me into the bush to show me where their ceremonies formerly took place. With Maino's assistance I could fairly well conjure up the past appearance of this tabooed *kwod*.

On entering manhood the boys were secluded in the *kwod* for one month, and might on no account see a woman, or be seen by any. A large stone was shown me, with which a long time ago seven boys had been killed for breaking this rule. These misguided youths, tired of the irksomeness of the discipline, broke away from the *kwod*, and seeing their mothers carrying some yams and sweet potatoes shouted out to them, and holding their left arms to attract attention, asked for food.

During the month of their seclusion the boys daily had charcoal made from charred coconuts rubbed into them; they might eat anything, except fat, and were in charge of their mother's brother. During the day the boys were covered with mats, sewn together to form little tents; so that when the boys sat down only the tents were seen, and when they walked their legs alone were visible. The whole day was spent in the sacred camp. After sunset the uncles took the boys to a house set apart for them, and before sunrise, when the "pigeon whistles," they were marched back to the clearing.

The old men taught the lads what they might and might not do as men. The code of morality so far as it went was very high, one quaint instruction being, "You no like girl first; if you do, girl call you 'woman'!" For it is the custom here for the women to propose marriage to the men.

SOME WESTERN ISLANDS

The accompanying sketch is an attempted restoration of the sacred area, or *kwod*, of about thirty years ago. The four large mats in the centre belonged respectively (from the foreground backwards) to the Shark, Crocodile, Dog, and Cassowary clans. The fires of the first two were close together at one end, the Cassowary's fire at the opposite end, and the Dog's fire on one side; on the side opposite the latter was placed the chief's mat. The fireplaces are still to be seen. At one end of each mat was a large crocodile-head mask; besides these were some leaf coverings used in initiatory rites. The drums occupied the centre. The fires were tended by lads already initiated; the

FIG. 21. RESTORATION OF THE KWOD IN TUT DURING THE INITIATION PERIOD

men sat on their mats, or sat and stood around; the boys to be initiated were grouped at each end of the *kwod*.

At the end of the month the boys were washed, gaily decked, and anointed with a pungent scent, thereby hoping to gain favour with the girls. They were marched towards the village with a large mat raised in front of them. On reaching an open space the mat was lowered, and the lads were then seen for the first time by their fathers, female relations, and friends. The mothers and aunts rushed forward, hugged, and cried over the lads. There were great rejoicings and feastings, for the boys were then acknowledged as men.

Amongst the relics Maino showed me the navel shrine (*kupai* or *kupor*) of Sigai, a great warrior and traveller of long ago. Before going to fight the men would stand around the shrine of large shells and dig their bows and arrows into the ground there, so that virtue might pass into them. The men also took a coconut, and broke it. If it broke evenly in two halves, they would have a successful foray; if the fracture was not straight, they would kill only a few men. Should a piece of the coconut shell break off, a close relative of the man who broke it would die soon. All the men who were consulting the oracle ate a small piece of the kernel of the broken coconut, and took up the broken halves and put "medicine" inside.

I believe I was the first European to whom these revered relics of the past had been shown, and I felt quite sorry for my friend when, looking at one of the memorable stones with tears in his eyes, he said, "I think of old men, and I sorry. All finish now."

Later Maino gave me the head-dress his father, "king" Kebiso, wore when on the war-path, and a boar's tusk ornament which he stuck in his mouth to render his appearance yet more terrible.

Like a true gentleman, Maino did not let me know at the time of his reluctance to part with these relics of his famous father. I did not ask him for them, seeing how highly he valued them, but he offered them freely to me. I then asked what he wanted in return, and gave him what he asked for—a small oval looking-glass, a pocket-knife, a blue bead necklace, and seven sticks of tobacco for the head-dress; and for the tusk ornament a pocket-knife, two clay pipes, and four sticks of tobacco. He wanted me to have these mementoes of his father, partly because of our real friendship for each other, but also partly because he wanted them exhibited in a big museum in England, where plenty of people would see them and would know to whom they once belonged. They are now in the British Museum.

YAM

To return to the narrative of the present Expedition. We reached Yam in the afternoon, and all landed to have a look round. Maino took me to the old *kwod*, and I made a rough plan of it, and obtained a description of what it looked like formerly. After dinner I sketched a restoration, and later, when Maino and Jimmy Tut came off to the steamer, I got them to criticise it; and Maino made some sketches to elucidate details, the result being that I can with confidence restore what possibly no white man ever saw, or, at all events, no one has recorded it. The following day I returned to the *kwod* to take some photographs, and further information was given me.

There was in the *kwod* a low fence surrounding a space of about thirty-five feet square, in which were the shrines of the two great *augūds* of the island. All that now remains are three heaps of shells, mainly of the gigantic Fusus.

Two of the heaps are about twenty-five feet long; the third is relatively small. Formerly, at the southerly end of each long row was a large turtle-shell mask, representing a crocodile and a hammer-headed shark respectively. These were decorated in various ways, and under each was a stone in which the life

FIG. 22. RESTORATION OF THE KWOD IN YAM

of the *augūd* resided; stretching from each mask was a cord to which numerous human lower jawbones were fastened; at the opposite end was a stone on which a skull rested.

The small heap is the shrine of the *augūd Ger*, or sea-snake, which originated from the hammer-headed shark (*Kursi*). These shrines were formerly covered over by long low huts decorated, like the fence, with Fusus shells.

Outside the fence were two heaps of shells which had a mystical connection with the shrines. These were the *augūdau kupar*, or navel shrines of the *augūds*.

Of course women and children might not come near the place, and, further, they did not know what the *augūds* were like. They only knew of the crocodile (*Kodal*) as "Maiau" and of the hammer-headed shark (*Kursi*) as "Sigai." These heroes were related to the equally legendary Malu of Murray Island, who also had a dual human-shark personality.

This discovery is another of the links found between totemism and hero-worship, which I have noted in Torres Straits. I am not aware whether this transition has been previously described as occurring among a living people, but it seems as if it may be possible to trace some stages at least between pure totemism on the one hand and hero-worship on the other, and a hero-worship that is suspiciously like the origin of a god. I have collected all the legends I could concerning the histories of the heroes Bomai, Malu, Sigai, Maiau, and Sau.

According to our usual custom we visited all the shrines we heard of in the island; of these not the least interesting was the small boys' *kwod*, in which were two small heaps of ruddled shells, and where the boys played at *augud*. All over the world boys mimic the actions of their fathers, and we came across several instances of this during our Expedition. At Veifaa, in the Mekeo district of British New Guinea, some boys imitated, as we shall see, the masked taboo officials. Here they went a step further, and played at *augud*, the most sacred of all their religious ceremonies. In this case they cannot be said to have exactly mimicked their elders, as they did not know what the real *augud* was like, nor how the ceremonies were conducted, but they "made believe" to their own satisfaction.

Returning from the *kwod*, Maino pointed out a shelter under a rock where formerly two skulls had been kept. Unfortunately one was burnt when the ground was being cleared for a garden, but the other was in good condition, and Maino allowed me to appropriate it. He did not wish me to take the lower jaw of the burnt skull which was lying close by, and was anxious that no one should know he had given me the whole skull, nor would he touch it himself.

The afternoon was mainly devoted to photography and the phonograph.

NAGIR

We made an early start the next day, and in the forenoon visited Nagir (Mount Ernest). Here we found only two old men and one old woman. There were a few other inhabitants out in shelling boats, but the islanders are on the verge of extinction.

As we could only have two hours on the island, and there were places on it we wished to visit, there was but little time to prosecute inquiries; still we got something done.

The old *kwod* and other sacred spots are in a shocking state. Jimmy Samoa, an enormous Samoan, has resided on the island for many years, and he has made his garden in the *kwod* and built his house close by it. "Ichabod" was writ large. There was nothing to see, and very little reliable information to be had. It was a poor set-off, so far as we were concerned, to find Jimmy Samoa in possession of a graphophone!

A few days after my arrival in Torres Straits in 1888 I visited Nagir, and recalling the fact that when H.M.S. *Alert* was surveying the district six years previously Dr. Coppinger had obtained at this island two decorated skulls, I tried to get another. My inquiries after "head belong dead man," aided by a sketch and emphasised by a promise of ample remuneration, elicited in time the information from Aiwŏli that he "savvied" and that he "got 'im." Forbidding me from following him, Aiwŏli disappeared round the corner, and in a very short space of time returned with a basket containing a skull wrapped up in two very old and dirty red cotton handkerchiefs. (Plate XI., B, No. 1, p. 139.)

The skull was that of a young, unmarried man, Magau, whose English name was "Billy," and who died about the end of 1887. His death was firmly believed to have been caused by the telepathic magic of a *maidelaig*, or sorcery man, then residing at Cape York, some twenty-five miles away.

When Magau died, Kuduma, his uncle, and Aina ("Harry Nagir"), his foster-brother, agreed, "Very good, we make him same as man long-time fashion. We take him head, but leave him body in ground." So they buried him. On the fourth day after interment all the *mariget*, or men whose particular duty it was, went very quietly in a crouching manner to the grave. When they arrived there they all suddenly and simultaneously stamped on the ground, clapped their hands once, and cried "Ah!" Then the *mari*, or spirit, finally departed from Magau, and his head would come off easily from his body. The earth was removed from the body, and one particular man took hold of the cranium and another seized the jaw, and the head was easily severed from the trunk. A special *mariget* kept the skull, washed it in the sea, and when it was quite clean and sweet he painted blue marks over the eyes, inserted pearl-shell eyes, and moulded a nose out of wood and beeswax, which he painted red. The length was accurate, for it was the custom to measure the length of the nose of a dead person with a piece of stick, which was carefully preserved to this end. The deficiency of teeth was supplied with half a dozen pieces of wood, the jaw was lashed on to the cranium, and seed and calico ear-pendants were attached. So it was made "flash."

After about three months a death-dance was held ("made him *merkai*"), at the same time a big feast was made, but in addition to the yams, sweet potatoes, coconuts, bananas, and so forth, of olden time this feast was said to be reinforced with four bags of flour, one case of gin, and one of schnapps. The adorned skull of Magau was placed on a mat in the middle of the assembly. The father and brother prepared food for the other *mariget*, and put food in front of the skull; the *mariget* also made food ready for the father and brother of the deceased, and placed it likewise before the skull. Then "all got d—d drunk all night; if woman sleep, wake him up, no make row."

Before the feasting commenced the skull was handed over to the father; at night-time it was covered over with a mat, and later on the family slept around it in memory of old times. After three nights the father kept the skull in its basket close by his pillow.

Magau's skull was sold to me by Aiwŏli, and another foster-brother, for one tomahawk and three fathoms of calico print. It is now in the Christy Collection at the British Museum.

It does not sound to us a very cheerful custom for people to keep the skulls of their friends, but it must be remembered that they could not make pictures of their dead friends and relations, and, since they loved them as we love ours, they liked to have something to remember them by. In the Murray Islands and Darnley they even modelled the whole face in black wax so as to represent their dead friend still more closely. I have previously stated how pleased the natives were to see photographs I took ten years ago of their friends and relatives who had since died, and both at Murray Island and Mabuiag we had to photograph a dead baby, as the father wanted a likeness as a memento.

Whenever they were in trouble they used to take the skull of a relative, put fresh paint on it, and cover it with scented leaves, then they would speak to it and ask advice from it. When they went to bed they would put the skull on their sleeping-mat beside their heads, and if they dreamt they thought it was the spirit of their dead friend talking to them and advising them what they should do. As they believed all this, it was by no means strange that they liked to keep and preserve the skulls of their dead relatives. This is a very different matter from collecting the heads of dead enemies, which was very common in many parts of New Guinea and was also done in Torres Straits.

In the early part of November, 1888, a few natives from Nagir and Muralug, then resident on Thursday Island, got up a dance to inaugurate the approach of the rainy season, or, as it is usually termed, the "nor'-west." Night after night they practised their chant, and in the daytime they manufactured their masks. These were all of the same pattern, and consisted of a lower portion in the form of the usual conventional crocodile's head, surmounted by a human face surrounded by a sort of frill of tortoiseshell fretwork; below was a fringe of frayed leaves. This portion entirely covered the head of the wearer, the mask being held solely by the teeth, which gripped a stick extending across the central cavity. Above the face was a representation of a sawfish five feet in length. Towering above its centre was a long, narrow, erect triangle covered with turkey-red and flanked with white feathers. Feathers from five different kinds of birds, from a bird of paradise to a pigeon, adorned this remarkable structure, which attained to a height of 4 feet 6 inches. The masks were painted with red, white, black, and a little blue pigment. In olden times such masks would be made of tortoiseshell; these were constructed out of pieces of old packing-cases and kerosene tins.

The dancing-ground was in front of a small screen (*waus*), behind which the performers retired in rotation for rest and refreshment. The first dance began on Saturday afternoon, and was continued nightly till the following Thursday. The date of the ceremony was fixed by the rising of a particular star. There was a great sameness in the dancing, which was practically confined to one man appearing on each side from behind the screen; the pair advanced forward with a sedately capering step, crossed to the opposite side of the dancing-ground, and ultimately retired to the end of the screen: then they crouched down and slowly waved their grotesquely masked heads from side to side. As soon as the chant was finished they disappeared behind the screen, when their places were taken by two other performers. A free translation of the sawfish chant is as follows:—

1. Now I can see my reflection in the pools on the reef.
2. You cut the shoot of the coconut palm for me.
3. Farewell, dead coconut palm leaves. Ho! there's the lightning.
4. Fish now approach the shore, and we must build fish-weirs in their route.

The following notes may serve to explain the allusions. The first line refers to the glassy surface of the sea during the calms of the "nor'-west." At this season vegetation becomes rampant, the dead leaves falling off at the end of the dry south-east monsoon. The sprouting leaf of the coconut palm is split into long narrow bands, of which frontlets, crossed shoulder-belts, and anklets are made; these are worn in the dances. The dance petticoats of the men are also made from these blanched leaves: so this is equivalent to saying that preparations for dances must now be made. Sheet lightning at night is a very characteristic feature of the rainy season, and it occurs only then. Sometimes the lightning is so frequent that there is a continuous glare in the north-west, recalling certain manifestations of the Northern Lights of higher latitudes. This is also the season when shoals of fish approach the shore. These are entrapped at some islands by means of large areas on the flat fringing reefs being inclosed by low walls which are about two feet or so in height, and are composed of loose stones. The fish come inshore with the high night tides, and, as the water recedes, are caught within the weirs.

There can be no doubt that this dance was not got up for amusement, but was a serious ceremony. As there was no invocation to or recognition of a spiritual being of any kind, this act cannot be strictly called "religious," but it was designed to directly influence the fish in the sea. It was thus a magical ceremony to ensure a good fishing season.

We brought Maino on with us from Yam to Thursday Island, so as to get further information from him in our spare time, and we "worked" him as much as possible; but the seductions of Thursday Island were too great for him to withstand, as they also prove to so many other men of varied nationalities. This was a great disappointment, as we had hoped during these last

SOME WESTERN ISLANDS

few days in the Straits to clear up some doubtful points, with the help of further information from Maino, but we were not able to do much, owing to the false kindness of his self-styled "friends."

Ray, however, got hold of a Prince of Wales Islander named "Wallaby"; he was a native policeman, and we obtained some interesting information from him. There was, unfortunately, no old man handy as a referee, for many things that interest us are known fully only to the older men.

We again saw something of our friends of the Sacred Heart Mission, as Archbishop Navarre and Father Cochard were here from Yule Island; apart from these no one in Thursday Island knows or cares anything about native customs.

One afternoon we sailed to the neighbouring island of Kiriri (Hammond Island) to examine some rock paintings. These proved to be of a very simple character, representing totems (hammer-headed shark, turtle, dugong, and so on). Two canoes were also represented; these were supposed to illustrate the canoes in which the spirits paddle about on calm nights when they want to catch turtle, dugong, or fish. Among the crevices of the boulders in the vicinity of these paintings several skulls and bones have been found. We brought away two skulls that were found beneath the painted rocks, and we found another close by. This was our last little pilgrimage to old sacred spots in the islands.

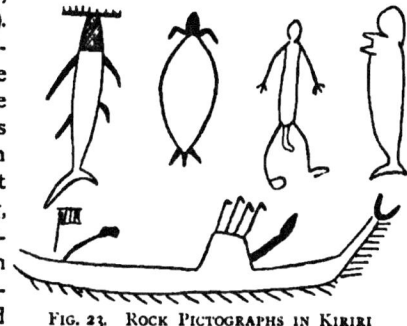

FIG. 23. ROCK PICTOGRAPHS IN KIRIRI

MURALUG

Towards the end of 1888 I paid a short visit to Muralug, commonly known as Prince of Wales Island. This is the largest island in Torres Straits, and it lies only a short distance from Cape York. I climbed one of the hills on the northern coast of the island, and obtained a good view of the country. Inland there were numerous timber-covered hills; towards the shore the hills came down close to the sea, and were interspersed with flat, low-lying mangrove swamps.

As dusk fell I strolled to the village, and found a family party seated on mats by the fire in an inclosure at the back of the chief's house; the inclosure served the double purpose of a wind-screen, and a fence to keep out obtrusive pigs. By the fire sat Serb, Tuigana's wife, while Tuigana (the chief) was playing cards with his three little nephews. In the background were Georgie and Pattie; they had not long been married, and they were quietly enjoying themselves in a way akin to that which is not unusual among newly married people at home. I joined the family party, and, lying on a mat, watched the group with interest. The card players were playing what was said to be a Malay game called "Jaro," and it was amusing to hear English names and phrases mixed with native language. Thus, in the midst of a chatter of words I could not understand, would come, "I have six tricks." "What are trumps?" "Spades." "That card will kill him." And so on. From time to time Serb replenished the bamboo pipe for her husband, and passed it to him for a "smoke." Altogether this was a pleasant little glimpse of real family life; the smoke of the wood fire was very pungent, however, and made my eyes smart, so that I soon left the happy group.

The day following I was entertained with a war-dance, a most interesting rehearsal of a dance which forty years ago would have commemorated some deed of valour or treachery. I gathered that such dances were never indulged in for mere amusement, and were quite distinct from what may be termed the festive dance.

It was evening, on a sandy shore. A gloomy mangrove swamp extended away to the right; to the left stretched a bay edged with a beach of white coral sand, against which the waves gently lapped. In the foreground were three fires. Near one was a native house of flimsy construction open to the wind, in which were the women and some children. The view behind was blocked by trees on rising ground; above was a clear blue sky studded with sparkling stars; and the moon, being in her second quarter, shed a soft silvery light on all.

Near a fire sat the primitive orchestra. The drums were beaten in a rhythmical monotone, and a wailing chant accompanied them. Gradually from the far distance swarthy forms came, as it were, into focus, and marched along in twos or threes; then, in sinuous course, they performed their evolutions, varying the celerity of their movements to the time of the weird singing. A mass of dried herbage thrown on a fire lighted up the scene and revealed a glowing picture of savagery.

The blackness of the dancers' nether parts was intensified artificially. The upper portion of their body was smeared with red ochre; the frontlets, crossed shoulder-belts, and anklets of pale yellow leaves gleamed brightly. The round shell ornaments stood out with opaque whiteness against the ruddled chests, while the pearly crescentic breastplates shone with a softer lustre. The loin-cloths and bits of red calico on the armlets or in the hair gave further colour; bunches of leaves inserted in the armlets, at the shoulders, appeared as verdant epaulettes; other bunches were inserted in a belt behind, the green showing up in vivid hue by the camp fires. The bizarre effect was enhanced by black cassowary plumes projecting from the gauntlet on the left arm, or stuck tail-wise into the belt at the back.

The yellow frontlet or chaplet was either a simple band or looped, or was prolonged into two streamers; again, white feathers were occasionally inserted into the black, frizzly hair, or a fine effect was produced by a coronet of cassowary feathers.

This dance illustrated the "war-path," the band of pretended warriors sometimes marching, more often skipping or stealthily stealing along, suddenly coming upon the foe with a "*Wahu!*" Then they skipped two or three times, usually raising the right leg, brandishing their weapons at the same time. Again and again the dread "*Wahu!*" resounded. This really effective manœuvre showed to yet greater advantage when, instead of being in rank, the men deployed in a semicircle facing the flaring fires, then, with their glittering eyes and gleaming teeth, and the waving of bows, arrows, and stone clubs, one realised how terrible to the lonely and surprised enemy must have been the "*Wahu!*" of such a foe.

The series of war-dances concluded with an evolution in lively measure, evidently indicative of military success, as, with exultant cries, the performers swayed their right hands,

The dire significance of this last movement was not difficult to discover. It represented what formerly occurred after a successful foray, for, after beheading the slain with their bamboo knives, the victorious warriors threaded the heads on the ratan slings which always hung on their backs when they went on the war-path, and as they returned joyously home they swung their ghastly burdens backward and forward with jubilant cries.

This dance finished, the old men begged off. They had walked thirteen miles that day to dance to me, and now they were tired and left further dancing to the younger men, who forthwith disappeared into the bush.

In due time they re-emerged, and treated us to an ordinary secular or festive dance or "*kap*." The dance, like all semi-realistic dances, is composed of "figures," which are, in fact, so many separate dances.

I gather that there is no set order for them. There is certainly considerable variety in the "movements," but, so far as my experience goes, one special "figure" always terminates the proceedings.

In one "movement" the whole company circles round and round, two deep, with all sorts of gestures. They might even be termed "antics"—cringing, swaying, leaping, tripping. It is noteworthy that the circling may be from left to right or from right to left. Thus there is no reminiscence of sun worship or other symbolism in their gyrations.

In the processions round the platform of turtle trophies, the men of Mabuiag, I was informed, marched invariably sun-wise, with whirling bull-roarers. Should one inadvertently march in the counter-direction the turtle would swim away from the island.

In one dance a man advanced singly and danced with stamping feet, illustrating the putting out of a fire; in another the men continually stood on one leg and rapidly moved the other up and down, or, it may be, jumped with both legs.

In the "crab dance" a man danced in a crouching attitude, with the upper-arms horizontal and the fore-arms vertical; the "iguana dance" represented the large local lizard (Varanus) whilst swimming. Some of the "figures" illustrated an action in real life, such as agricultural, nautical, or fishing employments; for example, a man would crouch and move his hands about as if he were planting yams or seeking for pearl-shell at the bottom of the sea.

The "pelican dance" concluded the evening's entertainment. The general body of the dancers stood together in the background, and from among these two men (or occasionally a single man) stepped forward and danced on the tips of their toes on the same spot. As the drum-beats became more rapid the jumping was accelerated, their legs keeping time, till with the quickened music their feet became almost invisible from the rapidity of their movements, and they seemed as if boring a hole in the ground, whilst the dust rose in clouds about them.

Naturally this could not last long; and when fatigued the pair retired, their places being taken by another two, till all had displayed their terpsichorean skill; and indeed it was a splendid exhibition of activity and *verve*. The spirit of emulation is largely evoked in this figure, and the onlookers admire and applaud the most vigorous and staying dancer of this particularly fatiguing step.

Not many years ago these islanders had a most unenviable reputation for ferocity, exhibiting a fierce determination to murder the encroaching white man. Now they will walk thirteen miles to dance for the amusement of an Englishman they have never seen, scenting tobacco and other largess from afar!

While the black man was dancing his *kap* in literal war-paint and decorated with shells and feathers, a channel only a mile in width separated him from a party of white ladies and gentlemen dancing together in civilised dance garb. Little thought the latter that the despised "nigger" would consider it indelicate for men and women to dance with one another, especially so closely together as the custom of modern "fast" dances permits, or that the figures of their square dances were relics of such realistic dances as were in actual force across the narrow channel.

CHAPTER XIII

CAPE YORK NATIVES

ON November 2nd, Ray, Seligmann, and I went with Mr. Douglas to Somerset, in Albany Pass, Cape York, to visit Mr. Frank Jardine. We reached Somerset early in the afternoon and left at ten next morning. Mr. Jardine is probably the oldest resident in the Straits, and has seen a great deal, but he does not care about the natives, and could tell us very little that we particularly wanted to know. We went prepared to measure and study the Australian natives of the Gudang tribe, of which Macgillivray wrote; but they have all died out, or at all events none now live in their own country, the same remark also applies to neighbouring tribes. We were greatly disappointed, as it was important to determine whether they had any relationship to the islanders. It was very saddening to be continually pulled up in our researches by the oft-repeated cry of "*Too late!*"

As an illustration of the way in which natives did their best to assist us in our work, I must mention the thoughtfulness of a certain policeman on Thursday Island named Jimmy Matauri, who was a native of Yaraikanna tribe of Cape York. On November 7th, Jimmy sent me four of his fellow-tribesmen who had come to Thursday Island on a shelling boat. We were very glad of this opportunity to measure them, as they filled up an annoying gap in our work, these people being virtually the same as the nearly extinct Gudang, whom we failed to meet at Somerset. Physically they are fairly typical Australians—the six men measured had an average height of 5 feet 4 inches, and they had long, narrow heads, and I should imagine there is extremely little if any Papuan blood in their veins.

As soon as the men were measured, I inquired about their

CAPE YORK NATIVES

bull-roarers. I led up to the question by referring to the middle upper front tooth which was absent in all of them, and which I knew must have been knocked out during initiation ceremonies. They acknowledged having the bull-roarer which they called *umbalako*, and promised to make some for me. There was a public holiday the following day as it was the Prince of Wales' birthday, and nearly all the white residents went for a picnic to Goode Island, where there were some sports for the coloured population. I had intended going to the picnic, but as our Cape York friends were coming again, Seligmann and I remained behind to see them.

In the afternoon they turned up with the promised bull-roarers. These were 5¼ inches in length and painted red, black, and white. There were no sticks as there should have been, so we supplied the men with a broken box-lid, a tomahawk, and a knife, and the omission was soon rectified. Whilst this was being done in an out-building, Sarah, the waitress, brought us out a cup of afternoon tea, and the natives deftly hid the bull-roarers. For a woman to see a bull-roarer would be a terrible sacrilege, and there was evident relief when the unsuspecting Sarah took her departure.

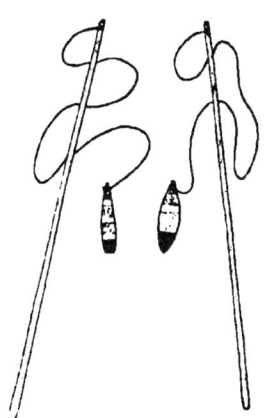

FIG. 24. BULL-ROARERS
Umbalako of the Yaraikanna tribe, Cape York. About one-thirteenth natural size

After taking their photographs we had a talk on their customs, and more particularly on their initiation ceremonies. When the boys have "little bit whiskers" they are taken into the bush about the end of the south-east monsoon, and the *langa*, as the lads are called, are isolated for a variable period lasting from a month to a year, apparently according to the age of each lad. Each *langa* is looked after by a *mawara* (his future brother-in-law) who anoints him with bush medicine in the hollow of the thigh (near the head of the femur), in the pits of the groin, the hollows above the collar-bones, the hollows of the temples, and at the back of the knee. This is done to make the boy grow.

During the period of seclusion the *langa* wears a short kilt;

he is not allowed to talk nor play, and has to remain all the time in the *tera*, which corresponds with the *kwod* of the islanders.

At the end of the period the real ceremonies are held, in which all the men participate. The *langa* are painted red, white, and black in a fearsome manner and otherwise decorated.

In the *Yampa* ceremony the *langa* sit in front of a screen, which has somewhat of a horse-shoe shape; the men of the tribe are stationed a good way off behind the screen, and quite out of sight of the initiates. A tall post is erected within the inclosure, and a man climbs up this and addresses the people beyond, stating that the *langa* have been well looked after, and asking for food. The people then throw food to him while he is still up on the post, the food being tied up in palm leaves or in baskets. If the *anachena* fails to catch one of the bundles, he comes down the pole and another climbs up, and so each take their turn till all the food has been thrown.

The swinging and exhibition of the bull-roarer follows this ceremony, but of course no women or children are allowed to witness this. Finally a front tooth is knocked out, and then the lad is recognised as a man. A year later the *okara*, or test for endurance, supplemented the earlier ceremony of initiation.

At this stage of our talk Seligmann and I were called to dinner, but our four friends said they would return later, when it was dark, as they wanted to paint themselves up and show me exactly how the bull-roarer was swung before the *langa*, and which they said no white man had ever seen before.

After dinner Jimmy Matauri came for us, and we went with him to an open spot behind some sheds and houses. There were our four friends, with very little on in the way of clothing, but with their bodies variously lined with whiting which I had previously given them. They swung the bull-roarers first, circling them round their heads, and produced the ordinary buzzing noise. Then they rapidly turned, facing the opposite direction, and at the same time swung the bull-roarers horizontally with a sudden backward and forward movement of the hand, which made them give out a penetrating yelping "Bow-wow!" It was a weird sound, and extremely incongruous in an environment of corrugated iron sheds, and not far from a steam merry-go-round, with its grating machinery, discordant whistles, and monotonous music, blatantly making merry on the occasion of the Prince of Wales' birthday! The contrasts which greet one constantly in such places as these are often most violent.

The four natives then gave a short exhibition of a dance, which consisted of a slow walk, strongly flexing each leg alternately, and occasionally standing still momentarily, bending the head from one side to the other, the men uttering low grunts all the time.

Next they gave a demonstration of the method used in knocking out an initiate's front tooth. The subject lies on the ground on his back, with his head resting on the operator's lap; the latter takes a kangaroo bone in his left hand, and a stone in his right, and inserts the former first on one side and then on the other of the tooth to be extracted, the bone being worked sideways; this is done several times till the tooth is loosened. The tooth is then smartly tapped, and with each tap the name is mentioned of one of the "countries" owned by the lad's mother, or by her father, or other of her relatives. These are given in order, and the name spoken when the tooth breaks away is the country to which the lad belongs in future. The lad is then given some water with which to rinse his mouth, and he gently lets the gory spittle fall into a leaf water-basket. The old men carefully inspect the form assumed by the clot, and trace some likeness to a natural object, plant, or stone; this will be the *ari* of the newly made man. So far as I know, this is a previously undescribed method of fixing the territory of an individual, or rather that land over which he has hunting, and root and fruit collecting rights. It is worth noticing that only the lands belonging to the mother's family were enumerated; that is, a boy inherits from his mother and not from his father. Thus the mother's land goes to her children, and a father's to his nephews and nieces. On November 10th the same natives came again for a talk in the afternoon, and we obtained some additional information from them. Tomari, one of the most intelligent of them, has three *ari* : (1) *aru*, a crab, which fell to him through blood divination at initiation in the manner just described; (2) *untara*, diamond fish; (3) *alungi*, crayfish. The two latter were given to him as the result of dreams. It appears that if an old man dreams of anything at night, that object is the *ari* of the first person he sees next morning; the idea being that the animal, or whatever appears in the dream, is the spirit of the first person met with on awakening. Tomari's father was a carpet-snake, his mother an oyster, and his wife a particular kind of fruit. The *ari* is very similar to the *manitu* or *okki* of certain North American tribes, or to the "personal totem," as Dr. J. G. Frazer terms it in his valuable little book on *Totemism*.

Women obtain their *ari* in the same manner as men. If it was true, as I was told, that men and women may not marry into the same *ari* in their own place, but may do so when away from home, its sanctity is local rather than personal. A wife must be taken from another "country," as all belonging to the same place are brothers and sisters; which indicates that there is a territorial idea in kinship and in the consequent marriage restrictions.

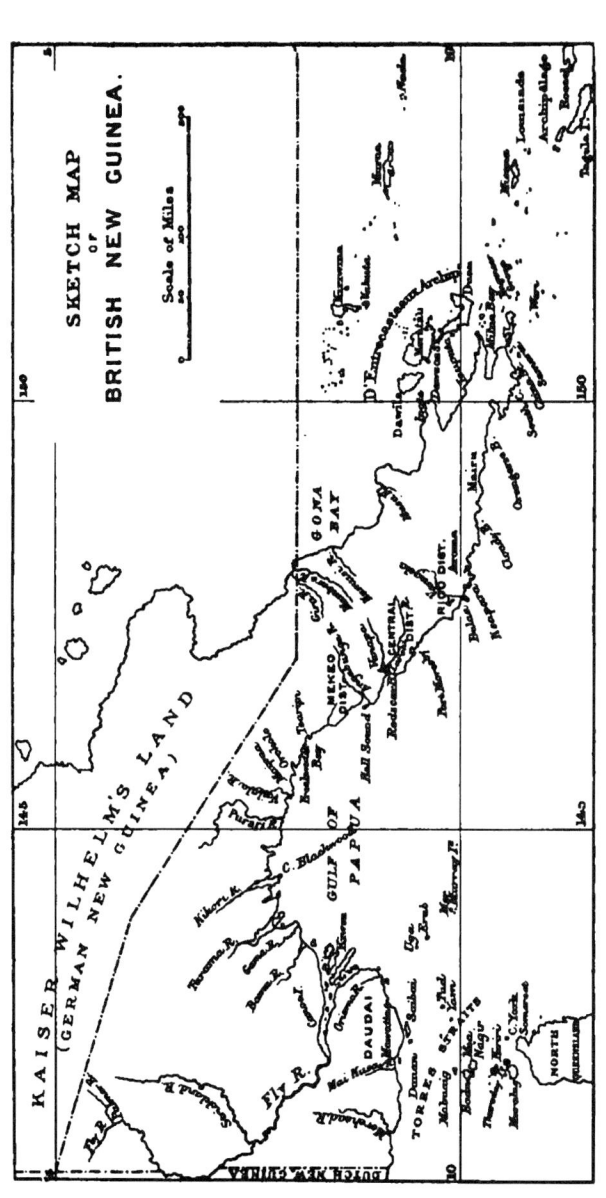

CHAPTER XIV

A TRIP DOWN THE PAPUAN COAST

AS explained in the Preface, I have not strictly followed a chronological order in this book, and the events narrated in this and the three following chapters took place from May 23rd to July 20th, during the whole of which time Rivers, Myers, and McDougall remained on Murray Island.

The Rev. James Chalmers had very kindly sent the *Olive Branch* to convey those of us who wanted to go to Port Moresby, and Ray, Seligmann, Wilkin, and myself took this opportunity to learn something about the natives of part of the south-eastern peninsula of British New Guinea. But for this timely aid it is most probable that we could not have got across the Papuan Gulf.

When the boat arrived, as is usually the case, we had to scurry round and put our outfit and apparatus together with as much expedition as possible. By the time we started we were all pretty well tired out and glad of a rest on this beautifully arranged and fitted-up boat. How I wished I could have her for the whole trip. It would have been perfect!

The *Olive Branch* is a fore-and-aft schooner 67 feet long—$16\frac{5}{10}$ beam; gross tonnage 45.96, registered tonnage 32.4; carvel built. She was built by Lane and Brown at Whangaroa, Auckland, N.Z., in 1895. The Rev. F. W. Walker, having been to sea before he became a missionary, was sent from New Guinea to superintend her building, and having a master's certificate he sailed her back when finished. The L.M.S. allowed £600 for her—far too little, it should have been £900—and she cost £1900! Walker with not unnatural enthusiasm tried to improve the boat as she was being built, and feeling his honour at stake he manfully determined to pay the balance himself, so he temporarily retired from the society and started trading in

New Guinea. I hear he is doing very well, as he deserves to, but I am afraid that fair trading with natives on Christian principles will not conduce to a rapid fortune.

We had the usual medley of races on board — European (skipper and passengers); Malay (ship's cook, Ali, from Penang, our cook, Ontong, from Batavia); Polynesian (first mate from Aitutaki, Hervey Group; a teacher from Rimatara, near Tahiti; a Samoan teacher, his wife and child); Melanesian (one boy from Keapara and three from Delena, British New Guinea); Negroid (a negro from St. Vincent, probably not full-blooded).

We made a quick passage through Flinders' Entrance, found rollers in the Gulf water, and as the wind was fresh most of us were *hors-de-combat*, and turned in very early, but had a broken night owing to a great deal of motion, noise, and rain.

Tuesday, May 24th.—A fair sea on and plenty of movement, dull sky and frequent squalls, and a heavy rain storm for an hour or so at noon. So far as the uninteresting sea and dull grey weather was concerned we might have been in English waters, but not as regards temperature — it was a pleasant temperature, neither hot nor cold, and the wind was warm. Not a very enjoyable day. Weather remained the same all day; too thick to see the New Guinea coast. Noon position: lat. 8° 57′, long. 145° 42′ E.; distance, 122 miles.

Wednesday, May 25th.—Weather looked squally in morning, and had slight puffs of wind with rain; but soon all wind dropped, and there we were at 11 a.m. lolling about the Papuan Gulf within sight of distant land, when the clouds permitted it to be seen, and the steersman vainly whistling for a wind. This kept on all day. We had a busy afternoon measuring anthropometrically some of the crew, and Seligmann tested the tactile sensibility of two of them. Noon position: lat. 8° 41′ N., long. 146° 5′ E.; distance, 27 miles.

Thursday.—Calm night; sails flapping in the wind and gear rattling. A quiet, soft morning; the continuous rain prevented bearings being taken. The captain thought we were about 19 miles off Yule Island. Cleared up later in the morning and had brilliant sunshine; sea perfectly calm, but with a long, steady roll. About one o'clock a little wind sprung up, and now, contrary to our fears, we began to hope we might anchor at Delena that night. Noon position: lat. 8° 53′ N., long. 146° 18′ 30″ E.; distance, 17 miles. The wind freshened slightly, which enabled us to get to our anchorage in Hall Sound, between Delena to the east and Yule Island to the west, about 4.45 in the afternoon. We had tea as soon as we could, and then landed; but the sun was setting, and it would rapidly be dark.

Delena is a small village of about twenty houses, situated on the sand beach at the end of a range of low wooded hills. On the high ground behind the beach are other houses, and here also is the L.M.S. Mission Station.

The Rev. H. M. Dauncey has a large house, which is very sensibly arranged, and must have been comparatively cheap to build. It consists of a large platform on posts covered by a corrugated iron roof. In the centre he has built large rooms with bamboo walls that do not go up to the roof. Thus there is ventilation above as well as through the walls, and instead of building the rooms in a solid block, one large room is detached so as to leave a broad gangway for a draught of air. The verandah is covered with creepers, and round the house are planted a large number of brilliant variegated crotons, hybiscus, and other shrubs, and the air was redolent with the sweet perfume of a grinadilla that was trained over an archway which sheltered one of the paths. The house is set in a large garden or plantation of bananas, coconuts, limes, and other fruit trees, and a short distance off are the teachers' and students' houses. Mr. Dauncey's energy and enthusiasm, backed by those of Matapo, have made themselves felt, and doubtless must have effect on the natives, though of this I was naturally unable to judge. Matapo is the native of Rimatara whom we had on board with us on the *Olive Branch*. He had been paying a visit to friends in Torres Straits, and was now returning home.

My first impression of the Eastern Papuans was that they are markedly different in several characters from the Torres Straits islanders, who are Western Papuans. They are shorter, lighter, and redder in colour, have less rugged features, and a somewhat more refined appearance. They are all tattooed. The younger men appear to tattoo their faces only, though some of the old men have patterns on the arms and legs and chest. The women are tattooed more or less all over. True tattooing, which consists in pricking pigment into the skin, does not show on very dark skins; indeed, the skin of most of the Eastern Papuans is often so dark that the tattooing does not readily show on it. Like the African negroes and the Australians, some of the Western Papuans ornament their body by means of severe scars. This practice of scarification has now ceased in Torres Straits and is diminishing on the mainland of New Guinea, where the influence of the white man extends; but we have seen many men amongst the Torres Straits islanders and Western Papuans who tattoo themselves slightly, in imitation of Polynesian or Eastern Papuans. It appeared to me that these people are less excitable than the Torres Straits islanders. We did not stay long on shore that evening, as we could do nothing in the dark.

We went ashore about eight o'clock the following morning and stayed till about four in the afternoon. We measured half a dozen men, and made records of their hair, eyes, skin, ears, etc. Seligmann tested the tactile sensibility of one or two natives, and got some interesting results. Ray gave a tune on the phonograph, and got some young people to sing a hymn on a blank cylinder. Wilkin took some photographs.

We saw the whole process of making pots except the baking in a wood fire. None of us had seen the manufacture of hand-made pottery before, and we were consequently much interested in it. Delena and Yule Island are the most northerly, or westerly, points at which pottery is made along this coast of British New Guinea. The pots are made of three shapes. The whole is done with clay, sand, water, a board on which the clay is mixed, a wooden beater, a stone, and a shell; no wheel is employed, but the pot is supported in an old broken pot and can thus be easily turned round. The women are very dexterous in using their hands and fingers, and they can make several pots in a day. The people have not much to trade with, and we did not see any decorated bamboo tobacco pipes.

What interested me most was a child's toy throwing-spear. It consists of a short, thin reed, in one end of which is inserted the mid-rib of a palm leaflet, to represent the blade or point; but the real interest consists in the fact that it is thrown by means of a short piece of string, one end of which is knotted and then passed twice round its shaft; the other end is passed twice round the index finger. The reed is held between the thumb and other fingers, with the index finger extended; when the spear is cast the string remains in the hand.

The use of a cord to increase the distance to which a throwing-spear or javelin can be hurled is an ancient, though not a common contrivance. The Greek and Roman soldiers employed a strap (ἀγκύλη or *amentum*), which was secured to about the middle of a javelin to aid them in giving it force or aim. In this case the strap left the hand of the thrower.

The only examples of this device I can find among recent peoples are in the Southern New Hebrides, New Caledonia, and Loyalty Islands. Captain Cook was the first to describe the practice, but it has been several times recorded since the great navigator's day. The short cord employed by these Melanesians is knotted at one end and has a loop at the other for the insertion of the tip of the forefinger of the right hand. The Maori, however, used a long-handled whip, *kotaha*, for hurling javelins.

Rigid wooden spear-throwers, or, as they are generally termed, throwing-sticks, are more widely distributed. They occur all all over Australia, and the Cape York variety was borrowed by the Western Islanders of Torres Straits. Strangely enough, in German New Guinea a distinct type of throwing-stick occurs sporadically. Another form of throwing-stick occurs in America among the Eskimo and among the Conibos and Purus of the Upper Amazon, and formerly among the ancient Mexicans.

This child's toy may yet prove to be a link in the chain of evidence of race migration.

These people also make very complicated string puzzles (cat's cradle); indeed, this amusement is widely spread in this part of the world.

There was great excitement in the afternoon over the catching of five goats, one of whom was a full-grown "billy." These belonged to Mr. Dauncey, and we had to take them to another mission station. What with the goats, ourselves, other passengers, our gear, bananas, and other food, we had a pretty good boatload on our return to the schooner.

Soon after our arrival at Thursday Island we met Mr. Dauncey, who was there on his way home on furlough; the only other time I had seen him was also at Thursday Island, ten years previously, when he had just arrived to commence his career as a missionary. Mr. Dauncey kindly said that when I went to Delena I could take some "curios" that were lying on his verandah. I did not forget his offer, and brought away with me three shields, a number of small masks from the Papuan Gulf, and, best of all, a sorcerer's kit, which consisted of a strongly-made round cane basket, about a foot in diameter and ten inches in height, which was lined with the cloth-like spathe of the coconut-palm leaf. It contained a cooking-pot, *uro* or *keke*, that from its appearance evidently came from Boera, inside which were the following objects :—

A small, pointed coconut receptacle (*biobio*), three inches in length, decorated with strings of grey seeds; the medicine inside was kept in place by a plug of bark cloth. When wishing to harm a person the coconut is pointed to the place where the patient sits. The patient may ultimately recover. Attached to this were the lower jaw of a baby crocodile (*auki*), this makes dogs kill pigs, and a small bamboo tube (*baubau*), containing a black powder which is used for decoration in a dance.

A spine of a sting-ray (*daiadai*), which is employed thus: When a man is enamoured of a girl from another village, who will have nothing to say to him, he takes the spine of the sting-ray and he sticks it in the ground where the girl has been, then he puts it in the sun for a day or two, and finally makes it very hot over a fire. In a couple of days the girl dies. Before dying she tells her father about the young man, and the bereaved parents instruct a sorcery man to kill the young man by magic.

A smooth ovoid stone, three inches in length, closely surrounded with netted string, has had pink earth rubbed over it, and was enveloped in a piece of black cloth which was part of a man's belt. This is taken into the garden at planting season and held over a yam, then water is poured over the stone so that it falls on to the yam. The stone is left on the ground in the garden till all the yams are planted; the stone is then returned to its bag.

Several pieces of resin were tied together with netted string in three little parcels, one having leaves wrapped round the resin. They were inside a small netted bag (*keape*). The bag with its contents is put on the top of a net that is to be used for catching a turtle in the night-time. This must be done by one man only, and no one else must see him do it. The charm must be put away before going out to fish the next morning. Another version was that the resin (*tomena*) is put in a fire so that the smoke of the ignited resin rises up into the net which is used to catch turtle or dugong. In either case it is a turtle or dugong fishing charm.

In the pot was also a broken skull of a small turtle; three

cassowary toe-nails, one of which was hollow, being used as a protecting sheath for a spear when hunting pigs or kangaroos, so that the point of the spear should not break when thrown on the ground; various fragments of a friable, whitish, shelly earth (*ănĭăninadina*), which comes from Toaripi, Lealea, and other places, and is eaten in the bush when no food is available.

Besides these there were also rounded pebbles of various sizes (*nadi*); two elongated ones, much larger than the others, were said to be yam stones, and the smaller ones may also be similar charms; some of the latter were in a bamboo tube (*baubau*), which had a protecting handle. In an old calico bag were nodules of iron pyrites and various stones, rounded pebbles, friable gritty rock, and a small piece of white coral (*ladi*), etc.

I should add that on subsequent occasions I showed one or two natives the contents of the sorcerer's basket, and the information I have given as to the nature of some of the objects was gathered from them. If we could get several sorcerers to tell the truth about their own practices much remarkable information would be obtained.

The Rev. James Chalmers gives a vivid sketch of the manner in which he obtained the death-dealing crystal and other magic stones of a renowned "Maiva" (Waima) sorcerer in his *Pioneering in New Guinea*.

We returned tired, hungry, and very happy.

Whilst we were at tea the Government schooner *Lokoko* came into Hall Sound and anchored close to Yule Island. As soon as we could, the skipper, Ray, and I paid her a visit, but found that Dr. Blainey and Mr. Monkton had gone ashore to visit the Sacred Heart Mission. So we went also. Archbishop Navarre was very courteous and friendly. He quite remembered about me, as his former colleague, Bishop Verjus, an old friend of mine, had often spoken to him of me. We learnt no European news, as Dr. Blainey had heard nothing later than we had, which was the attack on Manila by the Americans, and I think the Spaniards had capitulated. We heard of Sir William Macgregor's movements; he was then conducting the Governor of Queensland, Lord Lamington, and his party about the Possession.

The captain tried to sail next morning, but there was no wind. About midday he managed to crawl away, and we got a little wind outside; there was also a good roll, the remains of the late heavy wind. We sailed all night close hauled, but found next morning we had not at all advanced our course.

The next day a heavy sea was still running, and there was a fair amount of wind, but we only managed to cross the mouth of Redscar Bay, and get to anchor, just before sunset, in the lee of Redscar Head. The Vanapa and Laroki, two of the longest rivers in the central district of British New Guinea, flow into this deep bay, and the fertile alluvial plains of this region are dominated by the powerful Kabadi tribe.

We anchored the following afternoon off Borepada, in the lee of Haidana Island, and a long way from the shore. Here we landed a Samoan teacher, his wife, and their small boy, who had been paying a visit to her brother, "Jimmy Samoa," in Nagir. They were bound for Manumanu River, but they could not be landed in Redscar Bay owing to the swell. Just after we anchored, Seligmann shot a frigate bird. I particularly wanted one, as this is the sacred bird of the West Pacific, and enters so largely into the decorative art of the archipelagoes off the south-east end of New Guinea. The bird has a lordly flight, and it is a fine sight to see several of them sailing high in the air; it seemed cruel, however, to kill the poor thing. Unfortunately, the rats on board the schooner destroyed the skin.

As we could not land the previous night the captain gave us a chance next morning (May 31st); so we were called before 5 a.m., had cocoa and biscuits, and started before sunrise with the rest of the teacher's goods. The houses are of the ordinary Motu type, only slightly different from the Delena houses, and at high tide (as it was when we landed) some of the houses stand in the water with a long narrow gangway stretching to the beach above high water. We did a small trade in decorated lime gourds, bamboo pipes, and other objects. I found that the people made very little themselves, some of the specimens we bought came from Toaripi, over a hundred miles to the north-west, and others from Bulaa, seventy miles to the south-east! They apparently do not decorate the articles they make, and yet the women are very richly tattooed with various designs, but the men are only slightly so, and that chiefly a few broken lines on the face. I made a careful copy of the tattooing on the body and arm of one young woman; she posed excellently, and evidently felt very proud of her patterns being recorded, especially as a noisy crowd collected around us, and when I sketched a tattoo mark, the onlookers told her or touched the actual patterns as I drew them.

We also bought some flutes with two holes only, and one or two rounded stones which are used as charms to make the yams grow. We had great value for the hour and a quarter we were on shore; at leaving we saw several natives hacking away at a live turtle which was lying on its back, and happy children were collecting the blood in vessels. It was not an edifying spectacle. We parted in a very friendly spirit with the natives, and as the boat was leaving the shore I gave a scramble for bits of tobacco.

We entered the harbour of Port Moresby at one o'clock, and soon came to an anchorage off the Government offices. The Mission Station and village must be nearly two miles from the incipient township, and the Governor's Residency is between the two, but nearer the Mission premises.

As soon as the Hon. D. Ballantine, the Treasurer and Collector of Customs, had boarded us, we landed in his boat and called on the Hon. A. Musgrave, the Government Secretary. He received us very kindly, and promised to do all he could to forward my plans. He informed me that they were getting up a grand dance at Hula (Bulaa), and that as the harvest had been exceptionally good there was plenty of food, and the people had spare time. He expected inland tribes would come down, and that there would be a great crowd, perhaps a couple of thousand natives; but this proved to be one of those reports that arise one knows not where, and which disappear on inquiry like a morning mist. I gathered that the dance was got up for Sir William Macgregor and Lord Lamington. Naturally I was very keen to go, but as the *Olive Branch* would be delayed by having to be run up on the slip to be scraped and repaired, she would not be able to get down in time, so Mr. Musgrave very kindly offered me a Government schooner, which he immediately got ready, so that we might start as soon as possible.

I called on Mr. Gors, the manager of Burns, Philp, and Co., the great Queensland and New Guinea trading firm. He is a very pleasant fellow and a good man of business, who did what he could to help us. I noticed hanging up behind a door of the store a number of strings of worked shell, such as the natives wear round their necks all along the coast. As I was asking about them, two or three all but nude Papuan boys came into the store and bought a couple for one shilling each. It seemed so strange to see natives buying a native ornament, which is used as shell-money, in a large store with coin of the realm.

Had a busy time the following day arranging about our trip to the east and buying "trade" and "tucker." Everyone was very kind and helpful. Mr. Musgrave gave us dinner in the hotel, then we had afternoon tea in his house. I dined there in the evening, and later went on to Ballantine, who had an informal lantern show of local slides which were very interesting. A crew had been got together for us, so that we might start at daybreak the next day.

We got off early in the morning of June 2nd in the *Peuleule*, and arrived about four o'clock off Gaile, or Kaile (but the real name is Tava Tava), a marine pile village which is built perhaps a quarter of a mile from the shore on the fringing reef; but some houses are now built on the shore. Sir William Macgregor, the then Lieutenant-Governor, encouraged this innovation; but Mr. A. C. English, the very efficient Government agent for this district, states it is regrettable from a sanitary point of view, as the natives are far cleaner and healthier in their villages built over the salt water.

We were met by the teacher, a Port Moresby native, who accompanied us all the time and acted as interpreter. We photographed the village from the shore, with a group of natives on the sand beach. All the women were richly and thoroughly tattooed. We got off in a canoe paddled by girls, and clambered up the horizontal poles that serve as a ladder to one of the houses, and wandered from one end of the village to the other along the platforms. The planks of which the platforms are made are irregularly placed, often with spaces between them; and one has to cross from the platform of one house to another on poles which may be fastened or may merely be lying loose. The natives run along these easily with their bare feet, but we, with our boots on, found it a very different matter.

Crouching behind and beside the entrance of one house was a widow in mourning for her recently deceased husband; her head was shaved, her body smeared all over with charcoal, her chest was covered with netting, she wore a long petticoat, elongated tassels of grey seeds (*Coix lachrymæ*) hung from her

PLATE XIII

THE MARINE VILLAGE OF GAILE

BULAA

The largest of these plains is found in the Mekeo district, and here the natives seem to have advanced further from savagery in several respects than elsewhere on the mainland.

We arrived at Siruwai, or Kapakapa as it is generally called, about 12.30; after lunch we went ashore in a whale boat brought to us by the L.M.S. teacher, a native of Niue, an island in the South Pacific.

Kapakapa is essentially a marine village, but there are a few houses on the land, also several elaborately carved wooden platforms, or *dubus*. The *dubus* which are found in this region of New Guinea are taboo platforms, or stagings, on which the men sit and feast; here also they discuss private and public affairs. A *dubu* is, in fact, a sort of skeletonised club-house, which may not be approached by the women. (Plate XVII., A, p. 232.)

Close by, jutting above the level of the water, are a number of charred stumps which mark the site of the village of East Kapakapa, which was destroyed by a band of Bulaa men. All, or nearly all, the inhabitants were killed, and the village destroyed by fire, a repetition of the history of the Swiss pile dwellings. Wilkin photographed the burnt piles, and also some houses in process of manufacture. He and Seligmann stayed here while Ray and I walked a mile and a quarter to Vatorata (Vatororuata) to see Dr. Lawes, the revered L.M.S. missionary and well-known Papuan scholar.

There is a fair road along an alluvial valley-plain, through which a small river runs. Most of the plain is covered with a tall, coarse, broad-leafed grass, with clumps of trees. Dr. Lawes' house is situated on the spur of a moderately high steep hill. The Mission premises consist of 150 acres, all fenced in. The steep road immediately up to the house is lined by twenty students' houses, each of which is named by or after the donor. These comfortable little houses cost but £5 apiece to build. Beyond these is a well-built handsome church and school-house. The Mission residency is a large, comfortable, airy house, commanding a lovely view of mountains and lowland scenery.

Dr. Lawes, like most of the other white missionaries of the London Missionary Society, no longer does what may be termed ordinary evangelistic work in the midst of a village, this is performed by South Sea teachers, but he is practically solely occupied with the more important work of translating the Bible into Motu and in training native teachers, who here are all married men. The students, who come from various districts, can all read fluently, and are proficient in arithmetic up to fractions. They are well acquainted with the geography of Australasia, and are familiar with the position of Her Majesty the Queen with regard to the world and British New Guinea. Naturally they have mastered the main facts and principles of the Gospels. Their writing, as is generally the case in these native classes, is very good.

Mrs. Lawes superintends the domestic education of the teachers' wives. Each wife cuts out and sews the clothes of the family, plaits mats, does the washing, makes the starch and dresses her husband's shirts, prepares the food, and keeps the house clean and orderly. The husbands also work in their food-gardens, build the houses, and make the furniture. The advanced students conduct classes of younger ones.

I have gleaned most of the foregoing description from Sir William Macgregor's final report, and I cannot do better than quote his summing up. "As far as an experience of ten years can enable one to judge, the system of education and training initiated and now in force at Vatorata is so suitable to the circumstances of the country and to the character and condition of the natives, that it would be difficult to suggest any change that would be an improvement" (p. 50). No one has had a better opportunity of judging the value of the work done by Dr. and Mrs. Lawes than has the late Lieutenant-Governor of British New Guinea, and it would be unseemly for me to do more than add my testimony to the wisdom of their methods of training teachers.

In dealing with primitive peoples the problem is constantly arising how far it is wise that their mode of living should be altered seriously. I imagine that nobody objects to the humanising of natives, a term which I prefer to the somewhat ambiguous one of civilising. At the same time I cannot refrain from pointing out that, according to some whose opinion carries weight, the less primitive peoples are *Europeanised* the better it is for them.

Dr. and Mrs. Lawes gave us a very cordial reception—the former is a veritable patriarch, the latter is very bright, and from all we have heard and seen has proved herself to be a splendid missionary's wife. We had a most welcome shower-bath after the nearly as welcome afternoon tea. Dr. Lawes sent a note to

Mr. A. C. English, the Government Agent for the Rigo District, who lives a mile and a half inland, to come across to see us. A pencilled reply came that he was lying on the floor shivering with a temperature of 104°, and all his blankets atop of him. Scarcely had we finished dinner than in he walked, having adopted his usual plan of taking exercise to shake off an attack of fever. We had a very pleasant chat about British New Guinea, and I made some rubbings of two pipes from an inland tribe, the type of decoration of which was new to me.

We walked back to the village of Kapakapa, and happened on a dance. In most of the figures of the dance two parallel rows of dancers faced one another; the majority of the lads had drums, which they held in their left hand and beat with the extended fingers of the right. A number of lassies joined in the dance, and this was the first time in New Guinea I had seen both sexes dancing together. There was usually a girl between each lad, the girl on the boy's right hand put her left arm round his right arm.

CHAPTER XV

THE HOOD PENINSULA

WE started next day, and arrived at Hood Point at 4 p.m., but owing to the water being very shallow we anchored a long way from the shore. As we had no boat on board we were obliged to wait till someone took compassion on us, and it was not till after sunset that we were able to get away in a canoe with some of our gear. After a long paddle we passed between the land and the four hamlets of marine dwellings that constitute the village of Bulaa, or Hula, as it is generally called. These looked very picturesque. Dark stilted masses, upstanding from the silver-streaked calm sea, with its changing lights as the swell silently glided shorewards, the broken outlines of these strange homes were silhouetted by the bright moonlight, their blackness being occasionally relieved by the light of a fire.

On arriving at the beach near the London Missionary Society's Station we were met and most heartily greeted by the teachers, who proved themselves most cordial and hospitable. As one always finds in these Mission Stations, everything was tidy, in readiness, and beautifully clean; the table was covered with a cloth, and was decorated with flowers in vases, the four bedrooms fitted with mosquito nets and every requisite. These good people had not received any notice of our intended visit, but it is the common experience of travellers that the native teachers, like the missionaries themselves, are always ready for a casual traveller, and as invariably give him a warm welcome. It was very refreshing to have food served in a civilised manner after the rough accommodation of the boat. We were here much more comfortable and better fed, and vastly more nicely served, than in Murray Island. Seligmann visited and treated the chief's sick boy soon after we arrived, and the chief promised to send a canoe to fetch off Ontong, but his power was not strong enough to induce the men to go.

Sunday, June 5th.—We got up at 6.30, and found the teacher had made tea for us; the good man had also sent off a couple of boys in a canoe at 4 a.m. to bring Ontong and the rest of our goods. They arrived about seven o'clock. About 7.30, after a breakfast of hot soup and biscuits, we took a canoe to visit "German Harry," who was in charge of Mr. R. E. Guise's plantations while that gentleman made a trip to England. He took us in a two-horse buggy down the Hood peninsula, through the villages of Aruauna, Babaka, Kamali, to the very large and important village of Kalo.

The Hood peninsula has evidently been formed mainly by the Vanigela River. It is a low, level spit of sea sand and of alluvium brought down by the river, deposited in the salt water, and then heaped to leeward by the indirect action of the prevailing south-east wind. This combination makes a light, fertile soil. A considerable part of the peninsula consists of grass land, with scattered screw pines (Pandanus) and small trees, and here and there a few cycads. Occasionally there are patches of bush or jungle, and groves of coconut palms. There are also numerous gardens, which the natives keep in beautiful order.

The peninsula is divided into six lands, belonging to the Kalo, Kamali, Babaka, Makirupu, Oloko, and Diriga people. The last three villages were so decimated by sickness some three generations ago that there were few survivors, and the smaller numbers that still remain have been driven recently to Babaka by the Bulaa. The Bulaa people have planted many coconuts on the land, but the greater part belong to the three tribes mentioned. The Bulaa people now claim the land, and naturally this has been a cause of friction, as the Babaka and Kamali people resent the encroachment. The Government has taken the common-sense view, and recognised that it was necessary for Bulaa to have garden land; and as the Diriga land, which lies at the end of the peninsula, is practically unowned, the Government has had it surveyed and given Bulaa legal possession. The Kamali state they have been in occupation for ten generations, and that the land was unoccupied at the time of their first settlement on it.

The town of Kalo—for this is not too grand a term to employ in this instance—is situated at the base of the Hood peninsula close to the right bank of the Vanigela (Kemp Welch River) at its mouth. There are some magnificent houses here—all on piles, some of which are thirty feet in height and eighteen inches in diameter. It is very impressive to see great houses perched on such high and massive props. At the front of each house is a series of large platforms like gigantic steps. Some of the posts are partially carved, and occasionally the under surfaces of the house planks are also carved. I saw two representations of crocodiles and one of a man under a large steepled house. The planks employed for the flooring of the houses and platforms are often immense, and must represent a tremendous amount of labour, especially in the old days of stone implements; many of them are cut out of the slablike buttresses of great forest trees that grow inland. The wood employed for the great flooring planks is so hard that the boards are handed down from father to son as heirlooms, and the house piles last for generations.

Sir William Macgregor regards Kalo as the wealthiest village in British New Guinea. The people own rich alluvial gardens, and have a superabundance of coconuts, bananas, yams, sweet potatoes, and taro. They also grow numerous areca palms; the nuts of these palms are usually called betel nuts, and are in great demand for chewing with quicklime, and so constitute a source of wealth. The Kalo people also absorb the trade of the interior, as they command the mouth of the Vanigela. Feathers and feather ornaments, grass armlets, boars' tusks, bamboos, trees for canoes, wood for houses, and other jungle produce are retailed to the coast tribes, and fish, shell-fish, shell ornaments, and the like are traded in exchange.

It is interesting to note how the material prosperity of Kalo has made the people very conceited and not amenable to outside influence. Like Jeshurun of old, they have waxed fat and kicked, and they have readily listened on various occasions in the past to the counsels of their lusty neighbours of Keapara to oppose the Government. The story of the massacre of the Mission teachers in 1881 at the instigation of the chief is told by the Rev. James Chalmers in *Work and Adventure in New Guinea;* and in *Pioneering in New Guinea* he gives an account of how the massacre was punished by Commodore Wilson of the

Wolverene, on which occasion the chief lost his life. The marks of the bullets of the bluejackets in the palm-stems were pointed out to us.

So independent are the Kalo folk that they will not meet the Keapara people half-way for trade; so the women of the latter village have to trudge all round Hood Bay with their fish or other marine produce to barter for garden produce, and any day one may see Keapara women sitting in the village square of Kalo.

Hearing that there was to be a dance at Babaka, we walked there early in the afternoon of Monday, June 6th, accompanied by several boys and a couple of girls who carried our bags and cameras, and we were further escorted by four native police and a corporal. It was a hot walk down the peninsula for four and a half miles, across grassy plains, through the gardens and plantations of the natives. The bananas here are planted in regular rows, more evenly, we were informed, than anywhere else in the possession. We greatly appreciated the cool shade when the path meandered through the luxuriant bush.

On arriving at Babaka we climbed on the platform of a house, and rested in the shade and drank the cool, refreshing coconut water. A very disreputable-looking, dirty, aged ruffian came up and shook hands with Mr. English; his face was misshapen through disease, and one eye was bunged up. As is the custom here, his clothing consisted simply of a string. He has the reputation of being a successful dugong fisher and a great blackguard; the tattooing on his back shows that he has also taken human life. By the time I had copied his tattooing the dancing had commenced.

The men, carrying their drums, approached the dancing-ground with a prancing gait. Most of the men had a more or less yellow string as a garment; some had a nose skewer as well. In the crown of their black halo of frizzly hair was inserted a bunch of feathers, the most effective being a bunch of white cockatoo feathers, above which were reddish-brown and green, narrow feathers; from the midst of these arose a vertical stick covered with scarlet feathers. From the hair, and fastened to their armlets and leglets, streamed long ribands of crimped strips of pale yellow palm leaves. The cylindrical drums were also decorated with the same streamers and with seed rattles. They formed a brave show.

THE HOOD PENINSULA

In the first figure the men stood in three rows, the outer rows facing inwards; the third and middle row faced one of the other rows, and stood nearer to it than to the other. The men danced by slightly bending the knee and raising the heel, the toe not being taken off the ground, and as they bent their bodies their head-dresses nodded. A couple of girls danced at the end of two columns, facing the men. These girls were clothed with numerous petticoats of sago palm leaf dyed red, with flounces of white pandanus leaf; numerous shell necklaces with boars'-tusk pendants hung down their backs, and shell ornaments adorned their heads. 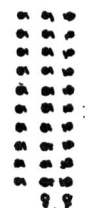 They placed their hands on their abdomen just above their petticoats, and swayed the latter from side to side without shifting their ground. I cannot describe the singing. The music consisted of paired drum-beats.

In the second figure, the central row of men all faced one way down the column except one end man, who faced them. The movements were the same as before; four girls now danced.

Next, the central men all faced the same way.

In the fourth figure the central men shifted their ground from side to side. The four girls at the one end grouped themselves into two couples, each pair took hold of hands, and all swayed their petticoats rhythmically from side to side. One or two girls had by this time joined the opposite end. Some girls swayed their petticoats more than others, and as the petticoats are fastened on the right side, the movement displays more or less of the thighs. A flighty girl often takes care that the two ends of the petticoat do not quite meet where they are tied, so as to increase the effectiveness of this swaying movement. Some girls kept their feet entirely on the ground, heels together, and toes separated; others moved the feet a little. They swung their arms backwards and forwards.

The fifth dance was a repetition of the first, and was repeated more than once, as were also some of the others.

Later, the men fell into seven rows of from four to six in each. All except those at one end faced one way, and these faced them.

There were now eight girls at one end, who stood in a row

and faced inwards, like the odd row of men. Two or three girls were at the other end dancing in the same way as girls, but one sidled up to a man and placed her arm round his, and danced demurely. I saw this done at Kăpăkăpă, and later on I saw it at Bulaa and Port Moresby. It is evidently the usual practice in ordinary dances, but I imagine the girl was not in order in introducing this style into this particular dance. All the men and the girls advanced and retreated slowly, moving their feet about three inches at a time; they covered only about a couple of feet of ground. In this figure the girls swung their petticoats forwards and backwards; the music consisted of a uniform series of beats.

In the next figure one end row of men defiled to the right of the others, and either danced up and down the column once and back to their places, or (as in B) they zigzagged up and down. The drums during most of this dance were held high up by the five or six men who were actively dancing.

The girls had rearranged themselves as in the diagram, and swayed their petticoats from side to side.

 In the last figure the two end rows left their places and faced one another as in the diagram, and after a little dancing all dispersed.

At the end of every figure the drums were beaten about a dozen times with relative rapidity, this being the signal that it was over. The same occurs in Torres Straits. The women's dancing appears to be subsidiary. I do not think that their exact position matters much. The variable number was, perhaps, due to their not being ready before.

This dance was one of a series which had been held in this village and in Kamali and Kalo. The last of the series was held the following morning.

After the dance a pig was caught by causing it to run its

snout into a coarse net, and then it was thrown down, several men sitting on it while others held its legs, which were next tied. The screaming and squealing of the pig and the shouts and laughing of the men were terrific; eventually the pig was fastened to a pole and left to await developments.

The fantastically dressed-up men who had been dancing collected on a sacred platform, or *dubu*, in the centre of the village; each carried a bunch of areca (betel) nuts. They then chanted a few sentences and finished off with a yell; and this was repeated two or three times, and an areca nut was thrown on the ground. This was a challenge to the other division of the village to make a similar dance next year.

This village, like so many others, is divided into two sections, each of which has its *dubu*. At these annual festivals only one division dances, the members of the other being spectators. If, for some reason, such as the death of an important man, a challenge is not taken up, there will be no dance the following year, which is a local misfortune.

A man of the other division stepped forward and picked up the areca nut; then those on the *dubu* broke up the bunches of the nuts and threw them among the spectators for a scramble, and a scene of hilarious excitement began. I joined in the scramble, and secured one or two nuts.

Shortly after this seven recently tattooed girls walked in a row up and down the broad open space in the village in front of the

FIG. 25. IRUPI DANCE, BABAKA

dubu. The *irupi* or *iropi* dance was to be performed by them, and the pigs for the feast had been provided by their relatives. The girls walked in a somewhat stately manner, and gracefully swung a cord of about three feet in length, to which a small netted bag was attached; the other end of the cord was attached to the waist-belt of the petticoat at the back. They swung it with the right hand, causing it to make a graceful sweep behind the back round to the left side, where it was caught by the left hand. During this manœuvre the whole body made a half turn. The action was then repeated with the left hand, the tassel being caught with the right hand. Up and down the little damsels walked, well pleased with themselves, and fully conscious that they were the centre of attraction; it was an elegant dance, and really quite charming. During the *irupi* dance some women sat on the *dubu* and beat the drums; this is the first time I have anywhere seen women beating drums, and it is only on this occasion that women may mount on a *dubu*. The movements of the girls were regulated by the staccato beats of the drums.

The same girls next ascended the *dubu* and stood in a row facing the village square. Two men then carried the pig, which was tied on to a pole, and stood in front of the girls. An old woman came and stood beside them; she was not ornamented in any way, whereas the girls wore numerous swagger petticoats; round their necks were as many necklaces and ornaments as they could muster, and some had wonderful shell head-dresses. The girls next took off all their petticoats and were anointed by the old woman, who dabbed each girl with a mixture of coconut oil and water by means of a bunch of wild thyme. As soon as the anointing was completed a drum was beaten, and the girls quickly dressed themselves and jumped down from the *dubu*. This ended one of the most interesting ceremonies it has been my lot to witness.

It is evident that the latter part of the ceremony is the most important, and that it is a fertility ceremony. I was told that it brought good luck to the plantations. It is interesting to note that here, as in India, and indeed in many parts of the world, the ceremony for ensuring a bountiful harvest is performed by the women.

The next day the pig was killed for the feast, and there was renewed dancing.

Mr. R. E. Guise, who has resided for over ten years in the Hood peninsula, has recently described this ceremony in the Journal of the Anthropological Institute (xxviii., 1899, p. 215). Apparently the second and principal part of the ceremony

PLATE XIV

GIRLS OF BABAKA DRESSED FOR THE ANNUAL
CEREMONY

GIRLS ON THE DUBU AT BABAKA FOR THE ANNUAL CEREMONY

(*kuiriga*) was somewhat abbreviated on the occasion when we witnessed it. As soon as the girls on the *dubu* have thrown their petticoats behind them, married women advance and place in front of each girl a basket containing a quantity of areca nuts, on the top of which are a few yams and a small knife. After the anointing, each girl takes a yam in her left hand and the knife in her right, and at each beat of the drum cuts off a piece of the yam, bends her knees, and slightly bows her head, causing the weighted head-dress to sway forwards. The whole effect is described as being wonderfully pretty. After each girl has cut up half a dozen yams the female orchestra give two sharp taps, and the drums cease beating. The girls immediately take up the baskets and pelt the crowd with the areca nuts; this part of the affair is much appreciated by the onlookers, who scramble for the nuts, tumbling over one another like children.

The girls quite enjoy the position, and do not show any shame. Very few, if any, men seem to care to look on the ceremony, old women, widows, and married women who have daughters constituting the majority of the bystanders.

I had previously known about this ceremony and understood that it was of an indecent character, but my experience quite corroborates these statements of Mr. Guise. I must confess to feeling surprised that the men took no notice at all of the girls, and it was perfectly evident that this was regarded by them as solely a woman's ceremony.

One day we started in the early morning to visit Keapara (Kerepunu). Mr. A. C. English, the Government Agent for the Rigo District, had followed us to Bulaa, and he took us in his whale-boat. After rowing for a long time in a heavy sea against a head wind Mr. English found that the wind and tide were too strong for us to cross Hood Bay; so the sail was set, and we ran down the bay to Kalo. To windward of the mouth of the Vanigela is a sand-bar, which deepens as it projects into the bay, and over this the breakers came rolling in with any amount of surf and flying spray. We had a few anxious moments as the boat was carried along through the seething water, but we got safely through into the quiet water beyond, and then rode into the mouth of the river, a vision of fairy calm and beauty. Nipa palms erected their rigid fern-like leaves directly from the water; they were banked by varied tropical foliage, and shooting skywards were the slender white stems of the coconut palms with their waving leafy crowns.

After a short spell we walked for eight miles along the sand beach round the bay till we came to the entrance of Hood lagoon, over which we were ferried in a canoe, and on arriving at Keapara we were hospitably received by Tau and his wife, the L.M.S. South Sea teacher, who gave us afternoon tea before we visited the village.

The sand beach in front of the village presented a busy scene; until now I had not come across such activity as was here displayed. Several canoes were being made, and not only was there a continuous succession of chopping noises, but the sense of smell was also affected, partly by the smoke of the fires, but mainly by the very disagreeable odour given out by the soft wood as it is chipped by the adzes.

The trees of which the canoes are made grow up the Vanigela River; they are cut down, and their trunks are floated down the stream to its mouth. The Kalo men sell the lumber to the Keapara men, who tow it to their village. The outside of the canoes is cut with steel tomahawks obtained from the white man, but the logs are hollowed out with stone adzes, the stone blade of which can be shifted round to any angle by turning the holder on the shaft. It seems strange that these primitive shipwrights should prefer stone implements to iron ones for hollowing out the canoes; perhaps it is because they are frightened lest the sharper iron blade should inadvertently cut through the thin side of the hull. After the canoes are dug out and trimmed down they are charred by fires lit outside and inside them; the effect of this is to harden the wood, and I suppose to somewhat fill up the pores so as to make the craft more seaworthy. I believe that one result of applying fire to the canoes is to make them open out more widely. Probably in precisely the same manner, save that no metal tool was available, our Neolithic ancestors manufactured their canoes. It was an unexpected pleasure to have this glimpse into the Stone Age.

Sitting on the sand beach was a man chipping out a wooden bowl from a piece of the same kind of wood as that of which the canoes were made. He employed a small adze, constructed on the same principle as that of the large adzes used in canoe making. In this instance the blade was made of iron, but so

PLATE XV

HOLLOWING OUT A CANOE WITH STONE ADZES AT KEAPARA

A BULAA GIRL BEING TATTOOED

fashioned as precisely to resemble the original stone blade; subsequently I procured a small stone adze. We photographed the man at work, and, as we have experienced often, he took no notice of us; but he appeared to be much surprised when I bargained for his implement and the unfinished bowl. A native cannot in the least understand why one wants to purchase an unfinished article and the tool with which it is being made.

The Keapara natives buzzed round us like flies, offering for sale "curios" of all kinds and sea shells; often the former were broken and worthless specimens. One did not know which way to turn, so persistent were they, and the din was deafening. Well did they maintain their reputation for being keen, and whenever possible, unprincipled traders; still we did very well and got our things reasonably enough. I understand that they live principally by barter, not only locally, but also doing some trading up and down the coast.

Next morning we paid a visit to the adjoining fishing village of Alukune, or Harukune, which is situated on the other side of the point of land on which Keapara stands. The natives, as is usually the case with fisher-folk in Europe, keep very much to themselves, but here they have good reason for this aloofness. The more powerful Keapara men have for generations been in the habit of levying toll from them in the shape of fish and other marine produce. The Alukune possessed no land, and were not allowed to acquire any, though the Keapara had more than enough for their own wants. Vegetable food being a necessity, the Alukune women either had to go to Kalo for it or had to buy it from their Keapara neighbours, giving fish in exchange, but the latter, being the stronger tribe, were able to obtain the fish at a very cheap rate. They were not only oppressed in this and other ways, but their women were seized and taken as wives by Keapara men. Some thirty-eight years ago half the village, driven to desperation by the oppressions of their neighbours, left in a body and settled at Hood Point, and built the village of Bulaa. The other half who remained were still held in subjection by Keapara, and their condition was but little improved since the old days until very recently, and even now they do not appear to be in a happy or thriving condition.

Although the inhabitants of Alukune are fisher-folk, they obtain their canoes from Keapara, and in return they have to pay half the catch; in other words, they have to trade on the half-profit system. We obtained very little in this village, but I cut some samples of children's hair, to the amusement of the onlooking crowd and to the great perplexity of the children themselves. The children were playing with toy miniature bows and arrows made from the mid-ribs of palm leaflets.

Just before we started in the whale-boat English arrested a man for petty larceny, and we had an exhibition of native grief. Men and women rushed up to the prisoner as he was being handcuffed and led off to the boat, rubbing noses and applying their mouths to his cheek, but I did not hear any actual kissing. On all sides was weeping and wailing; many clawed the sides of their heads and faces either on one or both sides; some beat their heads and faces, clasped hands were wrung alternately on each side of the head at the level of the ear, frequently the clasped hands were held at the back of the head. There was a great deal of tragedy for very little cause, as the man was going for only a week's imprisonment, or rather a week of forced labour on roadmaking. The comic element was that he had picked a policeman's pocket.

We had a spanking sail across the bay, and had a second breakfast on our arrival soon after eleven. About 12.30 Wilkin and I walked over to Babaka to take some more photographs. Ray worked that afternoon at languages, and Seligmann had a very profitable time testing the keenness of the eyesight of the natives.

During the next few days we got through a fair amount of anthropological measurements and other work. We persuaded some girls to demonstrate the process of tattooing, which we photographed. The girl to be tattooed lay on the ground, and the operator held a special clay vessel in one hand, in which was a black fluid paste made from burnt resin; this was applied on the skin by means of a little stick. When the design was finished a thorn was held in the left hand, while in the right hand was a small stick round which strips of banana leaves were wound. The thorn was lightly tapped with the stick until the pattern had been well punctured into the skin.

When a Papuan has a headache, or indeed any other kind of ache, an attempt is generally made to alleviate the pain by letting blood. Usually this is done by cutting the part affected with sharp shells or fragments of glass, or with anything handy

PLATE XVI

A NATIVE OF BULAA

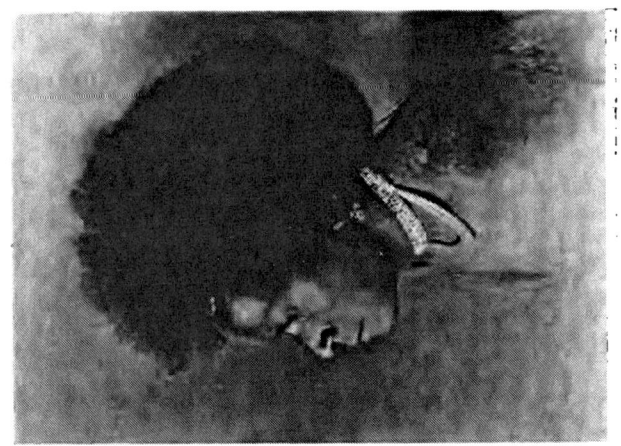

A BULAA YOUTH WITH RINGWORM

that has an edge; but here, and in a few other places, the phlebotomy is also performed by shooting with a diminutive bow and arrow. The bow is made of two or three pieces of the mid-rib of palm leaflets tied together, the string being a strand of vegetable fibre. The arrow is also a mid-rib of a palm leaflet tipped with a splinter of glass (originally a thorn formed the point); the shaft passes between two of the components of the arc of the bow, and the butt is tied on to the bow-string. Owing to this arrangement the arrow, when it is pulled rhythmically and let go, punctures the skin on or about the same spot.

Whilst in Bulaa I added very largely to my collection of samples of the hair of the natives. The Papuan belongs to the group of men who have dark skins and black woolly or frizzly hair. The hair is very much like that of the true negro, but it grows much longer. In some parts of New Guinea the hair is usually worn rolled into numerous cords, which hang down all round the head like a thrum mop, but among most of the people of the south-eastern part of the Possession the hair is combed out so as to form a very characteristic aureola, which is the glory of a Papuan dandy. It is astonishing, however, the number of people one finds in this part of New Guinea with curly, and even wavy hair. In a few cases the hair is almost quite straight, whereas, as I have remarked, the hair of the typical Papuan is frizzly or woolly, and so far as I am aware it is universally so among the hill tribes of the interior, among the inhabitants of the Papuan Gulf, and indeed all over the western portion of British New Guinea. This variability in the character of the hair evidently points to a racial mixture here. I was also surprised to find in this district the tips of the hair vary from dark to quite a pale brown or a tan colour, though the roots are black. I naturally put this down to bleaching, owing to the use of lime for sanitary purposes; but Mr. English assured me that it is a natural colour, a fact of some interest and perplexity.

The marine pile dwellings of the village of Bulaa probably present, at all events at a distance, much the same appearance as did the lake dwellings of Central Europe in prehistoric times. People have wondered how the primitive Swiss drove in the piles that supported their houses. This question can only be answered approximately by noting what people do nowadays. I therefore asked Mr. English to arrange to have the process of pile-driving exhibited.

A post was procured, one end of which was roughly pointed, and to the other extremity two long ropes were tied. One man scooped a hole on the reef at low tide with his hands; the pile was then propped up in the hole by several men. Two or three men steadied the post, while several caught hold of each guy and gently swayed it to and fro; the men who clasped the pole prevented it from overbalancing. Gradually by its own weight the pile is thus wormed into the ground. I was informed that when a pile is sunk actually in the sea a light staging is erected near the top of the post; two or three men stand on this framework, so that by their extra weight the pile may sink more readily.

One day we saw Neolithic men making canoes at Keapara, and here at Bulaa we saw the pile-dwellers at work with a marine pile-village in the background.

I spent a fair amount of time on various occasions in getting a number of small boys to make toys and play games, several of which we photographed. Very little is known about the toys and games of the children of savage peoples, and judging from the interest and anthropological value of the study of the amusements of our own children, these will prove an important field for research when more facts are available. I played a good deal with the children, to their and my amusement. I also showed them one or two of our games, such as cock-fighting and hand-slapping; but I think they were not sufficiently impressed by them to adopt them. I mention this, however, in case a future traveller should find them still practised.

Toys made of leaves were common. The small boys cut off pieces about ten to twelve inches in length from the origin of the leaves of a tall, coarse grass that is used in thatching houses. The blade is split off from each side of the mid-rib for about half its length; the two flaps are twisted round the index finger of the right hand, and the cleared mid-rib is held between the thumb and middle finger; the hand is jerked, and the tearing off of the remaining portion of the blade of the leaf gives a considerable impetus to the mid-rib, which thus flies away like a miniature javelin. This was the simplest method of playing, but there were three others, two of which necessitated the use of both hands; the principle of gaining the impetus was the same in all.

I was informed that this game is also played at Mawatta, a village on the Torres Straits coast of British New Guinea, but I do not know whether it occurs throughout the intermediate coast.

Rushes are twisted into diamond-shaped objects named *kuru*, they are said to be stuck in houses for play. A Mawatta man claimed that his people also made them, and said, "We look at hill, and make him all the same."

The following are all made of coconut palm leaves.

Lauga consists of two strips, each with three slits in them; the puzzle is to make or to undo the interlacing as shown in the figure (p. 226).

The simple whirligig *make* is a very widely spread toy. It is also found in the Solomon Islands in Melanesia, and in Funafuti (Ellice Group) and Rotumah in Polynesia.

A toy wind instrument is made of strips of palm leaf wound spirally so as to form a hollow cone or funnel, which varies from three inches to about a foot in length. Inserted in the cavity are two long narrow strips of leaf, or one long piece doubled upon itself; in either case two similar ends project through the narrow orifice to form a "reed."

It may not be amiss to explain that there are two main groups of simple wind instruments that are blown by the mouth. In one the lips are applied to the simple orifice, and it is their vibration intensified by the sounding chamber of the instrument that produces the noise. The conch shell and the trumpet are familiar examples of this group.

In the second group there is a vibrating arrangement which is technically termed a "reed." This group is divided into two classes: (*a*) the "oboe" or "shawm" series in which the fixed or removable mouthpiece is a tube, the ends of which are pinched together; (*b*) the "clarinet" series which has a single vibrating tongue. The Bulaa toy may be regarded as a kind of oboe.

I was delighted to find this musical toy, as I remembered that my friend Henry Balfour, the curator of the Pitt-Rivers Museum at Oxford, had recently written a paper on a very similar instrument, the "whithorn," which was made of spirally wound strips of willow bark. I have since learned from Mr.

Balfour that in Somersetshire these are called "Mayhorns," and very similar spirally twisted rude oboes (also of bark) have been recorded from France, Germany, and Finland in Europe. A spirally twisted palm-leaf trumpet (?) is found in West Africa, and similar instruments from Flores, Sumatra, and Celebes, but I am not quite certain of the exact nature of these latter. The Bulaa name for this instrument is *vili vili*. A Mawatta man at

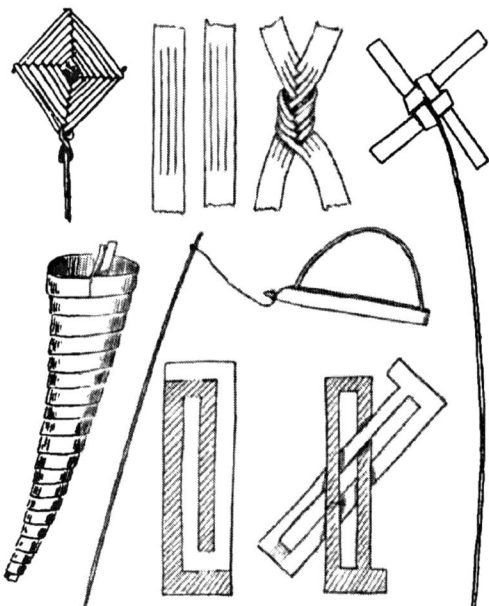

FIG. 26. PALM-LEAF TOYS, BULAA

Bulaa told me his people made it, where it was called *upa*, but I was not able to check this statement.

The occurrence of a reed instrument in this part of the world was so surprising that further inquiries were necessary, and Mr. English found out, after much questioning, that the toy was introduced by Johnson, a West Indian negro.

Hereby hang two useful warnings, whether this fact be true or not. First, not to assume an object is native to the district because it is found there, but always to make inquiries.

Secondly, the need for investigations, for in a few years all knowledge of the origin of this particular toy would be forgotten. These reflections hold good for other objects in all parts of the world. A few months later I found that at Mabuiag, in Torres Straits, a bent leaf of the *karbe* tree is used as a whistle by blowing with it between the lips.

Once I thought I was on the track of a bull-roarer, and was much excited thereby, as that remarkable implement has not been recorded south-east of the Papuan Gulf; but *kwari kwari* proved to be a new kind of toy that makes a noise like a fly buzzing, or the flying of a large grasshopper. It is made of a strip of palm leaf bent upon itself, one end of which is tied by a short bit of fine fibre to a long thin mid-rib. The two flaps of the strip are kept apart by a thin bent mid-rib of a palm leaflet. The whole is then whirled round.

A modification of the *lauga* puzzle is one in which the same strip of palm leaf is cut into two links. On looking closely, one finds that it is made thus: cut a piece of leaf (cardboard will do, but then the method of manufacture is too evident) right through the thick lines in the accompanying figure; cut half through the thickness of the leaf, or card, along the dotted lines, then split the material between these lines, and separate the upper and lower surfaces; the white portion will come away from the shaded link, as in the second figure; the two projecting spurs can be cut away if thought desirable. I cannot imagine how the natives found this out—that is, if it is their own invention; and they assure me such is the case.

Small cone shells are spun between the thumb and fingers like a teetotum.

Our old friend leap-frog is also a diversion for Papuan boys, as it occurs at such widely-spread places as Bulaa and Kiwai. A row of boys stand in a line some distance apart on their hands and feet; the last boy leaps over the others in succession, putting his hands on their backs in the usual way. He then takes his place in front of the others, and the now "last man" follows. This appears to be a very widely-spread game. In Korea and Japan it is called "jumping over," and the same attitude on all-fours is taken there as in New Guinea. In England we stand on our legs only, and "tuck in our tuppenny."

We also saw the children indulging in the familiar pig-a-back (*pĕkĕkau*), hopping (*kaikai*), jumping (*puri*), and skipping.

In the game called *evanena* two rows of boys face one another. Each boy takes hold of the arm of the boy opposite him at or immediately above or below the elbow with one hand, with the other hand he clasps his own arm, right hand may grasp the left arm or *vice versâ*. This position is similar to our "king's chair" or "queen's chair" with the exception that we clasp the wrist and not the arm. As all the boys stand close together they form a double row with a platform of arms between them. A small boy is placed standing on the arms of the last pair of boys, and he walks forward on those of the boys in front. As soon as he has left the last pair of boys they rush forward and place themselves in front of the others, and clasp their arms as before. In this way a continuous platform is maintained, and the game continues till the walker tumbles off. This game is also played at Elevara, Port Moresby.

A variant which I saw played at Elevara is called *omoro*, or "frog." In this case the boy, instead of walking on the arms, lies full length on his stomach, and is jerked up and down and at the same time forwards. Ray also saw this game played at Saguana, Kiwai Island, where it is called *mere kereme beretsi* ("boy-throwing").

The prettiest revolving game was that known as *maki gegelaki*. Four boys laid at full length on the ground at right angles to one another, so as to form a cross, with their feet touching; usually they placed a large piece of the husk of a coconut in the centre, against which they tightly pressed their feet. A small boy crouched on their feet to steady them. Four other boys stood between those lying down; they caught hold of their hands; this raised the arms and bodies of the latter. The standing boys walked round and round (right hand to centre), and the whole contrivance revolved like a four-spoked wheel.

Rapurapu. Four boys sit on the ground and interlock their legs in the form of a square in such a way that the instep of the right foot hooks over the pit of the knee of the boy to the right. They then stand up and hop round on the left foot, clapping their hands rhythmically and singing:—

> "*Rapu rapu tabai manu*
> *Roroiatĕ atĕ atĕ*
> *Roroiatĕ bada raita*
> *Eaiimo eai eaiimo.*"

As in Europe, the children have singing games, some of which I have observed are:—

Kwaito pinupinu. A number of boys form a circle, catching hold of each other's hands, facing inwards. Two run into the circle and under the arms of two other boys; when all the others have run under, the last two twist themselves under their own arms, and the circle is now complete again, but all the boys face outwards. They then revolve sideways as fast as they can, gradually accelerating their speed till one boy tumbles down. They all sing during the evolution:—

"*Maru gĕno o, ana kwaito o, pinupinu o, kwaito pinupinu o,—ai!*"

Mota ĕrĕmpto. A number of boys stand in a circle, each boy catching hold of his neighbour's wrists. One boy stands in the centre with arms folded over his chest. The encircling boys sing:

"*Mota erempto erempto
Bariva derempto derempto
Mota tim
Bariba tim
Pekuluoa waiau—o.*"

This sounds like a challenge, and immediately the rhyme is finished, the central boy rushes at the joined hands of any two boys and tries to burst through. The game is finished when he succeeds.

Korikini. Some half-dozen boys sit in a circle very close together; each holds the first or index finger of his hands upwards, closing the thumb and other fingers of one hand on the extended index of the other, or on that of another boy; in this way a column of hands is made, the uppermost having its free index finger pointing upwards. One boy alone has his right hand disengaged; with the forefinger he taps the uppermost index finger crosswise. The following is sung during the operation:—

Korikini korikini,   *papa raurirauri marire*
  Stick up finger   crossing one another
Agiana   *korikoana*   *karigămuai.*
  I look   take away finger   under armpit.

The top hand is then removed and placed under the armpit of the nearest boy. The tapping song is repeated for the next hand, which is similarly placed under the armpit of the boy that happens to be nearest. When all have their hands placed under the armpits, the same boy as before gently scratches each hand in rotation while singing:—

Pika pika kiaka pa
Gaule aule kiaka pa.

The first hand to be released is placed in the middle of the player's palm uppermost, and each succeeding hand is placed upon it in the same manner; sometimes the two hands of a player are placed side by side; the whole pile of hands is raised up and down. One boy with a disengaged hand gently taps the uppermost of the pile of hands three times, holding his index finger vertically downwards while he sings:—

Toitoi tutumu; keanai nunapakau.
Three times tap ear hold him.

At the end of the refrain the tapped hand is removed, and the nearest ear of the next player is held by it. When all the hands have been released and every ear is held by a hand, the players swing their bodies backwards and forwards, and pulling each other's ears with more or less vigour, all sing:—

Mekeri aria
Pull one another.
Kiko aria.

This continues until one of the players gives in.

The words for the ear-pulling may apparently be varied, as some children once sung:—

Wapuri poto
Kaia poto
i i i.

Mr. Ray saw the *korikini* game played at Saguane, where it is called *kuke*.

Kinimali. This is a very similar game to the foregoing. The players, however, pinch up the skin of the back of each other's hands, the slightly flexed hands being placed one on the top of the other. The whole column is swayed up and down to the following song:—

Kinimali lĕkwa lĕkwa
Pinch flesh let go
Malawa   kĕta kĕta
(name of a yam) (name of a yam)
Ana olio malauli
Run   a little boy
Polaia polai.
Yellow

When this is finished, the top hand is placed at the bottom of the column, palm uppermost, with extended fingers. The song is repeated until all the hands are placed the one on the top of the other. The Toitoi phase then finishes the game.

There appears to be considerable variation in these songs; we found it very difficult to write them down, and when we did, it was still more difficult to get a satisfactory translation; indeed, as with us at home, some words do not appear to have a meaning. This is also the case with many of the men's legendary songs, the meaning of which is now completely forgotten.

During our stay at Bulaa, we had one or two opportunities of seeing the young people amuse themselves by dancing on the sand beach. All those young men who had drums held them in their left hands and beat them with their extended right hands; one man rhythmically tapped the inside of his lime gourd with its spatula. The girls edged themselves between the men, linking their arms within those of the men. The drum-beats were in triplets (||| ||| |||). There was very little movement in the dancing. The men flexed their knees slightly, and the girls swayed their petticoats laterally; in some figures they swayed them backwards and forwards.

There were numerous figures, or separate small dances, in the Bulaa dances. In one that was often repeated the majority of the dancers formed a ⊓ shaped group, lads and lassies alternating; all these remained in their places. Other dancers, men only, advanced in couples, beating their drums and capering up the central space. In some figures the dancing men zigzagged across the space in a prancing manner as they proceeded up and down; in others they formed two parallel rows, all facing one side of the hollow oblong, and pranced sideways a few steps up and down the space. Then they jumped right round, so as to face the opposite way, and repeated the same process; then back again, and so on. In this dance the girls swayed their petticoats backwards and forwards.

In one figure groups of three—a man and two girls—stood in a series of rows. The active dancing men with drums came up and stood in a row along one side facing the others, and sang a song to the beats of the drums. After doing this three times, they ran round one end of the stationary column, and repeated the song on the other side, facing the others as before.

In another figure all the men and girls formed numerous short rows; this was, I believe, a Motu dance. The men in some of the figures formed a parallel row facing one another, with four others in the middle facing towards one end; the girls were at one end of the short avenue, and they swayed their petticoats laterally. The men then grouped themselves into two rows facing one another at right angles to the previous row. Then the first figure was repeated, only the two rows of men faced outwards instead of inwards, and the central pairs also reversed their previous position.

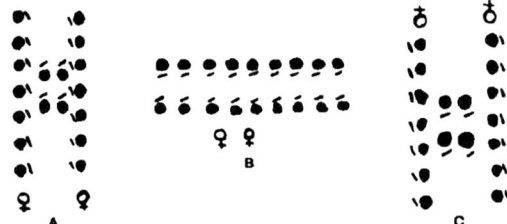

It is characteristic of some of the dances in the Hood peninsula for the girls to be, as it were, appendages to the dance rather than active participators in it. They make the minimum amount of movement, usually standing their ground, or else slowly advancing and retreating with the general movements of the men. They sway their petticoats sideways, or backwards and forwards; the latter is only a slight movement, but the former is more energetic, and (owing to the petticoat being tied on the right side and the two ends scarcely meeting) exhibits portions of the person which are ordinarily never exhibited, but the tattooing, which is liberally distributed all over the body, gives a half impression of clothing.

I noticed that one figure often merges into another, in which the positions of the dancers are reversed. It is difficult to

PLATE XVII

THE DUBU AT KAMALI

DUBU DANCE AT GOMORI DOBO

follow and record all the various movements, but I received the impression that if one could become familiar with the various figures one would find that there is a regular and fairly logical sequence of figures in each of the sets of dances.

There is a dance-leader, or master of ceremonies, and when he gives the signal the drums are rapidly beaten many times in succession to show that set is finished. The character of the dancing was quite similar to that we saw at Babaka, but it is entirely different from the dancing in Torres Straits and the neighbouring coast of British New Guinea. In the west, according to my experience, men and women never dance the same dance together; the single exception known to me was in the case of a particular war dance, *kawaladi*, at Mabuiag, after a successful foray. Only one or two drums are beaten, and that, so far as I saw, never by those actually engaged in dancing; indeed, the drum-men sit down to beat their drums. Further, only certain people have the right to beat drums, whereas in this part of New Guinea every male dancer may have a drum, which he holds in his hand and often flourishes about when he is dancing.

Although probably every religious ceremony has its appropriate dance or dances, I do not believe that all dancing has a magical or religious significance. I think it would be impossible to prove whether all dances arose from magical or religious dancing; if it be so, this must have been hundreds, or perhaps thousands of years ago; and all record, or even all suspicion of their origin must in some cases have long since disappeared. Here, as in Torres Straits, there are certainly play or secular dances—dances for pure amusement and without any ulterior design.

Some of the men looked very effective with their lithe figures and supple limbs of a bright, warm brown, almost copper-coloured skin, with shell and bead frontlets and a tall stick of scarlet and orange feathers starting up from their dark, bushy hair. Some had shell nose-skewers, most painted their faces in various devices with black paint; round their necks were bead and shell necklaces, sometimes with a pendant boar's tusk, and armlets and leglets decorated the limbs. The sole article of dress, in the usual acceptance of the term, is a narrow, yellow waist-belt, which also passes between the legs; streamers of a whitish leaf fluttered from various portions of the body.

The girls in these ordinary dances were not specially decorated, at all events in comparison with the men.

During our stay at Bulaa, Ray gave several phonograph demonstrations and recorded some of the local songs. The natives were never tired of listening to the machine, and fully appreciated singing into it, and were very delighted at hearing their songs repeated by it. Altogether we had a very pleasant and profitable trip to this district.

We left Bulaa on June 15th about 9 a.m., and had a fine sail to Kăpăkăpă, arriving there at 12.30. All of us went to call on Dr. and Mrs. Lawes at Vatorata in the afternoon, and received, as before, a kindly welcome. Had afternoon tea, and then on to a small neighbouring Ikoro village of Tagama Keketo, but there was not much to be done there. We saw here a tame white cockatoo, fastened by the leg to a ring chipped out of a coconut which slid along a horizontal pole; subsequently we found this was frequently done in New Guinea. As I have previously stated, the natives are very fond of decorating themselves with feathers, and they wear great bunches of white cockatoo feathers in their hair when dancing. These unfortunate tame cockatoos are periodically plucked to supply feathers for these occasions. After dinner, Ray exhibited the phonograph in the schoolhouse to the students, and continued his philological studies.

We got up early next morning, and Seligmann, Wilkin, and I went to breakfast with Mr. English. We saw his station, which is placed on a hill, and all around are thriving plantations of economic plants that he has introduced into the district, such as coffee, sisal agave, and rubber; the *makimaki* rubber has been named *Ficus rigo* by Mr. Bailey, the Queensland botanist.

Then we walked to Gomoridobo, where Wilkin took some photographs, one of which was of a man carving a post for their new *dubu*. We bought a few things, and I obtained two samples of hair; even here the wavy hair occasionally occurs, and there is a yellowish and brownish tinge in the hair at its tips, especially in young children. The wavy hair proves that there has been racial mixture at least five miles from the coast, or more probably a mingling with coast people, who must have been of mixed origin when they arrived.

Got back to Vatorata at 11.15, and shortly afterwards Dr. Lawes drove us down to Kăpăkăpă, and after a pleasant sail we reached Port Moresby at sunset.

CHAPTER XVI

PORT MORESBY AND THE ASTROLABE RANGE

I HAVE as yet said very little about Port Moresby. It is a commodious bay with an inner portion (Fairfax Harbour), which is land-locked. The double bay is surrounded by thinly wooded hills, and when these are brightened in places by the rising sun the effect is very beautiful. In full sunlight during the time we were there, there was generally a haze which greatly diminished the interest of the scene, but in the evening, especially a cloudy one, the hills again stood out clearly.

The small township lies on the north side of the neck of the promontory that forms the eastern limit of the bay; about a mile and a half off is the solitary Government House, and about half a mile beyond this again is the Mission Station. On the shore, below the hill on which the Mission stands, is the large stilted village commonly known as Hanuabada; off this is the rocky isle of Elevera, with its village of similar amphibious pile-dwellings, for at high tide they are completely surrounded by water.

The township or Granville, as it is officially termed (Ela is the native name for the locality), consists of a few Government offices and the houses of residents, most of whom are either Government officials or else connected with Burns Philp's Store. The jetty was built by Burns Philp at considerable expense, and at the foot of it lies their big store. This great trading company has ramifications all over Queensland and British New Guinea, and Port Moresby is naturally an important centre for their trade.

Apart from its remoteness from the world, the very bad postal arrangements, and the absence of a telegraph, Port Moresby is to my mind a much nicer place to live in than Thursday Island. The residents proved themselves very friendly and obliging.

Were it not for home-ties and duties I should very well like to make it my headquarters for a year or two. A certain amount of work could be done on the spot, and a very great deal by taking longer and shorter excursions from it. It appears to be a healthy locality, especially at the time of the year when we were there, and, what is of great importance in the tropics, we did not find the nights too hot.

Knowing that I was anxious to see a little of some inland people, Messrs. Musgrave and Ballantine arranged a three-days trip to the Astrolabe Range. Five horses were kindly loaned by the Government and the Vaigana Company. We packed our swags on Friday afternoon and fastened them on to the saddles before sunset. Each took with him a blanket, a spare flannel shirt, a pyjama suit, a tin of meat, some tobacco and handkerchiefs for trade wrapped up in a yard of American cloth. We also tied to our saddles a pannikin and hobbles for the horses, and carried bread and biscuits for the journey. Cameras, spare boxes of plates, and two water bottles were distributed among the party.

At three o'clock in the morning of Saturday, June 18th, Ballantine came to the hotel to wake us, and we dressed with despatch and went to Musgrave's to saddle the horses. This took some time, as it was quite dark, and there were several little details of girths and straps that required arranging. Musgrave was about and very kindly had cocoa made for us. We started about 4 a.m. in single file; the intense darkness was relieved by the shining of the stars. The positions of the constellations known to me presented a novel appearance, as one was not accustomed to be up so early.

We wended our way past the gaol and along the coast to the east, through occasional plantations and wooded country. After about an hour's walk we passed through a village, silent with the death of sleep, the only sign of life being two fires on the ground, the embers of which, fanned by the continuous breeze, were still glowing.

The calls of various birds were answered by the stridulation of insects as the eastern heavens gradually grew lighter, and we began to see something of the district in which we were travelling. The noises of nature became more marked as the dawn advanced, but there was little that can be described as singing made by the birds, though many of the cries were decidedly

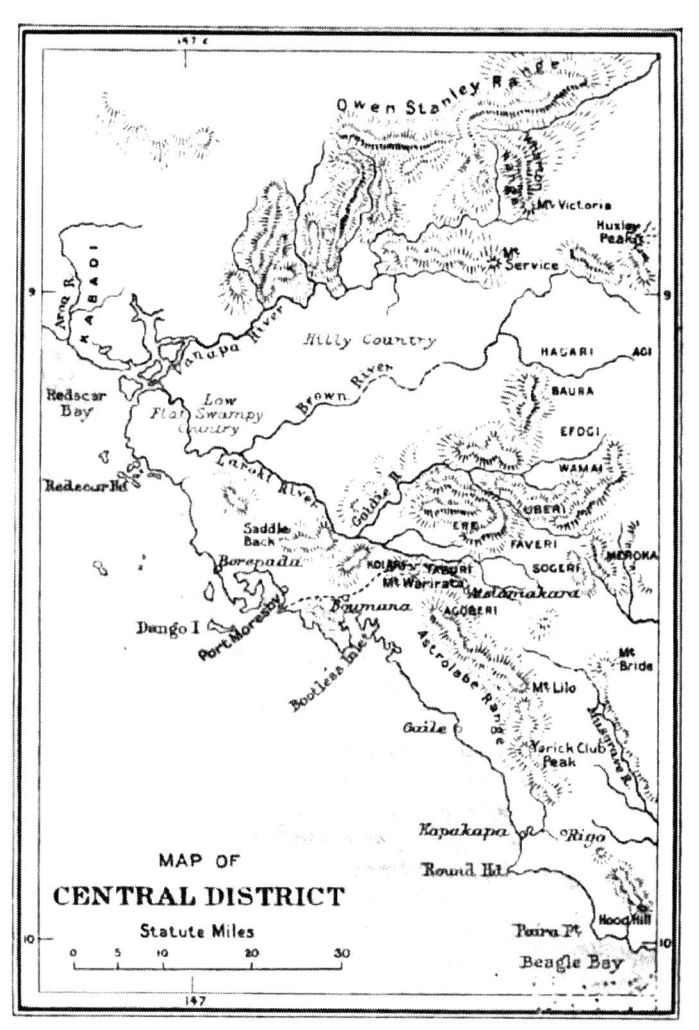

musical. Soon after sunrise we passed through Boumana, a plantation station owned by Peter Lifu, and situated nine miles from Port Moresby. It was only after passing this that we were able to trot or canter. Here the country consisted of grassy plains with scattered gum trees and occasional screw pines. In places the grass was as high as the horses, individual stems being as high as the rider as well. As we went inland cycads became more numerous; as a general rule these appear to die off when they reach a height of eight or ten feet, though I saw a few that exceeded that height.

In course of time we entered a more hilly country, and it was in places very rough on the horses, as there were steep gullies down which they cautiously picked their way, and up which they clambered like cats. On the plains there was a single track, but a road had been cut out of the side of the hills, or a broad avenue cleared through the dense jungle. Most of the country was sparsely wooded with a clothing of rank, coarse grass and had a very Australian aspect, as the trees were mostly eucalyptus, bastard gums, and a tree that looked like the Australian spotted gum, but with rather smaller leaves. An occasional wallaby hopping in the grass and small flocks of white cockatoos that screeched as they flew, gave a further Australian colour to the scene.

The ranges of mountains and hills in this part of New Guinea run as a rule in a north-west south-east direction—that is, roughly, parallel with the coast-line; geographically speaking, they are well-dissected, folded mountain chains. All are more or less wooded right up to their summits. As we were going obliquely across the trend of the hills we naturally had a lot of uphill and down-dale travelling, though the track took advantage of all available lateral spurs.

After the coast hills had been passed we saw looming in front of us the precipitous Astrolabe Range, rising abruptly from hilly ground and forming a huge rampart stretching away to the south-east, occasional peaks rising higher than the general level of the fairly uniform edge. On the flanks of this range, and indeed all the way up as far as the summit, were masses of volcanic breccia, which stood out black and sinister from the grass, some of the blocks being of enormous size. I was greatly exercised in my mind whether these blocks had weathered out *in situ* like the Devonshire tors and the granitic blocks one sees on the sides of the Dartmoor hills. This may be the case in some instances, but I noticed many blocks with distinct stratification, the plane of which was vertical or nearly so; these must either have been ejected fragments or boulders that had rolled down from some greater height, but the latter was by no means obvious, and I could not satisfy myself from whence they could have fallen. The breccia was remarkably coarse; the finest planes were about as rubbly as the coarsest volcanic ash of the Murray Islands. My impression was that there has been an enormous amount of weathering, and that it requires a combination of geological knowledge and imagination, which I do not possess, to reconstruct the physical features of the district at the time of the volcanic outburst. In any case a rapid horse-ride through a wooded country is not favourable for geological observations.

On the whole there is great uniformity in the vegetation; it is only in the occasional patches of dense scrub or in the gullies that there is much variation from the pendant, sad, greyish-green leaves of the eucalyptus. But in these exceptions it was a little relief to see nature freeing herself, so to speak, from the trammels of the Australian flora, and running riot on her own account. From the tangled undergrowth rose the tall tree stems, up which ran creepers, more particularly a climbing polypod, which had some resemblance to the foliage of ratan; swaying from the branches were festoons of creepers and aerial roots. One then felt that one was really in the tropics, though the forest trees were small compared with the giants of the Amazonian forests that Wallace, Bates, and other travellers describe, and such as we were destined to see later on in Borneo. Along the watercourses were clumps of bamboo. At home one always associates palm trees with tropical scenery, here they are conspicuously absent.

The last part of the ascent of Mount Warirata was very trying to some of us, as we had to drag our tired horses up a very steep, stony, zigzag road in the blazing vertical sun. The great rocks that walled the road in many places faced the sun, and instead of giving us the comfort of their shadows in the weary land they radiated superfluous heat to our further discomfort. We were immensely relieved when we reached the top of the north-easterly extremity of the Astrolabe Range, and then at a height of 2,615 feet we were in a better position to enjoy the magnificent panorama before us. Behind us, hidden by clouds, lay the main range of mountains that forms the backbone of the south-easterly portion of New Guinea. Below us was a gorgonised sea of land, ridges of sharp-crested hills running mainly in one direction, like the arrested rollers of a Titanic ocean. Rising like islands to the north-west from the general level of the lower hills were two conspicuous masses, "Fanny Peak" and "Saddle-Back." To the south-west lay the sea, and the coast-line was contoured as if on a map, the complex Bootless Inlet was the nearest portion of the coast, and the variable extent of the fringing reef off the headlands showed pale green against the blue of the sea. From this height Bootless Inlet and Port Moresby have the appearance of "drowned" bays, that is, of depressions of the coast which have permitted the sea to cover what would otherwise be fertile valleys. Around us were the same eucalyptus and cycads we had seen all day, but added to them were equally characteristic bottle-brush trees (banksias) of more than one species and a pink-flowered melastoma. A "cypress pine" gave the only mountainous touch to the vegetation.

With antipodean earthly scenery we had the sky of a glorious English summer, a clear deep blue, with massive fleecy cumulus clouds, whose brightness was contrasted with dark shadows. At the coast-level the sky is usually a greyer blue, often lavender coloured, owing to the moisture in the air which acts as a screen and lowers the blue tone of the sky. A haze pervaded the lower landscape, owing to the vapour-laden south-east breeze and the widely drifting smoke of numerous bush fires made by natives who were clearing the scrub for their gardens. This haze gave a softness to the view, and painted the shades with various shades of blue, but a little less "atmosphere" would, on the whole, have been better from a topographical point of view.

The purity of the air may be judged from the fact that Ballantine produced from under the shelter of a big rock a tin of fresh butter, which he had placed there six or seven weeks previously, and it was as sweet as when he cached it. The butter was actually fresh butter that he had put in a cocoa tin, and not an unopened tin of butter. This was at a height of about one thousand seven hundred feet, and the air was evidently practically free from putrefactive microbes, or at all events such as affect butter.

The top of Mount Warirata is composed of the volcanic

breccia *in situ*, and it formed imposing tors. I noticed several volcanic bombs in the blocks which weathered in concentric laminæ.

On passing the top we entered on a grassy plateau, or rather spur, along which we proceeded for a few miles. The plateau vegetation was very similar on the whole to that of the lower hills, with the addition, as I have already remarked, of the banksias, cypress pines, and melastoma. Among the smaller plants were a few ground orchids, one with a green flower somewhat resembling a listera, but with different leaves, and an umbrella fern. Remarkable streamers of a sulphur-green lichen depended from the boughs of the gums.

We next made a steep descent across a river gully, and after one or two clambers up and down wooded mountain valleys, we dismounted in a bamboo thicket close to a tributary of the Laroki River.

The horses were left here in charge of one of the party to be afterwards fetched by natives by a long détour. The rest of us had a steep climb up a detached hill, on the top of which was the small village of Atsiamakara. To the east of this hill is another higher one and with precipitous sides, but separated from it by a deep ravine; to the north and west is open, wooded, hilly country.

It is characteristic of these bush tribes to build their villages on the top of hills for the sake of safety from attack. Many of the villages formerly had tree-houses, but there are now very few of these left, as the country has been pacified. This village itself had some tree-houses, but no trace of them now remains. These tree-houses were used as places of refuge when the village was attacked. It might strike the reader that it would be very easy to chop down the tree and so destroy the refugees at one fell blow, but it must be remembered that these were designed by men still in their Stone Age, and it is by no means an easy or rapid matter to cut down a large tree with stone axes, especially when overhead foes are hurling down stones and spears. Savages are by no means fools, and they would not continue to build structures that experience proved to be useless; besides, it is against custom to fell these trees, thus, insecure as they appear to us, these tree-houses were real refuges.

At the time of our visit there were but eleven houses in the village. Two had verandahs along their sides on to which the

PLATE XVIII

UDIA AND DAUBE, TABURI, KOIARI

ELEVARA, PORT MORESBY, WITH THE LONDON MISSIONARY
SOCIETY'S STATION IN THE BACKGROUND

door opened, a type of house that was new to me as Papuan, but it is a characteristic type among the hill tribes. The four of us slept for two nights, and sat and had our meals and rested for nearly two days on the verandah of a house. Two natives slept inside.

This was a populous village before it was raided by the mountaineers of the main range, although these depredations have ceased in this particular district for ten years; two epidemics have since then reduced the population very considerably. We saw but five men, some half a dozen women, and a few children; this did not represent the entire population, as it is the custom for these bush tribes to reside but little in their own houses, the rest of the time being spent in the bush, making gardens and doing a little hunting. As a matter of fact, these people are good agriculturists; we saw some native tobacco growing in the village.

It was interesting getting a glimpse, for it was nothing more, of a real Papuan village, entirely unchristianised and scarcely at all affected by European civilisation.

Daube, our host, behaved very nicely; indeed, he was quite gentlemanly. He and a boy about the place looked after us in various ways, got water, made fires, and cooked yams and sweet potatoes. The ladies of the village were particularly shy, and consequently we took very little notice of them. They wore a common sort of leaf petticoat, not of so good a quality as is usually worn by the coast women. The men had the narrowest string of bark I have as yet seen worn—clothing it could not be called.

I measured the five men and made a few notes on them, and Wilkin took a few photographs. These natives are somewhat darker than the coast tribes, of more rugged countenance, and wear beards and moustaches. Ray obtained some information as to the nature of their language; like our Torres Straits friends they have names for only the numerals "one" and "two."

When strolling about we came across the old chief sitting on a log whittling saplings into spears with a boar's tusk for a knife. It was the first time I had seen this primitive knife in actual use, and much to the man's astonishment I bought the tusk after we had photographed him using it. Unfortunately for the picturesqueness of the photograph, he was wearing a shirt; the wearing of a shirt by a chief is the recognised symbol of loyalty in this district.

Our cooking was of a very primitive kind, and the results were not of a palatable quality. Every scrap that we dropped through the crevices of the verandah was immediately devoured by pigs. It was also a new sensation to hear pigs grunting and scrunching underneath one at night, and to feel the vibration of their rubbing against the verandah posts. The nights were comparatively quite cold; we all felt chilly, and my teeth chattered, but I doubt if the thermometer sank much below 55°.

This is a village of the Taburi tribe, who with others are called Koiari by the Motu, a name which simply means "bushmen," but it probably will be convenient to retain the latter as a general name for the small tribes of the whole district round about.

We rested all Sunday, but Ballantine walked on Saturday afternoon to Hogeri (Sogeri), a distance of seventeen miles. He returned from Hogeri on Monday morning, bringing along with him a crowd of inland natives amongst whom was Gewe, the chief of Agi, a noted warrior who a year previously would have been shot if he could have been caught, as he had more than once raided unoffending tribes; now the chief came of his own free will to visit Port Moresby. There were several men from Wamai and one or two from Hogeri and Ubere. Two of the natives carried a live pig tied to a pole, others had stone clubs, native food, and various articles.

We formed a long procession as we went back to Port Moresby in single file. For a long time the natives kept up well with us, but eventually they dropped behind. We had a very pleasant and by no means tiring ride home. At sunset we arrived at Boumana to find a liberal meal provided by Ballantine and prepared by Peter Lifu's wife. We had fresh wallaby-tail soup, stew, tinned raspberries, and coffee. Then we walked our horses in the dark to Port Moresby, arriving shortly before ten o'clock; we unsaddled at Ballantine's, and he invited us in to have a drink. We started with whisky and water and finished off with bread and cheese and beer. In fact, we had a "small-fellow Christmas." I had a good night, and woke up next morning in good form and not very stiff or sore.

The following day Ballantine took his visitors to Burns

PLATE XIX

GEWE, WITH HIS HAT RESTORED TO HIM

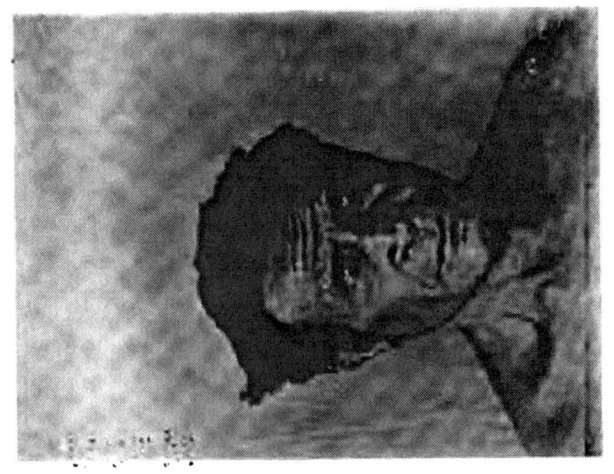

GEWE, CHIEF OF AGI, WHEN DEPRIVED OF HIS HAT

Philp's store, and showed them dozens of axes and tomahawks and cases of tobacco and other treasures, whereby they were duly impressed. Mr. Gors gave Gewe, the Agi chief, some turkey-red twill for a loin cloth, a belt, a cotton shirt, a second-hand guards-bandsman's tunic, and an ancient top hat, and the old fellow strutted about mightily pleased with himself.

Ballantine brought the party round to the hotel, as I wanted to measure and photograph them. I began with Gewe, and it was ludicrous to see his expansive smile of self-content. First we took him as he was, then by dint of gentle persuasion we divested him of his regalia, and it was evident that parting from his hat was the sorest trial. It appeared to be quite hopeless to get a side view of his face, as he kept turning round to see what we were doing, till Ballantine suggested that I should show him some pictures; so I produced a coloured plate of Torres Straits dances which so fascinated him that he became comparatively still immediately. But even so we could not get a satisfactory side-face portrait of him. I then measured his height, span, and head, and it was with great relief and transparent joy that he resumed his hat. I did not take all the measurements I should have liked, as he became restive and suddenly stalked off. I then measured a few other natives, who were duly photographed.

In the afternoon I went to where the natives were camped and witnessed one of those extremes of culture that are rarely met with, even in frontier colonies. My friend Gewe, clad in his medley of nineteenth-century garments, was solemnly chipping a hole in a stone club-head with a piece of flint! Close by was another mountaineer clad in his native fringed belt and sporran, holding a cheap mirror before his face, and shaving himself with a fragment of a glass bottle.

The following morning the natives again came to be investigated. I measured and Wilkin photographed some more, and Seligmann tested the keenness of their eyesight. He found the coast people at Bulaa, owing probably to their being sailors and fishermen, had even keener eyesight than Torres Straits islanders. The eyesight of our mountaineers, on the other hand, was much more like that of the average European landsmen. In the afternoon Seligmann tested their colour vision, but this did not show anything unusual. Altogether we got very good value out of the men, and it was a unique opportunity for us.

In the evening Ballantine gave his visitors a lantern show in the boat-shed, interspersed with phonograph songs and tunes by Ray. I think they did not understand the latter, but the pictures were thoroughly appreciated by them. I sat on a box next to Gewe in order to watch him, and I had a great treat. He had his hat on, but the military tunic was absent. Most of the lantern-slides were local, and the natives recognised them immediately. One slide was of especial interest, as it was the photograph of a village that Gewe and others had subsequently sacked and burnt. One wonders what was passing in the mind of the warrior, as in front of him was the representation of the "before," and in his mind's eye he must have seen the "after." I must say he did not look at all abashed, and why should he? He had only been following immemorial custom! Like the Torres Straits islanders and the coast Papuans, Gewe expressed wonder and admiration by a broad grin, glistening eyes, and by making various sucking and clicking noises with his lips. He also, like the others, flicked his teeth with his thumb-nail. Our glances often met, and we nodded and smiled and clicked to each other; once or twice with exuberant feeling, when a slide especially pleased him, he caught hold of my hand. I got quite fond of the old chap. He had a fine distinguished face. He held himself well, and behaved like a gentleman. When the portrait of Queen Victoria was on the screen, the phonograph played "Soldiers of the Queen," and I made Gewe take off his hat. He did so cheerfully, as if he understood the Queen should be respected, and directly the picture was changed I let him put it on again.

The evening was a great success, and must have considerably impressed the mountaineers, most of whom had probably not seen a white man before.

It was very interesting to come into personal contact with the raiders and the raided, to see individuals who were fighting each other a few months ago walking peacefully together, sharing the same food, and looking at lantern-slides of one another and of their villages. I would have given a great deal to know what they thought of it all. One thing is fairly certain, those who visited Port Moresby will remain pacific, as they must recognise what is to them the marvellous power of the white man. Next morning they started off home, and our friend Gewe had some hundred miles to walk.

Probably owing to their rich soil and fine climate, the mountaineers of the main range have a splendid physique, and are fine hardy men. They hunt the wild pig and other animals, but they are great gardeners, and have large plantations of indigenous sugar-cane, as well as of yams, sweet potatoes, and bananas. There is a superabundance of native food, and tons of it may be seen left to waste. Excess of food means plenty of leisure, and the energy begotten by such a country and good food must have an outlet. Naturally the people take to raiding their neighbours, and consequently there is a continual pressure, as it were, from the mountains towards the coast. It might be supposed that the intermediate belt of fertile hilly country would produce men strong enough to withstand the main range mountaineers; but it is not so, and the reason appears to be that they have no intertribal combination. The villages are usually small, from half a dozen to eighteen houses, and generally situated on the top of a steep hill or ridge. Most of them formerly had tree-houses as places of safety, and quite a number, especially towards the interior, were stockaded. The stockades might surround a village, or occur only as a close fence at each end, the object of which was to prevent the village from being rushed. Usually there was on the top of the stockade a projecting platform slanting upwards, up which the besieged rush to throw spears at the enemy.

Near Mount Bellamy, in the main range, five powerful tribes—Baura, Agi, Manari, Hagari, and Efogi—a few years ago entered into a sort of confederation, but only for aggressive purposes. A native, in describing this, illustrated his meaning in the following way: he was chewing sugar-cane at the time, and he gathered up the dry fibres into a heap, and then scattered them apart to express the dispersal of the tribes after a foray.

This confederation has harassed an extent of country that cannot be less than some fifty miles in length and thirty miles in breadth; over a large tract of this area the country has been depopulated and numerous villages entirely destroyed. The intermediate country being thus subjugated, the confederation had commenced operations quite close to the coast, when it was broken up by the Government; but it does not appear that even now the Hagari have been properly reduced, though their influence has been diminished.

The hill tribes of the interior have also played a similar game on the coast tribes. There was little to choose between them and the main range tribes, except that the latter were the more powerful.

We spent the rest of our time at Port Moresby in various ways. Wilkin went for a little trip inland, and photographed some tree-houses at Gasiri. Very few of these remarkable edifices are now extant, as the need for them has passed away in all places reached by the strong arm of the law. Seligmann wanted to see more of the country than would have been practicable had he stayed with us, so he left us on June 25th to visit Mr. English at Rigo; but before doing so he studied the collection of charms got together by Mr. Ballantine, and made notes on magic and native remedies, subjects that he investigated in other parts of New Guinea. Ray did what he could in studying the language of available natives, and made a collection of native potters' trade marks.

Port Moresby is the head-quarters of the pottery industry in the central district of British New Guinea, and when the season comes round great activity is displayed by the women, for pottery-making is entirely women's work. The men build up the *lakatois*, or trading boats, each of which consists of at least three ordinary canoes lashed together and provided with large crates to hold the pots in safety. The large sails, shaped like crabs' claws, and the flying streamers attached to the rigging give these strange craft a most picturesque appearance as they scud before the wind. It is not unusual for a fleet of twenty *lakatois* to sail with a crew of some six hundred men, each of whom would take about fifty pots.

These great trading voyages take place in October—that is, at the end of the south-east monsoon—and the *lakatois* wend their way up the coast, mainly to the Gulf of Papua, where the cargoes of pottery are exchanged for bundles of sago; as many as thirty thousand pots have been known to be bartered in one year for a hundred and fifty tons of sago. The voyagers return during the north-west monsoon with the sago and new canoes; they thus have a fair wind each way.

As no one had previously photographed the method of pottery-making, I was anxious to get a complete set of photographs, and Mr. Ballantine arranged for three women to go through the whole process in order that we might photograph

PLATE XX

TREE HOUSE AT GASIRI

POTTERY-MAKING AT HANUABADA, PORT MORESBY

it under favourable conditions. Wilkin and I also photographed various women at work in the native villages.

The villages of Port Moresby are composite in character, as two tribes, the Koitapu and Motu, live side by side, but apparently with extremely little mixture.

There is no doubt that the Koitapu are the original inhabitants; they are allied to the Koiari and other inland tribes, and hence are a branch of the true Papuans—that is, the essentially narrow-headed indigenous population of New Guinea. At the present time there is not much difference in appearance between many of the Koitapu and Motu, as doubtless intercourse has taken place at various times. The former are somewhat darker in colour, but there are quite a number of Koitapu, for example, who clearly have racial affinity with the hill tribes of the interior, while the Motu exhibit an equally strong resemblance to the main element in the coast population from Yule Island to Aroma.

The Koitapu are tillers of the soil, and the Motu are fisher-folks and potters. Chalmers says: "By no conquest do the Motu live here, but simply because the Koitapu allow them, saying, 'Yours is the sea, the canoes, the nets; ours the land and the wallaby. Give us fish for our flesh, and pottery for our yams and bananas.'"

There are many differences between the Koitapu and Motu that point to a difference of origin. The language is markedly different; Dr. Lawes long ago pointed out that there were very few words in common between these two tribes, and probably most, if not all, of these were borrowed. Ray, too, found that the affinities of the Koitapu language were with those of the true Papuan languages; while those of the Motu were unmistakably Melanesian. The Koitapu cook by means of the earth-oven, but the Motu mode of cooking by boiling in earthenware vessels is largely practised now. This is a borrowed custom. The Motu are more careful and nice in their diet, whereas the Koitapu devour anything edible. Their ornaments also differ, as do their mats and other handicrafts.

The Motu folk certainly look down on the Koitapu, but at the same time they fear the power of the sorcerers of their neighbours, and Lawes informs us: "The first thing a Motu man does, when anyone belonging to him is dangerously ill, is to go to a man, or oftener a woman, of the Koitapu, with large presents, that they may loose the power of the evil spirit over the sick man." As the Koitapu were the aboriginal inhabitants, they claim power over the elements, and rain and sunshine, wind and calms can be granted or withheld by them; consequently the Motu have to pay heavily for the weather that they happen to require. This is a very interesting example of what has often occurred elsewhere and at various times—a dominant people being dependent upon the magicians of the people they have subjugated.

Lawes also states that "The Motu are afraid to go out at night for fear of ghosts. The Koitapu have no such fear, but often travel inland at night. The coast tribes fear the gods of the land, and in case of calamity appeal to the owners of the soil to propitiate the gods, or wreak upon them their vengeance in revenge for what they have suffered." Chalmers says that he has "never heard of the two tribes fighting, but often the Motu has helped the Koitapu against their enemies, especially have they prevented the Hula (Bulaa) making raids on them."

We are not yet in a position to say definitely where the Motu originally came from.

The twenty-seventh of June was a red-letter day, as I received my first home letters since our departure from London on March 10th; these were forwarded from Thursday Island by the gunboat *Goldfinch*, which arrived in the morning. I was packing ethnographical specimens in a shed when she arrived, but I went off with Ballantine just as I was to hear the news, and we stayed to lunch. It was very pleasant to have fresh people to talk to, especially travelled men. Few things are more refreshing than intelligent chatting, when one is in one of the world's backwaters. We heard the news, not much more than we knew before, except the death of Gladstone. In the afternoon I continued my study of Ballantine's unique collection of stone clubs. After dinner we all, with Dr. Blaney and Ballantine, called at the *Goldfinch*, and took the captain and officers to Hanuabada to see a dance; the moon was young and the sky was cloudy, and there were no fires, so very little could be seen; indeed, we could smell more than we could see.

The third-class cruiser *Mohawk* arrived next morning fresh from the annexation of Santa Cruz and some of the Solomon Islands. The *Goldfinch* officers thought they would remain here for some weeks, and were planning shooting parties. Now they learnt they must go off the next morning to Melanesia, to annex more islands, and the *Mohawk* was to depart the same time for Thursday Island.

All the time I was visiting at Port Moresby I was hoping to hear some news about Sir William Macgregor, as I was looking forward to meet him once more; but he was at the other end of the possession, and there was no chance of my seeing him for a long time, so I decided to return to Murray Island as soon as possible. Burns Philp's boat, the *Alice May*, came in on July 5th, and Mr. Gors promised that she should take us back to Murray Island.

There happened to be a few days to spare, and as I was very desirous of seeing something of the Mekeo District, Mr. Musgrave kindly arranged that the Government ketch *Lokohu* should take us to Yule Island, where the *Alice May* would subsequently pick us up. Once again Mr. Musgrave's cordial co-operation enabled me to save time and accomplish something that I wanted to do, which otherwise might have been left undone; for this and for his hospitality he has earned our hearty thanks. Our stay at Port Moresby was also rendered more profitable than it might otherwise have been through the kindness of Mr. Ballantine. I much valued the opportunity he gave me of studying his very fine collection of Papuan stone clubs. Other friends too assisted us in various ways.

We left Port Moresby on the morning of July 7th.

CHAPTER XVII

THE MEKEO DISTRICT

WE arrived at Hall Sound at 6.15 p.m., Thursday, July 6th, and visited the Sacred Heart Mission, where we were cordially received by Archbishop Navarre and his colleagues. Although this Roman Catholic Mission has its headquarters at Issoudun, in Indre, in France, the executive may belong to any nationality, and thus it is not entirely a French Mission, though French is the language spoken among themselves.

After the evening meal I played "ludo" with the Archbishop, and we subsequently played the game several evenings. Ray, by request, had brought the phonograph ashore, and he gave a selection on it in the course of the evening, greatly to the delight of the Fathers and Brothers, none of whom had ever heard one before. Brother Philip, a kind-hearted, merry Dutchman, who is always smiling and laughing, and who is one of the musicians of the fraternity, was child-like in his enthusiastic appreciation of the machine. We persuaded some natives to sing into the phonograph, and, as usual, they were delighted at hearing their own voices echoed from the mysterious instrument.

Monseigneur kindly asked us to stay the night at the Mission, so we gladly sent for our kit bags. After a feverish night I was compelled to spend a quiet day, and Wilkin was only able to walk to the village of Ziria, which he photographed.

Ray was good enough to give another phonograph performance to the Fathers and the natives, and later we went to the nunnery and repeated the entertainment for the delighted Sisters. Ray spent all the rest of the day in philological brain-picking, and was very satisfied with the result of his day's work.

After another sleepless, feverish night I began to feel better, but decided to remain quiet, whilst Ray and Wilkin went to the village of Mohu on the mainland with Brother Alexis to visit Father Burke, the only "Englishman" (and he is an Irishman) in the Mission.

The day was a sad one for us, as Brother Edmond, who belonged to the station at Pokao on the mainland, and had come here for a visit, became very ill in the morning, and grew worse as the day wore on. Soon after 5 p.m. a little service was held in his room, when the Extreme Unction with the Pontifical Absolution and Benediction was given; the anointing with holy oil, which is performed in the early stages of an illness that may have a fatal termination, had been celebrated in the morning. All through the day we received numerous reports as to the progress of the disease.

The Brother had been in good health the previous day (Friday) and worked hard in the sun, but he drank water copiously, and probably had taken some from an infected source which brought on a malignant enteric disease (hæmaturia).

At 9 p.m., when all lights are put out and the Mission goes to bed, I heard the Sisters who were to keep the night watch arrive, for the patient's room was next to mine. At eleven o'clock I was awakened by a slight commotion, and turning out found Father Guis reading the prayers for the dying, and whilst they were being read Brother Edmond passed away. I retired again to bed whilst the Brothers and Sisters performed the last secular offices for the dead, and in a few minutes heard the suggestive "pwew, pwew" of the planing of boards, and later the hammering of nails. By 2.15 the body was lying in its last bed.

At 3 a.m., finding a service was about to be held in the chapel, I threw my dark blue bed blanket around me, and in pyjamas and with bare feet I attended the service. It proved to be a Communion service for those who had administered to the deceased. Father Guis, in broken voice, feelingly read the service, with a Brother as acolyte, to a congregation composed of three Sisters clad in their usual blue costume, four Brothers in workaday flannel shirts, and myself, a blanket-clad "heretic." The moral atmosphere was tense with emotion, and the service appeared to me to be not so much a communion with God, as a sacrament of renewed devotion under the most solemn circumstances. Of course I do not wish to imply that the first sentiment was not present, that is, the essential element in Holy Communion, but the other aspect appeared to predominate.

The impressiveness of the ceremony was enhanced by its being held in the depth of night.

Before finally retiring to rest I visited the coffin lying on the verandah of our hostel. Praying beside it were two of the indefatigable Brothers who had worked so hard, and two patient, statuesque Sisters.

The morning bell woke us at 5.30 o'clock, and I dressed in order to attend early morning Mass at six. During that service the sun rose, and a glorious tropical day commenced, joyous physically, but psychically sad. After Mass coffee was served, and at 7.30 the Mass for the Dead was solemnised in the chapel by the Archbishop.

The last time I attended a Catholic Requiem Mass was in Rome sixteen years previously.

There we witnessed the ceremony decked with all the pomp due to the rank of a high functionary of the Holy Catholic Church; here I participated in the same ceremony—the same, but how different!

There, a dignitary trained in ecclesiastical doctrine, dogma, and discipline, had worked his way up in the Church till heaven gave him a preferment. (I wonder whether it was a better one than his last on earth?) Here, a man who for fourteen years was a joint owner with his cousin of a fishing schooner in the North Sea, and who was making money in his venturesome calling, left all, like other fishermen we read of, and became a lay Brother, with no chance of promotion in this world, and volunteered to a fever-stricken country from which he knew he would never return. One day he worked hard, doing his duty heartily and manfully; the next, he was prostrated by a severe illness, and passed away before midnight, dying in perfect peace. His last words were that he was ready to die and be quit of suffering (for death had no terrors for him), or ready to live if God willed, and to continue his labours, although he knew full well that this meant a certainty of renewed sickness and pain.

As the procession was forming outside the chapel after the service, Ontong (who also had attended Mass) and I took the middle places, and helped carry the coffin to the grave, but after a short distance I was asked to desist, as I was taller than the others, and the equilibrium was disturbed.

The grave had been dug by natives, who stood by clothed in their usual fashion and decked with native finery, thus supplying a dramatic contrast between the ceremonial of an ancient Church and the religious and physical nudity of the savage.

At 8.30 a.m. we were back in the house for breakfast. By early afternoon Father Guis was groaning under an attack of fever. He was ill the previous Friday, and thought he was quit of it for a time; but his devotion to the deceased Brother had overtaxed his physical strength, and this, combined with the severe strain on his feelings, brought about a relapse. Truly the Fathers appear to be fighting against fate!

Soon after our midday meal I started on horseback with Father Guilbaud to the village of Ziria, where he was to conduct the Benediction. It is characteristic of the practical straightforward simplicity of this fraternity that the priest wore a large grey wide-awake hat, flannel shirt, corduroy trousers, and carpet slippers. We had a pleasant ride of somewhat under an hour, mainly along the sand beach.

After tea in the Mission house, Father Guilbaud and I went to the chapel, where a chair and *prie-dieu* were allotted me close to the altar rails, and in full view of the congregation. Opposite sat two Sisters, in charge of some small girls, and a third Sister presided at the harmonium. It was very pretty to see the naked little boys trotting hand in hand up the altar steps, bowing, and then darting to the right and squatting on the floor. Clothing among the males was almost a negative quantity; indeed, there was a marked absence of European dress of any description. Most of the bucks had painted their faces with red, black, and white pigments, the effect of which was certainly grotesque, and some were almost as much decorated with native finery as if they were going to a dance; one or two of the girls had freshly oiled themselves and were decorated with shell ornaments. The women folk all sat on the Sisters' side of the chapel, and the men on the opposite side. The youngest children sat in the front rows, and in increasing ages further back, so that the old people were near the door.

Father Guilbaud preached a sermon in the native language, evidently on the Communion, and he had on the altar rails a large coloured picture-card illustrating the Last Supper; in the upper corners were two small pictures, one of Elijah being fed by ravens, and the other of a Catholic Communion Service. From time to time the good Father pointed with a small stick to details in the pictures. Believing so firmly as I do in visual instruction, I was particularly pleased with this innovation.

After the sermon came the ceremonial part of the service, and it was charming to see two Papuan lads act as acolytes, with their mop of black frizzly hair, copper-coloured skins, long red cassocks, and short white cotta, going through the service in a most devout and seemly fashion. When service was over the acolytes disrobed behind the altar and stepped forth, two all but absolutely nude savage dandies with shell ornaments and painted faces. It is to be hoped the grace in their hearts was of a more permanent character than the brief adorning of their persons with the garments of Christian ceremonial. A pleasant ride back in the cool of early evening completed a most enjoyable day.

A little later in the week we again visited Ziria, when we took some measurements of the natives and bought a few "curios," mostly lime gourds. We exhibited the phonograph to the Sisters living in Ziria, and gave one rehearsal in the schoolroom, and another in the *marea* or club-house of the village, to excited audiences.

Ziria is quite an interesting village; some of its houses are similar to those lower down the coast, but others I recognised as belonging to a type characteristic of the Papuan Gulf. The people here certainly more resemble the coast people further east than those to the west, but they have a character of their own, and some appear to resemble the "typical Papuan" which Guillemard describes, and which he met with in the extreme north of New Guinea. This transitional area between the east and the west is marked, amongst other ways, by the men's costume more resembling that of the Gulf men. The bark-cloth belt trails behind on the ground, and the young men wear, when they are *ibitoe*, a rather narrow tight wooden belt. One lad I saw wore his so tight that above the wooden belt and below the breast-bone and ribs the abdominal wall protruded like an inflated pouter pigeon's crop; about an inch and a half below this belt was the tightly drawn ordinary bark-cloth belt, and in the interspace beween the two belts the flesh exuded as a prominent ring. Another example of tight-lacing is given in the accompanying photograph.

When a boy is about twelve years of age, the family council decides that he must be *ibitoe*, that is, of an age fit to marry,

PLATE XXI

MASKED MAN, KAIVAKUKU, OF WAIMA, MEKEO DISTRICT

A MEKEO IBITOE

and he is conducted to the *marea* of the *ibitoes*, or club-house of the young men. Thenceforth commences for him a life of unalloyed pleasure; nothing has he to do but to eat, drink, and be merry. But it is all harmless pleasure; intoxicant there is none. The only serious thing he has to do is to make his drum. Several lads will go into the jungle without saying anything to their friends, and will remain there, it may be a week or a month, until each has made his drum. A straight branch is selected and cut to the requisite size; this is next scraped with shells till the orthodox shape is arrived at; finally, the cavity is carefully and laboriously burnt out.

During this period the lads are taboo (*rove* in Roro, *ngope* in Mekeo)—they must have no intercourse with any man; the friend who brings them food must surreptitiously hide it in a secret spot previously arranged upon. Should they be seen by a woman or girl the drum would have to be destroyed, otherwise it would be certain to split, and would sound like an old cracked pot.

There are also restrictions as to food. If they eat fish, a fishbone will prick them, and the skin of the drum will burst; if red bananas are eaten, they will be choked, and the drum will have a dull sound; if they eat grated coconut, the white ants will destroy the body of the drum; should they cook food in an ordinary spherical earthen pot instead of a small high one, they will grow fat, and will not be able to dance, and the girls will mock them and call out, "Your stomach is big; it is a pot." Finally, they must never touch fresh water, but they may drink coconut milk, or the water which occurs abundantly in the stem of a banana; should they inadvertently touch water with feet, hands, or lips before the drum is completely hollowed out, they break it, crying, "I have touched water, my firebrand is extinguished, and I can never hollow out my drum." These prohibitions are interesting examples of symbolic magic: the sight of a woman destroys the tone of the drum, contact with water extinguishes the fire, a fishbone tears the tympanum, so the sorcerer informs them; everyone says so, no one has the temerity to prove it, but no one dares to deny it.

When a boy has been declared *ibitoe* he is told, "Now you are free look out for a woman and marry as soon as possible." At first the young man does not think about such things. He enjoys his absolute independence; he goes, comes, plays the fool as he pleases; he dances for the sake of dancing; decorates himself for his own delectation; but gradually other thoughts arise. The girls of his own age also grow up; his parents begin to talk about the girls, about the presents and marriage and so forth. Such suggestions soon have the natural result.

The lad becomes *rove*. It is difficult to find a proper English equivalent for this term: "holy" or "sacred" originally expressed this idea, now other meanings have been read into them; it is perhaps best to simply appropriate the Polynesian term "taboo." He ornaments himself more extravagantly, and tight laces till human nature can stand no more; he plays sweet, melancholy airs on his flute in a corner of the village, and the girls creep out to listen to the ravishing music.

The young men waylay the girls and offer presents. The weak damsels may cry out and run to their parents, the lusty will beat and scratch the adventurous youth, who never dares to resist lest he draw upon himself her parents' wrath. Should fair means fail, recourse is had to the sorcerer, and he generally brings the girl to reason.

It is against custom in the Mekeo district for a young man to make love to a girl of his own village, but each village is affiliated to another from which brides should be taken. In the Roro language the relationship between two villages is called *aruabira*, "part of our blood," and in the Mekeo tongue, *ufapie, auai*. The former word, according to Father Guis, means "the other side of the sky," in other words, as they would say, "The *ufapie* are our friends down below; they are like our own souls (*auai*); we are blood brothers." This friendship is carried out much further; for example, the people of Veifaa keep pigs and rear dogs for the village of Amoamo, their *ufapie*, and *vice versâ*. When there is a death at Veifaa the Amoamo people come and feast reciprocally. When the time comes to go out of mourning the *ufapie* is invited. They come, dance, eat, perform certain ceremonies, and the period of mourning is over.

There are one or two quaint customs of the *ibitoes* which may be noted. They must never walk down the main street of a village, though the girls at the corresponding period may do so. I noticed when we walked to Veifaa the young men who were with us slunk round by the backs of the houses in passing through a village or to get to the youths' *marea*. They are not constrained to work, but they are tacitly permitted to steal. If they are caught they will be punished, but it is no crime, and is not considered a disgrace, and will never be made the occasion of a quarrel as ordinary theft often is. Sometimes the lads will do a little perfunctory gardening, or if they want to combine amusement with business they will take a bow and arrow and go to the seashore to shoot fish.

It is tempting to go on writing about these interesting people, but those who desire further information are referred to Father Guis' charming account of them in *Les Missions Catholiques* (1898), Nos. 1,493–1,512.

Father Cochard gave me the following examples of belief in omens. When the hauba bird comes into a village and cries in the night, someone will die. If a kangaroo hops into a village when the men are out hunting, someone will die. Unfortunately I did not ask whether it was one of the hunters or of the people then in the village that would die, but I expect it was the former, and that the kangaroo was the spirit of the dead hunter. This interpretation is borne out by the following: If men are voyaging and a gale of wind suddenly springs up the mariners know that someone has died, as the gust of wind is the passage of the spirit.

An interesting example of what is known as the "life-token" occurs in Yule Island. When the men go to fetch sago from the Gulf a fire is lit, and if the fire goes out there will be bad luck for the voyagers, consequently care is taken to keep the fire alight during the whole time the men are away.

Very characteristic of this district is the custom of men wearing a large, plain, bark-cloth shawl, and the use of large mosquito nets, or rather sleeping bags (*ruru*), made from the net-like spathe of the leaf of the coconut palm. These contrivances are about ten to thirteen feet in length, and some six feet wide, and they afford a suffocating shelter from mosquitos for the whole family.

The women of Yule Island dress and tattoo from head to foot in a manner very similar to the Motu women; but in the neighbouring tribes the tattooing is less complete. According to Father Guis, at Waima only the face and breast are tattooed, and at Marehau, the village on the beach at Delena, the face alone; but when at Delena I certainly saw some tattooing on the legs of some women. The village of Delena is said to have a double origin. Some of the people belong to the Roro tribe, who claim to have originally come from Bereina, in the Mekeo district. The other inhabitants belong to the Motu stock, and migrated from Port Moresby. Hence one would expect ⁓ ⁓ a mixture of custom in this little village. One Nara woman I saw had characteristic tattooing on the body and legs, but not on the face and arms. I was informed that this custom was recently introduced from Delena; the spiral designs on her legs were certainly Mekeo and not Motu patterns.

Father Guis states that the women of Mekeo are not acquainted with tattooing. I do not know what particular villages he had in his mind, probably those far inland, for at Veifaa I sketched two women whose torsos were richly tattooed, and I

FIG. 27. TATTOOING IN THE MEKEO DISTRICT
Two Veifaa women and Maino, the chief of Inawi

saw women in Inawa with similar tattooing. He also states that each tribe has its distinctive pattern, and any infringement of copyright would be a valid reason for war.

There are three main groups of people in the region round Hall Sound, which are distinguished by marked dialectic as well as by various ethnographical differences. These are the Roro, Mekeo, and Pokao.

RORO.

The Roro plant their villages on the seashore or along creeks. The men live as much in their canoes as on their infertile soil. These fishermen collect in large numbers at the fishing seasons at the mouths of the Angabunga, Apeo, and other rivers. The fish are carefully smoked, and are bartered for the fine taro and enormous sweet potatoes grown by the Mekeo women.

According to the seasons, with their prevailing winds, these adventurous and trafficking mariners visit the coastal tribes to the north-west or to the south-east. In the Papuan spring,

THE MEKEO DISTRICT

October and November, they repair to Toaripi for sago, which grows in inexhaustible quantity in the neighbourhood of the great rivers. Here they exchange the thin pots of Ziria, the main village of Rabao (or Yule Island), which are celebrated all along the coast, for bundles of sago. On the return journey the packages of sago are stacked in the bottom of the trading canoes, the latter being four or half a dozen ordinary canoes lashed together.

In March or April, after the heavy rains, the annual visit is paid to the jewellers of Taurama and Pari, who excel in the manufacture of necklaces of small shells, *mobio* (called *taotao* by the Motu), and of polished shell armlets, *hoia*, or *ohea* (the *toea* of the Motu).

The art of pottery-making was introduced into this district by immigrants of the Motu stock, who appear to have reached their furthest western limit at Delena. Not very long ago only one woman in Pinupaka had acquired this art; now all the women make pottery, but the clay is obtained from Yule Island.

These merchant fisher-folk have the reputation of being roguish and cajoling, and with a pretty conceit in flattery. When boats arrive they are greedy for news. They have been described as the Athenians of Papua. Their language compares favourably with the guttural tongue of the inland folk, being clear, musical, and distinct, with neither strain nor ridiculous contractions.

MEKEO.

The Mekeo group of people live mainly in the villages that cluster round the Angabunga (St. Joseph) River. There are also villages on the upper waters of the Biaru, and on the Apeo, Laiva, and other streams that flow into Hall Sound near the mouth of the Angabunga. They are an intelligent, interesting, and well-to-do set of natives, who present marked differences from their Gulf neighbours.

There are two great divisions, the Vee and the Biofa. The prolific and skilful Biofa have devastated the villages of the Vee, and according to the Sacred Heart missionaries, they have also strengthened themselves by alliance with "the sea-warriors, Lokou and Motu-Motu" (Toaripi), in order to crush their rivals. Unfortunately I have no further information to give concerning these two factions. It would be important to trace out the history and significance of this feud; it rather looks as if the Biofa was an immigrant tribe that was dispossessing the indigenous Vee. I regret I cannot mention which are the Biofa and which are the Vee villages. It is, however, a matter of recent history that Eboa has attacked Inawabui, and later Inawaia followed their example; but these feuds have now been settled by the Government. Inawa, an offshoot from Inawaia, is (according to Sir William Macgregor) the smallest and fiercest tribe in this part of the district. The late Bishop Verjus urged the Inawaia and Eboa to cease their quarrelling, and prevailed on them to build a new village on the left bank of the Angabunga, in which the Vee and Biofa were to live amicably side by side. He named this village "The Peace of Jesus," *Jesu baibua*, or *Yeku ngangau*, according to two local dialects. The village is generally termed Yeku by the Government officials.

The Mekeo people are good agriculturists, and their rich soil yields them abundant harvests. Each of their villages consists of a single wide street, with houses on each side. Sometimes the houses are two or three deep, but in this case they are so arranged as to leave a regular street on each side of, and parallel to, the main street. There are usually two *mareas*, which are generally placed at opposite ends of the village. The *marea* is the club-house of the men; often it is highly decorated with carved and painted posts and boards and streamers of palm leaves. The *marea*, which is the equivalent of the *erabo*, or *eramo*, of the Gulf, the *kwod* of Torres Straits, and the *dubu* of further east, is the centre of the social, political, and religious life of the men.

The Government has had very great difficulty in getting the people to bury their dead in a cemetery away from the village, as they preferred their old plan of burying under the houses. The people are greatly in dread of the sorcerers, who have the reputation for very powerful magic.

POKAO.

The inland district south of Hall Sound is a dry, hilly country, with sparse woods and green swards, where grow the aromatic plants so dearly prized for personal wear by the natives of the whole district. The physical conditions of this

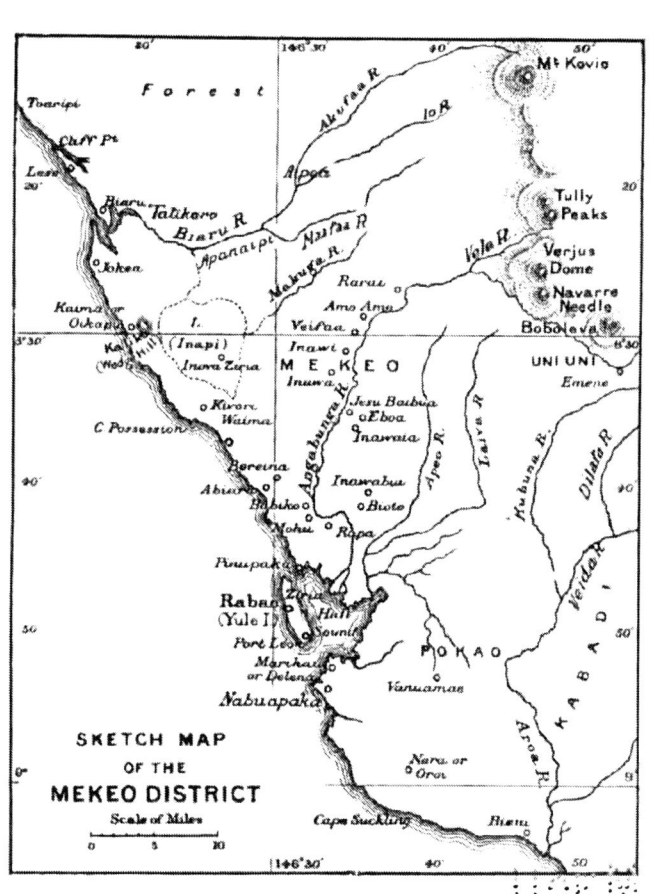

THE MEKEO DISTRICT

healthy land of eucalyptus and kangaroos do not appear to be favourable to agriculture, and so the inhabitants have become mainly hunters of the abundant game. On referring to a geological map, it is seen that this is a region of old volcanic rocks.

The Pokao people are an instructive example of the economic defects of a hunting existence. The necessity for getting fresh food every day fosters improvidence, for meat cannot be kept like yams or sago in this tropical climate. Hence these hunter folk are too lazy to send their meat to market. If the Mekeo people will fetch the meat they require, so much the better; if not, to use an expression employed nearer home, they "can't be bothered."

A hunting population, all the world over, is liable to periodic famines, and the Pokao people are no exception. But so ingrained is their laziness or indifference that they have been known to refuse to send for food which they could have had for nothing. They preferred to go hungry rather than take a monotonous tramp to obtain food.

Probably in no part of British New Guinea are markets so numerous as in the Mekeo district. As markets are important factors in the social evolution of a people, it would be well if some of the residents in this district were to make a special study of the origin and regulations of the various market-places.

Markets are held at Inawaia and Mohu every five days on the banks of the river, and at various intervals at Inawi, Inawa, and Jesu Baibua, to which the Bereina, Abiara, and Waima people come. During the crab and crayfish season in the northwest monsoon, these markets are also held every five days. Inawi and Inawa used to fight Bereina, and trouble consequently often arose in the villages on market days. To lessen this danger, the Government appointed a market to be held in the forest between Inawa and Bereina. Roro has no regular market, but there is a great market at the mouth of the little river of Oriki, near Abiara.

Owing to the physical features of the locality, the villages have a superfluity of some food, or have access to a speciality, or are experts in a handicraft; these naturally form their stock-in-trade. For instance, the Roro of the coast from Pinupaka,

Rabao (Yule Island), Marihau (Delena), and even the villages of Nabuapaka beyond Delena, trade in crabs, crayfish, and mussels, as well as pottery, for the taro, yams, sweet potatoes, sago, bananas, and areca nuts of the Mekeo tribes as far inland as Rarai, at the foot of Kovio (Mount Yule). Waima trade in coconuts; Waima, part of the Kivori, Bereina, and Babiko provide yams and some sago. If a big feast is approaching, the Mekeo people send for wallabies and cassowaries to the villages of the rich game district on the other side of Hall Sound, such as Pokao, Boinamai, Nabuapaka, and Biziu. Even the Waima and Kivori and Bereina will send to Pokao for game, although wallabies are obtained in the grassy plains round Bereina; sometimes they get game from Kaima.

The natives of Rabao buy nose-skewers and arm-rings and other shell ornaments from the Port Moresby villages, Pari, and other Motu villages; feather ornaments, gourds, and forks from Mekeo; petticoats from Kivori; and large bark belts from Toaripi. I believe these are plain bark belts, as the Toaripi men obtain the decorated bark belts which they wear from Vailala and Orokolo. The bows of the district are mainly manufactured at Kaima.

On July 14th a messenger arrived early in the morning, having very kindly been sent overland by Mr. Gors, of Port Moresby, to say that the *Alice May* had been delayed on her way to call for us; so I decided to make a trip inland, and had a chat with the Archbishop to arrange details. It was settled that Brother Alexis should take us to Veifaa, and we were to start by boat early in the afternoon with four native carriers, so we hastily got our things together.

Unfortunately there was the usual delay in starting, owing to the carriers not coming promptly from the village, but at last we got away, and then unluckily the wind slackened.

However, in due time we reached Pinupaka, which is the port of this district, owing to the shelter afforded by a sand spit jutting out from a monotonous coast-line of miles upon miles of mangrove swamps.

Pinupaka is a miserable village, and poor Brother George, who had lived in the district for twelve years, looked wan and worn, as well he may, living in this wretched fever-stricken hole. Two months later the devoted Brother died of hæmaturia. At high tide the sea comes up to the mission premises, not a clear healthy sea, but muddy water from mangrove swamps. Brother George offered us refreshment, but being desirous to push on we would not delay, for every minute was precious.

Off we started at a rapid pace along a sand beach flanked by mangroves. The sand was nearly black, and with but few shells or stones. The land here appears to be sinking, as there are stumps of mangroves exposed at low water, and many of the trees bordering the beach are dead. I may say that there are several species of mangroves, and those at Pinupaka are not the kind that encroach on the sea and accumulate land in their wake.

After about three-quarters of an hour we reached the first creek or mouth of a river, but in this part of the world the rivers themselves, far inland, are also called "creeks." We waded this bare-legged, and continued as fast as possible, for the sun was setting and the tide rising fast, and on a low, sandy, windward shore this combination has a sinister meaning. The second creek was known to be deeper than the first, and the tide was also higher, so we took off our scanty clothing, rolling it up into bundles to hold over our heads. Wilkin and I got along all right, but Ray, being shorter of stature, found himself getting out of his depth, walking on shifting sand and buffeted by breakers; so Wilkin and I each seized one of his arms, and this enabled him to hold his own, and we all safely gained the opposite side. In all these estuaries crocodiles abound, and we were very thankful to have escaped these brutes. In the muddy water their presence could not be seen, so there was no means of escaping them should they happen to be present; but usually crocodiles avoid noisy or numerous parties. By this time the sun had set, and the short tropical twilight was too quickly passing, whilst we still had a goodish bit of beach yet to traverse.

The tide was quickly gaining on the mangroves, and we had now to watch our opportunity to bolt forward as a wave retreated, and dodge up among the mangroves as it advanced; our progress was therefore slow and laborious, as fallen trees put further difficulties in our way. Eventually the high tide forced us altogether from the beach, and we then took to the scrub and wended our way in the dark till we came to another creek. After crossing this we halted and put on socks and shoes, for the swamp was here crossed by a "corduroy road," that is, a road made of logs placed transversely and kept more or less in position by upright stakes.

It was a comfort to get on firm earth again, and after a half-hour's walk through plantations we were right glad to reach the hospitable house of Fathers Cochard and Burke at Mohu.

A glass of white wine kept us going till dinner was ready. We had for dinner a mound bird (*Megapodius*), which Father Cochard had shot that morning, and we all thoroughly enjoyed our well-earned dinner. In the evening Ray gave a phonograph entertainment. On his visit a few days earlier he recorded a speech by Matsu, the chief, in which he exhorted the people to make the Government road, and finished off with a hunting song. This speech sounded very fine; it begins with the customary loud clearing of the throat, and the sentences come in bursts, the intervals of silence being evidently part of the orator's art.

As soon as it was sufficiently light next morning I strolled round to have a look at the village. There was a wonderful variety in the style of its houses, perhaps more so than in any other village in British New Guinea. On his previous visit Wilkin made notes of these and photographed some of them.

The *marea* had an enormously long projecting gable, which slants upwards. Suspended from various parts of the *marea* were long grass fringes, and carved and painted wooden boards.

After an early breakfast we again started on our travels. The path we followed was of dry mud and somewhat uneven, showing that it must be very swampy in wet weather. All the country for many miles round is low alluvial soil.

In forty minutes we reached Babiko, but had only time to glance at the interesting *marea*. Half an hour later we struck the Government road leading from the sea to Veifaa, the Government station of the Mekeo district.

The road passed over a plain covered with a tall, coarse grass, growing higher than our heads, and preventing any little wind there was from reaching us. Fortunately the sky was cloudy, or it would have been simply sweltering. There were numerous scattered trees, a kind of eucalypt, a few pandanus, and occasional cycads. After leaving this grassy plain our road lay through the forest. On first entering the forest we passed through one of the smaller market places which characterise this locality.

PLATE XXII

MOHU, MEKEO DISTRICT

MAREA AT MOHU

Women from different villages or districts meet at appointed places, usually at the boundary between two tribes, and there barter their specialities for commodities from other localities. The bartering is done by women only, but they are accompanied by a few armed men, who, however, do not go amongst the market women, but stand a little way off. The men bring a drum with them, which is beaten at the opening and close of the market.

The "market-place" we passed on this occasion was only a small one, but round about were remnants of the simple booths that the natives erect when trading. After traversing a small patch of forest and a grass plain, we crossed a river by a good wooden bridge, and shortly came to a large forest. There was another small market-place where the road entered the forest.

It was very enjoyable walking along the shady forest paths, and noting for the first time typical tropical scenery. The trees were tall, but by no means gigantic. Some had slab-like buttresses, which the natives utilise as boards; there were wild bread-fruit trees, with their beautiful foliage of a deep, glossy green, but in this species covered with inedible fruit; half a dozen different kinds of palms; ferns, bamboos, and a great profusion of shrubs and plants.

Our road passed at one point close to the Angabunga (St. Joseph River), a swiftly-running river of dirty water. It is a noteworthy fact that in this district many words have the *ng* (as in "singing"), but this peculiarity is scarcely found elsewhere in British New Guinea. Although very common in the western tribe of Torres Straits, it does not occur in Murray Island.

We had a short rest at Inawa. Whilst sitting on a platform of a house in process of construction I saw a man cutting wooden arrow points with a boar's tusk, and bought the lot, much to his amusement.

We reached Inawi at noon, and found there was to be a large gathering of the Sacred Heart Missioners to celebrate an anniversary of the founding of their mission at Inawi. After lunch Wilkin and I went to the village, which consists of one long street, with three rows of houses on each side, and a population of some four hundred people.

There are several different types of houses here. The chief's house is a picturesque pile-dwelling, built in the form of a cross, and adorned with long fringes of grass and carved and painted boards; from one of the latter, hanging in front of the house, depended a mask. Each chief in the Mekeo district builds a *marea*, and has his own designs on it, which no one may copy, as this would constitute a valid reason for a quarrel. The chief only has a right to hang a painted board in front of his house; it is, in fact, a sign of chieftainship, since when a chief is appointed he receives a board at the same time.

In the Mekeo district there appear to be two main divisions of family groups, each of which has its chief. I have more than once alluded to a dual division of a community in this part of the world, but here it seems to have been made the basis of a higher social development than has been hitherto recorded in New Guinea. The chief of one division is the war, or administrative chief; the other headman is *afu* (or taboo) chief. The office of the latter is hereditary.

A somewhat similar division of function has occurred elsewhere. To take two examples only: in ancient Gaul there were war chiefs and peace chiefs; the *sachem* of certain North American aboriginees was a peace chief. It is not improbable that in the *afu* chieftainship we have the commencement of a priestly dynasty after the order of Melchisedek, but at the Papuan stage of culture the secret of his power is probably a magical control over harvests rather than the authority due to purely religious functions. The mage has not yet become a priest.

On December 6th, 1897, the *afu* chief of Inawi put *afu* (taboo) on the coconuts and areca nuts, as these crops were failing in his district. Brother Alexis, who happened to be there, described the ceremony to me.

A small feast was made consisting of five pigs, five cassowaries, and plenty of native food, *i.e.* yams, sweet potatoes, taro, bananas, etc.; at about five o'clock Brother Alexis was invited to a place of honour on the *marea*, and one pig, one cassowary ham, and two banana leaves of native food were given him. The *Afu* chief of the village then made a speech proclaiming *afu*, stating that the coconuts and areca nuts would run short if this were not done. A piece of cassowary and pig meat with native food was placed in each person's *oro*, or cooking-pot, and then the *afu* was planted. This consisted of three bamboos, to the lower part of each was tied a leaf of the sago palm, and coconuts were tied to the bamboos. The bamboos were erected, grouped like a "Prince of Wales" feathers, to the noise of

THE MEKEO DISTRICT

conch shells and a wailing shout sounding like a siren. So far as I could discover, the bull-roarer is not known in this district. Leafy fringes, like women's petticoats, were put round the supports of the bamboos. (This *afu* still remained on the occasion of our visit, except that the central bamboo had disappeared.) In the evening there was a dance, and fifteen coconuts and a bunch of areca nuts were given Brother Alexis.

For the three days following the ceremony the nuts might be taken, but on the third day a small feast was held, and thenceforth no nuts could be picked.

FIG. 28. AFU, OR TABOO SIGNAL, AT INAWI

Another family than that to which the *afu* chief belongs (there seem to be only these two divisions or family groups in the village) has the responsibility of seeing that the *afu* is observed, and some fourteen or fifteen men of this group, called *fulaari*, form a sort of constabulary. Every evening they go round the village armed with clubs, and disguised either in masks similar to that which was hanging up before the chief's house, or they were so covered with leaves as to be unrecognisable. At Waima all the enforcers (*kaivakuku*) of a taboo wear masks (Pl. XXI., B, p. 256); at Inawa and Veifaa they paint the face and cover up part of the body, but they sometimes wear masks; at Aipiana they cover over the whole body with leaves. In the Gulf district there are several important ceremonies at which masks are employed; in the Mekeo district this custom is in the various stages of attenuation and disappearance.

All the time the *fulaari* are in office they may not chew the betel nut, nor drink coconut water, lest the areca and coco nuts should not grow. They may not live with their wives; indeed, they may not even look at a woman, and if they pass one they must keep their eyes on the ground. Women must not go outside their houses whilst the *fulaari* are going their rounds, but if a woman is seen, the *fulaari* places his club at her feet, and she must remain standing there until a fine has been paid for her. If the *fulaari* convict a man of eating the tabooed nuts he is tied to the tree from which he gathered the forbidden fruit, and is only released on the payment of a pig as a fine.

The village from time to time gives presents of food to the *fulaari*.

When there is again a good show of nuts the *afu* chief proclaims that on a particular day the restriction will be removed. We were at Inawi on July 15th and 16th, and the 18th the taboo would be removed from the nuts, after an interval of thirty-two weeks.

We saw the preparations for a big feast, for which eighty-six wild boars had been caught, besides numerous kangaroos and a large supply of native food. We were very sorry that we could not stay to witness the feasting and dancing.

During the afternoon and evening the missionaries arrived in detachments, and our unexpected party of four rather complicated Father Vitale's arrangements, but he was so hospitable and friendly and all were so kind that we did not feel *de trop*. We had two interesting phonograph exhibitions in the afternoon and evening, and one chief made a speech into it amid great excitement.

During our short stay at Inawi we bought a fair number of ethnographical objects, especially lime gourds with burnt designs and stone blades of the now obsolete stone adzes; no handles of these were to be had. These stone adze heads were ruder than any I had previously seen from New Guinea. The Papuan stone implements are usually characterised by being neatly ground and finely polished. These implements were roughly hewn and polished only at the cutting edge.

We also bought some whipping-tops; these are common here, and the following game is played. Two rows of four or five boys stand a considerable distance apart; each lad spins his own top, and they gradually increase the severity of the lashing, till the tops career in mid air across the space between the two rows, the object being to hit one of the opponent's tops. When this is accomplished the conqueror cries out, "*Ango ango angaia!*" ("My top has bitten you"). The tops (*ango ango*) are conical pieces of wood about two and a half to three inches in length.

The whips (*ngapu ngapu*) are ordinary pieces of stick or cane to which a lash is attached composed of a three-ply plat of strips of bark-cloth from the *ipi* tree. It is pretty certain that the whipping-top has not been brought to New Guinea by the white man, for Dr. Lawes has previously found it among the Kabadi tribe, where the natives had not been under the influence of the foreigner.

The following day, July 16th, some of the missionaries arrived, and all went to High Mass in the morning. We had so much else to do that we thought it was not necessary to show our sympathy to the extent of going to the service. We had quite a feast in the middle of the day, and all were very merry. Just before grace after meat, Brother Philip left the table, and in another part of the verandah played the air of our National Anthem in honour of the guests. This act of courtesy pleased us much.

In the afternoon we separated. Our party walked to Veifaa, a distance of forty minutes only, making a slight détour on the way to visit the village Aipiana. Veifaa was reached in good time for the evening meal. The boys' school-house was placed at our disposal, and three beds were put up for us in the inner room.

Sunday, July 17th.—We all went to early morning Mass, and Ray afterwards exhibited the phonograph to a very large audience of demonstrative, excitable natives and delighted missionaries. I was particularly struck with the calm, strong, sweet face of the Sister Superior. She is a Parisienne, with a narrow face and a finely-shaped nose. The two Savoyarde Sisters contrasted with her in having round faces and snubby noses; their more homely countenances were brimful of simple-hearted kindliness. An instructive demonstration of two European races when I was on the look-out for a lesson in Papuan ethnology! The phonograph selection was decidedly mixed, but that did not matter in the least. The Sisters appeared most pleased with the European orchestral marches.

T

The people about here wear native clothing almost exclusively, and it is, fortunately, quite rare to see a man or woman in European garments. The men of the Mekeo district wear a wider perineal band than is worn in the other places we visited, and these belts are here prettily painted in a manner quite new to me, and we were fortunate enough to secure several of them.

The women wear short black leaf petticoats, shorter than any we had previously seen. I was informed that their dress in the mountains is even scantier, as it consists merely of a broad perineal band.

The missionaries, wisely, do not care about introducing European clothing into ordinary use, but they expect the women and girls to wear calico gowns when attending the services. It was very comical to see the women and girls, just before a service, go to the girls' school-house, bring out their gowns, or throw gowns to other women waiting outside, and then proceed to dress themselves in the courtyard. It was still funnier when, after the service, the reverse process was gone through, and their native dress alone remained as the garments of civilisation were doffed. Here, as in most other parts of New Guinea, the women are extremely modest and virtuous, another of the many examples that the amount of clothing worn bears no relation whatever to modesty, though prudery is usually developed in direct proportion to dress.

Our host knew I was very anxious to obtain ethnographical specimens from this place, and made no difficulty whatever about our trading on Sunday, as "ours were not commercial transactions."

Indeed after service the good Father told his congregation to bring us things for sale, and thus we obtained a fair number of specimens, chiefly lime gourds and belts. Father Bouellat persuaded two girls to stand still whilst I copied their tattoo patterns.

In the afternoon I made friends with the children, who played some of their own games for us. For the first time I saw children playing games that mimicked the hunting expeditions of their fathers. In this instance a pig hunt and a kangaroo drive were very vividly acted. The "kangaroos" hopped about on the grass, some hid under bushes. They were stalked and surrounded by "men," and a rush was made, and the flying

THE MEKEO DISTRICT

kangaroos were chased all over the ground. "Man" and "kangaroo" would tumble about in a close embrace, the latter giving characteristic vigorous backward kicks with his legs.

The "pigs" walked about on all fours, hands and feet. They were chased by "men" with sticks to represent spears. When the men came close to the pigs, the latter jerked their heads sideways with an upward movement, as if trying to rip up the men with their tusks. One pig was eventually captured, and two boys got a pole and the pig clasped it with his hands and hooked his knees over it, his body hanging down, and so, like a tied-up pig, he was carried to a place where some boys had laid sticks across one another to represent a fire. The pig was placed on this amid much laughter. The shouting and noise during these games was considerable.

Various other games were played, and towards the end of the afternoon several boys ran off and stayed away some time. When they returned they presented a remarkable appearance. They had bound round their bodies and limbs green or sere banana leaves, and looked for all the world like miniature

FIG. 29. BOYS AT VEIFAA DRESSED UP AS FULAARI

knights of old in leafy armour. The head was entirely covered, the leaves in some cases being prolonged above into a long spike, like certain helmets. Flaps hung down from all the head-pieces like frilled capes. One or two boys had a fringe round the waist, and all had leaves radiating from their ankles, which gave them a very curious appearance, so that they looked like Cochin China fowls. Usually the hands were swathed in green strips, and the bandaging of the right arm was continued in some on to a stick held in the hand, so that it was uninterruptedly swathed.

The boys thus grotesquely accoutred chased the girls about and made them scream. These naughty little fellows were mimicking the *fulaari* of Aipiana !

I was immensely pleased to see an existing important social function imitated by children, and the game presumably also gave us an idea of what the real costume was like. We measured a few men in this village, and altogether had a most enjoyable and instructive time.

We started about 7 a.m. on Monday, July 18th, after breakfast, intending to visit Waima (Maiva) *viâ* Bereina; but at Inawi we received an urgent message from Yule Island that the *Alice May* had arrived there, and would sail on the 19th. This necessitated our giving up the much-desired visit to Waima, and returning instead to Yule Island. We therefore retraced our walk of Friday, except that we kept to the Government road leading direct to the sea. As it was low water the three creeks we had to cross presented no difficulties, but Brother Alexis was very exhausted when we reached Pinupaka at 4 p.m., after our eighteen miles' walk, as he was suffering from an attack of fever.

Brother George gave us a good meal, and we then had three and a half hours' beat to windward in the small Mission cutter, not arriving at the Mission on Yule Island till after 10 p.m. All had gone to bed by that time, but a frugal supper was somehow raked together, and we then retired, fairly tired out by our long day.

Next morning we spent in packing, as Captain Inman wished to start early in the day, and we left the good Fathers and Brothers, with very pleasant memories of the kindness and hospitality of all the members of the Sacred Heart Mission.

Before we left Yule Island for our little inland trip a Sister from Veifaa arrived very ill indeed. She was carried in a hammock by some natives, and shielded from the sun by a Sister holding an umbrella. So far as Father Guis could tell, she suffered from acute rheumatism, dropsy, and malarial fever. It seems a pity that with so many missionaries of both sexes there should not be one qualified medical man, or at all events one who has especially studied medicine. Father Guis has a very good practical knowledge of diseases and their treatment, but it is scarcely fair to expect an accomplished literary man to be responsible for the health and lives of his colleagues in so unhealthy a district. It would also seem desirable that the Brothers, who are often untutored working men, should be ordered to take more precautions, and especially to be careful as to the quality of their drinking water.

PART II

CHAPTER XVIII

JOURNEY FROM KUCHING TO BARAM

WE left Singapore at ten o'clock of the morning of December 10th, on the *Vorwärts*, and arrived at Kuching about 1.30 on the 12th. The voyage up the twenty-three miles of the Sarawak river was charming as the steamer glided along between the fringe of nipa palms and other luxuriant vegetation.

Immediately on landing I called on the Honourable C. A. Bampfylde, the Resident of the division, and who was acting for the Rajah, who was then in England. He kindly invited us to stay with him for a few days, and we had luxurious quarters in a most lovely garden, with a lawn that would not disgrace a Cambridge college, surrounded by choice shrubs and trees, conspicuous among the latter being a kind of areca palm that has a brilliant red stem.

The various members of the British population were very kind and hospitable, and did their best to render our stay in Kuching enjoyable, and we look back upon our visit to Kuching with considerable pleasure.

Dr. A. J. G. Barker, the principal medical officer of Sarawak, entertained Seligmann, and the two doctors had great talks about the tropical diseases in which they were both so keenly interested. Sarawak is to be congratulated on having so able and enthusiastic a medical officer as Dr. Barker unquestionably is. Seligmann took advantage of his stay in Kuching to visit a friend in the Land Dayak country.

Ray stayed at the hotel and spent most of his time in studying the Malay language.

Mr. R. Shelford put me up, and we both enjoyed talking

about Bornean natural history and over mutual Cambridge friends. As there was no chance of our getting away from Kuching for nearly three weeks, I devoted my time to work in the museum and in laying a foundation for a study of the decorative art of the natives of Sarawak. I photographed nearly a hundred Sea Dayak fabrics, and recorded the names of a large number of the designs on them.

The Resident gave his customary usual Christmas Eve dinner to his colleagues and friends, to which we were invited, and Mr. Smith, the then Manager of the Sarawak branch of the Borneo Company, invited us to his usual New Year's Eve dinner, when we again met "everybody," and saw the old year out in the orthodox fashion. Mr. Smith's garden is on a height that overlooks Kuching and the river. In a township of beautiful gardens this was noted for its orchids, and the plants in Mr. Smith's garden truly were a sight to behold, especially one avalanche of the trailing flower spikes of an *Arachnanthe Lowii*, which reached a length of some fourteen feet.

The annual regatta took place on Monday, the 2nd of January. The poop deck of the *Vorwärts* was the grand stand, and most of the white inhabitants were there.

It was a very gay and animated scene, on the shore crowds of quiet people in all kinds of gay dress and undress. On the water were boats of every size, from a tiny dug-out canoe that could scarcely support even a light native to canoes cut out of giants of the forests that would hold fifty to sixty men two abreast. These darted about hither and thither, smoothly gliding like fish or rampaging with flashing paddles and spurting spray.

The natives in the boats gave themselves up to exuberant pleasure, and there was no lack of shouting and merriment. There were large numbers of roofed boats in which one could get occasional glimpses of bedecked and bejewelled women and girls; nor were they ill provided with good things to eat. We could imperfectly see one gorgeously dressed woman in one of the covered boats eating her tiffin with a metal spoon. Some native nurses on board the steamer, who were looking after the children, were greatly interested to discover who could be showing off in this way by eating like a white woman, and they threw pieces of cake at the boat in order to attract the attention of the woman, who was hidden under the low roof of the boat.

PLATE XXIII

REGATTA AT KUCHING

VIEW FROM KABAN HILL, WITH THE BRUNEI HILLS
IN THE DISTANCE

KUCHING

At length their tactics were successful, and on her showing herself they made grimaces at her.

I took some snapshots of the scene and of some of the races, but the day was dull; in the morning there was rarely a gleam of watery sunshine, and it rained all the afternoon.

All the white inhabitants, the half-castes, and the more important Malays and Chinamen lunched in the court-house. The races lasted from 9 a.m. till 4.30 or 5 p.m. A sort of comic side-show was provided in the shape of a greased boom along which competitors had to walk in order to secure a small flag that was stuck at the end. The successful as well as the unsuccessful fell into the water, a matter of no moment to the amphibious people.

Kuching, the capital of Sarawak, is only a small town. On the left bank of the river, and situated in beautiful grounds, is the Astana, the simple residence of the Rajah. Separated from it by a gully are the fort and the barracks, the headquarters of the miniature Sea Dayak army of Sarawak. On the right bank of the river is the town itself. At the entrance to the wooden wharf at which the steamers tie up is the custom-house, beyond is a square in which are grouped all the Government offices. Immediately opposite the custom-house and for a short distance down stream is the large bazaar or Chinese quarter, where everything required for native or European use can be purchased at reasonable rates. The comparatively large establishment of the Borneo Company is at the extremity of the business end of the town. To the right, beyond the Government offices, is the Malay town.

The few Europeans, who are all Government officials or connected with the Borneo Company or the missions, live in the bungalow surrounded by charming gardens well stocked with varied and beautiful shrubs and trees. From most of the houses one obtains interesting views of distant isolated mountains uprising from the somewhat flat country, and the sunset effects with the lowering clouds of the rainy season are often very fine.

Despite the strange tropical vegetation, the township has a peculiar home-like appearance, due to the prevalence of carefully trimmed lawns, green hedges, and well-built roads. There is an air of neatness and quiet beauty which was very refreshing after much wandering on watery ways and the glare and bustle of some tropical towns and the frank unfoliaged ugliness of others. The rampant verdure of luxuriant vegetation is here kept within due bounds, though not without some difficulty. By day there is the sweet singing of birds, and at night myriad insects chirp with varied note, ranging from crude stridulation to what may be termed a musical song.

A very good native band plays twice or thrice a week in the evening in a public garden, and gives an excuse for social foregathering. The social centre for the white man is naturally the club. Deserted during the day, it wakes up in the evening, and about six o'clock members begin to drop in; but all leave shortly before eight, to bathe, and dress for dinner. There are a couple of tennis courts, but during the rainy season very little tennis is possible. Generally one or two members play billiards, but the great game is American bowls; this gives plenty of exercise, and is really a fine game for the tropics.

On the hill is a large reservoir, formed by a dam thrown across an irregular depression. The winding shore of this artificial lake, embowered with rank vegetation, makes a most lovely walk. By the side of the reservoir is the ice factory, which had only very recently been completed, but now ice is regularly supplied at a cheap rate by the Government.

On the slope of the same hill is the museum, and the picturesque house of the curator. Close by is the large demesne of the Anglican Church, with the bishop's house, rectory, and official buildings. A considerable part of the grounds is taken up with a cricket field for the Mission boys, and with golf-links; but new golf-links have recently been laid elsewhere.

Owing to the sporting proclivities and fondness of horses of the present Rajah, Kuching possesses one of the most picturesque racecourses in the Far East. The roads, too, in and around the town are in excellent condition, and they extend for a considerable distance into the country in various directions.

The museum is a very pet institution of the Rajah's, which he has wisely and liberally endowed. In his address on the occasion of the opening of the museum on the 4th of August, 1891, the Rajah admitted that it had cost a good deal both of trouble and money, "but," he continued, "I consider that every country worthy of being called a country should have a museum, and I hope that ours will be equal, at any rate in time, to any other country in the East, including even India. It has been for many years a great wish of my heart to see a good museum established here, and at last I hope that wish is accomplished."

The building is an attractive edifice, built in Queen Anne style, consisting of three lower and three upper rooms, built in the form of an H. It is very well lighted, and at the same time there is an abundance of wall space. The foundation of the ethnographical collections was the very valuable Brooke Low Collection, which the Rajah bought in England and re-shipped to its native land. This has been added to from time to time, and although there is a good deal to be done before all the arts and crafts of the natives of Sarawak are adequately represented, the museum contains the best and most instructive collection extant illustrating the ethnography of Sarawak. The fauna of Sarawak is also most fully represented. All the specimens are well labelled and attractively set out. Dr. G. D. Haviland was the first curator. He was succeeded by Mr. E. Bartlett, and Mr. R. Shelford, the present curator, was appointed in 1897.

The museum is a favourite resort for natives, and every day numbers of Chinese, Malays, and Dayaks come to have a look round. Often women and children come too, and very picturesque are some of the groups, as fortunately the natives retain their own costumes, and do not ape European clothing, which, whatever its effect when worn by ourselves, is ugly and incongruous when adopted by most native races. The Dayak men often have very little on, but that is an advantage, as one can then admire their shapely limbs. Their "chawats," or loin cloths, are varied in colour, and however bright they may be, they always harmonise with the beautiful deep cinnamon-coloured skin of the wearer.

Mr. Shelford has a Chinese clerk or assistant, who speaks English well and has a very good knowledge of the zoology of Borneo. He is a Catholic, and beats the big drum of the Catholic band with gusto. It is also amusing to see a Dayak boy, clothed only in a small chawat, sorting and drying bird skins. Several Dayak collectors are attached to the museum, and they continually bring in all kinds of zoological specimens. When I was working in the museum two of them got into trouble, one for carrying pig-meat through the bazaar, and the other for firing off crackers on Christmas Day at an unauthorised time. Pork may be carried along the high-roads, but not along the smaller streets of the bazaar, on account of the sentiments of the Mohammedans.

The enthusiastic curator had quite a menagerie in and under his house. On one occasion when I was staying with him he had nine hornbills in one cage, three different species being represented. In another cage were four lemurs (*Nycticebus*). He had also a binturong, and another small carnivore, three chained-up monkeys, one being a gibbon, and an owl. There were always a lot of live jungle insects about, and in the dining-room were a number of gigantic stick insects unceasingly munching away at leaves; the allied mantidæ are insectivorous. Mr. Shelford is anxious to induce the Rajah to add a small zoological garden to the other attractions of the museum.

We left Kuching early on January 4th in the *Adeh*, a small but comfortable coasting steamer. The morning was fine, but it rained all the afternoon when we were ascending the Rejang. As soon as it was dark we anchored, as it is against standing orders for the steamers to sail in the rivers between six o'clock in the evening and six o'clock in the morning.

By ten o'clock next day we reached Sibu, ninety miles up the river. On landing we called on the Resident, the Honourable H. F. Deshon. Mr. Johnson took us to the bazaar, the Malay town, and round the small, low island that forms the central station of the large and important Rejang district.

In the afternoon we went down river in a Government boat to see some Kanauit natives at Saduan who made beautiful baskets. I was anxious to see them at work, and to learn their names for the patterns; but our boatmen made a mistake, and took us to see a Sea Dayak house at Sanamari. It was a hopelessly wet afternoon, but still it was an enjoyable little trip.

We visited a native cemetery on the way back. Sheds were built over the graves, and under wall-less shelters were numerous pots, baskets, articles of clothing, and all sorts of objects that appealed very strongly to my collecting instincts, which, however, were rigorously kept under control. Most of the objects appeared to me to have been old and probably useless. Under one shed, or mausoleum as I suppose one ought to call it, was an old Kayan shield and a tiny model of another shield, also a mancala board. Mancala, the national game of Africa, is played with pebbles, or similar objects, on a board provided with parallel rows of depressions; the game has travelled nearly all over the world, the extent of its distribution depending upon negro or Arab influence. I think this is the first record from Borneo, though it is known in the Philippines.

Over another grave was an imitation parang with a wooden blade. A parang is a locally made steel sword, which is used for cutting down the jungle, chopping wood, and as a sword when fighting. Apparently the survivors considered that the spirits would be satisfied in some cases with the essence of things offered to them. The cemetery was bountifully decorated with parti-coloured red and yellow flags; there were also two long poles covered with what appeared to be straw decorations.

We had tea at Mr. Deshon's on our return to Sibu, and some Sea Dayak women came, by appointment, to show me some patterns. The remainder of the evening was very pleasantly spent at the Residency.

The steamer started at 5 a.m. next morning, and we reached the sea at one o'clock, and proceeded on our eastward journey.

Unfortunately, we had arrived at the season when it is impossible to cross the bar at the mouth of the Baram River, so we had to continue our journey to Limbang, and thence to proceed by a long overland détour to our destination.

The station at Limbang is situated at a bend of the river on its right bank below the range of the Kaban Hills. In coming up the river one first passes the Malay town, built as usual on piles, the houses being either near the water's edge or, as the Malays seem to prefer, actually over the running water. Here were several sago factories. Later we passed the bazaar, or Chinese quarter, for nearly all the shopkeepers in Sarawak are Chinamen. Then we arrived at the fort, a two-storied wooden building, in which are the Government offices; beyond were the barracks, stables, and other out-buildings.

On the spur of the hills behind and above the fort is the Residency, a commodious house, with a very large deep verandah, from which an extensive view is obtained of all the lower valley of the Limbang as far as the Brunei Hills.

Mr. O. F. Ricketts takes a great interest in his garden, and has laid it out very tastefully in well-mown grassy terraces with flower-beds, flowering shrubs, areca palms, and other tropical foliage. Mr. Ricketts has a large selection of cannas and hibiscus, so that there are always some bright flowers open. He has a delicate violet hibiscus brought from Celebes, which

I believe is a very rare variety; he has also raised a colias with deep brown leaves that do not show a trace of green. He procures all his canna seeds from England!

One evening we went up to the top of Kaban Hill, known popularly as Mount Pisgah, and had a magnificent panoramic view from Mount Mulu in one direction to Labuan in the other. The great swampy plains were intersected by the sinuous courses of several rivers. By the aid of a glass we could see part of the town of Brunei fringing Brunei Lake, and at the horizon were the Brunei Hills. (Plate XXIII., B, p. 280.)

A very considerable portion of Sarawak appears to be low-lying land; in some places the hills come down to the coast, but for about a hundred miles inland the country is flat and more or less swampy. Here and there solitary mountains rise above the level, and these are sculptured into peaks and precipices. It seems as if relatively recently the country as a whole has been slightly raised from the sea. Before this upheaval the isolated mountains had been islands which have since been embraced by the advancing land. Thus Sarawak would still be a land in the making, to which the rivers contribute their quota of alluvial soil.

The river banks in the interior, with their layers of pebbles, alluvium, and leaf beds, tell an unmistakable tale, and the spit at the mouth of Baram River demonstrates the gradual extension of the land into the sea. The innumerable gigantic tree trunks floated down by the river are deposited by the action of prevailing winds and currents mainly on the eastern or right side of the estuary, and river sediment and leaf deposits are entangled in the natural breakwater, and so by the conjoint efforts of the river and the sea the spit gradually grows. The swampy soil is soon rendered more coherent by the growth of casuarinas and other trees, and as the spit advances, so marches the appropriate vegetation behind it in marshalled order.

The river scenery in the low lands is somewhat monotonous. As far as the influence of salt water extends, palisades of nipa palms usually line the banks. These trunkless palms, whose long leaves spring from the water's edge, are of varied use to man, for their leaves are utilised as thatch, their sap produces sugar, and, when burnt, their ashes provide salt.

Behind the serried array of nipa palms are swamp trees, and beyond these again, on firmer soil, are tall jungle trees. When one paddles up the creeks a greater variety of vegetation manifests itself, and many beautiful vistas open out which the wealth and luxuriance of the tropical jungle tempt one to explore. We had our first experience of this at Sibu.

Immediately on our arrival Mr. Ricketts had sent messengers by jungle tracks to Mr. Hose, to acquaint him of our arrival, so that he might send boats to meet us on his side of the spur of Mount Mulu. As all this would take time we were obliged to remain at Limbang for some days, and a very enjoyable time we had there in the beautiful Residency, thanks to the kindness and hospitality of our host. I cannot refrain from once more remarking on the wonderful generosity and friendliness that was exhibited to us throughout our travels. Any verbal acknowledgment can but feebly express the gratitude we feel to those numerous friends who assisted and cheered us on our way.

We devoted one morning to visiting a small Malay sago factory by the side of the river. At the edge of the river bank were several lengths of the stems of sago palms, and beside them was a heap of bark that had been stripped off the trunks.

Under a shed, roofed with nipa palm leaves and supported on two horizontal poles, was a peeled log of sago, part of which had been scraped away by means of a long spiked rasp. A Malay showed us how their grating was done, and on the floor were two heaps of the triturated pith of the sago palm.

The man then removed some of the coarse powder to a mat on a neighbouring platform, which more or less overhung the river, and trod the grated pith, pouring water on it from a kerosene tin which was suspended by a cord from the end of a long, slender pole. This contrivance for scooping up water from the river is similar to the shaduf so extensively employed in Egypt and the East, and is doubtless another example of indirect Arab influence.

The dancing of the man separates, so to speak, the chaff from the wheat, and the farinaceous water pours into an old canoe that lies alongside of the platform. This canoe is covered over to prevent extraneous matter from getting into the sago, and the lower end is boarded up. The canoe thus forms a trough in which the sediment is deposited, while the superfluous water dribbles away from one end into the river.

The sago thus crudely manufactured by the Malays is sold to the Chinese factors, who give it extra washings and strain it through a fine cloth. The fine mud is spread out to dry in the sun. The white impalpable sago powder is packed in bags and shipped to Europe *viâ* Kuching. The granulation of the sago is a subsequent process. A considerable portion of the sago consumed at home must come from Borneo. The amount of sago flour exported from Sarawak in 1899 was 228,989 piculs (or over 12,000 tons), the value being $790,583 (or £79,058), which brought in an export duty to the Sarawak Government of $19,503.01 (£1,950).

The 14th of January was a memorable day for us, as the Resident invited us to accompany him to Brunei, which is one of the oldest of Malay towns. It was first described by Pigafetti, who visited "Bornei" in July, 1521. Even then the town was large and important, and the Sultan was powerful and wealthy; consequently the Malays must have been established in the country for at least five hundred years.

The former sultans held nominal sway over a considerable portion of northern Borneo; but though the Malays brought with them a relatively high civilisation, they only affected the coastal population, no influence was exercised for the improvement of the condition of the interior natives. The Malay traders have always been adventuresome, and they introduced various trade goods up the rivers; but the up-river tribes, such as the Kayans and Kenyahs, do not appear to have acknowledged the authority of the sultans, or to have paid them tribute.

The power of the sultans and of their subordinates, from the highest to the lowest, has for a long time been exerted to extract the maximum amount of revenue out of those unfortunate coastal tribes who, by their propinquity, could not escape from their cruel and rapacious neighbours. Whatever it may have been in the past, the history of the Brunei administration for the last half-century has been marked by rapine, bloodshed, extortion, injustice, and utter hopelessness.

The fall of the power of Brunei is probably owing to causes that have hastened the fall of other empires and cities. The State was founded by a civilised and even a polished people, expert in the arts of life; but success and power became undermined by wealth, luxury, and sensuality, which destroyed the energy that created those conditions in which alone they could thrive. Strength of character sunk into aimless cruelty.

The isolation of the town also prevented that intercourse with different peoples which affords the necessary stimulus for advancement. It is true that there were trading and diplomatic relations with China even in very early times, but that was in the days when Brunei was a living force, as it also must have been when centuries ago a Sultan of Brunei conquered the Philippines and the neighbouring islands.

Founded by a pagan, the State soon became converted to Islamism, and the religious fervour of the converts, backed by belligerent tenets of their faith, were doubtless important factors in the building up of the power of Brunei. But all that is now past, and Brunei has sunk into senile decay.

The name Brunei is variously spelt Bruni or Brunai; an old form of it was Brauni or Braunai, and another was Burni. Pigafetti called it Bornei. Voyagers applied the name of the town to the island as a whole; but the name of Borneo is unknown to the natives of Sarawak, who call it Pulo Kalamantan.

Most Europeans derive the term Kalamantan, or Klamantan, from an indigenous sour wild mango, which is called *Kalamantan;* but Hose believes this term is a corruption of *lemanta*, "raw sago." There is no obvious reason why Borneo should be known as the island of an inconspicuous wild fruit, while it is very appropriately "the island of raw sago."

Owing to an ineffective and rapacious system of government, great dissatisfaction with the Sultan has for a long time been felt by the natives, and as a result the Sultanate has shrunk to the small triangular area which constitutes the drainage basins of the Balait, Tutong, and Brunei rivers. At the present time natives of the Balait and Tutong have hoisted the Sarawak flag, and are urging the Rajah to take them over. It is obvious that the days of Malay dynasty in Borneo are numbered.

Owing to their having taken territory from him, the Rajah of Sarawak and the British North Borneo Company pay the Sultan a yearly tribute as cession money of about $30,000 (£3,000), paid half-yearly in advance, and practically this is the main source of his revenue.

Unfortunately we had for our excursion a dull day, unredeemed by a single glint of sunshine, and it drizzled during part of the morning. We went down the Limbang in the Government steam launch, the *Gazelle*, and owing to the tide being low we stuck for an hour and a half in a sandbank near the mouth of the river. When the tide turned we left the Limbang and entered the mouth of Brunei River. Owing to the hills on the left bank of the lower reaches of this river the scenery is much prettier than that of the corresponding portions of other rivers of Sarawak. The right bank is merely the coast of a large alluvial island deposited in the combined delta of the Limbang, Brunei, and Kadayan rivers.

About six miles from its present mouth Brunei River extends into a sort of elongated lake. The town is situated along the left or northern shore, and opposite to it is some high land. The waters of the Brunei and Kadayan rivers pass between this hill and the range of hills behind the town. In other words Brunei is situated at the conjoint mouths of the small Brunei and Kadayan rivers, and in close proximity to the large Limbang River. Originally this spot was on the coast of the Brunei Bay, but the growth of the largest of the delta islands, which is mainly due to the action of the Limbang, has made the site of Brunei appear as if it were actually up a river.

The situation of Brunei was extremely well chosen, as it is very sheltered, and would have been easily defended in the old days.

The town of Brunei has been so often described that there is no need to add one more account, especially as there is no reason to believe that it has essentially altered in its character since the days when it was first visited by Europeans, though it has probably become reduced in size, and it must surely have also become meaner of aspect.

At first sight one is wonderfully impressed with the town. Some houses are built on the bank, others on islets, but the vast majority form great compact masses standing in piles in the shallow estuary. The groups of pile-dwellings are intersected by broader or narrower waterways, along and across which dart small canoes like so many skaters or other aquatic insects that skim along the surface of our ponds.

On closer acquaintance, however, a good deal of the town presents rather a dilapidated appearance. This is, doubtless, partially due to the houses being built of wood, and thatched and usually walled with palm leaves. We saw it on a dull, damp day, however, and the impression on my mind was that it would take a great deal of time and material to put the town into a good state of repair.

PLATE XXIV

BRUNEI

A FAMILY BATHE

We rowed about the town and visited the small Chinese
[baz]aar, but we did not land for long as our time was limited
[and] there did not appear to be much that we could do. We
[took] several snapshot photographs, but were too low down
[on] the water to get very good views. Although the place
[look]ed poverty-stricken, I was informed there were a large
[num]ber of ancient and valuable objects in the houses of the
[imp]ortant people, such as gold, bronze, and brass work, Chinese
[silk]s and embroidery.

We should have greatly liked to call on the Sultan, but we
[were] prevented from doing so as we were on a Sarawak steamer,
[and] there had been recently a little friction between the Sultan
[and] the Rajah's Government. The Resident had on board the
[half]-yearly cession money and rent for Brooketon, which was
[then] due from the Rajah to the Sultan; but the cession money
[was] $1,000 short, for that sum had been paid by the Sarawak
[Gov]ernment as indemnity to some natives in the Limbang who
[had] been raided by some Brunei Malays.

[O]n our arrival at Brunei word was sent to the Chamberlain,
[and] soon that distinguished functionary came to receive the
[doll]ars. He was an elderly, fat man, with a clever, diplomatic
[face]. There was a good deal of conversation and documents
[were] read, and finally the rent for Brooketon was taken, as there
[was] no dispute about that; but the Chamberlain had to return
[to th]e Sultan to confer about the remainder. Finally the Sultan
[agree]d to accept the diminished cession money, as he still
[clai]ms ownership of the Limbang, and on that ground the
[raid]ed were his own subjects, consequently, according to his
[conten]tion, the Sarawak Government had no right to interfere.

[In] his recent life of Rajah Brooke, in the "Builders of Greater
[Brit]ain Series," Sir Spenser St. John writes (p. 216): "The
[Sult]an is the Suzerain Lord of all the possessions of the present
[Raja]h, with the doubtful exception of Sarawak proper, and
[tha]t Britain is the Protector of Sarawak and Brunei alike."

[T]he story of the first Rajah Brooke is most fascinating, and
[has] several times been told, so that it is superfluous to repeat it
[here], but I shall content myself by merely alluding to the most
[prom]inent events.

[Si]r James Brooke first landed at Kuching from his schooner
[yach]t *Royalist* on August 15th, 1839, and made acquaintance
[with] Muda Hassim, the Rajah of Sarawak. Pirates swarmed at

the mouth of the Sarawak river, the Rajah was not on friendly terms with his neighbours the Dutch, and the population of Upper Sarawak was threatening him with a hostile force. Trade was at a standstill, and people in and about the capital were subjected to oppression and extortion from every petty officer of the State.

As a friend of the Rajah, Sir James Brooke at once commenced his great work. His first achievement was a bloodless victory over the rebel army, which, after months of manœuvring and negotiation, was disbanded. For this assistance he was offered the Governorship of Sarawak, which, after some delay, he undertook, and at once set to work to clean out the Augean stables of wrong and oppression and to reform irregularities, always, however, regarding the customs and existing laws and rights of the people. He was confirmed as Rajah in 1842.

Warlike expeditions to protect and avenge his subjects had to be made against the wilder tribes of the interior, and to repress the pirates, who, whilst they existed, were a constant source of trouble, disorganising by one raid a whole district, which had perhaps taken years to settle down since a previous raid.

When all things seemed to be progressing favourably the great Chinese rebellion broke out in February, 1857, the story of which has been so well told by Sir Spenser St. John. One result of this calamity was to prove how well grounded Rajah Sir James Brooke was in the affection of the Malays and Sea Dayaks, and, thanks to their loyalty, zeal, and bravery the Chinese were completely routed after they had actually taken and burnt Kuching. The country soon settled down and became even more prosperous.

The "Old Rajah" died in England on the 11th June, 1868, and he was succeeded by his nephew Charles Johnson Brooke, Rajah Muda of Sarawak, who had long been in the country, and had distinguised himself in his uncle's service.

The Rajah is an absolute monarch who consults the Supreme Council on important matters. This Council is composed of the Rajah, three senior English officers, and four native chiefs of Sarawak proper. There is also a General Council composed of the more important chiefs of various districts and certain English officers. The General Council meets about once a year, and on this occasion the Rajah makes an address and states his policy and proposed changes in the administration or finance.

SARAWAK

The Raj is divided into five main districts under English Residents: Sarawak, Batang Lupar, Rejang, Baram, and Limbang. The mere enumeration of these names shows what accessions to the original Raj of Sarawak proper have been made in the progress of events. Limbang was annexed on the 17th March, 1890.

There are various Government officials in Kuching, each of whom has usually various duties to perform, but the practical administration of the country is in the hands of the Residents and Assistant Residents. A Resident is at the same time a governor and a magistrate, and his powers depend upon his rank; but his influence depends upon his personality. An energetic Resident who goes among the people can exercise an immense power for good, but for this is required a knowledge of the languages spoken in the district and a sympathy for the people themselves.

When Rajah Sir James Brooke first took over Sarawak it was with the intention of administering the country for the benefit of the natives rather than for personal aggrandisement, and ever since this has been the central idea of the Government.

It has often been objected to the rule of the late and of the present Rajah that they have not endeavoured to "open up" the country, and have thrown obstacles in the way of those who desired to develop it. To a certain extent this is true. So far as I understand it, the policy of the Government has consistently been to let the growth of the country take place slowly and, as far as practicable, naturally. Neither for the Civil List, nor for official salaries, nor even for administrative purposes and public works have the natives been exploited or the soil alienated. Probably few countries are financed so economically; perhaps in many cases the salaries of officials are too low, and there is at present a tendency to save a few dollars by petty economies; but these are faults of which the natives can scarcely complain. Life and property are safe, and there is perfect freedom in religion and custom, provided that the latter does not infringe on the life or belongings of others. These are advantages which the natives did not formerly possess and which are now thoroughly appreciated by them. The taxation, which is very light, is collected with discretion, and falls hard on no one. There is no difficulty in getting it paid by those heads of families who have but recently come under the Government, for they realise that the benefits of a settled government and of a secure outlet for their trade are more than compensated for by the annual payment of a couple of dollars. The amount of the "door" tax varies, but four shillings a year is what is usually levied. In certain cases, half or the whole of this is remitted in return for right to impress temporary labour. This system is very light, and is entirely suited to local conditions.

There would be a grave danger to the natives if Sarawak was "opened up" according to the desires of certain financiers or corporations whose sole idea is to make money. The "development" of a country does not necessarily mean the welfare of the original inhabitants; too often it spells their ruin or extermination. The hustling white man wants to make as much money as he can within the shortest possible time; but rapid exploitation is not development, and in many tropical countries it has meant that if the aborigines will not work as hard for the foreigner as the latter desires, their place must be taken by coolies from elsewhere.

According to one point of view, a country belongs to its inhabitants; but according to another, which is prevalent among Europeans, it should belong to those who can extract the most from it. The Sarawak government is based upon the former theory, and so far as I have observed it honestly endeavours to help the people to govern themselves and assists them towards a gradual bettering of their condition.

Sir Spenser St. John says: "The government of Sarawak is a kind of mild despotism, the only government suitable to Asiatics, who look to their chiefs as the sole depositary of supreme power. The influence of the old Rajah still pervades the whole system, and native and European work together in perfect harmony." This is the judgment of one whose opinion must always carry weight.

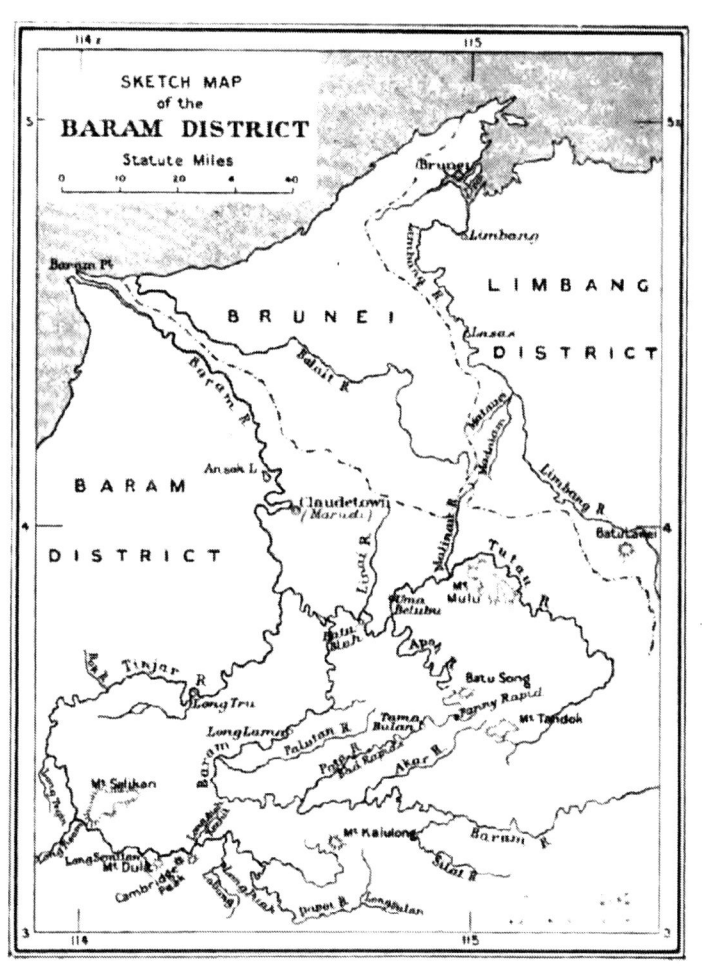

CHAPTER XIX

THE WAR-PATH OF THE KAYANS

HOSE had arranged for us to go up the Limbang and the Madalam rivers, to walk across a low watershed, and to come down the Malinau, Tutau, and Baram to Claudetown. The greater part of this route was the ancient war-path of the Kayans of the Baram, when they went head hunting in the river basin of the Limbang; it is also a route by which gutta hunters travel.

We left Limbang at eight o'clock on the morning of the 16th January in the *Gazelle*, and steamed up the river trailing three boats behind us. Each *goban*, or canoe, was about forty feet long, three to four feet wide, and was covered with a palm-leaf roof. Strips of nipa palm had been fastened together by ratan to form a kind of mat, or *kajang*; a number of these were laid over a bamboo framework. The hull of each boat was a large dug-out, the sides of which were heightened with boards.

For many miles up its course the river maintains the same general character that it has at Limbang, except that it narrows and the nipa palms which line the banks below the station are no longer to be met with.

We anchored that afternoon at Lasas, and search was made for fresh boats and more men. One of our canoes, which leaked considerably, we wished to replace, and we needed an extra one. Matters did not look promising at night, but next morning, about 5.30 a.m., the requisite boats turned up, and we started in them about eight o'clock, the steamer returning to the fort.

The heavy goods were packed in the middle of each boat, and behind these was the space reserved for each passenger. Four or five men paddled in front, and one or two behind. We arrived at Tulu at five. We established ourselves in the only house of the village, which was about a hundred and thirty feet in length. Like most of the houses in Borneo, it was situated on the bank of the river, and was built on piles, so that the floor of the house was some ten feet above the ground. A log with deep notches in it served for a ladder. On climbing up this we found ourselves in a long gallery or verandah on the outer, or river, side of which were placed mats. Along the verandah were one or two fireplaces, above each of which was a small staging, and at one end of the verandah was a raised platform used as a lounge and sleeping-place. The side of the verandah that faced the river was more or less boarded up, but a long, narrow opening was left of such a height that people sitting on the mats could conveniently look out. As we paddled up the river we always saw faces looking out at us through this opening in the various houses that we passed; sometimes there was a long row of buff-coloured faces without any body being visible.

On the other side of the verandah are the domiciles, each of which opens by a separate door on to the verandah. A long house averages from four to sixty or more distinct households, or "doors" as they are officially termed. On the low partition walls of the domiciles were stacked large quantities of firewood, and hanging from the rafters were loops of strips of palm leaves ready for plaiting into mats. On the floor of the verandah close to the walls of the homes were Chinese vases, gongs, and other valuables, and suspended from deer antlers were parangs, bamboo boxes, and various small articles.

The floor was composed of split bamboos placed a little distance apart, like lattice-work. This kept the floors clean, as rubbish fell through, and a little water spilt on the floor soon cleansed the smooth bamboo of any dirt.

Below the house were the pigsties. The pigs were fed in wooden troughs, which could be raised by a cord suspended from the floor of the house. If one pig tried to get more than its share it was poked away from the trough by a long bamboo, which passed through the flooring. When the trough was slightly raised above the pigs' heads the fowls could get their meal in peace.

After our evening meal Ray brought out the phonograph and gave a selection of Sea Dayak songs that he had obtained at Limbang. These caused great delight. We tried to get some of the natives of the village to sing into the machine, but they were too shy; at last one man made an attempt, which was both feeble and brief. Then a Brunei Malay, one of our crew, sang, but as he put his mouth too close to the trumpet the result was rather tinny. Altogether our hosts were satisfied, and we had the opportunity of seeing how these people express the emotion of pleasure.

We reached some rapids early the following morning; they were by no means formidable, and merely necessitated extra exertion in paddling or in poling. The excitement, however, was sufficient to cause the boatmen to shriek and call out to one another. When really excited the Sea Dayak is noisy, but not so much so, nor so demonstrative, as the Papuan. The natives are skilled boatmen, creeping along under the banks out of the swifter currents, and know how to take advantage of the lesser currents in the concave side of the bends, so that the boat takes a comparatively straight course, and as far as possible avoids the force of the stream.

On the morning of the nineteenth we entered the Madalam, an affluent which is distinctly narrower than the main stream, and our journey up it was more difficult, owing to the strength of the current and the numerous rapids. We landed in the afternoon on one of the shingle beaches or *karangang* that occur in the concavity of a bend of the river, or in other words, in the convexity of the bank, and immediately wood was chopped and a fire lit, a folding table was set up, and in a very short time a cup of afternoon tea was ready. After this we strolled about in the jungle and on the small beach, and shortly before sunset had a swim; there are no crocodiles to fear so far up the river. By this time our boatmen had finished making a sleeping-shed for us. It is surprising how quickly the natives will erect one of these huts. As there were three of us they made the hut about ten or twelve feet long and about six feet broad. A flooring of saplings or bamboos was raised two or three feet off the ground by poles running lengthwise; the roof was covered with *kajangs* from the boats; the ends were slightly walled with boughs, but the sides were open. This was of no consequence as the roof was low. To make everything more secure we threw our waterproof sheets over the *kajangs* and others over the floorings. With a couple of blankets and a pillow each, we had very comfortable quarters, safe from rain and damp.

We had a good dinner on the beach and turned in early.

The country we were passing through was a few years previously the scene of a little disturbance, and I have culled the following account of it from the *Sarawak Gazette* (vol. xxv., 1895) in order to illustrate some of the difficulties that the Government has had to contend against.

In December, 1894, Lahing, son of Orang Kaya Tumonggong Lawai, the chief of the Long Patas, went from the Tutau to the Pandaruan River with the avowed intention of collecting jungle produce, but when there, and only three hours' walk from the Government Station at Limbang, he murdered three Kadayans and, with two of their heads as trophies, returned to his father's house on the Tutau; the third man sunk in the river directly after he was killed, and so his head was not obtained. The heads were feasted in the house on their arrival, and news of this having reached the Resident of Baram, he at once ordered them to be given up and a deposit of $1,500 to be put in the fort. This was done, but the Rajah was not satisfied with the pledge, and ordered the Orang Kaya to pay a fine of $2,000, and to move back to the Baram District, for in the meantime he had shifted to the Madalam River. This the Orang Kaya refused to do, nor would he meet the Resident of Baram, but commenced building a house in the Madalam for himself and his people, who numbered about seventy families, to the annoyance of the peaceable inhabitants of the district, who had suffered on previous occasions from these men. The Resident of Limbang sent for the Orang Kaya to come down to the fort, but he refused to do so, and owing to the feeling of insecurity which was rife among the people of the Limbang, and the certain prospect of future disturbances should these men be allowed to settle in the Madalam, the Rajah decided that force must be employed to punish the aggressors, and restore tranquillity and confidence amongst the people in the Limbang.

The Rajah informed the Supreme Council on the 20th May, 1895, that Orang Kaya Tumonggong Lawai and his son Lahing in former times had been made use of by the Brunei Government for warlike purposes against the population of the Limbang. Since their arrival in the Madalam the Orang Kaya had on two occasions visited Brunei, where he was received in a friendly manner by H.H. the Sultan of Brunei and his Government.

Under these circumstances the Rajah did not consider it safe

ORANG KAYA TUMONGGONG LAWAI, CHIEF OF THE LONG
PATAS, IN WAR COSTUME, WITH A KENYAH SHIELD

A SLEEPING HUT IN THE JUNGLE

to permit this party to locate themselves in or near the Limbang and Brunei. He felt sure that if they were allowed to settle there further troubles and murders would ensue; he therefore intended to take steps to drive them out of the locality without delay. The Rajah further stated that the Resident of Limbang, Mr. Ricketts, had sent a message to call the Orang Kaya Tumonggong to come and see him, but that he declined to answer to the summons.

As regards the heads of the Kadayans murdered in Pandaruan, they were kept and feasted in the house of Lahing and his father, but were afterwards delivered up and sent to Baram fort with a deposit of $1,500, which the Resident of Baram, Mr. Hose, had required from them. These were to be detained in the fort as a guarantee for their future behaviour, until he could learn the Rajah's decision on the case. In a despatch to Mr. Hose the Rajah had given instructions that either Lahing, the murderer, or his father should be sent to Kuching to be dealt with. As far as their lives were concerned, the deposit of money and the delivery of the heads would render them safe, but some more certain pledge to ensure peace for the future would be required, such as one or other of the two men being detained as a hostage for some years in Kuching. Up to recently the principal thing against the Orang Kaya and his followers had been their untrustworthy characters, but now they were guilty of actual murder. The immediate danger was that, having once committed themselves, and having been well received since the commission of the offences at Brunei, with its weak and anarchical state of government, they would, if allowed to settle near Limbang, keep the peaceable inhabitants, who depend upon Sarawak for protection, in a state of discomfort and alarm, and this must be avoided at all hazards.

The members of Council gave their opinion that it was absolutely necessary that these murderers should be treated as enemies, and should be driven out of Limbang; and they hoped that the strongest representations would be made to the Brunei Government to prevent a recurrence of such conduct.

Towards the end of May a punitive expedition was organised, consisting of sixty Malay and four hundred and sixty Sea Dayaks and two or three white officials. They manned in all about forty boats.

The rebels held out a flag of truce, but the advance party on the opposite side of the river could not see it, and it was not without much trouble that the attacking force was checked. Only four men were killed, and these lives would have been saved if the people had remained in the house as they were ordered to do.

The Dayak portion of the expeditionary force having been restrained and stationed to the rear, the Malays and Europeans advanced. Orang Kaya Tumonggong Lawai was summoned to surrender himself, and warned that should he refuse to do so the house would be attacked. After considerable delay, during which he made several excuses, he came out and went to the boats. The force then at once retired.

Lahing was found to be absent with a body of men in Baram, whither they had gone to bring over the remainder of the property from their old house.

The rebels had received news of the advance of the expedition on the day previous to its arrival. There were evident signs of an intention of showing resistance, but the Government forces came upon the Orang Kaya too suddenly for this, as he was not properly prepared, and many of his men were away. The reason given for this attack upon the Pandaruan people was that they had killed two Punans who were under the Orang Kaya; but this story was false, the true reason being that the Long Patas heard that the Kenyahs had killed several Sea Dayaks before, and they followed their example.

Our men got up at daylight on Friday, January 20th, and lit fires. We had breakfast about 6.45, and started again a little before eight. About 8.35 we were stopped by a tree that had fallen across the river, and it took an hour to cut through it. Had tiffin about noon, as usual on a shingle beach. Shortly afterwards we passed some low cliffs, and at three were stopped by a karangang across the river; but the men by removing the bigger stones soon cleared a passage, through which they dragged the boats. Near here wild mangoes grow on the steep banks. The fruit has a pleasant aromatic odour, but I did not much care for the flavour. Still, a little fresh fruit was an agreeable change.

We had a very heavy day on Saturday, or rather the boatmen had, as the Madalam was little more than a succession of shallows, up which the boats had either to be poled or hauled.

At one place there was a steep, rocky rapid, indeed a cascade, where we had to unship all our baggage while the boats were hauled up a miniature waterfall. All day the men were nearly as often in the water as out of it; they worked very well and cheerfully. We stopped that afternoon at the junction of the Trunan (or Trikan) with the Madalam.

Sunday, January 22nd.—The Trikan is a very narrow river—practically a stream. We were now no longer bothered with shallows or rapids, but with trees that had fallen across the channel. Some of these we crept under, others were well above our heads, some we dodged round, while others had to be cut away.

We passed some durian trees, and the ripe fruit was floating in the water or had fallen on to the banks. Our men collected these with joy, and soon we had the extremely unpleasant odour of durian around us. Durian is a large fruit with long, hard spines. When ripe it is yellow and red externally; the thick rind has to be chopped open, and within four compartments are the large bean-like seeds, surrounded by a slimy paste which has a variable and indescribable taste. The first durian we tasted was on the steam launch going to Brunei; this was not quite ripe, and the stink of the fruit, combined with the hot oily smell of the engines, was not encouraging. We persevered, but the flavour was a mixture of slime, onions, and phosphorus, and all that afternoon and evening we had resurrection tastes of phosphorus. Wallace, in his *Malay Archipelago*, and others, have written in praise of durian; so there is another side to it, but our first experience was certainly not promising. The one I tasted in the Trikan was nothing like so unpleasant as the first two I tried. I made three attempts in all, and then gave up all hope of becoming a confirmed durian eater.

In about two and a half hours we came to a narrow channel, about five hundred yards long, cut by the Kayans for the passage of the war canoes, as the stream itself runs under a large rock. Shortly after passing this rock we heard a shout; we yelled, an answer was returned, and we were rejoiced to find we had made connection with the party sent to meet us.

It appears that Hose had left for the interior before hearing from Limbang that we had arrived. He took McDougall with him, as the famous and powerful chief, Tama Bulan, was very ill. Mr. R. S. Douglas, the Extra Officer of Baram, read Mr.

Ricketts' letter, and kindly came on himself with some men to meet us. He had started on Tuesday, the 17th, and arrived at the trysting-place half an hour before we did! He had gone about a hundred and ten miles by boat, and we had gone about ninety miles. The greater part of both our routes had been difficult travelling, and yet everything was so well arranged by Messrs. Hose, Ricketts, and Douglas that we synchronously arrived at the spot agreed upon in the depth of the jungle.

We soon settled our plans and then had tiffin. At two o'clock we started for our tramp across the watershed to the upper waters of the Malinau River. For about half-way we followed the track cut by the Kayans, along which they used to haul their canoes, and to facilitate this arduous labour they had lain trunks and poles transversely across the track. We had a rapid and interesting seven-mile walk through the jungle, and I made my first acquaintance with land leeches. We diverged from the main track to a narrower one, which led us several times over streams and small rivers, across which we had to wade.

About five o'clock we had reached the hut that Douglas had previously erected at the head waters of the Malinau. As the carriers could not transport the whole of our luggage on one trip we had to wait over the following day for them to fetch the remainder of our goods.

On the morning of January 24th we crossed the river and strolled in the jungle. Being what is known as "Old Jungle," it was much more easy to walk in than "New Jungle," as the tall forest trees, by cutting off light and air, prevent a dense undergrowth from springing up. Wherever land has been cleared and then allowed to revert to jungle the undergrowth has a chance, and a practically impenetrable tangled mass of vegetation results.

For the first time I saw various species of pitcher plants growing wild; some grow close to the ground, others climb to a height of about six feet. We also came across the forest paths made by wild pigs and by deer. Even in full sunshine the forests are dull and gloomy, and the lower vegetation reeks with moisture.

These jungles are inhabited by the simple nomadic Punans, who build rough shelters in which they sleep for a few nights, and then wander again in search of game and camphor trees.

As the last of our baggage did not come till midday, we

could not start till after tiffin. Douglas and I went in the smallest boat, and it was very interesting shooting the very numerous rapids. How different it was going down stream compared with the laborious journey against the current! The boatmen built in a remarkably short time a very large hut to accommodate the whole party for the night.

We started at 6.30 a.m. on Wednesday, January 25th, passing Batu Jilama about seven o'clock. The river here flows past fine vertical limestone cliffs five hundred feet in height. The Dayaks have a legend about a winged ghost-tiger (*remaung*), which is supposed to inhabit the caves in these cliffs, and to fly from one side of the river to the other. The Dayaks are very fond of these tiger stories, but as this is not the Sea Dayak country we need not believe this particular yarn.

A short distance before the Malinau joins the Tutau there is a bluff in which is an old burial cave called Lobang Tulang. Hose and McDougall had already visited it, and had brought away two skulls and a great many bones, which must have belonged to at least thirty individuals. Douglas and I clambered up the cave and had a look round. The cave was a small one; great stalactites depended from the face of the cliff, which was largely clothed with vegetation. There was a beautiful view of the bend of the river and of the Mulu range beyond. That evening we slept in a Long-Pata house on the Tutau opposite the entrance of the Malinau.

We left early the following morning, had a halt for breakfast at 7.45, and travelled steadily all day, not landing again till we reached the Umu Belubu house. This long house was very similar to those we visited on the Limbang River. In the evening we had some borak, a ginlike spirit made from rice, and Ray gave the inhabitants some native songs on the phonograph, and I copied some patterns. This was the first time I had come across people belonging to the Kayan group. Douglas and I were tattooed on the arm early next morning by Balu Long who is perhaps the best tattooer in the Baram District; she is the old mother-in-law of the chief. The pattern was printed on the arm in charcoal or rather soot by means of a wooden slab on which the design was cut in relief, and then the impression was gone over three times with a tattooing needle tapped by an iron rod. The whole process took a little over an hour. It was by no means painful, and as we had previously disinfected the ink with thymol, the punctured skin healed quickly with very little inflammation.

The Kayan men have a device tattooed on the fore-arm and thigh; very frequently there is a rosette or circular design on the shoulder. The back of the hand and fingers are tattooed when the man has taken a head. More than once up-country women have asked me when I was going to have my hands tattooed!

The Kayan women are tattooed all over the fore-arm and over the back of the hand. The thighs are richly tattooed and the upper surface of the foot and toes.

FIG. 30.
KAYAN TATTOO DESIGNS.
A little less than half natural size.

We left our friends in this house about ten o'clock, and reached Batu Blah about three o'clock. Here the natives were building a large long-house, and in the meantime resided in comparatively small houses. Close by the village was a small cemetery, in which was one pillar tomb boldly carved with spiral designs below a human face. It was the funeral post of a chief, whose body was pressed into a jar let into the top of the pillar.

We had tea here, and then proceeded on our journey. About six we reached the elongated house of the Orang Bukit at Long Linai. The Orang Bukits are a branch of the Kadayans, but, unlike the Kadayans of the coast, they are not Mohammedans. The *Lucille*, the Government river steamer for the Baram district, was waiting for us here.

After dinner we witnessed a most interesting Berantu ceremony, a magical ritual, which was employed in this instance to cure a sick woman.

Towards one end of the long verandah the floor was covered with mats, in the centre of which and depending from a rafter was a streamer (*lare*) of the frayed leaves of the areca palm; beneath, and partially covered by the ends of the *lare*, was a brass Brunei salver, on which were placed various folded cloths and garments.

PLATE XXVI

ASCENDING A RAPID

HOUSE OF THE ORANG BUKITS AT LONG LINAI, TUTAU RIVER

Around the salver were distributed the spathe of the blossoms of the areca palm containing the flower spikes, some leaves of the serimbangung and daunlong (a caladium), a wooden image of a woman (*anak jilama*), an empty whisky bottle, two small Chinese saucers, and a *maligai*, or house for the spirit.

To one side was a row of eight or nine gongs, suspended from a long horizontal pole raised three or four feet from the floor, and close by were several drums and a set of *geling*

FIG. 31. BERANTU CEREMONY OF THE ORANG BUKIT.

tamgan, or hand gongs, which were beaten with two sticks, one in each hand of the performer. At one end of the cleared space was a torch (*lutong*) of dammar supported in a ratan framework, and at the other end was a small lamp.

The chief medicine-man, whom we will call "A," came and sat with crossed legs in front of the altar, as the arrangement of the objects may be conveniently called. He hid his face behind a fan (*kipas*) and murmured incantations, every now and again calling the spirit by a chirruping noise.

He wore a *detta* as a turban, a white *blatchu* over the right shoulder, a Javanese *sarong*, and striped silk *seluar* (trousers).

After a little time another man and two women came. The man ("B") brought a salver containing some cloths. When he had deposited this near the other he lifted up some of the cloths and burnt incense (*kamanyan*) below them.

On his head he had a Javanese *detta*, a piece of red *kasumba*, and a piece of white cloth, the ends of which hung down his back; for the rest he was dressed like the other medicine-man, but had in addition a Sea Dayak bead belt (*tali pinggang marik*). The women were dressed in the Melanau fashion with Brunei sashes. One was a particularly beautiful example of gold brocade (*kain benang mas*). This woman, whom I will term "C," had also a kasumba round her head.

During all this time the drums and gongs were beaten by women.

The man "B" and the women "C" and "D" sat down in this order, and solemnly made their incantations with their fans in front of their faces. The man "A" stood up, and while continuing his incantations he slowly and gracefully waved his white cloth and fan, and occasionally put the edge of the latter to his lips and chirruped to the spirit. He then walked round the altar, left hand to centre, with a slow, dancing movement, the body being held upright but the head bowed. The other three sat still and covered their faces with their fans. To avoid repetition, I may here state that during the whole time the incantations were made there was an incessant booming, clanging accompaniment of drums and gongs.

The principal female attendant ("C") and the other two got up and faced "A," who was seated now and slowly fanning himself. The latter arose, and all gently swayed backwards and forwards, and very slowly processioned round the altar. The movement consisted of a sedate walk, the heel being slightly lifted two or three times at each shuffling step. After several revolutions all sat down; later they stood up again.

The chief magician ("A") took a mouthful of water and spat it over the chest of the sick woman, who was sitting close by. He had previously been chewing betel, so that he might be able to make a large red splash on the woman's bosom. He then patted her on the breast and head. He next took the areca blossom from the spathe and held it over her head, and made passes in front of her with it, ever and again stroking her head with it.

The attendants sat down while the chief woman ("C") stood by the operator ("A"); both then walked round the altar, the man still carrying the areca blossom, which he solemnly waved about.

The whole process was repeated with the green leaves from the altar by "B." The others sat down and chirruped frequently.

The second female attendant ("D") made passes over the chest of a boy who was also ill. The two men ("A" and "B") and the woman "C" then went round the altar. The latter went to the female patient, while the others continued their procession.

The medicine-man "A" took a knife and lightly pressed the edge of it along the throat and chest of the patient, and placed it on the wooden image. He then took the two saucers and, as it were, scraped the bad blood from the wound supposed to have been caused by the knife, off the chest of the woman with one saucer and poured it into the other. Eventually the pretended blood was caught between the two saucers, which were kept closed, the one on the top of the other, face to face. Having put the saucers down, he waved the fan about and made passes over the woman's throat and chest, and finally he appeared to pick up the sickness with the edge of the fan.

The two attendants ("B" and "D") retired; later the female magician ("C") felt herself all over, and looked as if she had just awakened. When her senses appeared to return to her, she took off her red and gold Brunei sash, and then retired for a minute or two.

The medicine-man ("A") next walked round the altar and took up the image and the folded white cloth on which it lay; the latter he tied into a sling which hung from his neck, and into this loop he placed the image, which meanwhile had been held by the chief woman. He then stood in front of the altar with his fan in front of his face.

The female magician ("C") gave "A" a kris with which to fight the evil spirit. His movements became rapid, and he jumped about flourishing the weapon. While this battle with the unseen powers was taking place, the woman put a pillow on the floor beside the altar, and placed on it the flower of the areca palm. In front of the pillow she placed a basket, and beside this the salver with cloths. "A" then placed the white cloth with the image beside the basket. By this time he had slowly walked round the objects and stood facing them on the far side. All the time the female magician had been talking to him, telling him to make his incantations thoroughly, so as to cure the patient; now she sat down and occasionally talked to him.

The man next sat down, and later stood up and danced a

little. He then caught the wandering soul of the sick woman in his scarf over the salver of cloths, and scooped it off the salver with his fan and poured it into his scarf.

All the objects being removed from in front of the pillow, the magician made a number of quick movements, advancing towards and retreating from the pillow. The pillow was next removed, and the man jumped over the spot where it had lain. He returned to where he was before, and then walked back to his original position on the other side of the altar, and went to the patient, made passes over and in front of her, and took the spirit from his sash and put it on her head.

The female magician tied a handkerchief round the patient's head and retired, the patient too slipped away into a private apartment.

As soon as he noticed the patient had gone, the medicine-man went about in a blind sort of way to look for her; then he rummaged among the objects which constituted the altar, and tossed the cloths about. The female magician gave him the image, telling him this was the patient. He dumped it up and down on the floor and flourished it about in a very excited manner, apparently not at all satisfied with the repeated assurances of the female magician that this was really the sick woman. At length the patient was recalled, and the medicine-man sat in front of her and gave her some charms.

What we saw was only one incident in a protracted ceremony. The whole operation extends over some three weeks. The chief woman magician ("C") was an expert, but the other two ("B" and "D") were admittedly learning the business.

Hose afterwards informed me that the Berantu ceremony belongs essentially to the coast tribes, and it is only near the coast that one sees it carried out with the most complete ritual.

Like other expert medical treatment, this "cure" was very expensive; probably the patient would have to pay as a fee a Chinese gong of a value of some three or four dollars, plates, cups, and other articles, to say nothing of numerous fowls.

It would require a prolonged study of the complete ceremony to understand the meaning of the ritual. The portion that I saw may perhaps thus be explained.

First the spirits who might assist in the cure were invoked; then the magician ripped open the neck and chest of the woman and collected the blood and picked up the spirit of the sickness with his fan. In the meantime I believe the spirit of the woman was resting in the *maligai*, the spirit, or soul, house.

With his kris the magician fought and conquered the evil spirits.

The patient's spirit was next caught by the magician in his scarf, and holding it safely he jumped across the spot where a pillow had lain, and beside which the wooden image was placed. I do not know what this act symbolised. Her own spirit was next returned to the patient.

The magician next appeared to be himself possessed by the spirit of the disease, and he blindly and clumsily searched among the paraphernalia of the altar, and tossed the cloths about, vainly endeavouring to discover the victim. The female magician then offered him the wooden image, telling him it was the patient herself, and, further to call his attention to it, she bounced it up and down, making the Chinese bell, which was tied round its waist, tinkle as she banged it on the floor. Eventually he appeared convinced against his will, and the spirit of the disease entered into the effigy.

The magician then came to himself, and going to the sick woman, who had just returned, gave her charms to keep the evil spirit from returning.

We left Long Linai early on the twenty-eighth in the steamer and arrived at Marudi (Claudetown) at eleven o'clock a.m.—very glad to be at our journey's end. The rest of the day was spent in unpacking, settling in and reading a heavy mail.

In the evening Aban Tingan, the brother of the great Kenyah chief Tama Bulan, and several of his countrymen turned up at the Residency, and we had a great drinking evening in true Kenyah style, chanting speeches while presenting a drink, moving the glass backwards and forwards till the time comes for the actual drinking. Whilst the glass is being drained at a gulp all shout in a peculiar manner. It was really a most effective performance, and might with advantage be introduced at home.

I felt it to be an appropriate, though quite an unarranged, welcome to Marudi. Ray gave a phonographic performance, and not very late in the evening Aban Tingan arrived at a well-known garrulous stage, and, later on, he did not realise that we should be glad if he departed.

CHAPTER XX

THE COUNTRY AND PEOPLE OF BORNEO

(a) THE GEOGRAPHICAL AND GEOLOGICAL FEATURES OF BORNEO

THE centre of Borneo does not appear to be occupied by one great central continuous range of old folded mountains, but by numerous more or less isolated peaks and ridges which rise in linear series from a medley of hills. These high mountain islands not only occur in the higher hill-land, but many rise up from the low hills that merge into great coastal plains.

The central mountains radiate from Gunong Tebang, which lies in lat. 3° N. and long. 115° 3′ 25″. From this central watershed an axial ridge proceeds north-eastwards, and culminates in Kina Balu, 4,175 m. (13,698 feet), the highest mountain in the island. A south-east ridge ends at Cape Kaniongan. An irregular southerly chain terminates in the Island Pulo Laut and in Cape Salatan. A broad south-westerly series of mountains stretches toward Cape Sambar; a more westerly branch of the latter system curves round to the north and terminates at Cape Datu. The latter watershed constitutes the boundary between Sarawak and Dutch Borneo.

On account of the peculiar configuration of mountain masses and divides, Borneo contains a number of extensive and distinct river basins, which radiate from the eccentric mountain centre.

The mountains proper are surrounded by hill-land, which gradually becomes lower towards the plains. Schwaner states that "these hills do not form ranges inclosing plains and valleys, nor are they very defined as regards height and form. They may be described as an aggregate of rounded or extended masses, often with very steep sides. Their usual height seldom exceeds 200 to 300 feet; only in the neighbourhood of the

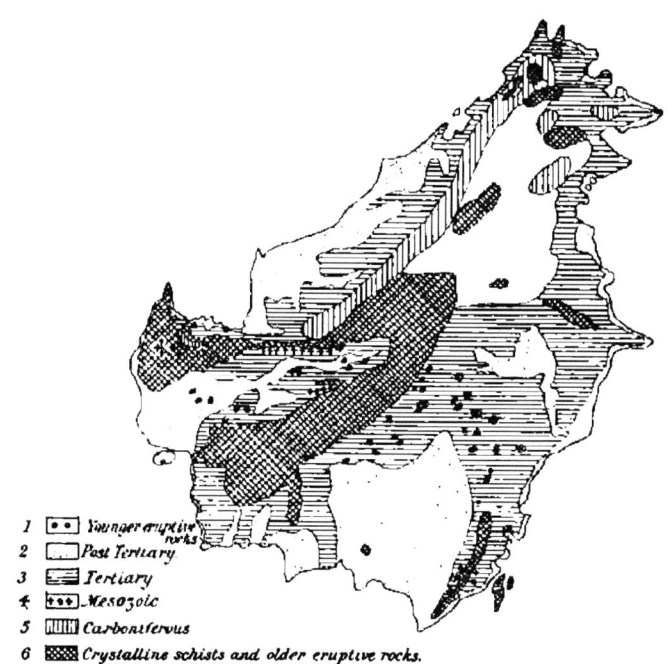

GEOLOGICAL SKETCH MAP OF BORNEO. AFTER POSEWITZ.

divide do they become higher and give the country a more mountainous character." The hill-land also sends spurs into the low-lying plains, which appear as outliers.

The great plains extend from the hill-land to the sea. Towards the hills there is dry flat land which gradually passes into swamps. Several travellers describe swamps and marshes at the foot of the hills and even in the mountain land. "On the other hand," as Posewitz points out, "outlines of the dry flat land stretch far into the swampy lowlands, and isolated high-lying districts are then formed in the middle of marshy low-lying plains."

THE GEOLOGY OF THE "MOUNTAIN LAND"

PALÆOZOIC

Very little is accurately known about the geology of the "mountain land" of Borneo. The mountain chains and their spurs are composed of crystalline schists, the so-called "old slate formations," which may be of Devonian age, and the igneous rocks; among the latter are granites, diorites, gabbros, and serpentines. The two latter appear to belong rather to the spurs.

Verbeek distinguishes in Sumatra between an "old slate formation" and a "younger slate formation" which he includes in the Lower Carboniferous Culm Measures. He is of opinion that perhaps part of the schists of the older group are of Archæan age, but that the greater part are Silurian or Devonian, or a mixture of both.

In Borneo there are hornblende schists, mica schists, and quartzites, which are likely to be Archæan, as there is no evidence for including these rocks as Devonian. A part of the quartzite schist and phyllites are perhaps Archæan, while another part may belong to the Devonian.

In Sumatra it is not always possible to separate the Culm Measures sharply from the slates of the "old slate formation." On the other hand, the unconformity between the limestone facies of the Lower Carboniferous and the "old slates" is clearly visible. Indeed, part of the "old slates" in Borneo perhaps belongs to the Culm Measures in such districts as British North Borneo and Sarawak.

The old crystalline rocks are very generally gold-bearing.

Deposits of the Carboniferous Formation usually form a broad zone flanking on their northern aspect the older Palæozoic rocks that constitute the backbone of the island. The Carboniferous rocks consist mainly of sandstones and limestones, which must not be confused with those of the Eocene Formation.

The older sandstone is coarse grained, and not very ferruginous: it rises to 4,000 feet; while the Tertiary sandstone, as far as is at present known, only constitutes a "hill-land" of very moderate altitude.

The older limestones are characterised by their hardness and bluish colour; usually they do not contain fossils, except in isolated localities; and the rocks are traversed by numerous calcite veins and by ore-bearing quartz veins. In Sarawak the veins mostly contain antimony; in Sabah iron pyrites and copper pyrites. Like the Tertiary coral reefs, the older bands of limestone are full of caves, which, by-the-by, contain edible swifts' nests; but while the Tertiary rocks only attain a height of 200 to 300 feet, the Carboniferous limestones reach as much as 1,200 feet. In places greenish or reddish slates are intercalated in the limestone, or the latter alternates with sandstone.

Although the Carboniferous Formation is clearly marked off from the Tertiary beds above it, this is not the case, as has been already noted, with its lower boundary. In many cases beds of the Culm type cannot at present be distinguished from the "old slate formation." There is much doubt as to the horizon to which in any given case a quartz schist or slate belongs, and the same is the case with the old sandstone. In Western Sarawak, which, with the "Chinese Districts" of West Borneo, forms an immense mountain island, the sandstone is certainly Devonian, and it may be of interest to note that these beds contain quicksilver.

MESOZOIC

No Secondary Formations have been described from Sarawak, though Jurassic and Cretaceous rocks occur in Dutch Borneo.

THE GEOLOGY OF THE "HILL-LAND"
CAINOZOIC

The Tertiary "hill-land" forms a belt round the mountain land, which in some places reaches to the sea, but in others is separated from it by wide alluvial plains. It has been mentioned that the hill-land not only surrounds the mountain land, but also penetrates within it, connecting the separate chains; and it also surrounds isolated mountain chains.

From a geotectonic standpoint, the Tertiary hill-land only averages 200 to 300 feet. Towards the border of the mountains the hills become higher where they are of Eocene Age; towards the plains their height diminishes, and they form low ranges of Miocene or Pliocene Age.

Verbeek systematised as well as added to the labours of Horner, Schwaner, and C. de Groot, and established a threefold division of the older Tertiary beds for the south of Borneo.

1. *Sandstone Stage.*—The lowermost beds are predominantly sandstones, and contain the "Indian coal" seams. The sandstones are usually of a white or yellow colour, and always contain flakes of a silvery-white mica; the cement is argilaceous. They are probably derived from mica schists. Alternating with them are bands of shale, carbonaceous shale, and coal. The sandstone beds are much pierced and faulted by younger eruptive rocks.

2. *Marl Stage.*—Among yellowish-white sandstones are the following beds: bluish-grey "Letten" and shales without fossils; bluish-grey "Letten" with crustacean remains; grey Marl, with marl-clay nodules, often of the large size and very full of fossils. The percentage of lime in these beds increases from below upwards.

3. *Limestone Stage.*—This stage consists of a hard whitish or bluish limestone rich in fossils, and contains numerous nummulites.

All the above strata are pierced in numerous places by basalts and hornblende-augite-andesites, the intrusion of which has disturbed their bedding. The andesites are always accompanied by widespread deposits of tuffs and volcanic agglomerates.

Verbeek[*] has recently recast his original allocation of these beds, and now he regards the "Sandstone Stage" as Eocene; the "Marl Stage" as Oligocene (Nari group of India); and the "Limestone Stage" to the later Miocene.

Above the andesites are later Tertiary shales and sandstones, which were previously regarded as of Miocene Age, but Verbeek now assigns them to the Pliocene. A lower band of shales and an upper series of sandstones can be distinguished; beds of a true brown coal are often present.

[*] *Neues Jahrbuch für Mineralogie*, etc., 1892, i. p. 65.

The Tertiary geology of Sarawak has chiefly been elucidated by A. H. Everett, but a great deal more remains to be done. In the district of the Sarawak River a hilly formation, comprising sandstones and limestones, extends from the coast to the mountains at the boundary. Exact details as to its composition are as yet wanting; we only know that the coal-bearing sandstone of the Eocene occurs, and that there are Tertiary coral reefs. The limestone beds, which appear to occur sporadically in Sarawak, are penetrated by numerous caves; they dip at a high angle and contain many fossils.

Intrusions of andesite have been found in the district of the Upper Sarawak River. These recent eruptive rocks have often disturbed the bedding of the coal-bearing strata. They are described as basalts and felspar-porphyrites, occurring in hills, or as dykes in the lowlands.

In the Bay of Brunei the Tertiary coal-bearing sandstone hills extend down to the coast. Coal is now worked at a mine close to Brooketown, whence it is exported.

The Limbang River, in its lower and middle course, traverses a hilly country, the elevations rising from 500 to 1,500 feet in height, and consisting of hard sandstone, which contains coal in places, as in the Madalam tributary. Limestone rocks are also found in the middle course of the Limbang. In part they are Tertiary coral reefs, in part older rocks.

On the island of Labuan the Tertiary beds are greatly developed and contain coal. The Rev. J. E. Tenison-Woods (*Nature*, April 23, 1885) has stated that "the Labuan coals are probably of Oolite age, and not connected with any marine formation, but apparently of Eolian origin." I am not aware that this view has received any support or confirmation.

Concretions of clay-ironstone are often present in the shales.

THE GEOLOGY OF THE PLAINS

QUATERNARY

Fringing the Tertiary beds almost continuously round Borneo, and often extending into broad bands, are the earlier Quaternary beds, which are to be regarded as shore deposits. These deposits constitute the great coastal plains of Borneo, and were laid down during the last partial submergence of the island. In part they form flat districts, in part gently undulating plains.

In general the composition is everywhere the same. The highest bed consists of a partly sandy clay, which towards the bottom becomes more sandy, the sand grains at the same time increasing in size. The conglomerates consist mainly of quartz pebbles, but also of pebbles of different igneous rocks, such as gabbro, diorite, granite, etc.; they also contain pebbles of the Tertiary strata, such as sandstones, coral limestone, etc. Between these pebbles there is more or less of a clayey earth, containing gold, diamonds, platinum, magnetic iron ore, and chromite. The pebbly bed is often united by a very hard siliceous cement.

Towards the sea these deposits merge into marshy lowlands. While flowing through the later alluvium the rivers have low banks, but in the earlier Quaternary beds they flow between high, perpendicular, clay walls, in a narrow gully. The bedding is horizontal, or, at the border of the hill-land, only slightly inclined.

THE GEOLOGY OF THE MARSHES

ALLUVIUM

The river deposits show their greatest development in south Borneo, where they form extended marshy plains. They are next best exemplified in west Borneo; while they are least developed in the east and north. They are composed of a dark brown, black, or bluish clay, which is often rich in humus in its upper layers; in the lower layers it is of a harder consistency. It is often mixed with, or traversed by, seams of sand; the latter, as a rule, occurring on a lower level. The boundary with the older Quaternary cannot be sharply drawn.

The bog formation and the marsh-land of the lower river courses of north Borneo are of less account than in the south and west owing to the great development of the sea sand, which hinders the formation of morasses. They occur only in the river deltas, some of which are of considerable extent. The great delta of the Rejang is a morass, and the swamps can only be travelled over by boats. On the Baram the alluvium extends for about a hundred miles from the coast.

The sea-sand formation extends from Sarawak as a long, broad strip of sand dunes, right along the coast, excepting the river mouths.

(b) A SKETCH OF THE ETHNOGRAPHY OF SARAWAK.

We have not at present sufficient precise information to be able to speak with certainty concerning the characters and affinities of all the races and peoples that inhabit Borneo. One of our objects in visiting Sarawak was the hope that by measuring a large number of people, and by recording their physical features, we might help towards a solution of the ethnic problems; we also hoped that further light might be thrown on the matter by a comparative study of their customs, beliefs, as well as of their arts and crafts. Our stay was of too short a duration, and the ground we covered was not sufficiently extensive for us to do much in this regard, and our physical results have yet to be fully worked out. Fortunately Hose has made a prolonged and careful study of Bornean ethnography, and when his voluminous manuscripts are published we shall be in a much better position to pronounce on the subject. In the meantime one must remain content with Ling Roth's great compilation, *The Natives of Sarawak and British North Borneo*.

In the following sketch of the ethnography of Sarawak I have purposely dealt with the subject on broad lines only, since if we understand the main features first we shall be the better able to formulate the real problems, and this is a necessary first step towards their elucidation. As most of the peoples that inhabit Borneo have representatives in Sarawak, this sketch may be taken to apply provisionally to the island as a whole.

Scattered over a considerable part of the jungle of Sarawak live the nomad Punans. They are a slender people, of moderate height, and paler in colour than most tribes. They were the lightest coloured of the indigenous people that we met with in Sarawak; many have a distinct greenish tinge. Those that we measured were slightly broad-headed, with an average cephalic index of 81. The Ukit may be allied to the Punan, but none of them have been measured as yet. Their mode of life is very similar.

The wild Punans are grouped in small communities, and inhabit the dense jungle at the head waters of the principal rivers of Borneo. They do not cultivate the soil, but live on whatever they can find in the jungle. There is so much that is edible in the jungle that there is no fear of starvation, especially as these people live on a very mixed diet.

PLATE XXVII

PUNANS

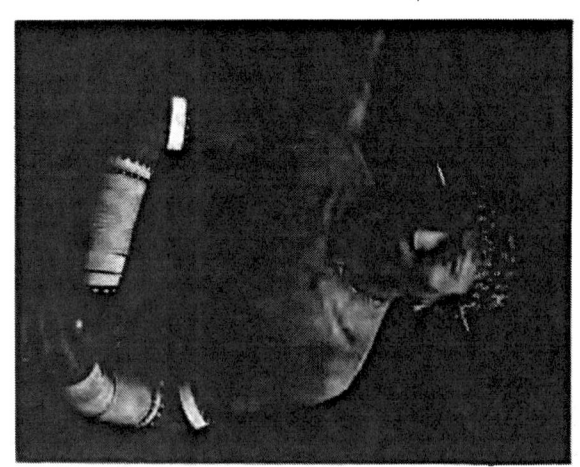

A LELAK MAN, WITH TYPICAL TATTOOING ON SHOULDERS AND UPPER ARMS

ETHNOGRAPHY OF SARAWAK

Their few wants are supplied by barter from friendly settled peoples, and in return for iron implements, calico, beads, tobacco, etc., they offer jungle produce, mainly gutta, indiarubber, camphor, dammar, and ratans. They do not live in permanent houses, but erect miserable shanties in which they sleep.

They are very mild savages, they are not head-hunters, do not keep slaves, are generous to one another, are moderately truthful, and probably never do an injury by purposely making a false statement. On first acquaintance they appear melancholy, and certainly shy and timid-looking, but when they have gained confidence they show themselves in their true colours as a cheerful, bright people, who are very fond of their children and kind to the women.

It is probable that eight hundred or a thousand years ago the greater portion of Sarawak, perhaps the whole of it, was occupied by a weak, agricultural people, who are now represented by the Land Dayak, Sĕbop, Malang, Kanauit, Mĕlanau, Narom, Kadayan, Kajaman, Lelak, Long Kiput, Batu Blah, Long Pata, Barawan, Kalabit, Dusun, and Murut. For this group Hose and I propose the term Kalamantan.

From the measurements we have made of some of these tribes there is no doubt that they were not all originally of one stock. Some are distinctly narrow-headed, others are inclined to be broad-headed. As Hose and myself propose dealing at some length elsewhere with the problem of the ethnology of Sarawak, I will not here anticipate our discussion further than to state that I believe it can be demonstrated that among this primitive population, as indeed in most, if not in all, of the larger islands of the Malay Archipelago, there are two stocks, one of which is distinctly narrow-headed, and to which we may restrict the name of *Indonesian;* the other being broad-headed, and to which the term *Proto-Malay* may conveniently be applied.

Hose states that the Muruts, according to their own traditions, migrated from the Philippines. They are essentially of Indonesian stock, as are also, I believe, the Land Dayaks. Probably it will be ultimately shown that this dual element existed in very early times in the country, but it has been blurred by intermarriage and by contact with immigrant peoples, some of whom belonged to one or other or even a mixture of these two stocks.

I do not intend to refer to even the main tribes of this

group of peoples; but I must allude to the Land Dayaks in order to emphasise their distinctness from the Iban or Sea Dayaks.

My acquaintance with the Land Dayaks is of the slightest, and I have had no opportunity of measuring any of them. Hose has given a Land Dayak woman's skull to the Cambridge Museum; its cranial index is 71·3. Apparently they belong to a native stock that has been crossed with Indo-Javan races; but they are not related in any way to the Iban. They occupy the western end of the Raj as far as the Upper Sadong River; they also extend into Dutch Borneo.

Brooke Low, who knew them well, gives a very favourable account of these people, and this opinion has been confirmed by other travellers. They are described as amiable, honest, grateful, moral, and hospitable. Crimes of violence, other than head-hunting, are unknown. It is uncertain whether the custom of head-hunting was indigenous to them, or adopted from the Iban; probably it was an older custom than the arrival of the Iban, but which had gradually increased until it was stopped by Rajah Brooke. The Land Dayaks, alone in Sarawak, permanently kept the heads in a separate house, which also served as the bachelors' quarters.

The following account of the dealings of the Malays with the Land Dayaks, which I have taken from *The Sarawak Gazette* (Vol. xxiv., 1894, p. 98), proves that the latter are rather easily imposed upon.

The Sarawak Malay can as a rule get on very fairly well with the Land Dayak—better, perhaps, than he can with the Sea Dayaks up coast; he can "*pèjal*," that is, he can force his wares upon those who really have no use for them, or who are not particularly in want of the goods hawked by the Malay pedlar. Whilst the Land Dayak is turning over his mind as to whether he will purchase or not, the seller sits patiently by smoking and singing the praises of his wares. A Land Dayak usually takes a considerable time in forming his mind in making a purchase, but time is of no particular object to either party, and the bargain is completed. The pedlar having obtained the customary cent. per cent. packs up his baggage and departs to the next house or village as the case may be.

But the present Malay system of trading with the Land Dayaks is rotten to the core. Land Dayak *bintings*, or

ETHNOGRAPHY OF SARAWAK

villages, are perpetually being visited, and the commonest articles of trade thrust upon them at exorbitant rates, which they could purchase ever so much cheaper at any of the numerous Chinese shops scattered through the river, and which are easily accessible in a day's journey, even from the remotest Land Dayak habitation; such commodities as waist cloths (*chawats*) and petticoats (*jamu*) trimmed with a little Turkey-red cloth are sold previous to the rice harvest to be repaid in *padi* at many times their respective values; nor does it end here, the purchaser being expected to deliver his payment at the house of the Malay merchant, entailing perhaps a long journey on foot or miles of boat travelling, and again he is expected to fully provide for those traders stopping in his house, such necessaries as rice, firewood, provisions, and the like, which he does without the slightest grumbling.

According to Hose, the Kenyahs and Kayans migrated into Sarawak from Dutch Borneo several hundred years ago, and he has previously published his opinion that the Kenyahs migrated into the Baram River some hundred years or so before the Kayans; they were the only people able to resist the constant raids made by the blustering and warlike Kayans, who almost exterminated the smaller tribes, and made slaves of the weaker ones. Naturally the Kayans occupied the best tracts of lands which lay in the undulating hills between the swampy low country and the mountains at the head waters of the rivers. They also confiscated all the caves of the esculent swifts, selling their nests to the traders whenever a Brunei Malay or Chinaman dared to venture up-river amongst them. Kayans often travelled as far as Brunei in their long boats, and some few even ventured as far as Singapore to sell the produce of these caves, taking passage in Chinese junks from Labuan.

All the tribes, except the Punans and Ukits, are agriculturists; they clear the jungle off the low hills that flank the tributaries of the large rivers, but always leave a few scattered trees standing; irrigation is attempted by the Kalabits only, as the *padi* (rice) is grown like any other cereal on dry ground; swamp *padi* is also grown in the lowland. In their gardens they grow yams, pumpkins, sugar cane, bananas, and sometimes coconuts and other produce. They hunt all land animals that serve as food, and fish, usually with nets, in the rivers, or spear the fish that have been stupefied with tuba; river prawns are also a favourite article of diet.

They all live in long communal houses, which are situated on the banks of the rivers. I have already described this type of dwelling, but although the different tribes have their own peculiar modifications, the same general plan is adhered to.

The social organisation is correspondingly higher than among Punans. Amongst the small Kalamantan tribes the headman has not much influence, unless he be a man of exceptional power and energy, but among the larger tribes, and especially among the Kayans and Kenyahs, the headmen are real chiefs, and exercise an undisputed sway. In some cases a pre-eminent man will be acknowledged as the head chief of a considerable district.

Of all these tribes the Kenyahs are perhaps the highest in social evolution. By their superior solidarity and their undoubted intelligence they were able to hold their own against the turbulent Kayans. They are the most expert boatmen of the Baram district, and, what is very significant, the women are less shy than is the case among other tribes. Indeed, some of the girls and young women—for example, those in Tama Bulan's house—are particularly friendly and lively, but always behave in a really ladylike way.

All these agricultural tribes are artistic, but in varying degrees. They are all musical people, and sing delightful chorus songs. Many of their utensils are decorated with no mean skill. In some tribes the ends of the beams of the houses are carved to represent various animals; in some the verandah is decorated with boldly carved planks, or with painted boards and doors. The bamboo receptacles are often carved in low relief in very effective patterns, and the bone handles of the *parangs* are always carved in an intricate manner. Lastly, the minor utensils of daily life are often decorated in a way that reveals the true artistic spirit, such, for example, as the plaited patterns on the rice baskets and winnowing trays. Nor must the neat and effective bead-work be overlooked.

The Kenyahs and Kayans smelt iron and make spear heads and sword (*parang*) blades; the former are especially noted for their good steel. The forge with two bellows is the usual form that is widely spread in Malaysia.

The Iban, or Sea Dayaks, formerly occupied only the Saribas,

ETHNOGRAPHY OF SARAWAK

Batang, Lupar, and Kaluka rivers and their tributaries, and they still remain there; but as the Kayans and other tribes on the Lower Rejang have retreated more into the interior, this river, for a considerable portion of its course, is also now populated by Iban, who have migrated at various times from the above-mentioned rivers. As the country became more settled these truculent people have rapidly increased, and now occupy most of the best farming lands.

In more recent years migrations of the Iban have taken place to the head of the Muka River, the Tatau, and lastly into the Baram, but in all cases with the sanction of the Government. Before the establishment of the present Government the Iban were unable to obtain a footing on the Baram River, as they were afraid of the Kayans and Kenyahs. They are also found in the head waters of many of the Kapuas tributaries on the watershed between Sarawak and Dutch Borneo.

The Iban is short (average stature 5 feet $2\frac{1}{2}$ inches) and has a broad head (average cephalic index 83). The colour of the skin of the men is, on the whole, darker than among the inland tribes. They have the same long, slightly wavy, black hair, showing a reddish tinge in certain lights that is characteristic of the Borneans generally. They are an active little people.

In Sarawak these people are spoken of consistently as "Sea Dayaks," or more generally "Dayak." It is customary for the Dutch and other Europeans to term all the interior tribes of Borneo "Dayak," with or without a qualifying designation. As there is such confusion of the terminology in the text-books, I consider it better to boldly face the situation and to introduce a new term to science to which a perfectly definite meaning can be applied.

Most of the Iban inhabit low-lying land; they prefer to live on the low hills, but this is not always practicable, and so they plant swamp *padi*. All those who settle at the heads of rivers plant padi on the hills in the same manner as the up-river natives. They also cultivate maize, sugar-cane, sweet potatoes, gourds, pumpkins, cucumbers, melons, mustard, ginger, and other vegetables. Generally groups of relations work together in the fields.

Although they are essentially an agricultural people, they are warlike and passionately devoted to head-hunting. The Iban of the Batang Lupar and Saribas in the olden days joined the

Malays in their large war prahus on piratical raids along the coast and up certain rivers. Although they probably never went out a very great distance on the sea, by coasting they were able to attack numerous villages round the coast, and they owe their name of Sea Dayaks to this practice. The great piratical forays were organised by Malays, who went for plunder, but they could always induce the Iban to accompany them on the promise that all the heads of the slain should fall to their share.

Of the Iban, the Balaus, who live in and about the Lingga River, are the most efficient in handling boats at sea. The inland Iban of the present day are usually inexpert boatmen in rough weather, and even in river work they are nothing like so reliable in emergencies as the up-river Kenyahs.

The Iban women make beautiful cotton cloths on a very simple loom. The intricate patterns are made by tightly tying up several strands of the warp with leaves at varying intervals and then dipping the whole into a dye. On removing the lashing the threads that were tied are found to be undyed. This process is repeated if a three-colour is desired. The pattern is produced solely in the warp; the woof threads are self-coloured, and are not visible in the fabric, which is therefore a cotton rep. I have accumulated material for a special study of the numerous designs woven and embroidered by Iban women, as well as of the elegant patterns engraved in low relief on bamboos by the men, but there has not been time to work them out. It is an interesting fact that the decorative art of the two sexes is entirely distinct in motive and style.

The Iban women did not tattoo, though a few may now be seen with a little tattooing; but most of the men have adopted the custom from the Kayans. They admit that the tattoo marks are Kayan designs, but it very rarely happens that the Iban transfer such a design to their bamboo decorations, and the Iban women never adopt Kayan or tattoo patterns for their fabrics.

It is probable that the Iban belongs to the same stock as the original Malay. If this view is correct, the Iban migration may be regarded as the first wave of the movement that culminated in the Malay Empire.

The Malay must have come to Borneo not later than the

early part of the fifteenth century, as Brunei was a large and wealthy town in 1521. Probably the Malays came directly from the Malay Peninsula, but they must have mixed largely with the Kadayans, Mĕlanaus, and other coastal people.

The Sarawak and Brunei Malays are probably mainly coastal Borneans with some Malay blood; but they have absorbed the Malay culture, spirit, and religion.

The movements of the different peoples which I have so briefly sketched have a sociological significance which is worth tracing in detail, but I do not propose to inflict on my present readers anything more than the merest outline of this interesting line of inquiry.

The Punans represent the lowest grade of culture in Borneo. They are nomad hunters, who combine with the chase the simple exploitation of jungle produce. Without social organisation they are incapable of serious combination, and are alike incapable of any real endemic improvement or of seriously affecting other peoples.

The purely agricultural tribes that cultivate *padi* on the low hills or in the swamps form the next social stratum.

The Kalamantans were evidently a weak people, as they have been repressed and often subdued by other peoples. For example, the Kadayans and the Mĕlanaus have been very largely affected by the Malays, and the Iban have harassed the Land Dayaks, and the latter had previously been influenced by the Javano-Hindu colonisation of Borneo. It is also probable that some of the tribes of this group of peoples have been modified by contact with the Chinese. It is suggestive that all the stone implements Hose has collected have been obtained from Kalamantans, either the pure or mixed stock.

These indigenous tillers of the soil have been hard pressed by various swarms of foreigners. The Kenyah-Kayan migration was that of a people of a slightly higher grade of culture. It is true they also were agriculturists, but their social organisation was firmer, and they were probably superior in physique. Possibly they introduced iron weapons; if so, this would give them an enormous advantage. At any rate they were clever smiths. These immigrant agricultural artisans, who were directed by powerful chiefs, had no difficulty in taking possession of the most desirable land.

From an opposite point of the compass in early times came another agricultural people, who strangely enough have strong individualistic tendencies, the usually peaceable habits of tillers of the soil having been complicated by a lust for heads and other warlike propensities.

Although inclined to raid their neighbours, the Iban do not appear to have made much headway—certainly not against the Kayans and Kenyahs. Conquest implies a strong leader, obedience to authority and concerted action. So far as I can gather, the Iban only became formidable when led and organised by Europeans, and at the present time the individualistic temperament of the Iban manifests itself, even under the leadership of an English civil officer.

The Malay was a yet higher social type. His political organisation was well established; he had the advantage of religious enthusiasm, for Islamism had no small share in the expansion of the Malay. In Borneo he is not a cultivator of the soil, but is a keen trader, and this is another factor in the Malay expansion, especially when coupled with pluck and enterprise. Although a trader, the Malay is essentially a pirate; he seeks to exploit the people with whom he comes in contact, and there is a sporting element in his character, as I understand it, which is not compatible with steady trade. It seems that it was chiefly the Malay in his rôle of pirate who incited and led the Sea Dayak in his raids on other tribes. While the glory and heads fell to the Iban, the valuable spoils of war and the slaves were the booty of the Malay.

Then appeared on the scene the Anglo-Saxon overlord. The quality of firmness combined with justice made itself felt. At times the lower social types hurled themselves, but in vain, against the instrument that had been forged and tempered in a similar turmoil of Iberian, Celt, Roman, Teuton, and Viking in Northern Europe. Now they acknowledge that safety of life and property and almost complete liberty are fully worth the very small price they have to pay for them.

I do not know what were the conditions of the early Chinese trade with Sarawak, but at present the Chinaman is a legitimate trader. Owing to the settled state of the country under the white men's rule, he is rapidly increasing his sphere of influence, and by his better business habits he is ousting the Malay. Even now the intrepid Malay trader will be found paddling his trading canoe in the upper waters of the rivers of Sarawak, where the Chinaman dare not venture; but wherever the Government builds a fort, Chinamen lose no time in erecting their stores, and proceed to absorb all the trade that previously was in the hands of the Malay.

The piratical cruises of the Malays have been stopped by the Anglo-Saxon overlord, and their exploiting trading has had to give way before the more legitimate commerce of the Chinaman.

NOTE.—For the most recent information on the geology of Dutch Borneo the reader is referred to Dr. G. A. F. MOLENGRAAFF'S *Geologische Verkenningstochten in Centraal-Borneo.* Leiden: E. J. Brill.

CHAPTER XXI

A TRIP INTO THE INTERIOR OF BORNEO

THE following is an account of some experiences on an up-river trip, when McDougall, Ray, and myself accompanied Dr. Charles Hose, the Resident of the Baram District of Sarawak, Borneo, on one of his administrative journeys.

The Baram is the second largest river in Sarawak; it rises about 3° 10′ north latitude in the unnamed and unexplored mountains which form the division between Sarawak and Dutch Borneo, and enters the China Sea at the end of a prominent spit at 114° east longitude.

The Government station and fort are situated at Marudi, or Claudetown, about seventy miles up the river; here is also a large Chinese bazaar. Hose and the Assistant Resident, Mr. Douglas, are the only two Europeans resident in a district that comprises at least ten thousand square miles.

About thirty miles above Marudi the Tinjar joins the Baram; this affluent is almost as large as the main stream, and for a hundred miles it runs a course roughly parallel to the sea coast, but distant from it about thirty to sixty miles, as the crow flies.

On February 6th (1899) we started for a trip up the Tinjar. Only three or four white men had previously been up this river, and practically nothing has been written about it; consequently we were to all intents and purposes breaking fresh ground. But my object in writing this account is not solely to describe a few incidents of our visit to some of the interesting and unspoiled aborigines of Borneo, but also to give an idea of the personal method of dealing with native peoples, which is the keynote of the Sarawak theory of government.

On the 7th of February we visited a Lelak village at Long Tru. The village, as is often the case, consisted of a single house of great length, and built on piles some ten feet high.

PLATE XXVIII

SIDE VIEW OF A KAYAN HOUSE

VERANDAH OF A KAYAN HOUSE AT LONG LAMA, BARAM RIVER

The long houses of this district of Sarawak are built along the banks of the rivers; usually a notched tree trunk is laid on the slope of the steep bank, and other logs are placed end-wise from this to the house to serve as a causeway across the slippery and often foul mud. A house consists of two portions —a verandah extending along the whole length of the river frontage, and a series of domiciles opening on to the verandah.

The verandah is entered at the end, and by two or three door-ways at the side. The ladder consists of one or more notched tree trunks, usually with a slight hand-rail, the use of which is as often as not dispensed with by the nimble, bare-footed inhabitants, and even the dogs have learnt to go up and down these precarious ladders. Sometimes light, broad ladders are erected, of which the rungs are quite far apart.

On entering a verandah the first thing that one sees is the long wooden partition, about eight to ten feet in height, that separates the verandah from the dwelling apartments; this is pierced at fairly regular intervals by wooden doors, each of which gives access to a separate house. Each house, which, by-the-by, is always spoken of as the "door," is divided into variously sized rooms or cubicles; generally a narrow passage opens into a central room, which is the living-room by day and a sleeping-room at night; the cooking may be done here or in a separate small kitchen. The wife has a separate bedroom, or if there are two wives, each has her own room, and the elder girls usually also have one. A long house numbers from ten to fifty, or even as many as eighty or ninety doors, so that there may be from fifty to five hundred people, men, women, and children, in one of these strange dwellings.

The privacy of the home is thoroughly respected, but the society of the neighbours can always be enjoyed on the verandah, which is a broad, open space that extends along one side of the house. This is practically divided into an inner common gangway on to which the doors open, and a portion that runs along the outer wall of the house, and is generally slightly raised above the general level of the floor. The space of this outer portion of the verandah opposite each house belongs to the owner of the house, and, according to his taste or means, he keeps the space in good order and lays down mats. It is here visitors are received, the public business transacted, and neighbours sit and gossip and smoke or chew betel.

Most interesting is it to lounge and watch the daily life of the village, the men and women going to or returning from their gardens, and girls bringing up water. In some tribes the pounding of the rice in heavy wooden mortars is done on the verandah, and one is never tired of watching the rhythmic movements of the nearly nude women as they husk the rice with long thick poles, and gracefully push the grain into the mortars with their feet; the sinuous motions of lithe damsels are particularly fascinating. After the husking is finished the rice is winnowed in plaited trays by standing or crouching women. Then there are the jolly children, half fearful of the white-skinned stranger, yet always ready for a game. Happy, contented little mortals they are, very rarely squabbling among themselves, and still more seldom troubled by their elders.

Hanging from the rafters of the verandah in most houses are trophies of human skulls. They may be fastened to a circular framework looking something like a ghastly parody on the glass chandeliers of our young days, or they may be suspended from a long board, which in one house that I visited was painted and carved at one end into a crocodile's head, and the board itself was suspended from carved images of men who represented captives taken in war.

The skulls are smoke-begrimed and otherwise dirty, and interspersed among them are streamers of dried palm leaves, which all over Borneo are invariably employed in all ceremonies connected with skulls. Usually close by the skulls are pronged skewers on which pieces of pig's meat may be stuck, and short sections of a small bamboo so cut as to form cups ready for the reception of borak (a spirit made from rice), when it is desired to feast the skulls or their spirits. Below the chandelier of skulls there is always a fire which is kept continually burning, for it is believed the skulls like to keep warm, and that if they are kept comfortable and their wants supplied, they will bring good luck to the house and ensure plentiful harvests.

The artistic taste of the people often manifests itself in the decoration, by painting or carving, of the doors or of the wooden partition of the verandah. On the latter are often hung shields, gongs, and the large ornamented women's hats, which have a really fine decorative effect.

When one is tired of the sights of the verandah one can turn round and look over the low-boarded parapet towards the river

THE INTERIOR OF BORNEO

with the prospect beyond. Sometimes jungle alone can be seen, but usually there are *padi* fields on the low hills, and perhaps some plantations of yams and clumps of bananas.

The word "Long," which enters into so many Bornean names of villages, means the mouth of a river, and as many villages are situated at the spot where one river enters another, they are named from the smaller stream. This village took its name from the Tru River, but it sometimes happens that when a village shifts its quarters the old name is retained, and some confusion may arise.

FIG. 32. BUTIONG IN A LELAK HOUSE

The domicile at one end of the Long Tru house had projecting from the partition into the verandah a queer wooden sleeping bunk with lattice windows; a notched pole served as a ladder. It is not uncommon to find sleeping bunks for men built on the verandah, but one attached to the wall like a meat-safe is very unusual. By the side of the door of the same dwelling stood a rudely carved wooden image (*butiong*), in this instance a female figure, which represented a goddess who protected the house from any harm or sickness, but should there be any illness previous to the placing of the *butiong* in the house, she would prevent it from becoming worse. Stuck on to the wall of another dwelling was a portrait of Lord Kitchener!

About twenty miles up the Tinjar is the Bok River, and we

left the steamer and paddled up this tributary in canoes to visit a small community of Punans. The Punans are, as I have already stated, essentially a nomad people, who inhabit the jungles of Sarawak and do not build permanent habitations. They do not cultivate anything, but they collect jungle produce which they sell and barter amongst the more settled tribes, who further trade these with Malays or Chinamen. The Punans are an interesting folk, and may be the remains of an ancient aboriginal population. The settled Punans were very dirty, and looked miserable; they lived in a tumble-down house. But

Fig. 33. Sarcophagus of a Boy in a Barawan House

one must not expect much from people who are making the first step out of absolute savagery.

The wilder Punans we saw later were a better-looking people, and compared with the settled Punans it really seemed as if the latter were paying rather dearly for their slight advance in civilisation; but probably a fixed though squalid home is preferable to a temporary leafy shelter.

On the night of February 8th we slept at Taman Liri's village at Long Tegin. On the verandah against the partition-wall was the sarcophagus of a child. It consisted of a sort of decorated wooden case with a lean-to roof of palm leaves. From one end of the case projected a gaily-painted board carved to represent a head, neck, and arms. The head with its upright ears looked very much like that of a tiger, but we were assured it was intended to be the effigy of the dead boy who lay in the hidden coffin; hanging over this was the boy's hat. Suspended from the eaves of the tomb were wooden models of a sword, knife, kris, paddle, spear-head, and other objects, and leaning against it were a couple of large gongs. On one side of the sarcophagus were hen-coops, a gong, a basket containing plates and a small bamboo vessel; on the other side were a gong and a jar. On the partition-wall were three hats, two fish traps, and a fishing net.

Although Taman Liri is a *penghulu*, or head chief, he complained that the Long Tobai people had left him and had gone to live with Aban Abit at Long Tisam, a little higher up the river, the latter chief having enticed them away. Hose questioned some of the friends of the Long Tobai people, who stated that the reason for the latter not wishing to live with Taman Liri was that he constantly shifted his house, and that he did not fulfil his annual promise of building a really good house. They were sick of living in this unsatisfactory manner, and therefore went to live with Aban Abit, who also was a Barawan, and who had a very good house at Long Tisam. Hose told Taman Liri it was unreasonable to expect people to shift their house every year, as the greater part of their time was taken up in house-building, and their plantations suffered in consequence.

We next visited Aban Abit, who certainly has a much better house than Taman Liri. Owing to the influx of people the house was being extended. When we walked over the framework of the extension we were cautioned to be careful not to fall through. This warning was not given solely to save us from injury, although a fall of some fifteen feet would not be particularly pleasant, but because if anyone fell off a house in process of building a new house would have to be built elsewhere, as would also be the case if a dog were killed in the house. We stayed here a couple of days and measured a number of men, and I made some sketches and photographs.

Soon after our arrival Aban Abit gave each of his new visitors a present, a nice spear falling to my lot. Before leaving I gave his two wives some white calico. On another occasion Tama Bulan, the most famous chief of the Baram district, gave me a large shield decorated with hair, and a Dayak fortman once gave me a musical instrument. But these were the only presents I received from natives; indeed they very rarely give presents, in our sense of the term, in any country I have visited.

It was here I first saw the ceremony of divination by means of a pig's liver. A live pig with its legs tied was brought on to the verandah. Aban Abit took a lighted brand and slightly scorched it, at the same time praying to the Supreme God, and the pig was asked to give the message to the god, who was

FIG. 34. PRAYING TO A PIG IN A BARAWAN HOUSE
On the partition wall are two large women's hats, with yellow and black beadwork

requested to make his will known by means of the liver of the pig. When the scorching was over the suppliant kept the fingers of his right hand on the flanks of the pig, so that he was in touch with the animal all through his address, at the same time slightly prodding it with his fingers to make the pig pay attention to what he was saying. Finally a spear was thrust into the neck of the pig, and as soon as all the kicking was over the side of the pig was ripped open, and the liver rapidly and dexterously extracted and placed on a dish. The old men crowded round and discussed the augury. The size and character of the various lobes of the liver, the appearance of the gall bladder, and the amount of fat and tendon, are objects of the closest scrutiny, and these all have a definite significance.

Divination by means of a pig's liver is resorted to on most important occasions. If anything special is wanted they inquire of the pig. If they fear any enemies are coming, or ill luck or sickness, they ask the pig whether it is a fact that this will happen. They tell the pig not to mislead them, and to convey the message to the Supreme Being. The pig may even be told that they are not going to kill it or eat it; but the pig is killed the instant they have finished talking, lest the message should be altered by the pig if it knew it was to be killed.

There is always great difficulty in arriving at the true explanation of any particular custom; probably in many cases there is no single explanation which is universally admitted by the natives themselves. It rather seems as if in this pig ceremony the soul of the pig was directly addressed, and that on the death of the pig it was liberated, and thus was able to convey the message to the Supreme Being. The application of the lighted brand may be a secondary custom, introduced from the analogy of the cult of the omen animals. I am indebted to McDougall for this latter suggestion, who also thinks that the primary proper function of fire in a rite is to carry the message to birds or distant powers in case no other messenger, such as a pig's soul, is at hand.

Knowing that I was very anxious to obtain some human skulls for the collection at Cambridge, Hose negotiated with Aban Abit for some. This was a very difficult matter, as skulls are sacred, and not only bring good luck if well treated, but contrariwise they may do harm if they are offended. It is no small matter to prevail upon a man to part with skulls under such circumstances, as he feels he is running great risks, and natives fully realise that wealth can be bought too dearly. What gain is it to have an extra gong if the harvests are bad, if sickness comes, if troubles accumulate?

The following is the way in which the skulls were propitiated. A fowl was obtained, a very little one, for these wide-awake people recognise that it is the idea at the back of the sacrifice rather than the worth of the victim that is efficacious, so there is no need to extravagantly make use of a full-grown fowl when a fledgling will do as well. The chirping chicken was waved over the skulls, and the skulls were told that those of them that were going to be taken away were given and not sold (for here, as in our folk-tales at home, it is very easy to deceive spirits), that they would be well taken care of, and they were entreated not to be angry, as everything was "quite correct," and that the white man would take the whole responsibility and bear all the risks. Then the head and wings of the luckless chicken were torn off, and the spurting blood sprinkled on the skulls and charms, and even on the notched pole which served as a ladder. Hose had to provide a piece of iron, an old spear-head in this case, as a gift to the man who took down the skulls. It was only the great influence that Hose has over the natives and his generous offer, combined with his knowledge of and deference to native customs, and their personal regard for him, which enabled him to obtain these and other skulls.

In the evening we had a performance on the phonograph, which gave great enjoyment to the natives of both sexes and all ages. As in New Guinea, the reproduction of their own songs pleased the people much more than hearing the band-music and songs on the cylinders we had brought with us from England. Later on several of the natives performed some of their dances for us.

We were informed that people were spreading a scare similar to that known as the *Panyamun* scare of five years previously. Reports of all kinds were rife as to the originators of the trouble; some said the Malangs started it, others that it arose among the Sĕbops or the Barawans, while some thought it had come from the Baram River.

Hose explained fully to the people the stupidity of circulating and believing in such rumours, which always caused them a great deal of trouble, and they could not have forgotten that, owing to the last *Panyamun* scare, several people lost their lives. It was, therefore, his intention during this visit to the Tinjar to trace the originators of the false rumours, and if the evidence was sufficient to convict them, they would be heavily punished. It was consequently to everybody's interest to assist in the discovery of these troublesome people.

During the greater part of the year 1894 a remarkable and widely distributed panic spread over Sarawak, and all the races of the Raj, Chinese, Malays, Sea Dayaks (Iban), and various inland tribes were alike affected.

The Malays of Sarawak and Brunei started a rumour all through the country that the Rajah was anxious to obtain a number of human heads to lay in the foundations of the new high-level reservoir at the waterworks at Kuching, and that men were sent out at night to procure them. Similar stories with accompanying panics have occurred elsewhere in the East during the execution of large public works; as, for example, in Singapore, when the cathedral was built.

Professor E. P. Evans states* that as the Siberian railway approached the northern boundaries of the Chinese Empire, and surveys were made for its extension through Manchuria to the sea, great excitement was produced in Pekin by the rumour that the Russian minister had applied to the Empress of China for two thousand children to be buried in the road-bed under the rails in order to strengthen it. He also informs us that some years ago, in rebuilding a large bridge which had been swept away several times by inundations in the Yarkand, eight children, purchased from poor people at a high price, were immured alive in the foundations. As the new bridge was firmly constructed out of excellent materials, it has hitherto withstood the force of the strongest floods, a result which the Chinese attribute, not to the solid masonry, but to the propitiation of the river god by the offering of infants.

I have elsewhere† alluded to this barbarous custom which has been widely spread over the "Old World," and which has left its mark in modern Greek folk-song, and can still be traced in the singing-game of "London Bridge" played by village children in the British Isles.

Sir Spenser St. John writes in his recent book *Rajah Brooke*: "Another intelligent native remarked that the English must have been a barbarous race, as formerly they sacrificed a human victim every time they prepared to take the Sacrament, but that in more modern days they had become more civilised, as now they only sacrificed dogs, a reference to the periodical destruction in British settlements of all stray animals. What a perverse interpretation of missionary teaching!"

Many Sarawak natives went so far as to assert that they had met with the head-hunters among the villages. Great anxiety was caused amongst all classes; at one time numbers of people left their plantations, refusing to do any outdoor work except

* EVANS, E. P., "Superstition and Crime," *Appleton's Pop. Sci. Monthly* (New York), vol. liv., December, 1898.
† HADDON, A. C., *The Study of Man*, 1898.

in large parties; even Chinese *padi* planters in some instances left their isolated houses and crowded into the bazaars.

Other equally absurd stories were circulated and believed in. About fifty Ulu Simunjan Land Dayaks came down in September the same year to the station at Sadong and stated that their district was infested with spirits and ghouls. They asked for leave to hunt down the *hantus* (spirits) in the jungle, as these came by night into the kampongs and shoved sticks and weapons through the walls of their houses, much to their alarm and fright. The Land Dayaks were warned against making this an excuse for molesting anyone without just cause, for it was by no means improbable that mischief would ensue if they were allowed to hunt down *hantus* indiscriminately. Thousands of people living many miles apart were panic-stricken simultaneously, and believed it was unsafe to walk about at night unless armed, and that death would result if a *hantu* caught a man. One result of this particular scare was that coolies refused to do any sort of work unless they could be safely back in their houses before nightfall, and married couples who lived by themselves crowded into the larger houses, which were already full.

Evilly disposed persons were not slack in utilising this *panyamun*, or "robber," scare for their own nefarious purposes, and numerous murders were perpetrated, the murderers pleading that they thought the victims were prowling round for heads.

It can be readily understood that the whole country was in an excited and unsettled state, and this feeling was more or less answerable for various crimes and tragedies. One example of each must suffice.

At the close of the year a man named Newa with four followers was killed at Long Balukun on the Apoh River. A Kenyah named Mawa Obat asked Newa, when sitting in his canoe, to give him some tobacco, and murdered him whilst he was in the act of complying with his request. The Resident believes that one Remau, a worthless Undup Iban, who had married a Kenyah woman residing in the Long Balukun house, was to a great extent the cause of the death of these five men. Remau made up a story about the spear being thrust through the floor of his room, which spear he said belonged to Newa, and afterwards, when it was proved that the spear could not reach the floor of the house, as it was built very high off the ground, he said it was through the wall that the spear was thrust. The Long Balukun people were very short of food at the time, and there is very little doubt that Newa and his party were murdered for the eight bags of rice and fifteen katties of tobacco they had.

In January, 1895, Kempieng, an Iban, and his wife, were visiting Radin, who had married Jerieng, the sister of Kempieng's wife, and who lived on the Beradong, an affluent of the Rejang River. One night, about 9 p.m., Jerieng left her room to go out on the *tanju*, or outside platform, her husband, who accompanied her, going first. Kempieng and his wife were sleeping in the *ruai* (verandah), and as Jerieng passed them he sprang up and speared her. Kempieng admitted the facts at his trial, but pleaded that the people in Radin's house were in a disturbed state, and kept their weapons handy owing to a scare of *panyamuns*, or *hantus* (robbers or spirits). On the night in question, hearing someone moving near him, he arose and took his spear down; whilst doing so he accidentally kicked the lamp over and it went out. He did not thrust with his spear, but held it before him, and the deceased ran against it. It is, however, more probable that he got up in a state of alarm, and, without calling out, blindly lunged with his spear, and thus killed his sister-in-law. For this he was sentenced by the Rajah to three years' imprisonment with hard labour.

I was informed that some Brunei Malays, who had grudges against people who owed them money, or who would not pay any longer the repeated calls which these piratical traders made for fictitious debts, stirred up the Kenyahs of the Baram against the Iban (Sea Dayaks). They said the Rajah had sent out Iban to kill people for the purpose stated above, and they pointed to the Iban who worked gutta near their villages, knowing full well that this had long been a grievance of the Kenyahs against the Iban. The Brunei Malays reminded the Kenyahs of one or two cases of assassination of their people by Iban, and even went below Kenyah houses at night and thrust spears through the flooring in order to make their report appear more real.

At last the Kenyahs were roused, and killed twelve Iban. The Sĕbops of the Tinjar followed suit and murdered two Chinamen, and the Long Patas, seeing the Kenyahs had commenced, took the opportunity to go over into the Limbang, and, as I have already narrated, killed three innocent Kadayans.

Trade was at a standstill, and everybody was miserable; but by being continually on the move up and down the river, and by going familiarly amongst the people, Hose with great difficulty managed to stop any further spread of the scare, and he effectively proved to the natives that the trouble did not arise from any action by the Government. Having thoroughly disgusted everyone throughout the district, the Brunei Malays bolted back to Brunei. By this time they owed a good deal of money in the bazaar at Marudi, and could not get any more credit.

It was no wonder, then, with the recollection of this unsettled and anxious time fresh in his memory that Hose was determined to stamp out what might prove to be the commencement of a similar panic.

Long Semitan was next visited. The Malangs who live in this village requested that a Bakatan, who lived all alone in a Chinaman's store, should be told to leave the village, as he had done no work for months and stole on every opportunity. The people described him as a savage brute, of whom they were afraid, and he constantly threatened to do harm to people if they refused him food, or indeed anything that he asked for. The man was sent for, and Hose inquired of him what he was doing there. He said he was waiting for a month or two before going into the jungle to look for gutta, and denied that he had stolen anything. Hose decided to send him down to Marudi, and told him he must follow a party of Bakatans, Iban, or other people when they went gutta hunting, or he must return by the first steamer to his own country up the Rejang River. He strongly objected to go, although the Malangs had provided him with a boat and food. Eventually he was ejected by force, and all had the satisfaction of seeing this worthless loafer paddle down stream. It was evident that he had done nothing for his own living for months past, and the Chinaman stated that Aban Abit turned him out of his house two months ago, when he shifted to Long Semitan with the intention of sponging on the Malang people. Most probably he had really stolen, but unfortunately there was not sufficient evidence to convict him.

We reached Long Aiah Kechil on the evening of the 13th. The headman of this Sĕbop village is termed Tamoing. On our arrival a great wailing was set up, because very shortly after Hose's last visit the chief of the village had died, and his return reminded his followers of their loss; but they were soon comforted. The Barawans and Balmali people in the neighbourhood appear to have had several quarrels with regard to farming lands. Taman Aping Buling, the Sĕbop *penghulu*, had done his best to settle their differences, but there was still a considerable amount of discontent. The Tinjar is rather crowded here, and Hose considers it would be a good thing if some of the people moved further down the river.

The Sĕbops probably belong to the aboriginal population of Borneo. Those we measured were distinctly narrow-headed, their cephalic index being about 75·5. These people are constantly chaffed by other tribes about their procrastinating habits. If a man has to go on a journey he gets ready and packs his basket, and when just about to go down to the boat he may suddenly turn round and say, "*Sagum*" ("to-morrow"), and then may go on for a number of days until he is perforce obliged to go. The Kenyahs are fond of telling the following fable to illustrate the dilatoriness of the Sĕbops:—

A monkey and a frog who were chums were sitting together in the jungle when it came on to rain very heavily. It rained all that day and night, and the monkey, cold and wet, said to the frog, "This is wretched weather; to-morrow let us beat out a bark cloth from one of those kumut trees." "All right," said the frog, "this incessant rain is very disagreeable." When daylight appeared the rain ceased and the sun shone brightly. The frog hopped on to a fallen stump and basked in the sun, and the monkey climbed to the top of a tree and felt jolly again. Presently the monkey called to the frog, "Oh, comrade, how about that bark cloth we were going to beat out to-day; let's start in and do it." "Oh," said the frog, being unwilling to move from his pleasant spot, "I'm not cold any longer." As night came on the rain began to pour down once more, and the friends, shivering with cold, agreed that to-morrow they must really get the bark cloth. This happened time after time, until at last the monkey became disgusted with the frog always putting off making the covering, and he said it was useless to be friends with a person of so little energy; so he cleared off and left his old friend. The frog still hoots and howls when the rain comes down, but sits silent in the sunshine.

It had long been arranged by our good friend Hose that one of the special features of this trip up the Tinjar was to be an ascent of Dulit, a mountain whose name is well known to those interested in the birds of Borneo, for reasons that I shall shortly narrate. As Hose had a good deal of administrative work to do, he did not intend accompanying us, and, indeed, it would have been no novelty to him, as he has ascended it four times, and spent at least six weeks on or near the summit during those visits.

We made an early start on the morning of February 14th from Long Aiah Kechil, which is the nearest village to the mountain. As we were paddling down the Tinjar, quietly enjoying the swift gliding between banks of rank verdure, a joyous shout and noisy exclamations startled my reverie, and quickly our crews paddled to the bank. To the uninitiated but a small thing had happened, merely that an inconspicuous little bird had flown across the river from right to left. But this was no commonplace bird; it was an "isit," one of the omen birds, who come as messengers from the gods to warn mortals of impending danger, or to encourage them in what they are undertaking.

This was fortunately a favourable omen, hence the delight with which it was hailed, and immediately on seeing it flashing into the open our boatmen called upon it by name, and asked it to "make everything clear and sweep away all difficulties and obstacles from the path, and to make the white men strong in the legs, so that they can climb up Dulit."

In this manner is a bird "owned," and on hearing the prayer the bird assumes all responsibility and takes the petitioners under its protection.

Our friends landed on the steep bank of the river, and, cutting down some undergrowth, whittled a couple of sticks, so that they had a frilled appearance. A match was struck, and as soon as the shavings flamed, they asked the fire to tell the bird to inform the gods of the message, which was then repeated.

An unexpected episode of this sort is very refreshing. Here was illustration of that religious spirit which is so universally distributed among mankind. Our men were encouraged by the knowledge of divine sanction, and, moreover, their petition was unaccompanied by sacrifice, gifts, or promises; the human words were simply wafted godwards by the smoke. It is easy to call this paganism, to sneer at it as superstition, but such practices are essentially religious ceremonies, and of a refined character too, which require no intermediary between the spiritual powers and the ordinary individual.

We resumed our way, and shortly entered a small river which Hose has named the Scott-Keltie River, in honour of the Secretary of the Royal Geographical Society. In the muddy banks at its mouth are immense quantities of leaves, which give the alluvium a very characteristic laminated appearance. When consolidated and turned into rock, these beds will form ligneous shales, or earthy coal beds, such as we constantly find in various geological formations.

We landed a short distance up this stream, and ran our boat high and dry in a creek. Hose then left us, and we started on our way; our party consisted of Aris, my Malay "boy," three Iban fortmen, three Naroms (a branch of the Mĕlanaus), and four Sĕbops from Long Aiah Kechil, McDougall, and myself.

At first we walked for an hour or so on the alluvial plain through plantations, some of which were abandoned and overgrown; then we struck the Scott-Keltie River, and waded some distance along its rocky and gravelly bed; later we forded it several times, as our direct route through the jungle cut across its sinuosities.

Our path for some distance lay through "New Jungle," but as we ascended we passed into "Old Jungle." In the earlier part of the day there was a good deal of rain; when this ceased there was an aftermath of continual dripping off the trees, and all the undergrowth was reeking wet, but this was of little moment, as we wore woollen garments, and the heat of the atmosphere and the continual exercise prevented our getting a chill. There was the usual profusion of fallen, rotting trees, over, under, and along which we had to pass. The soil was the yellow, slippery clay that is met with in so many places in Sarawak. This laterite, as it is called by geologists, is widely spread over the tropics. When our feet slipped we clutched at what was nearest to hand, sometimes it was a thorny climber, or perhaps a rotten sapling that looked strong enough, but which was as weak as touchwood, owing to its being permeated by corroding fungi. Our caps and clothes were continually caught by the fine thorny filaments of a species of ratan or by other prickly plants.

Several men always preceded me to cut down the lianas and other impeding vegetation, and they also served to collect on their legs some of the land leeches, which, reaching out from the leaves of low shrubs, seek whom they may devour. At every halt we overhauled ourselves, and pulled off these tough, elastic worms.

We soon reached a ridge-like spur of the mountain, on each side of which we could hear a river rushing over its stony bed. This spur had very steep sides owing to the cutting down of the streams, but it was covered with deep vegetation, which acted as a kind of umbrella, and so prevented the heavy rains from denuding it down to a low watershed between the two streams.

About three o'clock we went a little way down to the Scott-Keltie River, and followed it up as far as a fine waterfall, some three hundred or four hundred feet in height. Here we built a hut, and after a bathe and a good meal felt very comfortable, and all except myself passed a good night. Fortunately there was no rain.

We awoke early next morning, but it was nearly eight o'clock before we started, owing to the dilatoriness of the Sĕbops in taking up their burdens. Before starting, and also on the previous evening, I photographed the Scott-Keltie Falls. The upper part of the falls is hidden by trees; the central portion consists of two large quadrangular faces of rock, one above the other, with a combined height of a hundred to a hundred and fifty feet. Below the fall proper is a steep declivity of fallen blocks of rock, many of huge dimensions, over which the water pours. Indeed, for a considerable distance down the steep river-bed is a mass of boulders which practically forms a continuous cascade. The vegetation about the falls was lovely, the masses of ordinary forest trees being relieved by graceful palms and shrubs of varied foliage (Frontispiece).

We ascended the mountain, leaving the falls on our right. It was very steep walking, and at places we had practically vertical escarpments of rock to negotiate, which were slippery owing to recent rains. The roots of trees and the stems of creepers afforded secure grip and foothold, but at a few places I was glad of the assistance of a ratan. We were in a mist the whole day, and every now and again a rift gave us tantalising glimpses of the outer world that far below us stretched out in all its tropical luxuriance and beauty. Sometimes we saw a bit of the river, and could just distinguish a village, when the view dissolved; then a neighbouring wooded spur of the mountain would shape itself out of the mist, only to disappear in the steamy atmosphere.

We pitched our camp about three o'clock, and made a long hut on the crest of a steep ridge at an elevation of over four thousand feet. Fortunately there was no rain all day, so our clothes were fairly dry, and we had no rain during the night. Of course it was chilly, but it was only really cold when the wind rose.

We got up on Thursday morning at 5.30. As soon as breakfast was finished, McDougall and all the carriers except Aris and one Sĕbop, who had a sore leg, continued the ascent. I was

FIG. 35. MOUNT DULIT FROM LONG AIAH KECHIL

not very well, and did not feel equal to the climb, so I spent a quiet day, writing, and letting the influences of the jungle soak into me. It was a strange sensation perched high up on a narrow ridge in a tropical jungle and screened from the world by a mist!

McDougall returned about 3.30. He had ascended the highest point, which Hose has since named Cambridge Peak, but had not obtained a satisfactory view. He had some difficulty in climbing the uppermost escarpments. As the cliffs were absolutely vertical, the natives made ladders which they leaned against trees projecting from the cliff, and from one tree another ladder was raised to a tree above it, till the summit was reached. Mount Dulit is, in geographical terminology, a partially dissected block mountain of Carboniferous sandstone, the beds of which dip in a southerly direction.

There was rain early next morning, but it soon cleared for a short time, and we started on our homeward journey. We had a scanty lunch at the Scott-Keltie Falls. The water was now a thin stream, indeed we had noticed a difference in the amount on the Wednesday morning as compared with that which fell during our first evening there. We retraced our steps as quickly as possible, but I took several photographs of the falls and river. We got back to our boat about 3.30, and returned to Long Aiah Kechil before dark.

I was particularly interested in Mount Dulit, as it has been a happy hunting-ground for Hose during some years past. He was the first European to ascend the mountain, and he has made natural-history collections on it from top to base. Hose here discovered a high-altitude fauna, more particularly among the birds, which, like that of the famous Kina Balu in British North Borneo, has affinities with the fauna of the Himalayas.

The island of Borneo lies at one edge of an immense submarine bank, while the islands of Java and Sumatra are situated at its southern and western sides, and the island of Celebes and the archipelago that stretches from Java to Ombasi are annexes. The hundred-fathom contour line embraces this vast area, and indeed a considerable portion of the sea between Borneo and Java on the one hand, and Siam and the Malay Peninsula on the other, is only fifty fathoms deep. In other words, the trivial elevation of this area to three hundred feet would connect Borneo and Java with the mainland of Asia. This continental shelf may be termed the Malay shelf.

I have already pointed out that the physical features of Borneo prove that there are indications that it has undergone changes of level in recent geological times. The geological structure of the island shows that it formed part of a continent, as it contains formations of the Palæozoic, Mesozoic, and Cainozoic periods, and is thus very different from what are termed oceanic islands, that is, islands composed solely of recent volcanic rocks or built upon coral banks. As Wallace[*] points out: "A subsidence of five hundred feet would allow the sea to fill the great valleys of the Pontianak, Banjarmassing, and Coti rivers, almost to the centre of the island, greatly reducing its extent, and causing it to resemble in form the island of Celebes to the east of it."

About a hundred and forty species of mammals have been discovered in Borneo, and of these "more than three-fourths,"

---

[*] *Island Life*, second edition, p. 375.

according to Wallace, "are identical with those of the continent. Among these are two lemurs, nine civets, five cats, five deer, the tapir, the elephant, the rhinoceros, and many squirrels, an assemblage which could certainly only have reached the country by land."

The most interesting of those species peculiar to the island, that is not found elsewhere, are the long-nosed monkey and the tailless porcupine. These peculiar forms, which amount to something over thirty in number, "do not, however, imply that the separation of the island from the continent is of very ancient date, for the country is so vast, and so much of the once connecting land is covered with water, that the amount of speciality is hardly, if at all, greater than occurs in many continental areas of equal extent and remoteness." The same story is told by the birds, although one would imagine that possessing power of flight their distribution would be more uniform than it is. Wallace concludes that the majority of forest birds are restricted by narrow watery barriers to an even greater extent than mammals.

Mr. John Whitehead has made some valuable collections on Mount Kina Balu, the highest mountain in Borneo. "The Chinese Widow" is an isolated mountain mass which rises to a height of 13,698 feet; at an elevation of about 4,000 feet Mr. Whitehead began to find traces of a new fauna which linked that mountain with the Himalayas. Hose has made a similar discovery on Mounts Dulit and Mulu, so that Dr. R. B. Sharpe has stated (*Ibis*, 1894, p. 542): "it is evident that Mount Mulu belongs to the same system of the Himalayan offshoots, such as Kina Balu, Dulit, and Kalulong" (*The Geographical Journal*, i. 1893, p. 203).

Hose has stated that "the fauna of Mount Dulit resembles that of Kina Balu in a great number of instances, but it is a curious fact that all the species above 2,000 feet are found at a higher altitude on Kina Balu than they are on Mount Dulit. This, I think, can be accounted for by the fact that Mount Kina Balu has been cleared of all the old jungle, and farmed by the natives to a height of about 2,000 feet, whilst on the Dulit there are no traces of human habitation within miles of the mountain [this is a slight exaggeration on Hose's part]. I think it is reasonable to suppose that many of the Kina Balu birds and animals, which prefer to live in the old jungle, have been in this way driven to a higher elevation" (*Proc. Zool. Soc.*, 1889, p. 228).

In a paper on the mammals of Kina Balu, Mr. Oldfield Thomas points out the affinity of the mammalian fauna of the mountain at great heights with that of the Himalayan region. For example, a water-shrew (*Chimarrogale himalayica*) had previously been recorded from Sikhim, Assam, and the Katchin Hills in the north of Burmah. On the other hand, a certain mouse (*Mus musschenbroecki*) was previously known from Celebes, and its occurrence on Kina Balu suggests that other members of the Oriental element in the peculiar Celebean fauna may also prove to have survived on the tops of the Bornean mountains. Dr. R. B. Sharpe (*Ibis*, 1892, p. 430) also states that some of the Kina Balu species of birds have been obtained in high Sumatra.

There is evidence that during the Miocene Age Java was at least three thousand feet lower than it is now, and, as Wallace suggests, " such a depression would probably extend to considerable parts of Sumatra and Borneo, so as to reduce them all to a few small islands.

"At some later period a gradual elevation occurred which ultimately united the whole of the islands with the continent. This may have continued till the glacial period of the northern hemisphere, during the severest part of which a few Himalayan species of birds and mammals may have been driven southward, and have ranged over suitable portions of the whole area.

"Java then became separated by subsidence, and these species were imprisoned in the island, while those in the remaining part of the Malayan area again migrated northward when the cold had passed away from their former home," with the exception of those forms which were cut off on isolated mountain masses, where they survived in those places where the conditions were not very dissimilar from those they were accustomed to.

In other words, these more northern forms retreated from the deluge of the typical Malayan fauna up the mountains. The lower mountains were overwhelmed by the equatorial forests and the profusion of animals that are adapted for that peculiar condition of existence. The lesser spurs of the high mountains shared the same fate, but the struggle between the rival faunas became less keen at altitudes of three or four thousand feet.

Here the temperature is cooler, and so the conditions of life become less favourable for the tropical lowland fauna, and more so to the relic-fauna of the northern mountains, and in consequence we have these faunistic islands.

Somewhat later the Malay continental shelf was submerged, and Borneo and Sumatra became isolated.

CHAPTER XXII

A TRIP INTO THE INTERIOR OF BORNEO
CONTINUED

WE reached the Sĕbop village of Long Puah, up the Lobong affluent of the Tinjar, on the evening of February 19th. Jangan, the headman, made us comfortable in the large new house, which was not yet completed. Hose had insisted on going to the new house, as the old one was dirty and was falling to pieces. The first ceremony to be performed before the house could be inhabited was the removing of the skulls from a temporary hut to their new quarters. This was to take place early the following morning. The business to be transacted that day required the presence of some women, and no women may enter a new house until the skulls have been transferred to it.

At daybreak a number of men perched themselves on the ridge pole of the new house and chanted invocations to the omen birds. They shouted for joy as a propitious hawk duly flew away to the right after soaring, for unless the omen was favourable nothing could have been accomplished that day. Immediately the omen bird had given permission for matters to proceed, there was a great din of shouting and gong-beating for the purpose of preventing the people from hearing the hawk in case it should scream, for that would have been an unlucky omen, and would have necessitated a delay. At various intervals rice was thrown out of the house by the old men as offerings to the omen birds and prayers made to the Supreme Deity and to the lesser gods. Hose and I also sacrificed some tobacco and rice to the birds.

Several men, accoutred as if for the war-path, went to the temporary hut where the skulls were lodged. Most of the men had on a war coat, which is the skin of a goat or a clouded tiger-cat, decked with the white and black tail feathers of the hornbill, which feathers, by the way, may be worn only by men who have been on the war-path or who have killed a man. Each had on a war cap, with the long tail feathers of another species of hornbill, and they carried shields and spears. Standing outside the hut the men chanted songs while an old man removed the basket of skulls from the hut. It is considered a dangerous matter to meddle with skulls, as they resent liberties taken with them, and may perhaps harm him who handles them; this business was therefore relegated to an old man, as it did not much matter if harm befell him during his short remaining span of life.

The skulls were hoisted on to the verandah of the new house from the outside—as they must never be taken up the ladder and through the house—and immediately they were hauled on to a rafter. Then the women trooped up; in this instance they came up the ladder that was erected at the open end of the verandah, but according to rigid custom the women should only enter a new house for the first time through temporary doors made for the purpose in the back wall of the house, but as that part of the house was only in skeleton this could not be done.

Jangan, the chief, was quite an elderly man, who only two months previously had been presented by his wife with his first child. His old wife had died a couple of years since, but before her death she had instigated him to marry his present young and pretty wife.

After three years of wedded life a boy appeared, greatly to the joy and satisfaction of Jangan and his wife. As yet the boy had no name, and therefore was not considered to have any social status. Before receiving its name a male child is always spoken of as a *ukat* and a girl as *itang*. The Iban call such children *anak ulat*, or "young grub." Our visit was a convenient opportunity for the naming ceremony, and Hose arranged with Jangan that I should act as godfather. This necessitated the presentation on my part of a gong, for that is the recognised present on such occasions. I was able to get one from a Malay trader, who had a small store close by, and we all made additional presents of cloth, to which I added a looking-glass.

A pig with tied legs was brought up into the house. This was the offering of the father, who, squatting beside it, singed a few hairs with a firebrand, and put his hands on the pig's flanks, praying meanwhile as follows:—

"O spiritual pig [Balli Boin], tell Balli Penyalong [the god of child-naming] the reason of our meeting here to-day. We are here to name my child, and we request you to convey our message to Balli Penyalong. It is our intention to do all in the best manner possible. We are only a poor people, and cannot do things on this river on a large scale. We trust you will approve of our performances, and we hope that blessings will come to all present who meet as friends.

"We also request Balli Penyalong to let us know by the inspection of your liver whether the name which we intend to give this child is suitable, whether it will in any way be harmful to him, whether he will suffer sickness, and whether he will come to any harm through false reports. Tuan Resident is a witness, and all those who have done us the kindness of being present."

Then turning to us he continued: "You are visitors to this country, and we hope that you will not be displeased with our simple customs, which are the ways of our forefathers, and which I request Tuan Resident to explain to you as I am unable to speak your language."

Again addressing the pig, he said: "The name which we have chosen has been proposed by the old man with the beard.* The first name, Utang ["Good-luck"], is entirely suitable, as his grandfather bore the same name. The second name, Haddon, is also a name given by the old man with the beard; in fact it is his own name, and the event has been marked by suitable presents. We hope that all this is well, and that the augury given in the liver will be the true one.

"We also employ you, O pig, for another little ceremony, to which, of course, you will have no objection. We have here two peoples, the Lepuanans and the Punans, who have met one another for the first time since quarrelling, and who take this opportunity to square all grievances and to make *urip*."

The pig was then killed in the usual manner by a spear plunged into its neck. Scarce was the unfortunate animal dead before it was cut open and the liver carefully extracted and handed round for inspection. It was on the whole a pretty fair one, but one or two points were not particularly favourable; all

---

* When travelling about I let my beard grow.

the good points were, however, explained by Hose as belonging to the child, whereas the less favourable details he asserted referred to the recent hostilities between the Lepuanans and Punans. As Hose is recognised by the natives as an expert in liver divination, his interpretation was accepted. The blood of the pig was smeared on the breasts of numerous spectators, mainly on those of Lepuanans and Punans.

The second or "house" pig was brought and spoken over by an old man of the house. The liver, fortunately, was more propitious than the preceding one. Some of the blood of the pig was smeared on a parang blade and dabbed on my bare chest by Jangan, who said, "You have seen our customs and how we make *urip!* Do not misrepresent us when you go back to your own country, and do not tell lies about us." I then smeared blood from the same parang blade on the breasts of many of the people round about.

The Punans next killed a sucking-pig to ratify their friendship with the Lepuanans.

The final ceremony of naming Jangan's boy consisted in killing a chicken. Some of the blood of the fowl was rubbed on a parang blade, and, taking the gory iron, I applied it to the arms of Utang Haddon, saying to him in English that I wished him good luck, a long life, a wife, and plenty of children.

Hose made a speech, and everyone shouted and stamped.

Finally, the *borak* (rice spirit) was produced. Hose gave a drink to the mother. I gave one to the father, and made a small speech, wishing him more children and a long life for himself, his wife, and his children. The wife gave Hose and me a drink, thanking us for what we had done.

Drinks then became general, and there was much noise and enjoyment.

Lepuanans and Punans gave *borak* to each other; the ladies were not forgotten, nor did they omit to offer some to us and to the other men. Great hilarity was caused in succeeding, or failing, as the case might be, in making a few Mohammedans who were present partake of a liquid that was prohibited to them by the Prophet.

Everything was very human, and, alas! the after results were in a few cases very "human" too. The older men and the wiser of the younger men who had court business to transact later in the day partook but sparingly of the seductive drink, others were carried away by the infectious gaiety, and subsequently became sleepy or excited, according to their respective idiosyncrasies. One man was fighting mad, and had to be held down by several men. One somnolent youth was affectionately tended by three young women, one of whom nursed his head on her lap. Next morning several men had sore heads.

Some of the Punans complained of certain Malay traders interfering with their women, and also that their debts to the traders never came to an end. They had paid many times for the same thing, and still the traders produced their books and stated that the debts were not settled. Hose heard their grievances, and having summoned all the Malays that were about, he thoroughly investigated the matter. He took away with him when he left four Malays who admitted that they had interfered with some of the wives of the Punans, and cautioned the others as to their future behaviour,

Some Malohs who were staying in this village wished to marry Sĕbop girls, but the Sĕbop chiefs did not want this, as the Malohs are untrustworthy people, being suspected of divorcing their wives on some trivial pretext when they wish to return to their own country. Hose thinks the Malohs possibly originally came from Java; they and allied people inhabit the southern part of Borneo, but parties of them have penetrated into various places in the interior, and have begun to make their way down some of the upper branches of the tributaries of the Baram River. They are essentially a trading people, and hence have no special interest in settling down; they are also great workers in brass, and so are of great use to the other natives. The Sĕbop girls appeared to be anxious to marry the five Malohs, and as the latter had done no harm in the village and there was absolutely nothing against them, Hose found it somewhat difficult to prevent the marriages, though he appreciated the reasonableness of the objection of the chiefs. He thereupon thought of a plan which would probably prevent the marriages, but at the same time if the girls were anxious to marry they would be allowed to do so. Hose gave the Malohs permission to marry the girls provided they will come down to Claudetown with their wives and live at Tangjong Upah with those Iban who have married Kayan and Kenyah women. If the girls are really fond of the Malohs they will go; on the other hand, their relatives will do their best to dissuade them.

Hose has found from past experience that it is a very unsatisfactory arrangement for foreigners like the Iban or Malohs, or even more nearly allied peoples like the Mĕlanaus, to marry into and live amongst up-river tribes. Sooner or later trouble arises through a lack of solidarity between the aliens and the original inhabitants, cliques are formed, and the foreigner sides with the disaffected and the irresponsible men, such as are to be found in every community. Whenever possible he solves the difficulty by making the parties of these mixed marriages live together far from the wife's relations, and he has caused them to build a long house at Tangjong Upah on the Baram, about eight miles south of Claudetown, where, being isolated, they can work out their own salvation, but at the same time they are within easy reach of headquarters. Hose can thus see that nothing goes wrong, but nevertheless they are left, as in other native villages, to regulate their internal affairs.

In the evening we were entertained with a dance by the Sĕbops. A man who played a *kaluri*, or mouth organ, walked in front; he was followed by two men, and these by ten women, all in single file. They walked with their toes well out, and scraped the sole of the advancing foot along the ground, the body being swung slightly from side to side. None of the men were specially dressed up, except the third, who had on a war coat and carried a shield; the Sĕbop shield is similar to the plain, red shield of the Kayans, but broader and rather more clumsy.

Another movement consisted in advancing two steps with a striding motion, scraping the sole along the ground and stamping when bringing it to rest. A lesser backward movement was made for two steps, then forward as before.

A third consisted in walking slowly and placing one foot pointing outwards somewhat to the side, the other foot is brought up to it, the moving foot being stamped twice before coming to a halt. In a variant of this the whole body is alternately turned to the right and to the left. The regular double stamping forms a pleasing feature.

In a fourth dance a backward and forward "goose step" was made, touching the ground with the heel, but without shifting the position. Then two forward steps were taken. At one interval the body was turned to the right, at the next to the left, and so on alternately.

In the dance that followed one step was taken at a time, bringing up the other to it, with the sole dragging along the ground. The string of dancers moved forward in a serpentine course.

In the "Bird Dance" there was only a slight movement forwards, the feet tapped the ground, and the arms were moved in an angular manner up and down and backwards and forwards.

The performance concluded with a war dance by a single man dressed in a war coat decorated with hornbills' feathers, and wearing a long-plumed war cap. First he danced without his weapons, then he picked up his shield, and later his parang. The dance consisted of a series of indescribable crouching, jumping, squirming movements, in which the approved positions or attitudes of actual warfare were blended with the gyratory motions and posturing of more ordinary dancing. Crouching on the ground with war coat trailing behind and brandishing his shield in front, the warrior turned, or rather hopped like an amorous cock-sparrow, first to one side and then to the other, as if warding off blows from an unseen adversary; then as if perceiving an advantage he would leap to his feet and take the initiative.

The numerous and rapid graceful movements, the finely harmonising colours of the buff skin, the ruddled shield, the black and tawny clouded tiger's skin coat and red loin cloth, and the bold contrast of the white and black feathers of the hornbill, lit up by blazing fire and yellow flickering lamps against a dim background of eager semi-nude natives and spaces of outer darkness, made a fascinating picture of savagery, in which the beauty of dextrous movement with harmony and contrast of colour were combined with the deeply seated human passion for combat and bloodshed.

We returned down the Lobong and again ascended the narrowing Tinjar, and negotiated several rapids, one of which Hose has named after Ray. On one occasion we had to wait a couple of hours in a sheltered spot by the bank of the river, as the water suddenly rose and the force of the current was too strong for our crew to paddle against it.

The scenery was very pretty, the rushing water passing between low wooded hills, which were occasionally more or less cleared for *padi*. A few birds flew across the river, and numerous gorgeous butterflies flitted in the sunlight, and vermilion-bodied dragon flies darted in quest of their prey. Tropical vegetation is perhaps seen at its best along the banks of rivers, as the trees and bushes have full light and air on one side, and more variety is seen in foliage and tints; but here, as elsewhere in the tropics, there is a general absence of brightly coloured or conspicuous flowers.

Our next stopping-place was at Long Dapoi, a village that, as its name implies, is situated where the Dapoi joins the Tinjar.

Taman Aping Buling, the chief of Long Dapoi and *penghulu* of the Upper Tinjar, and his people were in great distress owing to the recent loss of their former fine house by fire. It was not known how the fire arose, as it occurred when most of the people were away working on their *padi* farms. The village house was exceedingly well built, and was the largest house in all the Tinjar District. We saw the mournful rows of charred piles, and there was no reason to doubt the statement of the people that they had lost a large proportion of their worldly goods. They now occupy makeshift huts until the harvest is gathered in, when they will rebuild. They however found time to erect a comfortable little house for us to stay in, and were very anxious that we should spend some time with them.

Hose had a good deal of business to do, and so on the following morning, while we measured heads, he went into the *penghulu's* house and settled a number of cases of various kinds. Amongst these was one assault case, and complaints of diverse natives with regard to land grabbing. Further information was also obtained respecting the *panyamun* scare. It appears that one Turing, a Sĕbop, came up river to Long Dapoi, about ten days ago, and told Ajang, Taman Gau, and Suran, of this village, that he had narrowly escaped being killed by *panyamun* (or "robbers"), and had he not been near the house he would certainly have lost his life. The robbers were armed with spears and other weapons. When closely questioned who the people resembled were, he said, "Kayans from the Baram"; and when asked if he could recognise any of their faces, he said, "No, I was too frightened." Here, then, was evidence that could be dealt with as regards the statement of Turing, as all three men were willing to swear that they heard Turing make the above statement. It was necessary for these three men and the *penghulu* to meet Turing. Hose therefore arranged with the *penghulu* that either Turing should be called here, or, if they wished it, they could accompany Hose when he went down river, as Turing was living in the Lower Tinjar; something in the way of expenses would, of course, be allowed should their statement prove correct. They were all not only willing but anxious to go with us on our return. All the people were glad to have this matter cleared up, and it appeared that there was every chance of the guilty parties being discovered.

When Hose had finished his business we continued our journeying by ascending the Dapoi, a beautiful affluent of the Tinjar. Along the greater extent of its banks are native plantations of bananas, sugar-cane, and other edible plants; the low hills between which the river flows are largely deforested for the cultivation of *padi*. This small, swift river is a favourite one with the natives, and is well populated.

We reached our furthest point, at a distance of some two hundred miles from Marudi, on the evening of February 24th, at Long Sulan, on the Dapoi River. This is the largest village I had yet seen in this district; probably about fifteen hundred men, women, and children live here, and wherever I went I was followed about by swarms of children. The people are Long Pokuns, and belong to the Kayan group.

In front of the main house and facing the river was a large wooden model of a man holding a shield and waving a spear. This was a representation of Balli Atap, whose function is to ward off all sickness and misfortune. Beside him was a roughly carved image of Tegulan, who also keeps off sickness from people, and by means of this image you can either curse a man or prevent him from cursing you.

Behind these were two wooden effigies of the tiger (*linjau*), facing different ways. The object of these figures is to impress the enemies of the village with the idea that the inhabitants are as fierce as tigers, and should not be meddled with. They were intended to serve the same purpose as the sentiment in the chorus of the famous music-hall song—

> "We don't want to fight,
> But by Jingo if we do!"

Near these symbols of ferocity was a framework on which were some curiously shaped stones. Usually similar stones are placed on separate posts outside houses, and as a rule these

THE INTERIOR OF BORNEO

are simply rounded boulders which the natives believe have the power of increasing in size with age. In several places the natives tell stories about the stones being originally very small when they were in another district, but since then they have grown, and you can see how large they are now. A sacrificial fire is lit near them, or even a flaming firebrand will suffice. Fowl's or pig's blood is on ceremonial occasions smeared on the stones. This is always done when it is necessary to consult the omen birds before making a long journey or before setting out on the war-path. The fire conveys to the god the

FIG. 36. LONG SULAN

messages and desires of the worshippers. I am not quite clear what part the stones are supposed to play in this ceremony. I was informed that the fire is entreated to tell the stones to inform the god of the desires of the sacrificers, but I would rather not commit myself to this statement until it has been verified.

Around the shrine of sacred stones were a number of frayed poles and sticks (*isang*). These play an important part in all ceremonies connected with the war-path and the consequent bringing home of heads. They are also erected when skulls are shifted from one house to another.

Not far off were a couple of very tall poles (*kelebong*) decorated with shavings, from the tapered end of which depended a long decorated rope, to the free end of which was fastened a round block of wood. This is now an innocent object; formerly (and not so very long ago either) it would have been a human head or skull. A *kelebong* is erected on the return from the war-path, or, as on the present occasion, when a new house is built.

There were two groups of curious upright boards (*kedaman*), with streamers attached. A rough or conventional face is

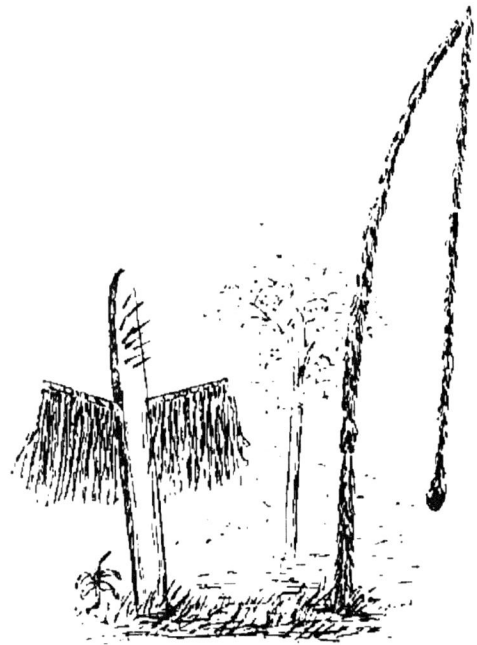

FIG. 37. KEDAMAN AND KELEBONG AT LONG SULAN

usually carved or painted at the end, and there project two slanting cross-boards that serve as arms. Indeed a *kedaman* looks at a distance for all the world like our familiar scarecrows, but their object is to attract and not to frighten away certain birds. On the upper part of the board were a number of spikes or thin skewers, on which were stuck small pieces of pig or fowl meat, to sacrificially feed the omen birds. Often, and that till quite recently, the flesh of enemies was offered in a similar manner.

On our way to Long Sulan we had picked up a Sĕbop chief, named Tingang, who had married the niece of Taman Balan Deng, the Long Pokun chief. Tingang had requested Hose to assist him in a little family matter. He had been married about four years, but his wife was still living with her relations, who refused to let her live with her husband in his present village, though she was not unwilling to live with him.

It appears that about a year after he was married it was arranged that he should send people to fetch his wife, and he agreed to pay over a sum of about a hundred dollars as dowry. He then returned home to make arrangements for his wife's arrival, and thinking that all was satisfactorily arranged and that there would be no difficulty or any necessity for much ceremony, he sent only a few of the low-class people of his house to fetch the lady.

It is usual on an occasion of this kind for some friendly chief with a number of influential people to go in a long boat decorated with flags, and to bring home the bride with a good deal of ceremony; this always takes place a year or so after marriage.

On the present occasion Tingang's wife expected something of this kind, and when the emissaries arrived in a small boat she was naturally much annoyed; her relations absolutely refused to allow her to go in such a manner, and coldness sprang up between husband and wife for about a year. Tingang, however, made repeated visits to the house, and now considered that sufficient time had elapsed, and wished to make another effort to get his wife away from her relations; therefore he asked Hose to assist him. Hose questioned him with regard to the *brian*, or dowry; he admitted there were about fifty dollars to pay, which, however, was of no importance, and he would pay it at once, his relative Tama Bulan and others having promised to help him.

On his arrival at Long Sulan, Hose, in the presence of Langat, a cousin of the lady, and son of Taman Balan Deng, said to Tingang that I asked where his wife was. Upon his answering that she was living in this house, Hose asked him, "Why haven't you taken her down to your house? You have been married a long time now." To which he replied, "I want to." Langat retired, and no doubt repeated the conversation to the relatives. Shortly afterwards Tingang's wife appeared, and asked Hose to go into her room. When there Hose asked her why she did not go and live with Tingang. Her answer was she was waiting for him to build a proper house. Hose did not let her know that he had heard the story of Tingang's sending for her, and no doubt she had no intention of telling him about it. As Tingang has really got a very wretched sort of house, Hose took the opportunity of his entering the room to tell him that really and truly it was hardly a suitable house to expect his wife to come to, and she had very good reason for not wishing to come if he did not choose to build a better one. He admitted that his house was unsatisfactory, and said that he had already settled on a new site, and the posts had been prepared. The wife stroked Hose and said, "That's right, make him build a good house, and then I'll go down." Later on in the day Hose spoke to Taman Balan Deng about it, and he said, "Oh yes, I have no objection; no doubt Tingang will make better preparation this time than formerly." Tingang had probably learnt his lesson.

The reason for Tingang having a poor house is a curious one. His house, which originally was a good one, had become old, and he determined the next year to rebuild it on the same site, but an Iban, who had been loafing about for a long time, and for whom his people had a strong objection, cursed some people of the house with whom he had trading transactions and killed a dog in the house. The killing of a dog in a house is a serious matter for Kenyahs and Kayans, and necessitates the breaking up of a whole house and rebuilding it elsewhere. This is the reason for the delay in the house-building, together with hindrances due to farming operations. Later on Hose brought this Iban down to Marudi, and on the charge being proved against him he was ordered out of the Baram district back to his own people. As he had some sixty dollars owing to him at the village he had injured, Hose told him that he could not recover the debt, which would thus stand over as compensation.

The following day some Madangs from the Silat River arrived with the news that Saba Irang, the Madang chief, who had conveyed messages from Hose to the important chiefs who live on the Upper Batang Kayan River, would return shortly, and that his mission had been most successful. The Batang Kayan is a large river in Dutch Borneo, inhabited by people allied to the Madangs and Kenyahs of the Baram district, but there has been some friction between some of the Batang Kayan and

Baram tribes, and it was to relieve this that Hose has entered into friendly relations with the foreigners.

Saba Irang reported that the chiefs of the Batang Kayan were very anxious to meet Hose, and would come very shortly to Marudi (Claudetown). It was also stated that some thirty "doors" (families) of Leppu Agas from the Batang Kayan had moved into the Silat, being anxious for a more settled life. Knowing that the Madangs had recently acknowledged allegiance to the Government of Sarawak, the Leppu Agas were anxious to follow their example, as they are related to the Madangs. This was good news, as Hose is getting more and more into touch with the people of the Batang Kayan, who, of their own accord, move over into the head waters of the Baram district, and by mixing with the Baram people quickly become loyal subjects of the Sarawak Government.

These Kenyah races are always the best workers of jungle produce, and quickly accumulate wealth whenever they find an outlet for their trade. They now fully realise that if they kill, or are at enmity with, the surrounding peoples their trade is at a deadlock. Traders are unwilling to enter their villages, and the natives are also equally unwilling to pass by the houses or territory of their enemies. The result is that trade is one of the most important civilising influences among these interior tribes. The necessity for salt, tobacco, and other luxuries is felt very severely when the supply is cut off, and they know well that when under a settled government they can have most of their requirements within easy reach.

We measured fifteen people here, and visited various houses and collected a few objects. Unfortunately Hose was ill in the afternoon with fever, in addition to the sore throat and cough from which he had been suffering for some time.

We returned the following day to Long Dapoi, and after Hose had received $200 for fines collected by the *penghulu*, went down river, the people who had charged Turing accompanying us. Our crew paddled hard all day, and at night reached Long Semitan. Here we found Turing, and when questioned he admitted that he had made the previously mentioned statement to Ajang, Taman Gau, and Suran, but said that he had been told about the *panyamun* by a Barawan woman named Obong. Obong was living a little further down the river in the house of Taman Ladang. Hose told Taman

Aping Buling that he must fetch Obong to-morrow, and that at Long Tisam he would make further inquiries.

There was a Punan medicine-man in the Long Semitan house, and Hose allowed himself to be operated on so that we might have an opportunity of witnessing native medical practice. Hose, who was really ill, was lying in an inner room, and the Punan was sitting on a gong Hose had given him for his fee. Like other inland natives he wore only a *chawat*, or loin cloth, his black hair hung down his back, and a string of blue beads encircled his right wrist.

The room was dark, save for the flickering of a distant fire and the glimmer of a small lamp. The weird jungle man sat close to Hose with his hands to the side of his own head.

He asked Hose what was the matter. Hose replied he had fever every alternate day. The medicine-man asked if Hose had a headache, and other details of his illness.

The Punan then requested the spirits not to allow the sickness to be too bad. He sang, or rather crooned, and occasionally breathed loudly, and wiped his head and hair and smoked a cigarette. Next he took the blade of a parang, and so held it that the shadow of the iron fell on Hose, and he attentively regarded the shadow. Again he blew, sang and smoked, looked at Hose, felt his abdomen, and stroked it, singing all the while and calling on the sickness to come out.

Once or twice he put his hands together so as to form a tube, through which he blew the abdomen. He next covered his own ears with his hands and blew on the pit of Hose's stomach. Again he stopped his ears and sucked at Hose's abdomen through a small tube made of the stem of the wild ginger; he had previously scratched the place with his finger-nail, and he sucked so hard as to make the skin rise in the tube. By a clumsy sleight of hand he brought a small ball of wax, from which projected a few hairs, out of the tube, this he pretended he had extracted from Hose's body. After having shown it round he carefully dropped the pellet of wax and the tube through the floor.

On Hose saying he had a headache the medicine-man pricked Hose's temples with his nails and proceeded as before. By this time the operator was perspiring profusely.

Again he sang and examined the parang. Next he paid attention to Hose's legs, and stroked them from the knee to the ankle; then he covered his head with a cloth and bent over the legs, pricked the skin with his nails and sucked hard through a tube as before, again producing a pellet of wax.

Once more he repeated the process on the leg, looked at the parang, sang, blew on the leg, and stated that Hose would be well on the morrow. The whole operation was again repeated.

After an interval the same operation recommenced. The man called on the different spirits by name: "Who has done this? Has —— done it? Has —— done it?" When he had exhausted the enumeration of the spirits he looked into the parang and saw that Hose's soul was better.

A fresh supply of ginger stems was placed in front of the doctor; he then took a hat, put it on, and pretended to cry. Once more he put a cloth over his head, which he scratched, and then looked through a tube of ginger at Hose's abdomen, and pricked it slightly above the navel. He looked inside the tube, smelt and tasted it, and applied it to the sternum. After sucking the tube for a short time he produced a small ball of wax from the ginger tube, which he examined and showed round; then he burst into song and dropped the wax and tube through the flooring.

The whole process was again repeated. After this the patient thought he had had enough of it, so he proclaimed himself much better, and we retired to rest.

The medicine-man was evidently very much in earnest, and he did not at all like Hose murmuring to me from time to time what was going on, nor was he too well pleased at my taking notes; but he performed his part with due seriousness and thoroughness. We clearly saw the man's finger-nails were coated with the wax, and under cover of the cloth a pellet could easily be transferred to the tube of ginger. There is in the stem of the wild ginger an inner tube, which can readily be pushed up and down the outer sheath. First the medicine-man pushed the inner tube down and inserted the pellet of wax in the larger aperture, with his finger he pushed up from below the inner tube, and this ejected the pellet from the stem of the ginger. The whole contrivance was very simple, and could not impose on any but the most credulous.

The following morning we reached Long Tisam at 10 a.m., and the reports about the *panyamun* scare were inquired into.

The truth then came out. Turing and Obong when brought face to face with the Lirong people admitted the whole thing. Turing stated that he had been told by Obong that she had seen robbers (*panyamun*) round about her house, and that she was afraid, and begged him to come down river to live with her and to protect her, and that he had lied to the Lirong people when he said he had himself seen the robbers.

Obong was then questioned, and admitted that the whole thing was false from beginning to end, and that she had started the report with the idea of frightening Turing into coming down river, for she was anxious for him to live with her, being a lorn lone widow. She had previously tried to persuade him to come, and he had refused, as he was busy with the harvest, so this had been her plan to bring about what she desired. She was fined fifty dollars, or in default six months' imprisonment, and Turing was fined twenty-five dollars, or three months' imprisonment. The fines were at once paid by their relatives, and Taman Aping Buling and others present who had been considerably inconvenienced by having had to come down river received compensation, and everybody appeared to be considerably pleased that disquieting rumours had been proved false and the guilty scandal-mongers punished.

I have already mentioned that we stopped at the Sĕbop village of Long Aiah Kechil (the mouth of the little Aiah River) on our journey up the river. On looking at the charms (*siap*) that were, as is always the case, hanging from the roof of the verandah, I immediately recognised a polished stone implement, half hidden amongst the sacred odds and ends and wholly encrusted with soot and dirt. I quietly drew Hose's attention to it, and, though at first somewhat sceptical as to its really being an implement, he at once began to negotiate for it.

This proved to be a very difficult and delicate operation, for the natives have an extreme regard for their charms as being ancient and sacred objects that bring good luck to the house. Hose reminded Tama Sorong, the headman, that he had never asked anything of him before, and gentle persuasion and patience prevailed when combined with the offer of a liberal gift. A chicken was next procured and waved over the *siap*, and an invocation made in which Tama Sorong said that the spirits were not to be angry and bring misfortune to the people, and that "Tuan Resident" was wholly responsible. The head

THE INTERIOR OF BORNEO

of the unfortunate bird was pulled off, and the spurting blood sprinkled over the *siap*. Then only did Hose become the proud possessor of his first stone implement.

This stone adze-head had been found long ago in the bed of the Upper Tinjar River. It is a narrow, thin slab of fibrolite, 7¾ inches (196 mm.) long, and 1½₀ inch (48 mm.) broad, ground to an edge at one end. This hard, tough stone is extremely suitable for making implements. But our friends the natives did not recognise it as an implement; they called it "Silun

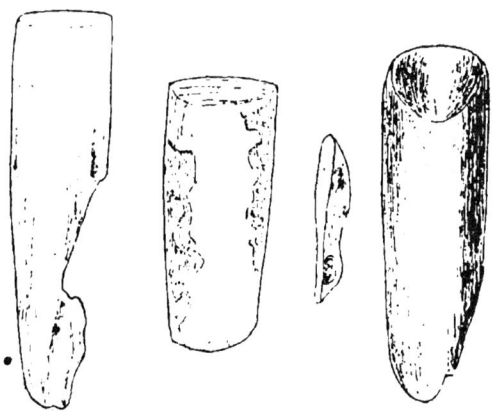

FIG. 38. STONE IMPLEMENTS FROM SARAWAK

Baling Go," that is, the toe-nail of Baling Go, the thunder god. It was also supposed by them to have fallen from the sky.

At every house we stopped at subsequently Hose made inquiries for Baling Go's toe-nails, and though he heard of the existence of other specimens, he did not come across any till we came to Long Tisam on our way back, where he obtained from Aban Abit a very typical adze-head (Fig. 38, B), which was made from a rather soft stone; it was 131 mm. in length.

These Seping Kenyahs brought it with them when they came from the Pliran River, a branch of the Upper Rejang. It was said to have been obtained in the Madang district, and to have been found in or near the Tiut River. The man who found it, several generations ago, said he had a dream that the good spirits (*hantus*) were going to give him a valuable present, and so he went to the river, and there he found this stone. On its being pointed out to them the people recognised that it had been used as an *asai* or adze-head.

The following night we stopped on our way down stream at the Lelak village of Long Tru, and another implement was discovered (Fig. 38, C). This is smaller (81 mm. long) and thicker than the others, one surface is smooth and slightly curved, the other is highly convex, somewhat rough, but the cutting end is ground to a sharp edge.

It was stated to have been found, with several others, three generations ago in the bed of the Lelak Lake by an old woman. One of the other specimens is said to have been exactly like the blade of a *biliong*, or axe. Unfortunately the other specimens were in a house that was accidentally burnt, and they were consequently lost, or at all events they were not carried away, as it is against custom to remove into a new house objects that have been burnt in this way. This implement is believed to be the front tooth of the lower jaw of Baling Go.

There was great difficulty in obtaining this specimen, but the old man who owned it brightened up considerably when Hose offered him a black silk *chawat* (loin cloth) to die in. It is the ambition of up-river natives to die respectably, and a man never feels easy at the thought of death until he has laid by an expensive *chawat* in which he can take his departure with becoming credit.

We also saw hanging up with the *siap* five abnormally curved boars' tusks, some crystals, and other objects, including one or two stone hooks. The latter were evidently mainly, if not entirely, artificially shaped; it was difficult to imagine their use, as it seemed impossible that they could ever have been employed as fish-hooks.

I was naturally very anxious to obtain a couple of these hooks, or one and a boar's tusk; the latter was precisely like the artificially deformed boars' tusks that are such valuable objects in Fiji and New Guinea, and of which I had recently collected several in Torres Straits. Insuperable difficulties were made; the several objects belonged to different people, and some of these were absent. I then had to play my trump card by asking Hose to offer a crystal sphere that I always carried with me for emergencies. When I handed the glass ball round it was fondled and passed from one to another; the old men

THE INTERIOR OF BORNEO

especially admired it immensely, and exhibited no surprise when they were informed by Hose that it was Baling Go's eyeball! One rhumous-eyed old gentleman directly it was passed to him rubbed his bleared eyes with it. It was evident that here was something they thoroughly appreciated. Hose told the men that I valued this very highly, but he would ask me to part with it as a favour, and that they were to give him two hooks or a hook and a boar's tusk for it. Nothing, however, could then be decided, as the owners of the hooks had first to be consulted and squared. In order to show how keen a man Hose is when on the scent for anything new, I cannot refrain from mentioning the fact that he was weakened from fever, and suffering from a bad sore throat, and yet he commenced these tedious negotiations at 4.30 a.m.

FIG. 39. MAGICAL STONE HOOK
About three-fourths natural size

A few days after our return to Claudetown we heard that one hook would be given for the glass ball. Although the price was relatively heavy, I agreed, as in trading one has usually to pay disproportionately for the first specimen, or even for the first few, after then the price falls considerably. When the barter was concluded we were informed that its origin was unknown, but the hook had been in the family for three generations, and that it was used in the ceremony that takes place before going on the war-path, and that it assists in obtaining another head where one had been previously obtained. In fact, it had the same function as the wooden hooks associated with skulls in the verandahs of the houses, the hook acts symbolically and by telepathy hooks in other heads.

Another type of implement of which Hose has obtained specimens is cylindrical and more or less oval in section, with an oblique polished face at one end, which may be either flat or more or less concave (Fig. 38, D, is 173 mm. in length). They were obtained from the Sĕbops and Muriks, who do not know their use, nor have they a name for them; like the old adze-heads, they were hung up along with other *siap*. My impression is they were formerly used for extracting the pith from the sago palm.

Stone implements have long been known from the Malay Peninsula and from most of the islands of the Malay Archipelago, including Borneo. Mr. A. Hart Everett found one "embedded at the bottom of a bed of river gravel exposed in a section on the left bank of the Upper Sarawak River. Sir Charles Lyell pronounced it to be of Neolithic type." This specimen is now in the Pitt Rivers Museum at Oxford.

The only specimen I had previously seen was an adze-head which was brought in to Mr. Shelford by one of his Dayak hunters one day when I happened to be working in the Sarawak Museum; it is now in that museum. Hose has generously given all the implements he collected to the Museum of Archæology and Ethnology at Cambridge.

There is nothing unusual in the sacredness of these stone implements. Nearly all over the world, wherever stone has been replaced by metal, the same reverence for the ancient objects is found, and not infrequently magical properties are ascribed to them. It is, however, rather strange that they are almost universally regarded as having fallen from the sky and usually as actual thunderbolts; a couple of examples of this belief will suffice out of the numbers that could be cited. Messrs. C. H. Read and O. M. Dalton, in their recently published sumptuous work on the *Antiquities from the City of Benin and from other parts of West Africa in the British Museum*, say, "Shango has many attributes, but is especially the god of thunder and lightning, in which capacity he is known as Jakuta, the stone-thrower; all aerolites are venerated as having been thrown by him. In some of the castings the king is represented as holding a ground stone axe-head in his hand, and reasoning on the analogy of similar beliefs all over the world, we can safely argue that this was a symbol of Shango. Such axes are venerated in various parts of Yoruba; they are still *ara oko*, and are frequently daubed with palm oil and blood" (p. 11).

But there is no need to go to Africa for superstitious beliefs concerning stone implements. In Europe there are many records that peasants regard them as thunderbolts, and ascribe magical qualities to them. In Denmark prehistoric stone hatchets or arrow-heads are termed "thunder stones" or "lightning stones"; they are often put by the side of the fireplace, in the thatch of the roof, over or under the door, and are regarded as charms that have supernatural power, the most important of which is protection from fire. Professor T. Wilson, in his address as president to the anthropological section of the American Association for the Advancement of Science, stated that he knew a man in Denmark who said he had seen a hatchet come down from heaven in a flash of lightning, that it struck the field adjoining his house, and that he went over to it and found the stone still hot. On no consideration would he part with it.

A similar belief occurs in our own country, the so-called celts are usually believed to be "thunderbolts," and stone arrow-heads are "fairy darts." I have seen stone implements in the north of Ireland which were used a year or two ago as a charm for curing cattle.

We are not in a position to criticise the Borneans when they regard similar implements as the teeth and toe-nails of the Thunder God, or as a tooth of Balli Taun, the God of Harvest, or the nail of the little toe of the huge river dragon Balungan.

On our next journey up the Baram, Hose obtained at Long Tamala, a Murik village, two stone implements and a brass gouge-like implement. There was great difficulty in getting them, and Bulieng, the owner, would not part with any other *siap*. I particularly wanted some hook-like stones, but these he could by no means be persuaded to sell, as he gave us to understand that they, as it were, hooked his soul to his body, and thus prevented the spiritual portion of him from becoming detached from the material. Another reason was that these charms had been handed down to him from his forefathers.

These three implements were contained in a basket which had not been opened for forty or fifty years, and on the present occasion the natives would not take it down from the beam where it was suspended, much less would they open it, but requested us to do so. Previously to the basket being touched by us, all the women and children were ordered out of the house, lest any evil should befall them. I climbed up a notched pole, which serves as a ladder in these parts, and unfastened the basket and handed it down to Hose. It contained, in addition to the three implements, three water-worn stone hooks, which appeared to me to be entirely of natural formation, two water-worn ferruginous sandstone pebbles, somewhat resembling phalanges in form, and which we were assured were human finger-bones, two irregularly shaped stones with natural perforations, and one spherical pebble about an inch and a quarter in diameter.

After the implements had been sold and taken out of the house, it was necessary to inform the spirits what had happened, and so a small chicken was killed by having its head torn off, and Hose, holding Bulieng's hand, took the bleeding bird and anointed the basket which contained the other stones and the neighbouring skulls with the blood; while the headman told the spirits no sickness or harm were to come to the house, as Hose was responsible for the removal, and the implements had been presented to him. As a matter of fact, Bulieng had just sold them for a brass gong; but he had no objection to deceive the spirits in this matter, their feelings would be less hurt by a donation than by a sale. It would be a pity to vex anyone when it can be avoided, especially a spirit who has various means at his command for retaliation. As Hose held the chicken, no iron was demanded, since the iron is the fee of him who performs this part of the ceremony.

When all had been duly accomplished the women and children returned, and Hose distributed tobacco as largess; but none of the women would take any, as Hose had previously touched the sacred charms, although he had subsequently taken the precaution to wash his hands in public.

On a subsequent occasion Bulieng, who accompanied us on our voyage, informed us that he could not have been cured of sickness by any medicine-man should he have parted with the hooks, and he would certainly have been struck down by sickness. Even now, he said, it would be necessary for him to go through a ceremony when he returned home. The medicine-man (*dayong*) would examine him to discover if anything out of the common had happened to his soul. If all is well with him, he will merely have to kill another fowl and smear the blood on the basket containing the remaining stones, explaining to them that he is pleased that everything has gone on all right, and that he will sit in his house for a whole day on their account, and also on account of his own soul. He positively declared that the night after he had sold the implements he dreamt he was sharing something of great importance with some male person, an augury which he did not consider unfavourable.

It is not known where these implements were found. Bulieng inherited them from his father, who brought them with him when he came from Long Sibatu, near the source of the Baram River.

A TRIP UP THE PATA

I had another up-river trip with Hose in order to visit Tama Bulan, the greatest of the Kenyahs, and one of the two or three inland chiefs who have been sworn members of the General Council of Sarawak. Tama Bulan lives on the Pata, a beautiful affluent of the Baram, whose swift course is often complicated with rapids, some of which are very formidable.

Unfortunately this trip, which promised to be so interesting, was marred for me by a bout of fever, and so I could not fully avail myself of the opportunities it afforded of studying this important and well-organised tribe of the Kenyahs.

Outside Tama Bulan's large village are the usual groups of carved posts, representing deities who have to be sacrificed to on important or critical occasions, and I took a photograph (Plate XXIX., A) of one group of carved and painted figures which were close to some sacred stones (*batu tulor*). I have previously alluded to the fact that stones perched on posts are generally to be found outside each house, and they are at times sprinkled with the blood of fowls.

Tama Bulan received us with friendly dignity, and his womenfolk soon prepared a palatable repast for us of rice and other native food served in banana leaves and laid out on the mats of the living-room, and we reclined on the floor and supped with princes.

Tama Bulan's house is about three hundred yards in length, and is supported some fifteen feet from the ground on huge posts of bilian, or "iron-wood," some of which are a foot and a half in diameter. The structure of the house is similar in general arrangement to those I have previously described, but it is famous for the size of the bilian planks with which it is floored, some of them being as much as five feet broad.

The young ladies of Tama Bulan's house proved to be the

friendliest and jolliest damsels I have met in all my travels. They were not shy, but sat with us after the meal and made themselves agreeable. I quite envied Hose his facility of chatting to them, but the girls tried to make me feel at home by pulling my fingers to make them crack—this appears to be a sort of delicate attention to pay to a friend. I could not help comparing the behaviour of these girls with that of a merry party of frank, wholesome girls in an English country-house. The non-essentials were as different as possible—features, dress, ornaments, and habits—but there was the same *camaraderie* and good breeding.

Bulan (Plate XXIX., C), whose name signifies "the Moon," was by no means so good-looking as several of her companions, and though dignified and friendly, she was not quite so genial. I do not think this was entirely due to her being weighed down by the fact of her being the eldest child of Tama Bulan; perhaps her domestic troubles had somewhat sobered her. I forget the details, but it was something like this. She had been married, or at least on the point of being married, three times. Once the omen birds foreshadowed such evil fortune that it would have been flying in the face of Providence to proceed further; and once, I think it was immediately after her marriage, a fire broke out in the kitchen, and this was regarded as an indication that the marriage should be null and void. The future writer of Bornean love stories will not have far to seek for obstacles in the path of true love. As Bulan was the firstborn, her father, following the custom of the country, changed his own name to Tama Bulan, "the father of Bulan."

The day after our arrival at the village I went with Hose a short distance up the Pata to visit the Leppu Lutong village. On our way we passed a lovely spot where two streams met, which has an historical interest. It was in the early days of Hose's administration, before he had fully acquired that influence over Tama Bulan which is now so marked, and which constitutes such a bulwark for the stability of the Rajah's government among the interior tribes of this district. It is a long story, but the gist of it is that Tama Bulan, with a host of Kenyahs who were spoiling for a fight, had decided to go on the war-path without permission. If they had done so it would have indicated to the neighbouring tribes that the Sarawak

PLATE XXIX

SHRINE OUTSIDE TAMA BULAN'S HOUSE

BULAN   SABA IRANG, THE HEAD CHIEF
                           OF THE MADANGS

Government could be flouted; so Hose put a brave face on it and, with a few followers, hurried to meet Tama Bulan and his warriors. They met at this rapid. Hose stood firm, and for a short time a game of bluff was played, at which the white man won, and Tama Bulan gave in; but it was a touch and go, and might very well have ended in a catastrophe. Unfortunately I was not well enough to photograph the spot, which I subsequently regretted, as the following year, when he published his new map of the Baram district, Hose named this rapid "Fanny Rapid," in honour of my wife.

We have already seen that a Resident who takes a sympathetic interest in his people is consulted about their private affairs, and in time he may possess an intimate knowledge of the domestic life of large numbers of natives. An example of the fatherly interest that Hose takes in his people came under my notice on the occasion of this visit to Tama Bulan.

Ballan, a pleasant young man about nineteen or twenty years of age, son of a Long Belukan Kenyah chief, spoke in a confidential tone to Hose, saying he had something to tell him. Ballan explained that he very much wanted to marry Laan, a nice-looking girl of about seventeen years of age, who was a niece of Tama Bulan's. He stated that the girl was willing to be married, and anxious for him to inform Tama Bulan and her father to that effect, but he was a little nervous of doing so.

As a matter of fact, a good number of youths in a similar predicament come to Hose to ask him to help them, and as he is constantly discussing such matters with Tama Bulan and other chiefs he is in a position to put in a word in season and smooth over any difficulties that may arise, for the course of true love does not always run smoothly even in Borneo. In the present instance not only had the girl's father to be approached, but it was necessary that consent should be given by the great chief Tama Bulan, who was also her uncle.

Hose questioned Ballan whether his was a genuine love affair, and the latter emphatically stated that the girl was quite willing. Hose then asked if he had slept in her room; and having been assured that he had done so, he further inquired if they had slept on the same pillow, and he said they had. Among these people it is customary for a young man to visit the sleeping-chamber of his sweetheart and sit and talk for several hours after the family has retired to rest. When friendly relations are well established the lover may enter within the mosquito curtains and sleep by the side of his beloved; but the sharing of the pillow is only accorded to him who has been accepted as a prospective husband. The young people behave with strict propriety, and I understand that there is little to object to in this custom, which may have resulted from the public life which everyone leads.

At all events we cannot criticise these good people very harshly, as the very similar practice of "bundling" was in vogue until recently in Wales, as Brand informs us in his *Antiquities* (vol. ii. p. 98): "In Wales there is a custom called 'bundling,' in which the betrothed parties go to bed in their clothes."

To return to my friend Ballan, Hose said he did not care to mention the matter to the relatives unless Ballan was in earnest, and that now he was assured of this he thought it was a very good and entirely suitable match, and he would be very pleased to help it on by speaking to Tama Bulan; if he waited on the verandah he would let him know the result.

Tama Bulan was in his room, and on entering Hose beckoned to him that he had something to say privately. Tama Bulan got up and went to one side and remarked, "Tuan?" "Oh, it's nothing important. Some of these young people want to get married, and as usual have asked me to put it through for them." "Who is it?" "Oh, Ballan wants to marry Laan, and they are afraid to tell you." "Oh yes, that's a good match; we are all connections. I'll go and tell the father. You wait here a bit."

Tama Bulan then went to consult Laan's father, Aban Tingan, who no doubt had seen what had been going on for the last few days, but he had held his peace. In a few minutes Tama Bulan returned. "Oh yes, Aban Tingan is agreeable; that's all right." Hose then put in a word for Ballan. "Will there be any *brian* [*i.e.* bride-price]?" "Oh no; we are all more or less related. Ballan is my relative; there will be nothing very much. There will be the usual *adat* [custom] of expenses for a feast in which we will all join; then there is the custom of depositing a *tarwak* at the time of proposal." Hose then said he would be responsible for the *tarwak*, for he had previously taken an interest in Ballan, and during the earlier part of my stay at Claudetown Ballan had visited him.

Hose then went into the verandah and found Ballan anxiously awaiting the result of the interview. Hose told him that Tama Bulan and Aban Tingan were agreeable. Ballan then said that according to custom he would have to find a *tarwak*. Hose reassured him by the information that he had already arranged this for him.

Aban Tingan's house, or rather suite of rooms, is next to Tama Bulan's, and that evening, when Hose retired into one of Tama Bulan's rooms, he heard the young people chatting in the adjoining room. Hose called out to Ballan to come round and talk to him; for a long time he was very unwilling, which was not unnatural, considering the circumstances. Having secured him Hose forced the conversation, so that Ballan sent round for his mat, and made preparations as if he were going to sleep in the same room as his tiresome benefactor. In the meantime the lady, weary of waiting, began to very softly play the usual lovers' tune on the *kaluri*.

Hose, of course, understood what the girl was playing, and chaffed poor Ballan about it; then, taking pity on the young people, he pretended to go to sleep, and when Ballan thought he was soundly off, he rolled up his mat and silently bolted. Next morning Laan came out to shake hands as Hose was going away, and told him that Ballan had told her all that he had done for them.

The subsequent history of this love affair was not quite such plain sailing. Preparations had been made for the marriage, and two days before the happy event a child, who was strolling in the farm, was killed by a tree falling on it. This incident was unlucky, and it was necessary for Ballan to return home and wait awhile.

Later they made a second attempt to get married, but it was first necessary to consult the omen birds. They did so, and one old man in the crowd said he saw a very bad omen. Ballan said to Taman Bulan he wanted to be married, the white man did not bother about omens, and why should he? A modern vernacular translation of one of his remarks to the great chief was that he wanted to "chuck those blooming birds."

It is really very doubtful how far Tama Bulan believes in

these things, but he is a statesman, and consequently always politic, so he replied to Ballan, "*You* may not mind, but your conduct may affect the whole family." Ballan had again to return home unmarried.

Subsequently Hose invited Ballan to come and stay for a month with him. Tama Bulan happened to come down during that visit, and Ballan asked the Resident to talk to Tama Bulan about his marriage. He did so, and Tama Bulan said he would arrange it after the next harvest.

CHAPTER XXIII

NOTES ON THE OMEN ANIMALS OF SARAWAK

THE cult of the omen animals is of such importance in the daily life of most of the tribes of Borneo that it is desirable that more attention should be paid to it by those who have the opportunity of studying it at first hand.

The Ven. Archdeacon J. Perham has given a full account of the Sea Dayak religion in the Journal of the Straits Branch of the Royal Asiatic Society (Nos. 1, 2, 3, 4, 5, and 8), which has been reprinted by Ling Roth in his book, *The Natives of Sarawak and British North Borneo*. Mr. Ling Roth has also compiled some other scattered references on omens (vol. i. pp. 221-31). Although the following notes are very imperfect, they contain some new facts derived from Hose, and also, thanks to information derived from Hose, I am able for the first time to give a fairly complete list of the omen animals of Sarawak with their scientific names.

I have taken the liberty of abstracting the following account of the way in which birds are "used," as the Iban (Sea Dayak) say, from Archdeacon Perham's most valuable papers, as it is the best description known to me of what is of daily occurrence in Borneo.

"The yearly rice-farming is a matter of much ceremony as well as of labour with the Dayaks, and must be inaugurated with proper omens. Some man who is successful with his *padi* will be the augur, and undertake to obtain omens for a certain area of land, which others besides himself will farm. Some time before the Pleiades are sufficiently high above the horizon to warrant the clearing the grounds of jungle or grass, the man sets about his work. He will have to hear the *nendak* (*Cittocincla suavis*) on the left, the *katupong* (*Sasia abnormis*) on the left, the *burong malam* (a locust) and the *beragai*

(*Harpactes duvauceli*) on the left, and in the order I have written them. As soon as he has heard the *nendak* he will break off a twig of anything near, and take it home and put it in a safe place. But it may happen that some other omen bird, or creature, is the first to make itself heard or seen; and in that case the day's proceeding is vitiated. He must give the matter up, return, and try his chance another day; and thus sometimes three or four days are gone before he has obtained his first omen. When he has heard the *nendak*, he will then go to listen for the *katupong* and the rest, but with the same liability to delays; and it may possibly require a month to obtain all those augural predictions which are to give them confidence in the result of their labours. The augur has now the same number of twigs and sticks as birds he has heard, and he takes these to the land selected for farming, and puts them in the ground, says a short form of address to the birds and Pulang Gana (the tutelary deity of the soil, and the spirit presiding over the whole work of rice-farming), cuts a little grass or jungle, and returns. The magic virtue of the birds has been conveyed to the land.

"For house-building, the same birds are to be obtained, and in the same way. But for a war expedition birds on the right hand are required, except the *nendak*, which, if it make a certain peculiar call, can be admitted on the left.

"These birds can be bad omens as well as good. If heard on the wrong side, if in wrong order, if the note or call be the wrong kind, the matter in hand must be postponed or abandoned altogether; unless a conjunction of subsequent good omens occur, which, in the judgment of old experts, can overbear the preceding bad ones. Hence, in practice, this birding becomes a most involved matter, because the birds will not allow themselves to be heard in a straightforward orthodox succession. After all it is only a balance of probabilities, for it is seldom that Dayak patience is equal to waiting till the omens occur according to the standard theory.

"These are the inaugurating omens sought in order to strike a line of good luck, to render the commencement of an undertaking auspicious. The continuance of good fortune must be carried on by omen influence to the end.

"When any of these omens, either of bird, beast, or insect, are heard or seen by the Dayak on his way to the *padi* lands, he supposes they foretell either good or ill to himself or to the farm; and in most cases he will turn back and wait for the following day before proceeding again. The *nendak* is generally good, so is the *katupong* on the right or left, but the *papau* (*Harpactes diardi*) is of evil omen, and the man must beat a retreat. A *beragai* heard once or twice matters not, but if often, a day's rest is necessary. The *mbuas* (*Carcineutes melanops*) on the right is wrong, and sometimes it portends so much blight and destruction that the victim must rest five days. The 'shout' of the *kutok* (*Lepocestes porphyromelas*) is evil, and that of the *katupong* so bad that it requires three days' absence from the farm to allow the evil to pass away; and even then a *beragai* must be heard before commencing work. The *beragai* is a doctor among birds. If the cry of a deer, a *pelandok* (*Tragulus*) be heard, or if a rat crosses the path before you on your way to the farm, a day's rest is necessary, or you will cut yourself, get ill, or suffer by failure of the crop. When a good omen is heard, one which is supposed to foretell a plentiful harvest, you must go on to the farm, and do some trifling work by way of 'leasing the work of your hands' there, and then return; in this way you clench the foreshadowed luck, and at the same time reverence the spirit which promises it. And should a deer or *pelandok* come out of the jungle and on to the farm when you are working there, it means that customers will come to buy the corn, and that therefore there will be corn for them to buy. This is the best omen they can have, and they honour it by resting from work for three days.

"But the worst of all omens is a dead beast of any kind, especially those included in the omen list, found anywhere on the farm. It infuses a deadly poison into the whole crop, and will kill some one or other of the owner's family within a year. When this terrible thing happens they test the omen by killing a pig, and divining from the appearance of the liver immediately after death. If the prediction of the omen be strengthened, all the rice grown on that ground must be sold; and, if necessary, other rice bought for their own consumption. Other people may eat it, for the omen only affects those at whom it is directly pointed. A swarm of bees lighting on the farm is an equally dreadful matter."

THE OMEN ANIMALS OF SARAWAK

Scientific Name.	Kayan.	Kenyah.	Punan.	Iban.
Cervulus muntjac	Telaau	Telauoh	Telauoh	Kijang
Tragulus napu	Planok	Planok	Planok	Pelandok
,, javanicus	Planok	Planok	Planok	Kamaya Panas
Arctogale leucotis	Munin	Munin	•	•
Haliastur intermedius (indus)	Niho	Flaki	Flaki	Senalong Burong
Carcineutes melanops	•	Asi	Asi	Membuas
Berenicornis comatus	Makong	Kong	Makong	•
Harpactes diardi	Upau	Pengolong Bioh	Pengiok	Papau
,, kasumba	•	Pengolong Bioh	Pengiok	—
,, duvauceli	•	Pengolong Lomit	Pengiok	Beragai
Lepocestes porphyromelas	•	Kieng or Usa Kieng	Kieng or Ratat	Pangkas or Kotok, or rarely Jaloh
Sasia abnormis	•	Ukang	Bukang	Katupong
Cittocincla suavis	•	•	•	Nendak
Orthotomus cineraceus	•	•	•	Briak
Platylophus coronatus	Pajan	Telajan	Telajan	Bejampong or Kajampong
Arachnothera longirostris	Isit	Isit or Sit	Sit	Enkrasak
,, modesta	Isit	Sit Asa	Sit	Enkrasak
,, chrysogenys	Isit	Sit Asa	Sit	Enkrasak
(Anthreptes malaccensis)	Isit	•	•	•
Coluber melanurus	—	Kusai	•	•
Simotes octolineatus	Batang Lima	•	•	•
Doliophis bivirgatus (flaviceps)	—	Semoi	•	•
,, intestinalis	—	Nawan	•	•
Lachesis wagleri	—	Laun Nangur	•	•
Gryllacris nigrilabris	•	•	•	Malam or Kundin
Chrysocoris eques	—	Turok Parai	—	—
Melipona vidua	•	•	•	Manyi

In the above table a blank space indicates that I am uncertain whether that people use the particular omen animal; the • means that it is not employed.

Omen animals are called *aman* by the Kayan, Kenyah, and Punan, and *burong* by the Iban.

OMEN ANIMALS OF SARAWAK

For the convenience of those who would like more precise information about these animals I give a table showing their position in zoological classification.

MAMMALIA

UNGULATA	. Artiodactyla	. Tragulina	. Tragulidæ	. Tragulus
,,	. ,,	. Pecora	. Cervidæ	. Cervulus
CARNIVORA	. Carnivora vera	Æluroidea	. Viverridæ	. Arctogale

AVES

FALCONIFORMES	Accipitres	. Falconidæ	—	Haliastur
CORACIIFORMES	Coraciæ .	. Alcedinidæ	. Halcyoninæ	Carcineutes
,,	. ,, .	. Bucerotidæ	—	Berenicornis
	Trogones	. Trogonidæ	—	Harpactes
—	Pici .	. Picidæ .	. Picinæ	. Lepocestes
—	,, .	. ,,	. Picumninæ.	Sasia
PASSERIFORMES	Oscines .	. Turdidæ	. Turdinæ	. Cittocincla
,,	. ,, .	. ,,	. Sylviinæ	. Orthotomus
,,	. ,, .	. Laniidæ	—	Platylophus
,,	. ,, .	. Nectariniidæ.	—	Arachnothera
,,	. ,, .	. ,,	—	Anthreptes

REPTILIA

OPHIDIA	. Colubridæ	. Aglypha	. Colubrinæ	. Coluber
,,	. ,,	. ,,	. ,,	. Simotes
,,	. ,,	. Proteroglypha	Elapinæ	. Doliophis
,,	. Viperidæ	—	Crotalinæ	. Lachesis

INSECTA

ORTHOPTERA	. Locustodea	. Gryllacridæ	—	Gryllacris
HEMIPTERA	—	Scutelleridæ	—	Chrysocoris
HYMENOPTERA	. Petiolata	. Apidæ .	—	Melipona

The "barking deer" (*Cervulus muntjac*) is very important as an omen to all peoples, but least so to the Iban. The bark of the deer prevents people from continuing their journey, and even divorces people who are newly married.

The little chevrotains, *planok* or *pelandok* (*Tragulus napu* and *T. javanicus*), have the same function as the muntjac so far as a journey is concerned, but otherwise they are not very important.

The Rev. W. Chalmers says: "If the cries of any of the three kinds of deer found in Sarawak be heard when starting on a journey, or when going to consult the birds by day or by night, it is a sure sign that, if the matter in hand be followed up, sickness will be the result. Also if a newly married couple hear them at night they must be divorced, as, if this be not done, the death of the bride or bridegroom will ensue. I myself have known instances of this omen causing a divorce, and I must say the separation has always been borne most philosophically by the parties most concerned; in fact, the morning of one of these divorces, I remember seeing an ex-bridegroom working hard at shaping some ornamental brass-work, which Dayak women are in the habit of wearing round their waists, and he said he intended to bestow it on a certain damsel whom he had in his eye for a *new* wife."

Sir Spenser St. John writes: "To hear the cry of a deer is at all times unlucky, and to prevent the sound reaching their ears during a marriage procession gongs and drums are loudly beaten. On the way to their farms, should the unlucky omen be heard, they will return home and do no more work for a day."

A Malay told me: If a Sarawak Malay was striking a light in the evening in his house, and a *pelandok* made a noise at the same time, the whole family would have to leave the house for three days; should they not do so, the house would catch fire and be burned down, or sickness or other calamity would overtake them.

On the second day of one of Hose's journeys through the jungle, the chief who was with him saw a *pelandok* rush across the path. Hose being behind did not observe it, but he saw all his party sitting on a log, and the chief informed Hose that he could not proceed that day as his "legs were tied up." This was most inconvenient, as Hose was in a hurry; but the men would not go on. Hose freely took upon himself all the responsibility, and said he would go first and would explain to the *pelandok* that he was the person in fault. The chief would not agree even to this, and did not budge, but said he would follow the next day. Hose went on with some of the men as far as he could, and then camped. Next day the chief caught Hose up at noon, and appeared very much surprised that no harm had befallen him. Hose chaffed him about his legs, and was "pleased to see that they had become untied"!

The small viverrine carnivore, *Arctogale leucotis*, is one of the most important omens for Kenyahs and Kayans, who, however, have a particular dread of coming in contact with it, lest it should produce sickness; they will never so much as touch a piece of its dried skin. It is not an omen for the Iban nor for the Punans, who even kill and eat it. After having obtained other omens the Kayans are glad to see the *munin*, as it is useful in conjunction with other omens, but they do not like to hear it squealing.

The screeching of the large hawk (*Haliastur intermedius*), which is closely allied to or a sub-species of Brahminy kite (*H. indus*), is a cautionary sign with the Kayans, and though it is not in itself a bad sign, they will generally return home from any enterprise on hearing it if they are still taking omens, or at all events they will remain where they are for the day. What the Kayan and Kenyahs most desire when "owning" a hawk is to see it skim silently, without moving its wings either to the right or to the left, as they wish it. Any other action than this, such as a swoop down or continued flapping of the wings, is considered unfavourable. Something bad is going to take place, they do not know what it may be or to whom it will happen, so everyone who sees the hawk do this turns away his face, or retires to some place out of the sight of the hawk, lest on being observed he should be the one on whom the misfortune will fall. On such an occasion no one speaks a word, and all return into the house and wait from ten minutes to half an hour. If they are very anxious to go on again that day they slip quietly out of the house so that the hawk may not see them, get into their boats, and start on their journey.

If the hawk appears on the wrong side when men are paddling a few days away from home and nearing another village, they immediately turn the boat right round and pull to the bank and light a fire. By turning round they put the hawk on the right side, and being satisfied in their own minds they proceed on their journey as before.

The hawk, or, as the Iban call it, *Sengalong Burong*, is a very important being. The little woodpecker (*Sasia abnormis*), *Katupong*, is his son-in-law, being married to Dara Inchin Temaga Indu Monkok Chilebok China, a poetical *hantu* who mentions in her songs the names of all the mouths of the rivers in their order, from Sarawak River to some distance up the coast. This is probably the remnant of a migration saga. The smallest of the trogons (*Harpactes duvauceli*), *beragai*, also married another daughter of *Sengalong Burong*.

Although this is the most important of any Iban omen bird, it is his sons-in-law that are most used. Food is offered to *Sengalong Burong*.

I believe that other large hawk-like birds are used as omens.

The Brahminy kite is popularly supposed in India to be the sacred Garuda, the mythical bird, half eagle and half man, which in Hindu mythology is the *vahana*, or "vehicle," of Vishnu. Whenever Bengali children see one of these birds they cry out—

"Let drinking vessels and cups be given to the *Shankar Chil*" (Brahminy kite); "but let the common kite get a kick on its face."

There is a kingfisher that lives in the jungle (*Carcineutes melanops*) which is not a particularly lucky bird. If, when they are making a trap, the Iban hear the long, mournful whistle of the *membuas* they know that although the trap will catch things, it will only be after an interval of ten or fourteen days that they will have any luck. On other occasions it is not unusual for them to catch little partridges, such as *Rollulus rouloul*, directly they have set up the trap, but often, under ordinary circumstances, it will be a day before they catch anything.

The Kenyahs apparently dislike this bird, which they call *asi*, as it is not very favourable; in fact, they would rather not see it.

The white-crested hornbill (*Berenicornis comatus*), which has a moderate-sized, black-keeled casque on its beak, and bare, blue orbits and throat, is an *aman*, that is sought for by Kenyahs and Kayans, particularly by the latter, when felling jungle for planting, and when going on the war-path. The Kenyahs use it slightly, and the Iban not at all; it is in any case an omen bird of secondary importance.

The trogon, called by the Iban *papau* (*Harpactes diardi*), is particularly useful to these people when hunting in the jungle for deer, pig, etc., as it is a sure sign that they will obtain something that day. The bird's note of "pau, pau, pau," infuses fresh energy into them. Supposing some Iban were making a spring-trap (*panjok*), the moment one of them heard the cry of the *papau*, or *beragai* (*H. duvauceli*), he would at once snap off or cut off a small twig with a *parang*—the small piece of wood thus cut or broken off is used for the release of the trap—the man would at the same time remark to the bird, "Here we are!"

Other tribes, such as the Kenyahs and Punans, use *H. diardi* as an omen, but it is not an important one; but *H. duvauceli* is of very considerable importance to the Kenyahs when going on the war-path, it being one of the omens of which it is imperative to obtain a sight or hearing. *H. kasumba* is employed indifferently with *H. diardi*.

Lepocestes porphyromelas is one of the most important of the omen birds, as it makes two perfectly distinct notes, one of which is favourable and the other unfavourable. On a rainy day it calls "tok, tok, tok," but when the sun comes out it bursts into a long "kieng, kieng." *Tok* is bad, but *kieng* is good.

When a Kenyah hears the *tok* cry he immediately stops, lights a fire, and takes the usual precautions in talking to it. He knows perfectly well that the same bird makes the two notes, and he waits for the *kieng*. His explanation is that when the bird calls "tok" it is angry, and in a good temper when it sings "kieng," and therefore it is well not to go contrariwise to the omen. The Iban behave in a similar manner. The Kenyahs regard it as a bird of warning, but not one that assists in getting anything. If a man was doing anything with a *parang*, or a knife, or other sharp-edged tool, and heard even "kieng," he would probably desist from further use of it for that day.

The little woodpecker (*Sasia abnormis*) is in high favour among the Iban; in fact, they consider it most important, as he represents his father-in-law, *Senalong Burong*. The *katupong* appears to produce whatever result they require. It is of less importance with other peoples of Sarawak.

Mr. Crossland informs us if a *katupong* enters a house at one end and flies out by the other, men and women snatch up a few necessaries, such as mats and rice, and stampede, leaving everything unsecured and the doors unfastened. If anyone approaches the house at night he will see large and shadowy demons chasing each other through it, and hear their unintelligible talk. After a while the people return and erect the ladder they have overthrown, and the women sprinkle the house with water "to cool it."

A kind of thrush (*Cittocincla suavis*) is particularly useful to the Iban when looking for gutta or other jungle produce. *Nendak* is a good bird to own, as it is a *burong chelap*, and on hearing it they would not be afraid of any sickness.

Before starting on a gutta expedition they would require to see something before *beragai* (*Harpactes duvauceli*), as this is a *burong tampak*, that is, an omen animal that is potent for hunting. What they like is: first to get *nendak*; then wait three days while they are "owning" it; finally, to get *beragai* on the right. This combination signifies certain success; not only would they find gutta, but would obtain plenty of it, and no harm or sickness would befall them. If, however, they went for gutta on *beragai* alone, and that perhaps appeared on the left, they would obtain a fair amount of gutta, but they would stand a good chance of some misfortune happening to them, and one of their party might fall sick or even die.

The tailor bird (*Orthotomus cineraceus*), although employed by Iban only, is of very little use, as it is only a secondary *burong*. It may be employed as an additional argument when deciding for *selam*, or trial by the water ordeal. This consists in the two disputants putting their heads under water, and the one who has the most staying power has right on his side.

The Bornean shrike, which has an erectile crest of long and broad feathers on its head (*Platylophus coronatus*), is used by the Iban as a weather prophet on account of its unerring faculty of foretelling a storm, for whenever its whistle is heard rain is always to be expected. It is very important for Kenyahs and Kayans in connection with tilling farms. When Kayans are clearing away undergrowth for a farm, after having offered to *niho* (*Haliastur intermedius*) and other *aman*, it is desirable they should hear *pajan*, the shrike, for then they know they will get plenty of *padi* of good quality, but there will be a good deal of hard work, and possibly a considerable amount of sickness and cuts and wounds. If they procure this omen they take the precaution of building very substantial graneries.

Three species of sun birds (*Arachnothera longirostris, A. modesta,* and *A. chrysogenys*) are very important to Kayans, Kenyahs, and Punans. Any one of these species is used impartially, and they bear the name of *sit* or *isit*.

The *sit* is always the first bird to look for when undertaking anything. Fortunately an individual of one of the three species is almost always to be seen crossing the river. It is one of the least important omen birds with the Iban. When Kayans, Punans, and Mělanaus go in search of camphor it is first necessary to see a *sit* fly from right to left, and then from left to right. A Mĕlanau who is intending to start on such an expedition sits in the bow of his boat and chants—

O Sit, Sit, ta-au, Kripan murip, Sit.
Ano senigo akau, ano napan akau.

("O Sit, Sit, on the right, give me a long life, Sit.
Help me to obtain what I require, make me plenty of that for which I am looking.")

An allied bird, *Anthreptes malaccensis*, is commonly mistaken by Kayans, but by them only, for *Arachnothera longirostris*, who then use it as an omen bird, but it is not so used by the Kenyahs, by whom it is called *manok obah*.

All the snake *aman* are bad omens, and in the case of a Kayan seeing *batang lima* (*Simotes octolineatus*) he will endeavour to kill it, and if successful no evil will follow; should he fail to kill it then "look out"!

I believe that the Sea Dayaks pay some regard to *sawa*, a large python (*Python reticulatus*), and to *tuchok*, a kind of gecko or house lizard (*Ptychozoon homalocephalum*), and to *brinkian*, another kind of gecko; but I do not know whether these are, strictly speaking, *burong*.

The omen *padi* bug, *turok parai* (*Chrysocoris eques*), is of importance to the Kenyahs alone, and that only because it injures the crops.

The bee *manyi* is an Iban *burong* only. If a swarm of bees settled underneath a house that had recently been built it would be considered a bad sign, and probably it would be necessary to destroy that particular section of the house or to leave the house altogether.

Many Land Dayaks, on the contrary, keep bees in their houses, and among most of the peoples of Borneo, including the Iban, it is most lucky in planting time to dream of an abundance of bees.

There are other creatures whose appearance, cry, or movements may signify good or bad luck, which are not omen animals (*i.e. burong* or *aman*) in the strict sense of the term. For example, the hawk owl (*Ninox scutulata*) makes a melancholy cry at night, on account of which it is very much disliked by the natives, who regard it as a foreteller of death. Its native name is *pongok*.

If the Malay bear (*Heliarctos malayanus*) climbs into an Iban's house it is a bad sign, and the house would have to be pulled down.

According to Perham, in answer to the question of the origin of this system of "birding," some Dayaks [Iban] have given the following. In early times the ancestor of the Malays and the ancestor of the Dayaks had, on a certain occasion, to swim across a river. Both had books. The Malay tied his firmly in his turban, kept his head well out of water, and reached the opposite bank with his book intact and dry. The Dayak, less wise, fastened his to the end of his waist cloth, and the current washed it away. But the fates intervened to supply the loss, and gave the Dayak this system of omens as a substitute for the book.

Another story relates the following. Some Dayaks [Iban] in the Batang Lupar made a great feast, and invited many guests. When everything was ready and arrivals expected, a tramp and hum, as of a great company of people, was heard close to the village. The hosts, thinking it to be the invited friends, went forth to meet them with meat and drink, but found with some surprise they were all utter strangers. However, without any questioning, they received them with due honour, and gave them all the hospitalities of the occasion. When the time of departing came, they asked the strange visitors who they were and from whence, and received something like the following reply from their chief: "I am *Sengalong Burong*, and these are my sons-in-law and other friends. When you hear the voices of the birds (giving their names), know that you hear us, for they are our deputies in this lower world. Thereupon the Dayaks discovered they had been entertaining spirits unawares, and received as reward of their hospitality the knowledge of the omen system."

Archdeacon Perham is perfectly right in his statement that "the sacredness of the omen birds is thus explained: they are forms of animal life possessed with the spirit of certain invisible beings above, and bearing their names; so that when a Dayak [Iban] hears a *beragai*, for instance, it is really the voice of *Beragai* the son-in-law of *Sengalong Burong*; nay, more, the assenting nod or dissenting frown of the great spirit himself. 'These birds,' says *Sengalong Burong*, 'possess my mind and spirit, and represent me in the lower world. When you hear them, remember it is I who speak for encouragement or for warning.' The object of the bird-cultus is like that of all other rites: to secure good crops, freedom from accidents and falls and diseases, victory in war, profit in exchange and trade, skill in discourse, and cleverness in all native craft."

We know that such very distinct peoples in Sarawak alone as the Iban, Land Dayaks, Muruts, Punans, Kayans, and Kenyahs pay attention to omen animals, and in most cases to the same animals. This points to a common origin of the cult, for in some cases there is no specially obvious reason why that particular species of animal should have been selected. In the three last-mentioned peoples the names of the omen animals are practically similar, but many of the Iban names are different.

There is no doubt that this cult is indigenous to Borneo; it is probable that it formed part of the fundamental religious equipment of the Iban, but it is also probable that the Iban have borrowed somewhat from neighbouring indigenous tribes. Much more information must be obtained before a satisfactory history of this interesting cult can be written.

The question may be asked whether the cult of omen animals in Borneo is connected with totemism. Personally I do not think this is the case, as there is in the omen cult no direct relationship between a species of animal and a group of men or a single individual. Neither does it enter at all into social organisation nor marriage restrictions. It is extremely probable that totemism, in the true sense of the term, is only one of several cults of animals; but this is not the place to enter into a discussion of these difficult and polemical problems.

CHAPTER XXIV

THE CULT OF SKULLS IN SARAWAK

A GOOD deal has been written on the subject of head-hunting in Borneo, and Ling Roth has collected together the available information about the practice in Sarawak.

There can be little doubt that one of the chief incentives to procure heads was to please the women. Among some tribes it was said to be an indispensable necessity for a young man to procure a skull before he could marry, and the possession of a head decapitated by himself seemed to be a fairly general method employed by a young man to ingratiate himself with the maiden of his choice. The fact of a young man being sufficiently brave and energetic to go head-hunting would promise well for his ability to protect a wife. This is, at all events, one sufficiently rational reason for the custom, and there may be others as yet not even guessed at.

The pride women feel in their men-folk who have taken heads is not confined to these people of Borneo; formerly amongst the western tribe of Torres Straits a young man who had taken a skull would very soon receive a proposal of marriage from some eligible young woman.

Some tribes believe that the persons whose heads they take will become their slaves in the next world. In this case head-collecting would mean for them a wise precaution for the future.

A desire for reprisal of injuries, the vendetta or blood feud is a very common reason for going on the war-path and bringing home the appropriate trophies.

The following incident was recorded in the *Sarawak Gazette* (vol. xxv., 1895, p. 91): A low-class Kayan named Boi Wan at Long Lama had taken a head from the Kayan graveyard and hung it up near his farm, and another Kayan named Jelivan said he had killed a man under the house, but this was

THE CULT OF SKULLS IN SARAWAK

a false statement, no one having been killed. The reason for these two men acting in this way was that they might wear hornbills' feathers, and have their hands tattooed, which is allowed by Kayan custom only to those who have taken a head. These two men caused a great deal of trouble, and the neighbourhood was in a very disturbed state. The Resident fined each man fifty dollars, and made them put the head in the grave whence it had been stolen.

It is the custom amongst the Kayans and Kenyahs that, before the people can go out of mourning for a chief or for one of a chief's near relations, either a new head must be taken or an old one, or some portion of one must be obtained.

If the people obtain an old head from some friendly community they go through the same ceremony as if they had recently taken the head of an enemy. The head, by-the-by, is always given, never sold. A head that has once been given in this way, or even only lent, is seldom returned to the place from which it has been taken. If a skull should be returned it is generally put under the house or in some separate shed. Kayans and Kenyahs, however, generally take skulls back into the house.

As Rajah Brooke will not permit the taking of a fresh head to enable a community to go out of mourning, and as there is sometimes great difficulty in borrowing a skull, or even a portion of one, the dilemma has been overcome and custom satisfied, I have been informed, by the village borrowing a skull from the collection kept at certain Government forts for this purpose. These skulls are labelled A, B, C, etc., and a record kept of each borrowing transaction. When all the ceremonies are over the skull has to be returned to the fort, where it is available for another occasion.

When a skull is given to a friend the following ceremony has to be gone through. A living chicken is waved over the man who takes down the head, over the ladder, the basket or framework that contains the head, as well as over the skull itself. The owner talks to the fowl, telling it to explain to the head that they are parting with it to friends who will treat it even better than it was treated in its own house. That the new owners will feast it, and it must not consider itself to be slighted in the least degree. All then present join in a war-whoop.

A piece of iron is taken, an old parang blade, or a spear-head, or anything made of *iron*, and the head and wings of the chicken are torn off with the iron, which thus becomes covered with blood. The hand of the owner of the skull, who is generally the chief or headman of the house, is next smeared with the bloody iron. This ceremony is called *urip*, that is, "life," and has for its object the prevention of harm coming to the original owner. Finally, some of the wing feathers of the fowl are pulled out, and stuck into the framework or basket containing the remaining skulls.

The skull is brought into the house of mourning with all the ceremony that would ensue if the head had been captured on the war-path, and the *urip* rite is again performed.

After the sprinkling ceremony everybody in the house and all relations in neighbouring houses take off their old mourning clothes, which are usually made of bark cloth; they then wash themselves and put on clean clothes. They also shave the hair round the crown and make themselves smart. Every "door," that is every family, kills a pig or a fowl, and all eat, drink, and are merry. Very often after this ceremony the head is taken out of the house, and hung up at the grave of the deceased chief.

After a good harvest, or after a successful head-hunting expedition, or when one or more skulls are added to the collection, a cube of cooked fat pork, with a skewer of wood thrust through it to keep it in position, is placed in the nose of each skull, and borak, the spirit made from rice, is put into a small bamboo receptacle about an inch and a half long, which is placed by the skull. Wooden hooks (*kawit*) are hung up near the skulls, with the idea that they will help the head-hunters to obtain more skulls on their forays. It is an example of sympathetic magic, the object of the wooden hooks being to hook in fresh heads.

I cannot refrain from mentioning what strikes one as being, to say the least of it, an illogical action on the part of the Sarawak Government. Head-hunting is rigorously put down, and rightly so; but when the Government organises a punitive expedition, say, to punish a recalcitrant head-hunting chief, the natives (generally Iban) comprising the Government force are always allowed to keep what heads they can secure. This is their perquisite. Surely it would be a more dignified position not to allow a single head to be taken away by anyone in the

PLATE XXX

SKULL TROPHY IN A KAYAN HOUSE

SKULL TROPHIES IN ABAN ABIT'S HOUSE AT LONG TISAM, BARAWAN TRIBE

THE CULT OF SKULLS IN SARAWAK

Raj under any pretext whatever, and to remunerate the punitive force in some more direct manner.

According to the Kayans and Kenyahs, head-hunting has been in vogue only for some eight to ten generations, certainly not earlier. Hose would put the time of its introduction to these tribes not more than two hundred years ago.

A Kenyah version of the origin of the custom is as follows; it was narrated by Aban Jau, a Sĕbop.

In olden days—and they still continue the practice—the Kenyahs took only the hair of a man killed on the war-path, and with this they decorated their shields.

One Rajah Tokong determined to retaliate on a neighbouring tribe that had killed some of his people, and having made all the customary preparations, he set out with his followers. They started, as is usually the case when going on the war-path, just after the *padi* had been planted, as this is a slack season, and paddled down the river and entered the jungle. On the third or fourth day, whilst they were cooking their rice on the bank of a small brook, they heard a frog croaking, "Wang kok kok tatak batok, Wang kok kok tatak batok" (*tatak batok* signifies "cut the neck," in other words, "cut off the head"). Tokong listened to the frog and said, "What do you mean?" The frog replied, "You Kenyahs are dreadful fools; you go on the war-path and kill people, and only take their hair, which is of very little use, whilst if you were to take away the whole skull you would have everything that you required—a good harvest and no sickness, and but very little trouble of any kind. If you do not know how to take a head, I will show you." Thus spoke the frog taunting them, and catching a little frog, he chopped off its head.

Tokong did not think much of this, but one of his *bakis*, or right-hand men, who was an elderly man, pondered long over the incident, and during the night he had a strange dream. He dreamt that he saw fields of *padi*, the plants being weighted down with their heavy grain, and in addition he saw an abundance of other food—sugar-cane, sweet potatoes, and what not. Next morning he said to Tokong, "I am very much concerned about what the frog said," and then he narrated his dream. Tokong still appeared to think very little of it, but the other men strongly advised him, if they were successful, to bring back one or two of the heads.

Eventually they attacked the hostile house and killed seven people. The old *bakis* put three of the heads in his basket with the consent of Tokong, who had been persuaded that no harm could be done in trying this new venture. They returned at the usual breakneck pace, and found that they were able to travel at a great rate without much fatigue. On reaching the river they witnessed a phenomenon they had never seen before; the stream, although it was far above the reach of the tide, commenced running up immediately they got into their boats, and with very little exertion in the way of poling they quickly reached their farms.

To their surprise they saw the *padi* had grown knee-deep, and whilst walking through the fields it continued to grow rapidly, and ultimately burst into ear.

The usual war-whoops were shouted as they neared their home, and were answered by a din of gongs from the house. The people, one and all, came out to welcome them, the lame commenced dancing, and those who had been sick for years were sufficiently energetic to go and fetch water, and everybody appeared to be in perfect health.

The heads were hung up and a fire lighted underneath to warm them, and everything was very jolly.

Seeing all this, Tokong remarked, "The frog was certainly right, and in future we must bring back the heads."

Suppose the members of a community of Kenyahs are intending to move into a new house and do not wish to take all the old skulls with them, it is necessary to devise some means for keeping the fact of their proposed removal from the knowledge of the skulls, for otherwise, should the skulls find out that they had been deserted, they would avenge themselves on the people of the house by causing many to go mad, and various other calamities would also ensue.

The skulls are deceived in the following manner. After the new site has been selected, and favourable omens obtained, but before any actual work has been commenced, a small hut is built close to the old house; this is well roofed, but only partly walled with leaves; a fireplace is made on the ground with large pebbles, and if necessary a new board or framework is suspended above it for the reception of the skulls. A fire is lit and the place made what they consider snug. The skulls

THE CULT OF SKULLS IN SARAWAK

that are to be left behind are then taken down by some very old man and with great care are hung up in the new hut. A pig or chicken is killed, and the usual ceremony (as described above) is performed.

The skulls are left in the hut, and each day a fire is lit beneath them, and apparently they are very comfortable and pleased with their new home; but at times suspicious skulls are heard to "kriak kriak," and they may even throw themselves down on to the floor. If this should happen the skulls are taken back again, for the people dare not run the risk of displeasing them; but if nothing takes place the people know that the skulls are quite contented with their lot.

A good deal of trouble is taken by the people to prevent the skulls from knowing anything that is going on, and no mention is made before them of a new house being built.

When the new house is completed, the skulls that remained in the old house are removed to the new one with great ceremony. Before they are actually moved, the headman touches them and speaks to Balli Pengalong, the Supreme Being, and to Balli Urip, who gives men long life, and likewise he brings in by name most of the other gods; they fear to leave them out lest the slighted gods should be annoyed and retaliate on the inhabitants of the house. Then fowls are killed and their blood sprinkled in the usual manner.

The men go into the new house by the front entrance, but the basket containing the skulls is hauled up outside the house, and then pulled in through the open space in front of the verandah; it may not be carried up the steps and through the main entrance. The *siap* (charms) are brought in afterwards.

On the morning of the day when the people enter the new house a fire is built up beneath the skulls that are left behind of wood that smoulders for a long time, and the people skulk away from the hut as if afraid.

After about three days the fire burns out, and the skulls begin to talk and grumble to one another. "Where are the people?" "How is it that no fire has been put here?" "It's fearfully cold." The roof then chimes in, "Oh, they are probably away at the farms; most likely they will be here in a day or two."

Day after day goes by. No one comes back, and the skulls begin to feel sure something is wrong. However, they live in hope for some time. After a month or so the leafy roof begins to leak; when the skulls feel the rain they say to the roof, "Why do you serve us so badly? Why do you allow the rain to fall on us? Why don't you make the people come and mend you." The roof replies, "Don't you know that you have been left. The people have gone long ago." Then the skulls begin to hustle around and seek to revenge themselves on the people who have deserted them. They look up river and down river and along the banks, but rain has obliterated all the tracks the people made when they flitted; and finding it hopeless to follow them they give themselves up to their fate, and gradually become bleached by the rain and the heat of the sun. Their ratan lashing rots, and they fall to the ground. So the people are saved from any serious harm coming to them.

It may be asked, Why do people ever leave skulls behind them when they move into a new house, as they are always very anxious to obtain new ones? There is a very common-sense reason for this apparently anomalous proceeding.

Although the skulls are very old, and those who obtained them are long dead and buried, they have to receive the same care and attention while they are still in the house as the more recent skulls. They have to be fed with pork and refreshed with *borak*, and the fire has to be attended to daily; unless all this is done the inhabitants of the house will have only bad luck. On the other hand, those in the house receive no benefit from these skulls, that is, assuming the owners to have died. Why, then, should they be put to all this trouble and even run a risk of ill luck should the skulls consider themselves slighted, but at the same time gain no advantage? The natives of Borneo are sharp enough to appreciate that this is not good business, and so they judiciously relieve themselves of their somewhat troublesome benefactors.

CHAPTER XXV

PEACE-MAKING AT BARAM

AT the close of our stay at Baram we had the good fortune to be present at a great gathering of chiefs and representative men, with their followers, from all parts of this large district. The festivities and competitions connected with the gathering commenced on April 8th, and lasted for several days. After these were over, taxes were paid in at the fort, and during the whole time that the visitors were in Claudetown a great deal of business was done in the bazaar with the Chinese storekeepers, for large quantities of jungle produce were brought down the river, and many goods purchased by the natives. To do them justice I must add that the leading Chinese storekeepers had volunteered a handsome donation towards the heavy expenses of the meeting, the remainder being met by private subscriptions from the white men then present.

It was not possible to count the number of people gathered together. Tama Bulan estimated the Kenyahs at about 2,500; there may have been 1,500 Kayans, and some 500 Madangs, including a few Batang Kayans; the Long Kiputs, Long Patas, Naroms, etc., probably numbered 1,500; thus making a grand total of at least 6,000 persons.

It was quite exciting seeing the canoes arrive and to welcome old friends, whom one had met in their own homes, and to make fresh acquaintances, as they come to pay their respects to the Resident.

From every part of the district they streamed in, and even from beyond. Deputations came from the Orang Bukits of the Balait River, and from the people of the Tutong River who are still under the authority of the Sultan of Brunei. Representatives also came from tribes on the upper waters of the Batang Kayan, or Balungan River, who are nominally under the Dutch Government. Besides all these settled peoples, numerous nomad Punans put in an appearance from different quarters.

In order to give a stimulus to the cultivation of *padi* of superior quality, a *padi* and rice competition was previously announced; unhusked rice is here referred to as *padi*. As this was the first attempt at a competition of this sort in the district, only the down-river natives were invited to compete. There were a hundred and fifty-seven entries in each class; for each class there were three prizes. The native judges unanimously awarded the first rice prize to Abit, an Orang Bukit.

On the morning of the 9th was a boat race, limited to canoes carrying a crew of fifteen men. The course was two and a quarter miles, and the time was eleven minutes five seconds. Tama Bulan's people, the Long Belukan Kenyahs, won the race, but they were hardly pressed by a Malay boat.

An obstacle race next took place, which caused great amusement. The competitors had to run up and down one or two hillocks, to jump over a hurdle, and then dive off a crazy staging into a pond; after swimming this there was a steep hill to climb, next a converging framework ended in two small orifices which led into two canvas tubes which had been coated internally with soot, and finally a pool had to be passed through. Those who came through presented a very bedraggled appearance, and received the good-humoured chaff of the onlookers.

The same evening we had a display of Chinese fireworks. The rockets and fire-balloon were greatly appreciated, but the cataract of Chinese crackers was rather trying to the nerves of some of the people. Unfortunately the following evenings were too wet to allow of more fireworks.

In the afternoon a large preliminary gathering was held in the temporary hall which Hose had erected for this purpose. The chiefs and Europeans sat on a raised platform, of which a portion was railed off for the separation of the more important personages. The meeting was opened by *borak* being handed round. Tama Bulan, in giving me a whisky and soda, made the usual speech in musical declamation, and repeated the performance to the other members of the party. Next he offered drink to and apostrophised Douglas, and finally Hose. The two officials received tremendous applause from the crowded throng. I then gave a drink to Tama Bulan, and delivered

a little recitative in the English tongue but in the Kenyah manner, and we cheered him again and again, and sang—
"For he's a jolly good fellow."

Tama Bulan gave drinks to most of the chiefs present, emphasising with appropriate speeches the more important of them. With some he was evidently on very friendly terms, sitting down and caressing them while speaking; he also made a point of being markedly friendly with the Madang chief whom he had recently visited with Hose.

Aban Tingan, the warrior brother of Tama Bulan, gave a drink to Taman Jaat Kirieng, a chief of the Lepu Agas who recently came to reside in the Silat. The latter chief formerly lived in the Batang Kayan, in Dutch territory, where a number of his people still remain. It was interesting to see these two men sit and cuddle one another and drink together, when one remembered that until very recently they were at enmity, and a few years ago Aban Tingan, when on the war-path, had thrust a spear through the thigh of Taman Jaat Kirieng, a wound which nearly proved fatal.

There was also a Kenyah-Kayan-Madang group of chiefs, who sat with their arms round one another and sipped from the same glass of *borak*.

That evening I was in a war-canoe that was engaged with two or three others in an exciting practice race. The vociferous effervescence of the rival crews, the exhilaration of rapid movement, and the stimulation of half-stifling showers of spurting spray, formed a striking contrast to the sweet tranquillity of a waning tropical day, as it folded itself to rest in the gorgeous robes of sunset.

But a new element of turmoil arose as the Lirongs dashed down the river in three canoes, chanting their war-song, and dressed in feathered war coats and caps. They were received with re-echoed shouts, which were merged into a continuous roar of sound. No sooner had they landed than they rushed up the hill, and before one could realise what was happening there was a rough-and-tumble, in which the Resident and Tama Bulan were mixed up, and everyone had his share of blows. Hose, as a matter of fact, had fully expected this encounter, as it is according to custom that people who feel aggrieved should make some display when first meeting those against whom they have a grudge. In this instance the Lirongs had a score to pay off on Tama Bulan, as two years previously he had led a Government punitive expedition against them, in which two murderers were attacked and killed. Tama Bulan did not know that the Lirongs had arrived, and was quite unprepared, although a number of his followers, seeing the Lirongs' canoes scudding down the last reach, had rushed to their huts and donned the panoply of war. No serious damage was done, and all friction ought then to have been over.

The next morning a public meeting was announced in the temporary hall, but whilst the people were assembling, the Lirongs, assisted by the Sĕbops, started another *jawa*, and there was a great hubbub and some scuffling as they attempted to drag the Kenyah chiefs from the platform on which they were seated. This was not according to lawful custom, and indicated spite, as the scrimmage of the previous evening should have settled the affair.

The people became mad with excitement when blood was seen flowing down Tama Bulan's face, owing to a blow over the left eye. This was the signal for less covert hostilities, and the Kenyahs and Kayans rushed to their several huts for weapons, and the Lirongs made for their boats, but the Long Kiputs and Sĕbops were nearer their huts, and soon armed themselves. Hose had wisely arranged that the Kenyahs and Kayans were encamped on the lawn near the Residency, while the Lirongs were located in the Bazaar, a good way off down the hill and beyond the Long Kiput encampment; between these and the camp of the Kenyahs and Kayans was a large unoccupied tract, in which was the fort.

Hose immediately grasped the situation, ran to the fort, and in a very short space of time had the two small cannon charged with shot, the one trained towards the huts of the Long Kiputs, and the other towards the main encampment. The fortmen and some of the crew of the *Lucille*, and one or two other trusted men were armed by Douglas with rifles.

No sooner had Hose given his orders than he rushed unarmed down to the Lirong boats, and after a great deal of trouble succeeded in quieting down the Lirongs and other natives, who had by this time armed themselves with spears, parangs, and shields. The din was awful, and the excitement intense; that Hose came out of it unharmed was due to the fact that the trouble was purely local, and had nothing to do with the Government, which, as represented by the Resident, was loyally respected. The esteem, not unmixed with fear, in which Hose is personally held by all the natives of his immense district, stood him in good stead, and the rapid quieting down of the overwrought, gesticulating crowd was a powerful argument in favour of a "personal Government."

Douglas had charge of the fort, and no one was allowed to pass from one side of the open ground to the other. He also succeeded in pacifying the Long Kiputs and Long Patas.

Beyond, there were angry and vociferating groups of Kenyahs and Kayans, and one or two men danced and brandished imaginary spears and shields as they harangued their several groups and clamoured for vengeance. Thanks to the good sense of the chiefs, assisted by the calming words of McDougall, they gradually simmered down.

All danger was now over, and Hose went about interviewing chiefs, and orders were issued that no one was to carry a spear, parang, or other weapon, on pain of its being confiscated temporarily.

In the afternoon, at Hose's instigation, the Lirongs presented Tama Bulan with two tawaks and three gongs. Tama Bulan wanted to make peace without compensation being made to him, and the Kenyah chiefs and Tama Bulan's followers were also disinclined to allow any sort of compensation to be made to Tama Bulan, but for a different reason, and suggested they should in any case wait to see how the wound progressed before anything was received. Fortunately for the sake of peace, McDougall was on the spot, and bound up Tama Bulan's wound directly, and under his treatment it rapidly healed, though the eye was black for some days. Tama Bulan was thoroughly at one with Hose, and was equally anxious to bring matters to a close, and said he was ready to accept apologies only.

Hose next went down to the Bazaar and suggested to Taman Aping Bulieng, the headman of the Lirongs, that he should call on Tama Bulan to inquire after him. He at once acquiesced, and immediately went to call on Tama Bulan, with whom he stayed a couple of hours. All through there was little friction between the chiefs themselves, the misunderstanding was principally due to the inferior men, who had nothing to lose by causing trouble.

This unfortunate occurrence put a stop to any further festivities for that day. The social atmosphere was too electrical for friendly rivalry, and there were great searchings of heart among the various combinations of natives, and many arrangements had to be made by Hose and Douglas to ease down the excitement.

The Lirongs admitted they were entirely in the wrong, as there was no custom that allowed a *jawa* to be done a second time. In order to quiet his followers, Tama Bulan immediately he was hurt gave out that he was hit by a fallen roof-pole of the hall and not by a blow from a Lirong. Later, when all was settled, the truth leaked out, and also with his customary good sense he was content to accept the apologies of the Lirongs, and to let bygones be bygones; but for politic reasons he accepted their presents.

It is occasions of this sort that test the loyalty and capability of men, and bravery and readiness in an emergency are bound to make themselves felt. It will be remembered that a few years before Orang Kaya Tumonggong Lawai was an ill-disposed warrior whom the Government had some little difficulty in bringing to reason. This former defier of the Government proved his loyalty by walking up and down among the excited people, armed only with a walking-stick, and he effectually exerted his influence to quiet them down.

A little incident like this proves that the present form of government is extremely suitable for the people. As in the case of Tama Bulan in the early days when the Baram was taken over, and in other instances, a little rough discipline served to develop what sterling qualities were lying latent in them. Indeed, trouble is usually given at first instance by those men of character who later on shape into loyal and capable adherents of the Government.

One great feature of the peace-making was a *tuba* fishing on an unprecedented scale, and a lake connected with Baram River was to be the scene of the attempt.

We started in the steamer at 6 a.m. on the morning of the 11th, and on our way down stream we passed numerous canoes that had started still earlier. On arriving at the scene of action we transhipped into a boat and entered Logan Ansok by a narrow waterway which meandered through a tropical jungle composed of divers trees of varied size, interspersed among which were screw pines, palms, ratans, and ferns, epiphytes clinging on to trunk and bough added to the complexity of the luxuriant foliage.

We stayed a little time in this verdant water-lane and allowed several canoes to pass us. First rounding the corner, and as it were peering through the foliage, would appear a grotesque head of what seemed to be a monstrous dragon with long, sharp tusks, goggle eyes, and erratic horns, but the long,

FIG. 40. FIGURE-HEADS OF CANOES, BARAM DISTRICT

thin neck soon resolved itself into the bow of a war-canoe, paddled by lithe-bodied, copper-coloured natives, in some instances wearing a hairy war-coat adorned with the black and white feathers of the hornbill, and on their heads ratan war-caps ornamented with the long tail feathers of another species of hornbill. Other men were clad solely in the usual *chawat*, or loin cloth; some wore in addition a white cotton jacket. The heads of nearly all were protected by large round hats.

At one spot the canoes had to be dragged in shallow water through the jungle, owing to a huge hard-wood tree having fallen and so blocked up the waterway, and the weirdness was enhanced by the cadenced hauling-cries of the men as they laboriously tugged their canoes. It is impossible to adequately describe the scene and the noise. The vivid colouring of some of the costumes was jewelled against the green background by the broken sunshine as it streamed through the tropical foliage, and all was instinct with human life and activity.

Eventually we found ourselves in a large lake entirely surrounded by trees; unfortunately the river was high, and so the water had overflowed its banks, and the lake had an apparent rather than a definite margin, as the water was spread out among the surrounding trees. The placid water shimmered in the sunshine, and the varied foliage lit by the early morning sun looked very beautiful, but the interest was greatly increased by the numerous canoes now paddling about in full sunshine, the high lights, catching the large, round palm-leaf hats or some unprotected portion of skin or clothing, being emphasised by deep shadows. The rows of hats alone constituted a striking decorative feature.

The boats were ultimately ranged round the lake, and were tied up to trees and bushes as far as possible in the shade. The next business was to cut logs and short billets from thick boughs to serve as mallets. The small packets of tuba root were separated from the large bundles with which every boat was well supplied, and these were beaten with the mallets on the logs which were placed in the canoes. Many men preferred to climb on to trees and beat the tuba on fallen trunks, or, perched aloft, they employed the branches for that purpose.

From all around the lake came the measured beating, varied by an irregular access of loudness and rapidity, reminding one somewhat of the company firing of a distant review or sham-fight.

Later the boats came into the open; in most several men were hammering away, while others baled water over the crushed roots. Then the bilge of discoloured water was ladled into the lake, and the clouds of the infusion gradually dispersed. The characteristic but indescribable odour of crushed tuba was wafted over the surface of the still waters.

In about an hour a few tiny fish were observed wriggling in an uneasy manner near the surface of the water; these were at

PLATE XXXI

BEATING TUBA AND BALING THE INFUSION OUT OF A CANOE

PENCHALLONG PREPARED FOR THE GREAT PEACE-MAKING

once netted. I was in a boat with the Resident, Tama Bulan, and Aban Batu, a Umo Poh chief, when the first little fish we saw was captured. This miserable firstfruit was offered to Balli Flaki by Tama Bulan, who said to the omen bird that he gave it the largest share and that we had kept the smallest for ourselves. This was strictly true, as hitherto we had caught nothing, and therefore a diminutive fishlet was a greater share than nothing at all. Aban Batu then lit a match and asked Balli Flaki to make the tuba strong that we might catch plenty of fish. It was rather a descent to the commonplace to burn a lucifer match instead of the shredded sticks that are used customarily, but doubtless the smoke was as effectual a medium for the conveyance of the prayer as if it were produced in the orthodox manner.

At one spot just within the jungle ten sticks were stuck in the water, the cleft upper end of each holding an egg. These were placed there by the Kayans, probably as an offering to the birds to secure good omens, and possibly, in addition, because some of their number had never been in the Lower Baram before, and it is customary for two eggs to be offered in this way on entering a river for the first time.

Unfortunately while the lake was being tuba'ed the river rose, and so the increase of the water prevented the operation from being a success, and only a few small fish were obtained. Some twenty-five piculs (over three thousand pounds) of tuba had been provided by natives from all over the district, and this would have proved sufficient for the purpose had not the heavy rains caused floods.

A very large number of men and boats were engaged, and we all spent an enjoyable day, for as a native chief remarked some time previously, when the arrangements were being made, "The scale on which the tubaing was done and the general excitement would please the people even if no fish were caught."

The second boat race took place early on the morning of the 12th; sixteen canoes started, seven of which belonged to the Kenyahs, four to the Kayans, and four to other up-river tribes; the Naroms of Baram had one canoe. The number of each crew was unlimited, and some boats carried as many as sixty or seventy men, so that there must have been about a thousand engaged in the race.

The first prize of fifty dollars was won by the Naroms by about two lengths; the Long Kiputs gained the second place and a prize of ten dollars. The course was about 3¼ miles and the time was 15 minutes 10 seconds. The Oxford and Cambridge course from Putney to Mortlake is 4¼ miles, and the average time for the last ten years is 20 minutes 34½ seconds. Thus the speed of these untrained natives is slightly faster than that of a trained University crew, but it is doubtful whether this would be the case if the Baram course were as long as that on the Thames; further, it must be remembered that in Borneo they paddled down a fairly large swift river, whereas on the Thames they row on a full tide.

Many of the Tinjar people were delayed by one or two deaths occurring, so they arrived too late to participate in the great race of war-canoes. But as they wanted to maintain the honour of their river, Taman Liri of Long Tegin and the Lelaks of Long Tru challenged the Naroms to a supplemental race. This was rowed on the evening of the 13th, the course being about a mile. The result was a dead heat, which was gratifying to the pride of the Tinjar folk.

The final public meeting took place on the morning of the 13th; by this time nearly everyone had arrived who was expected; amongst the late comers was Saba Irang, the head chief of the Madangs (Pl. XXIX., C., p. 376). On a low staging in front of the platform reclined three enormous pigs, with tied legs, which the Resident had provided for the purpose of swearing peace and friendship; one was primarily intended for the Baram tribes, one for the Lirongs of the Tinjar, and the third for the Madangs. At the other end of the hall was a gigantic gaily painted model of a hornbill, on which a very large number of cigarettes were suspended. The body was a large barrel; each wing consisted of two hairy Kenyah or Madang shields, and the head had been skilfully hewn out of a great block of wood by Iban fortmen. A model of a hornbill is the customary table-piece, so to speak, of an Iban feast, but this "Penchallong" or "Tenyalang" surpassed the usual effigy as much as this occasion transcended an ordinary feast (Pl. XXXI., B). A great quantity of borak was provided, which was duly despatched at the close of the meeting.

After a little preliminary talking the following representative chiefs crouched by the pigs: Saba Irang, a Madang; Taman Oding Silong, a Kenyah; Taman Balan Deng, an Upper Tinjar

Long Pokun; Taman Aping Bulieng, a Lirong; Jangan, an Upper Tinjar Sĕbop, and others. Saba Irang, taking a glowing brand, singed a pig and spoke to it, telling it to act as a witness in the ceremony of peacemaking. He solemnly swore that he and his people would be friends with those now assembled, and would not combine with outside enemies against them, and he himself, so far as he had the power, would endeavour to prevent others from breaking the peace. Should they break this solemn oath, they hoped that the gods would call down upon them all sorts of illness, and that they might be destroyed by crocodiles or other harmful beasts.

Tama Bulan then pointed out that the Baram people had formerly taken a similar oath, which they had kept. Now they were making friends with the Madangs, and were in future to be one people. Old scores had been wiped out, and there was nothing now to complain of. The Government had brought them together, and they had mixed with one another and had discussed old troubles; now was the time to speak if they had anything to say.

Dr. Hose stood up and said, "Now you have sworn the inviolable oath. This meeting was assembled that there should be a lasting peace in the district. There is nothing to gain by war, but everything to gain by peace. The difficulty in the past has been to make enemies meet one another with a view to settling their differences amicably; now this difficulty has been overcome, thanks mainly to the assistance of those chiefs who have supported me. Now all of you present! see this multitude, and bear in mind that whoever breaks this oath, which has been taken to-day in the presence of everybody, does so at his own peril. Who of you would dare after this to kill anyone if he thought what the consequences would be? It would be a matter of only a few minutes to wipe him and his people off the face of the earth. The Rajah's dogs will hunt, if it prove necessary to call them out; as is known to everybody, they require no hounding on. So remember the oath, and peace, I hope, is assured."

Several of the chiefs stated that they were very pleased the Resident had spoken so plainly, as they did not like to do so themselves. After this the pig was killed in the usual manner by sticking it in the neck with a spear, and the liver was duly examined amid great excitement.

The Madangs admitted the liver was everything that could be desired; they stated they had already felt that the Baram people had kept their promises to them, and now they had every confidence in them. Saba Irang, in a great speech, said he was pleased to see such unity among everybody in the district, and the Madangs all felt that this was everything to them. Not only were his people glad to join Baram, but he knew that many of the people of the Batang Kayan had already begun to appreciate this general good fellowship, and he had every reason to believe those chiefs were anxious to be on friendly terms with the Baram folk.

Another highly excited Madang chief made a vociferous speech, emphasising his points by violent jumping. "The Madangs," he said, "were anxious to have the same advantages as the others, and the Baram people would see that, after all, they were no worse than anyone else (jump). For years we had to hold our own on all sides; we now feel assured that our people will meet with no opposition when endeavouring to trade in the Baram district, and I will be responsible for any fault committed by my people, but I feel they will not be the first to break the peace (great jumping). I have finished" (jump).

Speeches in a similar strain were made by Tama Bulan and others. All said they were loyal to the Government; they would do what they were told to do even unto death. So the great palaver came to an end.

The meeting of the chiefs and principal natives of the Baram district was organised primarily for the sake of the Madangs. Last November, when Hose went into the Madang country, it was the first time a white man had visited them, and he received the adherence of a number of chiefs, some of whom promised to come shortly into the Baram district, a few having previously done so. Hose therefore deemed it politic to have a mass meeting at which the Madangs would be publicly acknowledged as Baram subjects, both by the Government and by the other natives.

The Madangs, who live in the healthy uplands of Central Borneo, have at divers times raided the inhabitants of the affluents of the Rejang and Baram in Sarawak, on the one hand, and those of the streams of the Batang Kayan in Dutch Borneo on the other. As they live in a country that is very difficult of access, they have hitherto practically been beyond the pale of the Government, and have had a disquieting effect upon the natives who have given their adherence to the Rajah. Certain of the Madang villages had already received some punishment in the Rejang district, but it was necessary that this unsettled state of affairs should cease, and these energetic agriculturists be brought in under the Sarawak Government. The up-river Baram people were pleased to make peace, as tranquillity is always more remunerative than hostility, and the men felt it to be irksome to be always in suspense when working in their gardens, or to be anxious about the folk at home when they are out gutta hunting.

The fact that Hose could collect all the important people from Miri on the sea coast on the one hand, to Silat, one of the head streams of the Baram, on the other, and from the as yet unvisited Kalabit country to the east to their own country in the interior, would naturally impress the Madangs with the far-reaching influence of the Government, and would give them confidence in the power of the Government to preserve peace and protect property.

The same argument would appeal to those chiefs who came from the Batang Kayan River across the border. Several houses have already come into the Silat and Lata Rivers, tributaries of the Baram, and more are prepared to come. Hose had hoped that a large contingent would arrive from the Batang Kayan, and he knew that the head chief Tama Kuling and several minor chiefs with a considerable following had actually made a start. It is probable, however, that at the last they were somewhat fearful of meeting such a large gathering of foreigners, many of whom were hereditary foes; and it was through the territories of the latter that they would have to pass to reach Claudetown. Small wonder, then, that they held back, though they promised to come down shortly afterwards when there were fewer people about. The few Batang Kayans who did come would tell their friends about the meeting, and there is no doubt it will have a tangible effect on those who feared to put in an appearance.

There are always local jealousies and feuds in every district, and the river-basin of the Baram is not exempt therefrom, as we have already seen in the fracas of the Lirongs with the Kenyahs. It is therefore of importance that representatives of all the larger villages from the various rivers should meet

INDEX

Aban Abit, 335, 337, 369
Acolytes, Papuan, 256
Adzes, stone, still used in canoe making, 220; in Mekeo, 272; Borneo, 368-70
Afu (taboo in Mekeo), 270, 271
Afu symbol at Inawi, 271
Agi, 244, 245
Agricultural ceremonies, 106
— charms, Torres Straits, 67, 86, 87, 107, 140; New Guinea, 104-7, 202, 205
Agriculturists, 212, 262, 323
Agu, turtle trophy, 154-6
Alexis, Brother, 252, 266, 270, 271, 276
Alluvium, 212, 319
Alukune, 221
Aman (omen animals), 384
Amentum, 201
Andersen, Neil, 4-8
Angabunga River, 261
Anglo-Saxon overlord, 328, 329
Anthreptes, 384, 385, 391
Arachnothera, 384, 385, 390
Archbishop Navarre, 185, 203, 252, 266
Arctogale, 384-6
Areca nut (betel), 217
Ari, chief of Murray Island, 8, 9, 20, 28, 29, 57, 72, 74
Ari (personal totem) at Cape York, 193, 194
Arrow-points, making with a boar's tusk, 269
Astrolabe Range, 239
Atsiamakara village, 242
Augŭd (totem), 132
Au kosker (big women shrine), 69
Australian aspect of vegetation, 239
— colour names, 24
— dance, 193
— languages, 30
— medicine-man, 90
Australians, Cape York, 190-4

Baby, paying for, 175
Balfour, Henry, 225
Baling Go (the thunder god), 369
Baling Go's eyeball, 371
— — front tooth, 370
— — toe-nails, 369
Ballantine, Hon. D., 205, 206, 236, 241, 244-6, 248, 251

Balli Atap, 360
Balli Flaki, offering to, 384, 409
Balli Penyalong (god of child-naming), 354
Balli Taun (god of harvest), 373
Balungan (river dragon), 373
Bamboo knife, 115
Bampfylde, Hon. C. A., 279, 280
Barawan, 321, 343
— house, 334, 336
Bark belts, 266
Bark-cloth shawl, 259
Barker, Dr. A. J. C., 279
Barking deer, 385
Bartlett, E., 283
Batang Kayans, 364, 365, 401, 403, 412, 413
Batu Blah, 306, 321
Beardmore, E., 111, 114
Bêche-de-mer, 2, 3
Beehive house in Murray Island, 58
Bees, 383, 391
Beheading knife, 115
Berantu ceremony, 306-11
Berenicornis, 384, 385, 388
Betel, 217
Biofa, 261
Bird dances, Sëbop, 358; Torres Straits, 49, 114, 189
Birding, 392
Blood-letting, 222, 223
Boar's-tusk knife, 243, 269
Boars' tusks, abnormally curved, 370
Boat races, 280, 401, 409
Boigu, the island of spirits, 90
Bok River, 333
Bomai, 46, 47, 80, 180
Brass-workers, 356
Broad-headed natives, Sarawak, 321; Torres Straits, 119, 120
Borepada village, 204
Bornean love stories, 376-80
Borneo, physical features of, 212, 348
Bouellat, Father, 274
Bow and arrow fleam, 223
Boys dressed up as Fulaari, 275
Boy-throwing, game of, 228
Brahminy kite, 388
Brother Edmond, death of, 253, 254
Bride-price, 363, 378

Bridge, sacrifice for a, 339
Brooke, Rajah Sir Charles. Cf. Rajah of Sarawak
Brooke, Rajah Sir James, 291-3
Bruce, John, 8, 9, 31-5, 77, 78, 84
Bruce, Robert, 168
Brunei, 288, 291, 300, 327
— Malay, 327, 338, 341, 342
Bulaa dances, 231
— village, 211, 212, 221-34
Bulan, 376
Bull-roarer, 42, 227; in Torres Straits, 33, 107, 140, 156, 157; in Kiwai, 104, 105; at Cape York, 191, 192
"Bundling" in Wales, 378
Burial cave, 305
Burke, Father, 253, 268
Burns Philp, 235
Burnt village, 208, 359
Burong (omen animals), 384
Burying under houses, 262
"Bushmen," Masingara, 111, 112
Butiong (wooden image), 333

Cainozoic rocks, 316
Cambridge Peak, 347
Canoe (Sarawak), 297
Canoe-making in New Guinea, 220
Cape York natives, 190-4
Carcineutes, 384, 385, 388
Card players (Papuan), 185
"Cat's cradle" games, 38, 39, 175, 201
Cave of skulls, Pulu, 141-3; Borneo, 305
Cemetery, 284, 306
Ceremony for the removal of skulls, 337, 352
Ceremony of child-naming, 353, 354
Cervulus, 384, 385
Chalmers, Mrs., 95, 128.
Chalmers, Rev. James, 95-8, 104, 107-109, 128-30, 197, 203, 213, 249, 250
Chalmers, Rev. W., 385
Chapel, service in Catholic (New Guinea), 255
Charms, agricultural (New Guinea), 104-7, 202, 205; (Torres Straits), 67, 86, 87, 107, 140
— curative, 107
— fishing (dugong), 133, 134, 153, 154, 202
— injuring people, 106, 202, 203
Chawat (loin cloth), 283
— to die in, 370
Chevrotains, 385
Character of Mabuiag people, 122
— of Murray Islanders, 72.
Chiefs, petty, in Sarawak, 414
Children's toys and games, 224, 231, 274
Child-naming ceremony, 353
Chinamen, 327-9
Chinese districts 316
Chorus songs, 324

Church at Saibai, 170; at Mabuiag, 122
Cicatrices, 110, 113, 200
Cittocincla, 381, 384, 385, 389
Clan houses, 99, 171
Clarinet, 225
Claudetown, 297, 311, 330, 357, 371, 379, 401-13
Club houses in New Guinea, 99, 100, 208, 256, 257, 262, 268, 270
Coal in Borneo, 318
Cochard, Father, 185, 259, 268
Cockatoo feathers for dances, 234
Cockatoos, tame, 234
Coconut palm, triple crowned, 172
Coconut shrine, 67
Codrington, Rev. Dr., 44
Colour blindness, 126
— vision of natives, 24, 25, 245
— vocabulary, Australian, 24; Kiwai, 24; Torres Straits, 24
Comet, 80-2
Confederation of mountain tribes, 247
Conscientiousness of Murray Islanders, 27, 29
Constabulary, for enforcing taboo, 271
Constellations, 139, 165-8, 381
Cooking in Torres Straits, 41
Copper Maori, 41
Copra, 3
Craniology, Torres Straits, 18, 119, 120
Cotton cloths of the Iban women, 280, 285, 326
Cowling, J., 117
Crocodile-man, 171, 172
Crystal sphere, 370
Culm measures, 315
Cult of skulls, 332, 394-400
Cuscus, 110
Customs of the Ibitoes, 258
Cyclone, 79, 80, 88
Cymodocea, 151

Dalton, O. M., 372
Dam, ceremony at, 61
Dance costume, 113, 187, 214, 233, 234, 358
Dances stopped by teachers, 35, 128
Dances:
  Australian, 193. Bornean, 357, 358. Papuan: Babaka, 214-19; Bulaa, 231; Kapakapa, 210; Mabuiag, 131, 139, 140, 233; Mawatta, 113, 114; Muralug, 186-8; Murray Island, 47-9, 60, 102; Nagir, 182. South Sea, 35; Rotumah, 36, 53
  Ceremonial: Agricultural dances, 215-19; death dances, 139, 182; fishing dances, 183, 184; Malu dances, 47-9, 102; war dances, 60, 131, 140, 186-8, 233, 358
  Festive, 188, 189, 210, 231-3
  Mimetic, 49, 114, 188, 189, 358

INDEX

Danilkau, a funeral buffoon, 139, 140
Danish thunderbolts, 372
Dapoi River, 360
Darnley Island (Erub), 5, 12, 51, 95
Daru, 95
Dauar, 12, 17, 18, 64-8
Dauncey, Rev. H. M., 199, 201
Death of a baby, 123
— of Brother Edmond, 253, 254
Decorated skull, 91, 181
Decoration, native, 332
Deer, 383-6
Delena, 199-201, 259, 260
Deshon, Hon. H. F., 284, 285
Devonian rocks, 315
Divination by means of a parang, 366
— by pig's liver, 336, 337, 354, 355, 411, 412
— in Murray Island, 54-6
Divining grasshopper, 92
— skull, Torres Straits, 91, 92, 182
— zogo, 91
Dog killing unlucky, 335, 364
Dogs, supposed by natives to be sacrificed by the English, 339
Doiom (rain charm), 32-5, 86
"Doors," 298, 331
"Door" tax, 294
Dorgai, 166
— constellation, 166
Douglas, Hon. John, 1, 4, 20, 123, 170
Douglas, R. S., 303, 304, 330, 337, 404-6
Dowry, 363
Dyeing patterns on cloth, 326
Dragon, river, 373
Drinking customs, 311, 402, 403
Drought, 84, 86
Drum-making, 257
Drums, 231, 233; sacred drum, 45
Drunkenness, 356
Dubu, 100, 208, 217, 234
— ascended by girls, 218
Dugong, 151
— charms, 133, 134, 153, 154, 202
— food of, 151, 152
— harpoon, 149
— methods of catching, 148-54
Dukduk, in New Britain, 51
Dulit Mount, 344, 347, 348, 349
Durian, 303
Dusun, 321

Earthquake in Murray Island, 78, 79
Eastern Papuans, 199
Economic defects of a hunting existence, 265
Edible earth, 203
Edmond, Brother, 253, 254
Elevera, 235
English, A. C., 206, 210, 214, 219, 226, 234, 248
Eocene, 317

Erabo (club house), 100
Erub, 5, 12, 51, 95
Eruptive rocks of Borneo, 318
Ethnography of Sarawak, 320
Evanena, 228
Evans, Prof. E., 339
Everett, A. Hart, 318, 372
Eyesight, defects of, among natives, 24
— of hill tribes, 245

Fable of the monkey and the frog, 343
Fairy darts, 373
Fanny Rapid, 377
Fauna of Mount Dulit, 348   [272
Feasts, Murray Island, 39-41; Mekeo,
Feeding skulls, 396
Fertility ceremony, 218
Figure-heads of canoes, 407
Fire, legend of origin, 108
Fire-making in New Guinea and Torres Straits, 108, 109
Fireworks, 402
First man, legend of origin of, 108
Fish, shooting with bow and arrows, 259
Fisher-folk in New Guinea, 207, 221, 260, 261
Fish, zogo, 68
Fleam, 223
Flutes, 205, 258
Food restrictions, 135, 257
Forge, 324
Frazer, Dr. J. G., 134, 135
Frigate bird, 204
Frog, fable of, 343
— game, 228
Fulaari, 271, 272, 275, 276
Funeral in Murray Island, 93; in Yule Island, 254

Gaile, 206
Games:
  Borneo, mancala, 284
  Papuan adults' games: hockey, 78; *iamar*, 40, 58, 59, 62; top-spinning (*kolap*), 40, 41
  Papuan children's games: balancing (*evanena*), 228; boy-throwing (*omoro* or frog), 228; hopping, 227; hunting kangaroo and pig, 274, 275; imitating ceremonies (*fulaari*) 275, (*kwod*) 180; jumping, 227; leap-frog, 227; pig-a-back, 227; revolving (*maki gegelaki* and *rapurapu*), 228; ring games (*kwaito pinupinu* and *mola erempte*), 229; round sitting games, played with the hands (*korikini*) 229, (*toitoi kinimali*), 230, 231; skipping, 227; top-whipping, 272, 273
Gapu (sucker-fish), 155, 156
Garden charms, Torres Straits, 67, 86, 87, 107; New Guinea, 104-7

Gasiri (tree houses), 248
Geigi's fish-spear, 68
Gelam, 16
Genealogies of natives, 124
Geographical features of Borneo, 312
— of British New Guinea, 207, 239-41
— of Sarawak, 286, 348
Geological features of Borneo, 312, 348
— of British New Guinea, 207, 239, 240
Geology of Sumatra, 315
George, Brother, 266, 267, 276
Gewe (chief of Agi), 244-6
Ghost (lamar), 89, 90
Ghost tiger, 305
Girls ascending dubu, 218; seclusion of, in Mabuiag, 135
God of Harvest, 373
Gold in Sarawak, 315; in Torres Straits, 4
Gomoridobo village, 234
Gope (charm), 103, 104
Gors, Mr., 205, 251, 266
Government of Sarawak, 292, 294
— of Torres Straits by Queensland, 19-21
Grammar of Torres Straits languages, 29, 127
Granville, 235
Grasshopper, divining, 92
Graves, New Guinea, 112
Great houses in New Guinea, 99, 213; in Sarawak, 298
Guilbaut, Father, 255
Guis, Father, 253, 258-60, 276, 277
Guise, R. E., 218
Gunboat, 249

H., Captain, 5, 6, 22, 80, 82, 95
Hair, 18, 119, 223, 234, 325
— wavy, among Papuans, 234
Haliastur, 384, 385, 387, 390
Hammond Island, 185
Hantus (spirits), 340, 369
Hanuabada village, 235
Harpoon, 148
Harpactes, 381-5, 387-90
Haviland, G. D., 283
Hawk omen, 387, 352
Hawk-owl, 391
Head-hunters, Kiwai, 107
Head-hunting, 322, 325, 328, 339; object of, 107
— origin of, in Borneo, 397
— in Sarawak, reasons for, 394
Hearing, acuity and range, 25
Heliarctos, 391
Hely, Hon. Bingham A., 95, 98, 103, 109
Hill-land of Borneo, 316
Hill tribes, colour-vision of, 245
— — keenness of eyesight, 245
History of Sarawak, 291, 292
Hockey in Murray Island, 78

Hoe, shell, 109
Hogeri, 244
Holiness, 67, 258
Hood Bay, 219
— Peninsula, 211-34
Hooks, magical, 370, 371, 373, 396
Hopping, game, 227
Hornbill, 410
— white-crested, 388
Hornbills' feathers, 395
Hose, Dr. C., 297, 301, 303-5, 320-415
Houses: Torres Straits, 58, 110; Kiwai, 99, 100; New Guinea, 204, 206, 208, 211, 213, 223, 224, 242, 243, 268, 269; Sarawak, 298, 290, 331-3, 335
Hula, 211. Cf. Bulaa
Human heads for foundations of Kuching waterworks, 339
Human sacrifice, 339
— skulls. Cf. skulls
Hunters, 265
Hunting games, 274
Huts, 110; sleeping hut in jungle, 299
Hurricane in Torres Straits, origin of, 79, 80, 82, 87, 88

Iasa (Kiwai), 98-108
Iban (Sea Dayak), 281, 283, 301, 302, 305, 322, 324-8, 338, 341, 381-93
Ibitoe, customs of, 256-9
Inawi village, 269, 272
Indo-Javan people, 322, 327
Indonesian, 321
Ingratitude of natives, 19
Initiation ceremonies, 42; in Murray Island, 44, 135, 140, 176, 191
Instruction of lads (Murray Island), 49, 50
Iriam Moris, 64
Ireland, stone implements used as charms in, 373
Iron, 338, 366, 395
Irupi dance, 217
Isang, 361
Isit, 344, 384, 385, 390
Islamism, 328

Jangan, 352-5, 411
Japanese in Thursday Island, 2, 3
Jar burial, 306
Jardine, Frank, 190
Javano-Hindu colonisation of Borneo, 322, 327
Javelin, miniature, 224
Jawa, 404, 406
Jesu baibua, 262
Jumping game, 227
Jungle, new, 304, 345
Jungle, old, 304, 345

Kadayans, 300, 301, 306, 321, 327, 341
Kaikai, origin of term, 39, 40

INDEX

Kaivakuku, mask at Waima, 271
Kajaman, 321
Kalabit, 321, 323, 414
Kalamantan, 289, 321, 324, 327
Kalo village, 212-14, 219, 220
Kalulong Mount, 349
Kaluri, 357, 379
Kamut (string puzzles in Murray Island), 38, 39
Kanauit, 321, 284
Kangaroo drive game, 274
Kap, 188. Cf. Torres Straits dances
Kapakapa village, 208, 210
Karangang, 299, 302
Kayan tattoo designs, 306
Kayans, 288, 297, 304-6, 323-5, 328, 357, 360, 364, 384, 386-93, 394, 395, 397, 401, 404, 405, 409, 414
— war-path of, 297, 304
Kawit, 396. Cf. Hooks, magical.
Keapara village, 219-22
Kedaman, 362
Kelebong, 361
Kenyah drinking songs, 311
Kenyah-Kayan migration, 327
Kenyahs, 288, 302, 323-5, 328, 340, 341, 364, 365, 384, 386-93, 395-8, 401, 402, 404, 405, 409, 413, 414
Kerepunu. Cf. Keapara
Kernge (lads during initiation), 140
Kersi (lads during initiation), 45, 48, 50, 61, 70
Kina Balu, Mount, 349, 350
Kingfisher, 388
Kinimali (game), 230
Kiriri Island, 185
Kiwai Island, 24, 96-109; natives of, 101
Knife, bamboo, 115
— made of boar's tusk, 243
Knocking out tooth, 193
Koiari, 244
Koitapu, 249; language of, 249
Kolap (top), 40, 41
Kôpa-kôpa, 175
Korikini (game), 229
Kwaito pinupinu (game), 229
Kwari kwari (toy), 227
Kwod (sacred ceremonial ground), 192
— in Mabuiag, 134
— in Nagir, 181
— in Pulu, 137-42
— in Tut, 176-78
— in Yam, 178-80
— small boys', 180
Kwoiam (the hero of Mabuiag), 136-47
Kuching, town of, 279-84
Kupor (navel shrine), 142, 177, 179
Kuru (toy), 225

Labuan Island, 286, 318
Ladies of Tama Bulan's house, 375

Lakatois, 248
Lamar (ghost), 89, 90
Land Dayak, 321, 322, 327, 340, 391, 393
Land inheritance, Cape York, 193
Land leeches, 304, 346
Langa (toy), 225
Lange, Mr. H. W. de, 95, 97
Language of Roro, 261
— Australian, 30
— Melanesian, 29, 30
— Papuan, 29, 30
Languages of Torres Straits, 28-30, 127
Lantern entertainment in Murray Island, 37, 38
— at Port Moresby, 246
Laterite, 345
Lawes, Dr., 208, 209, 234, 249, 273
Lawes, Mrs., 209, 234
Laziness of natives, 19
Leap-frog, 227
Legends: Gelam, 16, 155; of various shrines, 53-69; origin of man, 108; origin of fire, 108; the stone that fell from the sky, 138; of Kwoiam, 136-47; about dugong, 155
Lelak, 321, 410
— village, 330
Lepocestes, 383-5, 389
Lepuanans, 354, 355
Liberality of natives, 90
Life token, 259
Lifu, colour-blindness of natives, 126
— head-form, 126
Limbang, 285-90, 293, 297
Ling, Roth H., 320, 381
Linjau, 360
Lirongs, 403-6, 410, 413
Liver of pig, 336, 354, 355, 411, 412
Lobong River, 352
Logan Ansok, 406
Loin-cloth to die in, 370
London Missionary Society's stations: Murray Island, 9; Kiwai, 96, 97; Mabuiag, 117; Vatorata, 208-10; Delena, 199; Bulaa (Hula), 211; Port Moresby, 235
"Long," 333
Long Aiah Kechil, 342, 344, 348
— Kiput, 321, 401, 404, 405, 410
— Pata, 302, 321, 341, 401, 405
— Pokuns, 360
— Puah, 352
— Semitan, 342
— Sulan, 360
— Tegin, 334
— Tru, 330
Love affairs, Mawatta, 112; Mabuiag, 158-64
— charms, Torres Straits, 106
— letters, Papuan, 163, 164
Love-making in Mekeo, 258
— in Sarawak, 377-80

Lovers' tune, 379
Low, Brooke, 283, 322
Lower carboniferous rocks, 315

Mabuiag, 117-64
— church, 122
— language, 127
— social condition of, 118
— war dance, 233
Macfarlane, Rev. Dr. S., 7, 120, 127, 142, 143
Macgregor, Sir William, 97, 102, 203, 205, 206, 209, 213, 251, 262
Madangs, 364, 401, 410, 412, 413
Madub (garden charm), 106, 107
Madubu (bull-roarer), 104-6
Magic. Cf. Sorcery
— symbolic, 257, 133, 134
Magical ceremonies, 133, 134, 184
— stone hooks, 370, 371, 373, 396
Magur ("devil" belong Malu), 50
Maiau, 180
Maino (chief of Tut and Yam), 171, 174-80, 184, 185
Maki gegelaki (game), 228
Malangs, 321, 342
Malay Archipelago, 372
— bear, 391
— Peninsula, 372
— rule, 288
— traders, 356
Malays, 326-9, 338, 341, 342
Malohs, 356, 357
Malu, 46, 61, 180
— ceremonies, 42-52, 61-3, 102
— masks, 46-8, 92
— songs, 45, 46, 62, 63
Mammals of Borneo, 348, 349
Mamoose (Torres Straits chief), 8, 20, 21
Mancala game, 284
Mangoes, 302
Mangroves, 266
Manufacture of stone club, 245
Map of stones, 61   [270
Marea (club-house), 100, 257, 262, 268,
Mari, 181
Mariget, 181
Marine pile dwellings, 206, 223
Marital relations in Mabuiag, 161
— — in Murray Island, 20, 76, 78
Market-place, 269
Market women, 269
Markets in Mekeo district, 265
Marriage customs, Torres Straits, 158-64; Borneo, 363, 364, 377-80
Marsh land of Borneo, 319
Marudi. Cf. Claudetown
Masingara "bushmen," 111, 112
Mask, war ceremony, 59; Mawatta, 114; fishing dance, 183; Malu ceremony, 46-8
— in Mekeo district, 271

Mausoleum, 284
Mawatta, 111-116
May Meeting, 128-31
McDougall, W., 22, 23, 26, 28, 303, 305, 330, 337, 347, 405
Medicine-man (Australian), 90; (Bornean), 307, 374
Meeting, public, 402, 410
Mekeo district, 252-77
— — markets, 265, 269
— tribe, 261, 262
Mělanau, 321, 327, 357, 390, 391
Melanesia, secret societies in, 44
Melanesian languages, 29 30,
Melanesians, 18
Mer. Cf. Murray Island
Mesozoic rocks in Borneo, 316
Milman, H., 111-113, 175
Mimetic dances, 49, 114, 188, 189
Miocene in Borneo, 317
Mirror-writing, 25
Mission schools in New Guinea, 97, 98, 208, 209
Mixed marriages, 357
Modesty of New Guinea women, 274
Mohu, 252, 268
Monkey and frog fable, 343
Morality, code of in Torres Straits, 176
Mosquito nets, native Papuan, 259
Mota črěmpto (game), 229
Motu tribe, 249
Mountain ranges of Borneo, 312
— tribes, New Guinea confederation of, 247
Mount Ernest. Cf. Nagir
— Warirata, 240, 241
Mourning in Murray Island, 94
Mulu, Mount, 349
Mummies, Torres Straits, 91
Muntjac, 385
Muralug (Prince of Wales Island), 119, 185-9
Murder, 340
Murders in Sarawak, 300-2, 338-41
Muriks, 371
Murray Island (Mer), 8, 11-21; climate, 18; geology, 12-17
— Islanders, 18, 19, 118, 119, 127
Muruts, 321, 393
Museum, Sarawak, 282-4, 372
Musgrave, Hon. A., 205, 206, 236, 251
Myers, C. S., 22, 23, 25, 26, 28

Nagir, Island of, 180-3
Names, reluctance to mention, 103
Nara, tribe, 260
Naroms, 321, 401, 409, 410
Narrow-headed natives, Torres Straits, 18, 119, 120; Sarawak, 321, 343
Native cemetery (Sarawak), 284
— grief (Papuan), 222
Navarre, Archbishop, 185, 203, 252, 266

INDEX

Navel shrines, 142, 177, 179
Nĕĕt (dugong platform), 152, 153
New Guinea oratory, 268
— — vegetation, 239, 241
New Jungle, 304, 345
Ninox, 391
Numerals, Papuan, 30, 243
Nurumara (totem of Kiwai), 101-3

Oboe, 225
Obstacle race, 401
Offering of eggs, 409
— to Balli Flaki, 409
Old Jungle, 304, 345
Oligocene in Borneo, 317
"Olive Branch," 197
Omen animals of Sarawak, 381-93
— birds, 344, 352, 362, 379, 381-93
— — offerings to, 352
Omens, 259, 344, 352, 362, 379, 381-93
Omoro (game), 228
Oracles, 53-7, 178
Orang Bukit, 306, 401, 402
Orang Kaya Tumonggong Lawai, 300-2, 406
Oratory, Bornean, 411, 412
— Papuan, 268
Origin of fire, 108
Orthotomus, 384, 385, 390
Owning an omen bird, 344

Padi bug, 391
— competition, 401
— cultivation of, 323, 327, 360, 381-3
— swamp, 323, 325
Painted board, sign of chieftainship, 270
Palæozoic rocks in Borneo, 315
Panyamun scare, 338, 340, 359, 365, 368
Papuan Gulf, 198
— language, 29, 30
Papuans, true, or Western, 119, 249
Parang, 285, 324
Pasi, Mamoose of Dauar, 8, 28, 72, 74
Pata River, 375
Paying for a baby, 175
Peace-making at Baram, 401-15
Pearl-shelling industry, 2-4, 6, 85, 121
Pelandok, 383-6
Pelican dance, 114, 189
Penchallong, 410
Penghulu, 335
Pepker the hill-maker, 64, 65
Perham, Ven. Archdeacon J., 381, 392
Perineal band, painted, 274
Personal totem, 194
Petticoats (leaf), New Guinea, 111, 175, 274
Philip, Brother, 273
Phlebotomy, 223
Phonograph, 37, 100, 200, 234, 252, 256, 273 338 ; — in a marea, 256

Photographing natives, 28
— zogos, 66
Photographs (natives recognising friends), 9
Physical features of Borneo, 348
Pictographs, 137, 140, 185
Pig-a-back, game of, 227
Pig ceremony in Sarawak, 336, 353-5, 411, 412
— hunt (game), 274
— offering of for feast, 217, 270
Pigsties, 298
"Pigeons," 74
Pile dwellings: Kiwai, 99; Saibai, 173; New Guinea, 204, 206, 208, 211, 213, 235 ; Borneo, 290, 298, 330, 331, 375
— driving, 224
— village, marine, 206, 208, 211, 235, 290
Pinupaka, village of, 266, 267, 276
Piracy, 291, 326
Plains of Borneo, 315
Plantations of the natives, 214, 234
Platforms, taboo, 208
Platylophus, 384, 385, 390
"Play" in Murray Island, 36, 37, 63
Pleiades, 381
Pokao tribe, 262
Police (native), Torres Straits, 19, 20, 76, 77
Poles, frayed, 361
Port Kennedy. Cf. Thursday Island
Port Moresby, 205, 235, 246, 248, 249
Porpoises, 151
Posts, carved, 375
Pottery, manufacture of, 200, 248, 261
Prayer to an omen bird, 344
Praying to a pig, 336, 354, 411
Presents from natives, 10, 122, 130, 172, 335, 336
Prince of Wales Island. Cf. Muralug
Procrastinating habits of Sébops, 343, 346
Proposals of marriage, 158, 162-4, 377,
Proto-Malay, 321
Psychological laboratory, 23
Psychology, experimental, 23-8, 109, 126, 200, 222
Pulu, Island of, 136-43
Punan medicine-man, 366
Punans, 302, 304, 320, 323, 324, 327, 334, 355, 384, 389, 390, 393
Punishments in Torres Straits, 20, 21
Punitive expedition in Sarawak, 301
Purchasing a stone implement, 368-74

Quaternary rocks in Borneo, 318
Queensland. Cf. Australia

Rabao (Yule Island), 199, 200, 203, 252-61, 276
Race, practice, 402,

Raiding by New Guinea natives, 247
Rain-making in Torres Straits, 33-5, 86, 87, 134
— stopping, 87
Rajah of Sarawak, 279, 282, 284, 289, 291, 293, 300, 322, 338, 341, 411
Rapids, 299, 358
Rapurapu (game), 228
Ray, S. H., 28-31, 39, 126, 127, 243, 248, 249, 252, 267, 273, 279, 298, 330, 358
— Rapids, 358
Reaction experiments, 26
Read, C. H., 372
Reefs (coral), 1, 6-8, 12, 15-18, 117, 148
Regatta at Baram, 402, 409, 410
— at Kuching, 280
Relationship between two Papuan villages, 258
Relic-fauna in Borneo, 351
Remaung (ghost-tiger), 305
Requiem Mass in New Guinea, 254
— — in Rome, 254
Reservoir in Kuching, 282; scare about heads for foundations of, 339
Resident, 293
Restrictions in food, 135, 257
Reticence of natives, 32, 45
Revolving game, 228
Rice, cultivation of. Cf. Padi
Ricketts, O. F., 285, 287, 301, 304
River scenery, 286, 358, 359
Rivers, Dr. W. H. R., 23-5, 27, 39, 59, 123, 124
Rock paintings, 137, 140, 185
Roro language, 261
— tribe, 260
Rotumah dances, 36
Roth, H. Ling, 320, 381
Rove, 258

Saba Irang, 364, 365, 410-12
Sacred Heart Mission, 203, 252-6, 262, 266-77
Sacredness, 67, 258
Sacred stones, 360, 375; of Murray Island, cf. Zogo
— words or songs, 31, 32, 45, 46, 62, 63
Sago factory, 287
— trade (native) in New Guinea, 248
— — in Sarawak, 288
Saguane village, 96-9, 104, 109
Saibai, Island of, 170-4
Salter, Dr., 1
Samaria kosker (women of Samaria), 84
Sarawak, 293
— geographical features of, 286
— history of, 291-3
— Malay, 322, 327
— Museum, 282-4, 372
Sarcophagus, 334
Sasia, 381, 384, 385, 387, 389

Saw-fish chant, 184
Scarification, 110, 113, 200
Scott-Keltie Falls, 346, 348
— — River, 345, 346
Sea-cow, 151
Sea Dayaks. Cf. Iban
Sêbop, 321, 341, 343, 346, 357, 363, 371, 404
— chief, 363
— dances, 357, 358
— fable about, 343
— girls, 356
— head-form, 343
— village, 352, 368
Seclusion of boys in Tut, 176
— of girls in Mabuiag, 135
Secret societies in Melanesia, 44
Secular dances, 188, 189, 233, 357
Seligmann, C. G., 1, 23, 28, 62, 109, 135, 154, 200, 245, 248, 279
Sengalong Burong, 384, 385, 387-9, 392
Sensitiveness to pain, 26
Shaduf, 287
Sharpe, Dr. R. B., 350
Shelford, R., 279, 283, 284, 372
Shell hoe, 109
— ornaments, 261
Shields, 357, 358, 360, 410
Shirt as symbol of loyalty, 244
Shrike, 390
Shrines in Torres Straits: Rain, 34; Tomog Zogo, 54; Zabarker, 60; wind, 60; Iriam Moris, 64; therapeutic, 65; coconut, 67, 87; fishing, 68; turtle, 69; Au Kosker, 69; Waiad, 69, 70; yam, 86; constipation, 88; navel, 142, 177, 179; of Kwoiam, 136-145
Siap (charms), 368, 370, 372, 373, 399
Sibu, town of, 284
Siberian railway, sacrifice for, 339
Sigai, 177, 179, 180
Skipping game, 227
Skull collecting, 92, 93, 120, 121, 337, 338
— cult of, 394-400
— danger of meddling with, 337, 353, 374, 399, 400
— decorated, 91, 181, 182
— divination, 92, 182
Skulls: Mer, 91-93; Mawatta, 115; Mabuiag, 120, 142; Yam, 180; Kiriri, 185; Sarawak, 332, 337, 352, 394-400
— leaving old, 398
— loaning, 395
— preparation of in Kiwai, 107
Sleeping with a sweetheart, 377
Smell, sense of (Murray Islanders), 25
Smelling a dance, 250
Smith, Mr., 280, 283
Smoking, Papuan method of, 75
Snakes, omen, 391

INDEX

Social divisions in Mekeo, 270
Sociology of Torres Straits, 19-21, 77, 118-20, 125, 145, 146; of Kiwai, 99-109; of New Guinea, 207, 208, 212-14, 242, 243, 247, 248, 270-2; of Sarawak, 327-9
Sogeri tribe, 244
Songs, chorus, 324
Sorcerer's kit, 201
Sorcerers, Mabuiag, 154, 262
— of Koitapu, 249
Sorcery, New Guinea, 83, 202
— Murray Island, 128
Soul house, 311
— of a sick woman, 310
— of the pig, 337
South Sea dances, 35
Spear-throwers, 200, 201
Speeches, 354, 355, 411, 412
Spencer, Prof. Baldwin, 134
Spiral designs, 260
Spirits (lamar), 89, 90, 340
— of sickness, 366
Star myths (Torres Straits), 165-9
St. John, Sir Spenser, 292, 294, 339, 386
St. Joseph River, 261
Stockades in New Guinea, 247
Stone adzes in use (New Guinea), 220, (Mekeo), 272; — axes, Africa, 372
— club, manufacture of, 245
— clubs, 251
— implements in Kiwai, 108
— — in Sarawak, 327, 368-72
Stones, sacred, in Borneo, 360, 375
String puzzles and tricks, 38, 39, 175, 201
Sucker fish (Echeneis), fishing with, 155
Suggestibility of natives, 27
Sumatra, geology of, 315
Sun birds, 390
Sun, moon, and night (myth of), 168
Supreme God in Sarawak, 336, 337, 352
Sultan of Brunei, 288, 300
Swimming diving, 121
Symbolic magic, 257

Taboo, 257, 270, 272
Taburi, 244
Tagai constellation, 166
Tailor bird, 390
Tama Bulan, 324, 335, 375-80, 401-6, 409-14
Taman Liri, 335
Tamar, 40, 58, 59, 62
Tamate, 95, 128. Cf. Rev. J. Chalmers
Taste, 26
Tattooed hands, 306, 395
Tattooing, 199, 204, 214, 222, 259, 305, 306, 326
— process of, in New Guinea, 222; in Borneo, 305, 306
Taxation in Sarawak, 293
Teetotum, 227

Tegulan, 360
Thief, 222
Thomas, Oldfield, 120, 142, 350
Throwing-stick, 201
Thrush, 389
Thunderbolts, 372, 373
— in Europe, 372
Thunder god, 369
Thursday Island, 1-4, 183-5, 189-93
Tiger, effigy of, 360
Tight-lacing in New Guinea, 256
Time, estimation of, 25
Tingang, 363
Tinjar River, 330, 358
Tobacco, native, 243
— pipes, Papuan, 75
Toitoi (game), 230, 231
Tomb decorations, 285
Tomog Zogo, 53-7
Tooth, knocking out, 193
Top-spinning in Murray Island, 40
— in New Guinea, 227, 272, 273
Totemism, 43, 44
— in New Guinea, 101-3
— in Queensland, 193, 194
— in Sarawak, 393
— in Torres Straits, 102, 132-5, 138, 142, 171, 172
Toy bows and arrows, 222
— throwing spear, 200
Toys: Papuan children's toys: *kuru* (diamond), 225; *kwari kwari* (hummer), 227; oboe (*vili vili*) 225-7); palm leaf puzzles (*langa*), 225-7; spear (or javelin) throwing, 200, 201, 224, 225; teetotum, 227; tops, 272, 273; whirligig, 225; whistle, 227
Trade, native: Borneo, 321-3, 356, 365; New Guinea, 204, 213, 214, 222, 261, 265, 266, 269
— on the half-profit system, 222
— voyages, 248
Tragulus, 385. Cf. Pelandok
Tree-houses in New Guinea, 242, 248
Tripang, 3
Triple-crowned coconut palm, 172
Trogon, 388
Trumpet, 225
Tuba-fishing, 324, 406, 408, 409
Tuk (New Guinea sorcery), 83, 84
Turtle charms, 69, 134, 140
— cutting up, 205, 157
— fishing, 155-7
— tracks in sand, 67
— zogo, 69
Tut, Island of, 174-8

U zogo (coconut shrine), 67
Ufapie, 258
Ukit tribe, 320, 323
Umu Belubu, 305
Urip, 354, 355, 396

Vaccination marks, 172
Vanigela River, 212
Variability of native temperament, 27
— in character of the hair, 223
Vatorata, 208, 234
Vee, 261
Vegetation, 65, 118, 212, 219, 239, 240-2, 269, 280, 281, 286, 304, 359
Veifaa, 273-6
Verandah in New Guinea houses, 99, 242, 243
— in Sarawak houses, 298, 331
Vili vili (toy), 226
Villages on top of hills, 242
Visual acuity, 23
Vitale, Father, 272

Wag Zogo (wind shrine), 60
Waiad, 69
— ceremonies, 70
Waier, Island of, 12, 17, 18, 68-70
Waima, masked men at, 271
Waipem (turtle shrine), 69
Wallace, A. Russell, 303, 348, 349
Walker, Rev. F. W., 197
War dances, 60, 131, 140, 186-8, 233, 258
Waria, chief of Mabuiag, 123
Warirata Mount, 240, 241
Warpath of the Kayans, 297
Warrior Island, 174. Cf. Tut
Waterspouts, spirits of, 141
Wauri, 156, 157
Wedding in Mabuiag, 161
Weight, discrimination of, 26
West Africa, stone axe-heads, 372
Whipping-tops, Mekeo, 272; Kabadi, 273

Whirligig, 225
Whistle, 227
Widow in mourning, 206
Wife-beating and slanging, 20, 76, 83
Wilkin, A., 27, 28, 38, 100, 157, 248, 252, 267
Wilson, Prof. T., 273
Wind charm, 60, 82
— instruments, 225
— zogo, 60
Women beating drums, 218
Women's ceremony, 219
Wooden belt, 256
— bowl, 220
— hooks, 396
— images, 104-7, 333, 360, 375
Woodpecker, 389

Yam, Island of, 174, 176, 178-80
Yam charms, 104-7, 202, 203
— zogo, 86
Yaraikanna tribe, 190
Yeku, 262
Yellow earth, 172
Yule Island. Cf. Rabao

Zab Zogo (fishing-shrine), 68
Zabarker shrine, 60
Ziai Neur Zogo, 65
Ziria, 252, 256
Ziriam Zogo, 59
Zogo, 53-70; meaning of term, 67; coconut, 87; divining skull, 91; of Wiwar (constipation), 88, 89; yam, 86
— mer (sacred words), 31, 32, 45, 46, 63
Zogole (sacred men of Murray Island), 48, 61, 70, 88, 89, 92

A CATALOGUE OF BOOKS AND ANNOUNCEMENTS OF METHUEN AND COMPANY PUBLISHERS : LONDON 36 ESSEX STREET W.C.

CONTENTS

	PAGE
FORTHCOMING BOOKS,	2
POETRY,	12
BELLES LETTRES, ANTHOLOGIES, ETC.,	12
ILLUSTRATED AND GIFT BOOKS,	16
HISTORY,	17
BIOGRAPHY,	19
TRAVEL, ADVENTURE AND TOPOGRAPHY,	21
NAVAL AND MILITARY,	23
GENERAL LITERATURE,	24
PHILOSOPHY,	26
SCIENCE,	27
THEOLOGY,	27
FICTION,	32
BOOKS FOR BOYS AND GIRLS,	42
THE PEACOCK LIBRARY,	42
UNIVERSITY EXTENSION SERIES,	42
SOCIAL QUESTIONS OF TO-DAY	43
CLASSICAL TRANSLATIONS,	44
EDUCATIONAL BOOKS,	44

NOVEMBER 1901

MESSRS. METHUEN'S ANNOUNCEMENTS

Illustrated Books and Books for Children

THE BROTHERS DALZIEL: being a Record of Fifty Years of their Work, 1840-1890. With 150 Illustrations after Pictures by Lord LEIGHTON, P.R.A., Sir J. E. MILLAIS, Bart., P.R.A., Sir E. J. POYNTER, P.R.A., HOLMAN HUNT, DANTE G. ROSSETTI, Sir JOHN TENNIEL, JOHN RUSKIN, and many others. *Quarto.* 21s. net.

THE ESSAYS OF ELIA. By CHARLES LAMB. With over 100 Illustrations by A. GARTH JONES, and an Introduction by E. V. LUCAS. *Demy 8vo.* 10s. 6d.

This is probably the most beautiful edition of Lamb's Essays that has ever been published. The illustrations display the most remarkable sympathy, insight, and skill, and the introduction is by a critic whose knowledge of Lamb is unrivalled.

THE VISIT TO LONDON. Described in verse by E. V. LUCAS, and in coloured pictures by F. D. BEDFORD. *Small 4to.* 6s.

This charming book describes the introduction of a country child to the delights and sights of London. It is the result of a well-known partnership between author and artist.

The Little Blue Books for Children
Edited by E. V. LUCAS
Illustrated. Square Fcap, 8vo. 2s. 6d.

Messrs. METHUEN have in preparation a series of children's books under the above general title. The aim of the editor is to get entertaining or exciting stories about normal children, the moral of which is implied rather than expressed. The books will be reproduced in a somewhat unusual form, which will have a certain charm of its own. The first three volumes arranged are:

1. THE CASTAWAYS OF MEADOW BANK. By T. COBB.
2. THE BEECHNUT BOOK. By JACOB ABBOTT. Edited by E. V. LUCAS.
3. THE AIR GUN: or, How the Mastermans and Dobson Major nearly lost their Holidays. By T. HILBERT.

History

CROMWELL'S ARMY: A History of the English Soldier during the Civil Wars, the Commonwealth, and the Protectorate. By C. H. FIRTH, M.A. *Crown 8vo.* 7s. 6d.

An elaborate study and description of Cromwell's army by which the victory of the Parliament was secured. The 'New Model' is described in minute detail, and the author, who is one of the most distinguished historians of the day, has made great use of unpublished MSS.

Messrs. Methuen's Announcements

ANNALS OF CHRIST'S HOSPITAL. By E. H. Pearce, M.A. With numerous illustrations. *Demy 8vo.* 7s. 6d.

A HISTORY OF RUSSIA FROM PETER THE GREAT TO ALEXANDER II. By W. R. Morfill, Jesus College, Oxford. *Crown 8vo.* 7s. 6d.

This history, by the most distinguished authority in England, is founded on a study of original documents, and though necessarily brief, is the most comprehensive narrative in existence. Considerable attention has been paid to the social and literary development of the country, and the recent expansion of Russia in Asia.

A HISTORY OF THE POLICE IN ENGLAND. By Captain Melville Lee. *Crown 8vo.* 7s. 6d.

This highly interesting book is the first history of the police force from its first beginning to its present development. Written as it is by an author of competent historical and legal qualifications, it will be indispensable to every magistrate and to all who are indirectly interested in the police force.

A HISTORY OF ENGLISH LITERATURE: From its Beginning to Tennyson. By L. Engel. *Demy 8vo.* 7s. 6d.

A HISTORY OF THE BRITISH IN INDIA. By A. D. Innes, M.A. With Maps and Plans. *Crown 8vo.* 7s. 6d.

Biography

THE LIFE OF ROBERT LOUIS STEVENSON. By Graham Balfour. *Two Volumes. Demy 8vo.* 25s. net.

This highly interesting biography has been entrusted by Mr. Stevenson's family to his cousin, Mr. Balfour, and all available materials have been placed at his disposal. The book is rich in unpublished MSS. and letters, diaries of travel, reminiscences of friends, and a valuable fragment of autobiography. It also contains a complete bibliography of all Stevenson's work. This biography of one of the most attractive and sympathetic personalities in English literature should possess a most fascinating interest. The book will be uniform with The Edinburgh Edition.

THE LIFE OF FRANÇOIS DE FENELON. By Viscount St. Cyres. With 8 Portraits. *Demy 8vo.* 10s. 6d.

This biography has engaged the author for many years, and the book is not only the study of an interesting personality, but an important contribution to the history of the period.

THE CONVERSATIONS OF JAMES NORTHCOTE, R.A. AND JAMES WARD. Edited by Ernest Fletcher. With many Portraits. *Demy 8vo.* 10s. 6d.

This highly interesting, racy, and stimulating book, contains hitherto unpublished utterances of Northcote during a period of twenty-one years. There are many reminiscences of Sir Joshua Reynolds, much advice to young painters, and many references to the great artists and great figures of the day.

Travel, Adventure and Topography

HEAD-HUNTERS, BLACK, WHITE, AND BROWN. By A. C. HADDON, Sc.D., F.R.S. With many Illustrations and a Map. *Demy 8vo.* 15s.

A narrative of adventure and exploration in Northern Borneo. It contains much matter of the highest scientific interest.

A BOOK OF BRITTANY. By S. BARING GOULD. With numerous Illustrations. *Crown 8vo.* 6s.

Uniform in scope and size with Mr. Baring Gould's well-known books on Devon, Cornwall, and Dartmoor.

General Literature

WOMEN AND THEIR WORK. By the Hon. Mrs. LYTTELTON. *Crown 8vo.* 2s. 6d.

A discussion of the present position of women in view of the various occupations and interests which are or may be open to them. There will be an introduction dealing with the general question, followed by chapters on the family, the household, philanthropic work, professions, recreation, and friendship.

ENGLISH VILLAGES. By P. H. DITCHFIELD, M.A., F.S.A. Illustrated. *Crown 8vo.* 6s.

A popular and interesting account of the history of a typical village, and of village life in general in England.

SPORTING MEMORIES. By J. OTHO PAGET. *Demy 8vo.* 12s. 6d.

This volume of reminiscences by a well-known sportsman and Master of Hounds deals chiefly with fox-hunting experiences.

Science

DRAGONS OF THE AIR. By H. G. SEELEY, F.R.S., With many Illustrations. *Crown 8vo.* 6s.

A popular history of the most remarkable flying animals which ever lived. Their relations to mammals, birds, and reptiles, living and extinct, are shown by an original series of illustrations. The scattered remains preserved in Europe and the United States have been put together accurately to show the varied forms of the animals. The book is a natural history of these extinct animals, which flew by means of a single finger.

Theology

REGNUM DEI. THE BAMPTON LECTURES OF 1901. By A. ROBERTSON, D.D., Principal of King's College, London. *Demy 8vo.* 12s. 6d. net.

This book is an endeavour to ascertain the meaning of the 'Kingdom of God' in its original prominence in the teaching of Christ. It reviews historically the main interpretations of this central idea in the successive phases of Christian tradition and life. Special attention is given to the sense in which St. Augustine identified the Church with the Kingdom of God. The later lectures follow out the alternative ideas of the Church, and of its relation to civil society which the Middle Ages and more recent types of Christian thought have founded upon alternative conceptions of the Kingdom of God.

OLD TESTAMENT HISTORY. By G. W. WADE, D.D. With Maps. *Crown 8vo.* 6s.

This book presents a connected account of the Hebrew people during the period covered by the Old Testament; and has been drawn up from the Scripture records in accordance with the methods of historical criticism. The text of the Bible has been studied in the light thrown upon it by the best modern commentators; but the reasons for the conclusions stated are not left to be sought for in the commentaries, but are discussed in the course of the narrative. Much attention has been devoted to tracing the progress of religion amongst the Hebrews, and the book, which is furnished with maps, is further adapted to the needs of theological students by the addition of geographical notes, tables, and a full index.

THE AGAPE AND THE EUCHARIST. By J. F. KEATING, D.D. *Crown 8vo.* 3s. 6d.

THE IMITATION OF CHRIST. A Revised Translation, with an Introduction, by C. BIGG, D.D., Canon of Christ Church. With Frontispiece. *Crown 8vo.* 3s. 6d.

A new edition, carefully revised and set in large type, of Dr. Bigg's well-known version.

Oxford Commentaries

General Editor, WALTER LOCK, D.D., Warden of Keble College, Dean Ireland's Professor of Exegesis in the University of Oxford.

THE ACTS OF THE APOSTLES: With Introduction and Notes by R. B. RACKHAM, M.A. *Demy 8vo.* 12s. 6d.

The Churchman's Library

General Editor, J. H. BURN, B.D., Examining Chaplain to the Bishop of Aberdeen.

THE OLD TESTAMENT AND THE NEW SCHOLARSHIP. By J. W. PETERS, D.D. *Crown 8vo.* 6s.

COMPARATIVE RELIGION. By J. A. MACCULLOCK. *Crown 8vo.*

THE CHURCH OF CHRIST. By E. T. GREEN. *Crown 8vo.*

THE CHURCHMAN'S INTRODUCTION TO THE OLD TESTAMENT. Edited by ANGUS M. MACKAY, B.A. *Crown 8vo.* 3s. 6d.

The Churchman's Bible

General Editor, J. H. BURN, B.D.

Messrs. METHUEN are issuing a series of expositions upon most of the books of the Bible. The volumes will be practical and devotional, and the text of the authorised version is explained in sections, which will correspond as far as possible with the Church Lectionary.

ISAIAH. Edited by W. E. BARNES, D.D., Fellow of Peterhouse, Cambridge. *Two Volumes. 2s. net each.*

THE EPISTLE OF ST. PAUL THE APOSTLE TO THE EPHESIANS. Edited by G. H. WHITAKER. *1s. 6d. net.*

The Library of Devotion

Pott 8vo, cloth, 2s. ; leather, 2s. 6d. net.

'This series is excellent.'—THE BISHOP OF LONDON.
'Very delightful.'—THE BISHOP OF BATH AND WELLS.
'Well worth the attention of the Clergy.'—THE BISHOP OF LICHFIELD.
'The new "Library of Devotion" is excellent.'—THE BISHOP OF PETERBOROUGH.
'Charming.'—*Record.* 'Delightful.'—*Church Bells.*

THE THOUGHTS OF PASCAL. Edited with an Introduction and Notes by C. S. JERRAM, M.A.

ON THE LOVE OF GOD. By ST. FRANCIS DE SALES. Edited by W. J. KNOX-LITTLE, M.A.

A MANUAL OF CONSOLATION FROM THE SAINTS AND FATHERS. Edited by J. H. BURN, B.D.

THE SONG OF SONGS. Being Selections from ST. BERNARD. Edited by B. BLAXLAND, M.A.

Leaders of Religion

Edited by H. C. BEECHING, M.A. *With Portraits, Crown 8vo. 3s. 6d.*

A series of short biographies of the most prominent leaders of religious life and thought of all ages and countries.

BISHOP BUTLER. By W. A. SPOONER, M.A., Fellow of New College, Oxford.

Educational Books

COMMERCIAL EDUCATION IN THEORY AND PRACTICE. By E. E. WHITFIELD, M.A. *Crown 8vo. 5s.*

An introduction to Methuen's Commercial Series treating the question of Commercial Education fully from both the point of view of the teacher and of the parent.

EASY GREEK EXERCISES. By C. G. BOTTING, M.A. *Crown 8vo. 2s.*

GERMAN VOCABULARIES FOR REPETITION. By SOPHIE WRIGHT. *Fcap. 8vo. 1s. 6d.*

A COMMERCIAL GEOGRAPHY OF FOREIGN NATIONS.
By F. C. Boon, B.A. *Crown 8vo.* 2s.

JUNIOR EXAMINATION SERIES. Edited by
A. M. M. Stedman, M.A. *Fcap. 8vo.* 1s.

French Examination Papers. By F. Jacob, B.A.
Latin Examination Papers. By C. G. Botting, M.A.
Algebra Examination Papers. By Austen S. Lester, M.A.
English Grammar Examination Papers. By W. Williamson, B.A.

Fiction

THE HISTORY OF SIR RICHARD CALMADY: A Romance.
By Lucas Malet, Author of 'The Wages of Sin.' *Crown 8vo.* 6s.

This is the first long and elaborate book by Lucas Malet since 'The Wages of Sin.' It is a romance on realistic lines, and will certainly be one of the most important novels of the last ten years.

This novel, the scene of which is laid in the moorland country of the northern part of Hampshire, in London, and in Naples, opens in the year of grace 1842. The action covers a period of about three and thirty years; and deals with the experiences and adventures of an English country gentleman of an essentially normal type of character, subjected—owing to somewhat distressing antecedent circumstances—to very abnormal conditions of life. The book is frankly a romance; but it is also frankly a realistic and modern one.

THE SERIOUS WOOING: A Heart's History. By Mrs. Craigie (John Oliver Hobbes), Author of 'Robert Orange.' *Crown 8vo.* 6s.

LIGHT FREIGHTS. By W. W. Jacobs, Author of 'Many Cargoes.' Illustrated. *Crown 8vo.* 3s. 6d.

A volume of stories by Mr. Jacobs uniform in character and appearance with 'Many Cargoes.'

CLEMENTINA. By A. E. W. Mason, Author of 'The Courtship of Morrice Buckler,' 'Miranda of the Balcony,' etc. Illustrated. *Crown 8vo* 6s.

A spirited romance of the Jacobites somewhat after the manner of 'Morrice Buckler.' The Old Pretender is introduced as one of the chief characters.

A WOMAN ALONE. By Mrs. W. K. Clifford, Author of 'Aunt Anne.' *Crown 8vo.* 3s. 6d.

A volume of stories.

THE STRIKING HOURS. By Eden Phillpotts, Author of 'Children of the Mist,' 'Sons of the Morning,' etc. *Crown 8vo.* 6s.

The annals of a Devon village, containing much matter of humorous and pathetic interest.

MESSRS. METHUEN'S ANNOUNCEMENTS

FANCY FREE. By EDEN PHILLPOTTS, Author of 'Children of the Mist.' Illustrated. *Crown 8vo.* 6s.
A humorous book. Uniform with 'The Human Boy.'

TALES OF DUNSTABLE WEIR. By GWENDOLINE KEATS (ZACK). Author of 'Life is Life.' With Photogravure Frontispiece by E. W. HARTRICK. *Crown 8vo.* 6s.
A volume of stories after the style of 'Zack's' well-known first book 'Life is Life.'

ANGEL. By Mrs. B. M. CROKER. *Crown 8vo.* 6s.

THE PROPHET OF BERKELEY SQUARE. By ROBERT HICHENS, Author of 'Flames,' 'Tongues of Conscience,' etc. *Crown 8vo.* 6s.
A new long novel.

THE ALIEN. By F. F. MONTRESOR, Author of 'Into the Highways and Hedges.' *Crown 8vo.* 6s.

THE EMBARRASSING ORPHAN. By W. E. NORRIS. Illustrated. *Crown 8vo.* 6s.

ROYAL GEORGIE. By S. BARING GOULD, Author of 'Mehalah.' With eight Illustrations by D. MURRAY SMITH. *Crown 8vo.* 6s.

FORTUNE'S DARLING. By WALTER RAYMOND, Author of 'Love and Quiet Life.' *Crown 8vo.* 6s.

THE MILLION. By DOROTHEA GERARD, Author of 'Lady Baby.' *Crown 8vo.* 6s.

FROM THE LAND OF THE SHAMROCK. By JANE BARLOW, Author of 'Irish Idylls.' *Crown 8vo.* 6s.

THE WOOING OF SHEILA. By GRACE RHYS. *Crown 8vo.* 6s.

RICKERBY'S FOLLY. By TOM GALLON, Author of 'Kiddy.' *Crown 8vo.* 6s.

A GREAT LADY. By ADELINE SERGEANT, Author of 'The Story of a Penitent Soul.' *Crown 8vo.* 6s.

MARY HAMILTON. By LORD ERNEST HAMILTON. *Crown 8vo.* 6s.

MASTER OF MEN. By E. PHILLIPS OPPENHEIM. *Crown 8vo.* 6s.

BOTH SIDES OF THE VEIL. By RICHARD MARSH, Author of 'The Seen and the Unseen.' *Crown 8vo.* 6s.

A GALLANT QUAKER. By Mrs. ROBERTON. Illustrated by A. H. BUCKLAND. *Crown 8vo.* 6s.

MESSRS. METHUEN'S ANNOUNCEMENTS

THE THIRTEEN EVENINGS. By GEORGE BARTRAM, Author of 'The People of Clopton.' *Crown 8vo.* 6s.

THE SKIRTS OF HAPPY CHANCE. By H. B. MARRIOTT WATSON. Illustrated. *Crown 8vo.* 6s.

A FOOL'S YEAR. By E. H. COOPER, Author of 'Mr. Blake of Newmarket.' *Crown 8vo.* 6s.

This book, like most of Mr. Cooper's novels, is chiefly concerned with sport and racing.

THE YEAR ONE: A Page of the French Revolution. By J. BLOUNDELLE BURTON, Author of 'The Clash of Arms.' Illustrated. *Crown 8vo.* 6s.

THE DEVASTATORS. By ADA CAMBRIDGE, Author of 'Path and Goal.' *Crown 8vo.* 6s.

THE FORTUNE OF CHRISTINA M'NAB. By S. MACNAUGHTAN. *Crown 8vo.* 6s.

JOHN TOPP: Pirate. By WEATHERBY CHESNEY. *Crown 8vo.* 6s.

The Novelist

Messrs. METHUEN are issuing under the above general title a Monthly Series of Novels by popular authors at the price of Sixpence. Each Number is as long as the average Six Shilling Novel.

XXIII. THE HUMAN BOY.   EDEN PHILLPOTTS.

XXIV. THE CHRONICLES OF COUNT ANTONIO.   ANTHONY HOPE.

XXV. BY STROKE OF SWORD.   ANDREW BALFOUR.

XXVI. KITTY ALONE.   S. BARING GOULD.
                                                                    [*October*.

Methuen's Sixpenny Library

A New Series of Copyright Books.

THE CONQUEST OF LONDON.   DOROTHEA GERARD.

A VOYAGE OF CONSOLATION.   SARA J. DUNCAN.

THE MUTABLE MANY.   ROBERT BARR.

A CATALOGUE OF

Messrs. Methuen's
PUBLICATIONS

Poetry

Rudyard Kipling. BARRACK-ROOM BALLADS. By RUDYARD KIPLING. 68th Thousand. Crown 8vo. 6s. Leather, 6s. net.

'Mr. Kipling's verse is strong, vivid, full of character.... Unmistakeable genius rings in every line.'—*Times*.

'The ballads teem with imagination, they palpitate with emotion. We read them with laughter and tears; the metres throb in our pulses, the cunningly ordered words tingle with life; and if this be not poetry, what is?'—*Pall Mall Gazette*.

Rudyard Kipling. THE SEVEN SEAS. By RUDYARD KIPLING. 57th Thousand. Cr. 8vo. Buckram, gilt top. 6s. Leather, 6s. net.

'The Empire has found a singer; it is no depreciation of the songs to say that statesmen may have, one way or other, to take account of them.'—*Manchester Guardian*.

'Animated through and through with indubitable genius.'—*Daily Telegraph*.

"Q." POEMS AND BALLADS. By "Q." Crown 8vo. 3s. 6d.

"Q." GREEN BAYS: Verses and Parodies. By "Q." Second Edition. Crown 8vo. 3s. 6d.

H. Ibsen. BRAND. A Drama by HENRIK IBSEN. Translated by WILLIAM WILSON. Third Edition. Crown 8vo. 3s. 6d.

A. D. Godley. LYRA FRIVOLA. By A. D. GODLEY, M.A., Fellow of Magdalen College, Oxford. Third Edition. Pott 8vo. 2s. 6d.

'Combines a pretty wit with remarkably neat versification.... Every one will wish there was more of it.'—*Times*.

A. D. Godley. VERSES TO ORDER. By A. D. GODLEY. Crown 8vo. 2s. 6d. net.

J. G. Cordery. THE ODYSSEY OF HOMER. A Translation by J. G. CORDERY. Crown 8vo. 7s. 6d.

Herbert Trench. DEIRDRE WED: and Other Poems. By HERBERT TRENCH. Crown 8vo. 5s.

Edgar Wallace. WRIT IN BARRACKS. By EDGAR WALLACE. Crown 8vo. 3s. 6d.

Belles Lettres, Anthologies, etc.

R. L. Stevenson. VAILIMA LETTERS. By ROBERT LOUIS STEVENSON. With an Etched Portrait by WILLIAM STRANG. Third Edition. Crown 8vo. Buckram. 6s.

'A fascinating book.'—*Standard*.
'Unique in Literature.'—*Daily Chronicle*.

G. Wyndham. THE POEMS OF WILLIAM SHAKESPEARE. Edited with an Introduction and Notes by GEORGE WYNDHAM, M.P. Demy 8vo. Buckram, gilt top. 10s. 6d.

This edition contains the 'Venus,' 'Lucrece,' and Sonnets, and is prefaced with an elaborate introduction of over 140 pp.

'We have no hesitation in describing Mr. George Wyndham's introduction as a masterly piece of criticism, and all who love our Elizabethan literature will find a very garden of delight in it.'—*Spectator*.

MESSRS. METHUEN'S CATALOGUE

Edward FitzGerald. THE RUBAIYAT OF OMAR KHAYYAM. Translated by EDWARD FITZGERALD. With a Commentary by H. M. BATSON, and a Biography of Omar by E. D. ROSS. 6s. Also an Edition on large paper limited to 50 copies.

'One of the most desirable of the many reprints of Omar.'—*Glasgow Herald*.

W. E. Henley. ENGLISH LYRICS. Selected and Edited by W. E. HENLEY. *Crown 8vo. Gilt top. 3s. 6d.*

'It is a body of choice and lovely poetry.'—*Birmingham Gazette*.

Henley and Whibley. A BOOK OF ENGLISH PROSE. Collected by W. E. HENLEY and CHARLES WHIBLEY. *Crown 8vo. Buckram, gilt top. 6s.*

H. C. Beeching. LYRA SACRA: An Anthology of Sacred Verse. Edited by H. C. BEECHING, M.A. *Crown 8vo. Buckram. 6s.*

'A charming selection, which maintains a lofty standard of excellence.'—*Times*.

"Q." THE GOLDEN POMP. A Procession of English Lyrics. Arranged by A. T. QUILLER COUCH. *Crown 8vo. Buckram. 6s.*

W. B. Yeats. AN ANTHOLOGY OF IRISH VERSE. Edited by W. B. YEATS. *Revised and Enlarged Edition. Crown 8vo. 3s. 6d.*

W. M. Dixon. A PRIMER OF TENNYSON. By W. M. DIXON, M.A. *Cr. 8vo. 2s. 6d.*

'Much sound and well-expressed criticism. The bibliography is a boon.'—*Speaker*.

W. A. Craigie. A PRIMER OF BURNS. By W. A. CRAIGIE. *Crown 8vo. 2s. 6d.*

'A valuable addition to the literature of the poet.'—*Times*.

G. W. Steevens. MONOLOGUES OF THE DEAD. By G. W. STEEVENS. *Foolscap 8vo. 3s. 6d.*

L. Magnus. A PRIMER OF WORDSWORTH. By LAURIE MAGNUS. *Crown 8vo. 2s. 6d.*

'A valuable contribution to Wordsworthian literature.'—*Literature*.

Sterne. THE LIFE AND OPINIONS OF TRISTRAM SHANDY. By LAWRENCE STERNE. With an Introduction by CHARLES WHIBLEY, and a Portrait. 2 *vols. 7s.*

Congreve. THE COMEDIES OF WILLIAM CONGREVE. With an Introduction by G. S. STREET, and a Portrait. 2 *vols. 7s.*

Morier. THE ADVENTURES OF HAJJI BABA OF ISPAHAN. By JAMES MORIER. With an Introduction by E. G. BROWNE, M.A. and a Portrait. 2 *vols. 7s.*

Walton. THE LIVES OF DONNE, WOTTON, HOOKER, HERBERT AND SANDERSON. By IZAAK WALTON. With an Introduction by VERNON BLACKBURN, and a Portrait. *3s. 6d.*

Johnson. THE LIVES OF THE ENGLISH POETS. By SAMUEL JOHNSON, LL.D. With an Introduction by J. H. MILLAR, and a Portrait. 3 *vols. 10s. 6d.*

Burns. THE POEMS OF ROBERT BURNS. Edited by ANDREW LANG and W. A. CRAIGIE. With Portrait. *Second Edition. Demy 8vo, gilt top. 6s.*

F. Langbridge. BALLADS OF THE BRAVE; Poems of Chivalry, Enterprise, Courage, and Constancy. Edited by Rev. F. LANGBRIDGE. *Second Edition. Cr. 8vo. 3s. 6d. School Edition. 2s. 6d.*

'The book is full of splendid things.'—*World*.

Methuen's Standard Library

Gibbon. MEMOIRS OF MY LIFE AND WRITINGS. By EDWARD GIBBON. Edited, with an Introduction and Notes, by G. BIRKBECK HILL, LL.D. *Crown 8vo. 6s.*

'An admirable edition of one of the most interesting personal records of a literary life. Its notes and its numerous appendices are a repertory of almost all that can be known about Gibbon.'—*Manchester Guardian*.

Gibbon. THE DECLINE AND FALL OF THE ROMAN EMPIRE. By EDWARD GIBBON. A New Edition, Edited with Notes, Appendices, and Maps, by J. B. BURY, LL.D., Fellow of Trinity College, Dublin. *In Seven Volumes. Demy 8vo. Gilt top. 8s. 6d. each. Also Cr. 8vo. 6s. each.*

'At last there is an adequate modern edition of Gibbon.... The best edition the nineteenth century could produce.'—*Manchester Guardian.*

'A great piece of editing.'—*Academy.*

Gilbert White. THE NATURAL HISTORY OF SELBORNE. By GILBERT WHITE. Edited by L. C. MIALL, F.R.S., assisted by W. WARDE FOWLER, M.A. *Crown 8vo. 6s.*

C. G. Crump. THE HISTORY OF THE LIFE OF THOMAS ELLWOOD. Edited by C. G. CRUMP, M.A. *Crown 8vo. 6s.*

This edition is the only one which contains the complete book as originally published. It contains a long Introduction and many Footnotes.

Dante. LA COMMEDIA DI DANTE ALIGHIERI. The Italian Text edited by PAGET TOYNBEE, M.A. *Demy 8vo. Gilt top. 8s. 6d. Also Crown 8vo. 6s.*

Tennyson. THE EARLY POEMS OF ALFRED, LORD TENNYSON, Edited, with Notes and an Introduction by J. CHURTON COLLINS, M.A. *Crown 8vo. 6s.*

An elaborate edition of the celebrated volume which was published in its final and definitive form in 1853. This edition contains a long Introduction and copious Notes, textual and explanatory. It also contains in an Appendix all the Poems which Tennyson afterwards omitted.

Jonathan Swift. THE JOURNAL TO STELLA. By JONATHAN SWIFT. Edited by G. A. AITKEN. *Crown 8vo. 6s.*

Chesterfield. THE LETTERS OF LORD CHESTERFIELD TO HIS SON. Edited, with an Introduction by C. STRACHEY, and Notes by A. CALTHROP. *Two Volumes. Crown 8vo. 6s. each.*

The Works of Shakespeare

General Editor, EDWARD DOWDEN, Litt.D.

Messrs. METHUEN have in preparation an Edition of Shakespeare in single Plays. Each play will be edited with a full Introduction, Textual Notes, and a Commentary at the foot of the page.

The first volumes are:

HAMLET. Edited by EDWARD DOWDEN. *Demy 8vo. 3s. 6d.*

'Fully up to the level of recent scholarship, both English and German.'—*Academy.*

ROMEO AND JULIET. Edited by EDWARD DOWDEN, Litt.D. *Demy 8vo. 3s. 6d.*

'No edition of Shakespeare is likely to prove more attractive and satisfactory than this one. It is beautifully printed and paged and handsomely and simply bound.'—*St. James's Gazette.*

The Novels of Charles Dickens

Crown 8vo. Each Volume, cloth 3s. net; leather 4s. 6d. net.

With Introductions by Mr. GEORGE GISSING, Notes by Mr. F. G. KITTON, and Topographical Illustrations.

THE PICKWICK PAPERS. With Illustrations by E. H. NEW. *Two Volumes.*

'As pleasant a copy as any one could desire. The notes add much to the value of the edition, and Mr. New's illustrations are also historical. The volumes promise well for the success of the edition.'—*Scotsman.*

NICHOLAS NICKLEBY. With Illustrations by R. J. WILLIAMS. *Two Volumes.*

BLEAK HOUSE. With Illustrations by BEATRICE ALCOCK. *Two Volumes*.
OLIVER TWIST. With Illustrations by G. H. NEW.
THE OLD CURIOSITY SHOP. With Illustrations by G. M. BRIMELOW. *Two Volumes*.
BARNABY RUDGE. With Illustrations by BEATRICE ALCOCK. *Two Volumes*.

Little Biographies

Fcap. 8vo. Each volume, cloth, 3s. 6d.

THE LIFE OF DANTE ALIGHIERI. By PAGET TOYNBEE. With 12 Illustrations. *Second Edition*.

'This excellent little volume is a clear, compact, and convenient summary of the whole subject.'—*Academy*.

THE LIFE OF SAVONAROLA. By E. L. S. HORSBURGH, M.A. With Portraits and Illustrations.

The Little Library

With Introductions, Notes, and Photogravure Frontispieces.

Pott 8vo. Each Volume, cloth 1s. 6d. net, leather 2s. 6d. net.

'Altogether good to look upon, and to handle.'—*Outlook*.
'In printing, binding, lightness, etc., this is a perfect series.'—*Pilot*.
'It is difficult to conceive more attractive volumes.'—*St. James's Gazette*.
'Very delicious little books.'—*Literature*.
'Delightful editions.'—*Record*.
'Exceedingly tastefully produced.'—*Morning Leader*.

VANITY FAIR. By W. M. THACKERAY. With an Introduction by S. GWYNN. *Three Volumes*.

THE PRINCESS. By ALFRED, LORD TENNYSON. Edited by ELIZABETH WORDSWORTH.

IN MEMORIAM. By ALFRED, LORD TENNYSON. Edited, with an Introduction and Notes, by H. C. BEECHING, M.A.

THE EARLY POEMS OF ALFRED, LORD TENNYSON. Edited by J. C. COLLINS, M.A.

MAUD. By ALFRED, LORD TENNYSON. Edited by ELIZABETH WORDSWORTH.

A LITTLE BOOK OF ENGLISH LYRICS. With Notes.

EOTHEN. By A. W. KINGLAKE. With an Introduction and Notes.

CRANFORD. By Mrs. GASKELL. Edited by E. V. LUCAS.

THE INFERNO OF DANTE. Translated by H. F. CARY. Edited by PAGET TOYNBEE.

THE PURGATORIO OF DANTE. Translated by H. F. CARY. Edited by PAGET TOYNBEE, M.A.

JOHN HALIFAX, GENTLEMAN. By Mrs. CRAIK. Edited by ANNIE MATHESON. *Two Volumes*.

A LITTLE BOOK OF SCOTTISH VERSE. Arranged and edited by T. F. HENDERSON.

A LITTLE BOOK OF ENGLISH PROSE. Arranged and edited by Mrs. P. A. BARNETT.

SELECTIONS FROM WORDSWORTH. Edited by NOWELL C. SMITH, Fellow of New College, Oxford.

SELECTIONS FROM WILLIAM BLAKE. Edited by M. PERUGINI.

PRIDE AND PREJUDICE. By JANE AUSTEN. Edited by E. V. LUCAS. *Two Volumes*.

PENDENNIS. By W. M. THACKERAY. Edited by S. GWYNN. *Three Volumes*.

LAVENGRO. By GEORGE BORROW. Edited by F. HINDES GROOME. *Two Volumes*.

The Little Guides

Pott 8vo, cloth 3s.; leather, 3s. 6d. net.

OXFORD AND ITS COLLEGES. By J. WELLS, M.A., Fellow and Tutor of Wadham College. Illustrated by E. H. NEW. *Fourth Edition.*

'An admirable and accurate little treatise, attractively illustrated.'—*World.*

CAMBRIDGE AND ITS COLLEGES. By A. HAMILTON THOMPSON. Illustrated by E. H. NEW.

'It is brightly written and learned, and is just such a book as a cultured visitor needs.'—*Scotsman.*

THE MALVERN COUNTRY. By B. C. A. WINDLE, D.Sc., F.R.S. Illustrated by E. H. NEW.

SHAKESPEARE'S COUNTRY. By B. C. A. WINDLE, F.R.S., M.A. Illustrated by E. H. NEW. *Second Edition.*

'One of the most charming guide books. Both for the library and as a travelling companion the book is equally choice and serviceable.'—*Academy.*

SUSSEX. By F. G. BRABANT, M.A. Illustrated by E. H. NEW.

'A charming little book; as full of sound information as it is practical in conception.'—*Athenæum.*

'Accurate, complete, and agreeably written.'—*Literature.*

WESTMINSTER ABBEY. By G. E. TROUTBECK. Illustrated by F. D. BEDFORD.

'A delightful miniature hand-book.'—*Glasgow Herald.*

'In comeliness, and perhaps in completeness, this work must take the first place.'—*Academy.*

'A really first-rate guide-book.'—*Literature.*

Illustrated and Gift Books

Tennyson. THE EARLY POEMS OF ALFRED, LORD TENNYSON. Edited, with Notes and an Introduction by J. CHURTON COLLINS, M.A. With 10 Illustrations in Photogravure by W. E. F. BRITTEN. *Demy 8vo.* 10s. 6d.

Gelett Burgess. GOOPS AND HOW TO BE THEM. By GELETT BURGESS. With numerous Illustrations. *Small 4to.* 6s.

Gelett Burgess. THE LIVELY CITY OF LIGG. By GELETT BURGESS. With 53 Illustrations, 8 of which are coloured. *Small 4to.* 6s.

Phil May. THE PHIL MAY ALBUM. *4to.* 6s.

'There is a laugh in each drawing.'—*Standard.*

A. H. Milne. ULYSSES; OR, DE ROUGEMONT OF TROY. Described and depicted by A. H. MILNE. *Small quarto.* 3s. 6d.

'Clever, droll, smart.'—*Guardian.*

Edmund Selous. TOMMY SMITH'S ANIMALS. By EDMUND SELOUS. Illustrated by G. W. ORD. *Fcap. 8vo.* 2s. 6d.

A little book designed to teach children respect and reverence for animals.

'A quaint, fascinating little book: a nursery classic.'—*Athenæum.*

S. Baring Gould. THE CROCK OF GOLD. Fairy Stories told by S. BARING GOULD. *Crown 8vo.* 6s.

'Twelve delightful fairy tales.'—*Punch.*

M. L. Gwynn. A BIRTHDAY BOOK. Arranged and Edited by M. L. GWYNN. *Royal 8vo.* 12s.

This is a birthday-book of exceptional dignity, and the extracts have been chosen with particular care.

John Bunyan. THE PILGRIM'S PROGRESS. By JOHN BUNYAN. Edited, with an Introduction, by C. H. FIRTH, M.A. With 39 Illustrations by R. ANNING BELL. *Crown 8vo.* 6s.

'The best "Pilgrim's Progress."'—*Educational Times.*

F. D. Bedford. NURSERY RHYMES. With many Coloured Pictures by F. D. BEDFORD. *Super Royal 8vo.* 2s. 6d.

S. Baring Gould. A BOOK OF FAIRY TALES retold by S. BARING GOULD. With numerous Illustrations and Initial Letters by ARTHUR J. GASKIN. *Second Edition. Cr. 8vo. Buckram.* 6s.

S. Baring Gould. OLD ENGLISH FAIRY TALES. Collected and edited by S. BARING GOULD. With Numerous Illustrations by F. D. BEDFORD. *Second Edition. Cr. 8vo. Buckram.* 6s.
'A charming volume.'—*Guardian.*

S. Baring Gould. A BOOK OF NURSERY SONGS AND RHYMES. Edited by S. BARING GOULD, and Illustrated by the Birmingham Art School. *Buckram, gilt top. Crown 8vo.* 6s.

H. C. Beeching. A BOOK OF CHRISTMAS VERSE. Edited by H. C. BEECHING, M.A., and Illustrated by WALTER CRANE. *Cr. 8vo, gilt top.* 3s. 6d.

History

Flinders Petrie. A HISTORY OF EGYPT, FROM THE EARLIEST TIMES TO THE PRESENT DAY. Edited by W. M. FLINDERS PETRIE, D.C.L., LL.D., Professor of Egyptology at University College. *Fully Illustrated. In Six Volumes. Cr. 8vo.* 6s. *each.*

VOL. I. PREHISTORIC TIMES TO XVITH DYNASTY. W. M. F. Petrie. *Fourth Edition.*

VOL. II. THE XVIITH AND XVIIITH DYNASTIES. W. M. F. Petrie. *Third Edition.*

VOL. IV. THE EGYPT OF THE PTOLEMIES. J. P. Mahaffy.

VOL. V. ROMAN EGYPT. J. G. Milne.

VOL. VI. EGYPT IN THE MIDDLE AGES. STANLEY LANE-POOLE.

'A history written in the spirit of scientific precision so worthily represented by Dr. Petrie and his school cannot but promote sound and accurate study, and supply a vacant place in the English literature of Egyptology.'—*Times.*

Flinders Petrie. RELIGION AND CONSCIENCE IN ANCIENT EGYPT. By W. M. FLINDERS PETRIE, D.C.L., LL.D. Fully Illustrated. *Crown 8vo.* 2s. 6d.

'The lectures will afford a fund of valuable information for students of ancient ethics.'—*Manchester Guardian.*

Flinders Petrie. SYRIA AND EGYPT, FROM THE TELL EL AMARNA TABLETS. By W. M. FLINDERS PETRIE, D.C.L., LL.D. *Crown 8vo.* 2s. 6d.

'A marvellous record. The addition made to our knowledge is nothing short of amazing.'—*Times.*

Flinders Petrie. EGYPTIAN TALES. Edited by W. M. FLINDERS PETRIE. Illustrated by TRISTRAM ELLIS. *In Two Volumes. Cr. 8vo.* 3s. 6d. *each.*

'Invaluable as a picture of life in Palestine and Egypt.'—*Daily News.*

Flinders Petrie. EGYPTIAN DECORATIVE ART. By W. M. FLINDERS PETRIE. With 120 Illustrations. *Cr. 8vo.* 3s. 6d.

'In these lectures he displays rare skill in elucidating the development of decorative art in Egypt.'—*Times.*

C. W. Oman. A HISTORY OF THE ART OF WAR. Vol. II.: The Middle Ages, from the Fourth to the Fourteenth Century. By C. W. OMAN, M.A., Fellow of All Souls', Oxford. Illustrated. *Demy 8vo.* 21s.

'The whole art of war in its historic evolution has never been treated on such an ample and comprehensive scale, and we question if any recent contribution to the exact history of the world has possessed more enduring value.'—*Daily Chronicle.*

S. Baring Gould. THE TRAGEDY OF THE CÆSARS. With numerous Illustrations from Busts, Gems, Cameos, etc. By S. BARING GOULD. *Fifth Edition. Royal 8vo.* 15s.

'A most splendid and fascinating book on a subject of undying interest. The great feature of the book is the use the author has made of the existing portraits of the Cæsars and the admirable critical subtlety he has exhibited in dealing with this line of research. It is brilliantly written, and the illustrations are supplied on a scale of profuse magnificence.' —*Daily Chronicle.*

F. W. Maitland. CANON LAW IN ENGLAND. By F. W. MAITLAND, LL.D., Downing Professor of the Laws of England in the University of Cambridge. *Royal 8vo.* 7s. 6d.

'Professor Maitland has put students of English law under a fresh debt. These essays are landmarks in the study of the history of Canon Law.' —*Times.*

John Hackett. A HISTORY OF THE CHURCH OF CYPRUS. By JOHN HACKETT, M.A. With Maps and Illustrations. *Demy 8vo.* 15s. *net.*

A work which brings together all that is known on the subject from the introduction of Christianity to the commencement of the British occupation. A separate division deals with the local Latin Church during the period of the Western Supremacy.

E. L. Taunton. A HISTORY OF THE JESUITS IN ENGLAND. By E. L. TAUNTON. With Illustrations. *Demy 8vo.* 21s. *net.*

'A history of permanent value, which covers ground never properly investigated before, and is replete with the results of original research. A most interesting and careful book.' —*Literature.*

'A volume which will attract considerable attention.' —*Athenæum.*

H. de B. Gibbins. INDUSTRY IN ENGLAND: HISTORICAL OUTLINES. By H. DE B. GIBBINS, Litt.D., M.A. With 5 Maps. *Second Edition. Demy 8vo.* 10s. 6d.

H. E. Egerton. A HISTORY OF BRITISH COLONIAL POLICY. By H. E. EGERTON, M.A. *Demy 8vo.* 12s. 6d.

'It is a good book, distinguished by accuracy in detail, clear arrangement of facts, and a broad grasp of principles.' —*Manchester Guardian.*

Albert Sorel. THE EASTERN QUESTION IN THE EIGHTEENTH CENTURY. By ALBERT SOREL. Translated by F. C. BRAMWELL, M.A. *Cr. 8vo.* 3s. 6d.

C. H. Grinling. A HISTORY OF THE GREAT NORTHERN RAILWAY, 1845-95. By C. H. GRINLING. With Illustrations. *Demy 8vo.* 10s. 6d.

'Mr. Grinling has done for a Railway what Macaulay did for English History.' —*The Engineer.*

Clement Stretton. A HISTORY OF THE MIDLAND RAILWAY. By CLEMENT STRETTON. With numerous Illustrations. *Demy 8vo.* 12s. 6d.

'A fine record of railway development.' —*Outlook.*

'The volume is as exhaustive as it is comprehensive, and is made especially attractive by its pictures.' —*Globe.*

W. Sterry. ANNALS OF ETON COLLEGE. By W. STERRY, M.A. With numerous Illustrations. *Demy 8vo.* 7s. 6d.

'A treasury of quaint and interesting reading. Mr. Sterry has by his skill and vivacity given these records new life.' —*Academy.*

G. W. Fisher. ANNALS OF SHREWSBURY SCHOOL. By G. W. FISHER, M.A. With numerous Illustrations. *Demy 8vo.* 10s. 6d.

'This careful, erudite book.' —*Daily Chronicle.*

'A book of which Old Salopians are sure to be proud.' —*Globe.*

J. Sargeaunt. ANNALS OF WESTMINSTER SCHOOL. By J. SARGEAUNT, M.A. With numerous Illustrations. *Demy 8vo.* 7s. 6d.

A. Clark. THE COLLEGES OF OXFORD: Their History and their Traditions. Edited by A. CLARK, M.A., Fellow of Lincoln College. *8vo.* 12s. 6d.

'A work which will be appealed to for many years as the standard book.' —*Athenæum.*

T. M. Taylor. A CONSTITUTIONAL AND POLITICAL HISTORY OF ROME. By T. M. TAYLOR, M.A., Fellow of Gonville and Caius College, Cambridge. *Crown 8vo.* 7s. 6d.

'We fully recognise the value of this carefully written work, and admire especially the fairness and sobriety of his judgment and the human interest with which he has inspired a subject which in some hands becomes a mere series of cold abstractions. It is a work that will be stimulating to the student of Roman history.'—*Athenæum.*

J. Wells. A SHORT HISTORY OF ROME. By J. WELLS, M.A., Fellow and Tutor of Wadham Coll., Oxford. *Third Edition.* With 3 Maps. *Crown 8vo.* 3s. 6d.

This book is intended for the Middle and Upper Forms of Public Schools and for Pass Students at the Universities. It contains copious Tables, etc.

'An original work written on an original plan, and with uncommon freshness and vigour.'—*Speaker.*

O. Browning. A SHORT HISTORY OF MEDIÆVAL ITALY, A.D. 1250-1530. By OSCAR BROWNING, Fellow and Tutor of King's College, Cambridge. *In Two Volumes. Cr. 8vo.* 5s. each.

VOL. I. 1250-1409.—Guelphs and Ghibellines.

VOL. II. 1409-1530.—The Age of the Condottieri.

O'Grady. THE STORY OF IRELAND. By STANDISH O'GRADY, Author of 'Finn and his Companions.' *Crown 8vo.* 2s. 6d.

Byzantine Texts

Edited by J. B. BURY, M.A., Litt.D.

ZACHARIAH OF MITYLENE. Translated into English by F. J. HAMILTON, D.D., and E. W. BROOKS. *Demy 8vo.* 12s. 6d. net.

EVAGRIUS. Edited by Professor LÉON PARMENTIER and M. BIDEZ. *Demy 8vo.* 10s. 6d. net.

THE HISTORY OF PSELLUS By C. SATHAS. *Demy 8vo.* 15s. net.

Biography

R. L. Stevenson. THE LETTERS OF ROBERT LOUIS STEVENSON TO HIS FAMILY AND FRIENDS. Selected and Edited, with Notes and Introductions, by SIDNEY COLVIN. *Fourth and Cheaper Edition. Crown 8vo.* 12s.
LIBRARY EDITION. *Demy 8vo.* 2 vols. 25s. net.

'Irresistible in their raciness, their variety, their animation ... of extraordinary fascination. A delightful inheritance, the truest record of a "richly compounded spirit" that the literature of our time has preserved.'—*Times.*

J. G. Millais. THE LIFE AND LETTERS OF SIR JOHN EVERETT MILLAIS, President of the Royal Academy. By his Son, J. G. MILLAIS. With 319 Illustrations, of which 9 are in Photogravure. *Second Edition.* 2 vols. *Royal 8vo.* 32s. net.

'This splendid work.'—*World.*

'Of such absorbing interest is it, of such completeness in scope and beauty. Special tribute must be paid to the extraordinary completeness of the illustrations.'—*Graphic.*

S. Baring Gould. THE LIFE OF NAPOLEON BONAPARTE. By S. BARING GOULD. With over 450 Illustrations in the Text and 12 Photogravure Plates. *Large quarto. Gilt top.* 36s.

'The main feature of this gorgeous volume is its great wealth of beautiful photogravures and finely-executed wood engravings, constituting a complete pictorial chronicle of Napoleon I.'s personal history from the days of his early childhood at Ajaccio to the date of his second interment.'—*Daily Telegraph.*

A. Hulme Beaman. TWENTY YEARS IN THE NEAR EAST. By A. HULME BEAMAN. *Demy 8vo.* With Portrait. 10s. 6d.

Henri of Orleans. FROM TONKIN TO INDIA. By PRINCE HENRI OF ORLEANS. Translated by HAMLEY BENT, M.A. With 100 Illustrations and a Map. *Cr. 4to, gilt top.* 25s.

Chester Holcombe. THE REAL CHINESE QUESTION. By CHESTER HOLCOMBE. *Crown 8vo.* 6s.

'It is an important addition to the materials before the public for forming an opinion on a most difficult and pressing problem.'—*Times.*

'It is this practical "note" in the book, coupled with the fairness, moderation, and sincerity of the author, that gives it, in our opinion, the highest place among books published in recent years on the Chinese question.'—*Manchester Guardian.*

J. W. Robertson-Scott. THE PEOPLE OF CHINA. By J. W. ROBERTSON-SCOTT. With a Map. *Crown 8vo.* 3s. 6d.

'A vivid impression ... This excellent, brightly written epitome.'—*Daily News.*
'Excellently well done.... Enthralling.'—*Weekly Dispatch.*

S. L. Hinde. THE FALL OF THE CONGO ARABS. By S. L. HINDE. With Plans, etc. *Demy 8vo.* 12s. 6d.

A. St. H. Gibbons. EXPLORATION AND HUNTING IN CENTRAL AFRICA. By Major A. ST. H. GIBBONS. With full-page Illustrations by C. WHYMPER, and Maps. *Demy 8vo.* 15s.

A. H. Norway. NAPLES: PAST AND PRESENT. By A. H. NORWAY, Author of 'Highways and Byways in Devon and Cornwall.' With 40 Illustrations by A. G. FERARD. *Crown 8vo.* 6s.

In this book Mr. Norway gives not only a highly interesting description of modern Naples, but a historical account of its antiquities and traditions.

S. Baring Gould. DARTMOOR: A Descriptive and Historical Sketch. By S. BARING GOULD. With Plans and Numerous Illustrations. *Crown 8vo.* 6s.

'A most delightful guide, companion, and instructor.'—*Scotsman.*
'Informed with close personal knowledge.'—*Saturday Review.*

S. Baring Gould. THE BOOK OF THE WEST. By S. BARING GOULD. With numerous Illustrations. *Two volumes.* Vol. I. Devon. *Second Edition.* Vol. II. Cornwall. *Crown 8vo.* 6s. each.

'Bracing as the air of Dartmoor, the legend weird as twilight over Dozmare Pool, they give us a very good idea of this enchanting and beautiful district.'—*Guardian.*

S. Baring Gould. A BOOK OF BRITTANY. By S. BARING GOULD. With numerous Illustrations. *Crown 8vo.* 6s.

Uniform in scope and size with Mr. Baring Gould's well-known books on Devon, Cornwall, and Dartmoor.

S. Baring Gould. THE DESERTS OF SOUTHERN FRANCE. By S. BARING GOULD. 2 vols. *Demy 8vo.* 32s.

J. F. Fraser. ROUND THE WORLD ON A WHEEL. By JOHN FOSTER FRASER. With 100 Illustrations. *Crown 8vo.* 6s.

'A classic of cycling, graphic and witty.'—*Yorkshire Post.*

R. L. Jefferson. A NEW RIDE TO KHIVA. By R. L. JEFFERSON. Illustrated. *Crown 8vo.* 6s.

J. K. Trotter. THE NIGER SOURCES. By Colonel J. K. TROTTER, R.A. With a Map and Illustrations. *Crown 8vo.* 5s.

W. Crooke. THE NORTH-WESTERN PROVINCES OF INDIA: THEIR ETHNOLOGY AND ADMINISTRATION. By W. CROOKE. With Maps and Illustrations. *Demy 8vo.* 10s. 6d.

A. Boisragon. THE BENIN MASSACRE. By CAPTAIN BOISRAGON. *Second Edition.* *Cr. 8vo.* 3s. 6d.

H. S. Cowper. THE HILL OF THE GRACES: OR, THE GREAT STONE TEMPLES OF TRIPOLI. By H. S. COWPER, F.S.A. With Maps, Plans, and 75 Illustrations. *Demy 8vo.* 10s. 6d.

Travel, Adventure and Topography

Sven Hedin. THROUGH ASIA. By Sven Hedin, Gold Medallist of the Royal Geographical Society. With 300 Illustrations from Sketches and Photographs by the Author, and Maps. 2 vols. *Royal 8vo. 20s. net.*

'One of the greatest books of the kind issued during the century. It is impossible to give an adequate idea of the richness of the contents of this book, nor of its abounding attractions as a story of travel unsurpassed in geographical and human interest. Much of it is a revelation. Altogether the work is one which in solidity, novelty, and interest must take a first rank among publications of its class.'—*Times.*

F. H. Skrine and E. D. Ross. THE HEART OF ASIA. By F. H. Skrine and E. D. Ross. With Maps and many Illustrations by Verestchagin. *Large Crown 8vo. 10s. 6d. net.*

'This volume will form a landmark in our knowledge of Central Asia. . . . Illuminating and convincing.'—*Times.*

R. E. Peary. NORTHWARD OVER THE GREAT ICE. By R. E. Peary, Gold Medallist of the Royal Geographical Society. With over 800 Illustrations. 2 vols. *Royal 8vo. 32s. net.*

'His book will take its place among the permanent literature of Arctic exploration.' —*Times.*

T. H. Holdich. THE INDIAN BORDERLAND: being a Personal Record of Twenty Years. By Sir T. H. Holdich, K.C.I.E. Illustrated. *Demy 8vo. 15s. net.*

'Probably the most important work on frontier topography that has lately been presented to the general public.'—*Literature.*

'Interesting and inspiriting from cover to cover, it will assuredly take its place as the classical on the history of the Indian frontier.'—*Pilot.*

'A work that should long remain the standard authority.'—*Daily Chronicle.*

A. B. Wylde. MODERN ABYSSINIA. By A. B. Wylde. With a Map and a Portrait. *Demy 8vo. 15s. net.*

'The most valuable contribution that has yet been made to our knowledge of Abyssinia.'—*Manchester Guardian.*

'A book which will rank among the very best of African works.'—*Daily Chronicle.*

'A repertory of information on every branch of the subject.'—*Literature.*

Alex. Hosie. MANCHURIA. By Alexander Hosie. With Illustrations and a Map. *Demy 8vo. 10s. 6d. net.*

A complete account of this important province by the highest living authority on the subject.

'This book is especially useful at the present moment when the future of the country appears uncertain.'—*Times.*

E. A. FitzGerald. THE HIGHEST ANDES. By E. A. FitzGerald. With 2 Maps, 51 Illustrations, 13 of which are in Photogravure, and a Panorama. *Royal 8vo. 30s. net.* Also a Small Edition on Hand-made Paper, limited to 50 Copies, *4to, £5, 5s.*

'The record of the first ascent of the highest mountain yet conquered by mortal man. A volume which will continue to be the classic book of travel on this region of the Andes.'—*Daily Chronicle.*

F. W. Christian. THE CAROLINE ISLANDS. By F. W. Christian. With many Illustrations and Maps. *Demy 8vo. 12s. 6d. net.*

'A real contribution to our knowledge of the peoples and islands of Micronesia, as well as fascinating as a narrative of travels and adventure.'—*Scotsman.*

H. H. Johnston. BRITISH CENTRAL AFRICA. By Sir H. H. Johnston, K.C.B. With nearly Two Hundred Illustrations, and Six Maps. *Second Edition. Crown 4to. 18s. net.*

'A fascinating book, written with equal skill and charm—the work at once of a literary artist and of a man of action who is singularly wise, brave, and experienced. It abounds in admirable sketches.'—*Westminster Gazette.*

L. Decle. THREE YEARS IN SAVAGE AFRICA. By Lionel Decle. With 100 Illustrations and 5 Maps. *Second Edition. Demy 8vo. 10s. 6d. net.*

E. H. Alderson. WITH THE MOUNTED INFANTRY AND THE MASHONALAND FIELD FORCE, 1896. By Lieut.-Colonel ALDERSON. With numerous Illustrations and Plans. *Demy 8vo.* 10s. 6d.

Seymour Vandeleur. CAMPAIGNING ON THE UPPER NILE AND NIGER. By Lieut. SEYMOUR VANDELEUR. With an Introduction by Sir G. GOLDIE, K.C.M.G. With 4 Maps, Illustrations, and Plans. *Large Crown 8vo.* 10s. 6d.

Lord Fincastle. A FRONTIER CAMPAIGN. By Viscount FINCASTLE, V.C., and Lieut. P. C. ELLIOTT-LOCKHART. With a Map and 16 Illustrations. *Second Edition. Second Edition. Crown 8vo.* 6s.

E. N. Bennett. THE DOWNFALL OF THE DERVISHES: A Sketch of the Sudan Campaign of 1898. By E. N. BENNETT, Fellow of Hertford College. With a Photogravure Portrait of Lord Kitchener. *Third Edition. Crown 8vo.* 3s. 6d.

W. Kinnaird Rose. WITH THE GREEKS IN THESSALY. By W. KINNAIRD ROSE. With Illustrations. *Crown 8vo.* 6s.

G. W. Steevens. NAVAL POLICY By G. W. STEEVENS. *Demy 8vo.* 6s.

D. Hannay. A SHORT HISTORY OF THE ROYAL NAVY, FROM EARLY TIMES TO THE PRESENT DAY. By DAVID HANNAY. Illustrated. 2 *Vols. Demy 8vo.* 7s. 6d. each. Vol. I., 1200-1688.
'We read it from cover to cover at a sitting, and those who go to it for a lively and brisk picture of the past, with all its faults and its grandeur, will not be disappointed. The historian is endowed with literary skill and style.'—*Standard.*

E. L. S. Horsburgh. WATERLOO: A Narrative and Criticism. By E. L. S. HORSBURGH, M.A. With Plans. *Second Edition. Crown 8vo.* 5s.
'A brilliant essay—simple, sound, and thorough.'—*Daily Chronicle.*

H. B. George. BATTLES OF ENGLISH HISTORY. By H. B. GEORGE, M.A., Fellow of New College, Oxford. With numerous Plans. *Third Edition. Cr. 8vo.* 6s.
'Mr. George has undertaken a very useful task—that of making military affairs intelligible and instructive to non-military readers—and has executed it with a large measure of success.'—*Times.*

General Literature

S. Baring Gould. OLD COUNTRY LIFE. By S. BARING GOULD. With Sixty-seven Illustrations. *Large Cr. 8vo. Fifth Edition.* 6s.
'"Old Country Life," as healthy wholesome reading, full of breezy life and movement, full of quaint stories vigorously told, will not be excelled by any book to be published throughout the year. Sound, hearty, and English to the core.'—*World.*

S. Baring Gould. AN OLD ENGLISH HOME. By S. BARING GOULD. With numerous Plans and Illustrations. *Crown 8vo.* 6s.
'The chapters are delightfully fresh, very informing, and lightened by many a good story. A delightful fireside companion.'—*St. James's Gazette.*

S. Baring Gould. HISTORIC ODDITIES AND STRANGE EVENTS. By S. BARING GOULD. *Fifth Edition. Crown 8vo.* 6s.

S. Baring Gould. FREAKS OF FANATICISM. By S. BARING GOULD. *Third Edition. Cr. 8vo.* 6s.

S. Baring Gould. A GARLAND OF COUNTRY SONG: English Folk Songs with their Traditional Melodies. Collected and arranged by S. BARING GOULD and H. F. SHEPPARD. *Demy 4to.* 6s.

S. Baring Gould. SONGS OF THE WEST: Traditional Ballads and Songs of the West of England, with their Melodies. Collected by S.

BARING GOULD, M.A., and H. F. SHEPPARD, M.A. In 4 Parts. Parts I., II., III., 3s. each. Part IV., 5s. In one Vol., French morocco, 15s.

'A rich collection of humour, pathos, grace, and poetic fancy.'—*Saturday Review.*

S. Baring Gould. YORKSHIRE ODDITIES AND STRANGE EVENTS. By S. BARING GOULD. *Fifth Edition. Crown 8vo. 6s.*

S. Baring Gould. STRANGE SURVIVALS AND SUPERSTITIONS. By S. BARING GOULD. *Cr. 8vo. Second Edition. 6s.*

Marie Corelli. THE PASSING OF THE GREAT QUEEN: A Tribute to the Noble Life of Victoria Regina. By MARIE CORELLI. *Small 4to. 1s.*

Cotton Minchin. OLD HARROW DAYS. By J. G. COTTON MINCHIN. *Cr. 8vo. Second Edition. 5s.*

W. E. Gladstone. THE SPEECHES OF THE RT. HON. W. E. GLADSTONE, M.P. Edited by A. W. HUTTON, M.A., and H. J. COHEN, M.A. With Portraits. *Demy 8vo. Vols. IX. and X., 12s. 6d. each.*

M. N. Oxford. A HANDBOOK OF NURSING. By M. N. OXFORD, of Guy's Hospital. *Crown 8vo. 3s. 6d.*

'The most useful work of the kind that we have seen. A most valuable and practical manual.'—*Manchester Guardian.*

E. V. Zenker. ANARCHISM. By E. V. ZENKER. *Demy 8vo. 7s. 6d.*

Emily Lawless. A GARDEN DIARY. By the Hon. EMILY LAWLESS. *Demy 8vo. 7s. 6d. net.*

S. J. Duncan. ON THE OTHER SIDE OF THE LATCH. By SARA JEANNETTE DUNCAN (Mrs. COTES), Author of 'A Voyage of Consolation.' *Second Edition. Crown 8vo. 6s.*

W. Williamson. THE BRITISH GARDENER. By W. WILLIAMSON. Illustrated. *Demy 8vo. 10s. 6d.*

Arnold White. EFFICIENCY AND EMPIRE. By ARNOLD WHITE. *Crown 8vo. 6s.*

'Stimulating and entertaining throughout, it deserves the attention of every patriotic Englishman.'—*Daily Mail.*
'A notable book.'—*Literature.*
'A book of sound work, deep thought, and a sincere endeavour to rouse the British to a knowledge of the value of their Empire.'—*Bookman.*
'A more vigorous work has not been written for many years.'—*Review of the Week.*

A. Silva White. THE EXPANSION OF EGYPT: A Political and Historical Survey. By A. SILVA WHITE. With four Special Maps. *Demy 8vo. 15s. net.*

'This is emphatically the best account of Egypt as it is under English control that has been published for many years.'—*Spectator.*

Chas. Richardson. THE ENGLISH TURF. By CHARLES RICHARDSON. With numerous Illustrations and Plans. *Demy 8vo. 15s.*

'As a record of horses and courses, this work is a valuable addition to the literature of the Turf. It is crammed with sound information, and with reflections and suggestions that are born of a thorough knowledge of the subject.'—*Scotsman.*
'A book which is sure to find many readers; written with consummate knowledge and in an easy, agreeable style.'—*Daily Chronicle.*
'From its sensible introduction to its very complex index, this is about the best book that we are likely for some time to see upon the subject with which it deals.'—*Athenæum.*

Philip Trevor. THE LIGHTER SIDE OF CRICKET. By Captain PHILIP TREVOR (DUX). *Crown 8vo. 6s.*

A highly interesting volume, dealing with such subjects as county cricket, village cricket, cricket for boys and girls, literary cricket, and various other subjects which do not require a severe and technical treatment.

'A wholly entertaining book.'—*Glasgow Herald.*
'The most welcome book on our national game published for years.'—*County Gentleman.*

Peter Beckford. THOUGHTS ON HUNTING. By PETER BECKFORD. Edited by J. OTHO PAGET, and Illustrated by G. H. JALLAND. *Demy 8vo. 10s. 6d.*

'Beckford's "Thoughts on Hunting" has

long been a classic with sportsmen, and the present edition will go far to make it a favourite with lovers of literature.'—*Speaker.*

E. B. Michell. THE ART AND PRACTICE OF HAWKING. By E. B. MICHELL. With 3 Photogravures by G. E. LODGE, and other Illustrations. *Demy 8vo.* 10s. 6d.
'No book is more full and authoritative than this handsome treatise.'
—*Morning Leader.*

H. G. Hutchinson. THE GOLFING PILGRIM. By HORACE G. HUTCHINSON. *Crown 8vo.* 6s.
'Without this book the golfer's library will be incomplete.'—*Pall Mall Gazette.*

J. Wells. OXFORD AND OXFORD LIFE. By Members of the University. Edited by J. WELLS, M.A., Fellow and Tutor of Wadham College. *Third Edition. Cr. 8vo.* 3s. 6d.

C. G. Robertson. VOCES ACADEMICÆ. By C. GRANT ROBERTSON, M.A., Fellow of All Souls', Oxford. With a Frontispiece. *Pott 8vo.* 3s. 6d.
'Decidedly clever and amusing.'—*Athenæum.*

Rosemary Cotes. DANTE'S GARDEN. By ROSEMARY COTES. With a Frontispiece. *Second Edition. Fcp. 8vo.* 2s. 6d. Leather, 3s. 6d. net.
'A charming collection of legends of the flowers mentioned by Dante.'—*Academy.*

Clifford Harrison. READING AND READERS. By CLIFFORD HARRISON. *Fcp. 8vo.* 2s. 6d.
'An extremely sensible little book.'—*Manchester Guardian.*

L. Whibley. GREEK OLIGARCHIES: THEIR ORGANISATION AND CHARACTER. By L. WHIBLEY, M.A., Fellow of Pembroke College, Cambridge. *Crown 8vo.* 6s.

L. L. Price. ECONOMIC SCIENCE AND PRACTICE. By L. L. PRICE, M.A., Fellow of Oriel College, Oxford. *Crown 8vo.* 6s.

J. S. Shedlock. THE PIANOFORTE SONATA: Its Origin and Development. By J. S. SHEDLOCK. *Crown 8vo.* 5s.
'This work should be in the possession of every musician and amateur. A concise and lucid history and a very valuable work for reference.'—*Athenæum.*

A. Hulme Beaman. PONS ASINORUM; OR, A GUIDE TO BRIDGE. By A. HULME BEAMAN. *Second Edition. Fcap 8vo.* 2s.
A practical guide, with many specimen games, to the new game of Bridge.

E. M. Bowden. THE EXAMPLE OF BUDDHA: Being Quotations from Buddhist Literature for each Day in the Year. Compiled by E. M. BOWDEN. *Third Edition.* 16mo. 2s. 6d.

F. Ware. EDUCATIONAL REFORM. By FABIAN WARE, M.A. *Crown 8vo.* 2s. 6d.

Sidney Peel. PRACTICAL LICENSING REFORM. By the Hon SIDNEY PEEL, late Fellow of Trinity College, Oxford, and Secretary to the Royal Commission on the Licensing Laws. *Second Edition. Crown 8vo.* 1s. 6d.

Philosophy

L. T. Hobhouse. THE THEORY OF KNOWLEDGE. By L. T. HOBHOUSE, Fellow of C.C.C., Oxford. *Demy 8vo.* 21s.
'The most important contribution to English philosophy since the publication of Mr. Bradley's "Appearance and Reality."'—*Glasgow Herald.*

W. H. Fairbrother. THE PHILOSOPHY OF T. H. GREEN. By W. H. FAIRBROTHER, M.A. *Second Edition. Cr. 8vo.* 3s. 6d.

'In every way an admirable book.'—*Glasgow Herald.*

F. W. Bussell. THE SCHOOL OF PLATO. By F. W. BUSSELL, D.D., Fellow of Brasenose College, Oxford. *Demy 8vo.* 10s. 6d.

F. S. Granger. THE WORSHIP OF THE ROMANS. By F. S. GRANGER, M.A., Litt.D. *Crown 8vo.* 6s.

Science

E. H. Colbeck. DISEASES OF THE HEART. By E. H. COLBECK, M.D. With numerous Illustrations. *Demy 8vo.* 12s.

W. C. C. Pakes. THE SCIENCE OF HYGIENE. By W. C. C. PAKES. With numerous Illustrations. *Demy 8vo.* 15s.

'A thoroughgoing working text-book of its subject, practical and well-stocked.'—*Scotsman.*

A. T. Hare. THE CONSTRUCTION OF LARGE INDUCTION COILS. By A. T. HARE, M.A. With numerous Diagrams. *Demy 8vo.* 6s.

J. E. Marr. THE SCIENTIFIC STUDY OF SCENERY. By J. E. MARR, F.R.S., Fellow of St. John's College, Cambridge. Illustrated. *Crown 8vo.* 6s.

'A volume, moderate in size and readable in style, which will be acceptable alike to the student of geology and geography, and to the tourist.'—*Athenæum.*

J. Ritzema Bos. AGRICULTURAL ZOOLOGY. By Dr. J. RITZEMA BOS. Translated by J. R. AINSWORTH DAVIS, M.A. With an Introduction by ELEANOR A. ORMEROD, F.E.S. With 155 Illustrations. *Crown 8vo.* 3s. 6d.

The illustrations are exceedingly good, whilst the information conveyed is invaluable.'—*Country Gentleman.*

Ed. von Freudenreich. DAIRY BACTERIOLOGY. A Short Manual for the Use of Students. By Dr. ED. VON FREUDENREICH. Translated by J. R. AINSWORTH DAVIS, M.A. *Second Edition, Revised. Crown 8vo.* 2s. 6d.

Chalmers Mitchell. OUTLINES OF BIOLOGY. By P. CHALMERS MITCHELL, M.A. *Illustrated. Cr. 8vo.* 6s.

A text-book designed to cover the new Schedule issued by the Royal College of Physicians and Surgeons.

George Massee. A MONOGRAPH OF THE MYXOGASTRES. By GEORGE MASSEE. With 12 Coloured Plates. *Royal 8vo.* 18s. *net.*

'A work much in advance of any book in the language treating of this group of organisms. Indispensable to every student of the Myxogastres.'—*Nature.*

C. Stephenson and F. Suddards. ORNAMENTAL DESIGN FOR WOVEN FABRICS. By C. STEPHENSON, of the Technical College, Bradford, and F. SUDDARDS, of the Yorkshire College, Leeds. With 65 full-page plates. *Demy 8vo. Second Edition.* 7s. 6d.

'The book is very ably done, displaying an intimate knowledge of principles, good taste, and the faculty of clear exposition.'—*Yorkshire Post.*

C. C. Channer and M. E. Roberts. LACE-MAKING IN THE MIDLANDS, PAST AND PRESENT. By C. C. CHANNER and M. E. ROBERTS. With 16 full-page Illustrations. *Crown 8vo.* 2s. 6d.

'An interesting book, illustrated by fascinating photographs.'—*Speaker.*

Theology

W. R. Inge. CHRISTIAN MYSTICISM. The Bampton Lectures for 1899. By W. R. INGE, M.A., Fellow and Tutor of Hertford College, Oxford. *Demy 8vo.* 12s. 6d. *net.*

'It is fully worthy of the best traditions connected with the Bampton Lectureship.'—*Record.*

Lady Julian of Norwich. REVELATIONS OF DIVINE LOVE. By the LADY JULIAN of Norwich. Edited by GRACE WARRACK. *Crown 8vo.* 6s.

A partially modernised version, from the MS. in the British Museum of a book which Dr. Dalgairns terms 'One of the most remarkable books of the Middle Ages.' Mr. Inge in his Bampton Lectures on Christian Mysticism calls it 'The beautiful but little known *Revelations*.'

R. M. Benson. THE WAY OF HOLINESS: a Devotional Commentary on the 119th Psalm. By R. M. BENSON, M.A., of the Cowley Mission, Oxford. *Crown 8vo.* 5s.

'His facility is delightful, and his very sound and accurate theological sense saves him from many of the obvious dangers of such a gift. Give him a word or a number and at once there springs forth a fertile stream of thought, never commonplace, usually both deep and fresh. For devotional purposes we think this book most valuable. Readers will find a great wealth of thought if they use the book simply as a help to meditation.'—*Guardian.*

Jacob Behmen. THE SUPERSENSUAL LIFE. By JACOB BEHMEN. Edited by BERNARD HOLLAND. *Fcap 8vo.* 3s. 6d.

S. R. Driver. SERMONS ON SUBJECTS CONNECTED WITH THE OLD TESTAMENT. By S. R. DRIVER, D.D., Canon of Christ Church, Regius Professor of Hebrew in the University of Oxford. *Cr. 8vo.* 6s.

'A welcome companion to the author's famous "Introduction."'—*Guardian.*

T. K. Cheyne. FOUNDERS OF OLD TESTAMENT CRITICISM. By T. K. CHEYNE, D.D., Oriel Professor at Oxford. *Large Crown 8vo.* 7s. 6d.

A historical sketch of O. T. Criticism.

Walter Lock. ST. PAUL, THE MASTER-BUILDER. By WALTER LOCK, D.D., Warden of Keble College. *Crown 8vo.* 3s. 6d.

'The essence of the Pauline teaching is condensed into little more than a hundred pages, yet no point of importance is overlooked.'—*Guardian.*

F. S. Granger. THE SOUL OF A CHRISTIAN. By F. S. GRANGER, M.A., Litt.D. *Crown 8vo.* 6s.

A book dealing with the evolution of the religious life and experiences.

'A remarkable book.'—*Glasgow Herald.*
'Both a scholarly and thoughtful book.'—*Scotsman.*

H. Rashdall. DOCTRINE AND DEVELOPMENT. By HASTINGS RASHDALL, M.A., Fellow and Tutor of New College, Oxford. *Cr. 8vo.* 6s.

H. H. Henson. APOSTOLIC CHRISTIANITY: As Illustrated by the Epistles of St. Paul to the Corinthians. By H. H. HENSON, M.A., Fellow of All Souls', Oxford, Canon of Westminster. *Cr. 8vo.* 6s.

H. H. Henson. DISCIPLINE AND LAW. By H. HENSLEY HENSON, M.A., Fellow of All Souls', Oxford. *Fcap. 8vo.* 2s. 6d.

H. H. Henson. LIGHT AND LEAVEN: HISTORICAL AND SOCIAL SERMONS. By H. H. HENSON, M.A. *Crown 8vo.* 6s.

J. Houghton Kennedy. ST. PAUL'S SECOND AND THIRD EPISTLES TO THE CORINTHIANS. With Introduction, Dissertations, and Notes, by JAMES HOUGHTON KENNEDY, D.D., Assistant Lecturer in Divinity in the University of Dublin. *Crown 8vo.* 6s.

Bennett and Adeney. A BIBLICAL INTRODUCTION. By W. H. BENNETT, M.A., and W. F. ADENEY, M.A. *Crown 8vo.* 7s. 6d.

'It makes available to the ordinary reader the best scholarship of the day in the field of Biblical introduction. We know of no book which comes into competition with it.'—*Manchester Guardian.*

W. H. Bennett. A PRIMER OF THE BIBLE. By W. H. BENNETT. *Second Edition. Cr. 8vo.* 2s. 6d.

'The work of an honest, fearless, and sound critic, and an excellent guide in a small compass to the books of the Bible.'—*Manchester Guardian.*

C. F. G. Masterman. TENNYSON AS A RELIGIOUS TEACHER. By C. F. G. MASTERMAN. *Crown 8vo.* 6s.

'A thoughtful and penetrating appreciation, full of interest and suggestion.'—*World.*

William Harrison. CLOVELLY SERMONS. By WILLIAM HARRISON, M.A., late Rector of Clovelly. With a Preface by 'LUCAS MALET.' *Cr. 8vo.* 3s. 6d.

Cecilia Robinson. THE MINISTRY OF DEACONESSES. By Deaconness CECILIA ROBINSON. With an Introduction by the Lord Bishop of Winchester. *Cr. 8vo.* 3s. 6d.

'A learned and interesting book.'—*Scotsman.*

E. B. Layard. RELIGION IN BOYHOOD. Notes on the Religious Training of Boys. By E. B. LAYARD, M.A. 18mo. 1s.

T. Herbert Bindley. THE OECUMENICAL DOCUMENTS OF THE FAITH. Edited with Introductions and Notes by T. HERBERT BINDLEY, B.D., Merton College, Oxford. *Crown 8vo.* 6s.

A historical account of the Creeds.

H. M. Barron. TEXTS FOR SERMONS ON VARIOUS OCCASIONS AND SUBJECTS. Compiled and Arranged by H. M. BARRON, B.A., of Wadham College, Oxford, with a Preface by Canon SCOTT HOLLAND. *Crown 8vo.* 3s. 6d.

W. Yorke Fausset. THE *DE CATECHIZANDIS RUDIBUS* OF ST. AUGUSTINE. Edited, with Introduction, Notes, etc., by W. YORKE FAUSSET, M.A. *Cr. 8vo.* 3s. 6d.

J. H. Burn. THE SOUL'S PILGRIMAGE: Devotional Readings from the published and unpublished writings of GEORGE BODY, D.D. Selected and arranged by J. H. BURN, B.D. *Pott 8vo.* 2s. 6d.

F. Weston. THE HOLY SACRIFICE. By F. WESTON, M.A., Curate of St. Matthew's, Westminster. *Pott 8vo.* 6d. net.

À Kempis. THE IMITATION OF CHRIST. By THOMAS À KEMPIS. With an Introduction by DEAN FARRAR. Illustrated by C. M. GERE. *Second Edition. Fcap. 8vo.* 3s. 6d. Padded morocco, 5s.

'Amongst all the innumerable English editions of the "Imitation," there can have been few which were prettier than this one, printed in strong and handsome type, with all the glory of red initials.'—*Glasgow Herald.*

J. Keble. THE CHRISTIAN YEAR. By JOHN KEBLE. With an Introduction and Notes by W. LOCK, D.D., Warden of Keble College. Illustrated by R. ANNING BELL. *Second Edition. Fcap. 8vo.* 3s. 6d. Padded morocco. 5s.

'The present edition is annotated with all the care and insight to be expected from Mr. Lock.'—*Guardian.*

Oxford Commentaries

General Editor, WALTER LOCK, D.D., Warden of Keble College, Dean Ireland's Professor of Exegesis in the University of Oxford.

THE BOOK OF JOB. Edited, with Introduction and Notes, by E. C. S. GIBSON, D.D., Vicar of Leeds. *Demy 8vo.* 6s.

'The publishers are to be congratulated on the start the series has made.'—*Times.*

'Dr. Gibson's work is worthy of a high degree of appreciation. To the busy worker and the intelligent student the commentary will be a real boon; and it will, if we are not mistaken, be much in demand. The Introduction is almost a model of concise, straightforward, prefatory remarks on the subject treated.'—*Athenæum.*

Handbooks of Theology

General Editor, A. ROBERTSON, D.D., Principal of King's College, London.

THE XXXIX. ARTICLES OF THE CHURCH OF ENGLAND. Edited with an Introduction by E. C. S. GIBSON, D.D., Vicar of Leeds, late Principal of Wells Theological College. *Third and Cheaper Edition in One Volume. Demy 8vo.* 12s. 6d.

'We welcome with the utmost satisfaction

a new, cheaper, and more convenient edition of Dr. Gibson's book. It was greatly wanted. Dr. Gibson has given theological students just what they want, and we should like to think that it was in the hands of every candidate for orders.'—*Guardian.*

IN INTRODUCTION TO THE HISTORY OF RELIGION. By F. B. JEVONS, M.A., Litt.D., Principal of Bishop Hatfield's Hall. *Second Edition. Demy 8vo.* 10s. 6d.

'The merit of this book lies in the penetration, the singular acuteness and force of the author's judgment. He is at once critical and luminous, at once just and suggestive. A comprehensive and thorough book.'—*Birmingham Post.*

THE DOCTRINE OF THE INCARNATION. By R. L. OTTLEY, M.A., late fellow of Magdalen College, Oxon., and Principal of Pusey House. *In Two Volumes. Demy 8vo.* 15s.

'A clear and remarkably full account of the main currents of speculation. Scholarly precision . . . genuine tolerance . . . intense interest in his subject—are Mr. Ottley's merits.'—*Guardian.*

AN INTRODUCTION TO THE HISTORY OF THE CREEDS. By A. E. BURN, B.D., Examining Chaplain to the Bishop of Lichfield. *Demy 8vo.* 10s. 6d.

'This book may be expected to hold its place as an authority on its subject.'—*Spectator.*

THE PHILOSOPHY OF RELIGION IN ENGLAND AND AMERICA. By ALFRED CALDECOTT, D.D., *Demy 8vo.* 10s. 6d.

'Singularly well-informed, comprehensive, and fair.'—*Glasgow Herald.*

'A lucid and informative account, which certainly deserves a place in every philosophical library.'—*Scotsman.*

The Churchman's Library

General Editor, J. H. BURN, B.D., Examining Chaplain to the Bishop of Aberdeen.

THE BEGINNINGS OF ENGLISH CHRISTIANITY. By W. E. COLLINS, M.A. With Map. *Cr. 8vo.* 3s. 6d.

'An excellent example of thorough and fresh historical work.'—*Guardian.*

SOME NEW TESTAMENT PROBLEMS. By ARTHUR WRIGHT, M.A., Fellow of Queen's College, Cambridge. *Crown 8vo.* 6s.

'Real students will revel in these reverent, acute, and pregnant essays in Biblical scholarship.'—*Great Thoughts.*

THE KINGDOM OF HEAVEN HERE AND HEREAFTER. By CANON WINTERBOTHAM, M.A., B.Sc., LL.B. *Cr. 8vo.* 3s. 6d.

'A most able book at once exceedingly thoughtful and richly suggestive.'—*Glasgow Herald.*

THE WORKMANSHIP OF THE PRAYER BOOK: Its Literary and Liturgical Aspects. By J. DOWDEN, D.D., Lord Bishop of Edinburgh. *Second Edition. Crown 8vo.* 3s. 6d.

'Scholarly and interesting.'—*Manchester Guardian.*

EVOLUTION. By F. B. JEVONS, M.A., Litt.D., Principal of Hatfield Hall, Durham. *Crown 8vo.* 3s. 6d.

'A well-written book, full of sound thinking happily expressed.'—*Manchester Guardian.*

The Churchman's Bible

General Editor, J. H. BURN, B.D.

Messrs. METHUEN are issuing a series of expositions upon most of the books of the Bible. The volumes will be practical and devotional, and the text of the authorised version is explained in sections, which will correspond as far as possible with the Church Lectionary.

THE EPISTLE OF ST. PAUL TO THE GALATIANS. Explained by A. W. ROBINSON, Vicar of All Hallows, Barking. *Fcap. 8vo.* 1s. 6d. net.

The most attractive, sensible, and instructive manual for people at large, which we have ever seen.'—*Church Gazette.*

ECCLESIASTES. Explained by A. W. STREANE, D.D. *Fcap. 8vo.* 1s. 6d. net.

'Scholarly, suggestive, and particularly interesting.'—*Bookman.*

THE EPISTLE OF PAUL THE APOSTLE TO THE PHILIPPIANS. Explained by C. R. D. BIGGS, B.D. *Fcap. 8vo.* 1s 6d *net.*

'Mr. Biggs' work is very thorough, and he has managed to compress a good deal of information into a limited space.'
—*Guardian.*

THE EPISTLE OF ST. JAMES. Edited by H. W. FULFORD, M.A. *Fcap. 8vo.* 1s. 6d. *net.*

The Library of Devotion

Pott 8vo, cloth, 2s.; leather, 2s. 6d. net.

'This series is excellent.'—THE BISHOP OF LONDON.
'Very delightful.'—THE BISHOP OF BATH AND WELLS.
'Well worth the attention of the Clergy.'—THE BISHOP OF LICHFIELD.
'The new "Library of Devotion" is excellent.'—THE BISHOP OF PETERBOROUGH.
'Charming.'—*Record.* 'Delightful.'—*Church Bells.*

THE CONFESSIONS OF ST. AUGUSTINE. Newly Translated, with an Introduction and Notes, by C. BIGG, D.D., late Student of Christ Church. *Third Edition.*
'The translation is an excellent piece of English, and the Introduction is a masterly exposition. We augur well of a series which begins so satisfactorily.'—*Times.*

THE CHRISTIAN YEAR. By JOHN KEBLE. With Introduction and Notes by WALTER LOCK, D.D., Warden of Keble College, Ireland Professor at Oxford.

THE IMITATION OF CHRIST. A Revised Translation, with an Introduction, by C. BIGG, D.D., late Student of Christ Church. *Second Edition.*
A practically new translation of this book, which the reader has, almost for the first time, exactly in the shape in which it left the hands of the author.

A BOOK OF DEVOTIONS. By J. W. STANBRIDGE, B.D., Rector of Bainton, Canon of York, and sometime Fellow of St. John's College, Oxford.
'It is probably the best book of its kind. It deserves high commendation.'—*Church Gazette.*

LYRA INNOCENTIUM. By JOHN KEBLE. Edited, with Introduction and Notes, by WALTER LOCK, D.D., Warden of Keble College, Oxford.
'This sweet and fragrant book has never been published more attractively.'—*Academy.*

A SERIOUS CALL TO A DEVOUT AND HOLY LIFE. By WILLIAM LAW. Edited, with an Introduction, by C. BIGG, D.D., late Student of Christ Church.
This is a reprint, word for word and line for line, of the *Editio Princeps.*

THE TEMPLE. By GEORGE HERBERT. Edited, with an Introduction and Notes, by E. C. S. GIBSON, D.D., Vicar of Leeds.
This edition contains Walton's Life of Herbert, and the text is that of the first edition.

A GUIDE TO ETERNITY. By Cardinal BONA. Edited, with an Introduction and Notes, by J. W. STANBRIDGE, B.D., late Fellow of St. John's College, Oxford.

THE PSALMS OF DAVID. With an Introduction and Notes by B. W. RANDOLPH, D.D., Principal of the Theological College, Ely.
A devotional and practical edition of the Prayer Book version of the Psalms.

LYRA APOSTOLICA. With an Introduction by Canon SCOTT HOLLAND, and Notes by H. C. BEECHING, M.A.

THE INNER WAY. Being Thirty-six Sermons for Festivals by JOHN TAULER. Edited, with an Introduction, by A. W. HUTTON, M.A.

Leaders of Religion

Edited by H. C. BEECHING, M.A. With Portraits, *Crown 8vo. 3s. 6d.*

A series of short biographies of the most prominent leaders of religious life and thought of all ages and countries.

The following are ready—

CARDINAL NEWMAN. By R. H. HUTTON.
JOHN WESLEY. By J. H. OVERTON, M.A.
BISHOP WILBERFORCE. By G. W. DANIELL, M.A.
CARDINAL MANNING. By A. W. HUTTON, M.A.
CHARLES SIMEON. By H. C. G. MOULE, D.D.
JOHN KEBLE. By WALTER LOCK, D.D.
THOMAS CHALMERS. By Mrs. OLIPHANT.
LANCELOT ANDREWES. By R. L. OTTLEY, M.A.
AUGUSTINE OF CANTERBURY. By E. L. CUTTS, D.D.
WILLIAM LAUD. By W. H. HUTTON, M.A.
JOHN KNOX. By F. MACCUNN.
JOHN HOWE. By R. F. HORTON, D.D.
BISHOP KEN. By F. A. CLARKE, M.A.
GEORGE FOX, THE QUAKER. By T. HODGKIN, D.C.L.
JOHN DONNE. By AUGUSTUS JESSOPP, D.D.
THOMAS CRANMER. By. A. J. MASON.
BISHOP LATIMER. By R. M. CARLYLE and A. J. CARLYLE, M.A.

Other volumes will be announced in due course.

Fiction

Marie Corelli's Novels

Crown 8vo. 6s. each.

A ROMANCE OF TWO WORLDS. *Twenty-Second Edition.*
VENDETTA. *Seventeenth Edition.*
THELMA. *Twenty-Fifth Edition.*
ARDATH: THE STORY OF A DEAD SELF. *Thirteenth Edition.*
THE SOUL OF LILITH. *Tenth Edition.*
WORMWOOD. *Eleventh Edition.*
BARABBAS: A DREAM OF THE WORLD'S TRAGEDY. *Thirty-seventh Edition.*

'The tender reverence of the treatment and the imaginative beauty of the writing have reconciled us to the daring of the conception, and the conviction is forced on us that even so exalted a subject cannot be made too familiar to us, provided it be presented in the true spirit of Christian faith. The amplifications of the Scripture narrative are often conceived with high poetic insight, and this "Dream of the World's Tragedy" is a lofty and not inadequate paraphrase of the supreme climax of the inspired narrative.'—*Dublin Review.*

THE SORROWS OF SATAN. *Forty-Fourth Edition.*

'A very powerful piece of work. . . . The conception is magnificent, and is likely to win an abiding place within the memory of man. . . . The author has immense command of language, and a limitless audacity. . . . This interesting and remarkable romance will live long after much of the ephemeral literature of the day is forgotten. . . . A literary phenomenon . . . novel, and even sublime.'—W. T. STEAD in the *Review of Reviews.*

THE MASTER CHRISTIAN.
[160*th Thousand.*

'It cannot be denied that "The Master Christian" is a powerful book; that it is one likely to raise uncomfortable questions in all but the most self-satisfied readers, and that it strikes at the root of the failure of the Churches—the decay of faith—in a manner which shows the inevitable disaster heaping up. . . . The good Cardinal Bonpré is a beautiful figure, fit to stand beside the good Bishop in "Les Misérables". . . . The chapter in which the Cardinal appears with Manuel before Leo XIII. is characterised by extraordinary realism and dramatic intensity . . . It is a book with a serious purpose expressed with absolute unconventionality and passion . . . And this is to say it is a book worth reading.'—*Examiner.*

Anthony Hope's Novels

Crown 8vo. 6s. each.

THE GOD IN THE CAR. *Ninth Edition.*

'A very remarkable book, deserving of critical analysis impossible within our limit; brilliant, but not superficial; well considered, but not elaborated; constructed with the proverbial art that conceals, but yet allows itself to be enjoyed by readers to whom fine literary method is a keen pleasure.'—*The World.*

A CHANGE OF AIR. *Sixth Edition.*

'A graceful, vivacious comedy, true to human nature. The characters are traced with a masterly hand.'—*Times.*

A MAN OF MARK. *Fifth Edition.*

'Of all Mr. Hope's books, "A Man of Mark" is the one which best compares with "The Prisoner of Zenda."'—*National Observer.*

THE CHRONICLES OF COUNT ANTONIO. *Fourth Edition.*

'It is a perfectly enchanting story of love and chivalry, and pure romance. The Count is the most constant, desperate, and modest and tender of lovers, a peerless gentleman, an intrepid fighter, a faithful friend, and a magnanimous foe.'—*Guardian.*

PHROSO. Illustrated by H. R. MILLAR. *Fifth Edition.*

'The tale is thoroughly fresh, quick with vitality, stirring the blood.'—*St. James's Gazette.*

SIMON DALE. Illustrated. *Fifth Edition.*

'There is searching analysis of human nature, with a most ingeniously constructed plot. Mr. Hope has drawn the contrasts of his women with marvellous subtlety and delicacy.'—*Times.*

THE KING'S MIRROR. *Third Edition.*

'In elegance, delicacy, and tact it ranks with the best of his novels, while in the wide range of its portraiture and the subtilty of its analysis it surpasses all his earlier ventures.'—*Spectator.*

QUISANTE. *Third Edition.*

'The book is notable for a very high literary quality, and an impress of power and mastery on every page.'—*Daily Chronicle.*

Gilbert Parker's Novels

Crown 8vo. 6s. each.

PIERRE AND HIS PEOPLE. *Fifth Edition.*

'Stories happily conceived and finely executed. There is strength and genius in Mr. Parker's style.'—*Daily Telegraph.*

MRS. FALCHION. *Fourth Edition.*

'A splendid study of character.'—*Athenæum.*

THE TRANSLATION OF A SAVAGE. *Second Edition.*

'The plot is original and one difficult to work out; but Mr. Parker has done it with great skill and delicacy.'—*Daily Chronicle.*

THE TRAIL OF THE SWORD. Illustrated. *Seventh Edition.*

'A rousing and dramatic tale. A book like this, in which swords flash, great surprises are undertaken, and daring deeds done, in which men and women live and love in the old passionate way, is a joy inexpressible.'—*Daily Chronicle.*

WHEN VALMOND CAME TO PONTIAC: The Story of a Lost Napoleon. *Fifth Edition.*

'Here we find romance—real, breathing, living romance. The character of Valmond is drawn unerringly.'—*Pall Mall Gazette.*

AN ADVENTURER OF THE NORTH: The Last Adventures of 'Pretty Pierre.' *Second Edition.*

'The present book is full of fine and moving stories of the great North, and it will add to Mr. Parker's already high reputation.'—*Glasgow Herald.*

THE SEATS OF THE MIGHTY. Illustrated. *Eleventh Edition.*

'Mr. Parker has produced a really fine historical novel.'—*Athenæum.*

'A great book.'—*Black and White.*

THE BATTLE OF THE STRONG: a Romance of Two Kingdoms. Illustrated. *Fourth Edition.*

'Nothing more vigorous or more human has come from Mr. Gilbert Parker than this novel. It has all the graphic power of his last book, with truer feeling for the romance, both of human life and wild nature.'—*Literature.*

THE POMP OF THE LAVILETTES. *Second Edition. 3s. 6d.*

'Unforced pathos, and a deeper knowledge of human nature than Mr. Parker has ever displayed before.'—*Pall Mall Gazette.*

Jane Barlow. A CREEL OF IRISH STORIES. By JANE BARLOW, Author of 'Irish Idylls.' *Second Edition. Crown 8vo. 6s.*
'Vivid and singularly real.'—*Scotsman.*

Jane Barlow. FROM THE EAST UNTO THE WEST. By JANE BARLOW. *Crown 8vo. 6s.*

J. H. Findlater. THE GREEN GRAVES OF BALGOWRIE. By JANE H. FINDLATER. *Fourth Edition. Crown 8vo. 6s.*
'A powerful and vivid story.'—*Standard.*
'A beautiful story, sad and strange as truth itself.'—*Vanity Fair.*
'A singularly original, clever, and beautiful story.'—*Guardian.*
'Reveals to us a new writer of undoubted faculty and reserve force.'—*Spectator.*
'An exquisite idyll, delicate, affecting, and beautiful.'—*Black and White.*

J. H. Findlater. A DAUGHTER OF STRIFE. By JANE H. FINDLATER. *Crown 8vo. 6s.*

J. H. Findlater. RACHEL. By JANE H. FINDLATER. *Second Edition. Crown 8vo. 6s.*
'A not unworthy successor to "The Green Graves of Balgowrie."'—*Critic.*

J. H. and Mary Findlater. TALES THAT ARE TOLD. By JANE H. FINDLATER, and MARY FINDLATER. *Crown 8vo. 6s.*
'Delightful and graceful stories for which we have the warmest welcome.'—*Literature.*

Mary Findlater. A NARROW WAY. By MARY FINDLATER, Author of 'Over the Hills.' *Third Edition. Crown 8vo. 6s.*
'A wholesome, thoughtful, and interesting novel.'—*Morning Post.*
'Singularly pleasant, full of quiet humour and tender sympathy.'—*Manchester Guardian.*

Mary Findlater. OVER THE HILLS. By MARY FINDLATER. *Second Edition. Cr. 8vo. 6s.*
'A strong and wise book of deep insight and unflinching truth.'—*Birmingham Post.*

Mary Findlater. BETTY MUSGRAVE. By MARY FINDLATER. *Second Edition. Crown 8vo. 6s.*
'Handled with dignity and delicacy.... A most touching story.'—*Spectator.*

Alfred Ollivant. OWD BOB, THE GREY DOG OF KENMUIR. By ALFRED OLLIVANT. *Fifth Edition. Cr. 8vo. 6s.*
'Weird, thrilling, strikingly graphic.'—*Punch.*
'We admire this book.... It is one to read with admiration and to praise with enthusiasm.'—*Bookman.*
'It is a fine, open-air, blood-stirring book, to be enjoyed by every man and woman to whom a dog is dear.'—*Literature.*

B. M. Croker. PEGGY OF THE BARTONS. By B. M. CROKER, Author of 'Diana Barrington.' *Fifth Edition. Crown 8vo. 6s.*
'Mrs. Croker excels in the admirably simple, easy, and direct flow of her narrative, the briskness of her dialogue, and the geniality of her portraiture.'—*Spectator.*

B. M. Croker. A STATE SECRET. By B. M. CROKER, Author of 'Peggy of the Bartons,' etc. *Second Edition. Crown 8vo. 3s. 6d.*
'Full of humour, and always fresh and pleasing.'—*Daily Express.*
'Ingenious, humorous, pretty, pathetic.'—*World.*

H. G. Wells. THE STOLEN BACILLUS, and other Stories. By H. G. WELLS. *Second Edition. Crown 8vo. 6s.*
'The impressions of a very striking imagination.'—*Saturday Review.*

H. G. Wells. THE PLATTNER STORY AND OTHERS. By H. G. WELLS. *Second Edition. Cr. 8vo. 6s.*
'Weird and mysterious, they seem to hold the reader as by a magic spell.'—*Scotsman.*

Sara Jeannette Duncan. A VOYAGE OF CONSOLATION. By SARA JEANNETTE DUNCAN, Author of 'An American Girl in London.' Illustrated. *Third Edition. Cr. 8vo. 6s.*
'The dialogue is full of wit.'—*Globe.*

Sara Jeannette Duncan. THE PATH OF A STAR. By SARA JEANNETTE DUNCAN, Author of 'A Voyage of Consolation.' Illustrated. *Second Edition. Crown 8vo. 6s.*

C. F. Keary. THE JOURNALIST. By C. F. KEARY. *Cr. 8vo. 6s.*

W. E. Norris. MATTHEW AUSTIN. By W. E. NORRIS, Author of 'Mademoiselle de Mersac,' etc. *Fourth Edition. Crown 8vo. 6s.*
'An intellectually satisfactory and morally bracing novel.'—*Daily Telegraph.*

W. E. Norris. HIS GRACE. By W. E. NORRIS. *Third Edition. Cr. 8vo. 6s.*

W. E. Norris. THE DESPOTIC LADY AND OTHERS. By W. E. NORRIS. *Crown 8vo. 6s.*

W. E. Norris. CLARISSA FURIOSA. By W. E. NORRIS. *Cr. 8vo. 6s.*
'As a story it is admirable, as a *jeu d'esprit* it is capital, as a lay sermon studded with gems of wit and wisdom it is a model.'—*The World.*

W. E. Norris. GILES INGILBY. By W. E. NORRIS. Illustrated. *Second Edition. Crown 8vo. 6s.*
'Interesting, wholesome, and charmingly written.'—*Glasgow Herald.*

W. E. Norris. AN OCTAVE. By W. E. NORRIS. *Second Edition. Crown 8vo. 6s.*

W. Clark Russell. MY DANISH SWEETHEART. By W. CLARK RUSSELL. Illustrated. *Fourth Edition. Crown 8vo. 6s.*

Robert Barr. IN THE MIDST OF ALARMS. By ROBERT BARR. *Third Edition. Cr. 8vo. 6s.*
'A book which has abundantly satisfied us by its capital humour.'—*Daily Chronicle.*

Robert Barr. THE MUTABLE MANY. By ROBERT BARR. *Second Edition. Crown 8vo. 6s.*
'Very much the best novel that Mr. Barr has yet given us. There is much insight in it, and much excellent humour.'—*Daily Chronicle.*

Robert Barr. THE COUNTESS TEKLA. By ROBERT BARR. *Third Edition. Crown 8vo. 6s.*
'Of these mediæval romances, which are now gaining ground, "The Countess Tekla" is the very best we have seen. The story is written in clear English, and a picturesque, moving style.'—*Pall Mall Gazette.*

Robert Barr. THE STRONG ARM. By ROBERT BARR, Author of 'The Countess Tekla.' Illustrated. *Second Edition. 8vo. 6s.*

C. J. Cutcliffe Hyne. PRINCE RUPERT THE BUCCANEER. By C. J. CUTCLIFFE HYNE, Author of 'Captain Kettle.' With 8 Illustrations by G. GRENVILLE MANTON. *Second Edition. Crown 8vo. 6s.*
A narrative of the romantic adventures of the famous Prince Rupert, and of his exploits in the Spanish Indies after the Cromwellian wars.

Mrs. Dudeney. THE THIRD FLOOR. By Mrs. DUDENEY, Author of 'Folly Corner.' *Second Edition. Crown 8vo. 6s.*
'One of the brightest, wittiest, and most entertaining novels published this spring.'—*Sketch.*

Andrew Balfour. BY STROKE OF SWORD. By A. BALFOUR. Illustrated. *Fourth Edition. Cr. 8vo. 6s.*
'A recital of thrilling interest, told with unflagging vigour.'—*Globe.*

Andrew Balfour. TO ARMS! By ANDREW BALFOUR. Illustrated. *Second Edition. Crown 8vo. 6s.*
'The marvellous perils through which Allan passes are told in powerful and lively fashion.'—*Pall Mall Gazette.*

Andrew Balfour. VENGEANCE IS MINE. By ANDREW BALFOUR, Author of 'By Stroke of Sword.' Illustrated. *Crown 8vo. 6s.*
'A vigorous piece of work, well written, and abounding in stirring incidents.'—*Glasgow Herald.*

R. Hichens. BYEWAYS. By ROBERT HICHENS. Author of 'Flames,' etc. *Second Edition. Cr. 8vo. 6s.*
'The work is undeniably that of a man of striking imagination.'—*Daily News.*

R. Hichens. TONGUES OF CONSCIENCE. By ROBERT HICHENS, Author of 'Flames.' *Second Edition. Crown 8vo. 6s.*
'Of a strange, haunting quality.'—*Glasgow Herald.*

Stephen Crane. WOUNDS IN THE RAIN. WAR STORIES. By STEPHEN CRANE, Author of 'The Red Badge of Courage.' *Second Edition. Crown 8vo. 6s.*
'A fascinating volume.'—*Spectator.*

Dorothea Gerard. THE CONQUEST OF LONDON. By DOROTHEA GERARD, Author of 'Lady Baby.' *Second Edition. Crown 8vo.* 6s.

'Bright and entertaining.'—*Spectator.*
'Highly entertaining and enjoyable.'—*Scotsman.*

Dorothea Gerard. THE SUPREME CRIME. By DOROTHEA GERARD. *Crown 8vo.* 6s.

'One of the very best plots we have met with in recent fiction, and handled with that quiet unerring realism which always distinguishes the author's best work.'—*Academy.*

C. F. Goss. THE REDEMPTION OF DAVID CORSON. By C. F. GOSS. *Third Edition. Crown 8vo.* 6s.

'Dramatic instinct and a vigorous imagination mark this soul history of a Quaker mystic.'—*Athenæum.*
'A really fine book.'—*Public Opinion.*
'A powerful and original book, and unusually striking.'—*Pilot.*
'Worthy to stand high in the ranks of modern fiction.'—*Literature.*

OTHER SIX-SHILLING NOVELS

Crown 8vo.

A SECRETARY OF LEGATION. By HOPE DAWLISH.
THE SALVATION SEEKERS. By NOEL AINSLIE.
STRANGE HAPPENINGS. By W. CLARK RUSSELL and other Authors.
THE BLACK WOLF'S BREED. By HARRIS DICKSON. Illustrated. *Second Edition.*
BELINDA FITZWARREN. By the EARL OF IDDESLEIGH.
DERWENT'S HORSE. By VICTOR ROUSSEAU.
ANNE MAULEVERER. By Mrs. CAFFYN (Iota).
SIREN CITY. By BENJAMIN SWIFT.
AN ENGLISHMAN. By MARY L. PENDERED.
THE PLUNDERERS. By MORLEY ROBERTS.
THE HUMAN INTEREST. By VIOLET HUNT.
THE KING OF ANDAMAN: A Saviour of Society. By J. MACLAREN COBBAN.
THE ANGEL OF THE COVENANT. By J. MACLAREN COBBAN.
IN THE DAY OF ADVERSITY. By J. BLOUNDELLE-BURTON.
DENOUNCED. By J. BLOUNDELLE-BURTON.
THE CLASH OF ARMS. By J. BLOUNDELLE-BURTON.
ACROSS THE SALT SEAS. By J. BLOUNDELLE-BURTON.
SERVANTS OF SIN. By J. BLOUNDELLE-BURTON.
PATH AND GOAL. *Second Edition.* By ADA CAMBRIDGE.
THE SEEN AND THE UNSEEN. By RICHARD MARSH.
MARVELS AND MYSTERIES. By RICHARD MARSH.
ELMSLIE'S DRAG-NET. By E. H. STRAIN.
A FOREST OFFICER. By Mrs. PENNY.
THE WHITE HECATOMB. By W. C. SCULLY.
BETWEEN SUN AND SAND. By W. C. SCULLY.
SIR ROBERT'S FORTUNE. By Mrs. OLIPHANT.
THE TWO MARYS. By Mrs. OLIPHANT.
THE LADY'S WALK. By Mrs. OLIPHANT.
MIRRY-ANN. By NORMA LORIMER.
JOSIAH'S WIFE. By NORMA LORIMER.
THE STRONG GOD CIRCUMSTANCE. By HELEN SHIPTON.
CHRISTALLA. By ESMÉ STUART.
THE DESPATCH RIDER. By ERNEST GLANVILLE.
AN ENEMY TO THE KING. By R. N. STEPHENS.
A GENTLEMAN PLAYER. By R. N. STEPHENS.

CPSIA information can be obtained at www.ICGtesting.com
Printed in the USA
LVOW051720161111
255294LV00011B/174/P

9 781142 531461